AF469752

GREETINGS FROM THE BARRICADES

ВЫСОЧАЙШІЙ МАНИФЕСТЪ.

Божіею милостію,

МЫ, НИКОЛАЙ ВТОРЫЙ,

ИМПЕРАТОРЪ И САМОДЕРЖЕЦЪ ВСЕРОССІЙСКІЙ,

царь польскій, великій князь финляндскій,

и прочая, и прочая, и прочая.

Смуты и волненія въ столицахъ и во многихъ мѣстностяхъ Имперіи Нашей великою и тяжкою скорбью преисполняютъ сердце Наше. Благо Россійскаго Государя неразрывно съ благомъ народнымъ, и печаль народная—Его печаль. Отъ волненій, нынѣ возникшихъ, можетъ явиться глубокое нестроеніе народное и угроза цѣлости и единству Державы Нашей.

Великій обѣтъ Царскаго служенія повелѣваетъ Намъ всѣми силами разума и власти Нашей стремиться къ скорѣйшему прекращенію столь опасной для Государства смуты. Повелѣвъ подлежащимъ властямъ принять мѣры къ устраненію прямыхъ проявленій безпорядка, безчинствъ и насилій, въ охрану людей мирныхъ, стремящихся къ спокойному выполненію лежащаго на каждомъ долга, Мы, для успѣшнѣйшаго выполненія общихъ преднамѣчаемыхъ Нами къ умиротворенію государственной жизни мѣръ, признали необходимымъ объединить дѣятельность высшаго Правительства.

На обязанность Правительства возлагаемъ Мы выполненіе непреклонной Нашей воли:

1. Даровать населенію незыблемыя основы гражданской свободы на началахъ дѣйствительной неприкосновенности личности, свободы совѣсти, слова, собраній и союзовъ.

2. Не останавливая предназначенныхъ выборовъ въ Государственную Думу, привлечь теперь же къ участію въ Думѣ, въ мѣрѣ возможности, соотвѣтствующей краткости остающагося до созыва Думы срока, тѣ классы населенія, которые нынѣ совсѣмъ лишены избирательныхъ правъ, предоставивъ, засимъ, дальнѣйшее развитіе начала общаго избирательнаго права вновь установленному законодательному порядку,

и 3. Установить, какъ незыблемое правило, чтобы никакой законъ не могъ воспріять силу безъ одобренія Государственной Думы и чтобы выборнымъ отъ народа обезпечена была возможность дѣйствительнаго участія въ надзорѣ за закономѣрностью дѣйствій поставленныхъ отъ Насъ властей.

Призываемъ всѣхъ вѣрныхъ сыновъ Россіи исполнить долгъ свой передъ Родиною, помочь прекращенію сей неслыханной смуты и вмѣстѣ съ Нами напрячь всѣ силы къ возстановленію тишины и мира на родной землѣ.

Данъ въ Петергофѣ, въ 17-й день октября въ лѣто отъ Рождества Христова тысяча девятьсотъ пятое, Царствованія же Нашего одиннадцатое. На подлинномъ Собственною Его Императорскаго Величества рукою подписано:

„*НИКОЛАЙ*".

Къ сему листу Свиты Его Величества Генералъ-Маіоръ Треповъ руку приложилъ.

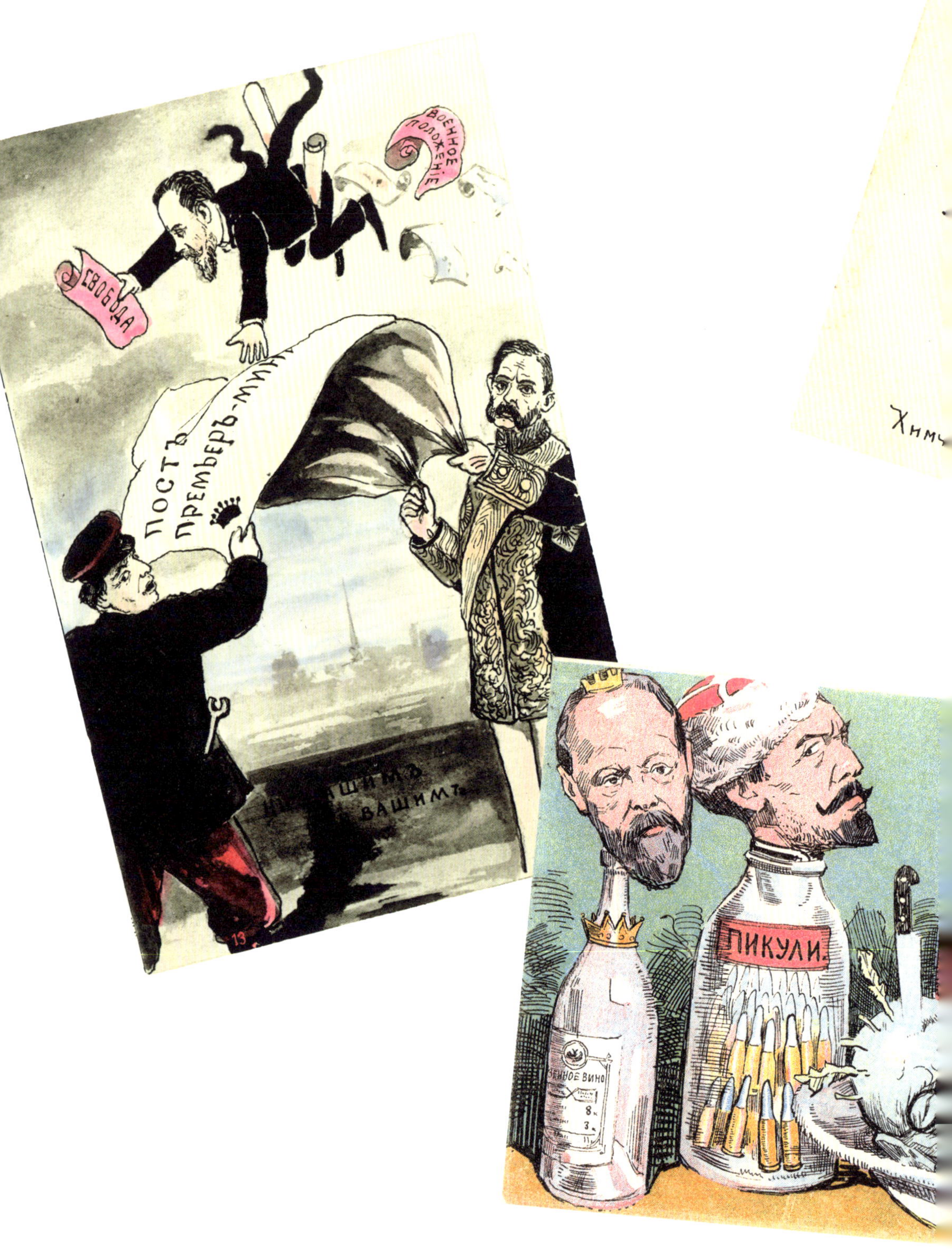
ВОЕННОЕ ПОЛОЖЕНІЕ
СВОБОДА
ПОСТЪ
ВАШИМЪ
ПИКУЛИ.

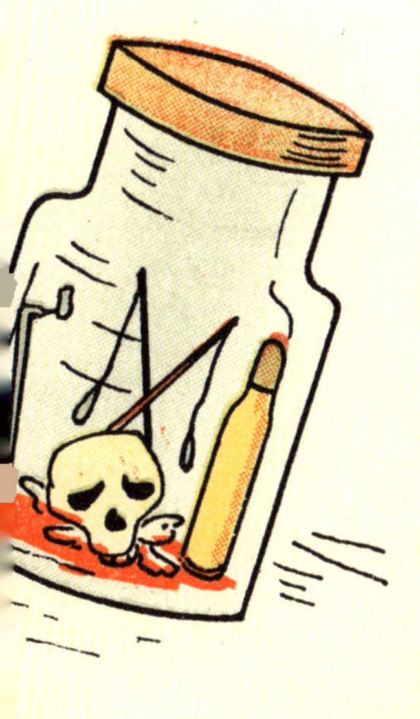
въ русской своводы.

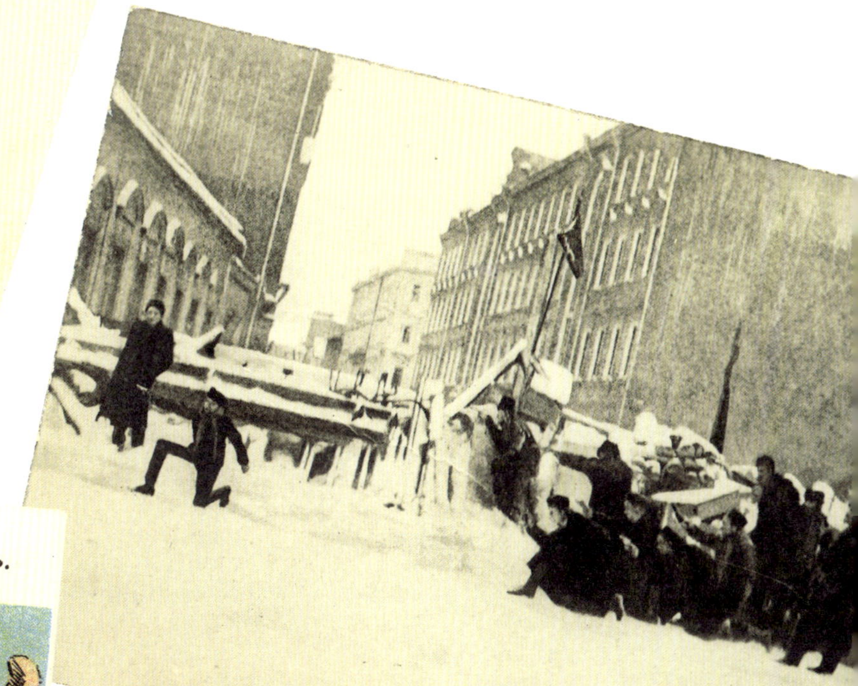

мыя кушанья русскихъ.
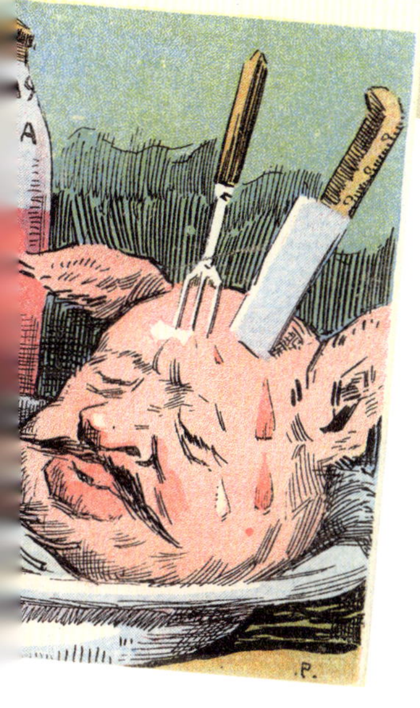

GREETINGS FROM THE BARRICADES

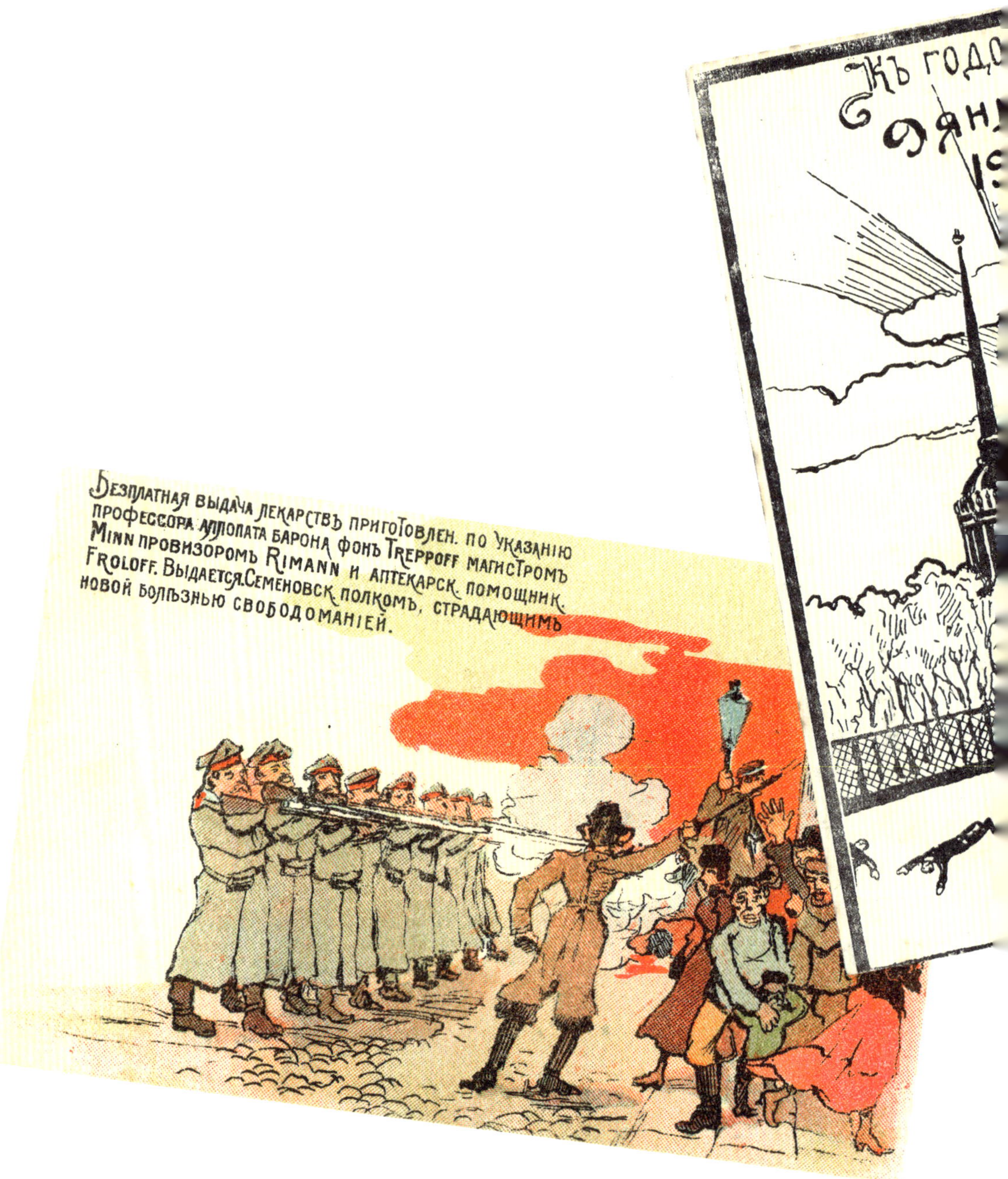

REVOLUTIONARY POSTCARDS IN IMPERIAL RUSSIA

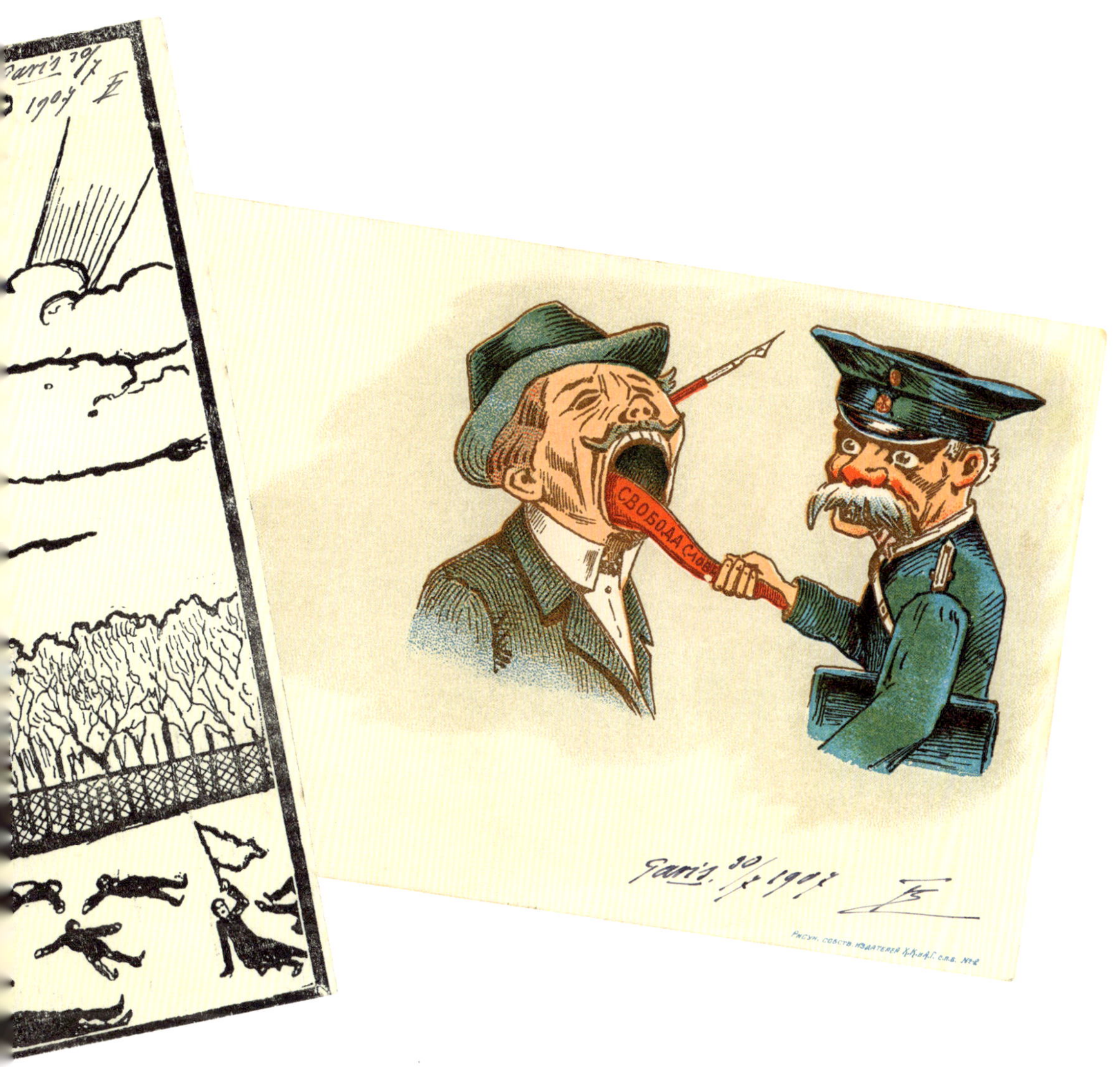

TOBIE MATHEW

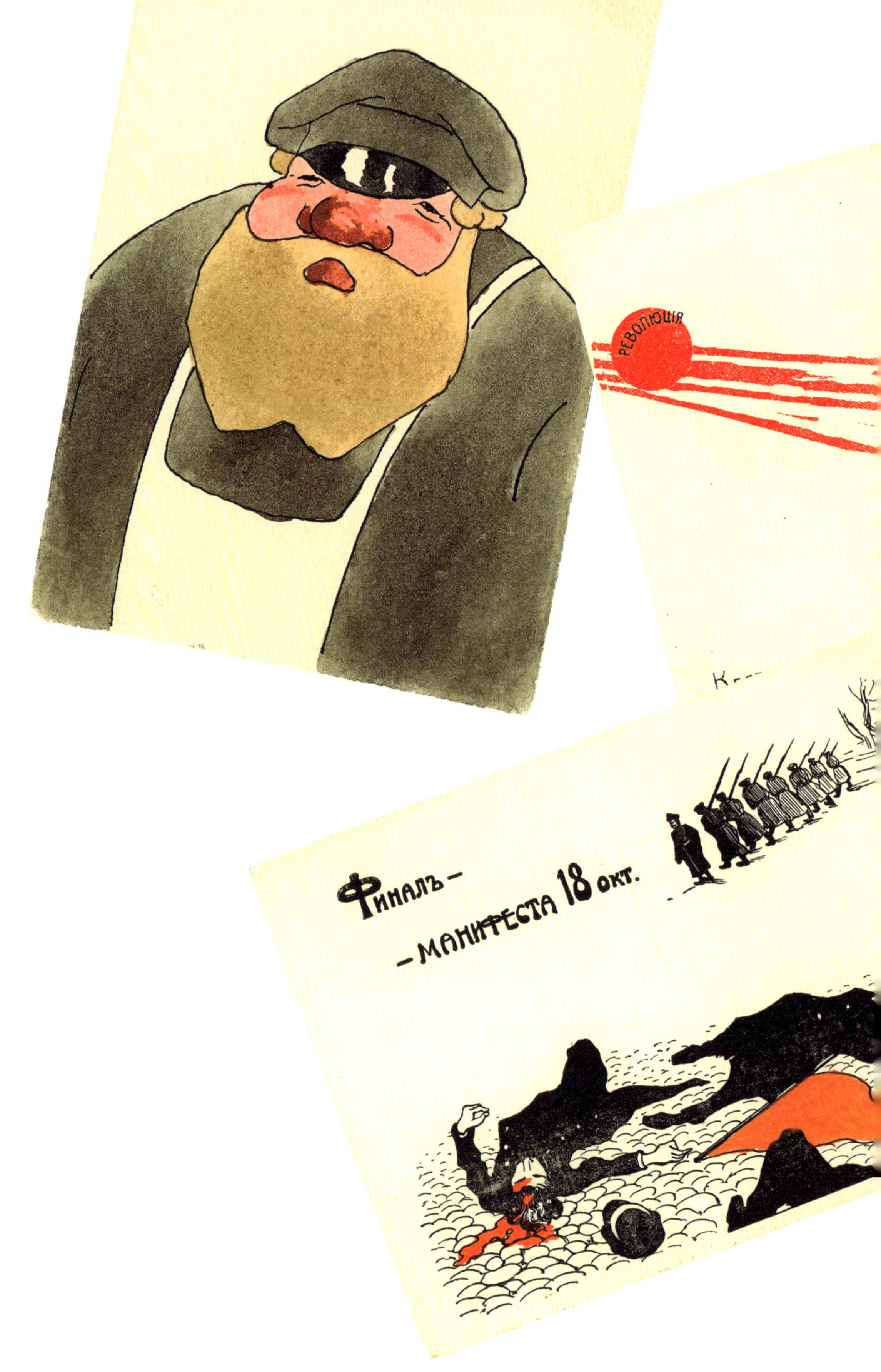
РЕВОЛЮЦІЯ
Финалъ -
- МАНИФЕСТА 18 окт.

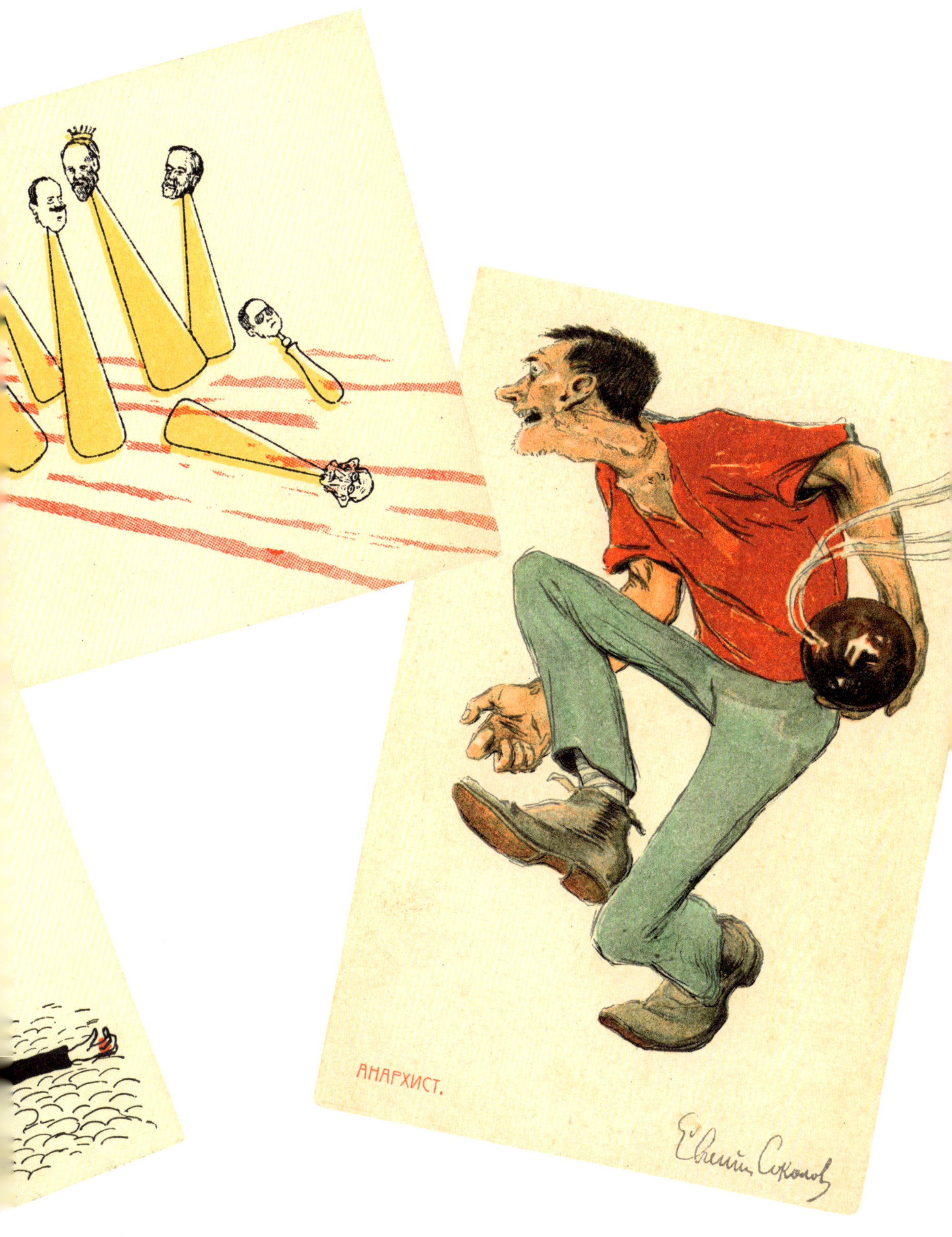

FOUR CORNERS BOOKS

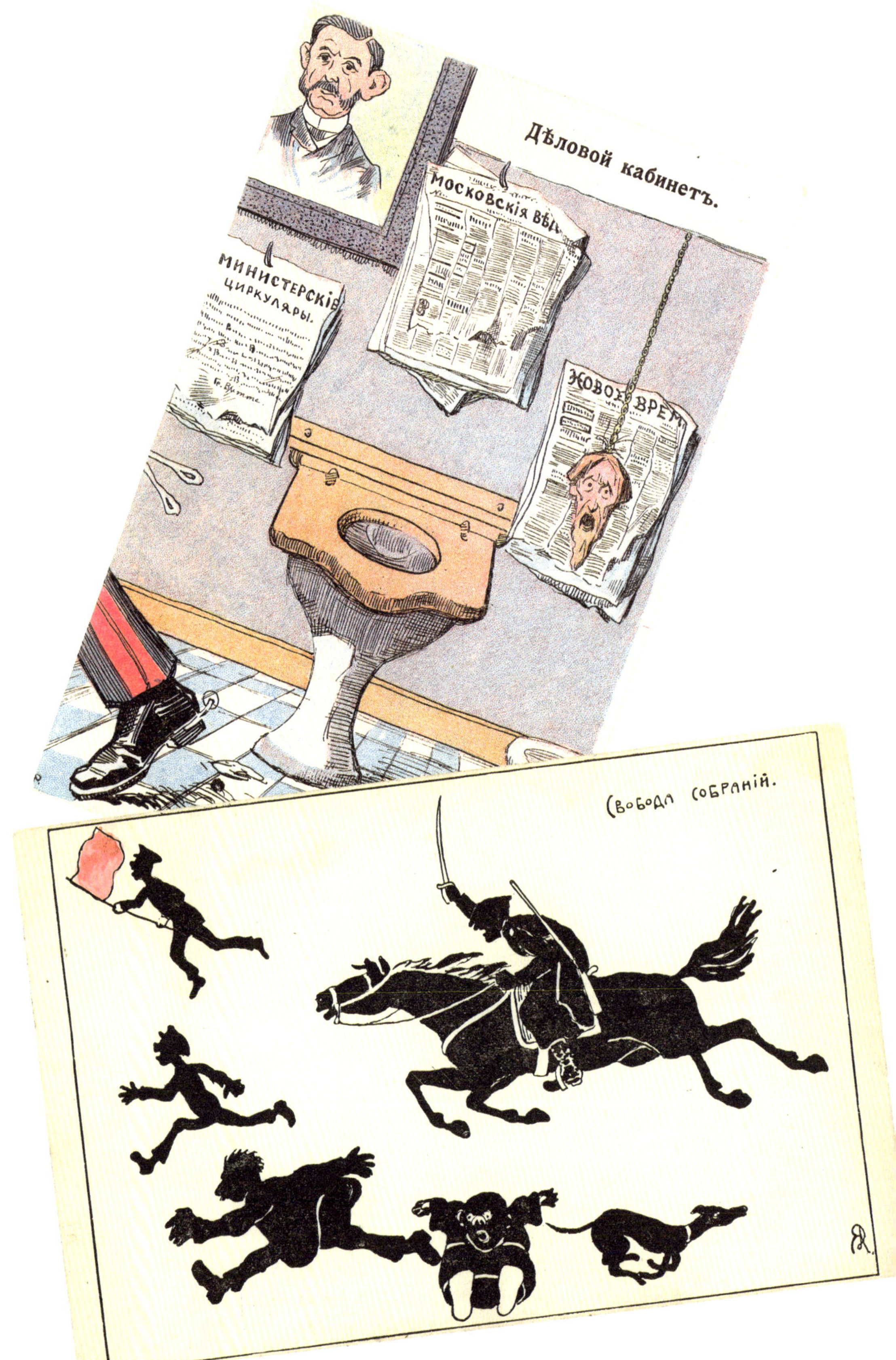
Дѣловой кабинетъ.
МОСКОВСКІЯ ВѢД
МИНИСТЕРСКІЕ
ЦИРКУЛЯРЫ
НОВОЕ ВРЕМ
Свобода собраній.

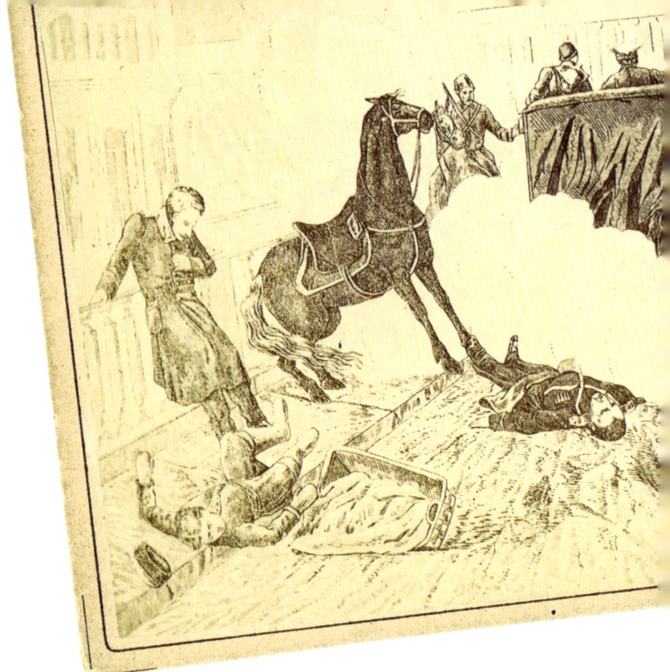

Author's Note

Prior to February 1918, Russia used the Julian Calendar, which in the twentieth century was 13 days behind the Gregorian Calendar used in the West. All dates are given according to the former.

Names have been transliterated according to the Library of Congress system, with the exception of those that have more familiar English-language alternatives, such as Tolstoy rather than Tolstoi, and Witte rather than Vitte. The names of the Tsars have been given in their anglicised forms and, for the ease of the reader, soft signs have been omitted in the main body of the text.

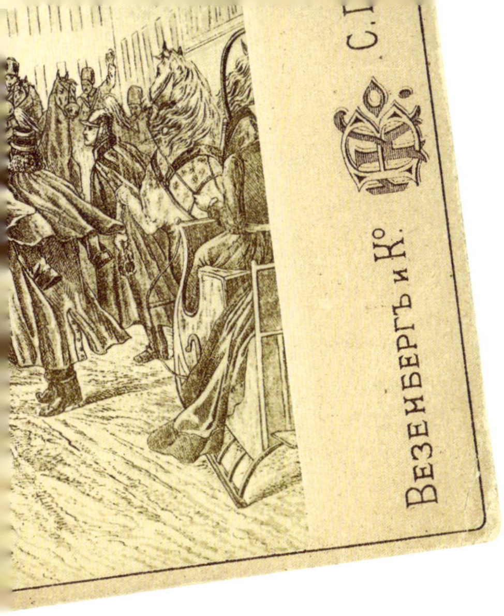

It seemed as if the air itself was filled with tiny, invisible clock hammers, ready to strike at a moment's notice to sound the alarm that would wake the people from their slumbers.[1]

V. Pakhomov

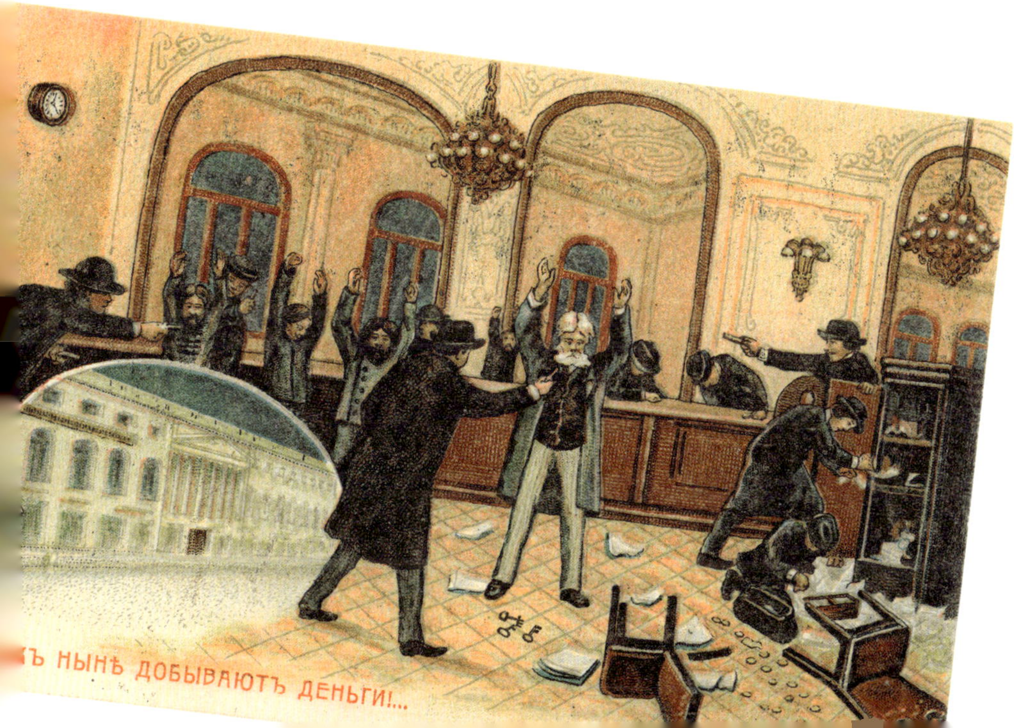

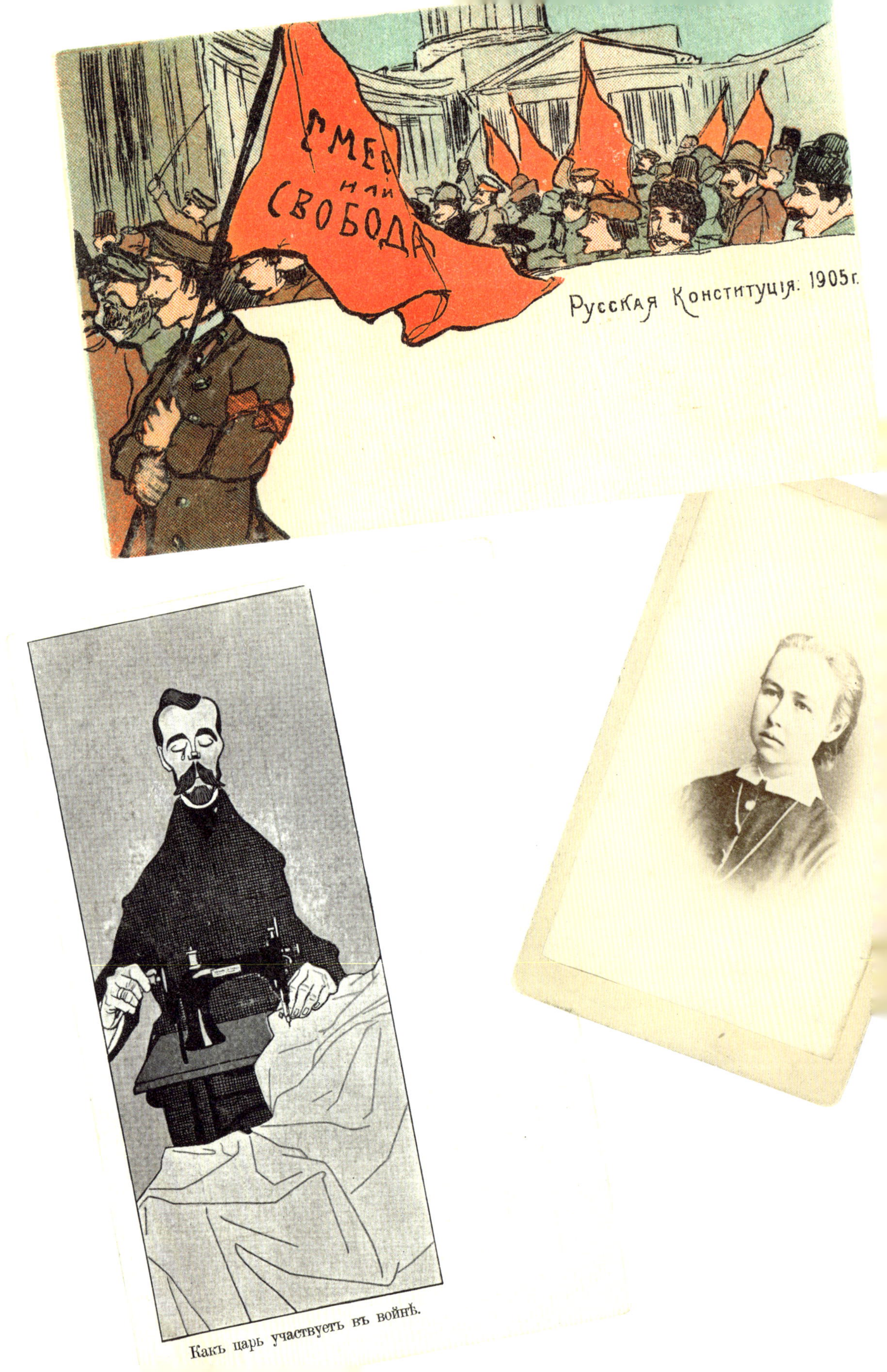
СМЕ
или
СВОБОДА
Русская Конституція: 1905г.
Какъ царь участвуетъ въ войнѣ.

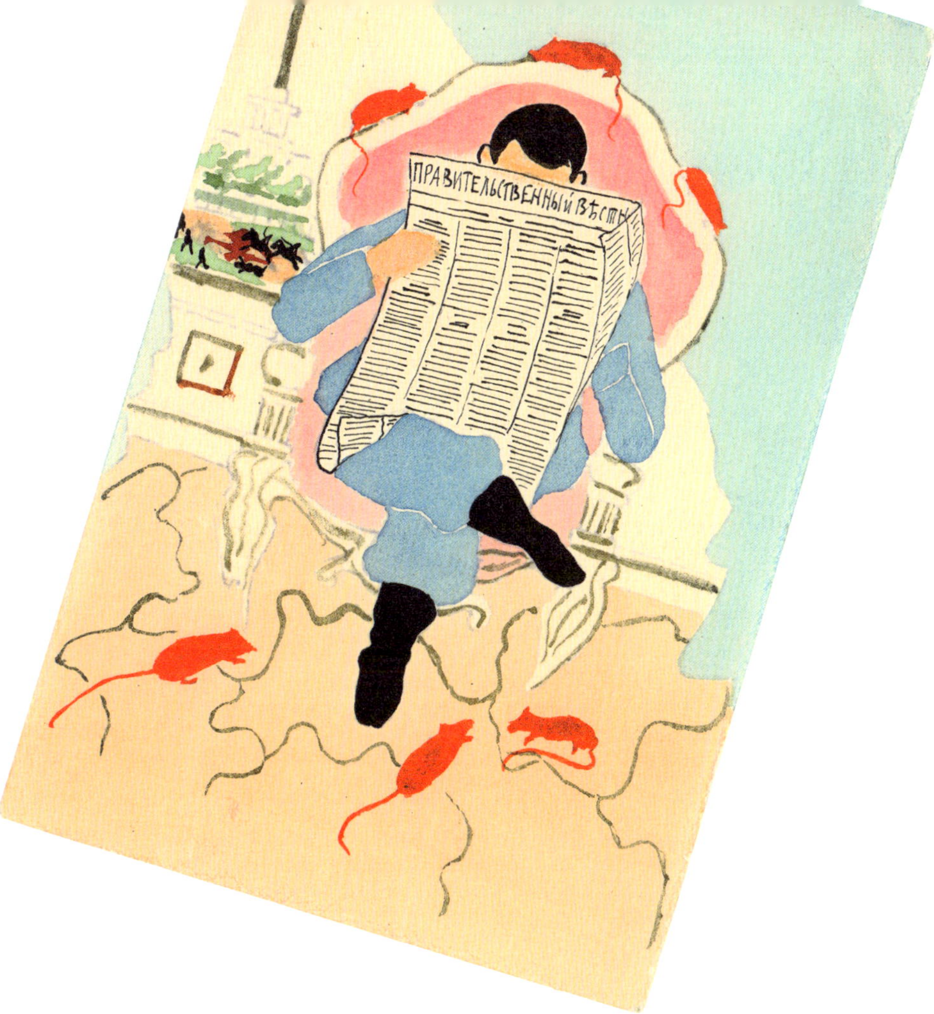

ПРАВИТЕЛЬСТВЕННЫЙ ВѢСТН

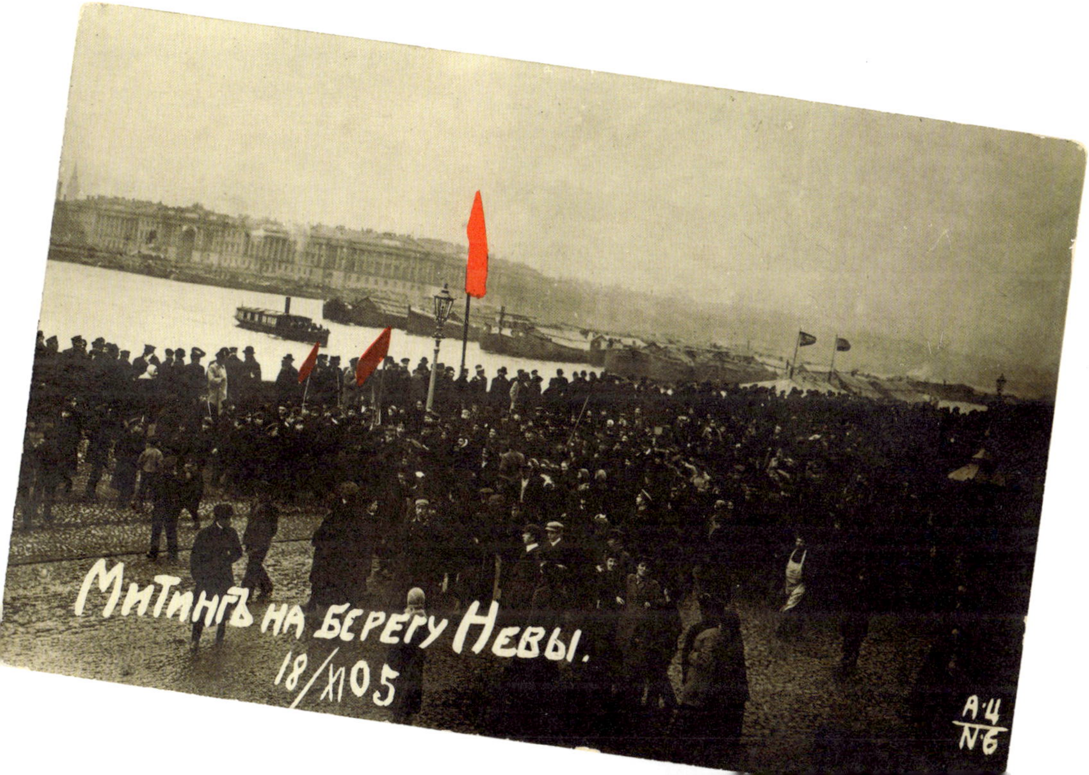

Митингъ на берегу Невы.
18/XI 05

А·Ц
N6

Timeline

1855 Tsar Alexander II accedes to the throne

1856 Crimean War ends, Alexander II embarks on a series of reforms

1861 Emancipation of the Serfs

1865 New Russian press laws unveiled

1866 Dmitrii Karakozov attempts to assassinate Alexander II

First revolutionary cartes de visite printed

1869 Austro-Hungarian Empire starts issuing postcard blanks

Hectography invented in Russia

1870 First propaganda postcards printed during Franco-Prussian War

1872 Russian government starts issuing postcard blanks

Germany becomes first country to allow private postcard production

1874 'Going to the People' movement reaches apogee

1879 Narodnaia Volia formed

1881 Alexander II assassinated, Alexander III accedes to the throne

Okhrana formed

1890 Statute on Censorship and the Press enacted

First May Day postcards printed in Austria

1894 Nicholas II accedes to the throne

Russia allows private postcard production

1895 Earliest known picture postcards bearing censorial marks printed in Moscow

1898 Russian Social Democratic Labour Party formed

Society of Saint Eugenia starts printing picture postcards

1901 Socialist-Revolutionary Party formed

1902 Stepan Balmashev assassinates Interior Minister Dmitrii Sipiagin

1903 Social Democratic Party splits into Bolshevik and Menshevik factions

1904 *February*

Russo-Japanese War starts

Russia allows messages to be written on postcard backs, alongside the address

First Russian cartoon postcards published

April

First Russian postcard journal launched in Saint Petersburg

July

Egor Sazonov assassinates Interior Minister Viacheslav von Plehve

1905 *January*

Father Gapon leads march to Winter Palace, resulting in Bloody Sunday

February

Ivan Kaliaev assassinates Moscow Governor Grand Duke Sergei Alexandrovich

March

Aleksei Belgard appointed head of Main Administration for Press Affairs

May

Vera Vodovozova starts publishing postcards in Kiev

June

Potemkin Mutiny takes place

Satirical journal *Zritel* launched

c. July

Iosif Belopolskii founds Vpered in Odessa

September

Russo-Japanese War ends

October

Constitutional Democratic (Kadet) Party formed

Saint Petersburg Soviet formed

October Manifesto enacted

Sergei Witte appointed Chairman of the Council of Ministers

Petr Durnovo appointed Interior Minister

August Tsenter starts printing anti-government postcards in Saint Petersburg

November

Temporary regulations for periodical press enacted

First legal anti-government satirical postcards published

Lieutenant Petr Schmidt leads uprising in Black Sea Fleet

December

Saint Petersburg Soviet broken up

Moscow Uprising put down, period of repression starts

1906 *January*

Maria Spiridonova shoots Tambov official Gavril Luzhenovskii

Utro founded in Saint Petersburg

c. February

Dmitrii Peschanskii starts printing Mikhail Chemodanov's drawings in Moscow

March

March Changes and Supplements enacted to combat satirical journals

Maria Spiridonova tried and convicted

Petr Schmidt executed

April

Ivan Goremykin replaces Sergei Witte as Chairman of Council of Ministers

Petr Stolypin replaces Petr Durnovo as Interior Minister

First Duma inaugurated

Temporary regulations for non-periodical press enacted

Shipovnik founded in Saint Petersburg

Vpered founded in Saint Petersburg

Volia founded in Nagasaki, Japan

July

Petr Stolypin replaces Ivan Goremykin as Chairman of Council of Ministers

First Duma dissolved, Vyborg Manifesto issued

November

Vasilii Metalnikov starts printing satirical postcards in Saint Petersburg

December

Mikhail Chemodanov arrested

1907 Second Duma (February–June)

1908 Viktor Zheglinskii publishes series of socialist portrait postcards in Vologda

Mikhail Chemodanov dies

1912 Striking workers shot at Lena Goldfields, leading to period of unrest

Luka Zlotnikov publishes series of anti-Semitic postcards in Saint Petersburg

1914 First World War starts, military censorship brought in

1917 Tsar Nicholas II overthrown, censorship nominally abolished

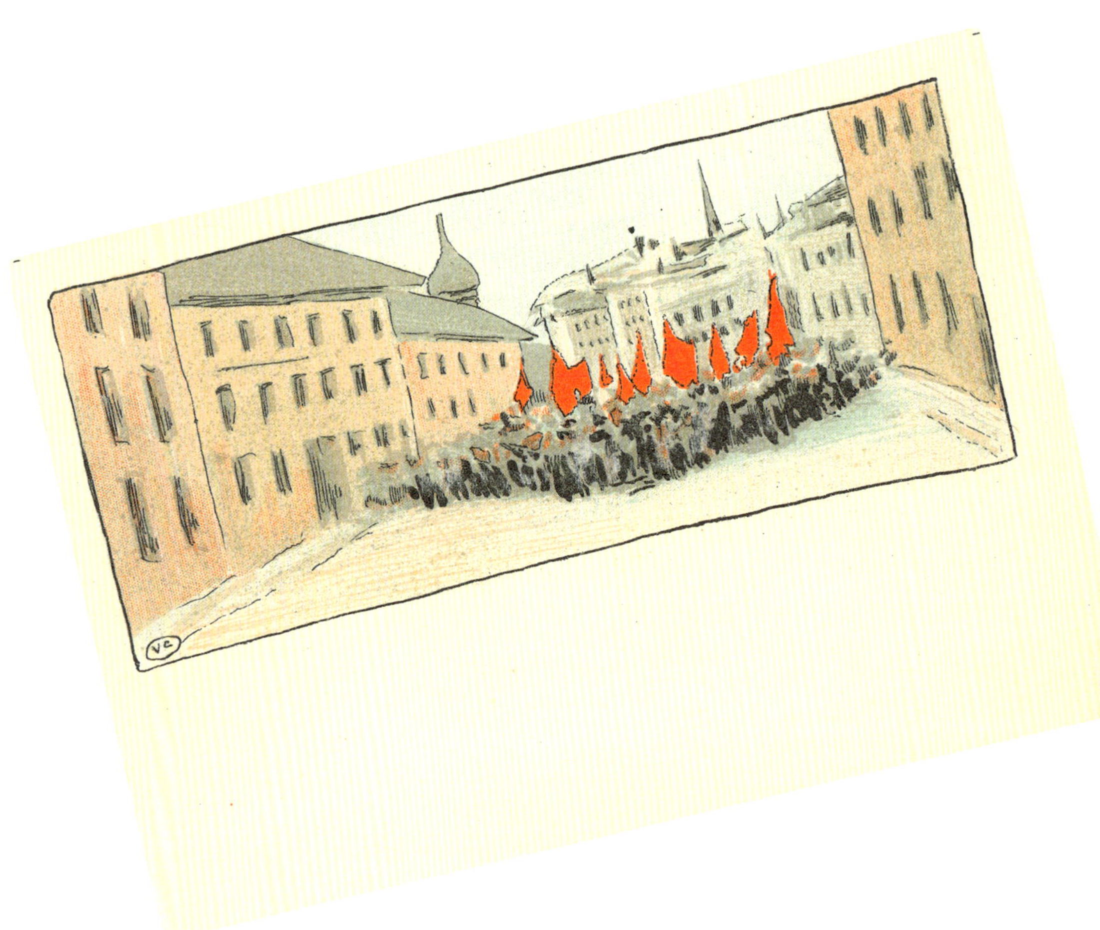

PROLOGUE

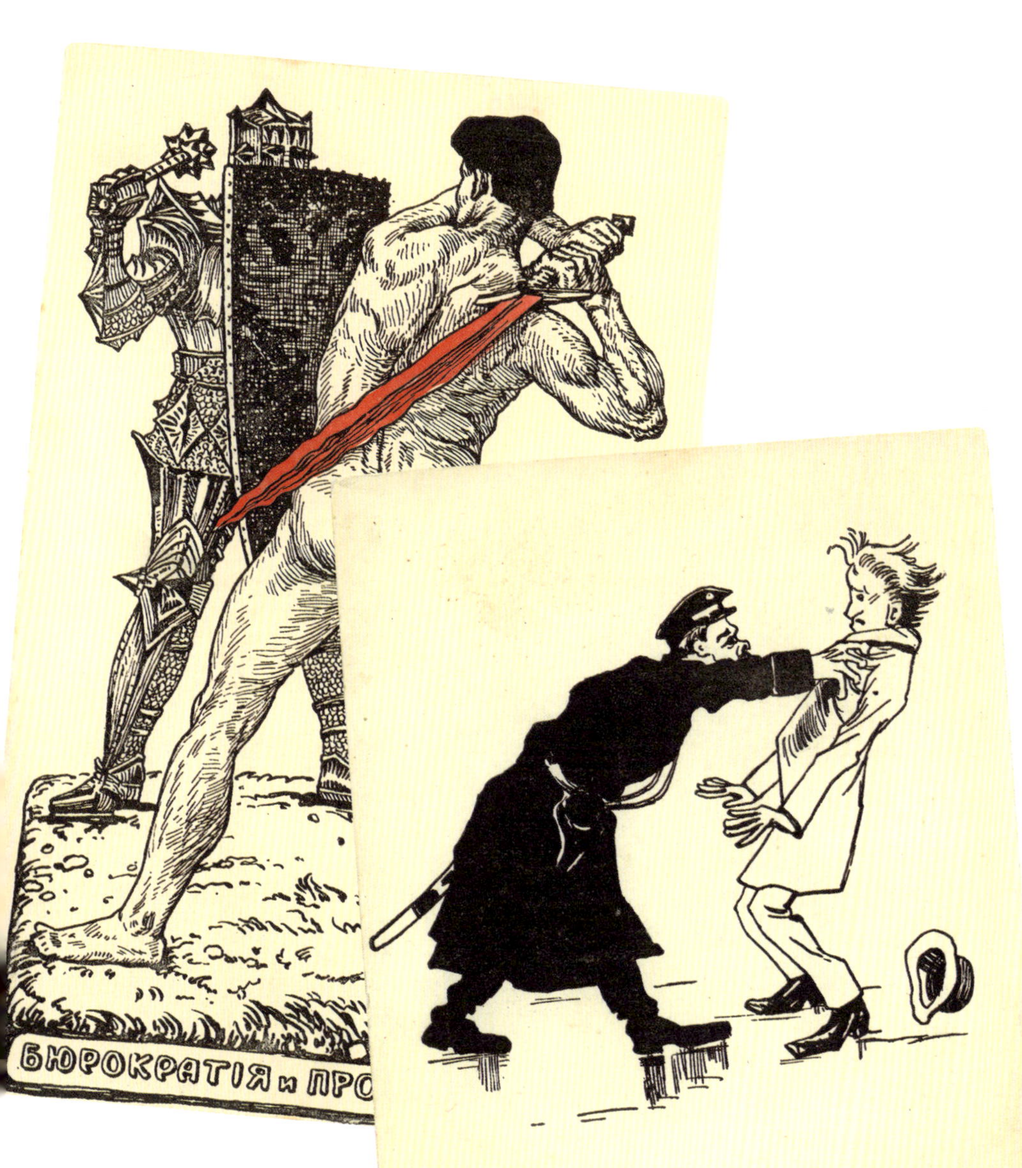

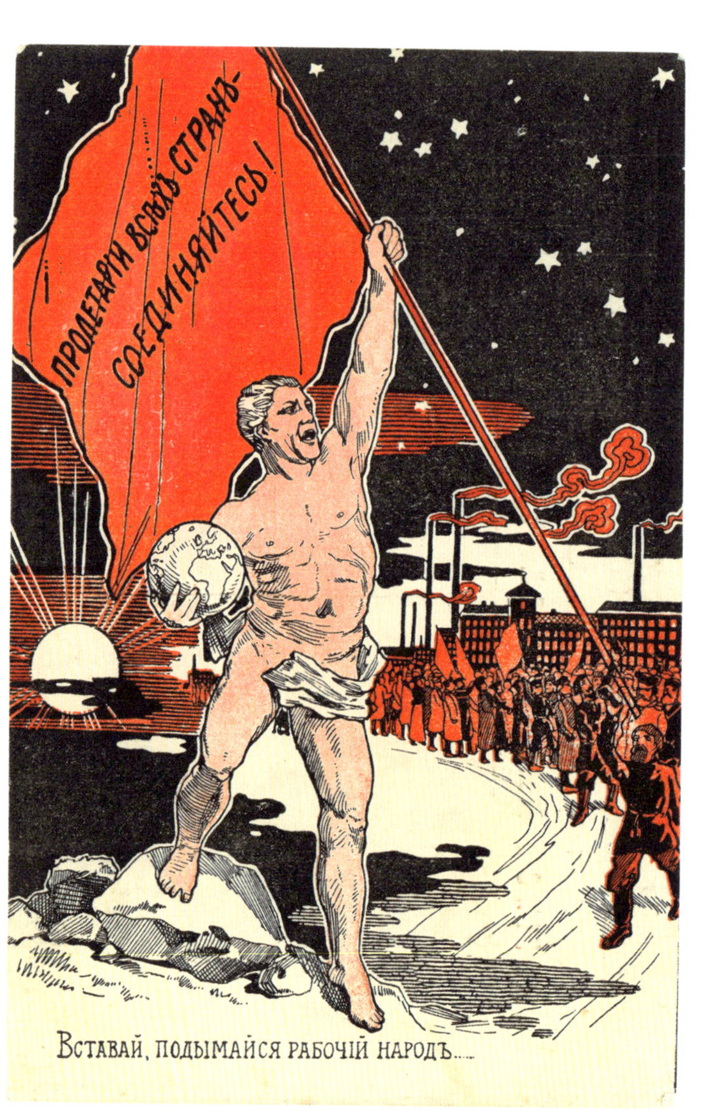
ПРОЛЕТАРІИ ВСѢХЪ СТРАНЪ-
СОЕДИНЯЙТЕСЬ!
ВСТАВАЙ, ПОДЫМАЙСЯ РАБОЧІЙ НАРОДЪ.....

At four thirty in the afternoon on 3 June 1906, a small team of policemen arrived at an inconspicuous residential building in central Kiev. Acting on a tip-off from the security services, they had come in search of revolutionaries.

Upstairs, in flat fifteen, three young students were hard at work, oblivious to the danger outside. When the knock on the door came there was no time for them to hide, and although one was later found to be carrying a loaded revolver, all three were swiftly detained. With the situation under control, the flat search could begin. It went on until nine o'clock that evening.

Even by the standards of the day, the haul from the raid was impressive. Laid out on tables and concealed in boxes, bins, and trouser pockets, the police discovered: 285 printed pamphlets, 125 revolutionary proclamations, forty-one copies of an anti-government journal, fifty-six sheets of cartoons, a box of screws, blue and red printing inks, over a hundred bullets, enlargers for developing photographs, two lamps, various chemical solutions, a small red flag, and 1,022 anti-government postcards.[1]

Many of these postcards reproduced images of a massacre that had taken place in Saint Petersburg around eighteen months previously. On that day, tens of thousands of unarmed workers and their families had set out for the Winter Palace to petition the Tsar for greater social and political rights. But as the columns of marchers approached the city centre, Imperial soldiers had opened fire, killing hundreds. Bloody Sunday, as it became known, was the trigger for a nationwide rebellion, releasing a long-suppressed wave of revolutionary activity that threatened to sweep away Russia's centuries-old tradition of autocratic government.

Amid the strikes, demonstrations, and terrorist attacks that followed, all sides competed for popular support – the state through patriotic appeals and short-lived legal reforms, their opponents through anti-government agitation and rhetoric. Hampered by the censor and limited in the ways that they could circulate their incendiary messages, the groups battling against autocracy were forced to develop their own methods of political communication. Established couriers of the printed word, such as newspapers, pamphlets, and leaflets were used extensively. But postcards became their key method of disseminating visual propaganda.

Postcards were originally conceived as a cheap form of written correspondence, but the ease with which they could be printed, small size, and their great popularity made the medium an ideal conduit for political ideas, as well as a convenient way of generating income. The production of opposition postcards was initially the preserve of committed revolutionaries, many of them based in Western Europe, but the breakdown of Imperial authority in 1905 led to the creation of a vibrant commercial market inside

Previous spread from left to right

Valerii Karrik. Untitled depiction of a revolutionary demonstration. No publication details, circa mid-1906.

Anonymous artist. *Bureaucracy and the Proletariat.* No publication details, circa 1906–1910.

Anonymous artist. *Inviolability of the Individual.* No publication details, late 1905.

Opposite

Anonymous Artist. *Arise, Workers…* No publication details, late 1905. The figure holds aloft a flag emblazoned with the slogan: 'Proletarians of the World Unite'.

Russia itself. During a short-lived period of open revolt, numerous publishers joined the fray, manufacturing millions of images for ideological and financial gain.

Over recent years the internet has transformed the organisation of subversive activity. Through Facebook, Twitter, and YouTube, opposition parties and terrorist groups have acquired instant access to citizens the world over. A hundred years ago the Russian revolutionaries were not so very different from today's militants and freedom fighters – a small band of committed individuals who needed to convince a nation to act against what they perceived to be a morally bankrupt regime. The medium they used may have been less technologically advanced, but it was no less effective in communicating partisan tales of popular resistance.

In an environment of rising literacy and increasing political awareness, postcards repackaged the 1905 Revolution for popular consumption, bringing the drama of the street into the safety of the home, and allowing the defining events of the era to live on and fester in the mind long after they had taken place. Once the preserve of the law-abiding town dweller, they were transformed during this period into political message-bearers, spreading stories of oppression and heralding the change that many hoped might one day be upon them. Long before the advent of television and the internet, postcards were a potent form of mass communication, transmitting ideas of opposition across the Russian Empire.

Research and Writing

This book owes its existence to my collecting habits. As a young visitor to Russia in the 1990s, I used to spend hours trawling through the many street markets selling souvenirs of the Cold War. Soviet posters, heavily braided uniforms and discarded political ephemera all caught my eye, the jetsam of a once-glorified empire now the prey of a passing tourist.

In due course, I started coming across older pieces, including items associated with the early revolutionary movement. Among them were often small groups of anti-government postcards dating to before the fall of the last Tsar. These images, once the seditious vehicles of a forbidden mindset, were at that time cheap and relatively plentiful. It seemed extraordinary, and it still does, that one could pick up an original revolutionary document for the price of a hamburger. And what's more, without the queue.

I did not at first seek out political postcards, but after a few years of disorderly purchases the beginnings of a collection had formed. A passing interest has since become an obsession, and I have spent much of the intervening period gathering whatever information I could find, all the while revelling in the excuse of research to make yet more acquisitions.

However haphazardly found, it is rare to come across a novel vantage point from which to survey territory as well trodden as revolutionary Russia. Numerous works have already recounted how the battle between the Tsar and his people was fought on the streets and in the political arena, and this book makes no claims to correct the established narrative. My aim instead is to show how the many social and legal changes that took place in the late nineteenth and early twentieth centuries affected the production of anti-government postcards. In doing so, I hope to shed new light on the dissemination of revolutionary ideas, and to offer a fresh perspective on late Imperial Russia as a rapidly modernising society with a diverse and vibrant public sphere.

Discussions of opposition imagery in late Imperial Russia have traditionally focused on the profusion of satirical journals printed between late 1905 and mid-1906. By comparison, little space has been given to postcards. This is in many ways surprising; postcards were the most geographically, socially, and pictorially diverse form of anti-government visual propaganda produced during the reign of Nicholas II, and likely also the most numerous. Quite apart from the information they provide on early revolutionary organisation and ideology, opposition postcards offer a remarkable insight into the way in which the regime lost its sacred lustre. And yet, since they were made there have been only a handful of related articles, and thus far no book-length study.[2]

Since the 1990s, research into Russian postcard production and design has grown considerably, aided in great part by the collecting community.[3] In recent years, academic historians have also started to pay more attention to the medium, rightly seeing it as an important source of information on early twentieth-century popular culture.[4] Nonetheless, the oft-repeated charge that anti-government postcards have been unjustly neglected still stands.[5] There has been no new archival research carried out in this area for nearly forty years, with the inevitable result that our understanding of the subject is still coloured by the salient but often dogmatic work of Soviet scholars, who largely ignored the work of non-revolutionary publishers.

Recent articles have been strongly weighted towards pictorial analysis; this book intends to even out the balance by focusing on production. Given the broad range of individuals who became involved in opposition postcard publishing, and the fast-evolving circumstances under which they were operating, there is a critical need to look in greater depth at the identities and principal motives of the dramatis personae, as well as to construct a clear chronology of their activities. A more detailed understanding of production practices serves in turn to pave the way for a more informed study of the images themselves. The outcome is a view of anti-government postcards that is at once less ideologically-centred and more heterogeneous than has hitherto been suggested.

Postcards, like the revolutionary crusade, came into being through efforts to better address the needs of a fast-changing world, and at heart this work is about the correlation between two key strands of Russian modernity – the rise of the commercial print industry and the growth of the liberation movement. These developments, which both emerged from the debris of mid-nineteenth century social and political reforms, together proved integral to the mass production of leftist material. Their alignment in 1905 led to the widespread commodification of anti-government thought, resulting in a barrage of opposition propaganda that stretched the boundaries of Imperial power and for a short time forced leftist publishers of all types into a market dynamic.

Anonymous artist. *In Commemoration of 9 January 1905.* No publication details, January 1906.

This fleeting outburst of popular defiance met with a fierce response, and within a few years the liberation movement and its printed offshoots had been largely suppressed in Russia. But however brief its duration, the temporary unshackling of the print industry served to greatly exacerbate a loss of popular trust in the autocratic regime, a loss that would come back to haunt the Tsar less than a decade later. Indeed, while the exact causes of the 1917 Revolution lie elsewhere, the long-term public abasement of the regime came about largely through printed propaganda. In an era of rapid social development and chronic political unrest, the erosive power of anti-government pamphlets, leaflets, and postcards proved impossible to contain.

Parameters

This has not been a straightforward book to write. The main complication of researching anti-government postcards lies in the complexity of determining the many different groups and individuals who stood behind the imagery. Although the objects themselves survive in some numbers, the majority do not carry publication details, meaning that the waters through which any historian must wade are very murky. There are stylistic characteristics that can be used to identify certain publishers and artists, but unless firm evidence is available, it is impossible to write with certainty about the origins of a particular postcard. New information continues to be uncovered, but this remains an imperfect science.

Much of the material for the book has come from archives in Europe and North America. In Russia, documents from the Main Administration for Press Affairs and the Department of Police have been instrumental in illuminating the changing nature of official approaches towards anti-government postcards, as well as the various efforts that the regime made to combat production. On the other side, the Socialist-Revolutionary Party papers held at the International Institute of Social History in Amsterdam have allowed for a more detailed understanding of the role that postcards played

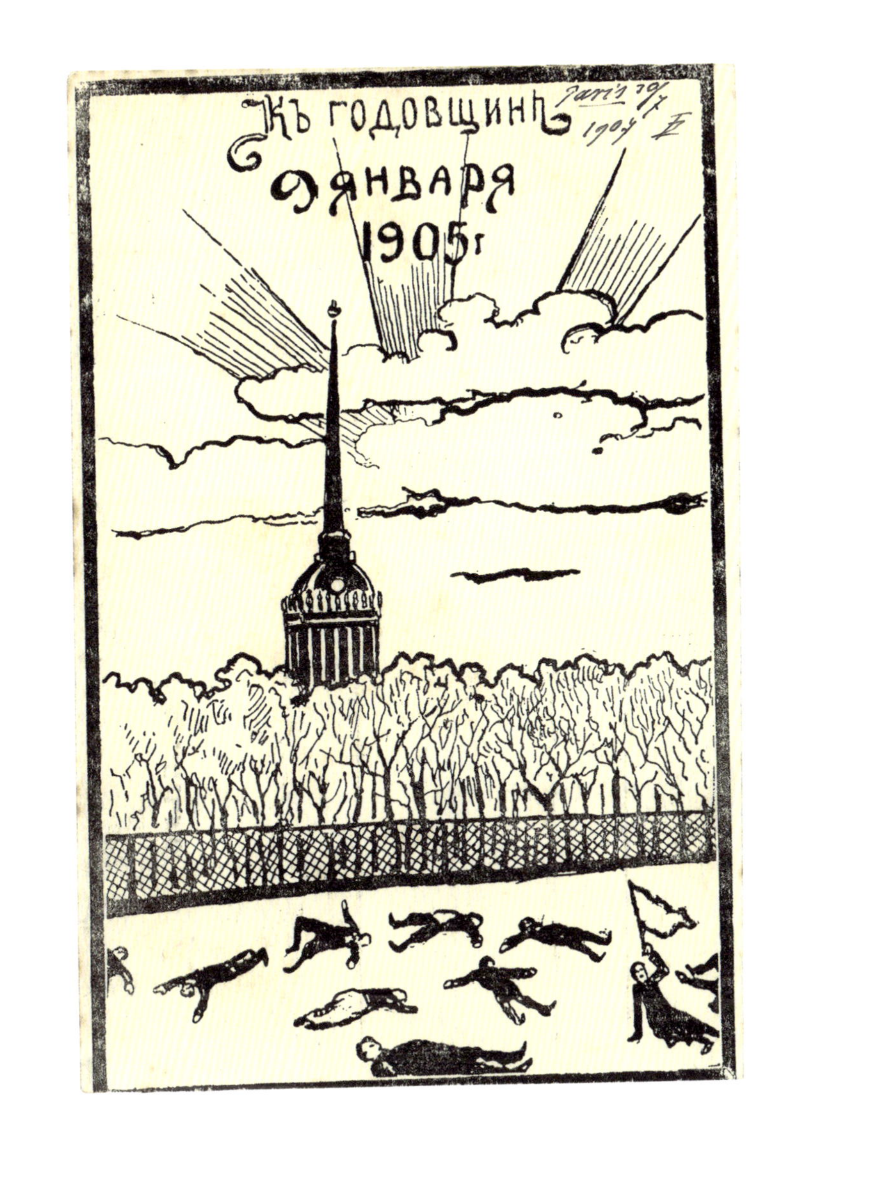
Къ годовщинѣ
9 января
1905 г

in funding the revolutionaries, and laid the groundwork for a less Bolshevik-centric study.

Party newspapers and postcard journals have filled out some of the evidence and occasionally helped to reveal the cost of anti-government postcards, as well as the places where they were sold. But most importantly, extensive examination of the postcards themselves has yielded the names of several publishers and artists, and offered written clues as to how buyers related to opposition imagery. Although in most cases intended to serve as anti-government propaganda, postcards took on a new life once released into the wild. Here, as private possessions, they were exposed to myriad different uses and interpretations, reflecting the subjective nature of all responses to the reproduced image.

Most anti-government postcards were never sent through the post; they were instead passed from hand to hand or kept for personal use. The question therefore arises as to whether they should be called postcards at all. This is an argument that stretches back well over a hundred years. As late as 1907, some collectors were still insisting that a picture did not become a postcard until it had been written on, and travelled through the mail, yet for every proponent of this line, there were many others who were happy to enjoy the pictorial content at face value.[6] I have taken as my guide the revolutionaries themselves, who referred to all small format pictures, whether they had plain or printed backs, as either postcards or cards.[7]

This study spans the reigns of the last three Tsars, but focuses primarily on the 1905–1907 period, when the overwhelming majority of anti-government postcards were produced. The main text comprises four separate but overlapping sections. The first and largest of these offers a chronological survey of the legal and political circumstances under which the postcards were printed and distributed. The second looks at the organisations and individuals behind the cards, paying close attention to the differing reasons for their involvement. The third examines the images, analysing their content and interpreting the ways in which they endeavoured to convey an opposition narrative, and the final section considers postcard usage.

My concern throughout is with leftist images printed by Russian manufacturers or intended for a Russian market – foreign, nationalist, and Yiddish-language postcards lie outside the realm of this work.[8] Within these parameters the scope is relatively wide. The small number of contemporary collections that have survived intact contain a wide range of opposition subject matter, often from publishers with greatly differing political beliefs. This, and the broad brush that Tsarist officials used when referring to anti-government postcards, suggest that any attempt to restrict analysis to particular types of imagery would limit appreciation of the phenomenon as a whole.

The picture that has emerged is significantly more complex and mercantile than previously envisaged. Production and distribution was not always united in practical, geographical or ideological terms. Within the purview of a single postcard, a number of different organisations and individuals may have been involved, sometimes linked only by the loosest of common motives. Even the subject matter itself was fluid. Revolutionary groups, liberal activists, and private firms all reproduced images of the same events and the same people, and it follows that the reasons for purchase were as many as the postcards themselves. This was a period of both great opportunity and great opportunism.

The 1905 Revolution was never a clear-cut fight between the opponents and proponents of autocracy. Some were waging personal battles for better pay and working conditions, others were agitating for the overthrow of the regime, and others still wanted the Tsar to remain but with his powers checked. The opposition was pulled back and forth between all these different opinions, its sallies and retreats made between the margins of practicality and opportunity. Anti-government postcards embody this complicated blend of politics and circumstance, reflecting the wide range of opinions and aspirations that were held at a time when Russia stood on the brink of revolution and reform.

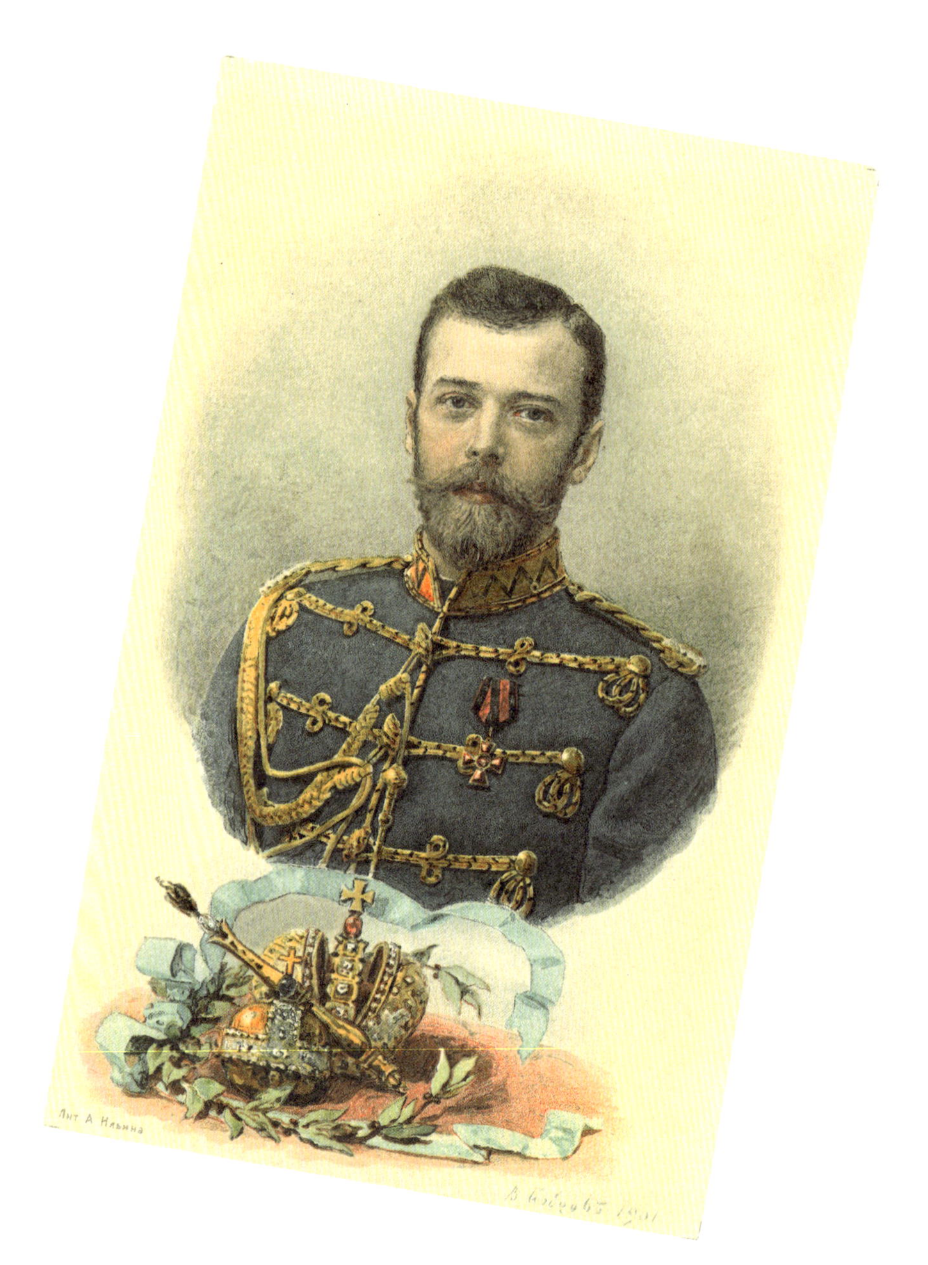
Лит А Ильина

THE PICTURE POSTCARD

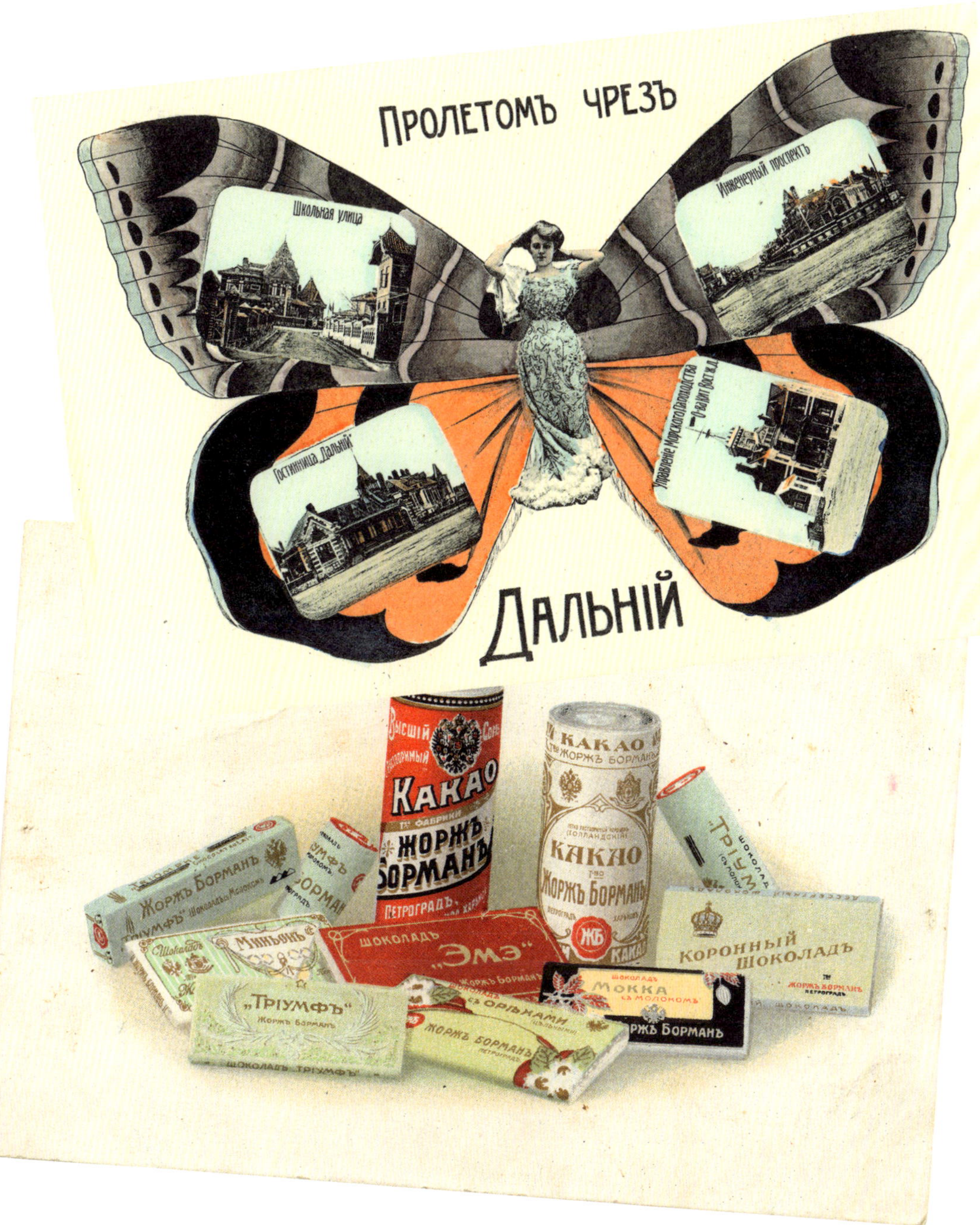

1869–1905

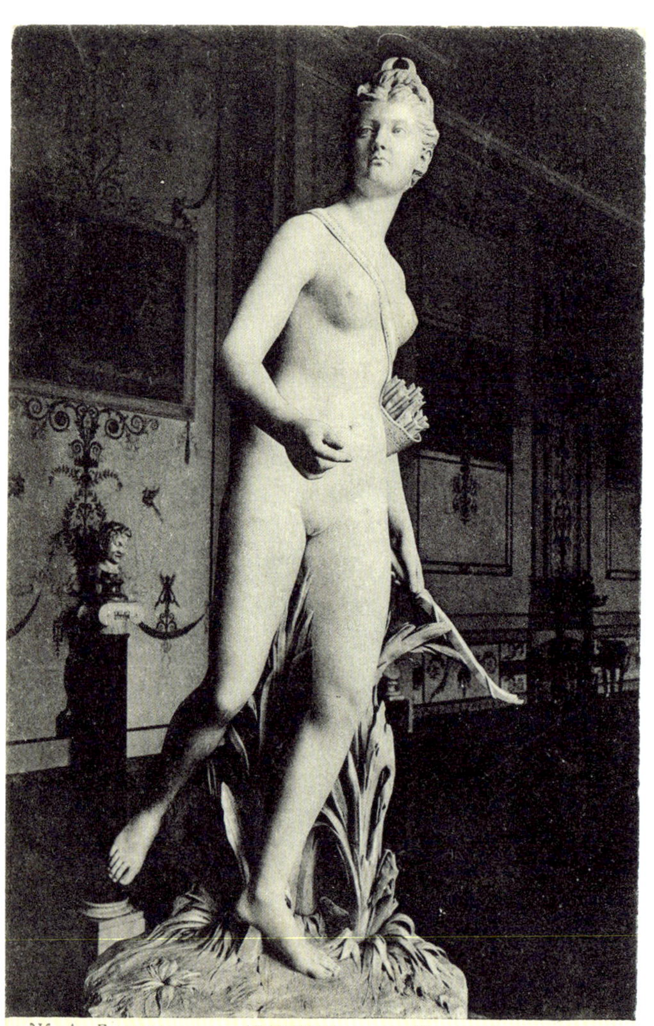

Ж. А. Гудонъ. 1740-1828. Діана. Эрмитажъ.
J. A. Hondon. Diane. Ermitage.
5-е изданіе. impérial.

Prison

On 8 December 1906, Russia's leading dental expert sent a letter to the country's prime minister, begging to be released from Moscow's Butyrka Gaol. Four days earlier, Doctor Mikhail Chemodanov had been apprehended for disseminating illegal postcards, but now, over three sides of ruled notepaper, he insisted that his detention and subsequent imprisonment had been the result of a colossal misunderstanding. It was, Chemodanov wrote, a complete mystery as to why he had been arrested in the first place. 'I do not belong to any political party, nor have I been a part of any political organisations or even meetings,' moreover, he added, 'from morning till night I have been stuck behind my dentist's chair.'[1]

One week later, Chemodanov was still waiting for a response. Sick and exhausted from long hours treating his fellow prisoners, he sent a follow-up telegram to the prime minister's office in a last-ditch attempt to secure his freedom. With the cold of a Russian winter bearing down upon him, it amounted to little more than a plea for his life: 'My chronic bronchitis has developed into pneumonia. If I remain in gaol even for one more night then my days are numbered.'[2] Chemodanov was released on bail two days later, but it was already too late. His health had been fatally compromised, and he passed away a little over a year later at the age of fifty-one.

Picture postcards are commonly associated in the popular imagination with short thank you notes and bouts of vacational gloating from foreign climes; however, the message that Doctor Chemodanov and his fellow activists were looking to convey was not one of gratitude, good weather, or touristic glee, but of social and political rights. Theirs was a pictorial missive that was intended to expose the injustices of day-to-day existence in Imperial Russia, an ideological cause for which Chemodanov ultimately gave his life. The question is: how did the postcard get here, so far from its roots, to arrive in a place where a person might die for the crime of creating it?

Origins of the Postcard

Despite the many roles that it would later assume, the origins of the postcard owe more to developments in the social sphere than they do to art and politics. The first postcards, which went on sale in the Austro-Hungarian Empire on 1 October 1869, were intended to serve as a more efficient way for individuals to send short, non-private messages. The pre-stamped blanks were cheaper to post and easier to compose than the average letter, and they quickly proved popular with both private and commercial customers. In the first three months, an average of 250,000 postcards were sold every week, and from this starting point, they soon spread

Previous spread from left to right

Viktor Bobrov. Untitled portrait of Tsar Nicholas II. Published by the Society of Saint Eugenia, Saint Petersburg, 1901.

Anonymous artist. *Flying through Dalnii.* Published by Rosenfeld and Schtscholokow, Harbin, 1910s.

Anonymous artist. Untitled advertisement for George Borman Chocolates. Published by George Borman Cooperative, 1910s.

Opposite

Jean-Antoine Houdon. *Diana.* Published by the Society of Saint Eugenia, Saint Petersburg, 1900s. This postcard was initially prohibited by the censor in 1903 as 'improper'.

to other nations, reaching Germany, the United Kingdom and Switzerland the following year.[3]

The postcard came about as the offshoot of more wide-ranging efforts to bring postal services into line with the developments of preceding decades. Population growth, increased access to education, and the expansion of railway networks all contributed towards the necessity of revamping delivery systems, as well as providing more affordable forms of written correspondence. In Russia, a large empire in the throes of great change, the requirement for improvement was particularly acute. An exponential rise in population, literacy, and social mobility, brought about in part by wide-ranging political reforms, had created ever-greater demand for postal communication, placing serious pressure on an outdated mail service once used solely by government officials and the elite.

In October 1870, Interior Minister Alexander Timashev sought to address these issues with a complete overhaul of the Russian post. 'Many of the existing forms of mail operations, including postal regulations and tariffs, do not meet the needs of contemporary society,' he reported to the Tsar, adding that, 'compared to those in place abroad, our procedures are completely out of date.'[4] In order to function efficiently over such a vast territory, the Russian state required a well-run postal system, and in common with other measures enacted after defeat in the Crimean War, this move towards reform was less a response to the country's social needs than it was an attempt to restore Russia to the position of a great power, competitive with the rest of Europe.

Alexander II gave Timashev permission to draw up a set of temporary regulations aimed at streamlining postal operations across the Empire. These measures, which centred on more rigid, European-style postal classifications and pricing structures, were to be trialled for three years before a final decision would be taken on their suitability for Russia. Among the initial suggestions was the proposal to introduce postcards: 'As has been done in Prussia and Austria, it might also be possible to establish in Russia a special form of correspondence that allows private individuals the possibility of exchanging messages openly.'[5] The Interior Ministry authorised the new regulations in June 1871, and the first postcards went on sale on 1 January the following year.

Similar changes in countries across Europe and North America were replicated on an international level with the establishment of a General Postal Union. Russia, again looking to play an integrated role on the European stage, was one of the twenty-two founder signatories of the so-called Treaty of Bern. This agreement, signed on 9 October 1874, brought parity between the many different national postal services, introducing standardised rates, and ensuring that all mail could be sent without hindrance between member countries.[6] Once largely restricted to domestic usage, postcards now started travelling en masse through international borders. In 1875, 231.5 million postcards were sent in countries represented by the Union. By 1900, this had risen to 2.8 billion.[7]

In Russia, as in other countries, the state initially retained a monopoly on postcard production. The government-issued blanks, which were only available at designated sales points, were printed on plain paper and lacked any pictorial elements other than a small double-headed eagle. No other forms of open letter could be sent legally through the internal mail, and this included illustrated postcards. In July 1872, Germany became the first country to allow private firms to print their own postcards, and over the decade many other countries followed suit. But there remained notable exceptions to this free market trend, including Russia, the United States and the United Kingdom, whose governments were reluctant to surrender such an easy source of income.

In countries where private production was legalised, capitalist competition helped drive the rapid development of the picture postcard. The need to attract new customers provided publishers and manufacturers with an ongoing financial incentive to create ever-more vibrant and varied images, leading to an increase in the diversity of subject matter and the aesthetic refinement of the medium. Within the space of a few years, simple sheets of printed card once intended only for epistolary exchange had been reconfigured into sophisticated pieces of commercial propaganda appealing to the cultural and ideological prejudices of the masses. No longer simply a good value message carrier, postcards became primary purveyors of art, titillation, travel and politics.

This democratisation of visual imagery could not have taken place without the great advances in paper production and printing made over previous decades. The invention of wood pulp paper in 1847 had allowed the basic material with which the printed word was distributed to become available to a hugely expanded audience, and at the same time the development of steam-powered rotary presses improved printing speeds and productivity. There were analogous inventions in the visual arena, particularly in regard to chromolithography, and towards the end of the century, collotype printing, which significantly eased the process of photographic reproduction. Publishers, once limited by the state, could now begin to play a greater role in shaping it.

Abuses

Not everyone in Russia thought that postcards were such a great idea. Despite the restrictions on the involvement of private enterprise, the medium aroused considerable trepidation among officials wary of any

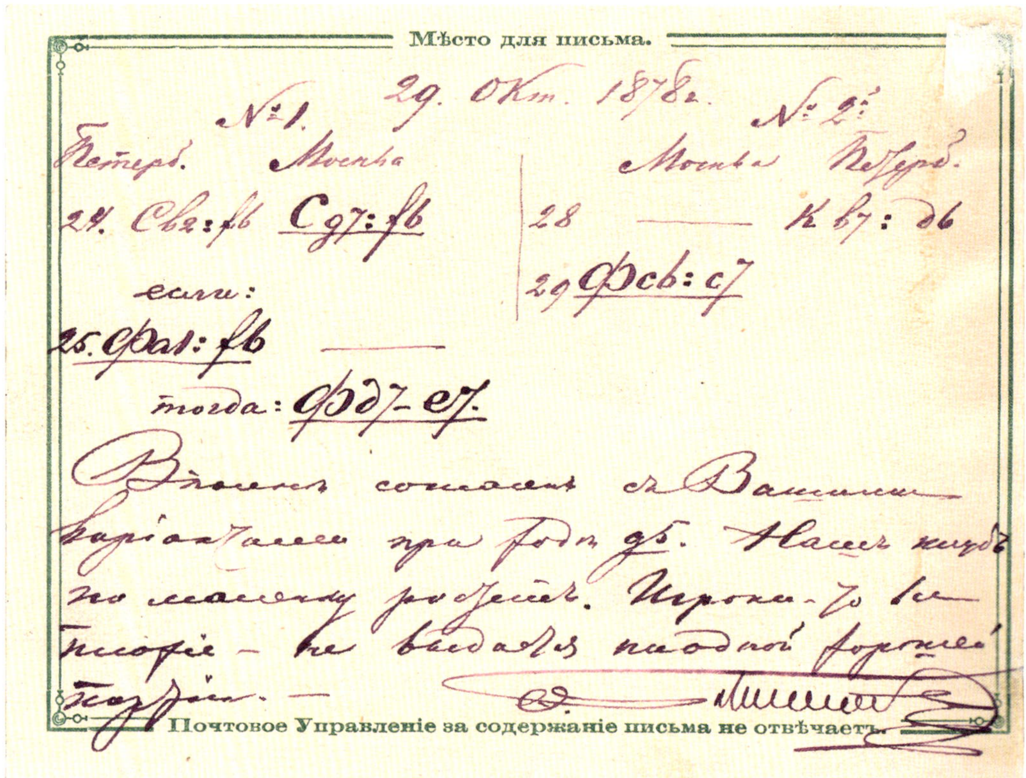

Postcard carrying suspicious content intercepted by the secret police. Moscow, 1878.

innovation that might threaten the government's stranglehold on dissemination of information. In an empire where word was often law, writing held a particular power; it was admired and feared as a dangerous weapon, all the more so when backed by personal opinion. No surprise then that when the proposal to introduce postcards was initially put forward, officials from two regional postal departments expressed the concern that they might increase the likelihood of 'unpleasant confrontations between officials and members of the public.'[8]

Fears that postcards would be used for subversive ends were soon realised. In July 1873, the secret police, known at the time as the Third Section, sent a letter to the Interior Minister reporting that, 'postcards [with messages] lampooning women and government officials have started to appear, as have those indicating that the addressee belongs to some type of secret society.'[9] When questioned, postal officials acknowledged the issue, admitting that they had already received similar complaints from regional governors. The problem was what to do about it. Reading every single postcard was considered, but soon dismissed as impractical due to the number of languages used across the Empire, and the disruption it might cause to delivery times.[10]

The eventual outcome was an official circular issued on 13 August 1873, titled 'On the Inspection of Postcards'. It begins with a précis of the situation: 'From the very start [postcards] have been subject to misuse. People started sending postcards to private individuals and government officials with the most insulting and immoral content, and sometimes even with unsavoury illustrations. This has caused serious annoyance to those on the receiving end of such letters ... At first the Interior Ministry ascribed the appearance of significant quantities of improper postcards to the novelty of this form of correspondence, and suggested that it would die down of its own accord, but after a year and half, the misuse of postcards has not in the least abated.'[11]

The proposed solution was two-fold. First, an amendment was made to the postal regulations to include a specific injunction against any content contravening 'the law, public order, morals or decency.' Postcard senders were warned that any messages found to be violating these precepts would not be delivered. Second, officials were instructed to inspect as many postcards as they could without delaying delivery times. Suspicious items were to be sent to the main Postal Department on the 1st and 15th of each month, and from there they would be forwarded to the political police. These packages, the circular added, should be marked 'secret', an indication that the authorities had no wish to alert the public to the fact their mail was anything but.[12]

Inflammatory cards, including those with revolutionary content, were soon unearthed.[13] In autumn 1878, postal workers intercepted four postcards sent from Moscow to Saint Petersburg. Each contained a short note and coded figures purporting to relate to chess moves: 'I completely agree with your suggestions for moving D5,' reads one message dated 29 October. 'Our club is growing bit by bit, but the players are all bad – we haven't yet been able to have a single decent game.' These missives may have been entirely innocent, but the Third Section certainly did not think so. Across a covering note describing the postcards as suspect, an agent has scrawled: 'Chess!!!' – the three exclamation marks sufficient to suggest contempt for the very idea that they might have anything to do with the game.[14]

But despite repeated attempts by the Imperial authorities to prove the existence of a nationwide revolutionary conspiracy, it would be at least another twenty-five years before one materialised. While it is likely that these four postcards were written by political radicals, the majority of seditious postcards discovered by the police and postal workers in the late nineteenth century were sent not by revolutionaries intent on overthrowing the government, but by disgruntled individuals with little or no redress against an all-powerful state staffed by an incompetent and self-serving bureaucracy. With extraordinary rapidity, the postcard had become a vehicle for popular dissent – a much-needed steam-valve in the Russian pressure-cooker.

Taxation and social injustice were a particular source of anger, as is shown by an incident involving a fifty-nine-year-old townsman from Voronezh

Province. In December 1898, Pavel Evstifev sent a postcard to the head of his local council complaining about having to pay for grazing rights: 'Why are we not given grass and forest land for free? You are rich and stuff your pockets, while we get nothing at all.'[15] More seriously, Evstifev also made disparaging comments about the Tsar. The police, however, came to the conclusion that the message had been composed 'without malicious intent,' and they blamed the content, which the illiterate townsman had dictated to his 12-year-old neighbour, on the 'coarseness and ignorance of the accused.' For this lack of refinement, Evstifev was sentenced to seven days in gaol.[16]

As officials had foreseen, postcards undoubtedly did lead to an increase in the number of direct confrontations between state and society, but it would be many years before the pictures on the front could catch up with the writing on the back. Nevertheless, their subversive worth was already clear. For the revolutionaries, postcards were cheap and convenient aids to conspire, narrowing the distance between like-minded souls, but for the nation at large they heralded something far more momentous; they brought the popular voice within earshot of the regime. It had been mere decades since access to printed material had begun to extend beyond the elite, but already powerful new public spaces were being created over which the state was struggling to exert full control.

Russian Picture Postcards

The Russian government lifted the ban on private production in October 1894. Earlier images are known, but the first picture cards to carry the imprimatur of the censor are a set of Moscow views dated 18 November 1895.[17] These are of comparatively good quality, but in common with many contemporary Russian postcards, the designs are strongly derivative of European 'Gruss aus' ['Greetings from'] counterparts. Printing facilities were still under-developed, and it would be some time before Russian cards acquired either the decorative refinement or mass character of the images being produced in other, more industrialised countries. In the first few years after the restrictions were lifted, few Russian printers were capable of creating anything other than small runs of simple photographic town views.

This gap in manufacturing capability was filled by non-native publishers, who became a dominant force in Russia's postcard industry in its early years. Many foreign firms set up offices in Saint Petersburg through which to offer their own designs, and process commissions from local publishers.[18] Given the advantage provided by access to better-equipped printing facilities abroad, particularly in Germany, few Russian enterprises could challenge their supremacy. Indeed, prior to the 1900s, only one came close. Founded in 1882 as a charitable organisation for destitute nurses from the Russo-Turkish

War, the Society of Saint Eugenia became both the first and the foremost indigenous enterprise to publish artist-drawn picture postcards.[19]

The Society started producing decorative envelopes in 1896 and, encouraged by its success in this venture, published its first postcards in April 1898 (four watercolours on Russian themes by the artist Nikolai Karazin).[20] From fourteen works in the first year, production more than doubled in the second, and thereafter continued to expand at a steady pace until 1902. In May that year, Chairwoman Evdokiia Dzhunkovskaia wrote to the Interior Minister to solicit a monopoly on Russian picture cards and a ban on the sale of all foreign-made images. This bold request was refused, but the charity, which already had the unique privilege of publishing postcards of the Imperial Family, was instead given exclusive rights to artworks housed in the royal palaces.[21]

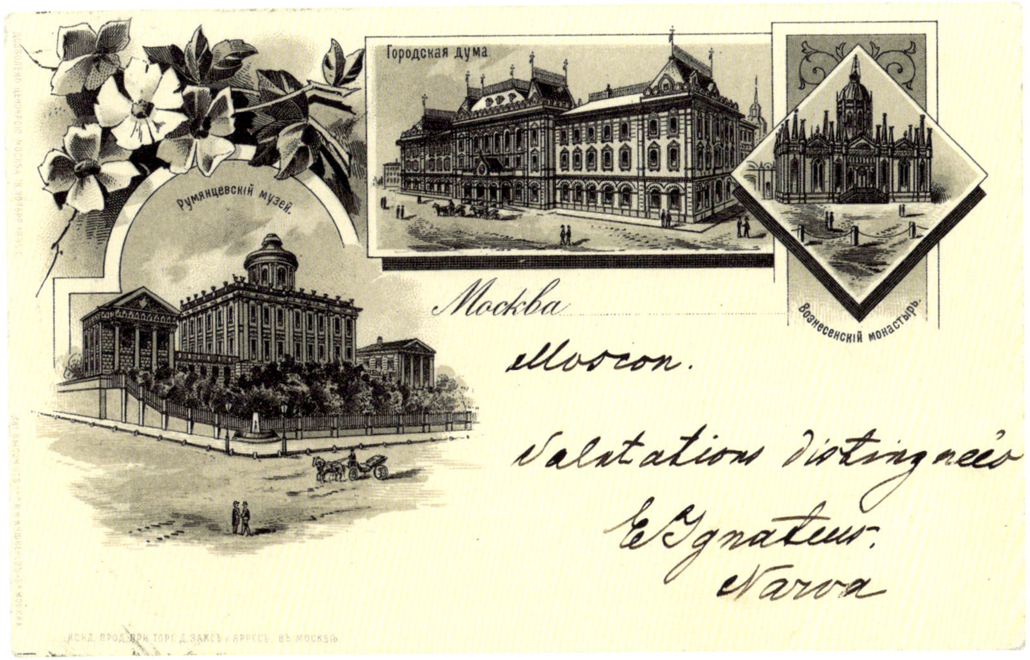

Anonymous artist. *Moscow.* Printed by I. N. Kushnerev and Co., Moscow, 18 November 1895. This is the earliest known postcard to have been approved by the censor.

This proved a decisive turning point, leading the Society to broaden its repertoire far beyond artist-drawn postcards to include photographic images of Imperial buildings, paintings, and numerous other items of national patrimony. Its output, further boosted the following year by images relating to the 200th anniversary of the founding of Saint Petersburg, would go on to comprise over 6,400 different designs. The charity had no real competitors in Russia during the first years of its existence, either to rival the quantity and quality of its production, or to replicate the high standards of artistic design. Nevertheless, it blazed a bright trail, and many firms were quick to try to follow in its footsteps.

Many of the earliest postcard publishers had existing links to the print trade. Book and print sellers were particularly active, among them Datsiaro, which had been in operation since the first half of the nineteenth century, and Felten, another well-established firm. Printers, notably including Levenson, and Sytin in Moscow, and Golike and Vilborg in Saint Petersburg (established in 1902) also published, as well as manufactured postcards. The same was true of photographic studios. The long-running firm of Scherer, Nabholz and Company started publishing extensive series of town views and character types from 1896 onwards. As the market took off, independent entrepreneurs also became heavily involved, as did charities and artistic institutions, particularly in the later 1900s.

Production was concentrated in Saint Petersburg, followed some way behind by Moscow, Kiev, Warsaw, and Riga. Few printers in these towns restricted themselves to postcards. The largest enterprises manufactured items ranging from books to posters, while many of the smaller firms were often local photographers with a modest sideline in postcards. Some issued their own original designs, but the majority were produced on commission. Postcard runs varied from a few hundred copies up to the high thousands, but outside the bigger cities, where production was limited by the availability of printing facilities, large editions were rare. The resulting works were sold across the Empire – through peddlers, bookshops, kiosks, stationery shops, chemists, at exhibitions, museums, telegraph offices, and railway stations.

Since a revision of the country's press laws in 1865 (another element of Alexander II's Great Reforms), the print industry had grown briskly, its partial release boosted by ongoing social and industrial development.[22] As the century drew to a close, the pace of expansion began to speed up, with technology and the coal of commercial competition feeding the rapacious engines of public appetite. By way of example, if in 1870 (its first year of publication), the circulation of Russia's foremost illustrated newspaper *Niva* [*Cornfield*] stood at 9,000, then by 1900 it was over 230,000.[23] Postcard publishers benefited greatly from this industry-wide surge, and as capitalist enterprise accelerated across Russia, new publishers and audiences emerged at all price levels.

Advances in printing processes helped to drive down production costs, and savings were in turn passed on to consumers. Colour postcards were still comparatively expensive, often double the price of black-and-white images, but by the mid-1900s there was a range of cards on offer, with prices tailored to suit most pockets. It was possible at this time for a specialist journal to talk about the postcard being as much the property of a 'dandy writing to his beautiful lover,' as it was of a 'poor soldier sending a letter to home to his peasant parents.'[24] Illiteracy was still an obstacle to mass-usage, particularly in the countryside, but writing services were available in urban areas, and the image itself could serve in place of a detailed message.

In 1904, Russia followed Britain and France in lifting a proscription against writing messages on the address side of postcards. A dividing line was added, and the whole of the front left free for the illustration. This allowed for more elaborate artistic designs, as well larger photographic images, and the move proved popular with publishers and collectors, who were fast becoming a prominent force in the postcard world. In April that same year the first dedicated Russian postcard journal appeared in Saint Petersburg. Much of *Domashnii muzei* [*The Home Museum*] was filled with advertisements promoting the wares of its proprietor, Nikolai Merder, but alongside elements of shameless self-promotion, room was also found for a few articles on postcard artists and collecting.

Merder, who had been printing postcards for around a year before he launched the journal, gives an indication of the attractive proposition that the medium must have presented to an ambitious young publisher. When he applied for permission to launch *Domashnii muzei*, he already had a number of failed magazine ventures behind him, and at the time was registered as the editor-publisher of the journals *Teatr i pesy* [*Theatre and Plays*] and *Zolotopromyshlennik* [*The Gold Industry Entrepreneur*]. Press industry officials noted drily that the former did not come out on time and the latter had yet to appear, but such trifling considerations were clearly no barrier to Merder and his next big business opportunity.[25]

Publishing Aims and Consumer Desires

Many Russian publishers were content to reproduce run-of-the-mill greetings cards, town views, landscapes, and portraits of popular figures, and the public was only too happy to buy them, but from the late nineteenth century onwards, progressive publishers and critics argued that postcards should be used to promote a carefully cultivated artistic and social agenda. In one of the earliest Russian discourses on picture postcards (published in 1899), the ethnographer and collector Natalia Shabelskaia pushed the idea that the postcard was a new form of aesthetic endeavour that should be taken seriously by artists, publishers and consumers alike. Its great advantage, as she saw it, was the ease with which the medium could be distributed among the masses.

Shabelskaia's plea for the postcard to be seen as a work of art was not simply a case of art for art's sake, but a reflection of her conviction that the postcard was a commodity that could be used as a force for the intellectual and aesthetic good of the nation. In 'A New Branch of Artistic Industry' she writes primarily about postcards from more established markets in Germany, Austria and France, but imagines how practices there might be applied more widely in Russia: 'Because of their affordability, postcards can be made available to everyone, penetrating into the deepest, most remote provinces and even villages, and in this way teach many people and develop artistic taste.'[26]

Mass production, however, threw up aesthetic as well as political challenges and Shabelskaia's suggestion that postcards be used as a way of promoting 'good' art was not universally popular. While acknowledging the merit of many of the illustrations, the influential critic Vladimir Stasov argued that postcards were an unsuitable method of artistic distribution because of the risk of them being postmarked, written on, dirtied, or simply treated without the respect that he believed fine art was due. 'It always seemed to me,' he wrote, 'that the extent to which many of the drawings are accomplished, elegant and interesting is reflected in equal measure by the unaesthetic and anti-artistic method of their dissemination.'[27]

Stasov's claim that mass-produced art was a contradiction in terms reflected wider concerns in Russia that commercialisation was beginning to erode the traditional boundaries between 'high' and 'low' culture. In the minds of the intelligentsia, the emergence of a consumer society was causing both art and literature to become vulgarised.[28]

Irrespective of these objections, the belief that postcards could be used to influence the cultural sensibilities of the Russian population became an article of faith, repeated down the years in the editorials of every pre-revolutionary postcard journal. 'Apart from its convenience, elegance and interest, the postcard has one other important advantage, or more correctly – virtue: in reflecting our material needs it unnoticeably fosters our aesthetic feelings and develops our artistic taste,' declared Merder in 1904.[29] Three years later, the editor of the provincial journal *Otkrytka* [*Postcard*] described postcards in an almost identical manner as: 'one of the best and most wonderful methods of developing a feeling for aesthetics, artistry and taste in the most diverse strata of society.'[30]

In Russia, this idea was almost single-handedly pioneered by the Society of Saint Eugenia, for whom Shabelskaia's article might have stood as a manifesto.[31] The charity's primary aim was to raise money for humanitarian purposes – Dzhunkovskaia made it clear in her letter to the Interior Minister that the Society's postcards provided an invaluable source of income for its work – nevertheless, the overall thrust of her argument for awarding the Society a monopoly was based not on the organisation's philanthropic deeds, but on what she perceived as the importance of its role in promoting Russian art. 'In engaging the finest artists to work in the sphere of postcard design, the Society brings a noted benefit in elevating the artistic taste of the masses,' she declared.[32]

In 1904, the charity launched its own journal, edited by the artist Fedor Bernshtam, who also served as the librarian of the Imperial Academy of

Arts. *Otkrytoe pismo* [*The Postcard*] contained information on new publications, postcard artists and collecting, all of which was geared towards fostering demand for high-quality, well-designed cards by leading Russian artists. In the first issue of the new journal, the Society laid out its ethos, arguing forcefully for the need to combat 'anti-artistic publications done in a coarse and rudimentary, and at times debauched manner.'[33] It is evident from this that the Society saw itself as far more than just a charitable publisher; it was a self-proclaimed arbiter of 'good taste' with a firm duty to educate the masses.

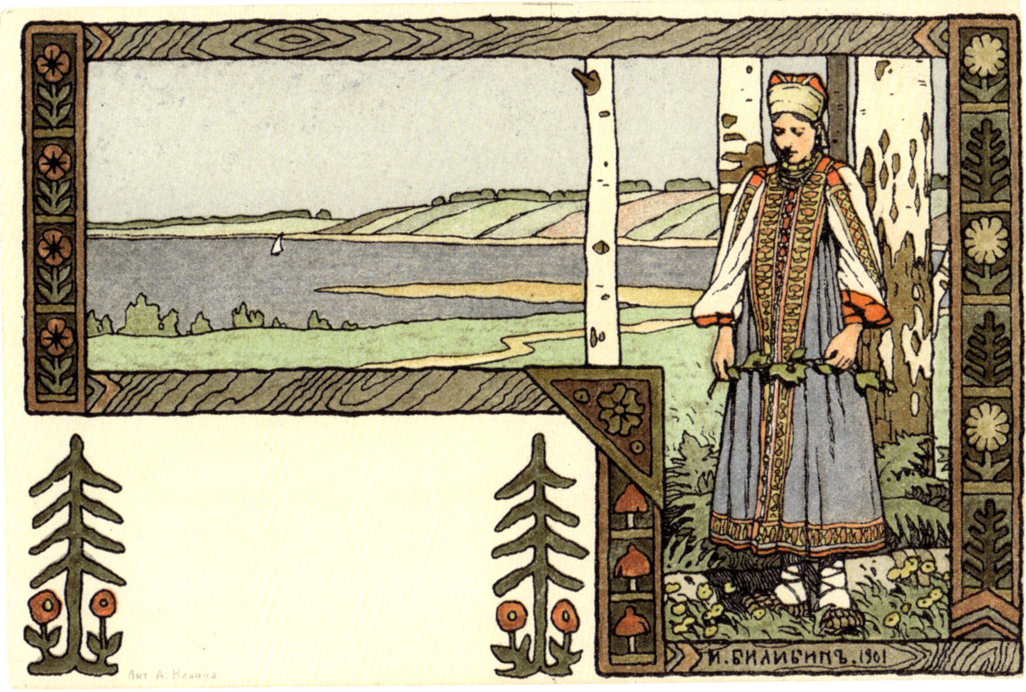

Ivan Bilibin. Untitled depiction of a peasant woman. Published by the Society of Saint Eugenia, Saint Petersburg, 1901.

Its first, and most critically acclaimed postcards were original artist-drawn images, many commissioned from painters associated with the World of Art Group, a loose affiliation of artists influenced by European Art Nouveau. Under the direction of the Society's secretary, Ivan Stepanov, leading adherents of the movement, including Leon Bakst, Ivan Bilibin, and Mstislav Dobuzhinskii, created a range of highly refined images that fused stylistic influences from Europe with a nationalist thematic orientation. In the Society's earliest postcards, galloping troikas, chocolate box children, and romanticised visions of peasant life abounded, while in 1899, the anniversary of the birth of Alexander Pushkin served as the pretext for one of the charity's first themed groupings.

The home-grown subject matter of the Society's postcards tied in with a rising sense of national awareness, providing consumers with appealing, decorative objects to use and collect, while at the same time promoting the various achievements of the country's artistic, literary and historical past. On the international stage, the postcards served as ambassadors, highlighting Russia's accomplishments to foreign audiences, but within the country itself, they were items of cultural indoctrination consciously designed to popularise what was deemed to be proper art and correct civic identity. And in this respect, they can be seen as an integral part of the Slavic Revival movement.

The draw of these postcards may have lain in their decorative appeal, but what consumers were actually buying was a sophisticated piece of ideological propaganda, promoting Tsarist nationalism, aestheticism and philanthropy. The Society's influence extended deep into all three areas; it upheld an idealised conception of the country's Imperial past and present, popularised the work of Russian Style Moderne artists and, crucially, showed that postcards could be used effectively as vehicles for charitable fundraising. The latter custom was later copied by many other organisations in Russia, including revolutionary groups.

The Society of Saint Eugenia's role as a national tastemaker reflected its exalted position among the social elite. The charity's patron was Nicholas I's granddaughter, Princess Eugenia Maximilianovna of Leuchtenberg, and Empress Alexandra was among the readers of its journal.[34] Furthermore, Princess Eugenia, and Grand Duchesses Elizaveta Fedorovna and Olga Alexandrovna also contributed designs for its postcards. This fact, allied with the quality and comparative expense of the images, which cost between five and twenty-five kopecks, naturally conferred a sense of exclusivity on their output. This was reinforced by the knowledge that many of the cards were used and collected by members of the Imperial Family.

Collecting had begun to take off in Russia around the turn of the century – a few years after the pastime had first caught on in Europe. Off the back of this burgeoning interest, many publishers started tailoring their wares towards collectors, numbering their postcards in sequences and issuing themed sets. Collecting was restricted by the need for a disposable income, but among the better-off the hobby became a fashionable pursuit, particularly among women. According to one journal, it was 'very much the done thing in so-called 'high society', where it is considered a sign of good taste … It is a must for every young woman or lady from 'society' to have a few albums of postcards, which can serve as a good adornment to a living room.'[35]

Postcards may have been marketed as an opportunity for cultural improvement, but what this meant for many was an opportunity for social improvement. Like paintings on a wall, they were seen as reflections of a person's educational standing and refinement, by extension serving as a physical representation of their ideological outlook on the world. In common with a gentleman's library, a well put-together collection of postcards was appreciated as the mark of a civilised mind. One contemporary commentator remarked that it was rare 'to find a person claiming to be cultured who did not possess even the most limited collection of postcards, bought haphazardly or received through the post.'[36]

An indication of the various interests of Russian collectors can be found in specialist journals, which regularly included sections for individuals who were looking to exchange images through the post. Many wanted copies of famous paintings or town views. Countess Brevern in Saint Petersburg, for example, asked for postcards of buildings, especially churches, and pictures by well-known artists. Others, such as engineer Franz Stanevich from Tiumen, had baser needs. He placed an advertisement in the same journal asking for correspondents to send him 'pictures of beautiful women,' a preference echoed by Nikolai Nikitin, who wrote that he was looking to 'feed a weakness for pretty female portraits.'[37]

Then as now, members of the public were rather less concerned than the critics about the importance of exercising 'good taste'. Indeed, original artist-designed postcards were not nearly as popular among the masses as might have been hoped. This was in part due to their expense, but a letter sent to the Society of Saint Eugenia in 1905 indicates that publishers regularly fell out of sync with the wants of their consumers. 'Might it be possible for the committee to swap certain cards,' asked a regional agent, 'for ones with greater popular appeal, such as, pictures of horses, cows, dogs and other similar images?'[38] Unsurprisingly, many firms were only too happy to oblige the banality of public taste – Merder, never one to miss an opportunity, had a special section devoted to 'beauties'.[39]

Although late in emerging and still embryonic, Russia was becoming a consumer society. Popular taste was becoming a force, and in response publishers were looking both to reflect and shape demand.

For the purchaser, postcards were appealing because their format was accessible and their content subjective. The sheer range of different designs and themes on offer allowed the medium to serve in any number of different roles: a method of communication to break down geographical barriers, a way of sharing experiences and marking significant dates, or on a more intimate level, a reflection of personal belief, cultural interests or inner desires. Postcards were pocket-sized vehicles for social, intellectual, and sexual exploration, all contained within an attractive, affordable and widely available set-up. Dependent on one's outlook, they could provide entry into a world of artistic finesse or serve as a pass into a den of aesthetic iniquity.

Whatever the reason for their acquisition, the practice of collecting postcards reinforced a change in perception about the role of the medium in contemporary society. A number of early aficionados, particularly of townscapes, maintained that postcards were not worth collecting, indeed, should not even be called postcards, unless they had been sent through the post.[40] A different type of collector, however, came to predominate, one who saw them not principally as items of written communication, but as decorative objects that could be admired and purchased for their aesthetic merits alone. As one enthusiast wrote, 'I value my postcards more when they are unmarked rather than received through the post, usually all stained and crumpled.'[41]

Education and Advertising

The Society of Saint Eugenia was described in one journal as being near unique among Russian publishers for its maintenance of a dedicated artistic programme.[42] This may be true, but it glosses over the fact that the dissemination of 'aesthetic culture' in postcard form went far beyond the production of expensive original designs. Those who could not afford to commission new works instead reproduced images from the art historical canon. Merder, for example, made his money by offering 'the finest works of art by Russian and foreign artists.'[43] His stock included pictures by the popular European painters Franz Stuck and Sascha Schneider, as well as works by Leonardo and Raphael, and Russian artists such as Vladimir Makovskii, and Ilia Repin.

Long after most Western nations had moved on to better quality reproductions, cheap photographic copies of celebrated artworks remained widespread in Russia. Articles in *Domashnii muzei* repeatedly emphasise the importance of such postcards as 'affordable distributors of artistic taste and knowledge,' with one writer gushing: 'what a space in which to express artistic taste, and to develop and educate it.'[44] Such postcards served an important role, enabling those who could not travel abroad to become acquainted with the history and culture of the world, and in a nation as large as Russia, help to spread imagery of the country's treasures and triumphs to people living outside the major cities.

At ten kopecks a piece, Merder's images were not especially cheap, but even further down the price scale postcards were still seen as possessing an invaluable facility for instruction. Their relative affordability, compared to other methods of pictorial reproduction, presented an opportunity for teaching the masses that was stressed by all early admirers.[45] 'The essential significance of the picture postcard is clear to everyone, but it is of even greater benefit to people who do not have the means to give their children a proper education,' wrote Shabelskaia.[46] Postcards, therefore, were not solely a way of improving taste; in the absence of decent schools, critics hoped that they might serve as an 'educational guide to all branches of art and knowledge.'[47]

This emphasis on the importance of the postcard as a 'tool for spreading knowledge' prompted publishers to produce sets of images specifically designed for schoolchildren. The Society of Saint Eugenia, for example, took part in a special commission to publish a series of postcards for young students learning history, geography, zoology and botany.[48] This use of the medium as an educational device directly paralleled similar efforts in book publishing, particularly by Ivan Sytin, who pioneered the introduction of popular prints and cheap illustrated pamphlets into the classroom. Print industry expansion had enabled the production and distribution of printed material to become democratised, and with it the power to educate and influence the population.

The didactic intent of many publishers during this era reflects a larger shift in Russian politics, which saw the state begin to loosen its grip a fraction in order to make way for a limited degree of civic involvement in the administration of the Empire. Prior to the nineteenth century, philanthropy was the sole preserve of the elite, operating under the direct patronage of the Tsar, but Alexander II's local government and municipal reforms had aided the creation of new social institutions, notably including schools and voluntary associations. The deployment of postcards as educational devices can be seen as evidence of the gradual replacement of the state as the sole actor capable of ensuring the good of the people.[49]

Postcards were also used to educate taste in its most literal sense. The primary focus of early imagery was on fine art, scenic views, and popular culture, but it rapidly became apparent to retailers that postcards could be deployed to sway people financially, as well as aesthetically. The earliest advertising cards, which first appeared in the 1880s, were no more than messages printed on the back of government blanks, but within a few years many enterprises, notably including the Singer Sewing Company and the chocolate factory Einem, started producing branded picture cards.[50] The practice was particularly prevalent among the food and drink industry, where postcards were often given away as free promotional gifts or used as prizes.

The custom of using postcards as a means to advertise was in part an attempt to hijack a popular print medium, but their ability to communicate a message directly, and in a more intimate setting than could be achieved through posters and advertising hoardings proved deeply alluring. Many years before the invention of television, picture postcards were a way for commercial firms to gain entry into the home, and moreover to remain in situ for months and even years afterwards. On a conscious level these postcards reflected the personal and aesthetic interests of the consumer, but at the same time they worked to advance the aims of the publisher, steadily pressing their cause with each admiring glance.

In early twentieth-century Russia, postcards were seen as far more than cheap communication devices for the masses, or frivolous playthings for the upwardly socially mobile. For a significant proportion of purchasers, publishers, and commentators the picture postcard was an artistic object with a serious social and cultural role to play in the life of all classes. Long before revolutionaries started printing anti-government images in Russia, the medium was regarded as a device for furthering particular ideas and beliefs, be it in matters of taste or knowledge. And if postcards could serve as a commercial and ideological conduit for art, food and learning, then why not also politics?

Political Imagery and Censorship

On 16 July 1870, one day after the Prussian army's mobilisation for war against France, a bookseller named Augustin Schwartz printed one of the very first illustrated postcards. The image was simple: a stereotype of artillerymen printed on the reverse of a standard correspondence card.[51] A few months later, in besieged Paris, a system of balloon post was introduced to enable the population to communicate with the world outside. As they weighed considerably less than letters, pre-printed agitational postcards (carrying rousing patriotic messages) became the city's main form of postal correspondence. Together, these examples set a precedent for mixing postcards and politics that would be taken up by many others during the Franco-Prussian War and beyond.

Early political postcards reflected national causes, whether through portraits of heads of state, depictions of armies, or commemorations of historic events. Most were photographic or realist images, but in the mid-1890s, caricatures and cartoons also started appearing on the market. Within a few years, satirical postcards had grown to encompass all the major news events, from conflict – particularly the Boxer Rebellion and the Boer War – to anti-Semitism, which received an unwelcome boost during the second trial of Captain Dreyfus in 1899. Whatever their mode of depiction, most of these political postcards were consciously patriotic; oppositional images, especially those that espoused alternative forms of governance, were much rarer and far more problematic.

The first postcards to advocate socialist ideas openly are believed to be a set of two May Day pictures printed in Vienna in 1890, one an excoriation of capitalism, and the other a celebration of labour.[52] Earlier that year, draconian Anti-Socialist Laws in Austria and Germany had been allowed to lapse, leading to a near instantaneous outpouring of leftist printed works. May Day postcards lauding the heroism of the proletariat and advancing the cause of an eight-hour working day quickly proved popular among workers in both countries, offering them a simple and attractive way of keeping in touch with their families, while at the same time helping to raise awareness of the key issues that affected their daily working lives.

Latitude in the realms of socialist imagery did not, however, mean complete freedom for publishers in all areas. In 1900, the Russian Post and Telegraph Journal published a translation of an Austrian article reporting that the authorities in the capital had confiscated 'many postcards with political caricatures, photographs and drawings of indecent content.' Such were the number of subversive cards in circulation that the Viennese censor had issued the police with a special album containing over 200 different illegal images.[53]

This report was printed in the journal without comment, but the very fact of its reproduction in Russia shows a deep wariness of the postcard medium on the part of Imperial officials. Postcards were a platform from which to pass comment on the social and political issues of the day; they presented the public with an alternative to the official narrative, and while most were legally produced, their potential for subversion kept all governments on their toes. In Russia, where a tight lid was kept on any form of dissent, unease about the dangers of postcards had not diminished.

With very few exceptions, all forms of printed material, from works of literature down to designs for caramel wrappers, were subject to a system of preliminary censorship. Until the system was overhauled during the 1905 Revolution, the Russian Legal Code's 'Statute on Censorship and the Press' of 1890 defined the legal circumstances under which picture postcards could be printed.[54] This decree made it a requirement for all prints and drawings to be submitted to the regional censorship committee before publication. If approved, the printer was then mandated to add the date the work had passed the censor, and the name of the firm, and city of manufacture.[55] This whole process was overseen by the Main Administration for Press Affairs, a subsidiary department of the Interior Ministry.[56]

If postcards carrying political and religious imagery were published relatively freely in other countries, then in Russia both were liable to arouse the ire of the censor. Cartoons on Russia-related subject matter were printed abroad from the late nineteenth century onwards, but inside the country itself anything that opposed the status quo was strictly forbidden. Before the outbreak of hostilities with Japan in 1904, even pro-government imagery was circumscribed, largely limited to ceremonial events and portraits of long dead heroes. Pictures of the Imperial Family were about the closest postcards ever came to making a direct political statement, yet while freely printed in the rest of Europe, their production was prohibited in Russia before 1900 and remained partially restricted until 1910.[57]

Publishers and printers had a good understanding of what the Administration would and would not allow; nevertheless, the authorities still found reasons to refuse permission for certain images. The censorship committees were sticklers for the regulations, which provided them with generous scope to prohibit any work that aroused their disapproval.[58] Sometimes, as with the decision in 1904 to ban a postcard illustrating Russian coinage for fear that it might be mistaken for real currency, the censorial thought process is easily understood, especially in a country with such high rates of illiteracy.[59] But other cases, such as a ban that same year on a postcard depicting Vasilii Surikov's painting *Boyarina Morozova* (1887), only serve to illustrate the regime's stifling hold over all printed matter.

As the censor pointed out, Morozova was against the doctrinal changes brought in by Patriarch Nikon in 1653, and in Surikov's picture the crowd displays unambiguous sympathy towards her. The censor, however, was just as troubled about the method of its reproduction as he was about the painting, which had first been exhibited back in 1887: 'In view of the fact that this picture is clearly meant for popular publication, the censor does not consider it possible to allow its manufacture, since it might fall into the hands of Old Believers and be used by them as a tool for spreading their teachings.'[60] The censor thus saw the postcard not only as a weapon for propagandising seditious opinions, but also as a threat to the regime's ability to maintain popular authority.

At times, the harshness of officials surprised even seasoned publishers. In August 1903, the Main Administration for Press Affairs wrote an apologetic letter to the Society of Saint Eugenia to let them know that the censor had refused permission for reproductions of three statues of female nudes in the Hermitage collections. These were all celebrated works, not least the *Tauride Venus* – the first Classical sculpture brought to Russia; nevertheless, the purse-lipped morality of the censor dictated that it was 'improper' for images of naked women to be reproduced in postcard form. The Administration did, however, say that if these images had been published in an art history book they would have been allowed.[61] Again, the danger lay as much in the medium as in the message.

Few of the images submitted to the censor during this period were intended to subvert, even those that carried notionally controversial subject matter. Witness, for example, the outrage that greeted the decision in 1903 to ban a set of images of Chita on account of their inclusion of two buildings constructed by a group of rebellious army officers exiled to the town some eighty years previously. The publisher fired off an indignant letter, arguing that, 'talking or writing about the Decembrists stopped being considered a crime a long time ago,' and insisting, therefore, that the ban was 'illegal and incorrect.'[62] But however tenuous their suspicions, the Administration was ever alert to the potential for popular revolt and the role that postcards might play in encouraging it.

These examples provide a vivid illustration of the various limits imposed on postcard production in Russia; nevertheless, they are comparatively uncommon. The threat of administrative punishment and financial loss was sufficient to make most publishers operate their own system of self-censorship, and as a result the prohibition of images was only an irregular occurrence. As far as can be ascertained, the Saint Petersburg Censorship Committee forbade postcards on fewer than five separate occasions in 1904, and only once for overtly political reasons.[63] Anti-government pictures could still be printed underground, but as long as the press laws stood firm and publishers remained compliant, there was no way for seditious imagery to be mass produced.

If most enterprises obeyed the spirit of the law, then not all were as diligent in adhering to the letter. Postcards do not appear in the censor's records nearly as often as one might expect, suggesting that as the industry expanded manufacturers became increasingly lax about submitting their wares.[64] This does not, however, mean that publishers and printers sought to, or could easily get away with producing or selling anti-government imagery.

A further line of defence against subversion was provided by the Inspectorate of Printing Houses and the Book Trade, which was responsible for monitoring the manufacture and sale of printed works across the Russian Empire.[65] A licence was required to operate a printing facility, and to sell printed material, and the Inspectorate, which was attached to the regional governor's office, carried out regular checks on all registered individuals and enterprises.

Backed up by the police and their informants, officials from the Inspectorate fought an ongoing battle to eradicate illegal postcards of all types, notably uncensored works, unauthorised portraits of the Tsar, and anything containing pornographic, religious, or revolutionary content.[66] Although there were undoubtedly many images, particularly ones imported from abroad, that did slip through the net, the combined forces of the Interior Ministry constituted an effective guard against any individual brave or foolish enough to consider the possibility of printing or distributing seditious postcards.

Revolutionary Usage

Restricted from using postcards as pictorial propaganda, the revolutionaries continued to deploy the medium as an epistolary weapon. In the thirty years since their introduction, frustration at the state of Russia had grown to such an extent that some were now openly predicting a revolution. In June 1903, postal workers in Minsk Province came across an unstamped postcard carrying an unsavoury, but increasingly commonplace message. On one side was scrawled: 'Nicholas II is an impostor, an evil-doer and a thief.' And on the other: 'Hooray, Hooray, political freedom, hooray. You know how it was in Serbia, and so it will be with Nicholas II.'[67] The culprit was never found, but it was not as if a police investigation were required to divine the meaning.

Since 1873 the government's toolbox of repressive measures had expanded considerably. By the early 1900s, the postal departments of Saint Petersburg, Moscow, Warsaw, Kiev, Odessa all contained so-called 'black offices' – secret departments set up to perlustrate mail.[68] The multi-lingual staff in these offices monitored post travelling through these areas from the standpoint of internal and external security.[69] Although the task was an overwhelming one, years of experience, and no doubt a highly suspicious mind, enabled them to see trouble in the most innocent-looking of white envelopes. Even if a postcard with an incendiary illustration or message was concealed from view, there was still a very real possibility of discovery.

One way to get around the black offices was to employ cryptic allusions, but this method also had its shortcomings. At times the code words used by the revolutionaries were all-too easily deduced, the cipher more suitable to fooling schoolboys than agents of the Imperial police. 'The huntsman we spoke about is alive and well and living in Riazan and is prepared to sell us some hunting dogs,' reads one letter intercepted in 1905. 'The dogs are fantastic, although they are not pure breeds – that is to say they are petit bourgeois rather than aristocratic ... good luck with the hunt you have organised for the spring.' Beneath the excerpt a well-informed policeman has written: 'Obviously they are talking about printing presses.'[70]

Messages were also written in cipher and invisible ink, but a more secure method was to use the postcard illustrations themselves as a code. It was best to send 'anodyne greetings on birthdays, name days or on the occasion of a marriage,' wrote the Socialist-Revolutionary leader, Viktor Chernov, 'the text meant nothing, but the illustration, say for example if it was of male figures, this would signify that the task had gone well, but if it was of female figures then this would mean difficulties and failure.'[71] Sexual politics aside, Chernov shows that by the early years of the new century, the postcard had become a familiar and valuable tool in the revolutionary armoury.

For reasons of convenience as much as security, the majority of postcards sent by the revolutionaries in Russia in the early 1900s were not used to communicate political messages, but rather more prosaically, to relay everyday information to friends and family. The primary contact that most activists had with the medium was therefore practical rather than ideological, and in this respect at least, they were no different from the rest of the population. Even as dedicated a rabble-rouser as Vladimir Lenin used to send regular messages to his mother and sisters, most containing nothing more than mundane updates on his wellbeing, and occasionally, news of the odd Swiss walking holiday.[72]

Internal exiles and political prisoners also relied on postcards as an easily available and above all cheap method of communication. Picture cards and the messages they carried were very often the only tangible link that detainees and exiles had to the world outside, and as such they provided a significant source of comfort, connecting them in real terms with day-to-day events in areas beyond their immediate area of confinement. For the radicals therefore, postcards were not only devices for insulting the regime and supporting political networks, but also emotional crutches that helped to sustain them during their long and bitter fight for change.

⁂

In the early years of the twentieth century the modern world was gripped by a mania for sending and receiving picture postcards. From prosaic beginnings as a form of postal communication, the postcard evolved into an object of high fashion and fine artistry. Patronised by all social classes, the medium became celebrated across the globe for its ability to entertain and educate in matters of culture, commerce and current affairs. 'In our age, picture postcards have been distributed extremely widely,' observed Nikolai Merder in 1904; 'you will find them everywhere, in Europe and in Australia, in capitals and provincial backwaters, in all shops and kiosks, on railway stations and in hotels, in expensive guesthouses and village huts.'[73]

In Russia, as elsewhere, postcards rose in tandem with the print trade as a whole, driven forward by unprecedented social and industrial change. By the early 1900s, access to printed wares had improved to such an extent that they had now begun to constitute a viable force of influence within the emerging public sphere. Strong measures were still in place to restrict the distribution of inflammatory material, but the extraordinary growth of private enterprise had critically undermined the regime's ability to control the flow of information to its people. Few legal publishers were yet willing to test the state's defences, but underground, postcards were steadily being transformed into messengers of popular discontent.

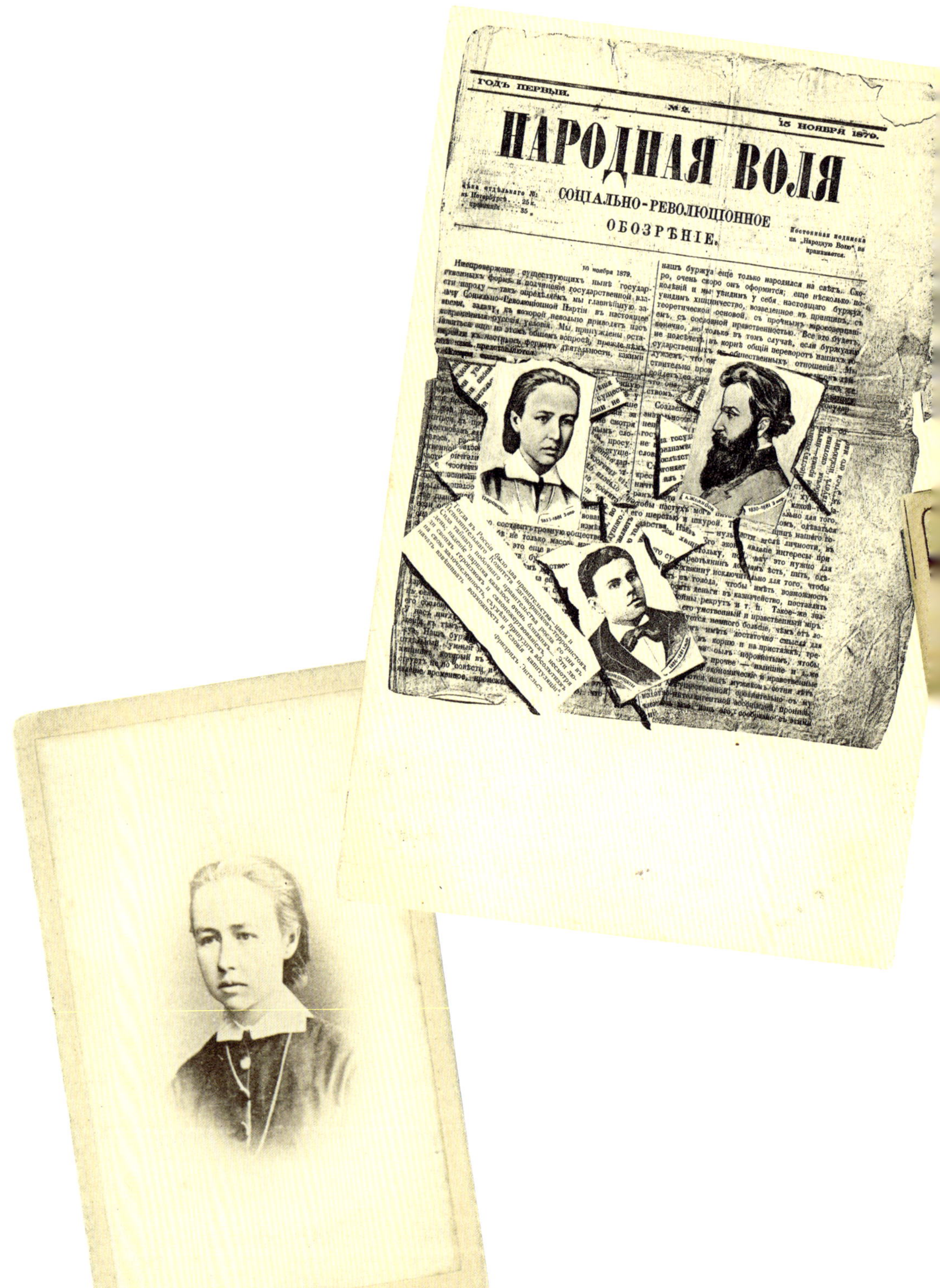

ГОДЪ ПЕРВЫЙ. № 2. 15 НОЯБРЯ 1879.

НАРОДНАЯ ВОЛЯ

СОЦІАЛЬНО-РЕВОЛЮЦІОННОЕ ОБОЗРѢНІЕ.

Цѣна отдѣльнаго №: въ Петербургѣ . . . 25 к. „ провинціи . . . 35 „

Постоянная подписка на „Народную Волю" не принимается.

10 ноября 1879.

Ниспровержение существующихъ нынѣ государственныхъ формъ и подчиненіе государственной власти народу — такъ опредѣляемъ мы главнѣйшую задачу Соціально-Революціонной Партіи въ настоящее время, задачу, къ которой невольно приводятъ насъ современныя русскія условія. Мы принуждены останавливаться еще на этомъ общемъ вопросѣ, прежде нѣмъ перейти къ частнымъ формамъ дѣятельности, какими ...

... нашъ буржуа еще только народился на свѣтъ. Скоро, очень скоро онъ оформится; еще нѣсколько поколѣній и мы увидимъ у себя настоящаго буржуа, увидимъ хищничество, возведенное въ принципъ, съ теоретической основой, съ прочнымъ міросозерцаніемъ, съ сословной нравственностью. Все это будетъ, конечно, но только въ томъ случаѣ, если буржуазію не подсѣчетъ въ корнѣ общій переворотъ нашихъ государственныхъ и общественныхъ отношеній. ...

OPPOSITION VISUAL PROPAGANDA

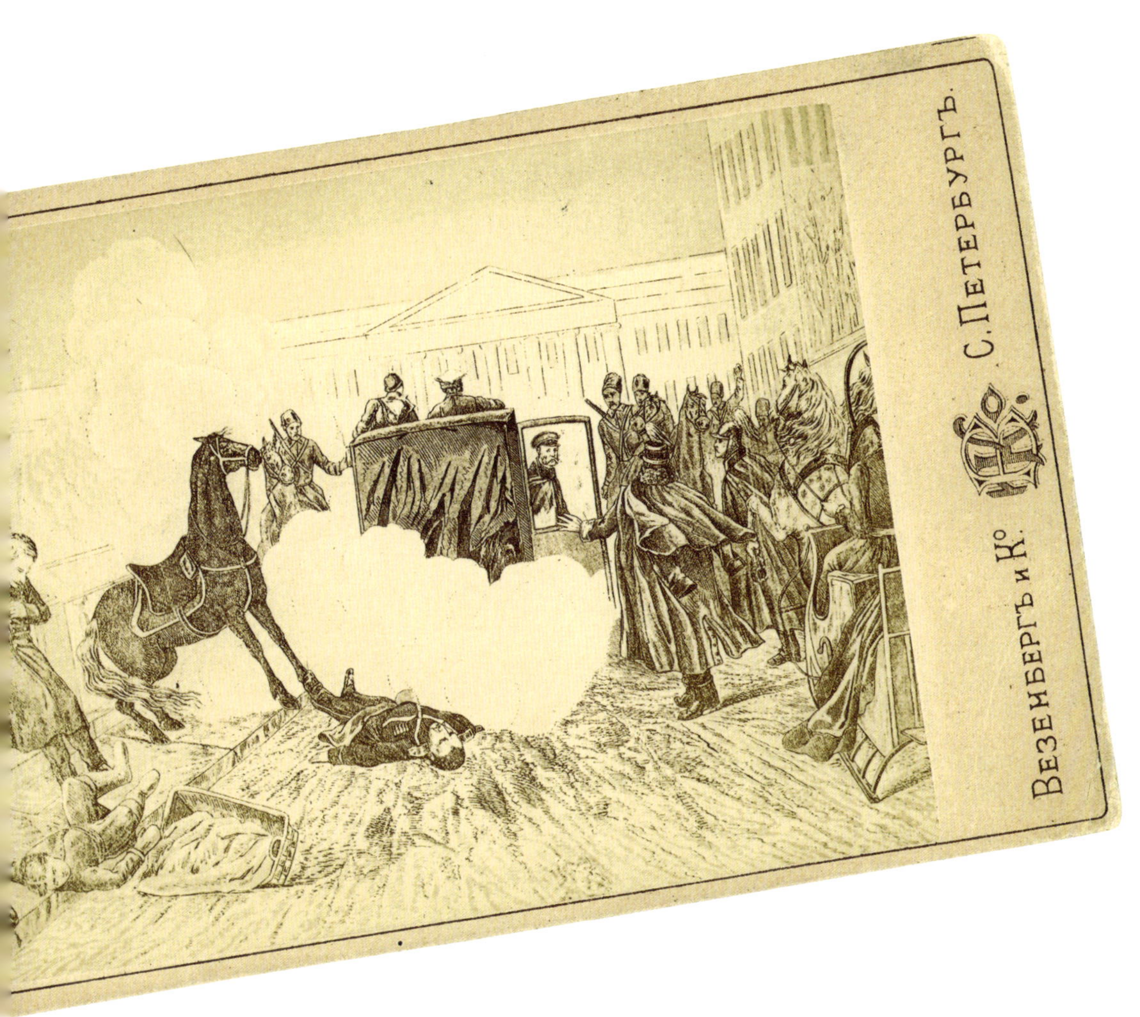

1866–1905

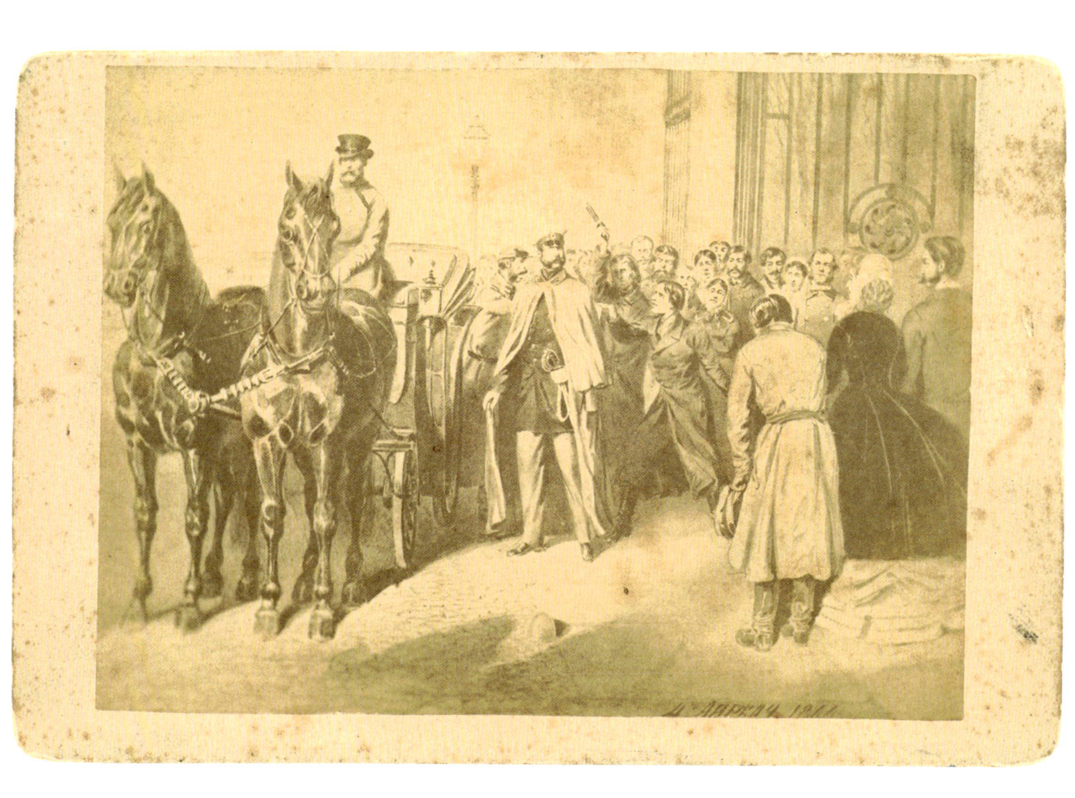

On his accession to the throne in 1894, Nicholas II inherited an unstable and under-developed country, beset by deep-rooted social and political unease. The task that lay before him, of steering Europe's last absolute monarchy safely through the waters of industrial and legislative reform, would have presented a challenge to any monarch, let alone a man of his political ability. Nicholas's views, however, never stretched much beyond his family and a firm belief in his own divine right to rule, and he was quick to disappoint all those who had hoped for progress. Early refusal to countenance the dilution of Imperial power set a rigid pattern for his reign during which dissent was dealt with brutally and reform was seen as a dirty word.

Over the preceding fifty years, the Russian Empire had undergone enormous social and economic upheaval. After defeat in the Crimean War, the government embarked on a decades-long, deeply inconsistent process of modernisation, kick-started in 1861 with Alexander II's decision to abolish serfdom. Change led not only to greater social opportunities, but also to increased resistance against the old ways. Discontent had been simmering among the upper echelons of Russian society for years, but the promise of reforms and their eventual stagnation helped to galvanise opposition to autocracy, first in disappointment at the terms of the Emancipation Act and later in response to the lack of any substantial developments within the political domain.

In its earliest incarnation, the liberation movement had no firm organisational structure, consisting largely of idealistic noblemen, who relied solely on the power of the written word to express their discontent. As the century progressed and Russia embarked on a period of rapid industrialisation, opposition to the state expanded in size and social composition, while at the same time, the Tsar's adversaries became more ideological and more radical in their struggle. Illegal revolutionary parties were formed to foment anti-autocratic sentiment, and at the dawn of the new century the need to sustain and subsidise their growth led to an increase in political coherence and organisation, as well as the advent of new fundraising activities, including postcard production.

For the revolutionaries to establish a viable following, they needed an effective way to spread their creed. Isolated attempts to set up propaganda operations had got underway in the earliest days of the movement, but the difficulty of accessing machine presses, noise and constant bustle, made mechanised printing a precarious activity.[1] As a result, most revolutionary material was manufactured abroad.[2] Inside Russia itself, output was largely restricted to leaflets and short proclamations, often printed by hectography, a homespun method of duplication invented in 1869. The resulting propaganda was poor in quality and limited to runs of around 200 copies, but the process caused minimal racket and demanded little by way of equipment and supplies.

Previous spread from left to right

Anonymous photographer. Carte de visite depicting Sofia Perovskaia. No publication details, Western Europe, 1880s.

Anonymous designer. Postcard depicting Sofia Perovskaia, Andrei Zheliabov, and Ignacy Hryniewiecki. Published by the Socialist-Revolutionary Party, Zurich, 1902.

Anonymous artist. Legally printed carte de visite depicting the assassination of Alexander II. Published by Wesenberg and Co., Saint Petersburg, 1880s.

Opposite

Pro-Tsarist carte de visite depicting Osip Komissarov saving the life of Tsar Alexander II. No publication details, circa 1866. Revolutionary cartes de visite were also produced of the would-be assassin Dmitrii Karakozov.

Visual propaganda was less common, even if in principle it held great promise. Pictures, cartoons, and caricatures were an uncomplicated way of conveying revolutionary ideas to a largely illiterate population, moreover one that already had a long tradition of absorbing religious and historical information through illustrated narrative. Their decorative appeal and comparatively light tone provided a valuable alternative to the heavy theoretical texts that characterised the majority of revolutionary propaganda. But even if this was appreciated at the time, and it is not always clear that it was, practical considerations often hampered output, not least a chronic lack of funds and personnel, as well as the absence of any established contacts among proficient artists willing to produce subversive imagery.

Modern technology was an essential prerequisite for the emergence of mass opposition parties in Russia, for without the ability to produce and disseminate their ideas in quantity, the revolutionaries had no way of reaching the country's vast and scattered population. In the 1860s machine printing still lay largely beyond their reach, but photography, which was becoming widely available through cartes de visite, offered a potential alternative propaganda apparatus. Following the first attempt on Alexander II's life in 1866, portraits were printed both of the Tsar's alleged saviour and of his would-be assassin.[3] Although the latter were illegal and very finite in number, their appearance was a clear warning to the state that the Imperial narrative would no longer go uncontested.

The revolutionaries started making more concerted efforts to produce and use photographic propaganda in the 1870s. Around this time, a new generation of Russian radicals started to agitate for a more practical approach to social activism, arguing that the peasants were already on the road to revolt and that something now needed to be done to help them. In the summer of 1874, waves of idealistic young men and women travelled into the countryside in a largely spontaneous crusade that became known as 'going to the people.' Here, they attempted to speak directly to the rural multitude, whom they hoped to enlighten about the injustices of their existence. The peasants, however, met these Populist romantics with hostility and incomprehension, and most were soon rounded-up.

When police searched the detainees, some of the activists were discovered to be carrying cartes de visite adorned with photomechanical portraits of opposition political figures. A certain Lev Dymskii, for example, had images of the socialist philosopher Nikolai Chernyshevskii, and the peasant insurrectionist Emelian Pugachev, while fellow radical Leonid Popov was caught with a portrait of Maximilien de Robespierre.[4] The latter image was unmarked, but both of Dymskii's portraits carried the imprint of the Wesenberg Photographic Studio in Saint Petersburg, an enterprise well-known for its cartes de visite of prominent literary, artistic and historical figures.[5] Although such works were often manufactured underground, it appears that this was a case of legal material being put to illegal use.

Dymskii and Popov's cartes de visite, while no doubt also valued personal possessions, were intended to be used as portable instruction manuals through which to educate the masses in the history of political rebellion. Activists always placed a major emphasis on ideological tuition, and local peasant and worker study circles formed a vital part of their efforts to raise levels of political awareness. However, even with guided explanation, the problem of how to make revolutionary doctrine relevant to the everyday lives of the people remained a constant headache.[6] In the memorable phrase of one leading subversive, theoretical ideas 'bounced off the Russian masses like peas off a wall.'[7] Most visual propaganda therefore remained in the hands of those already committed to the cause.

For the activists themselves, revolutionary cartes de visite were an aid to enlightenment. Hidden away from prying eyes in desks and drawers, portraits of revolutionary heroes were kept as objects of personal contemplation, the secret totems of a very dangerous creed. Here, they served as ideological comfort rags, creating an outlet for caged thoughts, and helping to establish, sustain and reinforce political belief. Revolutionaries isolated through political misdeeds found them a particular source of solace. Lenin, for example, had with him an album of portraits while in Siberian exile in the early 1900s, which included images of Emile Zola, Alexander Herzen, Dmitrii Pisarev and Chernyshevskii.[8]

The emergence of photomechanical propaganda marked the beginnings of a more structured approach, not only towards the production of anti-government visual material, but also towards the process of opposition itself. In the following decades, vague ideas that something must be done hardened around the fates of martyr-revolutionaries and theoreticians, whose deeds and doctrines were perpetuated through photographic portraiture.[9] The significance of revolutionary cartes de visite therefore lies both in the semi-industrialised method of their production, which set a clear precedent for later mass distribution, and in what they said about the movement itself: from a loose gathering of individuals, the liberation movement was acquiring a history, as well as a form and a face. In short, it was becoming self-aware.

New Revolutionary Parties

The ongoing failure of attempts to convert the peasantry, and the excessive response of the government, pushed many Populist activists into taking a more extreme stance against the autocratic regime. This eventually led to a schism in the early liberation movement between those who believed that violence constituted an admissible form of attack against the regime and those who saw it as an aberration. In 1879, a new, more radical organisation emerged from this division. Named Narodnaia Volia or The People's Will, the Party distinguished itself by an impassioned belief in bringing about revolution through violent means. Its small cadre of fanatic adherents soon determined that their first and most important political objective was the death of the Tsar himself.

In March 1881, Narodnaia Volia succeeded in assassinating Alexander II. The killing was widely condemned, even by opponents of autocracy. Public speeches were made, poems composed and several lithographic broadsides produced commemorating the Tsar's life and untimely death.[10] Much of the public's initial goodwill, however, was lost with the decision to execute the perpetrators. To a concentrated hub of sympathisers, the revolutionary assassins were transformed into reformist martyrs, and none more so than leading conspirator Sofia Perovskaia. Fervent commitment and youthful features made Perovskaia an appealing figurehead, and for a movement in need of inspiration, she came to embody all the ideals of political sacrifice.[11]

Following the Tsar's murder, the secret police (now renamed the Okhrana) was reorganised and a major crackdown initiated against revolutionary groups.[12] Narodnaia Volia was destroyed and opponents of the regime fled the country in their droves, choosing a life of exile over possible execution or imprisonment. Under the rule of Alexander III, political reforms were shelved and further restraints brought to bear against the press and free society. None of these measures, however, could help solve the problem of how to modernise the country. In the eyes of the new autocrat, attempts to recharge the system through social and political reform had only ended in disaster. Nonetheless, something now had to take their place. The answer was partly found in industrialisation.

As a new age beckoned, small workshops, mills and factories sprung up across the country, drawing in vast numbers of people from the surrounding towns and villages. Between 1890 and 1900 the population of Saint Petersburg rose by forty percent, and that of Moscow by thirty percent.[13] But in the rush to embrace industrial change, the welfare of those who were doing the work was all too often neglected. Cramped and unsanitary housing was the norm, and most workers were forced to endure low wages and long hours. The mass aggregation of former peasants in towns and cities across the country de facto led to the creation of a new social force in Russia. Strikes were illegal, but the very possibility of economic opposition provided a way of exerting pressure on the state in a manner hitherto impossible.

By the turn of the century, Russia had developed a small industrial centre, but the majority of its population was still rural. Here, the situation remained dire, incentive enough for many to leave the countryside in search of a better life. The peasantry as a whole was enveloped in poverty, unable to cope with heavy taxes or meet redemption payments for land that they had always thought of as their own. Barren soil and outdated agricultural methods resulted in low yields, while poor weather conditions left farmers beholden to the mercies of the seasons. Widespread alcohol abuse and indolence had a further effect on productivity. A few enterprising smallholders prospered, but most were desperate, and outbreaks of violence and famine were common.

Inequality, poverty and economic development provided a fertile backdrop for the increase of revolutionary activity under Nicholas II. In the late nineteenth and early twentieth centuries, two new political parties were born, each with very different ideas about how to hasten the downfall of autocracy. The first to form, the Russian Social Democratic Worker's Party, was founded in Minsk in 1898. This organisation, firmly rooted in Marxist theory, held that economic factors were the ultimate determinants of change. Despite the overwhelmingly rural make-up of the Empire, the Social Democrats took it for granted that it was the proletariat and not the peasantry who would be at the vanguard of the country's soon-to-be-realised social and political transformation.

Their rivals in the Socialist-Revolutionary Party came together piecemeal around three years later. While acknowledging the importance of economic considerations, the Socialist-Revolutionaries took up the mantle of Populist tradition, maintaining a staunch faith in the peasantry as a revolutionary force. The Party was influenced by Marxist ideas but was less determinist in outlook. Its leading lights argued that revolution could come about through a range of factors, and be driven by all of Russia's social estates, from the peasants to the intelligentsia.[14] Arguments over the merits of these two creeds played out endlessly, and although both organisations collaborated at times against a common enemy, they remained steadfast opponents, rarely missing an opportunity to exchange ideological insults.

Each party had their own small cells of activists in localities across Russia, but the majority of their planning, theorising and fundraising was carried out in Western Europe, where the leadership of both groups was based. The European continent had long provided a haven for dissidents, but over recent decades the Russian communities in exile had been dramatically boosted by large numbers of students, Jews and revolutionaries. Here, radical activists had a much freer hand, as well as a ready audience among the expatriate diaspora. Outside the confines of the Empire, there was less risk of arrest, printers were easily found and, crucially, access to the retail infrastructure of the publishing industry was a matter of money, not politics.

Growth Propaganda Production in Russia

As strikes increased and elements of the population became more receptive to opposition ideas, revolutionary propaganda, including visual material, started becoming more commonplace in Russia. Much of the latter was

After Nikolai Lokhov. *The Pyramid.* Hectograph published by the Socialist-Revolutionary Party, Ekaterinoslav, early 1900s.

unoriginal – works were often copied from foreign publications or from cartoons made abroad by revolutionary exiles – but increasingly, subversive images were being reproduced and sold inside the country itself. One individual who became tangentially involved was a lawyer from Vitebsk named Genrikh Teodorovich. While on a trip to Saint Petersburg in January 1902, Teodorovich paid a newspaper vendor seventy-five kopecks for a photo-card titled *The Pyramid*, and on returning home, he asked a friend at a local photographic studio to make six duplicates.

The Pyramid, a satire of Imperial rule made in 1901 by the political émigré Nikolai Lokhov, illustrates the socialist view of the autocratic state, showing in detail how all elements of Russian society, from the Tsar to the bourgeoisie, combined to oppress the masses. The drawing was originally published in Geneva by the Union of Social Democrats Abroad, and it is commonly seen as the Social Democratic Party's first political cartoon.[15] In Russia, both its content and its revolutionary origin were deeply contentious, not to mention illegal, and soon after receiving the prints, Teodorovich and his photographer friend were arrested, apparently as the result of an informer at the studio where the images were reproduced.[16]

Small-scale underground production such as this enabled revolutionary imagery to circulate between close acquaintances, but there is evidence in Teodorovich's original manner of purchase to suggest both more organised circles of dissemination and the growth of a market in socialist propaganda: the card's price reflects demand as well as danger; moreover, its sale through a newsagent indicates the existence of established retail networks. The use of private enterprise to reproduce the cartoon is also notable. Although the quantities involved were insignificant, it signals the gradual alignment of two by-products of Russia's push towards the modern age whose convergence would prove key to the mass production of anti-government material: the rise of commerce and the growth of revolutionary thought.

The increase of seditious propaganda in Russia was due, not only to a shift in political mood, but also to greater application by the revolutionaries themselves. In the early 1900s, activists had become conscious of the relative inefficiency of their organisations and had set about professionalising their activities on a political and practical level.[17] The first notable step in this direction came in 1901 with the formation of the League of Russian Revolutionary Social Democracy Abroad.[18] This umbrella organisation was essentially the foreign editorial board of the newspaper *Iskra* [*The Spark*], but its broader aim was to exert political control over the movement and to ensure material and financial support for Party cells in Russia and abroad.

At the same time, moves were made to expand printing operations inside the Russian Empire. In 1900 and 1901, the Northern Union of Socialist-Revolutionaries succeeded in publishing two issues of the newspaper

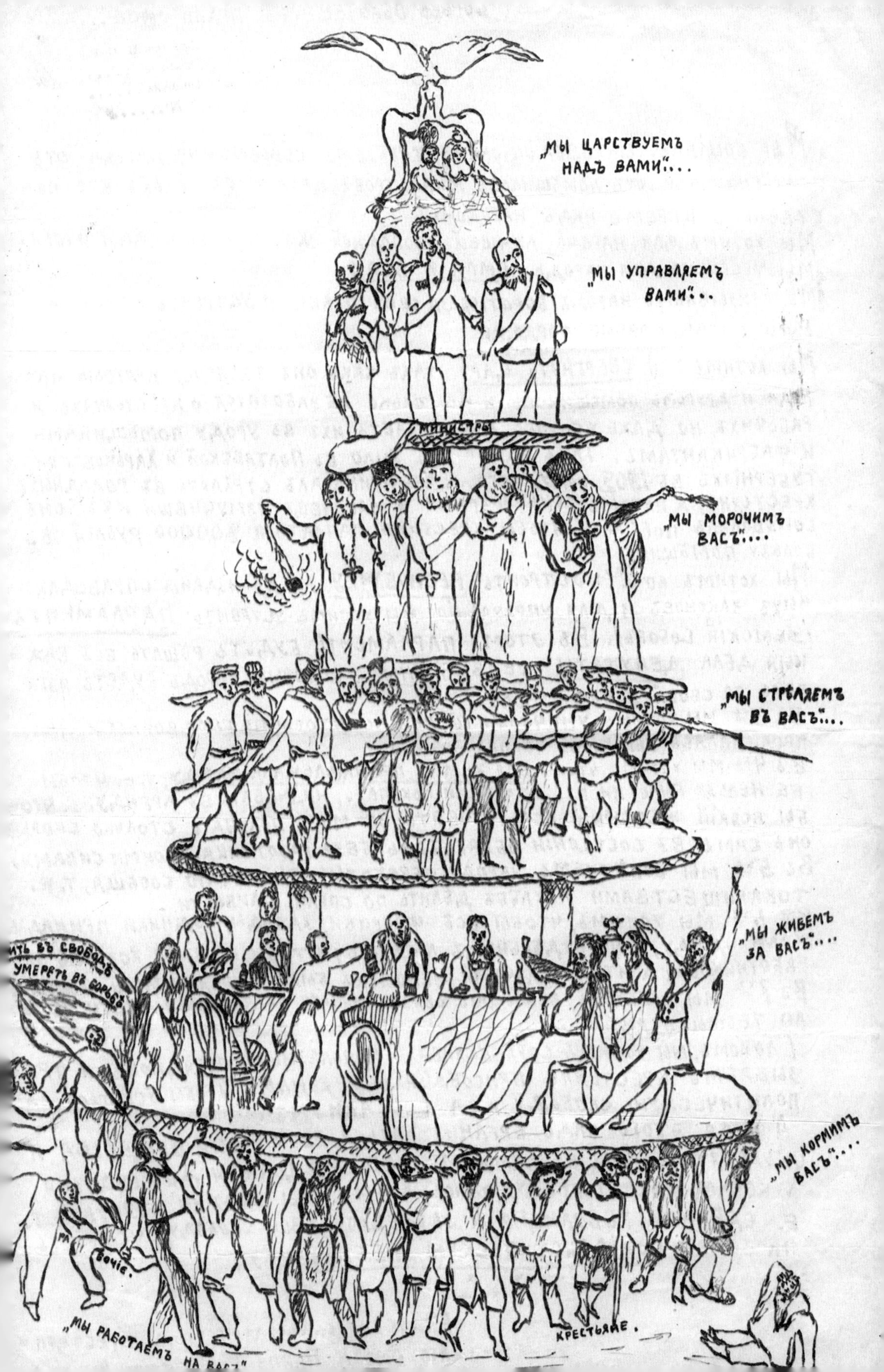
„Мы царствуемъ надъ вами"...
„Мы управляемъ вами"...
Министры
„Мы морочимъ васъ"....
„Мы стрѣляемъ въ васъ"....
„Мы живемъ за васъ"....
ить въ свободѣ
умереть въ борьбѣ
„Мы кормимъ васъ"....
бочие.
„Мы работаемъ на васъ"
Крестьяне.

Revoliutsionnaia Rossiia [*Revolutionary Russia*], the first in Finland and the second in the Siberian town of Tomsk. Attempts to establish a more permanent bridgehead, however, were thwarted when local gendarmes were tipped off about the Tomsk printing house by a government double-agent. Publication thereafter continued in Geneva. Social Democrat activists linked to *Iskra*, meanwhile, set up a secret printing house in Baku in July that same year. Nicknamed 'Nina', the enterprise continued to operate on and off until January 1906.

Propaganda production and distribution, however, remained a deeply precarious undertaking, and as such, it was still characterised as much by opportunism as by organisation. Both the main revolutionary parties were distinguished by their leaders' demands for rigorous centralised control, but this vertical system regularly broke down through distance, absence of personnel, and lack of professionalism. Thousands of leaflets, newspapers and pamphlets were now both coming into the country and being printed domestically in underground facilities, but while a significant amount of this material did reach its intended targets, the inherent dangers of being caught with illegal wares meant that distribution was frequently left to chance, and here, high drama was often the bedfellow of absurdity.

One excellent example of erratic delivery practices comes courtesy of Semyon Belozerov, a twenty-three-year-old sailor based in Sebastopol. On 21 March 1902, Belozerov absented himself from duty to go on a drinking binge. Two days later he was headed to a bordello with two friends when he came across five hectographic drawings lying in the street. Apparently unbeknown to the group, these were items of revolutionary propaganda, containing what the police later described as 'appeals to the nation to rise up against the crown.' Belozerov, addled with drink, picked up the cartoons, and on his arrival at 'Moisei Geld's House of Tolerance,' distributed them among the attendant prostitutes. He was reported to the authorities, and a short while later was detained.[19]

In his defence, Belozerov claimed that he had taken the cartoons unwittingly and had no interest in their content. Whether this was true or not, involvement in political issues had until comparatively recently been the preserve of the upper echelons of society; however, amid great social and industrial upheaval this situation was now rapidly changing. In particular, the huge growth in opportunities for public education over previous decades had played a vital role in expanding the range and number of individuals who became susceptible to modernising ideas. Students, whose overall number had risen to unprecedented levels, were the pillars of the revolutionary campaign, the enthusiastic backbone of a movement driven by a youthful belief in the possibility of transforming the world.

As the social composition of the educated population broadened, so too did the make-up of the revolutionary parties. By the early 1900s, workers and peasants alike were consuming anti-government imagery and starting to play a greater role in its dissemination. One young revolutionary caught in police nets was a twenty-two-year-old peasant from Voronezh named Nikolai Gorodnichev. During a search of his home in March 1903, gendarmes discovered several illegal pamphlets, a lithographic print of *The Pyramid*, and a photographic portrait of the Socialist-Revolutionary terrorist, Stepan Balmashev.[20] Further investigation revealed the existence of three underground study circles, each comprising around five to six young peasants, who met regularly to read illegal literature and discuss revolutionary ideas 'under the pretext of self-education.'

Gorodnichev, who was the leader of the second group, was described by the authorities as an 'energetic and bold young man, who would stop at nothing to achieve his aims.' An orphan, he had initially been educated with the help of the Voronezh Provincial Zemstvo, and was now studying at the local medical school.[21] And therein lay the rub. In order to modernise, the Russian state needed a professional workforce, but without associated reforms, every newly educated member of the population simply added to the potential for popular revolt. The fundamental problem faced by the regime at the start of the twentieth century was that the development of its population was fast outpacing the development of its political system.

The Imperial regime responded to the problem of political dissent in time-honoured fashion, using harsh deterrents and arbitrary repression. For minor offences, the penalties varied from a few days in prison up to three months or more. Gorodnichev was first gaoled, and then shortly afterwards released under police surveillance.[22] Teodorovich, who was deemed guilty of harbouring seditious imagery, was put under police surveillance for a year, while his friend Vladislav Ostrovskii, the owner of the photographic studio where the cartoon was reproduced, was imprisoned for five days.[23] Belozerov, whom the police believed when he claimed that he had been so drunk that he had not even looked at the hectographs, was given ten days' close confinement.[24]

These punishments were less than they might have been in previous decades, but they were still unduly severe. None of these individuals threatened the entity of the regime, but in many cases, the Justice Minister himself signed the charge sheets.[25] This reveals both how seriously the offences were taken and how rarely they occurred. Although social discontent was widespread in Russia, the sum total of committed revolutionaries was still vanishingly small; in a population of over a hundred million, they numbered in the thousands. Continual overreaction and a rigid refusal to differentiate between serious danger and trivial dissent only increased resentment against Tsarist rule, and over the long term alienated the government from its people.

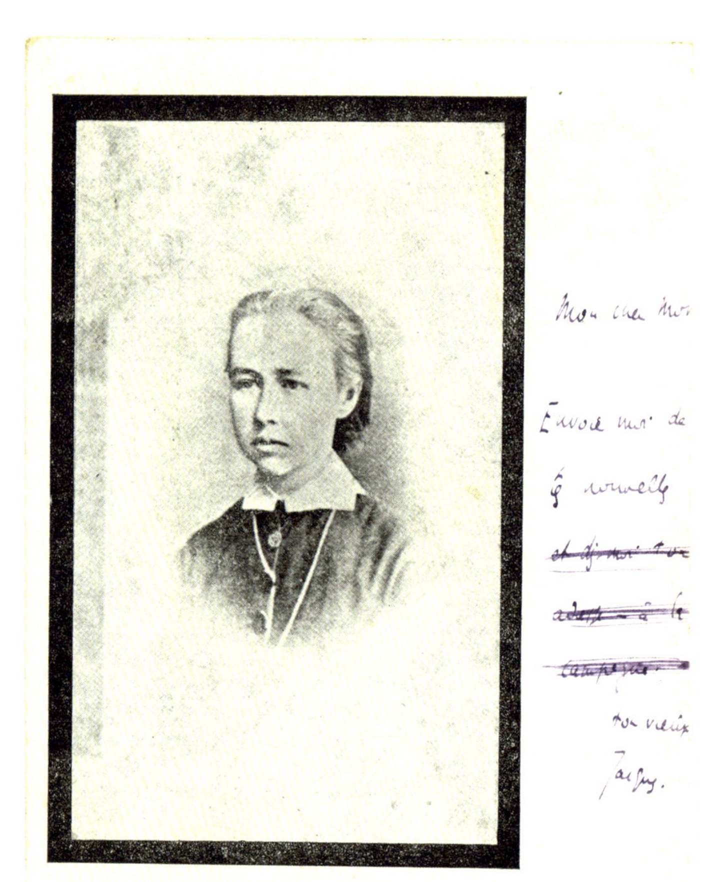

Софья Львовна ПЕРОВСКАЯ
† 3 апрѣля 1881 г.

The need to solve the fundamental issues of labour, land and political representation increased in urgency as the new century progressed, propelled by ongoing government repression and the absence of any legal outlet for popular discontent. In the early 1900s, Russia suffered a serious knock-on effect from a recent economic crisis in Europe. Credit dried up, and inflation led to a rise in the cost of raw materials. Thousands of small businesses were forced to close, and workers suffered from wage cuts and mass redundancies. Town and countryside rumbled with the sounds of unrest, giving rise to further opportunities for agitation, and in turn helping to attract more support to the liberation movement.

Anonymous photographer. *Sofia Lvovna Perovskaia † 3 April 1881.* No publication details, circa 1901.

The growth of anti-government feeling and a related expansion in propaganda production generated the need for greater sources of income, both to sustain the organisations themselves, and to cover the burgeoning costs of printing and dissemination. These financial imperatives brought increased discipline to revolutionary propaganda operations and accelerated an ongoing change in approach. From their inception, increasing support in Russia and abroad had enabled the new revolutionary parties to charge for their printed output. Where once leaflets had been left lying about in the street, Party literature was now becoming a more targeted, economic proposition, requiring highly organised channels of production and distribution to achieve its political and financial objectives.

Revenue came from many different sources, but publishing proved to be one of the most consistent. The focus of revolutionary propaganda printed in Western Europe was primarily on books and pamphlets, but groups abroad also manufactured and sold visual responses to the repression back home.[26] As in Russia, cartes de visite formed the initial mainstay of their pictorial output, but towards the turn of the century, the revolutionaries turned to postcard production as a new way of boosting support and income. Already a popular medium among other European socialist groups, the decision to start manufacturing postcards (which were cheaper to print than cartes de visite) was an obvious next step.

The earliest Russian anti-government postcard that I have discovered is a portrait of Sofia Perovskaia, likely issued in aid of a Socialist-Revolutionary group based in Paris.[27] This simple photographic image, encased in a black memorial border, contains no publishing details, but it was almost certainly made around April 1901 to commemorate the twentieth anniversary of Perovskaia's execution.[28] The group's choice of a nineteenth-century terrorist was no coincidence. Although controversial, the glorification of revolutionary violence would become one of the Party's principal unifying devices, serving to link the modern incarnation of the movement to its Populist past, as well as to ordain heroic figureheads around whom the ideologically disparate organisation could rally.

On its foundation, the Socialist-Revolutionary Party had set up a semi-autonomous attack group. Named the Combat Organisation, it was tasked with carrying out assassinations of prominent government functionaries. In common with his Populist forerunners, the thirty-two-year-old leader of the Organisation, a pharmacist named Grigorii Gershuni, believed the use of terror to be a legitimate means of advancing the revolutionary cause.[29] In theoretical terms, the Party saw violence as a quickening agent – a catalyst that could be deployed to aid the bubbling fermentation of revolution. It was not intended as a catch-all solution, but as an irregular method, sparingly employed, that might help to speed along political developments when no other options were available.[30]

Anonymous artist. Commemorative postcard depicting Stepan Balmashev and Foma Kachura. Published by the Socialist-Revolutionary Party, Zurich, 1902. This is the earliest known postcard directly attributable to a revolutionary party.

The self-perpetuating nature of violence meant that attacks were rarely so disciplined, but in the early years, killing government officials became a way for the Socialist-Revolutionaries to propagate their name in the most spectacular manner possible. As the only group to formalise its stance on terrorism, the Combat Organisation became central to the Party's fame and reputation. Indeed, one of the arguments used in validation of terror was the attention that it brought to the group and its aims.[31] The Party therefore sought to capitalise on Organisation actions with whatever methods came to hand. Books, pamphlets, leaflets, and postcards all lauded its murderous feats, pushing the impact of blast and bullet far beyond their immediate killing fields.

On 2 April 1902, a 'young and extremely impressionable' Socialist-Revolutionary named Stepan Balmashev shot and killed Interior Minister Dmitrii Sipiagin in Saint Petersburg.[32] The assassination was the first notable success of the Combat Organisation and a great coup for the Party. Overnight it became the most talked about revolutionary group in Russia and support rose accordingly. Leaflets hailing the assassination as a defining achievement in the revolutionary struggle were distributed in the capital the following day, and later that same year a black-and-white postcard of the recently executed Balmashev was printed in Zurich. This photomontage image is the earliest postcard I have found that can be linked unequivocally to a specific revolutionary party.

Gershuni, the guiding light of the Combat Organisation and the man who wrote the Saint Petersburg leaflets, was keenly aware of the need to justify and humanise terrorism through sympathetic representations of its perpetrators.[33] The Zurich postcard, which includes portraits of the twenty-year-old killer and a statement dedicating the attack to the suffering masses, was a way of personifying a tenet of Party theory that the Socialist-Revolutionaries believed to be fundamental to their make-up. In presenting Balmashev as an individual, the viewer is given a human framework through

ПАРТІЯ СОЦІАЛИСТОВЪ-РЕВОЛЮЦІОНЕРОВЪ.

РЕВОЛЮЦІОННАЯ РОССІЯ

Въ борьбѣ обрѣтешь ты право свое.

1902 г. Августъ. № 10

ДВА ПИСЬМА РАБОЧАГО-РЕВОЛЮЦІОНЕРА *)

I. Письмо къ рабочимъ.

Товарищи! Завтра я иду выполнять приговоръ Боевой Организаціи нашей Партіи надъ однимъ изъ деспотовъ — харьковскимъ губернаторомъ. Мнѣ потомъ уже нельзя будетъ говорить съ вами, а я хочу, чтобы вы знали, почему я рѣшилъ идти и почему я нахожу, что это дѣло, которое стоитъ, чтобы за него жертвовать жизнью. Много говорить мнѣ некогда, скажу только … чтобы вы меня поняли.

Я тринадцать … при- нимаю участіе … тыре тому назадъ … коро свернетъ само… ждую стачку мы сч… стачекъ ничего не … прп- смагриваться … что мы уже смот… скоро начали прекр… стачкахъ не могутъ ду… ться к… мѣстѣ, и нам… стач- ками …

Тут… товар… встрѣча… чаровался и … мы на демонстраціяхъ … что только подставляемъ спи… новы подъ кулаки и ружейные … нулся съ одной демонстраціи, я … обиды. На насъ на- летѣли казаки … другую, и потомъ разбѣжались … а казаки насъ догоняли, били нагайками … хохоталъ — „ишь зате… дали!“ А потомъ … въ Екатеринославѣ демо… въ участкахъ били и всячески издѣвались на… все молчали, и правительство почувствова… но, и что напрасно съ нами церемони…

Стыдно мнѣ стало за себя, стыд… рищей. Мы хотимъ порядокъ всего … а даемъ себя бить, какъ самые пропащіе люди. … лагаю, что, если мы идемъ на борьбу, то должны бо… какъ полагается честнымъ рабочимъ. И раньше всего мы должны такъ держать себя, чтобы насъ уважали друзья и враги. А вр… не только чтобы уважали бы, но и боялись. И когда … тора тому назадъ встрѣтился съ рабо- чими … что они соціалисты-революціонеры, … такъ какъ и они смотрѣли такъ … почти годъ, пока наконецъ … образовалась Боевая Органи- … бы туда попасть, но … послѣ того, какъ Бал- … приняли; мнѣ … вскаго губер- натор… продѣлы- валъ … нашимъ царемъ … на- хожу, что … етъ правильный …

Я самъ, какъ и … и мнѣ всегда больно бы… слова интеллигентовъ, что… что крестьяне всегда … правда, и говорятъ … жизни не … рабочему … такъ что … янство с… горсть … оставить … губер… но вол… но и х… рабо… вильно … Но крестьяни … чѣмъ намъ: … ихъ такъ безчел… Насъ-то … нельзя … которые … вправъ, … скапра- … товъ, … дились, … губерніи, … войска … Со- … она же … палачей. … кому … одно, … интеллиген- … ился … братья, что … друга стоять, … него весь … я, рабо- … какъ интел- лигентъ … народъ.

Я, конечно, … кого, какъ я убью харьковскаго губер… не будутъ избивать. Но вѣдь мы совершен… не думаемъ, что послѣ одной демонстраціи мы уничтожимъ самодержавіе. Если

*) Нашъ товарищъ, членъ Боевой Организаціи Партіи Соціалистовъ-Революціонеровъ, взявшій на себя выполненіе приговора Боевой Организаціи палачу харьковскихъ крестьянъ, кн. Оболенскому, оставилъ два письма — одно къ рабочимъ, другое — къ крестьянамъ. Опубликовывая эти письма, мы по конспиративнымъ соображеніямъ вынуждены пока воздержаться отъ сообщенія какъ имени товарища, такъ и свѣдѣній о его жизни, цѣликомъ отданной дѣлу служенія революціонному соціализму.

Въ пользу рабочихъ и ихъ семействъ, пострадавшихъ во время стачекъ въ гг. Ростовѣ, Новороссійскѣ и ст. Тихорѣцкой въ ноябр. дни 1902 года.

«Я приношу свою жизнь въ жертву великому дѣлу облегченія участи трудящихся и угнетенныхъ.»
Изъ письма С. В. Балмашева къ родителямъ.

which to understand the use of violence – as a rational response to repression, rather than as an abstract theoretical concept with which one either did or did not agree.

During this period, the Socialist-Revolutionary Party also published one other postcard celebration of terrorism, very similar in design, only this time containing portraits of Perovskaia and her co-conspirators Aleksandr Zheliabov and Ignacy Hryniewiecki. When seen alongside the image of Balmashev, the Party's aim of using political violence and the notion of individual action to establish the Socialist-Revolutionaries as the rightful heirs of the Populist movement becomes explicit. Just as it was beginning to gain support in the regions, the group was looking to reinforce the legitimacy of its actions by stressing the Party's theoretical links to its revolutionary predecessors. Both literally and metaphorically, terrorists were being made the public face of the Party.

As with other forms of propaganda, the purpose of anti-government postcards was not only to inculcate ideas, but also to generate money. An inset note reveals that the Balmashev image was sold in order to raise funds for 'workers and their families who suffered during the strikes in Rostov, Novorossiisk, and Tikhoretsk Station in November 1902.'[34] A corresponding entry in the accounts of the Zurich Socialist-Revolutionary group shows that between 1 January and 15 February 1903, sales of the postcard brought in just over forty-one francs.[35] Right the way through the pre-1917 period, postcards continued to occupy this dual role: although intended as propaganda, they were seldom given away for free.

In common with their counterparts, the Social Democrats started printing postcards just as they began to impose greater organisation on Party propaganda and administration. Following the establishment of the League of Social Democracy Abroad, Iosif Bliumenfeld, an experienced printer active in revolutionary circles since the mid-1880s, took over the technical side of the Party's propaganda output.[36] Among his papers are two handwritten financial statements covering a period between 17 November and 17 January 1902. In the first there are entries for membership fees, reports, literature, subscription lists, and at the very end, one for income derived from selling 'portraits of Marx'. In the second, there is an entry reading simply 'cards'. I believe that both refer to postcards.[37]

Other documentation relating to early Social Democratic postcard production is scarce, but there is still enough evidence to show that the portraits of Marx were not a one-off. Bliumenfeld's archives also contain an invoice from the Edouard Pfeffer Printing House in Geneva, dated 30 April 1902, which records an order for two Russian-language pamphlets, and a thousand postcards.[38] There is no mention of who or what the latter depict, but the quantity is by no means insignificant. Later the same year, a set of accounts from the Social

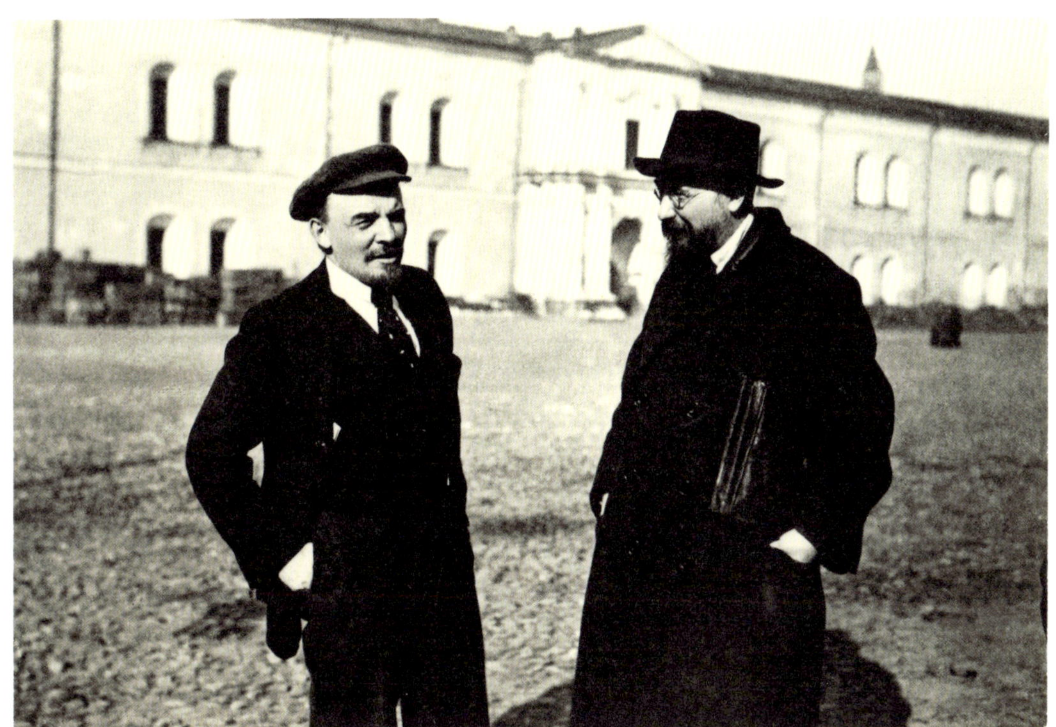

A. F. Vinkler and A. A. Levitskii (Cameramen). Still from film of Vladimir Lenin and Vladimir Bonch-Bruevich. Moscow, 1918.

Democratic group in Zurich, which were published in *Iskra*, record income derived from selling 'cards of Balmashev published by the circle of N and R.'[39]

I have not succeeded in identifying the 'N and R' cell, but the use of Latin initials suggests that it may have been formed by a group of Swiss sympathisers. This would help explain why postcards depicting a Socialist-Revolutionary terrorist were being printed to raise money for a rival party. Whatever the reason, it is an early example of a practice of political appropriation that became widespread during the 1905 Revolution, when postcards of popular revolutionaries were printed with little heed to the parties they represented. Here, the Balmashev postcards show the Social Democrats content to absorb the financial gain, even at the ideological profit of their political rivals.

Postcard Production in Exile

The Social Democrats' Second Congress in the summer of 1903 was most notable for the Party split that gave birth to the Bolshevik and Menshevik factions, but in propaganda terms it was significant for the many discussions that took place over the production and dissemination of socialist material.[40] The Party's shortage of trained propagandists and agitators was recognised as being a particular problem, as was the arbitrary nature of illegal deliveries to Russia. The result was a resolution to set up a technical bureau for propaganda production and distribution, with the Central Committee tasked to provide a unified programme for its implementation.[41]

In the months ahead, the Mensheviks gained ascendancy over *Iskra* and the League, while the Bolsheviks were left in control of the practical side of the Party's propaganda activities.[42] Following an agreement at the Congress, the latter was completely reorganised and a new technical and transportation office set up in Geneva, with the Bolshevik Vladimir Bonch-Bruevich at its helm. Bonch-Bruevich had only just turned thirty, but he was already skilled in the art of revolutionary printing, having acquired extensive experience both in Russia and abroad. As a man of great organisational capacity and deep commitment, he would prove an invaluable asset to Bolshevik publishing in the years leading up to 1917.

Social Democratic propaganda was still nominally united under a single Party banner, but after the split, the Bolsheviks made increasing efforts to separate their activities from those of their Menshevik rivals. Under Lenin's direction, Bonch-Bruevich looked to co-opt the resources of the Party's technical and transportation office for the group's own ends, printing leaflets and pamphlets aimed against their ideological adversaries within the Party. Perhaps inevitably, the Mensheviks eventually lost patience with the Bolsheviks and completely forbade them from using the office to distribute factionally-partisan works. As a result, Lenin and Bonch-Bruevich decided to set up their own publishing house.[43]

According to Bonch-Bruevich, money for the new venture was collected 'literally kopeck by kopeck, by taxing ourselves, gathering all possible subscription lists, selling photographic cards and so on and so forth.'[44] The 'cards' to which he refers here were phototype postcards reproducing scenes from Maxim Gorky's play *The Lower Depths*. This overtly political drama, which premiered at the Moscow Arts Theatre in late 1902, was a major success among the public, prompting many publishers to issue photographic postcards depicting the main characters. During the Second Party Congress, friends of Bonch-Bruevich in Saint Petersburg sent him a set of these images, published by the Moscow firm J. Kornitzki.[45]

The Bolsheviks soon set about printing their own set of *Lower Depths* postcards in Geneva. According to Bonch-Bruevich, the suggestion to reproduce the images originally came from Lenin.[46] 'When I showed Vladimir Ilich the photographs, he pored over them for a long time with evident pleasure, admiring the poses of the actors. Then, he said that, without fail, we must publish some of our own in order to familiarise the Russian émigré and student communities with this Arts Theatre production.'[47] In the spring of 1904, Bonch-Bruevich published a set of twenty-five cards, the majority of which were direct copies of Kornitzki's images.[48] The print run of 30,000 reportedly sold out in under a month, all to buyers based in Western Europe.[49]

Bonch-Bruevich later described the venture as 'hugely successful,' noting that the money raised from the postcards had 'contributed greatly to our meagre resources.'[50] These comments underscore the economic significance of postcard production, which in the early years of the twentieth century provided a small but useful addition to revolutionary coffers. However, if the practically-minded Bonch-Bruevich regarded the enterprise primarily in terms of profit, then Lenin's initial response to the images serves as a reminder that the central motivation for their production was ideological.

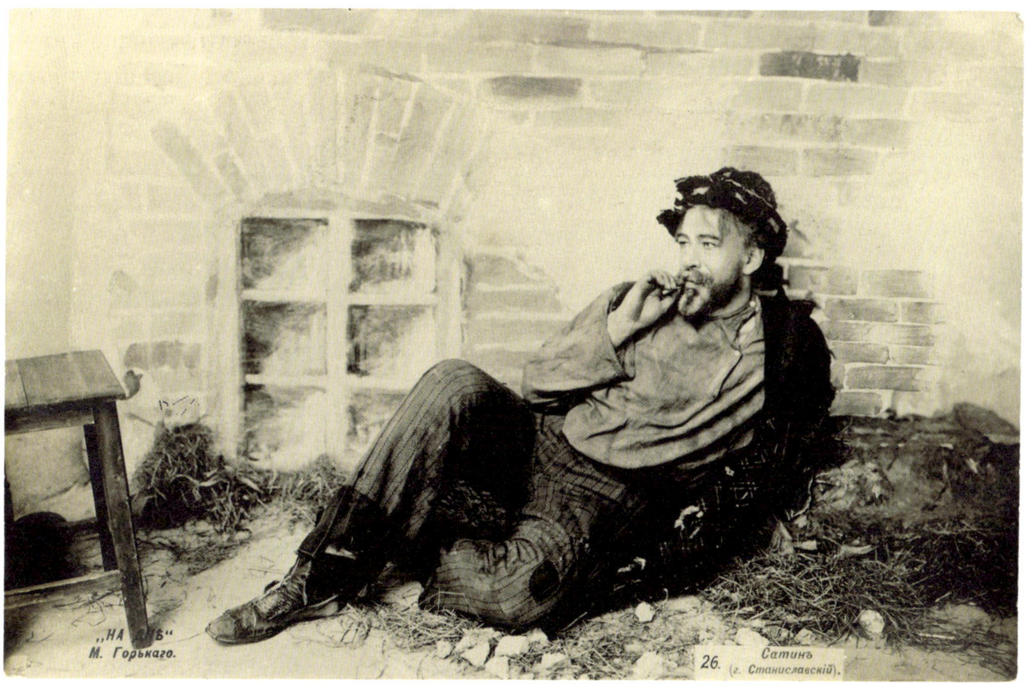

In the early years of the Soviet period, Lenin remarked that the people did not need 'chocolate box picture postcards, but those that tell the truth about life.'[51] He praised the Moscow Arts Theatre in precisely the same manner, as an institution that 'truthfully reflected life.'[52] The *Lower Depths* cards, which provided close-ups of the characters in all their downtrodden glory, offered Lenin an opportunity to expose the evils of capitalism in a manner that exemplified the purported truthfulness he had so admired in Gorky's play. He understood that the postcard was essentially a megaphone, and that by transforming words and events into simplified visual memes, the revolutionaries could disseminate core ideas quickly and efficiently among large swathes of their supporters.

Anonymous photographer. *Lower Depths. M. Gorky. Satin (Mr. Stanislavski).* Published by J. Kornitzki, Moscow, 1904.

This Bolshevik endeavour aside, Party accounts suggest that the majority of early Social Democratic postcards were either produced or distributed by the Menshevik-dominated League of Social Democracy Abroad. Financial statements printed in *Iskra* in the run-up to the 1905 Revolution show that money raised from postcard sales was regularly being sent back to the League by Party groups in Bern, Berlin, and London.[53] There is no information available on what these postcards depicted or where they were printed, but given the centralised structure of the organisation, it is likely that many of the images were published by the League itself in Geneva, before being distributed to regional cells for onward sale.[54]

The Socialist-Revolutionary Party followed a broadly similar structural set-up. In 1903, the Party created its own association for groups abroad, called the Foreign Organisation. Similar in purpose to the League of Social Democracy, it was created to impose ideological unity on Party cells in Europe and to help source money and men for the movement. The Foreign Organisation's involvement in printing and disseminating postcards appears to have been analogous to that of the League, with a comparable degree of centralised control over production and distribution. From early 1904 onwards, postcards appear often in the accounts of the Foreign Committee (the Party's central authority) suggesting that they were sent to regional cells as a matter of course.[55]

Little is known about where the postcards were sold, but propaganda was regularly offered at lectures and other special events, as well as through the offices of the various revolutionary organisations. Lenin reports having arranged the sale of Bolshevik material to over a hundred different bookshops in Europe and America, and it is likely that postcards were also disseminated in this manner.[56] Cards were sometimes also displayed and sold in local Party libraries, where they proved a great temptation for light-fingered visitors. A report on the reading library of the Socialist-Revolutionary Foreign Committee, complained that: 'Not only books, but newspapers, magazines and portraits have also disappeared (three cards of [Revolutionary terrorist Ivan] Kaliaev that were laid out on the table have now gone).'[57]

The market for revolutionary propaganda was predominantly to be found among Russian expatriates, particularly students. The Social Democrat Dmitrii Sverchkov reported that, even though many of these would-be radicals had never 'smelt the powder of revolution,' it was fashionable among Russian men and women studying at European universities to support one or other of the main revolutionary parties. Political allegiance, he noted, was often the first question that new arrivals were asked. Sverchkov dismissed many of his fellow countrymen as ideological philistines, but there is no doubt that students proved an indispensable source of income and manpower for Russian political groups in exile.[58]

In response to the threat posed by the revolutionaries, many of whom fled to Europe after the assassination of Alexander II, the Okhrana had set up a secret outpost in Paris. For much of its existence the so-called Foreign Agency was underfunded and constrained by a lack of cooperation from foreign governments. Nevertheless, using spies, mail interception and good tradecraft, Tsarist agents abroad did all they could to disrupt the work of those intent on bringing change to Russia. From the Agency's inception in 1883, activists and their illicit cargoes were regularly tailed back into the country by operatives from the Paris office, unwittingly leading the Imperial police to safe houses in Moscow, Saint Petersburg and other major cities of the Empire.

The revolutionaries in exile suffered from many of the same issues as their Tsarist adversaries. They were few in number, constantly short of money, and often hassled by the police forces of their suspicious hosts. What they did have, however, was a total conviction in the justice of their cause, and a tenacious, almost messianic will to succeed. This extraordinary sense of self-belief sustained many of the leading revolutionaries through years of exile and imprisonment. There were casualties along the way – traitors, suicides and others who simply abandoned the cause – but it was largely sheer force of personality that kept the intellectual side of the movement alive through troubled times.

Until the 1890s, émigré revolutionary publications did not reach Russia in great abundance, but this began to change towards the end of the century, not least due to more organised efforts by the revolutionaries themselves.[59] The steady growth of propaganda imports caused great concern in the Russian Interior Ministry, which sent regular missives back to the Paris Okhrana office, urging them to do more to prevent incendiary material from being smuggled into the country. 'Shipments of illegal literature have become very frequent over the last few years,' reads one Ministry note. 'I am therefore once again pleading with you to take measures to find out about them in advance, and to pass on prompt warning to the Department of Police.'[60]

The borders were penetrated by several different routes. One of the most popular was to send items by mail. An Okhrana report from 1904 complains of a proliferation of items being dispatched, 'not just from Switzerland, but also Belgium, France and Germany.'[61] Bonch-Bruevich, for his part, claims a one hundred percent success rate on posting Social Democratic leaflets, which he concealed from officials by gluing them to the back of prints reproducing famous paintings.[62] Easiest, however, was to use a plain envelope and trust one's luck. However, nothing was fail-safe. Suspect post was regularly perlustrated, and anyone receiving regular deliveries of foreign mail was liable to be put under surveillance.

As they became bolder in their actions and intent, the radicals abroad thought up ever more elaborate methods of transportation. These ranged from hiding illegal works in barrels of herring to shipping them in industrial pipes.[63] But despite the obvious creativity of the revolutionaries, the most reliable procedure remained the simplest – conveying illicit material through the border by hand. This work was often carried out by professional agents and activists, but vacationing Russians were also roped into helping, as were sympathetic students, who proved an invaluable source of propaganda mules.[64] Border guards, however, were constantly on the alert, and for some young activists, this precarious enterprise had life-changing consequences.

In the spring of 1903, guards on the westernmost fringes of the Russian Empire caught sight of a young student approaching the Imperial border carrying what appeared to be a very heavy suitcase. When the traveller nervously proffered what the officials suspected might be false papers they took him to one side and carried out a thorough search of his belongings. Carefully concealed in the man's luggage, they discovered two illegal political pamphlets, and 1,687 picture postcards decorated 'with revolutionary verses and songs', many of them in Polish. During the subsequent investigation the police identified their detainee as Jan Wleklinski, a twenty-four-year-old native of Warsaw and a hereditary member of the gentry.

Wleklinski, who was then studying at the Technological Institute in Saint Petersburg, was accused of smuggling anti-government propaganda and deliberately concealing his true identity. For what was considered to be a crime against the state, he was summarily exiled for three years to the far north of Russia. This sentence had a significant impact on his young family. His doctor wife Wanda, who was ill and short of money, was forced to live many miles from her husband in order to find work to support herself and their young son. After several appeals for clemency, Wleklinski was finally released under special dispensation in late 1904, and allowed to return to the capital to resume his studies.[65]

This pitiful episode shows that large-scale attempts to import illegal postcards into the Russian Empire were undertaken. Most smuggling runs, however, were far more modest – the postcard's convenient size meant that travellers could easily conceal a small cache of images about their person, and these could then be reproduced in greater numbers once inside the country.[66] Nevertheless, hard evidence of illegal postcard trafficking in the years prior to 1905 is difficult to come by. A Socialist-Revolutionary report detailing items of revolutionary propaganda smuggled through a single border point in 1903 and 1904 mentions 5,914 copies of fifty-one different pamphlets, and 1,364 copies of *Revoliutsionnaia Rossiia*, but no postcards.[67]

Perpetual shortages of money, manpower and facilities had a deleterious effect on the quantity of opposition material that could be printed and delivered. But even when the resources were available, it is clear that the focus of the revolutionaries was elsewhere. Although postcards outnumbered all other forms of visual propaganda being produced in Western Europe, they are only mentioned on around twenty occasions in the revolutionary financial accounts published in *Iskra* and *Revoliutsionnaia Rossiia*, and only once in relation to sales inside Russia.[68] This, unquestionably, does not reflect the full extent of their production; the paucity of references in comparison to text-based propaganda is nonetheless significant.[69]

The overriding concern for both the main revolutionary groups was to strengthen theoretical links between the party leaders in exile and the activists on the ground, and thus to increase support for the organisation in general and their faction specifically. Most revolutionaries believed that the best way to achieve this was through a newspaper, which could be used as a tool for gathering support as well as enforcing ideological unity. Lenin, who was quicker than most in realising the importance of this, wrote in reference to the Social Democratic Party that: 'The production of a political newspaper for the whole of Russia must serve as the crucial underlying thread that would enable us to progressively develop, and extend this organisation.'[70]

Portrait postcards, which comprised the bulk of production during this period, were relatively blunt instruments. While they could be effectively used to propagandise heroes and heroines, and to confront the monolithic power of a repressive government, they were of less use in the all-encompassing doctrinal disputes that continuously absorbed the adherents of both parties. Postcards, such as those of Marx and Perovskaia, did advance key aspects of party theory, but most images would still have required some form of ideological explanation among the politically ignorant, particularly in Russia. Thus, prior to the 1905 Revolution, the ideological role of postcards was more to solidify opinion among supporters than to actively convert the unenlightened.

In the final reckoning, it came down to whether the medium represented an economically and ideologically worthwhile use of the party's money and resources. For mass circulation to take place, it required an environment with secure channels of production and distribution, and just as importantly, a ready market of politically conscious consumers with the income to spend on propaganda. In the early 1900s, these conditions were more present in Western Europe than they were in Russia, and although considerable numbers of postcards did make it past the border guards, most were sold outside the Empire, where they played a small but notable role in generating income and diffusing party ideology among exiles, students, and vacationing Russians.

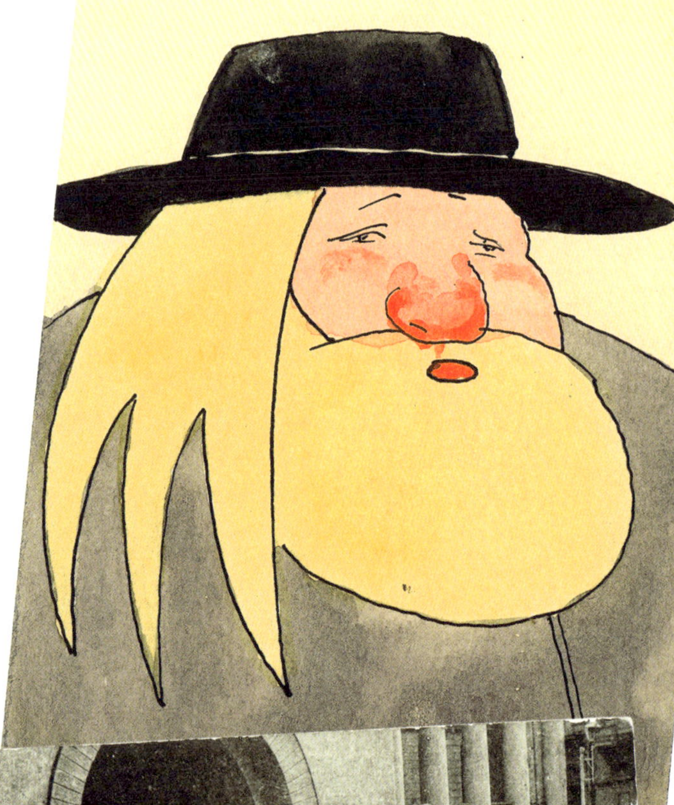
Типы „Истинно-русскихъ людей

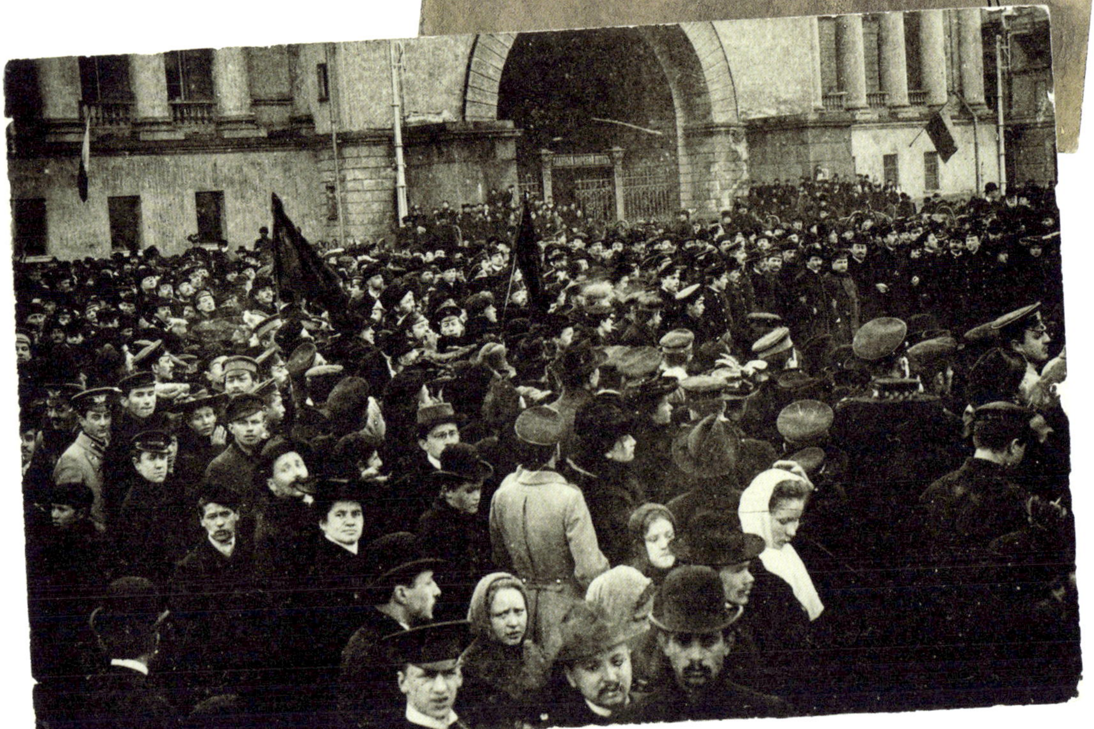

REVOLUTION AND REFORM

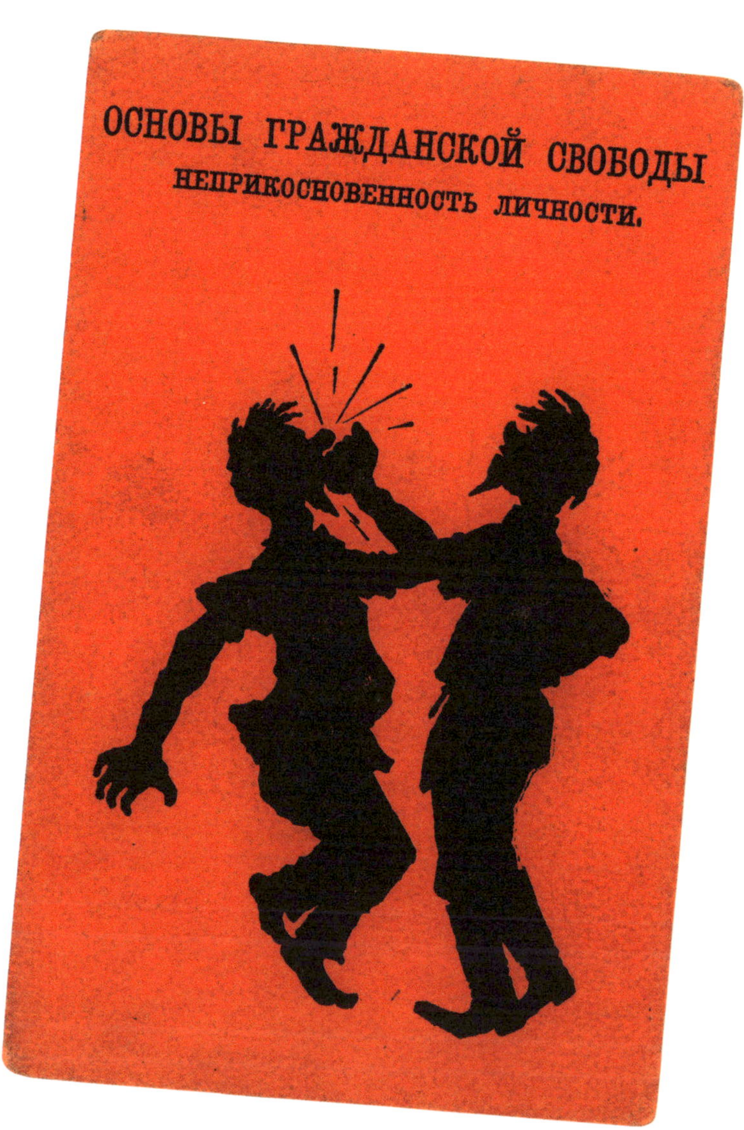

1904–1905

Отчетная карта
Кореи и прилегающих частей сосѣднихъ государствъ.
Масштабъ 1/7500000
въ дюймѣ 180 верстъ.

Karte vom ostasiatischen Kriegs-
-schauplatz zu Gunsten des
roten Kreuzes – Herzlich
23.II.1904 – Onkel Alex

The Russo-Japanese War

By early 1904, Russia's restricted environs were becoming increasingly intolerable to many of its more politically progressive citizens. In January, a revolutionary named Leonid Baron sent a letter from 'enslaved Saint Petersburg' to 'free Paris' in which he railed against the suffocating and false atmosphere in the city. Baron described the situation as being like an 'episode of general drunkenness,' commenting: 'Everyone wears a mask in public, hiding away, pretending and trying to convince themselves that they're having a good time ... This is how my life is; I have something bright in my soul, but it is being crushed to death by deception, lies, artificiality and falsehood.'[1]

The great changes wrought upon the country over previous decades had brought with them calls for a profound reconfiguration of the political and social lives of all classes. Now, the absence of meaningful reform was sending ripples of discontent through the many different layers of Russian society: professionals and intellectuals frustrated at the political torpor, workers wanting higher wages and shorter hours, peasants unable to break free from the bonds of their existence – all were eager for substantial concessions. The Tsar, however, saw little need for compromise, convinced that the grievances had been instigated by Jews and foreigners.

The pervasive disquiet in Russia did not often erupt into overt political defiance, but behind the country's regimented facade, the forces opposed to autocracy were beginning to stamp their feet with increasing vigour. The autocratic government, meanwhile, had no real plan or understanding of how to calm its restless population. When in January Japan launched a surprise attack on the Russian navy at Port Arthur, heralding the outbreak of war, the reactionary interior minister Viacheslav von Plehve is reported to have breathed a sigh of relief, seeing it only as a much-needed distraction to deflect the people from revolution.[2]

The mood of the regime at the outset of the conflict was one of jingoistic patriotism, with ministers all-too-confident in the country's inevitable victory over the 'treacherous' Japanese. Geared up by the state's nationalist rhetoric, commercial enterprises moved accordingly, printing vast quantities of postcards, posters and brightly-coloured broadsides, all glorifying in the spectacle of a major European power exerting its might over an 'inferior' Eastern neighbour.

Filled with triumphant songs and racist sentiment, many at first greeted the war and its commercial by-products with great enthusiasm. 'The traitorous attack by the yellow-faced barbarians gave rise to an immense, unprecedented surge in the popular mood, and prompted extraordinary unity across the vast Empire ... and we, losing no time in meeting the legitimate demands of the public, published [an extensive series of images] in the now

Previous spread from left to right

Karl Bulla. Untitled photographic postcard depicting crowds celebrating the October Manifesto. Saint Petersburg, October 1905.

Anonymous artist. *Types of 'True Russian People'*. Hand-drawn postcard, circa 1905.

Vasil Gulak. *The Principles of Civil Freedom. Inviolability of the Individual.* Printed by I. N. Kushnerev, Moscow, 9 November 1905.

Opposite

N. Kononov. *Reference Map of Korea and the Adjoining Parts of Neighbouring States.* Published by the Society of Saint Eugenia, Saint Petersburg, 27 January 1904. This postcard was published one day after the outbreak of war, and was sent to Vienna about two weeks later.

hugely popular postcard medium,' wrote Nikolai Merder, in his usual ebullient form.[3]

By April, he was advertising eighty different postcards relating to the conflict, including: diagrams, bird's-eye views, ships, portraits of military commanders, scenes of the fighting, and portraits of Japan's leaders. Merder claimed that these patriotically-minded images were being sold in the tens of thousands, with demand rising by the day.

The immediate clamour for postcards was such that the Society of Saint Eugenia was forced initially to rely on stock pictures of the Far East; moreover, several of its earliest images of the fighting were drawn by artists located miles from the front lines. As befitted an enterprise so closely connected to the establishment, the Society's total output on the Russo-Japanese War was vast. Indeed, the charity printed so many postcards that when peace was eventually declared, it was forced to commission new subject matter to make up for the corresponding loss in revenue.[4]

On an international level, there was considerable interest shown in the first modern war against an Asian country. This was one of the great spectacles of the new age and, as in Russia, the postcard was the lens through which much of the world chose to view it. Brightly coloured cartoons, caricatures, photographs, portraits, and reproductions of paintings all served to depict Russia's fight for an empire in the East. From Asia to America, consumers were handed their own postcard-sized view of the conflict, the bias of the image dependent on the political outlook of each respective nation. War had always been a spectator sport, but it could now be viewed from the comfort of one's own living room.

The popularity of scenes depicting the conflict demonstrated the lucrative potential of current events to many Russian publishers, and as the overall numbers of images increased, so too did their variety and subject matter. The genre of postcard portraiture in Russia now began to encompass depictions of senior officers and war heroes, particularly from the cruiser Variag, which in February 1904 had launched a glorious but doomed attack against a far larger Japanese squadron. Representations of real events, once confined to natural disasters and state pageantry, were also increasingly prized away from the historic past or Imperial present to cover as never before incidents involving the lives and deaths of ordinary people.

The advent of hostilities not only served to extend thematic boundaries, but also to expand the modes of depiction. Unlike the rest of Europe, Russia had no prior history of postcard cartoons, but this changed within days of the war getting underway.[5] Naturally, the Saint Petersburg Censorship Committee remained vigilant in its efforts to maintain the official war narrative. A depiction of a Japanese soldier taking aim at a dozing Russian sprawled across a map of the Far East was among the images banned. But the fact that satirical cartoons could be published at all marked a notable advance.[6]

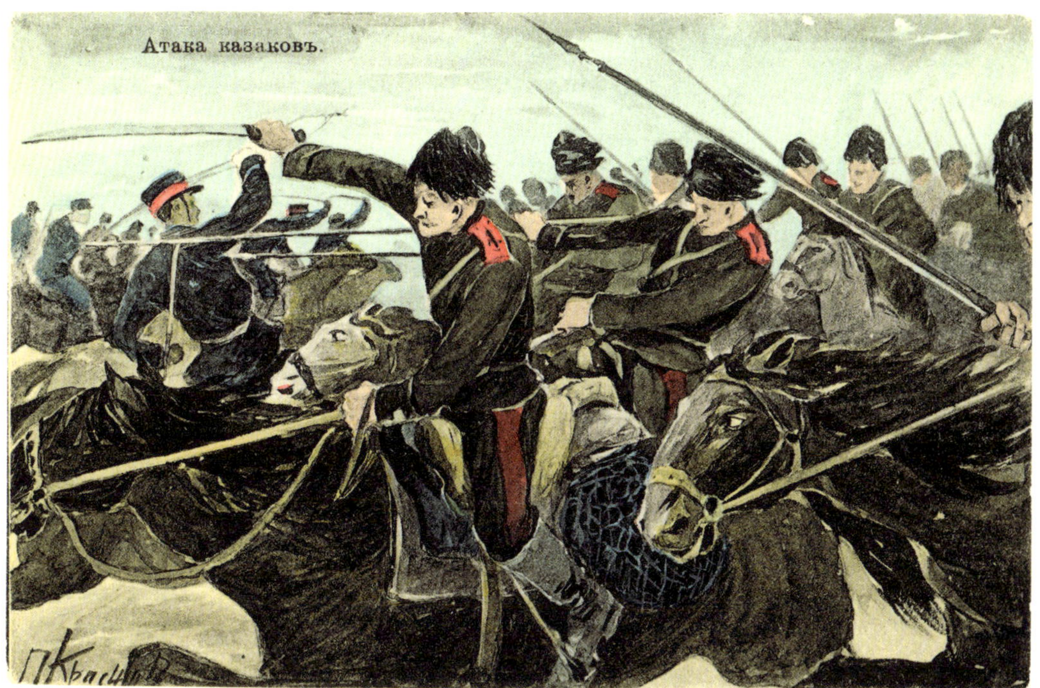

P. Krasnov. *Cossack Attack*. Published by M. P. Posanov, Saint Petersburg, mid-1904.

Since at least the eighteenth century, satirical imagery had been the domain of the lubok, a popular broadside relaying political, religious, and social events to the masses. During the war, the medium was given an artistic and technological make-over, its simple sentiments and pared-down aesthetic modernised and mass produced.[7] The more refined poster-style illustrations and satires that resulted were published in considerable quantities, but they were largely superseded at this time by postcards, which had fast become one of the primary ways in which the population absorbed patriotic sentiment on issues affecting the national consciousness.

Inspired by the lubok, Russian postcard cartoons deploy folk imagery and popular verse to promote the country as a superior racial and military power. Among the earliest to appear was a set of images by N. Kazachkov, which use humour, satire and stereotype to contrast the 'wild' Japanese with Russia's own strong and crafty natives.[8] In one card, a mighty warrior (bogatyr) towers over his quaking opponent. In another, Japanese saboteurs are sent fleeing by valiant lancers. Many of the cartoons circulating in Russia, however, were printed in Europe, particularly France and Germany. Foreign artists followed an even more predictable line than their Russian counterparts, throwing about galloping Cossacks and raging bears with reckless abandon.

As well as expanding the range, quality and quantity of picture postcards in Russia, the war boosted the numbers who came into contact with them. An increase in production and a corresponding decrease in cost had made postcards available to the poorer members of society, tens of thousands of

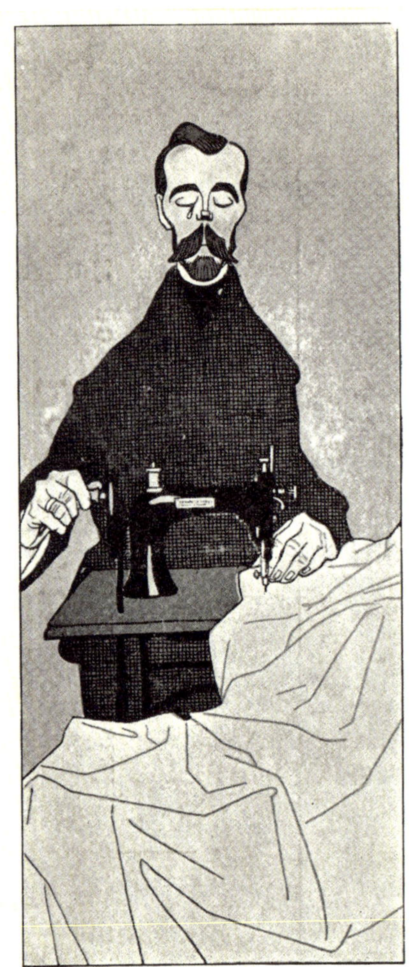

Какъ царь участвуетъ въ войнѣ.

whom now found themselves fighting an unfamiliar enemy far away from home. There was considerable demand for postcards among soldiers in the field, for whom they provided a much-desired link to relations and loved ones back home. When Russia's progress in battle became bogged down, many of these same men became prisoners, and once again postcards were widely used as a way of keeping in touch.

Postcards played their part in augmenting nationalist fervour during the Russo-Japanese War, but it would be wrong to see them solely as objects of government propaganda. Some publishers, such as the Society of Saint Eugenia were, unquestionably, close to the powers-that-be, but postcards relating to the war are nevertheless better understood as an example of private enterprise reflecting, and taking advantage of, the perceived mood of the nation. Publishers may have taken their primary lead from the state, but they were still dependent on consumers to buy their products. Patriotic postcards were thus financial propositions aimed at popular feeling, and when this withered, so too did their production.

Olaf Gulbransson. *How the Tsar Participates in the War.* No publication details, Western Europe, circa 1904. This caricature was originally published in *Simplicissimus* in 1904.

Revolutionary Postcard Production in Russia

Few appreciated all the implications that the war might have for Russia. The artist Alexander Benois recalled that nobody took the campaign particularly seriously at first, treating it as though it were a 'trivial adventure from which Russia could not but emerge victorious.'[9] When news of Russian defeats started to trickle through, this mindset made them all the harder to absorb. In April, the death of the well-regarded Commander of the Pacific Fleet Admiral Makarov, and losses on land in the months that followed were profoundly shocking to many, undermining trust in a state that had assured its people of a swift and certain triumph.

The government now found itself in an uneasy predicament, needing victory abroad in order to bring about peace at home. In July, Egor Sazonov assassinated von Plehve, another widely lauded success for the Socialist-Revolutionary Combat Organisation that prompted recognition among more moderate government circles that concessions were needed. His replacement, Petr Sviatopolk-Mirskii, made it clear to the Tsar that reform was the only way of bringing about reconciliation between the state and society.

Over previous decades, the phenomenal growth of the press had severely weakened the regime's control over the dissemination of information. In the absence of political representation, newspapers had become one of the only legal ways of influencing what the people thought and how the government acted, and as such, they had assumed critical significance. Public opinion was now a force, and much as the censor tried to curtail the promulgation of defeatist views, sceptical reporting on Russia's progress against Japan played an important role in feeding opposition both to the conflict and the government itself.

Throughout the year confidence in the regime and its handling of the war deteriorated. Few could understand the purpose of the conflict. It was just too far away and too remote from the everyday concerns of the people, and as the cost in men and money became ever more apparent, the public began to lose its enthusiasm for the fight. By late 1904, with a negative outcome no longer in any real doubt, much of the intelligentsia had turned against the regime, and among the educated classes as a whole there was a fundamental loss of trust in the system. Many now looked for political alternatives, both temperate and extreme.

Under Sviatopolk-Mirskii's more tolerant rule, liberalism, a movement aimed at achieving civil rights and a constitutional monarchy through peaceful means, gained considerable exposure and support among the educated classes, boosted first by the Zemstvo Congress in November, and then by the so-called Banquet Campaign, a remarkable two-month long series of dinners aimed at uniting moderate opposition to the regime.

New avenues also opened up for the revolutionaries, who printed off thousands of leaflets decrying the 'imperialist war', and everywhere they could, whipped up popular opinion against the government. Some even privately cheered on the enemy: 'Each Japanese victory brought joy to my soul,' recalled the Social Democrat Dmitrii Sverchkov. 'It felt as if it were not the Russian people who were suffering defeat but autocracy, and that each tiny Japanese bullet that passed through the body of a Russian soldier would go on to hit the Russian throne.'[10]

Visual propaganda could not yet reflect the more nuanced political debate that was being conducted across the major cities, but on the peripheries of the Russian Empire illegal postcards were beginning to emerge in greater quantities. In their accounts for late spring and early summer 1904, the newly created Socialist-Revolutionary group in Baku record expenditure and income derived from printing and selling 'photographic cards'.[11] And later that same year, the Party cell in Nizhnii Novgorod also reported a small return from selling postcards.[12] Both were industrialised areas that had been heavily affected by strike action over the previous few years.

The expansion of postcard production correlates to the rapid growth of the Party, particularly in the south and south-east of Russia. Between 1903 and 1904, the Socialist-Revolutionaries had risen notably in number and influence. Several new groups and committees had been formed, including in Nizhnii Novgorod and Baku, all of which immediately started carrying out propaganda work in their respective regions.[13] The spread of illegal postcard propaganda in Russia was thus both a consequence of greater political awareness, that is to say better market conditions, and also increased numbers of experienced activists who had the know-how, and more importantly, the initiative to print illegal material.

The police were quick to respond. In early 1904, gendarmes in Voronezh raided the home of a twenty-year-old suspected Socialist-Revolutionary named Nikolai Felten. Here, they uncovered several hectographic proclamations and cartoons, and over fifty photomechanical postcards – ten depicting *The Pyramid*, fourteen reproducing Mihály Munkácsy's painting *Strike* (1895), and thirty titled *Finland*, a cartoon criticising Russian dominion over the country.[14] When questioned about the postcards, Felten admitted to an amateur interest in photography, but denied having printed the images himself.[15] He instead claimed to have received them from an acquaintance, whom he considered it 'awkward to name.'[16]

Although none of these postcards was openly revolutionary, they were all subversive images, communicating a narrative of Imperial exploitation that tied in with rising social and economic discontent. Depictions of strike action and profiteering at the expense of the masses served to affirm and politicise the prevailing discord, and the spread of such a compelling new form of direct pictorial marketing indicates both the growth of the liberation movement, and the revolutionaries' greater efficiency in reaching the wider population. The government's suppression of the population was old news, but the radicals' increased ability to publicise it marked a step forward in their struggle.

Among the other frequently found postcards from this period are a group of Socialist-Revolutionary photomechanical cartoons, printed sometime between August 1904 and January 1905.[17] These images, which deal with proposals for a new constitution, corruption, and repression, were designed to tap into the underswell of unease among students and the intelligentsia, further undermining the foundations of autocracy and those who administered it to the people. Only one names the Party directly; nevertheless, these were its calling cards, generating much-needed funds and increasing support for the revolutionaries, while at the same time endeavouring to co-opt that sentiment in its own favour.[18]

But, for all its political significance, revolutionary postcard production was still far from widespread in Russia. Few groups had the necessary equipment to print photographic images, which required either getting hold of an enlarger, chemicals and light sensitive paper, or forming an alliance with a sympathetic local photographic studio. The latter option was possible, but represented a risky enterprise for both parties. And this was assuming that the group had the funds to pay for all the manufacturing costs. It was far easier and safer to print off a few hectographic leaflets and dump them by the side of the road in the hope that they might be picked up by a curious passer-by.

Even if the inclination was there and the money and manpower available, there was a further problem that affected the production of all revolutionary

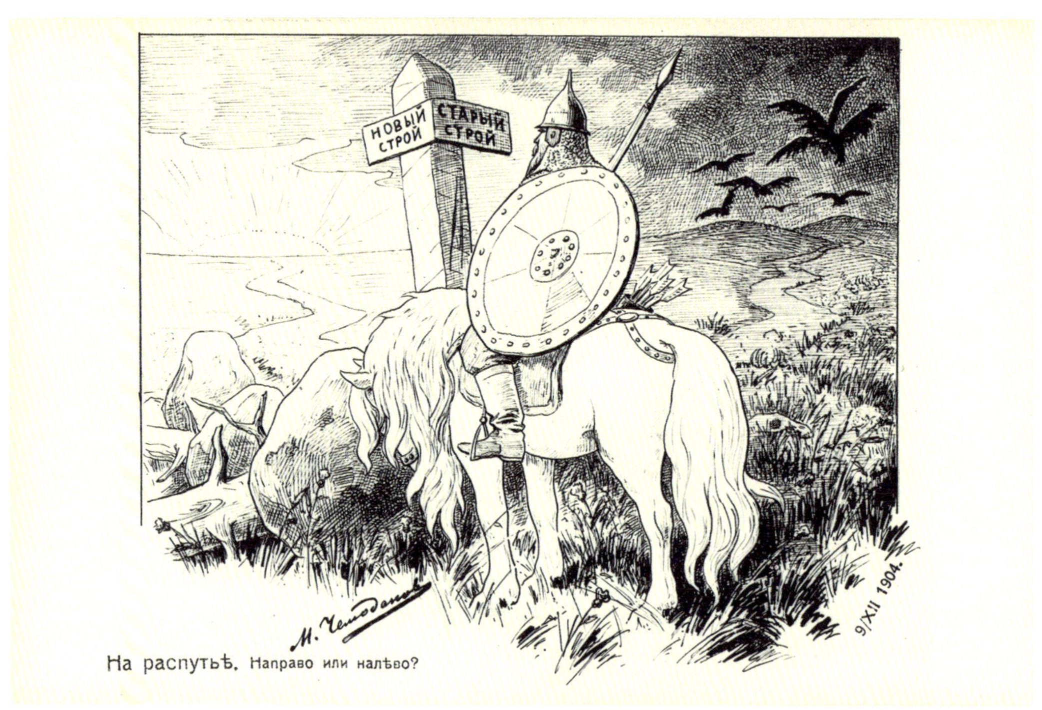

Mikhail Chemodanov. *At the Crossroads. Right or Left?* Printed by A. A. Levenson, Moscow, drawn in December 1904 but published around August 1905.

material – indifference on the part of those to whom they most wanted to appeal. In the cities, much of the workforce resented political issues getting in the way of their economic concerns, while in the countryside, the peasantry as a whole had an insular perspective and a pronounced tendency towards conservatism. Although the distribution of anti-government material among worker and peasant circles had been common practice in Russia since the 1870s, its overall effect on the wider population was modest.

The comparative scarcity of pre-1905 postcards reflects the problems faced by the revolutionary parties as a whole: danger, absence of popular demand, sheer size of the target area, and lack of skilled propagandists. The radicals may have had groups of activists dotted throughout Russia, but they could not in any way be said to have comprised a mass movement. Police inefficiency was rife, but officials still carried out regular arrests, and the average lifespan of a revolutionary cell was measured in weeks. Conditions were ripe for change, but it would take a series of calamitous events to transform the revolutionaries from a small band of extremists into the vanguard of a movement that could and would unseat the Tsar.

The revolutionary parties followed an uncertain trajectory in the lead-up to 1905. Police activity posed a constant threat, and economic depression, which made workers fearful for their jobs and less inclined to partake in unrest, worsened towards the end of the year.[19] The Bolshevik cell in Saint Petersburg, which put out fifty-five leaflets in 1903, could only manage eleven in the first year of the war.[20] But although revolutionary progress was uneven, there was no escaping the fact that the population was simmering with discontent, and as Russia's military progress stalled and impasse over reform continued, ever greater numbers of people were pushed towards the left.

Mikhail Chemodanov was one of many revolutionary sympathisers influenced by the deteriorating situation. A large bearded man, with a generous sense of humour, he was admired by his friends and patients alike for his kindness, humanity and professional ability. While not a member of any political party, he had worked in his youth as a satirist, and had long been an ideological opponent of autocracy. In late 1904, as discontent with the war reached unprecedented levels, Chemodanov determined to resume his activities against the regime. 'I've decided to start drawing again,' he told friends, 'it's too late for me to fight on the barricades, but I can still provide overhead fire.'[21]

Among Chemodanov's first cartoons of the new era was a drawing of a mythical knight halted before a fork in the road. Ahead lie two routes; one, a bright sunlit path, signposted 'the new regime'; the other, a trail beset by crows and bruised by clouds, marked 'the old regime'.[22] On the eve of the New Year, Chemodanov was presenting his country with a stark choice: follow the path of enlightened reform or be condemned to darkness forever.[23]

Bloody Sunday

At around ten a.m. on 9 January 1905 several large columns of workers and their families set off for the Winter Palace. It was a cold but sunny day and the ground was covered in a light frost. Many later recalled a holiday atmosphere, the huge crowds of men, women and children singing as they walked towards the centre of Saint Petersburg.[24]

Over previous days, strikes protesting against the dismissal of four metal workers had gathered momentum, prompting more than two-thirds of the city's workforce to down their tools. Now, under the guidance of Father Georgii Gapon, a charismatic priest who presided over the country's largest workers' union, tens of thousands of people were making their way towards the Winter Palace in order to deliver a petition to the Tsar, begging for his consideration of their plight.[25]

The soldiers who lined the streets did little at first to stop the procession, but as the bands of different marchers began to converge, orders were given for the crowds to stop and disperse. When one of the groups approached the Narva Gates, nervous troops opened fire. 'I heard groans, cries and shouts for help. I fell, my head spinning,' recalled a factory worker. 'One young woman lay on her front, a fountain of blood seeping from her mouth – raising her eyes, she stared blankly, shaking her head from side to side.'[26] Similar scenes were repeated across the capital.

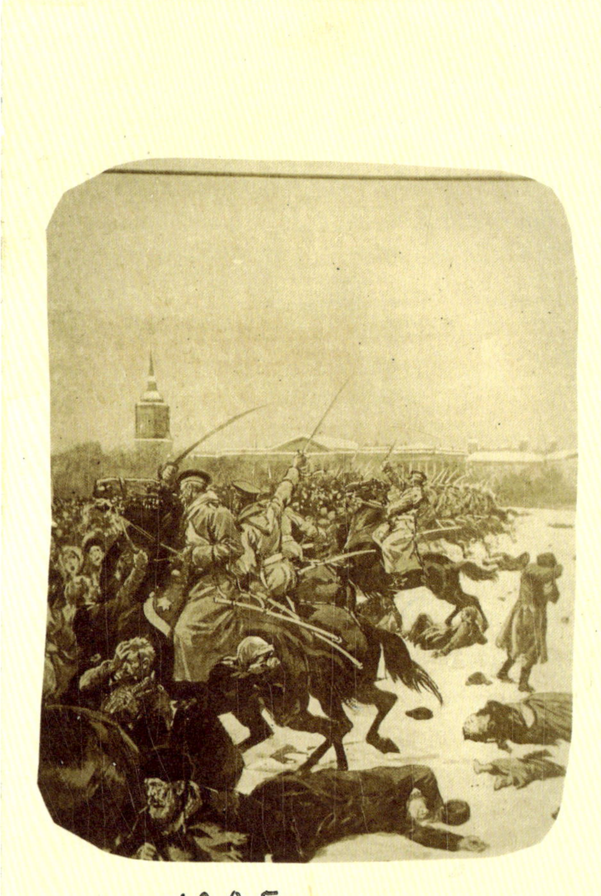

1905 г.
9 января

Hundreds were killed and many more injured on a day that would thereafter be known as 'Bloody Sunday'.[27] The revolutionaries abroad, most of whom had been decidedly ambivalent about the march itself, were in uproar at the result. In Geneva and Paris, exiled émigrés openly delighted in what was already being referred to as a revolution.[28] 'The bloody day of 9 January showed the whole world what wild beasts, murderers and villains we are dealing with in the Tsarist government,' wrote the Menshevik Iulii Martov. 'If the revolution is to triumph,' he added, 'it must use the most decisive means possible against this bestiality.'[29]

Georges Scott. *The Cossacks' Onslaught.* No publication details, circa 1905. The handwritten caption reads: '9 January 1905'. Originally published in *L'Illustration* on 28 January 1905.

All the revolutionaries pushed a similar line, and much of the propaganda that followed was aimed at goading the workers into violent insurrection. 'The government gave you a harsh lesson and showed you ... that the path of humble petitioning will never achieve anything,' read one Socialist-Revolutionary leaflet.[30] On the streets, this incendiary material found a ready audience. In Saint Petersburg, 'shouts of 'executioners, scum, robbers, murderers', now greeted the police when they asked people to disperse.'[31] A statement by the Tsar absolving all those who had taken part in the march did little to help. 'I don't want his forgiveness,' one worker said, 'it's him who should be asking for our forgiveness.'[32]

The lack of press freedom in Russia had proved both troubling and troublesome to many progressive journalists during the Russo-Japanese War, but it became absurd after Bloody Sunday. There had been no serious reforms since 1865, and in the intervening period the regime had shown little interest in enlightening the people as to the true state of affairs in the Empire. Indeed, from its point of view, the less they knew the better. In this dark state, any issues that related even remotely to the political and economic life of the country were taboo. Workers' rights, strikes, pogroms, revolutionaries and repression could neither be reported in serious newspapers, nor illustrated in popular journals.

By the end of January 1905, periodical editors had been banned from discussing clashes between soldiers and demonstrators, and ordered not to print any 'sharp or provocative articles or stories' on the labour question.[33] Thus, fundamental issues that had led to the killing of hundreds of unarmed civilians could not be discussed openly or even mentioned in the nation's newspapers and journals.[34] These restrictions infuriated the liberal press, and as the turmoil grew, journalists started to kick back against what one editor described as, 'a grievous crime against the Russian people, which dooms them to live without rights, forever residing in ignorance and darkness.'[35]

While the public record was silent, the revolutionaries were shouting from the rooftops. Bloody Sunday provided a focal point for discontent across the country, and the radical opposition was determined to channel this into political anger against the regime. With little possibility of publicising news of the government's repressive actions in the press, illegal publications were one of few ways that the population could hear the other side of the story. Russian cities were inundated with leaflets pouring out invective against the 'bloody Tsar' and his ministers, and many who had not previously thought to read such material were now brought into the circle of revolutionary influence.

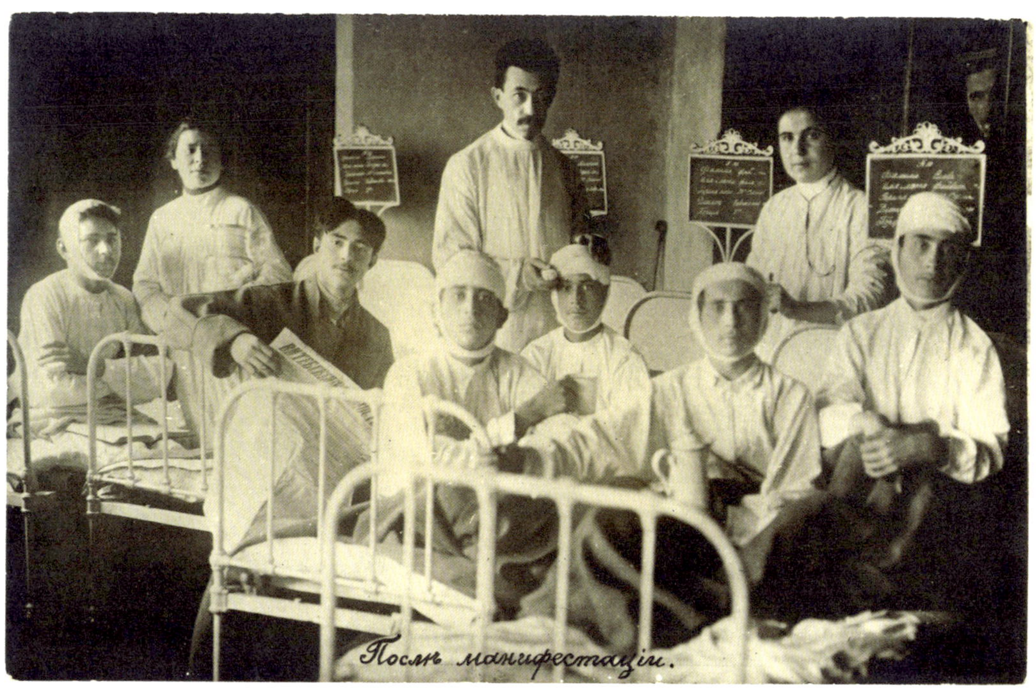

Anonymous photographer. *After the Demonstration* [Vitebsk]. No publication details, circa 1905.

In the push to get their message out, the revolutionary parties looked to other forms of propaganda, including those previously considered impractical, due to the insufficient ideological and financial returns they were thought to offer. Anti-government postcards had long been used for propaganda and fundraising purposes in Western Europe, but the medium had not yet fully taken hold in Russia because the difficulties – danger, cost, personnel, and audience – had always been considered too great. However, the significant increase in public donations and support that the revolutionaries received after Bloody Sunday now made their production in Russia a far more viable and attractive option.

'Dear Colleague, please send cards and photographs now – as many as you can, without delay,' wrote a Kursk-based revolutionary just under a month after the massacre. 'Everyone is already asking me for them. Don't send anything else. Send more examples showing the events in Saint Petersburg. Are there any of the 'Russian Revolution' postcards? I am expecting your parcel by the 25th.'[36] This unsigned letter, which was sent to Kiev Polytechnic student Vasilii Miller on 21 February 1905, demonstrates the speed with which postcards came into service after Bloody Sunday and how quickly they spread, not just across cities, but whole provinces.

The revolutionaries in Western Europe also ramped up their postcard output, churning out images relating to the events in Saint Petersburg.[37] But propaganda could now be made and distributed far closer to the source of the action. In March, a raid on a flat occupied by a group of Social Democrats in Kiev netted a large haul of revolutionary material, as well as what appears to be a mobile propaganda kit. Inside a neatly packed suitcase was a man's grey summer coat, a towel, two pairs of woolly long johns, socks, a flask of ink, over 1,000 seditious leaflets, and 1,761 copies of *Iskra*. The police discovered other items hidden in a satchel, and elsewhere in the apartment, twenty-one postcards, all of which related to 9 January.[38]

Ready money and a willing audience oiled the wheels of postcard production in Russia and abroad, but the importance of Bloody Sunday was not only to have put the necessary practical conditions in place, but also to have begotten the subject matter on which the imagery could be based. Newspapers and pamphlets continued to provide ideological cohesion for individual groups, but the focus of opposition to the Tsar was now not an idea but an event, and this was most powerfully described in visual form. From this moment onwards much of the content of anti-government postcards would be driven by real-life situations – political and practical occurrences that affected the fate of the nation at large.

Some postcards transmitted factual information; a number, for example, reproduced the text of Gapon's petition. But they were at their most compelling when conveying a single, hard-hitting idea. The best showed events on Palace Square, where against a backdrop of the Winter Palace, the mighty worked to crush the meek. Then as now, depictions of government troops killing women and children were hugely effective evocations of state brutality, requiring little explanation or knowledge of the circumstances. These images belied the complications of the movement, their aesthetic accessible and appealing to all who might be inclined to sympathise with the idea that the Russian state was a repressive regime with no interest in the wellbeing of its citizens.

The events of 9 January broke the Tsarist creed, fatally damaging popular belief in the sacred mystery of autocracy. Nicholas may still have believed in his divine right to rule, but the population was never again quite so sure of his benevolence towards them.[39] Postcards widened this disjoint, driving a wedge between Imperial ideology and the reality of everyday life in Russia. Forced to contend with imagery that purported to show the visual truth of events, the government no longer had the possibility of simply denying the facts. With devastating effectiveness, postcards exposed the lie that autocracy was justified because it served the best interests of its citizens.

Bloody Sunday was one of the first occasions that pictorial works were used en masse by the revolutionary parties to depict a contemporary event, and part of its legacy was to convince them of the huge potential of visual media, and by extension the postcard. The massacre not only confirmed the medium as the pre-eminent form of revolutionary visual propaganda, it also helped to establish a canon of imagery that would be used throughout the 1905 period. From this moment onwards, the idea that the postcards embodied – of trust betrayed and innocence killed – was repeated continuously in opposition photographs, paintings, and cartoons.

For foreign humourrists in Western Europe, the unrest in Russia also proved a rich source of inspiration. From Prague to Barcelona, and Milan to Rotterdam, satirical journals were filled with images characterising Nicholas as a ruthless tyrant. In France, the artists Orens (Charles Denizard), Mille (Félix-Antoine Marmonier), and A. Molynk became notorious for their politically charged postcards condemning Tsarist repression, the majority of which were issued in small collectors' editions.[40] Around the same time, Russian-language postcard cartoons also became more widespread, both in Russia and abroad. And all the while, portraits of revolutionary terrorists kept on selling.[41]

The post-Bloody Sunday period ended with a bang. On 4 February, the Tsar's uncle, Governor of Moscow Grand Duke Sergei Alexandrovich, was blown-up in another attack organised by the Socialist-Revolutionary Party. The bombing, carried out by a twenty-seven-year-old radical named Ivan Kaliaev, was the first successful assassination of a member of the Romanov Family since the death of Alexander II.

The postcard journal of the Society of Saint Eugenia expressed the charity's shock at the 'villainous' murder of a royal who had been so supportive of its activities, but many others, including liberal reformers, refused to condemn the attack.[42] For their part, the Socialist-Revolutionaries were jubilant: 'The well-aimed bomb that was thrown by our heroic comrade has removed one of the most repugnant pillars of autocracy from the historical stage,' crowed one Party leaflet shortly afterwards.[43] Following Kaliaev's execution, hagiographic portraits were widely disseminated, conferring eternal glory on this thirty-something activist, amateur poet, and policeman's son.[44]

The Spread of Anti-Government Postcards

At the end of January 1905, a special commission was set up to revise the country's press laws, but work was slow.[45] Violence, strikes, assassinations and open discussion of political issues continued all the while, emboldening many to push harder for more immediate change. Newspapers and journals, which depended for their existence on their ability to convey and interpret current events, were at the forefront of this battle, taking risks and liberties wherever they dared. The censorship committees did their best to frustrate the lunging flurries of the press, but the sheer amount of bad news made the task a near impossibility.

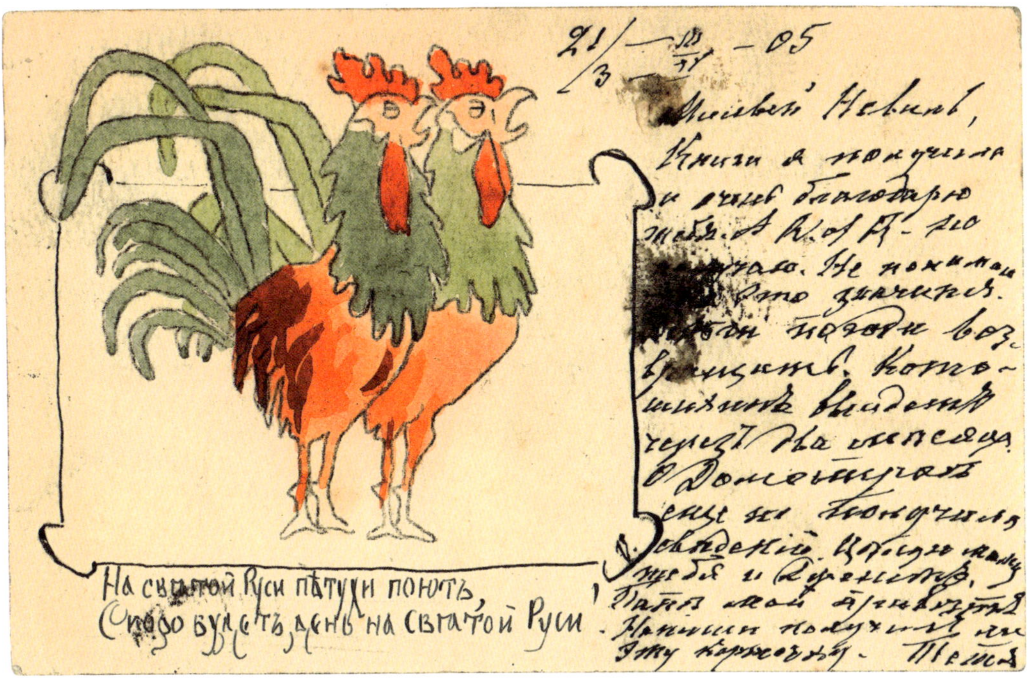

Valerii Karrik. *In Holy Russia the Cocks Are Crowing. It Will Soon Be Day in Holy Russia.* Hand-coloured postcard, Saint Petersburg, 1905. This postcard was sent by a cousin of Karrik's to her nephew in March 1905.

Anti-government postcard production was still largely the preserve of the revolutionary parties, but the spirit of unrest was beginning to spread. In March, Chemodanov, who had begun regularly attending opposition meetings, displayed a series of subversive drawings on the sidelines of a large medical conference in Moscow.[46] He was now more convinced than ever, both of the need for seditious imagery and its power. 'It is vital to discredit the government,' he told a friend, adding that, 'a well composed picture can persuade far more effectively than an article.'[47]

The Russo-British artist Valerii Karrik, a softly-spoken but deeply-engaged illustrator and writer close to revolutionary circles, was also making anti-government cartoons at this time. Karrik's works were all hand-drawn on postcard blanks, a widely available medium, popular among amateur enthusiasts. By avoiding the need to use a registered printing house, he was able to side-step official censorship of political imagery. His cartoons were comparatively mild nonetheless, deploying zoomorphism to herald the coming of a new order, rather than satirising the government directly. As he put it in one postcard: 'In Holy Russia the cocks are crowing. It will soon be day in Holy Russia.'[48]

Spring brought forth a rash of printed works relating to social issues and political theory. The reluctant, if dutiful new head of the Main Administration for Press Affairs, Aleksei Belgard later wrote that on his appointment in March it was clear that, 'under the existing circumstances, the press laws that I had been called upon to oversee had almost completely lost their sense, and their active power.'[49] Under a continuous drip of new material, the censorship committees were forced to concede ground, and as a result some more moderate leftist political texts were permitted. Encouraged by these changes, a few more assertive publishers now made moves to bring anti-government imagery into the open.

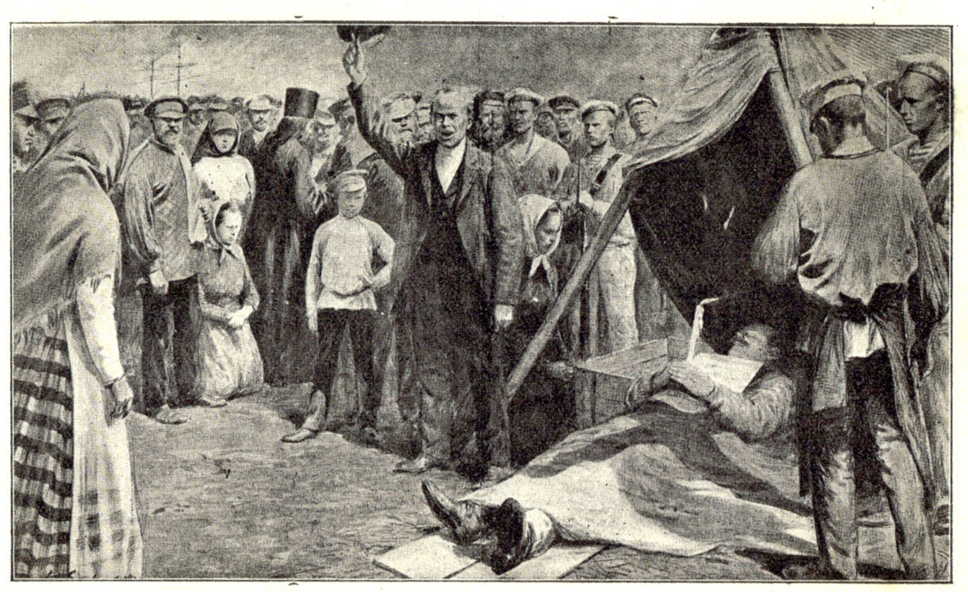

Louis Sabattier. *Vakulinchuk's Corpse on the Odessa Embankment. Sold in Aid of the Crew of the Potemkin.* Published by Iskra or Iskry, Western Europe, mid-1905.

In May 1905, the Press Administration looked at a set of portraits of Russian writers and thinkers, among which was an image of the revolutionary theorist Petr Lavrov. Apparently unbeknown to the censor, Vera Vodovozova, the individual who had put forward the images, was a member of the Kiev Committee of the Socialist-Revolutionary Party.[50] Vodovozova, who already had a rich revolutionary past, was evidently seeking to use publishing as a legitimate and sustainable way of fundraising. The outcome of the endeavour was a partial victory for the opposition. The Administration forbade the image of Lavrov, but allowed publication of the rest of the series to go ahead.[51]

The following month, the Saint Petersburg Censorship Committee received an application for two postcards, one reproducing a painting by Pavel

Svedomskii titled *The Terror during the French Revolution* (date unknown) and the other a copy of Iakob Kalinichenko's *Before the Search* (1895), which depicts a revolutionary burning his papers. Although the pictures had been painted some years earlier, the postcards were turned down by the Committee, 'in view of the fact that their content might have an agitational effect on the public, who are currently in an extremely turbulent state of mind.'[52] Both publishers and the censor were keenly aware that historical images could resonate just as powerfully as their contemporary counterparts.

The Press Administration was not yet willing to loosen its grip over printed imagery, but the very fact that a publisher thought to submit these works at all is significant. Attempts to disseminate anti-government pictures legally were still rare, but these two incidents are important for providing evidence of the growing commercial trade in leftist material, and of the increasing boldness of publishers as they strove to access a developing market.[53] Over previous months, anti-government postcards had become a viable and attractive financial proposition, and little by little individuals were beginning to look for legitimate ways to reap the potential rewards.

The majority of anti-government postcards, however, were still being processed through the underground, and officials, meanwhile, were doing their best to suppress them. In May, Warsaw's head of police wrote to the Main Administration for Press Affairs to complain about four photographic postcards depicting the unrest in the city.[54] These were duly banned, but one might well ask to what effect. Government initiatives helped to limit the scope, quantity and quality of leftist postcards, but they could neither stop them from appearing, nor fully curtail their distribution. Even if the authorities in one area knew about a particular postcard, the speed with which it could be distributed often far outpaced the wheels of state.[55]

Later that month, the Baltic Fleet was defeated by the Japanese at Tsushima, a decisive event that increased opposition to the war and contributed to a further lowering of morale in the navy. In June, sailors on the Battleship Potemkin revolted over a batch of rotten food. The mutiny was quickly suppressed, but it unnerved the government and opened up the possibility of further disturbances in the armed forces. Postcards reflecting the mutiny, however, were not widely produced.[56] Bloody Sunday still dominated the imagery of the main opposition parties, and it was not until the later Soviet period that the mutiny assumed its exalted place in the revolutionary visual sphere.

Over the summer, the revolutionaries continued to print enormous quantities of propaganda. Between May and July, the Moscow committee of the Socialist-Revolutionary Party issued 80,000 copies of 40 different leaflets. Many called openly for an armed uprising to overthrow the regime, reflecting ongoing preparations for an eventual showdown.[57] Postcard

Next Spread

Anonymous artist. *Freedom of Assembly*. No publication details, late 1905.

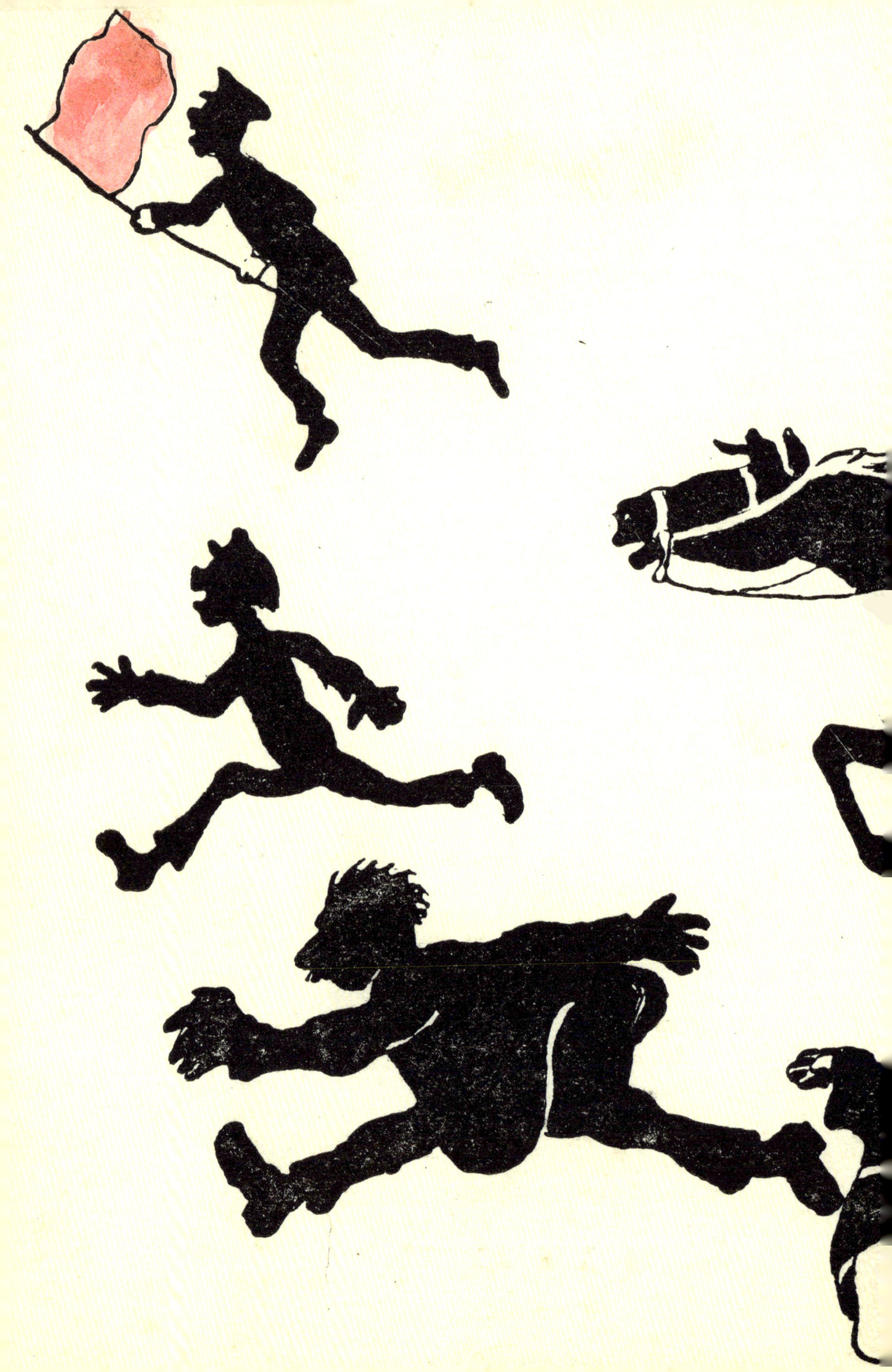

Свобода собраній.

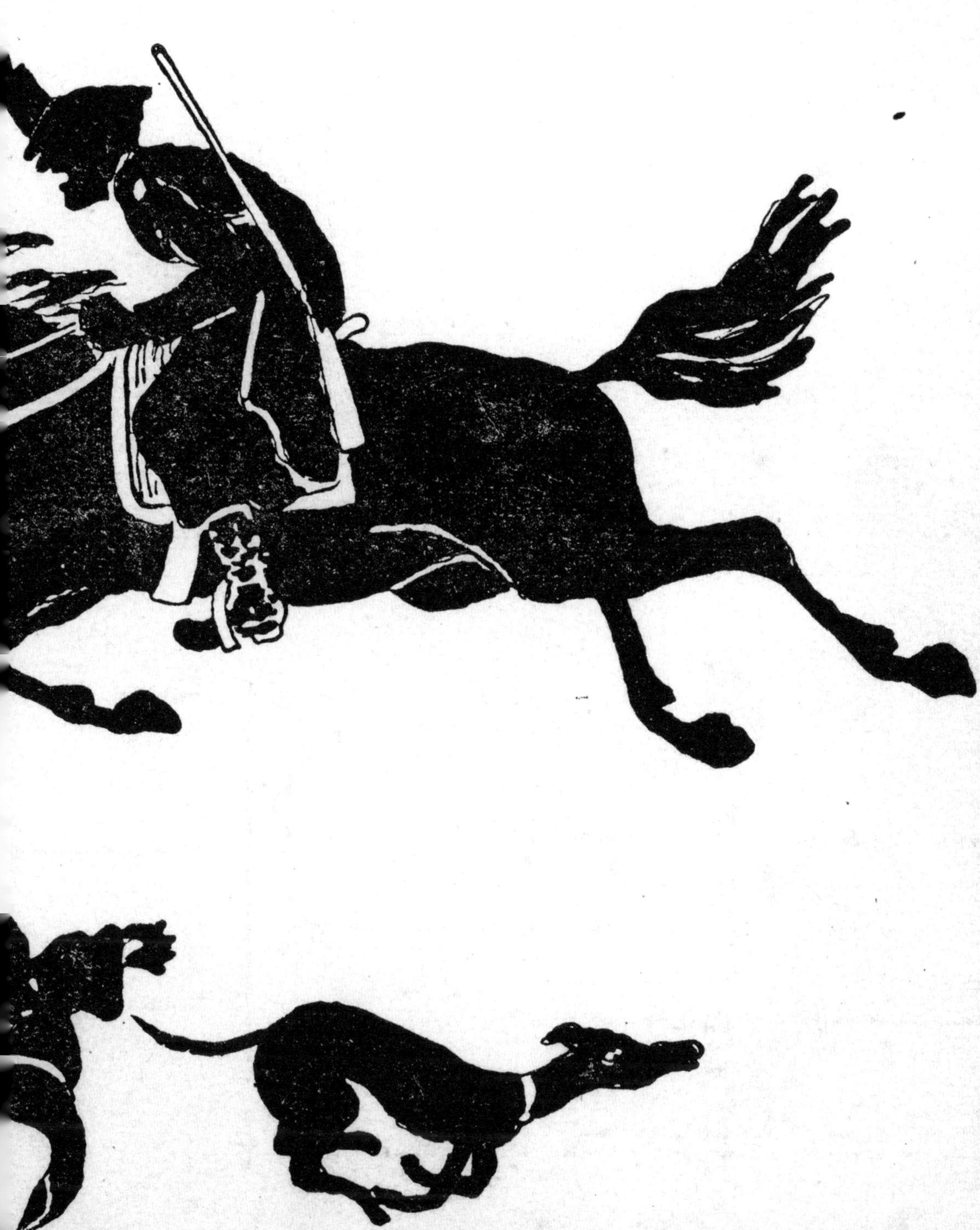

production during this period was slight compared to pamphlets and proclamations, but proof of its continuing influence can be found in the police archives, where reports of items found during official searches show that ownership of anti-government postcards was becoming a common occurrence, particularly among revolutionary activists.

One such incident took place in June 1905, when a guard at the Trekhgornyi Textile Mill in Moscow overheard pistol shots coming from a nearby sand quarry. When the perpetrator, a former peasant named Petr Iakovlev was detained he was found to be carrying a Smith and Wesson revolver and three anti-government postcards (two depictions of Bloody Sunday and a portrait of Kaliaev). Iakovlev, who worked at the mill, had joined the Socialist-Revolutionary Party just a few months previously. He told the police that he had bought the postcards on the banks of the River Moskva for five kopecks each.[58] This is no more than one might pay for a regular postcard, proof that opposition images were no longer the coveted rarity they had once been.

Throughout the summer, editors, publishers and booksellers continually harried at the sidelines of the permissible, putting yet more pressure on the Main Administration for Press Affairs. That same June, a twenty-seven-year-old former architecture student turned artist named Iurii Artsybushev was given permission to start up an illustrated periodical, the first in what would become a new wave of liberal-minded satirical journals. From the moment it first appeared, *Zritel* [*The Spectator*] caused a furore. Although highly suggestive rather than openly defiant, its boldness startled the public, a position shared by officials on the Saint Petersburg Censorship Committee, who prepared lengthy reports on its various transgressions.

The Administration relied for its mandate on adherence to the principle of preliminary censorship, but through cartoons, caricature, prose and verse, the journal exposed the weakness of a censorial system that was dependent on goodwill and limited resources. When loyalty to the crown slipped, as it did in 1905, its authority was fundamentally undermined. There were simply not the personnel available to stop a campaign of mass disobedience, and by the summer, officials were all too aware that they were losing control over the industry. At a meeting in July, it was acknowledged in reference to *Zritel* that 'preliminary censorship is completely powerless to fight against the current direction, and moreover, the mood of the periodical press.'[59]

August finally brought a negotiated peace to end the Russo-Japanese War and the promise of a consultative assembly – considered inadequate by most liberals and a waste of time by the revolutionaries.[60] The Moscow censor, meanwhile, passed Chemodanov's first postcards for publication. All were based on drawings completed around seven months previously, covering the rise of the liberation movement and the dire predicament in which Russia now found itself.[61] The reason for the delay is unknown, but it is an indication of the extent to which the political situation had moved on that it was now possible, and moreover made financial sense, for Chemodanov to publish his drawings in postcard form.

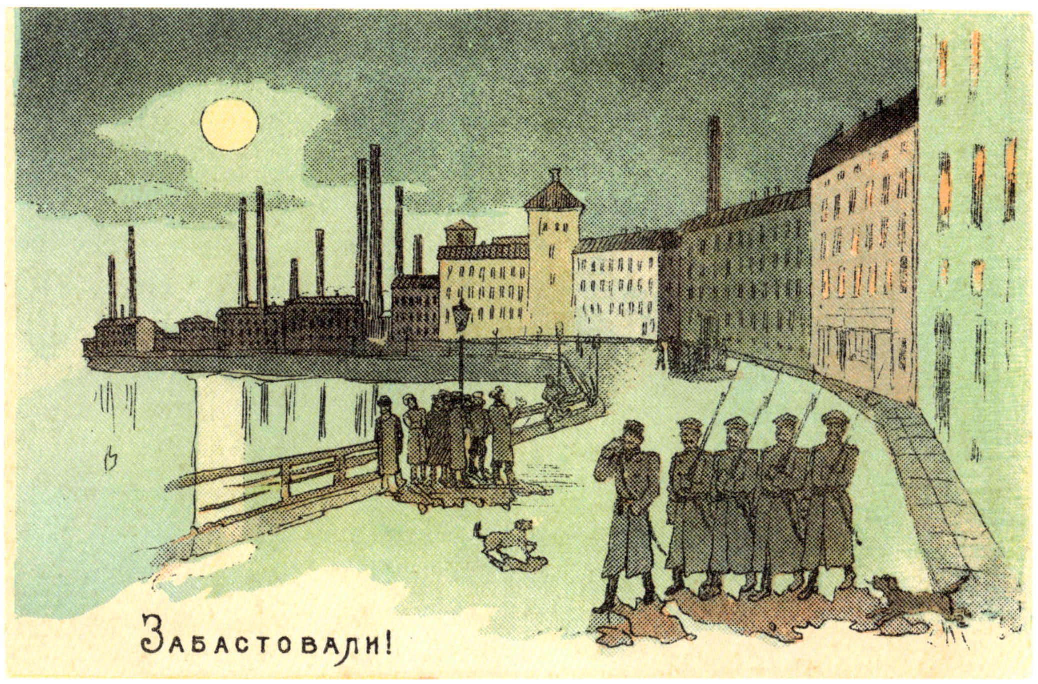

Anonymous artist. *They've Gone on Strike!* No publication details, late 1905.

The same month, 'in view of the length of time that has passed since his death,' the Saint Petersburg censor allowed the Society of Saint Eugenia to print a postcard portrait of revolutionary theorist Alexander Herzen. It was not only significant that such a comparatively conservative organisation should want to print an image of a celebrated opposition figure, but also that the censor should acquiesce.[62] With discussion over how to solve Russia's political future now a near universal pastime among the country's elite, ideas of reform and revolution were slowly edging towards mainstream acceptability, and with them, the once outlawed imagery of their historical proponents.

The October Manifesto

On 20 September 1905, employees of the Sytin printing plant staged a walk-out in demand of better pay and working conditions. They were soon joined by other printers, stopping the production of newspapers and journals across Moscow. The city's bakers and workers from other industries went on strike in solidarity, and over the coming days there were regular clashes on the streets between workers, students and police. In early

Next spread

Anonymous artist. *The Russian Constitution. 1905.* No publication details, late 1905. The flag is inscribed 'Liberty or Death'.

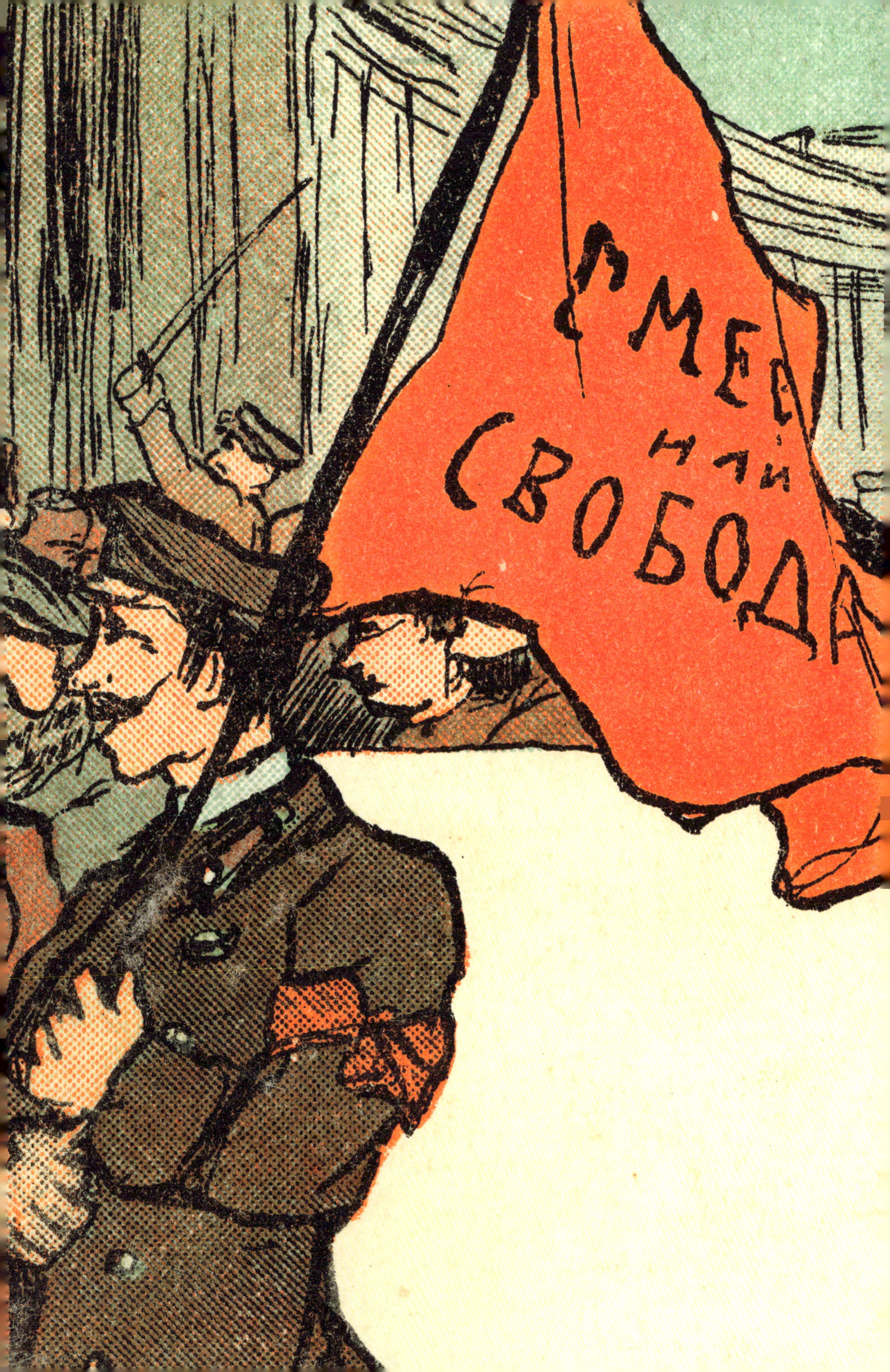
СМЕ
или
СВОБОДА

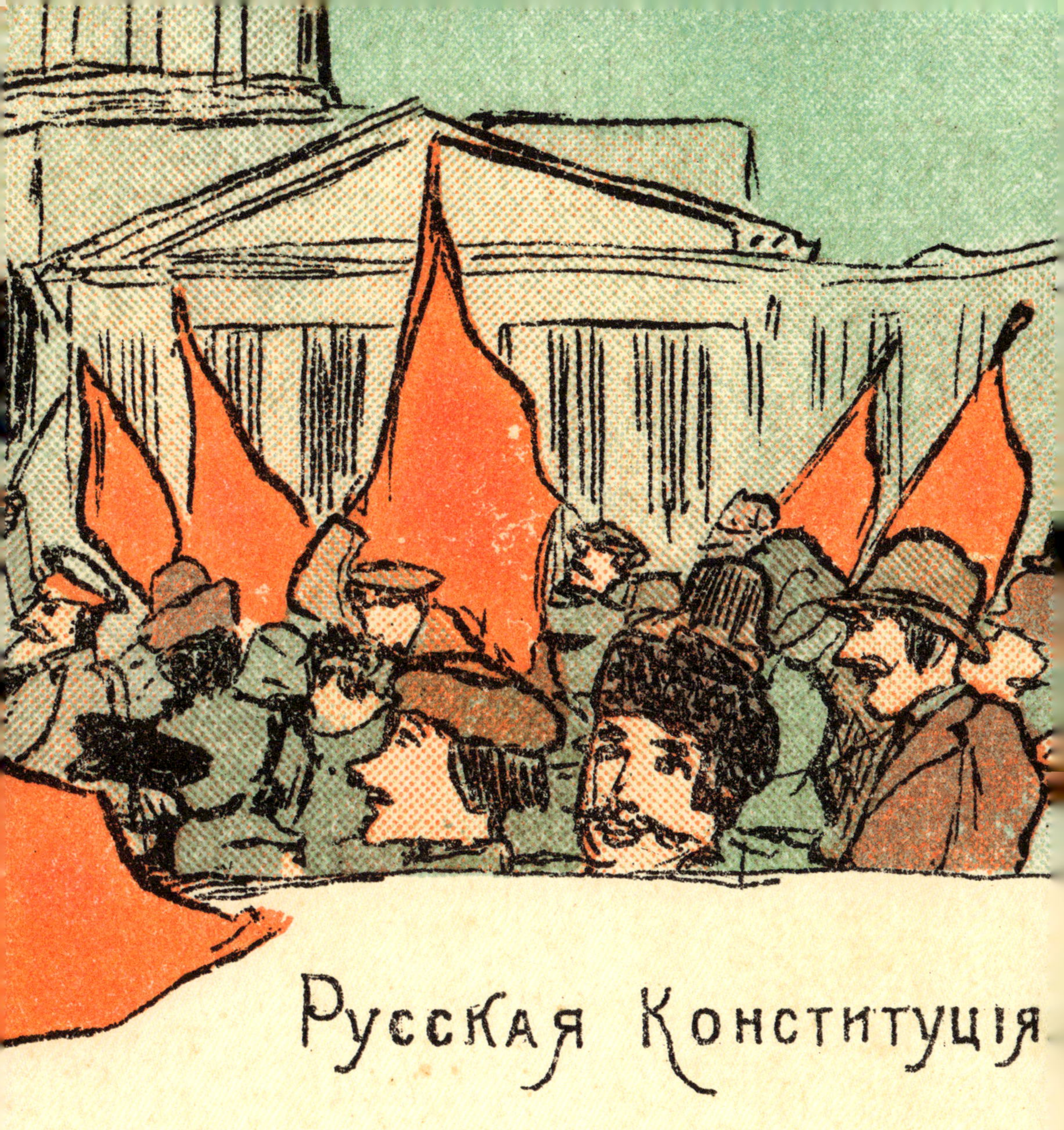
Русская Конституція

October, just as enthusiasm in Moscow started to ebb, momentum picked up in Saint Petersburg. A general strike on the railways was called for, and with the ball now fully rolling, more and more workers joined the boycott.

On the evening of 13 October, a Soviet [Council] was formed in order to direct and coordinate the strike action. This became the centre of the movement, with its own armed detachment, the ability to negotiate with the city authorities, and pretensions to rival state power. By 16 October, every transport line in the country had been stopped. Food prices went up, medical supplies started running low, and the lights on the streets went out.[63] In the face of a united opposition, the Tsar at last agreed to act. Sergei Witte, the former finance minister who had recently made a triumphant return from peace negotiations with Japan, was instructed to draw up a document outlining political reforms.

The resulting proclamation was short but its implications were far-reaching. Russia's citizens were promised a legislative assembly or Duma, and awarded 'inalienable freedoms based on the principles of personal inviolability, freedom of conscience, speech, assembly and association.' On paper at least, the Tsar and his ministers would now be answerable to the people.

The announcement, known as the October Manifesto, was greeted with genuine popular enthusiasm. On the morning after it was signed, large groups flooded the streets of Saint Petersburg and Moscow, singing songs and waving red flags. But that evening, in a harbinger of things to come, a demonstration in the capital was forcibly broken up by government troops, with several people killed and wounded.

In the days that followed, right-wingers known as Black Hundreds attacked anyone they suspected of revolutionary sympathies: mostly students, intellectuals and Jews. These individuals were blamed for forcing the Tsar into making what were seen as unnecessary and un-Russian reforms, a political and national loss for which the Black Hundreds were keen to exact revenge. Demonstrators were beaten up and murdered, drunken mobs fired guns into crowds, and in turn the revolutionaries fought back, leading to bloodshed on all sides. Promises of personal inviolability and freedom of assembly were now overwhelmingly countered by state violence. The revolutionary parties professed to be little surprised by the government's duplicity, but the liberal opposition felt bitterly betrayed.

The Manifesto greatly exacerbated the polarity of political opinion, not only between autocracy and its enemies, but also between the many groups opposing the Tsar, who could not agree on whether the solution to their woes lay in reform or revolution. On one side of the divide were the militant revolutionary parties, and on the other were the liberals, the majority of whom clustered around the banner of the newly formed Constitutional Democratic or Kadet Party. As violence consumed the country, a multitude

Anonymous artist. Untitled caricature of Dmitrii Trepov surmounting a pyramid of shells. No publication details, late 1905.

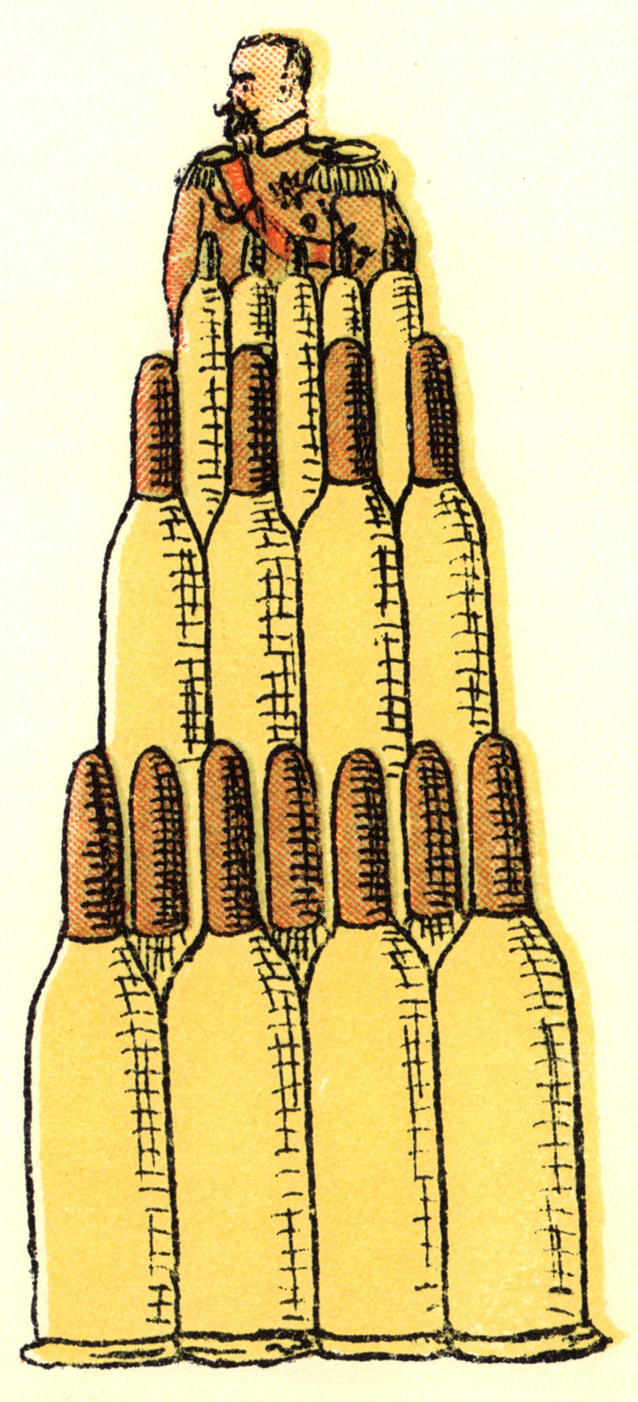

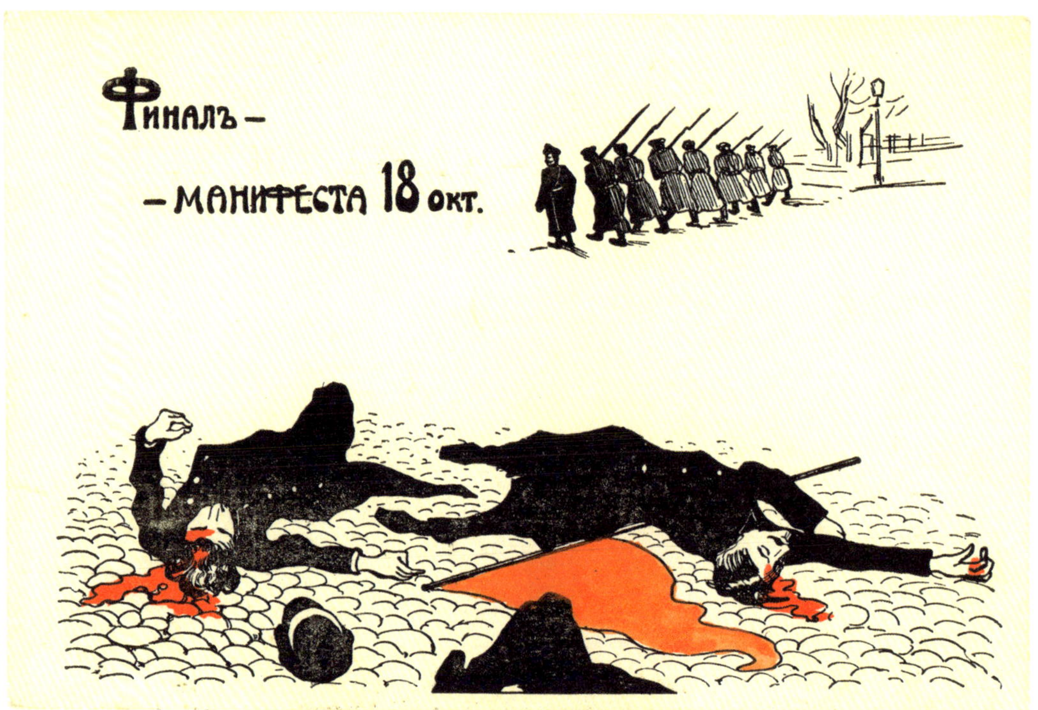

Anonymous artist.
The Conclusion of the 18 October Demonstration.
No publication details, late 1905.

of different opinions on how Russia should be ruled poured out from the presses and into the streets.

Among the censorship committees, the unexpected possibility that the Tsar had, with one stroke of his pen, granted complete press freedom gave rise to confusion, not to say panic. Two days after the Manifesto was announced, Belgard was forced to send a circular to all governors and censors making it clear that until new press laws were drawn up, the committees should continue to adhere to the existing regulations. The circular also gave notice that even after the implementation of new regulations, certain restrictions would remain in place: 'Every country in the world has specific punitive laws to circumscribe the freedom of the press, and that is why in Russia as well, the freedom of the press will always be legally constrained.'[64]

Belgard's only acknowledgement of demands that censorship be abolished was a vaguely worded provision that censors should 'take into account the new conditions in which the press now operates.' Nonetheless, the circular did contain one important concession: with immediate effect, all violations would now be made subject to the courts rather than dealt with according to administrative whim. Belgard, a former lawyer, cautioned censors that, henceforth, they were firmly obligated to follow due process: 'The censor must comply with the new requirements that have been put in place for the press, and with their own tact and a complete disregard for any demands not provided for by law, avoid the possibility of any kind of legitimate censure.'[65]

Despite his implacable belief in Imperial rule, Belgard was a conscientious and practical man; he was clearly receptive to arguments coming from reformist circles that randomly applied repressive measures had caused widespread resentment among publishers. The transferal of disciplinary responsibility to the judiciary can therefore be seen as an attempt to reflect the overall spirit of the October Manifesto, and to ensure that the government was seen to be acting in a uniform and principled manner. The courts were naturally biased and the parameters for punishment wide, but Belgard intended that mutual respect of the law would provide the basis on which the government and the print industry could co-exist.

The problem, however, was that while the political ground had shifted, publishers were being asked to carry on as if nothing had changed. Opposition-related subject matter was still heavily restricted, and until new laws could be enacted preliminary censorship remained in place. Few were in the mood to obey. On the same day that the circular was issued, the Soviet's official organ *Izvestiia* [*News*] ordered Saint Petersburg's printers not to work for any publisher that continued to submit their output to the censor.

Over the summer, printers in the city had formed their own union and in the weeks on either side of the Manifesto many publishers and booksellers followed suit. These unions became a powerful force for change, their defiance of the censor often driven forward by agitating employees, who had far less to lose than their more cautious masters. The front was never

Anonymous artist. *The Union of True Russian People.* No publication details, late 1905. This is a satire of the Black Hundreds organisation 'The Union of True Russian People', founded in 1905.

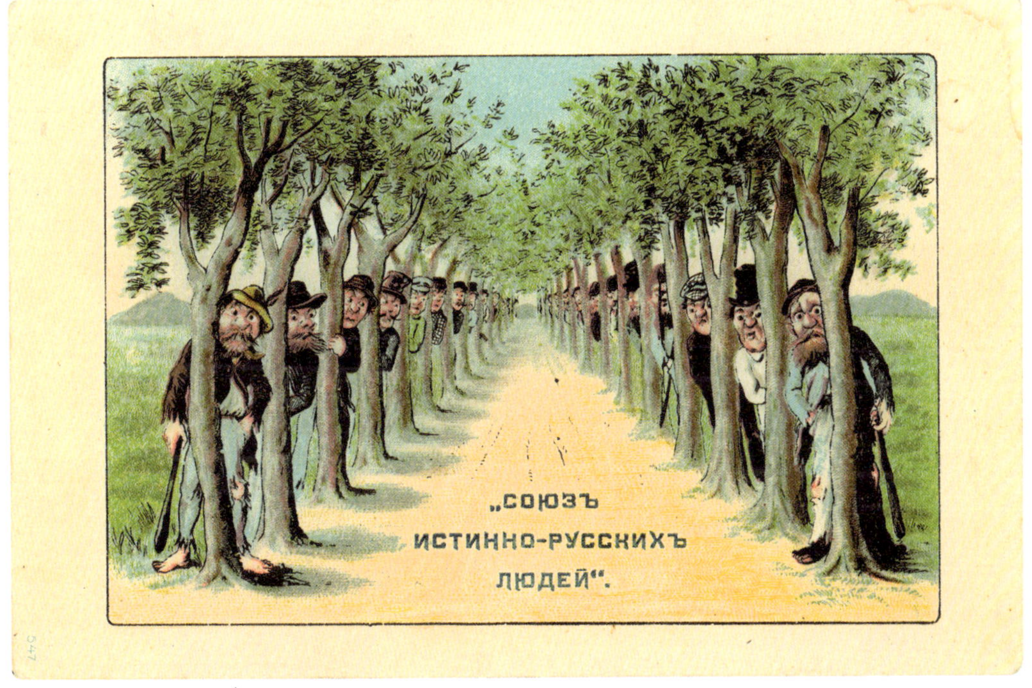

Типы „Истинно-русскихъ людей

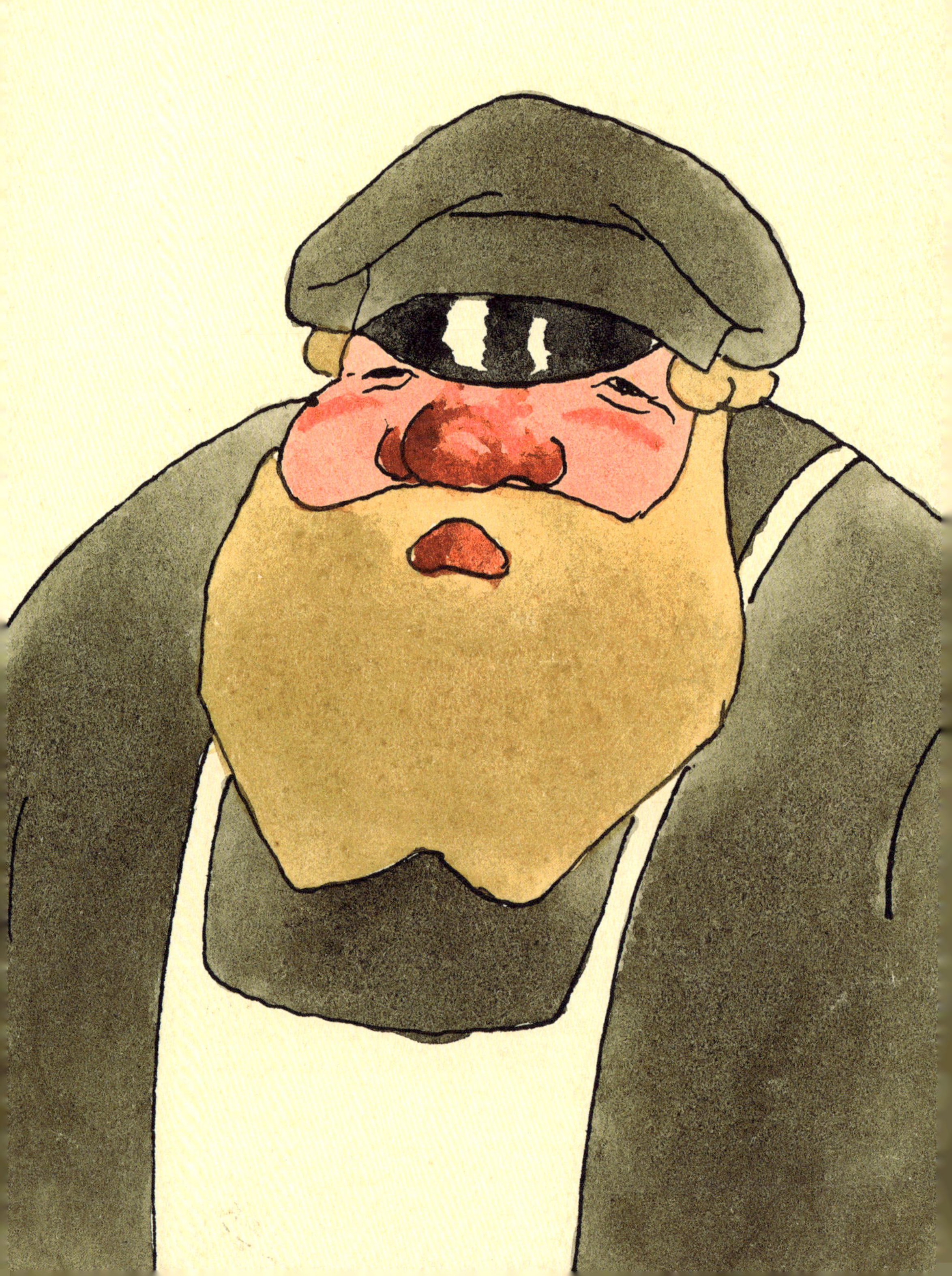

completely united, but the already overburdened machinery of censorship eventually broke down under the pressure.

According to the journal *Knizhnyi vestnik* [*The Book Herald*], press freedom had been a fully ripened apple waiting to fall. In October the winds blew, and in a situation of near anarchy individuals of all types moved to take advantage. Throughout the Empire, pornographers displayed their wares openly, revolutionaries distributed leaflets on the streets, and liberal journalists wrote without care for the consequences. A writer for the journal reported admiringly: 'Freedom of the press has been brought into being by society itself, which refused to wait while the government deigned to chuck them a few scraps of the full freedom it had promised in the Manifesto.'[66]

In this heady environment, editors displayed an unprecedented rebelliousness. *Zritel* had been officially banned on 2 October, but following the Manifesto Artsybushev decided to ignore the ruling and simply restart the journal. The first uncensored issue appeared later that same month. The Administration could do little in the face of such open defiance. Belgard described the task of stemming the onslaught as being akin to trying to fight against revolution with cardboard swords.[67] In the weeks that followed, ministers wrung their hands in despair, continually asking the question, 'what are we to do with the press?' But a lasting solution needed time, both to plan and to implement.

Anonymous artist. *Types of 'True Russian People'.* Hand-drawn postcard, circa late 1905.

November Press Regulations

On 24 November, the government took its first concrete steps towards solving its predicament with the announcement of new procedures governing periodicals. The November, or Temporary Regulations provided a legal framework for the promise of freedom of speech made in the October Manifesto, and comprised the regime's boldest attempt yet to reform and re-establish control over the press. Although it contained far more detailed provisions, the decree was essentially confirmation of the changes put forward in the previous month's circular. Requirements for starting up new periodicals were relaxed, preliminary censorship for newspapers and journals was abolished (except in the provinces), and the promise to make punishments a matter for the courts confirmed.

There is no question that the Regulations constituted an improvement on previous circumstance, but Russia still did not have freedom of speech in its most literal sense. Launching a periodical was now a relatively straightforward matter, but while the route to publication may have been eased, running a newspaper or journal was still fraught with difficulty. There was no greater leeway given on content; indeed, quite the opposite; the Regulations widened the scope for suppression, making it a relatively simple matter to confiscate and shut down any publication that was deemed to have broken the law. The government had granted freedom of speech, but it was still unwilling to grant freedom after speech.

The contradictory nature of the Regulations, which swung between reform and repression, was the result of a careful balancing act between what Belgard characterised as the opposing forces of 'revolution and reaction'.[68] Although a sincere attempt to convert the Tsar's broadly-worded promises of civil freedom into law, Belgard was always clear that the ultimate purpose of the regulations was not to introduce more freedoms per se, but to create enough breathing space to enable the Administration to reassert its full authority.[69] The Regulations were a compromise, made not to grant the press greater licence but to defuse its anger, and in the end they pleased no one. More seriously, they failed in most of their more immediate aims.

Anonymous artist. Untitled depiction of a Black Hundred mob throwing a revolutionary off a bridge. No publication details, circa late 1905.

In the long term, the November Regulations helped to establish new legal parameters for publishing and paved the way for an eventual crackdown on all forms of opposition print media. But in the short term the government's lack of control over the industry, and the ease with which publishers could now get new periodicals into print, ensured that the production of anti-government works continued unabated. With the outcome of the Revolution still far from certain, publishers, writers and artists were not about to hand back their hard-won concessions without a serious fight. The shortlived period that followed was anarchic; not for nothing is it known to posterity as the 'Days of Freedom'.

A few weeks after the Regulations were announced, a 'deluge' of satirical journals rained down on the major cities of the Empire. No longer emasculated by preliminary censorship, 'they were everywhere, pouring forth like stars on an August night, some witty and sharp, others coarse and blunt; they were confiscated on the streets and shredded in the printing houses but they only grew and grew in number.'[70] Another journalist wrote that, 'it was as if someone had accidentally opened the floodgates and a wave of something completely new and sharply satirical surged over the city's stunned inhabitants ... there was not enough paper in the warehouses, printing presses worked day and night, and red ink, in the bloodiest of shades, glowed from every page.'[71]

These journals opened up a platform for writers and artists, providing new outlets and revenue streams for opposition activists. With the forced closure of the main art schools in the late autumn, the major cities had become awash with young men itching to paint the town red.[72] Periodicals made regular calls for contributors, and many of those who stepped up to fill the artistic breach were students.[73] More experienced illustrators, such as Chemodanov and Karrik, were in great demand, but such was the need for satirists that even untrained amateurs threw their hats into the ring.

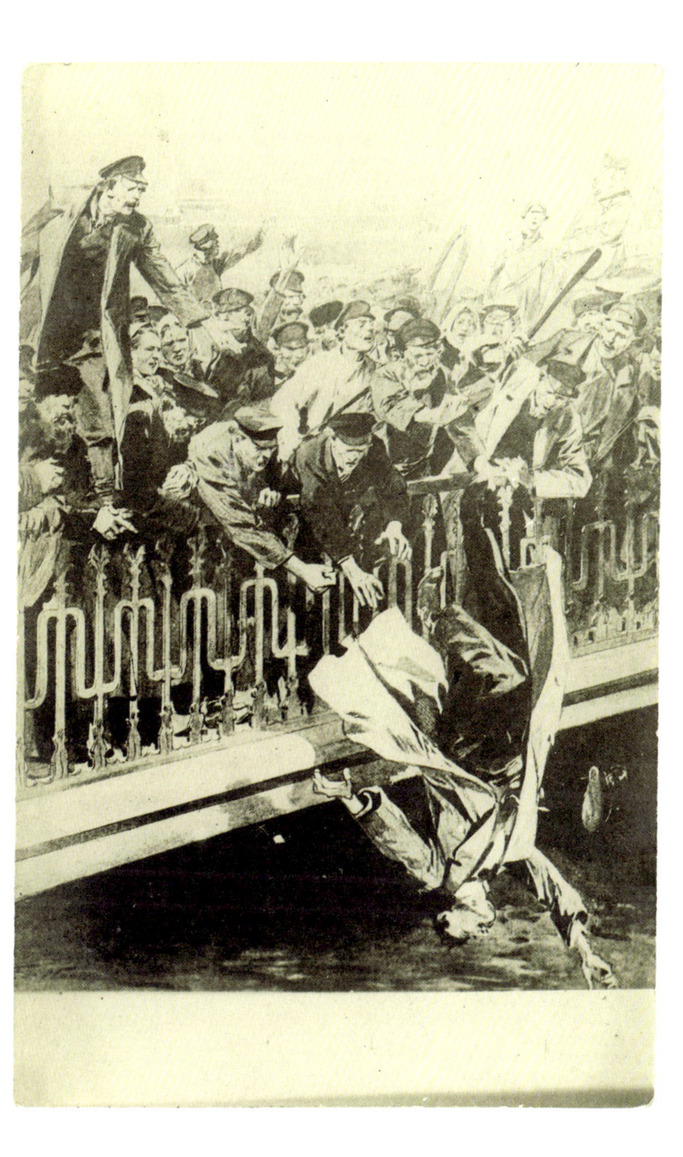

As one contemporary reported: 'Anyone who could wield a pencil and direct a rubber across the page could consider himself capable of somehow or other creating something.'[74]

The November Regulations applied only to periodical publications, but the atmosphere of abandon quickly spread across the whole of the print trade. When the regulations were announced, the Administration had given assurances that new laws covering books, pamphlets, prints and postcards would also soon be worked out. In the event, it was five months before they were unveiled. Until that time, all these media were still officially subject to preliminary censorship. It is almost absurd to think that as opposition newspapers and journals flooded the streets, the government expected the rest of the industry simply to stand by and watch. Quite apart from anything else, it would have been financial madness for publishers to have ignored such an opportunity.

Anonymous photographer. *Tableau Vivant: 'Freedom of the Press'. Days of Freedom. Political Review.* No publication details, late 1905.

The post-October period was described by one contemporary critic as 'a bacchanalia of publishing activity.'[75] According to the bibliographer Nikolai Rubakin, ninety-three new publishing houses were created between late 1905 and April 1906. The popularity of all forms of socialist literature, and the ease with which amenable printers could be found, attracted a wealth of both experienced publishers and speculators, some motivated by politics, others by commerce, and others still by a mixture of the two. There were ideological gains to be made from the disarray, as well as money to be had. In Rubakin's words, 'it seemed as though every Russian with a spare hundred roubles or so, was determined to turn a profit by becoming a publisher.'[76]

Illegal material carried a financial premium, and for printers as well as publishers the motivation to manufacture anti-government works was not always ideological.[77] All the same, printing house owners were often left with little choice in the matter, coming under considerable pressure from their clients and employees. As the Inspector of Printing Houses in Saint Petersburg pointed out: 'They were placed in an extremely difficult situation: either go without work and refuse to submit to demands from publishers and workers to break the law, or commit transgressions and be forced to deal with consequences.'[78] Naturally, many held opposition views, but the motivation to produce illegal works was not always as clear-cut as it may seem in retrospect.

As a result of the publishing binge, the number of book titles went up by around a third. Where once religion and literature had headed content lists, most of the new works were factual, their content often political and economic. Cheaply produced pamphlets now replaced large-format books: even serious tomes on political science were split up, with individual chapters published in separate, more digestible chunks.[79] All were easily read and quickly circulated. This was both the politicisation of the print industry, when feuilleton and partisan opinion became the way in which news and fact

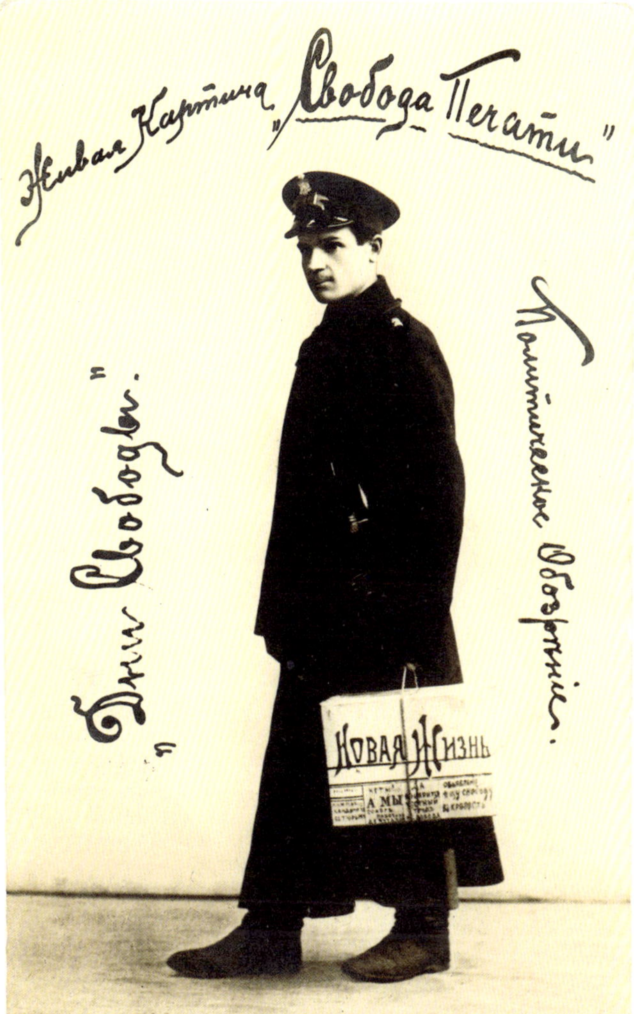

Живая Картина „Свобода Печати"

„Дни Свободы."

Политическое Обозрение.

НОВАЯ ЖИЗНЬ

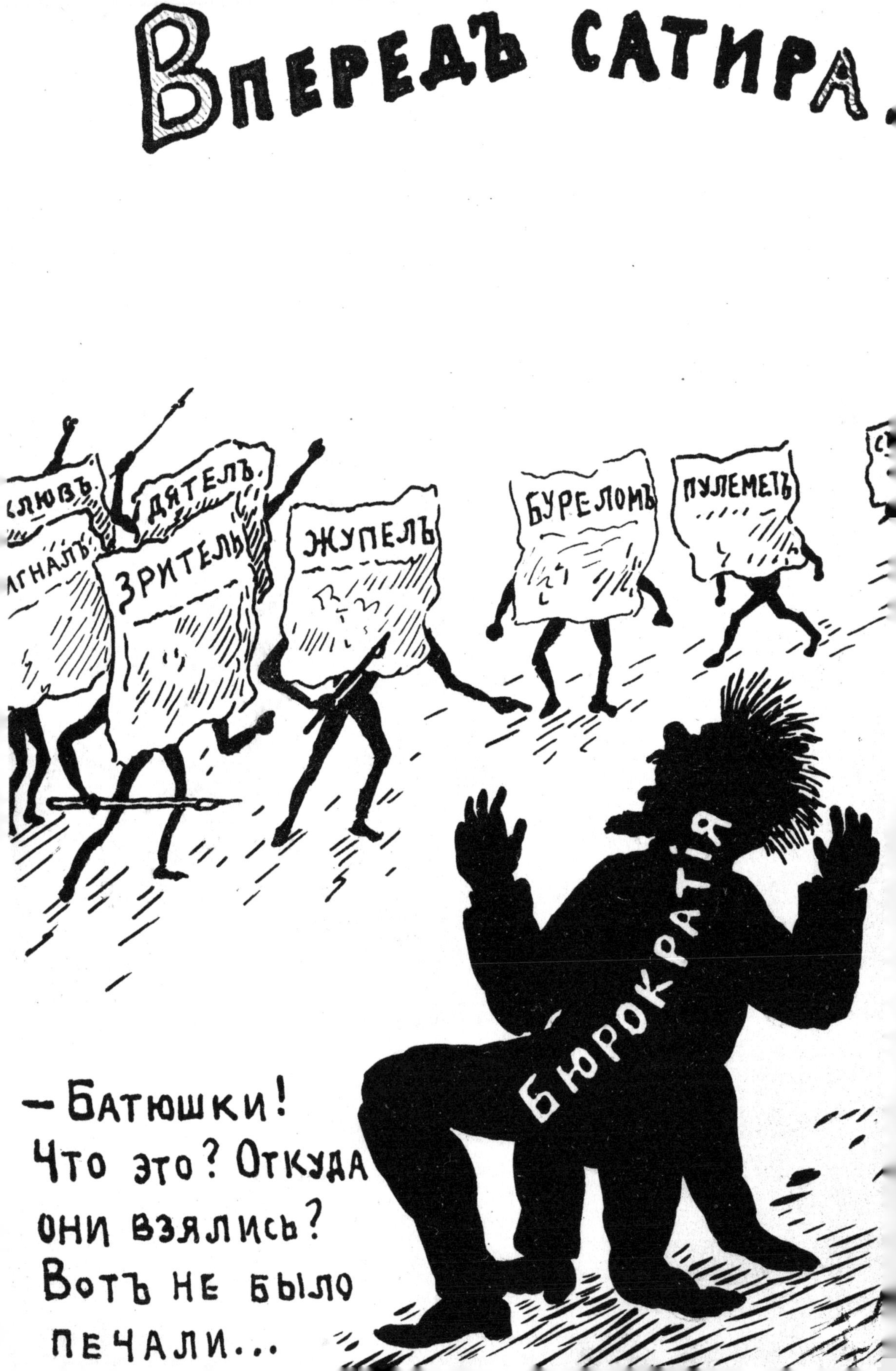

Впередъ сатира.

Дятелъ
Зритель
Жупелъ
Буреломъ
Пулеметъ
Бюрократія

— Батюшки! Что это? Откуда они взялись? Вотъ не было печали...

was absorbed, and the commodification of the propaganda industry, when the market became the only real barometer of success.

Stores were inundated. 'Before spring last year, it was difficult to find a book in any shop that had not passed the censor,' reported Vilnius' Inspector of Printing Houses, 'then at the start of autumn a whole range of small, extremely cheap pamphlets of varying orientation and character started to appear in the central book markets of Saint Petersburg, Moscow, Warsaw, Odessa and Kiev, and other major towns.' At first, many of them were submitted to the censor, but after the Manifesto huge numbers of publications, 'most of them of extremist content and orientation,' appeared for sale without having been approved. The Inspector claimed that the appetite for these editions was enormous: 'Bookshops have literally been trading in nothing else.'[80]

Vasil Gulak. *Satire on the March*. Published by Dmitrii Markov, Kiev, late 1905. The figure, labelled 'Bureaucracy' exclaims: 'Cripes! What's this? Where did they come from? As if we don't have enough problems already…'

The government's loss of control and the slow movement of the justice system had created an air of impunity. One commentator wrote in reference to satirical journals: 'Some editors have already been sentenced to prison, others have been arrested or exiled, and many have had criminal cases opened against them … but none of this has intimidated anyone, nothing has been stopped … despite everything, they're still laughing.'[81] There were countless examples of repression in the months that followed, but political disorder, public demand, and campaigning ahead of the Duma election, created an ongoing incentive to publish, reflecting in turn the vastly expanded numbers of people who now had a say in Russia's political future.

Postcards during the Days of Freedom

On 9 November 1905, the Kiev censor approved the publication of six satirical postcards by the Ukrainian artist Vasil Gulak.[82] These silhouette images, which satirise the regime's betrayal of the October Manifesto, were the first anti-government postcard cartoons legally printed in Russia. Eight days later, another publisher in Saint Petersburg submitted the same designs to the censorship committee there, which also deemed them fit for publication.[83] Further versions soon appeared in Moscow and Odessa in runs of up to 10,000 copies.[84] The speed of their dissemination was extraordinary. Within just a few months, postcards had helped to spread opposition ideas and beliefs across the Russian Empire.

Gulak's silhouettes, although reflective of greater government dispensation towards the print industry, were very much the exception to a prevailing atmosphere of rule-breaking, in which the majority of postcards were published with scant regard to the law. Imperial officials, already under enormous pressure, found it impossible to keep up. In mid-December, the Press Administration issued a circular to regional governors

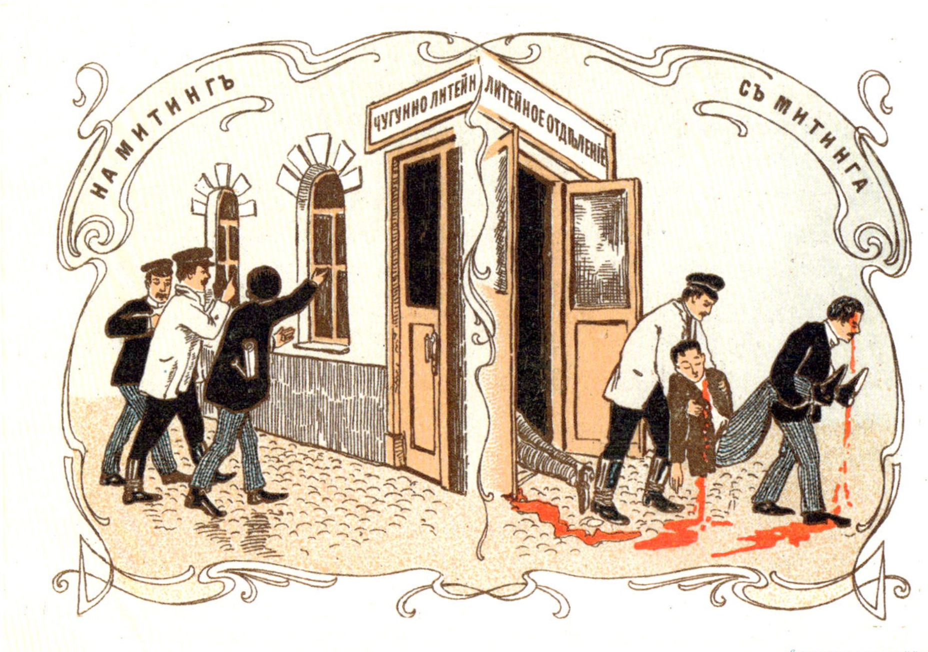

Anonymous artist. *To the Meeting / From the Meeting.* Published by Kh. K. and A. G., Saint Petersburg, late 1905.

complaining that uncensored images were being disseminated 'everywhere and in unprecedented quantities.'[85] Reaffirming the continuing existence of preliminary censorship for all non-periodical material, the Administration demanded that checks on printing houses be strengthened. Many were subsequently closed down, but with publishers in defiant spirit, the onslaught continued.

In concert with other forms of publishing, private firms played a substantial role in the production of anti-government postcards. Across the industry, political collapse and widespread support for change had made the mass production of leftist material a highly lucrative prospect, and while publishing motivations are often opaque, postcards unquestionably became major vehicles for profit as well as ideology. Perhaps inevitably the publisher Nikolai Merder was one of those who jumped aboard the gravy train, printing a range of silhouette cartoons satirising the October Manifesto. Many more established firms were still reluctant to run the political gauntlet, but there were plenty of others only too happy to take their place.

With the situation still so uncertain, it made little sense to risk a business that might be shut down within weeks. Many industry newcomers therefore set up what were known as 'flying publishers' – often one-man enterprises that swooped in to test the market, and then quickly withdrew when the heat became too much to bear.[86] Few succeeded in printing more than one or two sets of satirical postcards. This characteristic trait of 'publishing and running' comes down to the financial, as well as the political risks of publication. Ideology was the main impetus for involvement, but as during the Russo-Japanese War, this did not remove the need to make a profit. The rewards were great, but so too were the potential losses.

Just as capitalist competition aided the development of the postcard in the nineteenth century, so too it enriched the variety and quality of anti-government images in the twentieth. Where once the revolutionaries had seen postcards solely in terms of ideology and profit, entrepreneurial publishers now also looked to the medium as a vehicle for art and design. This approach is most clearly reflected in the more refined chromolithographic cartoons and caricatures that poured onto the market in late 1905 and early 1906. Their appearance heralded the emergence of anti-government postcards from the revolutionary underground, and signalled a broader change in production from cottage industry to professional enterprise.

The revolutionary parties, meanwhile, continued with their own endeavours.[87] Following the Manifesto, a wide-ranging amnesty on political crimes had been passed, and by the end of the year, government spies were reporting that most revolutionary exiles had already returned home. Morale was sky-high; in the words of the Okhrana, the radicals were 'certain both of their own inviolability and of the extensive possibilities for agitation.'[88] The epicentre of revolutionary publishing now moved from Western Europe to Russia itself. 'Abroad practically everything went into temporary shutdown, and in Russia the publication of books and newspapers started at a blistering pace,' wrote the Socialist-Revolutionary Viktor Chernov.[89]

Creating new firms and distribution networks was time-consuming, so initially the revolutionaries relied on partnerships with pre-existing commercial publishers and retail outlets. Alliances of convenience were also formed with photographic studios, printing houses, artists, and middlemen. Underground production continued throughout this period, but in the big cities it was now possible to print postcards covertly in commercial printing houses. Despite this shift in production methods, the revolutionaries continued to concentrate on cheap photomechanical and typographical images. For them, high turnover was preferable to high quality, and unlike some private publishers who channelled their resources into content and design, the radicals remained focused on output and distribution.

Partisan opinion, whether delivered through word or image, had become the way in which much of the population digested Russia's new reality, and in an environment where anything small, rousing and politically subversive gained an audience, postcards held a particular appeal. With official oversight weak, and extensive manufacturing facilities already in place, postcards became a highly convenient and near instantaneous way for publishers from across the political spectrum to relay topics that were being discussed on every street corner of the Empire. Newspapers and journals were a relatively

Next spread

Anonymous artist. *Christmas Tree Gifts for Free Citizens.* No publication details, December 1905. Caricature of Sergei Witte and Aleksei Ignatiev (on tree).

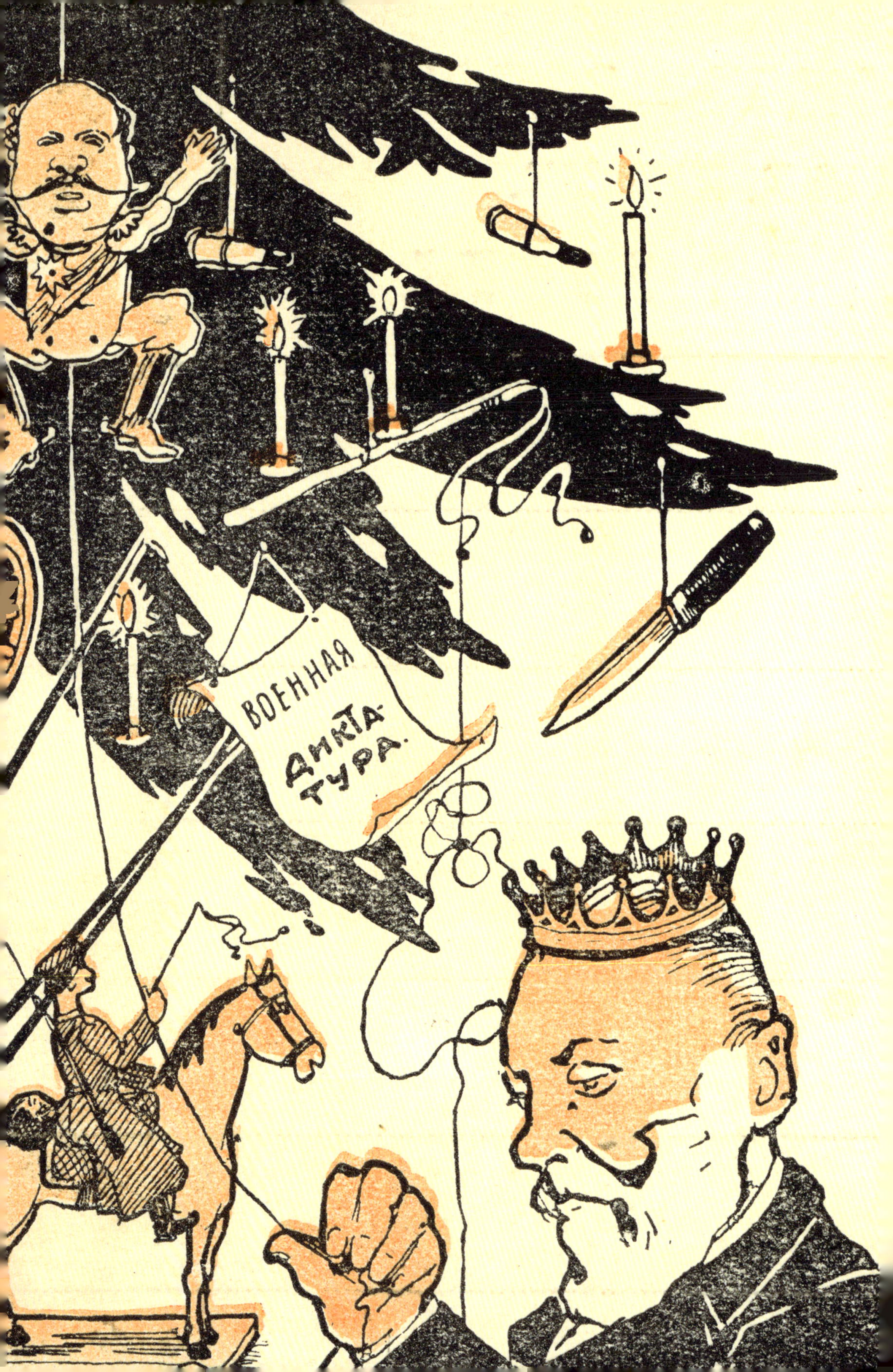

ВОЕННАЯ
ДИКТА-
ТУРА.

ПОДАРКИ ЗАГОТОВЛЕННЫЯ НА
ЕЛКУ СВОБОДНЫМЪ ГРАЖДАНАМЪ

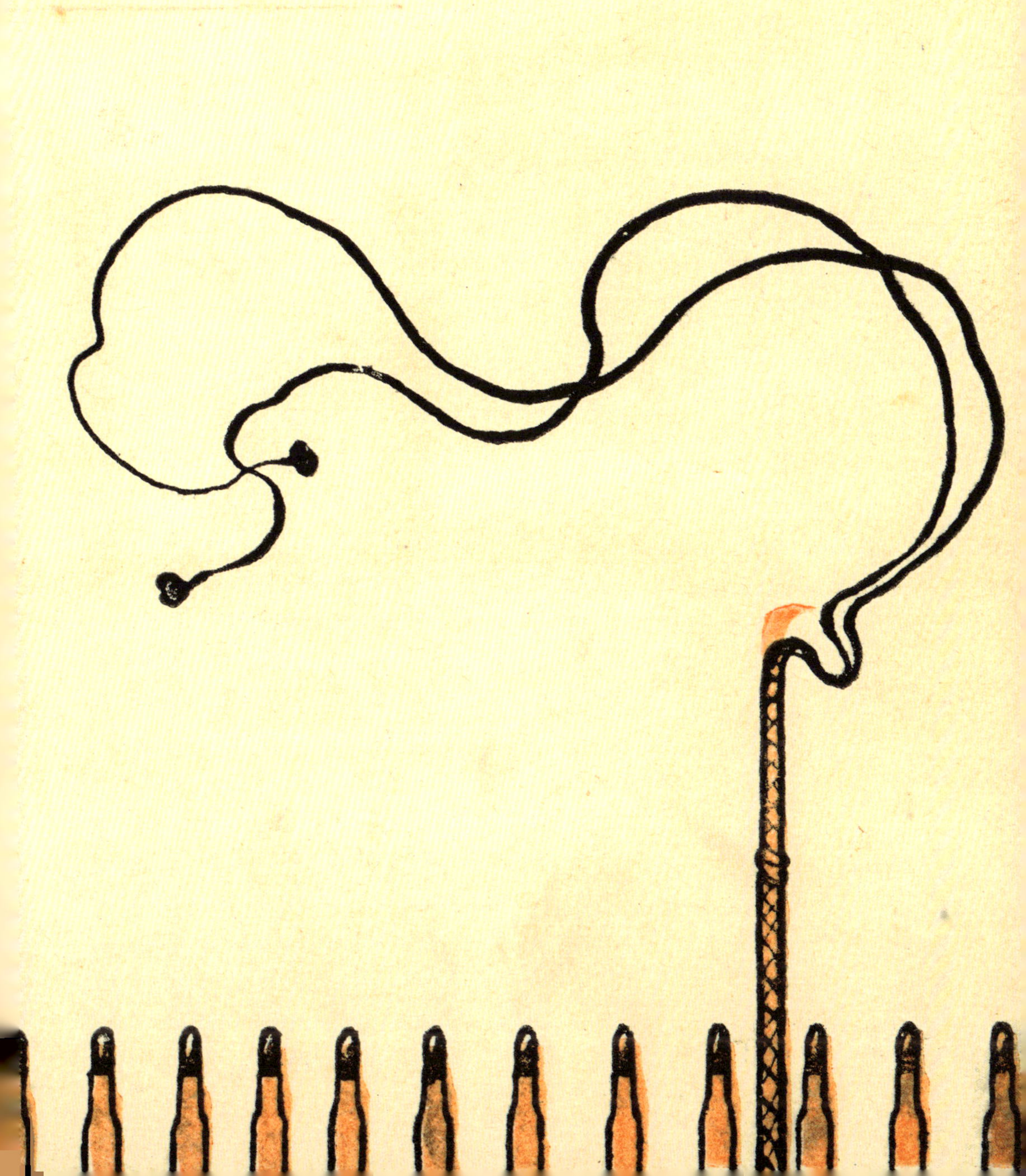

expensive and time-consuming undertaking, but postcards required less start-up capital, took less effort to compose, and once away from the printer, were easily distributed.

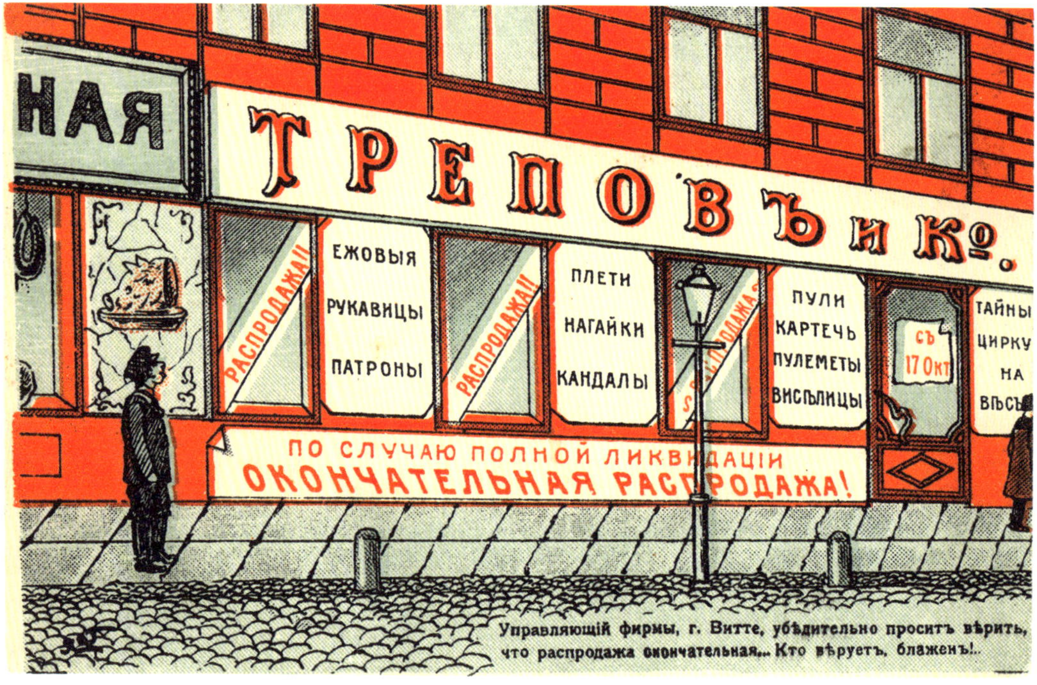

Anonymous artist. *Trepov and Co. Closing Down Sale. The Director of the Firm Mr. Witte Implores You to Believe That This Is the Final Clearance Sale… Blessed Are They Who Believe.* No publication details, late 1905. The signs in the windows read: 'handcuffs, ammunition, whips, fetters, bullets, buckshot, machine guns, gibbets, etc.'

Opposite

Anonymous artist. *Souvenir from the Muscovite Cannibal Dubasov.* No publication details, late 1905.

The Moscow Uprising

In the months after the October Manifesto there was no let-up in the violence. Haphazard repression and political inaction had emboldened and radicalised protesters, so that by the time the concessions had come they were too late to make any real difference. What had been intended as a gesture to mollify the opposition had the reverse effect, giving rise to mutinies, strikes and increased violence. In November, a naval officer named Petr Schmidt led an uprising in the Black Sea Fleet. The insurrection was quickly suppressed and the ringleaders executed, but the incident again raised the spectre of revolt in the armed forces.

The government's ineptitude was all too clear: 'When revolution has appeared in the lives of the people, there is nothing more dangerous than half-measures, delay and hesitation,' wrote the writer and liberal activist Vladimir Korolenko.[90] The regime, however, believing that it had already gone far enough and seeing no results from its lacklustre attempts at reform, grew impetuous and started applying violence ever more freely. An armed confrontation between the government and the radical opposition was by no means inevitable, but it was made more likely by the lack of alternatives.

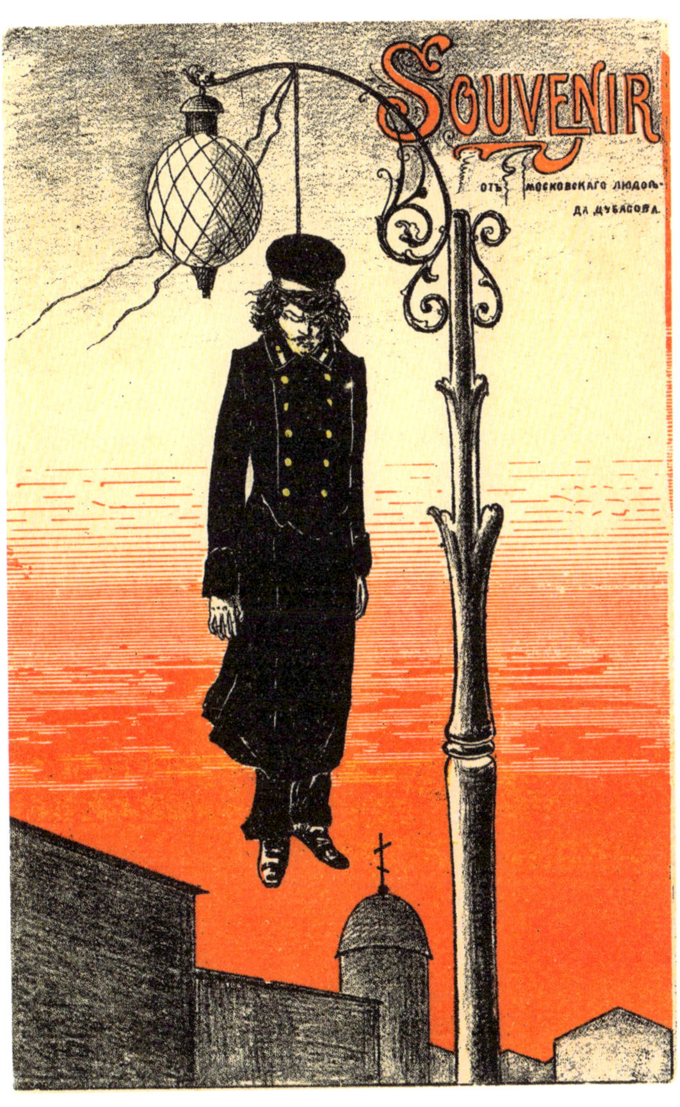
SOUVENIR
ОТЪ МОСКОВСКАГО ЛЮДОѢ-
ДА ДУБАСОВА.

Since at least the autumn, the revolutionaries had been actively smuggling weapons into Russia in preparation for a fight. The Okhrana reported in December that male students studying in Western Europe had been ferrying in revolvers and bullets, while female activists had been bringing in weapons, including bombs, concealed in their underwear.[91] Many revolutionary activists, however, were still reluctant to call for armed revolt, fearful that it would end in a massacre. In the event the uprising took place largely spontaneously, and not in the capital where it had been expected, but in Moscow.

On 7 December a general strike was declared in the former capital. The first few days were largely peaceful; crowds of demonstrators and striking workers milled about in the streets, and armed detachments roamed more or less freely. But after a confrontation with government troops, barricades were erected across town. 'House gates, railings and fences, hoardings, empty barrels, crates and boxes, coal and flour sacks, sawn off telegraph and telephone posts, trees felled from the boulevard, anything that came to hand went into building the barricades, all of it bound together and reinforced using strands of cable.'[92]

With neither side willing to challenge the other, a tense stand-off developed. Soldiers surrounded factories and occupied the main squares, while militiamen took pot shots from the side streets. Sporadic street fighting took place over the coming days, but it was not until the arrival of troop reinforcements on 15 December that the tide turned decisively in the government's favour.

The workers' stronghold of Presnia, a textile-producing district in the west of the city, was the last to hold out. Overwhelming force was used to suppress the remaining gunmen, many of whom had little or no military training. By the time the last pockets of resistance had been extinguished, around 700 people had been killed and up to 2,000 wounded.[93]

The uprising prompted a string of postcard cartoons, most deploring the excessive violence used to put down the revolt. One, depicting a student hanging from a lamppost, is drily titled 'A Souvenir from Moscow'. The majority of postcards, however, were souvenirs of a more literal kind – photographic images of the aftermath, most of them published legally. Although a few private enterprises had printed postcards depicting the post-Manifesto demonstrations, this was the first revolutionary spectacle to attract the widespread involvement of commercial publishers. Several large series were printed, their intention not only to satisfy political demand, but also to sate public appetite for images of death and destruction.

The uprising marked a turning point. The revolutionaries had shown themselves unable to unite to bring about a revolution, and as a result the government felt its hand greatly strengthened. Under the direction of the

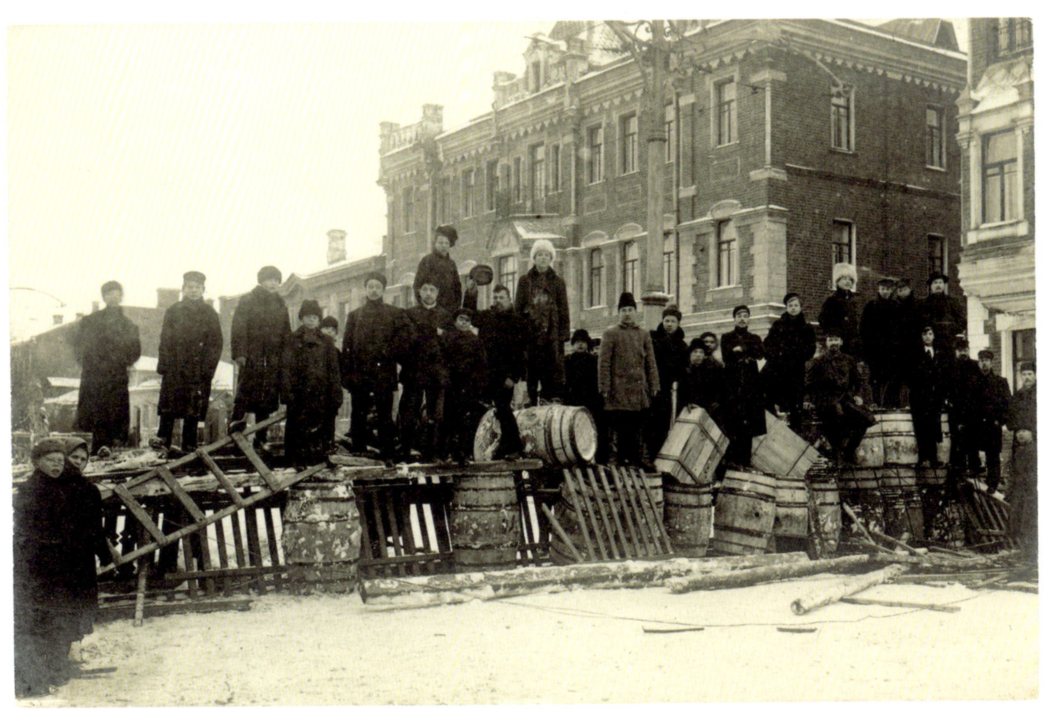

Attributed to Aleksei Zavadskii. Untitled photographic postcard depicting a barricade during the Moscow Uprising. No publication details, Moscow, late 1905.

reactionary Interior Minister Petr Durnovo, officials now moved to extinguish the liberation movement once and for all. A brutal period of repression followed. Punitive expeditions were sent out into the countryside, and the military was used extensively to put down unrest in town and country. In this manner, the Days of Freedom were brought to a violent close.

Meanwhile, the publishing industry also came under heavy scrutiny. In one of the government's first decisive moves against the production of opposition publications, raids were carried out on printing establishments across the major cities. Belgard later remarked that the regime's efforts to stem the flow of material at source proved highly effective, not least because 'without the printing houses it is impossible to commit the crime.'[94] An audit ordered by the Interior Ministry in mid-December led to over thirty printers being temporarily closed down in Saint Petersburg alone.[95] Over the next few months, many more suffered the same fate.

After the rout of the Moscow Uprising, the use of force was largely discredited among the broader opposition, and throughout the following year, the focus of revolutionary activity would gradually move away from plans for armed insurrection and back towards propaganda production. Thus, in early 1906, the tempo of violence fell and a new phase of the Revolution commenced, with politics at its fore. The attention of the country as a whole, and the liberation movement in particular, now turned to the State Duma. All hopes of political reform rested with the new legislative assembly.

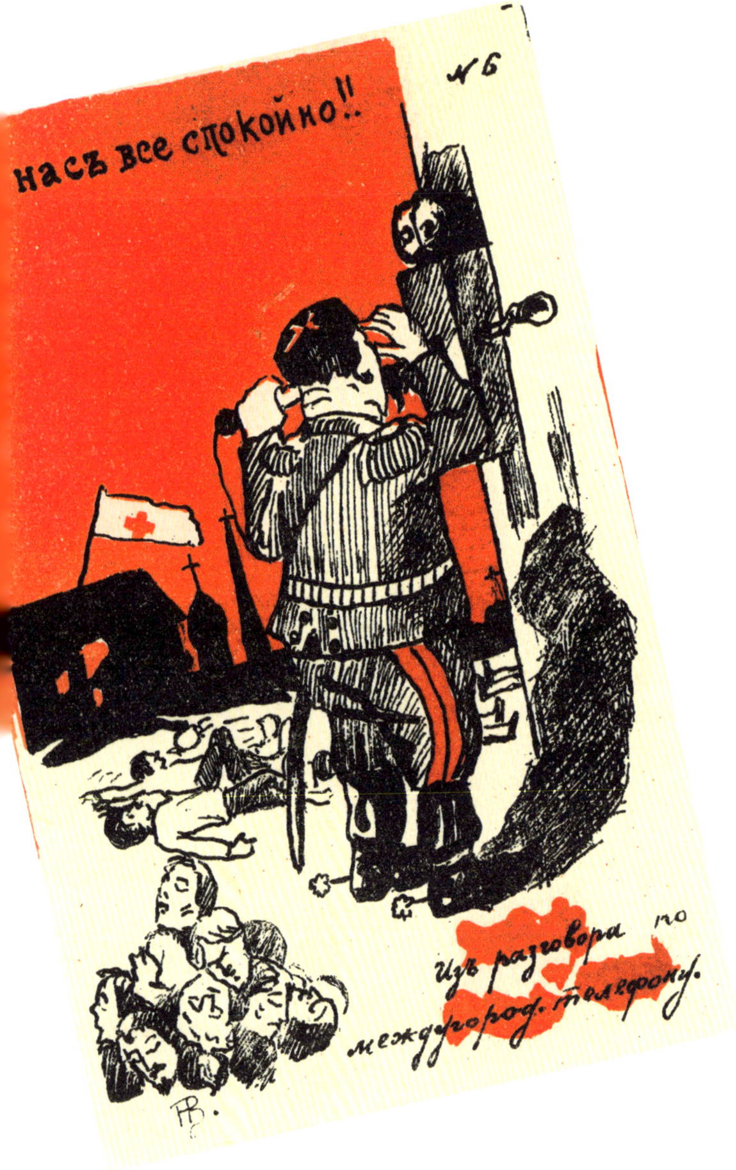

№6

насъ все спокойно!!..

Изъ разговора по междугород. телефону.

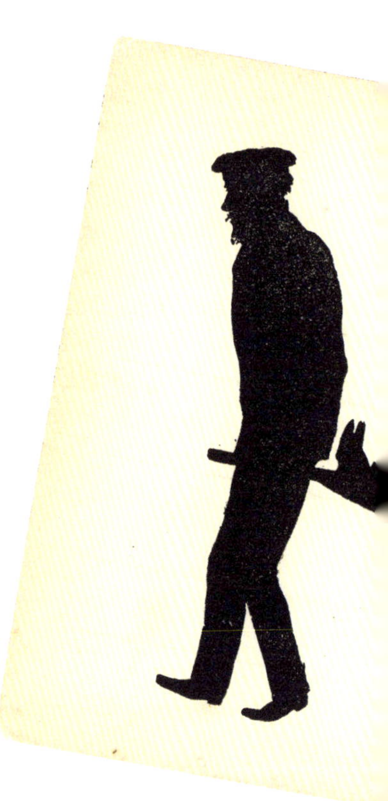

CONCESSION AND REPRESSION

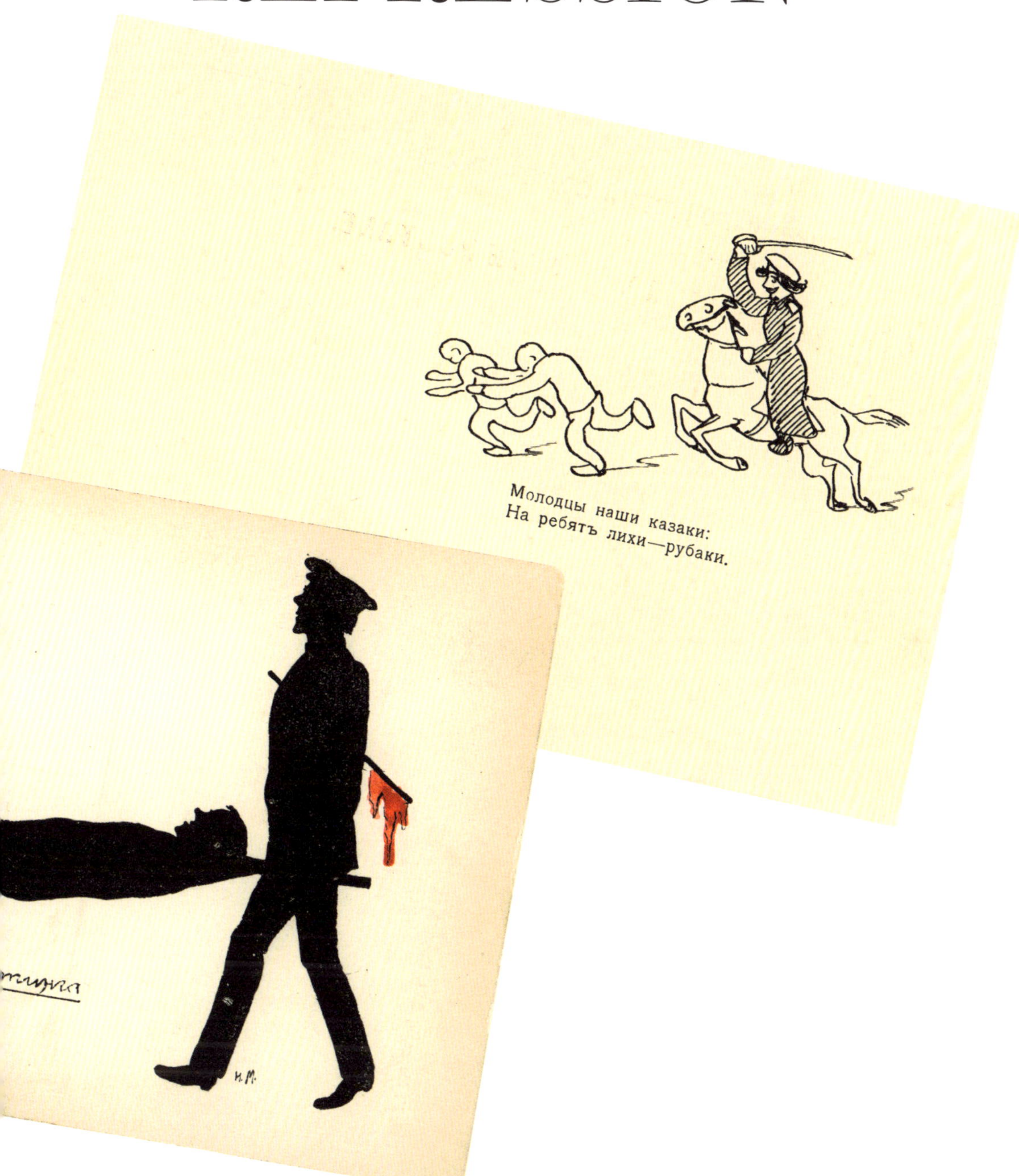

JANUARY–APRIL 1906

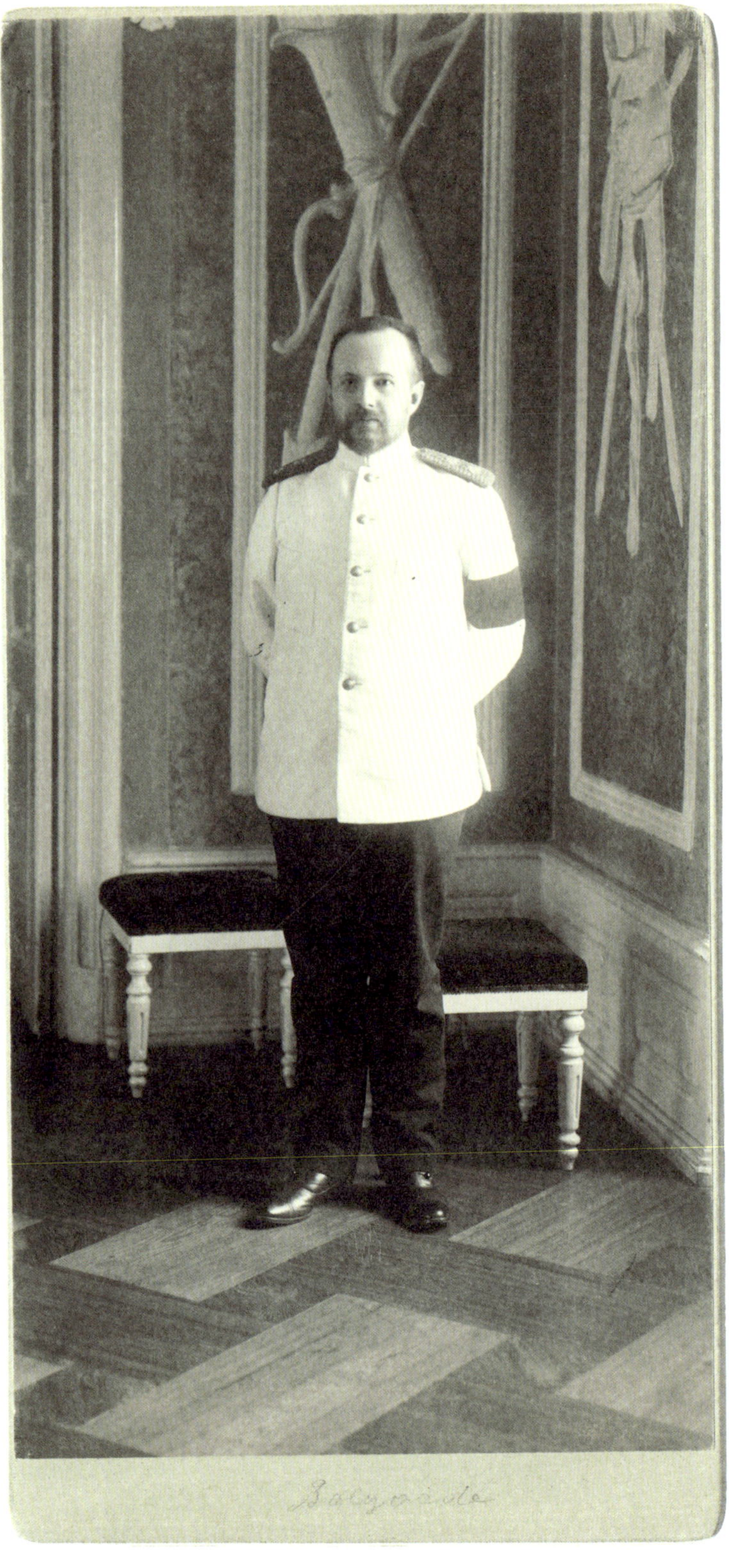

Applying New Press Regulations

Previous spread from left to right

N. V. *'It's All Quiet Here!!' Excerpt from an Intercity Phone Call.* No publication details, late 1905.

N. M. *Returning from the Protest.* Published by Nikolai Merder, late 1905.

L. Ch. *Good Fellows Our Cossacks. They Go after the Guys like Swashbuckling Heroes.* No publication details, circa late 1905.

Opposite

I. Teterina Photographic Studio. Carte de visite depicting Aleksei Belgard. Reval, circa 1902.

The crackdown that followed the Moscow Uprising dampened the flames of revolution and heavily impinged on the production of opposition propaganda, but for all the sharp edges of government repression, the state could never hope to succeed in erasing all the political and social gains of the previous year. Russia was not the same country it had been just twelve months before. It had new laws and political parties, the promise of a legislative parliament, and partial press freedom. Socialism was the concern of far greater numbers than at any previous time, and a say in politics was now the prerogative of all Russia's adult male population.

The transformation could be seen all around, and nowhere more so than in the changing content of Russia's illustrated journals. Throughout 1905, the mainstream newspaper supplement *Iskry* [*Sparks*] had deliberately overlooked all revolutionary events, but following the October Manifesto it started carrying pictures of popular demonstrations, mutinies, the Moscow Uprising, and even pogroms.[1] Its pages had previously been dominated by photographs of the Russo-Japanese War; now, with the acquiescence of the censor, the journal had adjusted its orientation to conform to readers' expectations of a new era in which discussion of internal affairs and violent dissent had become part and parcel of everyday life.[2]

The public's appetite for subversive material and the readiness of the print industry to serve it placed considerable pressure on the Main Administration for Press Affairs, whose workload had grown dramatically since the introduction of the November Regulations. The censorship committees, which previously held meetings once a week, now convened every day, often working late into the night to get through the piles of confiscated material that landed on their desks each evening.[3] The Administration's role was fraught with complications, both due to the volume of works being printed and also to the manifold practical difficulties of applying a new set of regulations in an uncertain political environment.

Between October and December 1905, only a handful of anti-government postcards were submitted to the Saint Petersburg Censorship Committee, but in early 1906 it received a whole array of different applications for revolutionary portrait cards.[4] The first of these, which came in just before the New Year, was a request to print an image of the lawyer Georgii Khrustalev-Nosar. Nosar was the former chairman of the Saint Petersburg Soviet, and a man whom the regime considered a state criminal. Similar postcards put forward earlier in the year had been banned outright.[5] This time, however, the Committee first postponed making a decision, and then early the following year, gave the go-ahead for publication.[6]

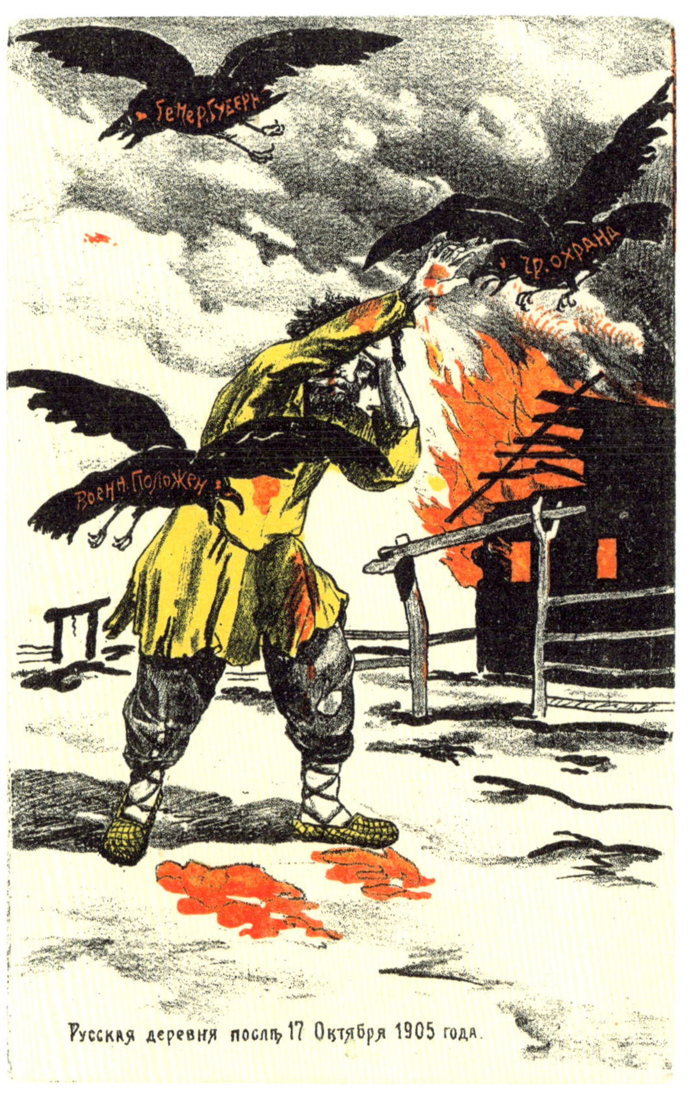

Русская деревня послѣ 17 Октября 1905 года.

For years, the censorship committees had adopted an uncompromising attitude towards all leftist imagery, but the October Manifesto had shaken many of the political certainties to which they had become accustomed. What followed was a period of experimentation; publishers probed to see what they could get away with and the Administration scrabbled around to find a compromise that might loosen the noose a little but still allow for a substantial degree of government control. The various censors worked fast to adapt to the new realities, but many were still in need of regular guidance on how to deal with images that were notionally oppositional but not obviously illegal.

Anonymous artist. *The Russian Countryside after 17 October 1905*. No publication details, late 1905. The circling ravens are labelled: 'Governors', 'Extraordinary Security', and 'Martial Law'.

A few months after the publication of Nosar's portrait, the Saint Petersburg Committee sent several communiqués to the Administration asking questions about what anti-government images might be legal to print. The first of these reads: 'Five portraits of state criminals have been submitted: Balmashev, Gershuni, Sazonov, Antonov and Ivanov. In view of the fact that these are intended to be issued as separate publications, the Saint Petersburg Censorship Committee has the honour of presenting them for inspection to the Main Administration for Press Affairs, and asks for direction in this matter.' Two days later, Belgard replied to say that there were no legal objections to their appearance in print.[7]

Again, on 11 March 1906, the Committee asked the Press Administration about another postcard of Nosar, and one of the naval mutineer Lieutenant Schmidt, who had been executed just five days previously. The response was duly given that there were 'no legal grounds to prevent the publication of these portraits.'[8] Queries about other individuals followed later in the month, but the answer remained the same in all cases. This amounted to a marked change in attitude towards the nature of the images that could be published in postcard form. Revolutionary and socialist pictures that had been considered illegal several months previously could now be printed freely.

Press officials remained cautious, however. On 7 April, the Committee wrote to inquire about the legality of postcards depicting Eugène Delacroix's *Liberty Leading the People* (1830), Ernest Pichio's *The Communards Wall* (1875), Auguste Couder's *The Tennis Court Oath* (1789), and Alfred Roll's *The Miners' Strike* (1880). The Committee was troubled about the potentially seditious nature of the images, pointing out to the Administration that, 'although the pictures are all by well-known Western artists, the reproductions are undoubtedly being published in Russia with the aim of inciting the public.' Belgard, however, was unpersuaded, writing in his reply that there were 'no legal grounds to stop the publication of these pictures.'[9]

Next spread from left to right

Anonymous artist. *G. S. Khrustalev*. No publication details, 1906.

Anonymous designer. *Doctor Grigorii Andreevich Gershuni*. No publication details, 1906. The vignette below depicts Shlisselburg Fortress, where Gershuni was imprisoned between 1904 and 1905.

Judging by contemporary advertisements, the Administration's concessions also applied to paintings depicting political events in Russia itself.

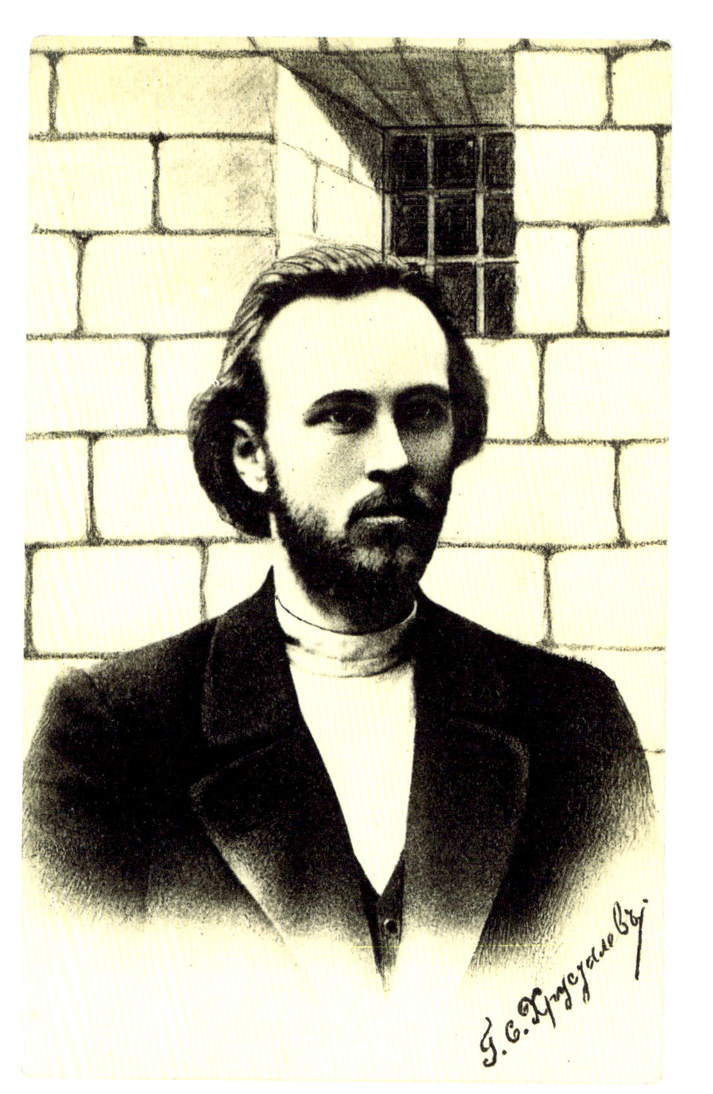
Г. С. Хрусталевъ

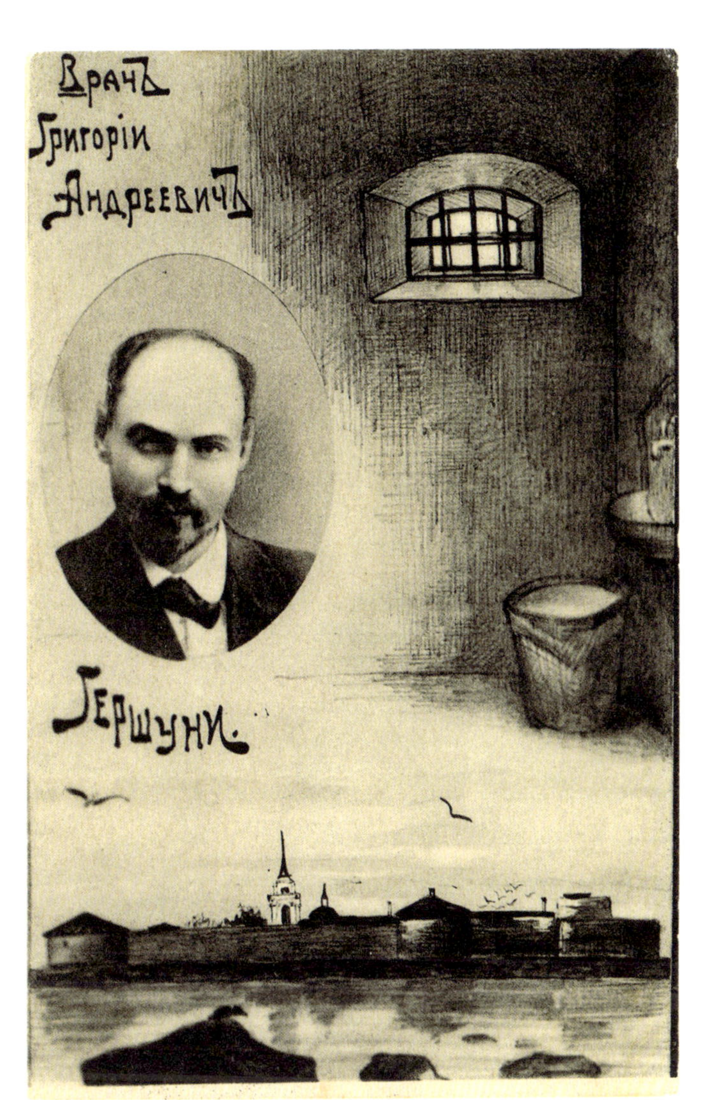
Врачъ
Григорiи
Андреевичъ
Гершуни.

Indeed, Belgard's insistence that no work could be banned unless it specifically contravened the criminal code allowed for the publication of a rather broader sweep of images than many of his fellow officials might have liked.[10] In March 1905, for instance, he authorised seventeen photomechanical postcards, despite the fact that many of them reproduced paintings that 'had been removed from exhibitions.' There is no mention of why the paintings were removed, but given that the police subsequently questioned the legality of the postcards, their subject matter was undoubtedly anti-government in tone.[11]

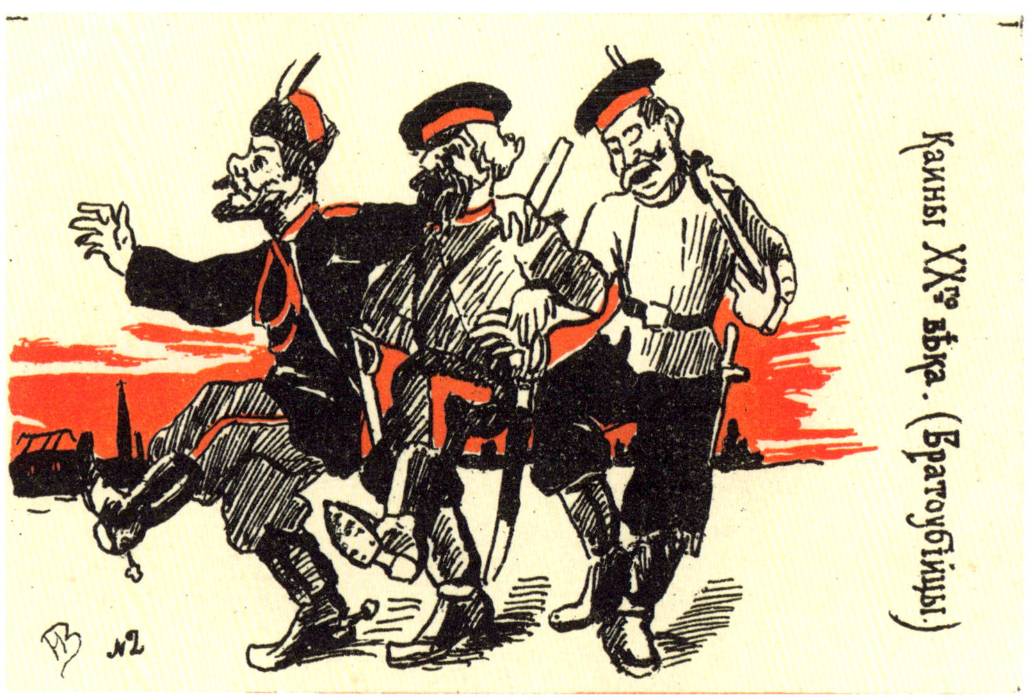

N.V. *Twentieth Century Cains (Fratricides)*. No publication details, late 1905.

Far from every postcard submitted to the censor during this period was passed – to the irritation of many publishers, satirical works criticising the government directly were still considered beyond the pale. In early February, for example, Nikolai Martynson wrote to the Administration to complain that the Saint Petersburg Committee had turned down eight of the twelve postcards that he had submitted the previous month. These were described in an official report as being 'scurrilous satires on the government's stance towards the revolutionary movement.' Despite their obviously subversive nature, Martynson argued that the Committee's decision was 'incompatible with the freedom of the press introduced on 17 October.'[12]

The tenor of Martynson's objection illustrates widespread confusion over the status of press regulations in the months after the Manifesto was issued, with many publishers still believing, or at least hoping, that they had been given free rein to print whatever they wanted. Naturally, the Administration had a very different understanding of the situation. While ready to allow revolutionary portraits and reproductions of paintings, officials remained concerned about the possibilities offered by the postcard medium as a vehicle for spreading subversive thought, particularly in cartoon form. In response to Martynson's complaint, the Administration concluded that the Censorship Committee had been right to ban the postcards, commenting that 'such illustrations can incite the population.'

Despite the modesty of the concessions, many provincial governors were displeased with the adjustments in postcard production that Administration officials had helped to bring about. While some wrote to complain about the changes, others simply ignored them.[13] But on the streets there was surprise and joy that a person could be considered a criminal one day and have their face emblazoned across the city the next. On the back of a postcard depicting the revolutionary Maria Spiridonova, a young woman named Vera wrote to her 'dear Mama' to express her amazement: 'I bought this postcard because I thought that it was forbidden to sell it, but now they're selling cards of Spiridonova and Schmidt everywhere.'[14]

March and April Publishing Regulations

Between autumn 1905 and spring 1906, the Saint Petersburg Censorship Committee passed around three quarters of the seventy-odd anti-government postcards that came up for discussion.[15] Many others were likely also approved (and banned) by individual censors, without the need for Committee-level scrutiny. This runs counter to the accepted view of the period, which characterises leftist publishing after the Days of Freedom as a steady descent into oblivion. Circumstances had certainly become more arduous for publishers, with fierce and indiscriminate repression taking place across the Empire, but it is clear, at least in regards to postcards, that the Press Administration was still searching for a middle ground between outright dissent and moderate criticism.[16]

There is no question that the Administration's concessions towards publishers constituted a stumble backwards in the face of the anti-government onslaught. Nevertheless, they should also be seen as a conscious attempt to play a difficult hand. No one in government circles was in any doubt that leftist imagery was harmful to the autocratic state, but Belgard believed that the Administration had a duty both to adhere to the law and to ensure that the Tsar's promises of civil freedom were properly implemented. Indeed, as he had earlier instructed officials: 'The censor's very relation to press publications should be changing in a fundamental

Next spread

Anonymous artist. *Freedom of Speech.* Published by Kh. K. and A. G., Saint Petersburg, circa late 1905.

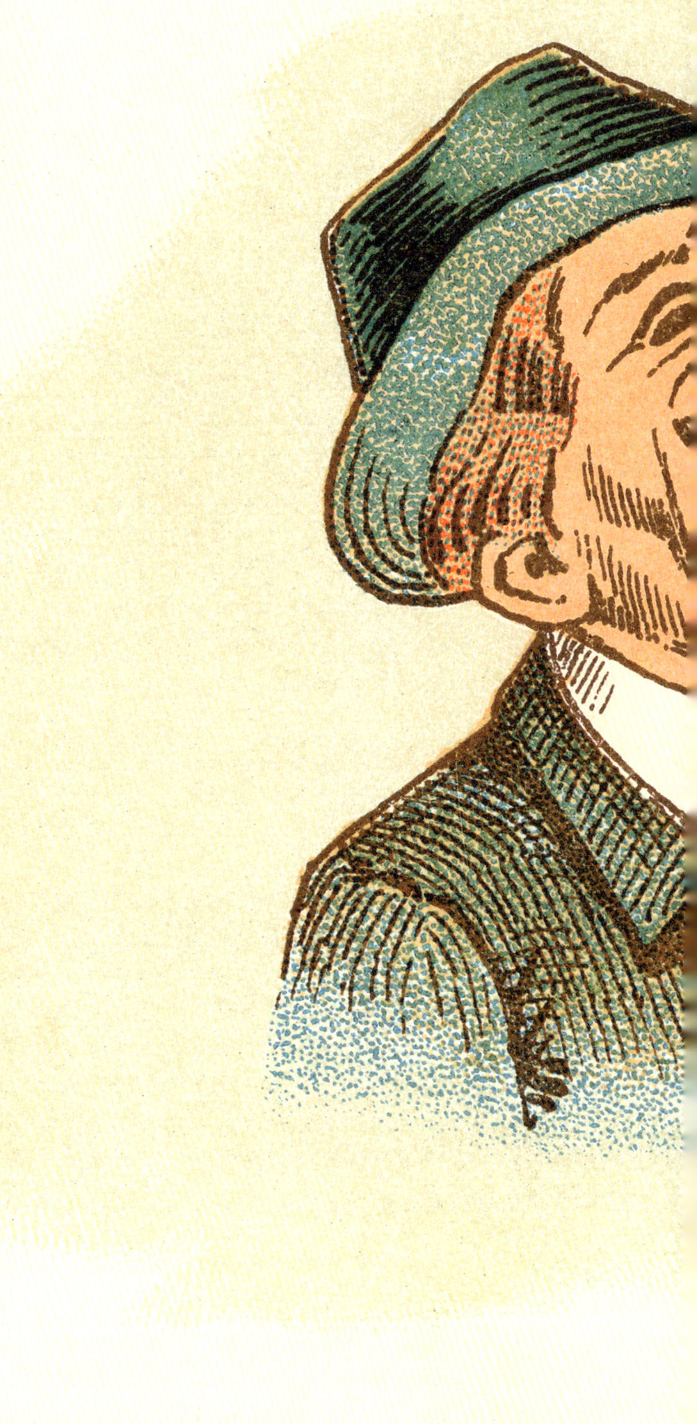

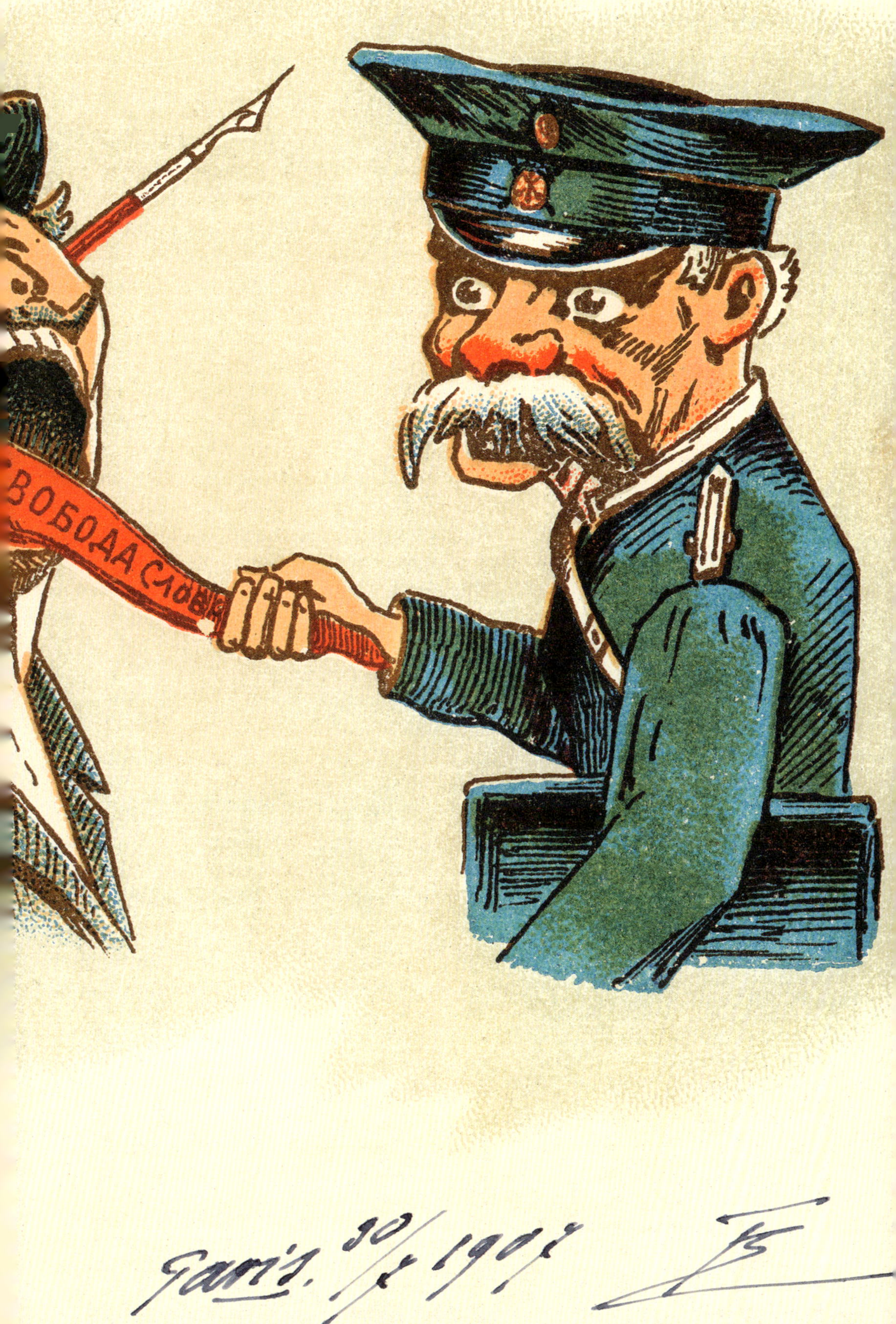
ВОБОДА СЛОВ
Paris. 30/x 1907

way, conforming to the clear and definite will of the Sovereign Emperor, as expressed in the Manifesto.'[17]

Belgard saw his task as finding a balance between the necessity of implementing reform, and the requirement of reimposing order. Or as he put it, 'the need to realise those freedoms that had been assured in the Imperial Manifesto, and the need to somehow put a stop to the rampant abuse of these freedoms and resurrect the wavering significance of government power.'[18] The struggle over how best this could be achieved was played out at all levels of the ruling elite, waged between those who understood the need for reform and those who preferred to muddle through using the old ways. Although a steadfast opponent of revolution, Belgard understood that if things were to stay the same, they would first have to change.

At the same time as the Press Administration was yielding ground over portraits and paintings, endeavours continued in parallel to clamp down on all more subversive forms of opposition material. Since late the previous year, officials from the Administration and the Inspectorate had maintained efforts to eradicate seditious and revolutionary wares, working hand in glove with the police, regional governors, and the courts to close publications, arrest editors and carry out raids on booksellers and printers. Newspapers and satirical journals were seen as a particular menace, and *Zritel* was one of many such periodicals that were shut down during this time. Printing houses were again heavily targeted, and owners became increasingly unwilling to run the risk of breaking publishing regulations.

Even these measures, however, proved insufficient, as the government itself admitted in the introduction to a new decree on the press, published on 18 March. The so-called March Changes and Supplements, which comprised a series of restrictive amendments to the November Regulations, were primarily aimed at reigning in the glut of satirical journals. They reintroduced preliminary censorship for illustrated periodicals, further expanded the government's range of confiscation powers against them, and increased the accountability of printing houses. This marked the start of the regime's attempt to dial back on the promises of the October Manifesto through legal means. Publishers still had a few months' grace, but this was a sign that the repressive mood was gaining ground.

The focus of government legislation and repression may have been on the periodical press, but both had a notable effect on postcards. Illegal satires were still in wide circulation, but the stifling of the printing houses meant that the bold, chromolithographic cartoons that had been produced so freely in the wake of the Manifesto largely dropped away during the first few months of 1906. In the damning words of one postcard journal: 'Production and content reached its apogee during the days of flourishing Russian political satire, before degenerating quickly under the influence of the rising forces of reaction.'[19] The dangers and potential financial losses were simply too great for either publishers or printers to carry on producing high-end cartoons and caricatures.

On 26 April 1906, preliminary censorship for non-periodical publications was nominally abolished. Postcards and short pamphlets, however, still had to be submitted to the censor before they could be put on sale, a reflection of the concern that such easily disseminated and frequently incendiary publications aroused. But, for all that the April Regulations helped to maintain the government's grip on the print industry, they marked the final stage in implementing the promises of the October Manifesto. Publishers were now, within the strict confines of Imperial law, free to print what they wanted, when they wanted, and the next few months, far from ushering in the end of anti-government postcards, instead bore witness to their continued growth.

Impact of Events and Press Regulations

In late 1905, when the political situation was at its most uncertain, the turmoil of events inflicted considerable damage on the print industry. Strikes and general disarray affected postcard production and distribution, and domestic publishers of all types were badly hit. Foreign companies that had once all but monopolised the sale of better quality picture postcards in Russia also grew increasingly wary over the course of the Revolution, scaling down their involvement and in some cases withdrawing from the market altogether. 'More than once I have had a [printing] order cancelled with a short note decrying the lamentable situation,' complained one Russian publisher, writing in a German postcard journal.[20]

In his letter, the publisher attempted to reassure nervous readers about the Russian postcard market, claiming that the foreign media, looking only for 'sensational news', had painted the state of affairs in the country in 'the darkest colours'. Nevertheless, even he was forced to acknowledge that, 'the disorder in November and December of last year [1905] seriously harmed trade, and in some cases Christmas sales fell through entirely.'[21] The repercussions of the revolutionary tumult were not only limited to the logistical difficulties caused by the chaos; unrest also harmed the economy, limiting the public's desire and ability to purchase non-essential goods, including postcards.

Order was gradually restored to the major cities in early 1906, and with this the situation began to improve. 'Everything somehow came to a stop and it's only now that we are starting to see small signs of movement,' wrote the Society of Saint Eugenia's publications manager in February.[22] As the industry chugged back into action, publishers of all types were confronted

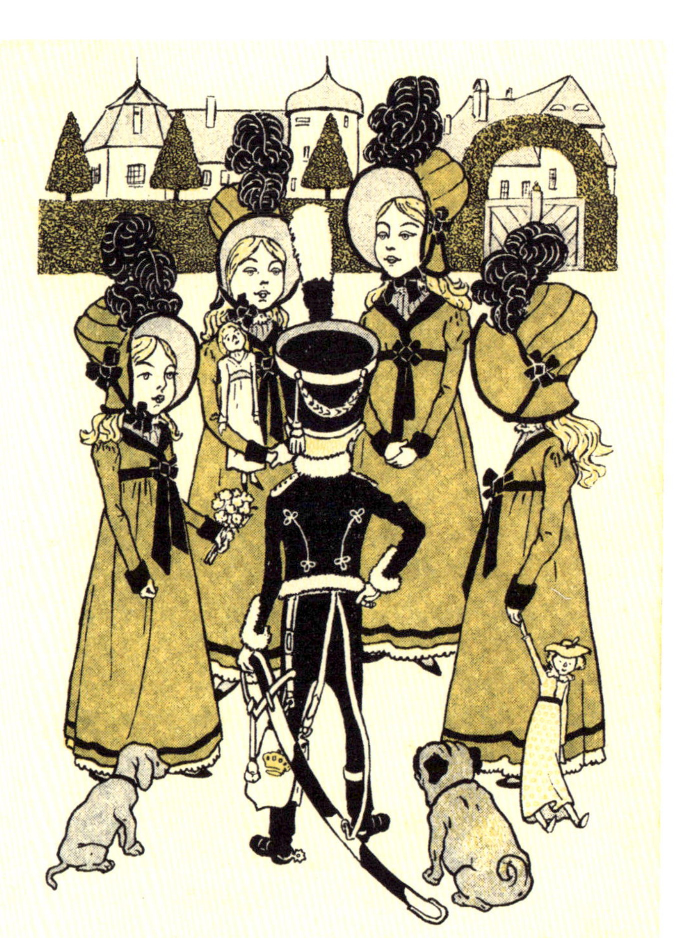

(*Рис. Т. Т. Гейне*)

НАСЛѢДНЫЙ ПРИНЦЪ.

— Когда мою куколку нажмешь, она кричитъ: „мама"...
— Это что! Вотъ, когда я буду большимъ, я получу шестьдесятъ милліоновъ куколъ, которыя кричатъ „ура", когда имъ наступишь на животъ.

with a decidedly changed landscape, both in respect of press regulations and public taste. The overwhelming majority of postcards being produced at this time were not remotely political, let alone leftist, but in what was already a cut-throat market, anti-government content continued to provide a way for publishers to offer their customers novel, and at times sensational subject matter.

Thomas Theodor Heine. *The Crown Prince. – I Have a Doll That Cries 'Mama' When You Squeeze It. – That's Nothing. When I Grow up I'll Get 60 Million Dolls That Will Cry 'Hoorah' When You Punch Them in the Stomach.* Published by Shipovnik and printed by Golike and Vilborg, Saint Petersburg, May 1906.

The initial phase of anti-government postcard production in the immediate aftermath of the October Manifesto had been spearheaded by a small group of committed activists and opportunists, but in the months that followed the market moved to embrace a broader range of publishers. The political yield of the Revolution, notably the government's promise of freedom of the press and subsequent postcard concessions, had taken the sting out of milder forms of leftist imagery, safeguarding the financial incentive to produce revolutionary portraits and picture reproductions in the run-up to the Duma elections. Several new publishers and printers now started dipping their toes into the water, both to test the political temperature and to take advantage of continuing demand.

The Administration's concessions made no difference to radical publishers intent on printing anti-tsarist satires in underground facilities, but for those willing to compromise, the gates to anti-government production had been left ajar. Ongoing government repression ensured that by spring 1906 opposition postcards were no longer as colourful or politically daring as they had once been, but images with milder leftist content could still be run off the presses in enormous quantities, attracting huge swathes of the population due to their low prices and moderate subject matter. Publishers also continued to print humorous cartoons on political themes, tolerated by the Administration so long as they did not venture to critique the government directly.

The ebb and flow of repression can be hard to follow, not least because it was rarely applied in a uniform manner, but it is evident that after an initial period of heavy constraint following the Moscow Uprising, the pressure on publishers eased up in the run-up to, and over the course of the First Duma. At the same time, the liberation movement regained some of its former confidence, and together these factors helped to bring about a steady increase in publishing tempo. The figures speak for themselves. In late 1905 and early 1906, publishing activity in Russia slowed, but in February it began to pick up again. That month 960 books and pamphlets were legally published, in March the figure was 1,335, in April 1, 664, and in June 2, 711.[23]

Postcard publishing also benefited. Among the more notable firms established after the announcement of the April Regulations was Shipovnik, a liberal enterprise founded by Zinovii Grzhebin and Solomon Kopelman. Shipovnik's postcards, which reproduce cartoons and caricatures published in the German magazine *Simplicissimus*, are unusual for the period in their use of political satire and emphasis on quality. Nevertheless, it is telling that Grzhebin and Kopelman operated in strict accordance with official regulations and avoided all overtly Russian subject matter.[24] Their aims were broadly ideological, but Shipovnik remained a commercial endeavour, and as such its owners had an economic interest in working with, rather than against the law of the land.

Vast quantities of postcards were still being printed illegally, but the need for publishers to find a workable compromise between political aims and the risk of repression saw a modest trend towards legitimisation – the beginnings of what might have become an accommodated settlement between the government and more temperate sectors of the print industry. Not only were more leftist images now being submitted to the censor, more firms also started following requirements to include publication details.[25] Prior to this, most had either not bothered or had used initials in order to avoid the danger to which full exposure might subject them. In a further sign of openness, several publishers also started advertising their wares in newspapers and journals.[26]

In the contemporary political climate, where subterfuge was still widespread, the main reasons for a publisher to comply with press regulations were to gain unrestricted access to commercial printing houses, and to ensure that their output could be sold on the open market without fear of confiscation. With many still neglecting to do so, submitting oneself to inspection

Viktor Mazurovskii. *Clearing the Square.* Published by Vpered, Saint Petersburg, 1906.

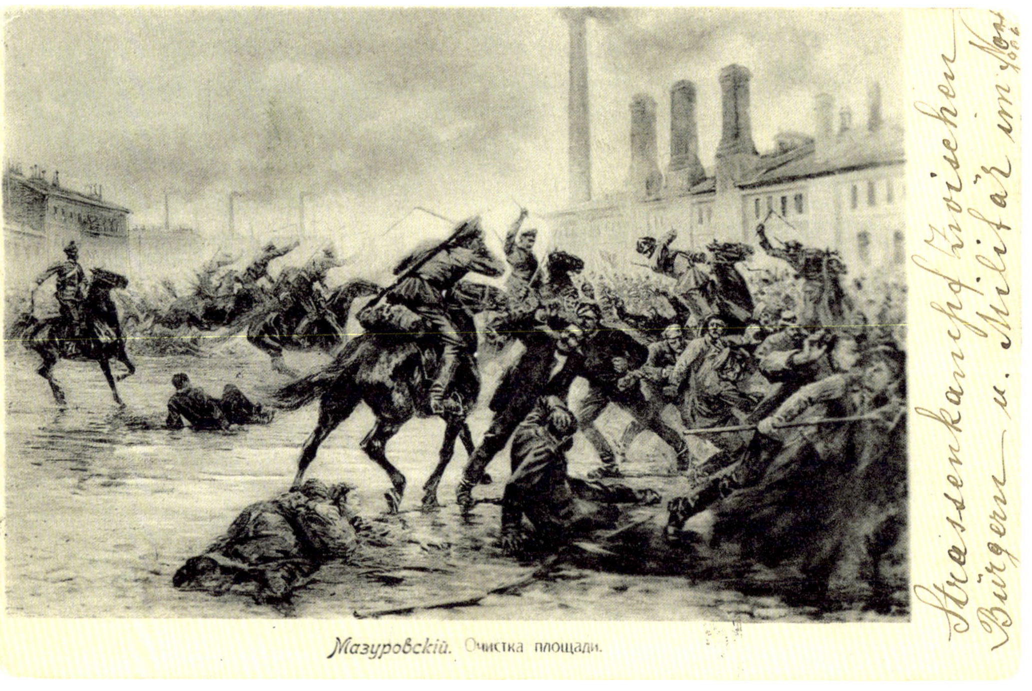

was a calculated act, done not so much out of necessity as in the interests of guaranteeing financial and political returns. Every anti-government postcard that either included publishing details or was advertised openly therefore reflects the gradual encroachment of legal retail publishing practices into an area once dominated by the revolutionary underground.

Anti-government postcard publishing was still heavily circumscribed and its position precarious, but in the spring of 1906 firms of all stripes were giving consideration to longer-term aims. Printing political images was no longer solely a case of charging in and charging out, but of establishing a legal foothold and loyal customer base within a highly competitive field. After a jumpy start, the market in anti-government postcards was beginning to settle down: advertising was the most visible evidence of this, but branding and attempts to legalise production also spoke clearly to the future, showing the extent to which many believed, or at least hoped that the broader political and social changes that had taken place over previous months were there to stay.

The revolutionary parties, while continuing to print images underground, also furthered their efforts to develop legal lines of production, in part to avoid reliance on fickle private firms, and in part to exploit continuing opportunities. The revolutionaries had once dominated the market in anti-government postcards, but following the October Manifesto they were forced to contend not only with larger numbers of fellow radicals, but also with commercial enterprises, which often had greater resources at their disposal. As the market in socialist material heated up, the revolutionaries realised that unless they learnt how to mass-produce, advertise and sell party propaganda along commercial lines, their sources of publishing income and influence would soon dry up.

An article published in the Socialist-Revolutionary organ *Partiinye izvestiia* [*Party News*] in late 1906 gives a lucid, if bleak view of the situation. After first remarking that the Manifesto had 'completely rewritten the rulebook,' the author went on to explain that where once the revolutionary parties had distributed agitational literature for free, this now only made financial sense where leaflets were concerned.[27] 'The producer who does not tailor his organisation to the demands of the market will be left trailing in the wind, risking bankruptcy, and will be forced to endure the unpleasant experience of seeing others take over.'[28] And this, according to the article, is exactly what had happened to the Socialist-Revolutionaries over previous months.

The Social Democrats appear to have been more successful in adapting. The diminished powers of the Press Administration had enabled revolutionary organisations to use commercial establishments to print and distribute their postcards since at least autumn 1905, but in early 1906, the Bolshevik Iosif Belopolskii established a Party-run publishing house in

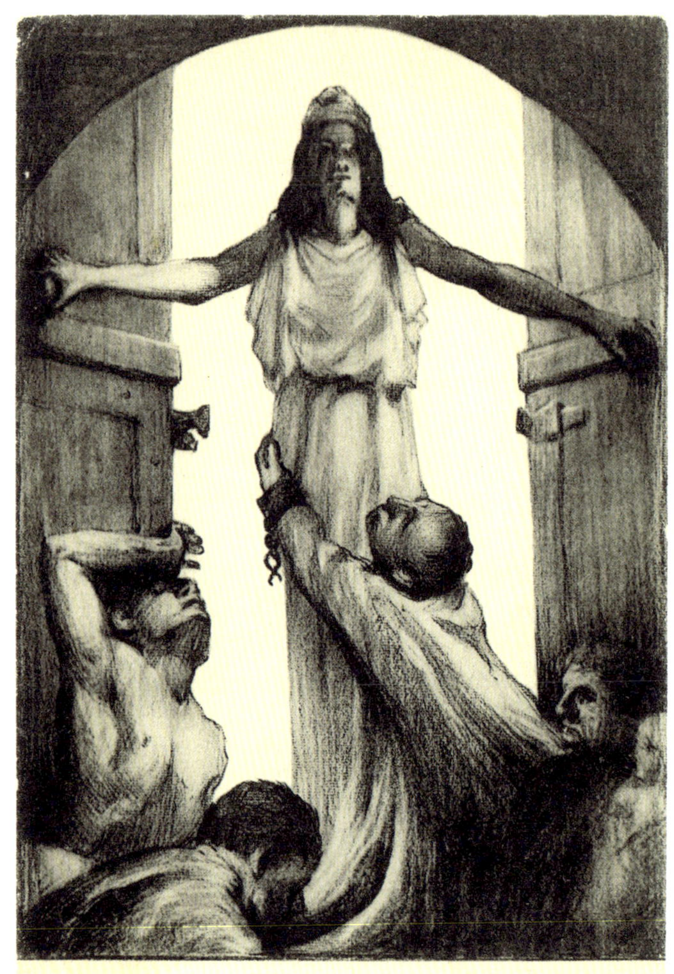

МАЙ НЕСЕТЪ СВОБОДУ.

Saint Petersburg, named Utro [Morning]. It was one of, if not the first revolutionary enterprises to mass produce anti-government postcards legally. In April, Bonch-Bruevich set up a new firm named Vpered [Forward], the result of a merger between Utro and two other Social Democratic publishers. It would go on to become the largest and most extensive revolutionary publishing operation created in Imperial Russia.

Postcards, which had long played a role in retail advertising, were used by the revolutionaries at this time to sell a very different form of ideology to the people, one that purported to reject capitalism but which still borrowed heavily from its entrepreneurial playbook. The collapse of Imperial authority late the previous year had brought together two great offshoots of Russia's drive towards modernity – opposition to autocracy and private enterprise – both of which had emerged in the wake of the Emancipation Act. For a period of several months, commercial publishing and anti-government ideas were able to travel openly aboard the same political train, leading at last to the mass production of revolutionary postcards in Russia.

Anonymous artist. *May Brings Freedom.* A. Freinkel, Saint Petersburg, April 1906. This copy of a German postcard (originally published in 1896) was one of a series of May Day postcards advertised by the Novyi mir bookshop in April 1906.

Expansion of the Print Industry

The first third of 1906 was a contradictory period marked by concession and repression. Following reformist rollbacks in the wake of the October Manifesto, the March Changes and Supplements heralded the start of an attempted return to the status quo ante. The April Regulations that followed can fairly be said to have struck a balance between the two, confirming the government's wide arsenal of repressive measures while still allowing a small degree of leeway in production practices. Although the regime was flailing, and as a result becoming increasingly vicious, there was some method in the madness; in postcard terms at least, the aim was to replace contentious satire with images that if not exactly desirable, were at least tolerable.

The hope was that repression would push publishers away from seditious imagery, while concessions would pull them towards the legal alternatives. However, as with other forms of printed material, the measures proved largely ineffective: the threat of punishment and the creation of a pressure valve meant that while some existing publishers did turn to more moderate political imagery, new firms also became involved, and more seriously, the revolutionaries already printing anti-government portraits and paintings were effectively given a free pass. The result was that more radical types of postcards were reduced but not altogether eradicated, and production as a whole rose, a consequence that, however mild, was inherently damaging.

The Manifesto had effectively led to the partial deregulation of the print trade, giving publishers far greater scope to take advantage of the many advances in technology and commerce that had been made over previous years. In the short term, this led to a torrent of anti-government material, but over the longer term, the publishing reforms served to entrench the power of the industry as a whole. The overall number of book titles shot up and print runs rose in tandem.[29] Similarly, while between 1900 and 1905, officially registered newspaper sales in Saint Petersburg grew from 20,715,406 to 37,400,200, and journals from 90,388 to 588,255, then in 1906 alone, they accelerated to totals of 45,357,802 and 773,455.[30]

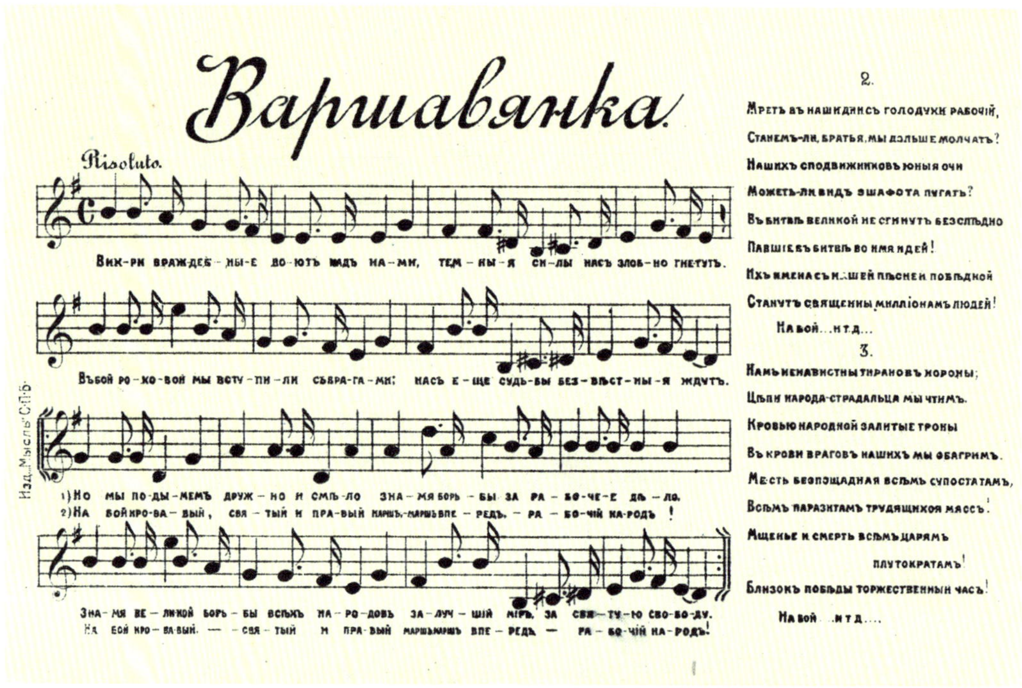

Anonymous designer.
Varshavianka.
Published by Mysl,
Saint Petersburg,
circa 1906.

These numbers do not tell the full story, for it was not just that overall quantities of printed material had risen, but that there was also far greater penetration, particularly in the regions. Prior to the Russo-Japanese War, very few newspapers and periodicals had reached rural settlements, but one study of villages in Moscow province found that by 1906 they were available in seventy-nine percent of them.[31]

The Revolution came at an equally pivotal point in the evolution of the postcard, just at the moment when production was moving beyond the elite and into the mass market. Writing in 1907, one commentator remarked: 'Over the last two to three years the picture postcard has made huge strides in its development, both with regard to artistic refinement and to the huge quantities in which it is now being distributed.'[32] In 1900, 91.1 million postcards were sent through the post; in 1904 it was 142 million; six years on, the total stood at 337.3 million.[33]

A perfect storm of technological capacity, distribution networks, and public demand came together in late 1905, right at the point that government dominance over the print industry was weakened by political events. A comparison between the quantities of postcards printed following the Potemkin Mutiny and the numbers printed after Schmidt's execution in March 1906 shows the transition that had taken place. Nine months separates the first incident from the second, but the extraordinary proliferation of images of Schmidt stands in marked contrast to the pitiful few of the mutiny. There is no ideological reason for this; the momentous developments in political, legal and commercial circumstance had simply enabled the market to respond more fully to the changing tastes of the population.

The mass production of anti-government postcards was a political phenomenon, but underlying it was a more long-term economic trend, whereby the rise of free enterprise had forced the autocratic government into competing against private firms in order to gain an audience for its ideological output. The expansion of the postcard market and the ensuing enlargement of the public sphere had enabled an alternative line of figures to perform on the national stage, first from the world of popular culture, then from the military and the government, and finally from the ranks of the opposition. When the floodgates were opened, the Imperial message was drowned out, unable to shout down public opinion when it was backed by commercial muscle.

These changes could not easily be undone. The population as a whole was now more engaged with the contemporary world than they had ever been, and henceforth it would become far harder for officials to sweep bad news under the carpet. This was a delicate situation for such an inflexible regime to find itself in. The government might survive through repression in the short term, but it was now presiding over a fundamentally changed nation, and without continuing reform, its rule was by no means guaranteed.

Combating Postcard Publishers and Printers

Throughout the revolutionary period, the Press Administration conducted lengthy battles against seditious and uncensored postcards, carrying out regular checks on both the establishments where they were produced and the places where they were sold. In the major cities of the Empire, responsibility for this difficult task came under the auspices of the Senior Inspector of Printing Houses and the Book Trade, who worked in close cooperation with the offices of the local governor and the police.

On coming across a subversive work, members of the Inspectorate had the power to 'arrest' the entire print run, a decision that would then be put before the courts to determine its validity. The procedure was in principle

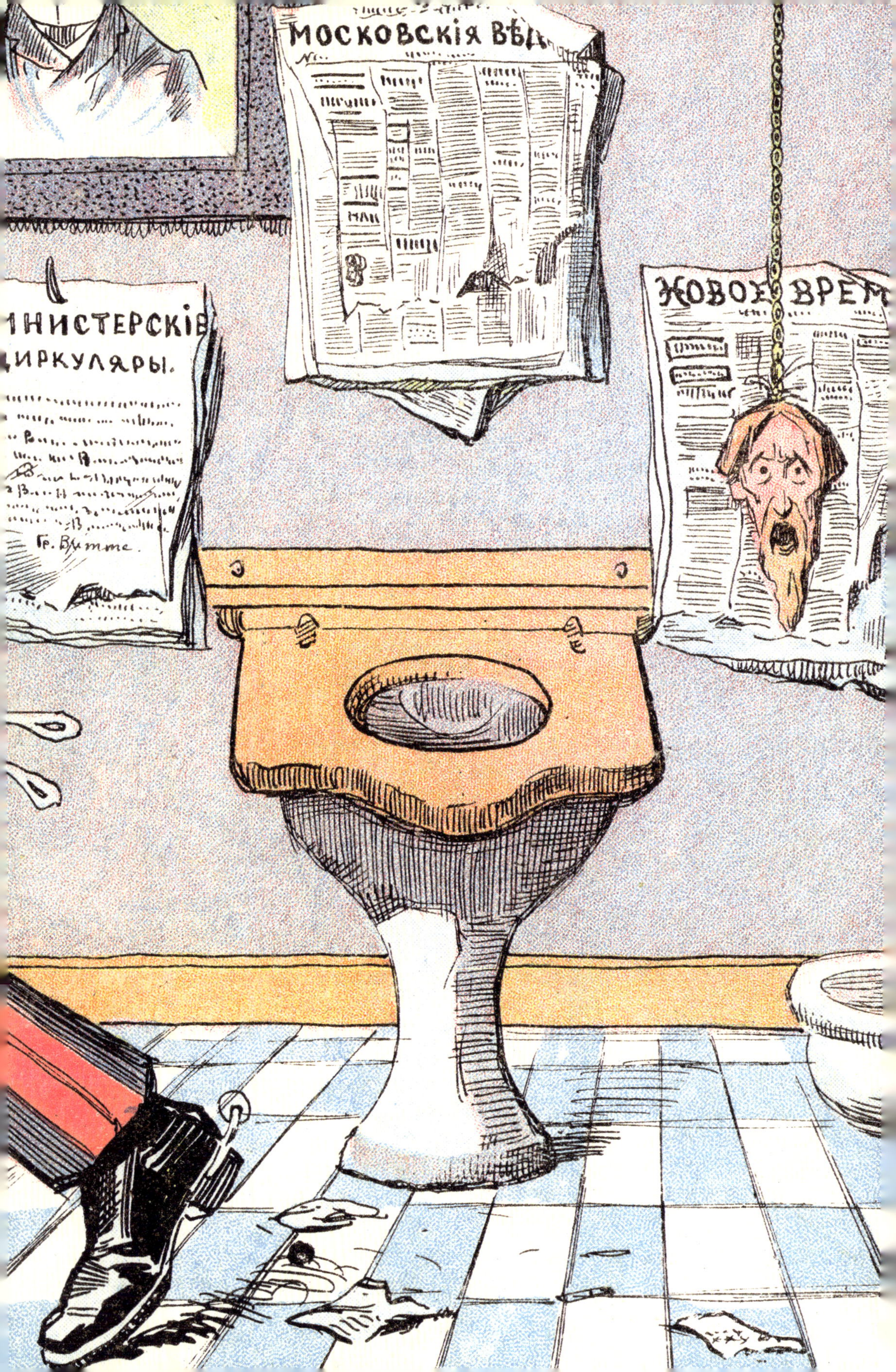

МОСКОВСКІЯ ВѢД
ИНИСТЕРСКІЕ
ЦИРКУЛЯРЫ.
Гр. Витте
НОВОЕ ВРЕМ

straightforward, but putting it into practice was anything but. Ideally, officials would find the whole edition still at the printing house, but in reality this was an uncommon occurrence. Printers would rarely keep contraband on site for long and by the time the Inspectors arrived, there would often be little to find.

Anonymous artist. *The Office.* No publication details, late 1905.

Fighting against illegal works in this way was akin to a game of whack-a-mole; it was reactive rather than proactive and as the Okhrana acknowledged, it was a battle that the authorities could never hope to win outright: 'Experience has shown that it is simply not possible to remove harmful publications from circulation. Publishers issuing, for example, a tendentious work in tens of thousands of copies will usually remove the vast majority of the edition from the printing house as a precaution, leaving just 200–300 copies in case the edition is 'arrested'.'[34] Many publishers also lied about the print runs of editions they knew would be banned, surrendering the declared amount while keeping back the extra.

Because of the difficulty of catching the culprits red-handed, much of the Administration's power was predicated on its ability to trace illegal works back to their original creators. However, the problem in regards to postcards was that there were still a great many printers and publishers who either refused to submit their wares to the censor, or who operated under a mask of obscurity. Moreover, in 1906 many of the anonymous postcard cartoons that had been produced during the Days of Freedom were still in circulation. The consequence of this was to ensure that once subversive images were out in the open, officials had little hope of finding the individuals ultimately responsible.

The difficulties faced by the Press Administration are amply demonstrated by an incident that took place in Saint Petersburg in 1906. On 6 April, the Senior Inspector wrote to the Administration to inform them that a former peasant from Livonia province named August Tsenter had been caught selling uncensored anti-government cartoons.[35] As the Administration did not believe that Tsenter was himself responsible for producing the postcards, an inquiry was launched to find the guilty party.[36] However, after a month-long probe the Inspector was forced to report that he had drawn a complete blank: 'Despite a thorough investigation … it has not been possible to uncover where these postcards could have been printed, or to discover the individuals responsible.'[37]

The Inspector went on to add that he thought it likely that the postcards had been printed abroad. (Although there were anti-government images produced in Western Europe at this time, there is no evidence to support the idea that high-quality Russian-language cartoons were manufactured beyond the confines of the Empire.)[38] Whatever the truth of the matter, the conclusion that the postcards were foreign-made had significant consequences. Not only did it absolve the Inspectorate of any responsibility for having failed to stop production, it also meant that the perpetrator would not be further pursued. Once it was confirmed that the Committee on Foreign Censorship had no record of the postcards, the matter was quietly laid to rest.

There was one further complication that the lack of publication details created for the authorities. Many of the anti-government postcards being published legally by private firms in 1906, in particular, socialist portraits and picture reproductions, were indistinguishable from those being produced by the revolutionary parties. Moreover, the postcards were often sold in the same bookshops, and occasionally even manufactured by the same printing houses. The legitimacy of a postcard, however, depended not only on the image, but also on the publisher. The picture itself may have been legal to print, but whereas the profit from one went towards enriching an apparently blameless individual, profit from the other funded an organisation intent on destroying the state.

The problem was that officials on the ground had no real way of telling which was which, except through the circumstances of their discovery. On occasion this was enough, say for example, if they were uncovered during a police raid, but on the streets and in the shops the Administration's attempt to draw a line between the products of the revolutionary parties and those of commercial publishers proved fruitless, an issue that was further compounded by the advent of ostensibly legal revolutionary publishers such as Utro and Vpered. Thus, while concessions towards some forms of leftist imagery were still in play, revolutionary postcards carrying nominally legal content could hide in plain sight.

The revolutionaries were further assisted by the susceptibility of many Imperial officials to bribery. The Senior Inspector of Printing Houses in Saint Petersburg, State Counsellor Dmitrii Butovskii, was one of the more notably corrupt individuals working during this period. 'For us revolutionaries, this was not a person, but an investment,' wrote Bonch-Bruevich in his memoirs, adding, 'thanks to his uncontrollable weakness for money, our printing houses, bookstores, and newspapers lasted for a significantly longer time than they might otherwise have done if the Saint Petersburg governor's office had not employed such an accommodating official.'[39]

Between 24 November 1905 and 1 February 1906, there were 276 criminal cases brought against publishers in the capital, and a further 763 in the provinces. These are substantial numbers, but as far as can be ascertained, none related to postcards.[40] The Press Administration's near total failure to root out the problem of illegal postcards in the commercial arena is laid bare in the official index of banned works, printed annually from 1906 onwards. Between 1906 and 1910, the *Alphabetic Index of Books and Pamphlets under Court-Ordered Arrest* lists just six different groups of postcards.[41] Two of these relate to designs reproducing banknotes, one to a set of pornographic pictures, and only three to anti-government images.[42]

Suppression of Commercial Retailers

Opposition printed wares were regularly sold on the streets, but the majority of commercially-produced anti-government postcards were channelled through legitimate retail enterprises. Many publishers chose not to get too closely involved in this side of the business, instead preferring to market their goods wholesale to bookshops and middlemen. Although in most cases this was because they lacked the requisite facilities to receive, distribute and sell their output, it also helped minimise risk: the merchandise was distributed quickly, and if lacking publishing details, its provenance was disguised. The latter was particularly important, given that it was at the point of sale that the authorities enjoyed their greatest success in combating illegal imagery.

As of 1 January 1906, Saint Petersburg had eighty-one bookshops, 123 small shops, ten stalls, seventy stores, and twenty-seven kiosks where printed works could be sold, as well as another 200 places offering various goods 'including postcards'.[43] While subversive images were often offered

Anonymous artist. *Free Distribution of Medicine Prepared under the Orders of Physician Professor Baron Von Trepov, Magister Minn, Pharmacist Rimann, and Chemist's Assistant Froloff. Distributed by the Semenovsk Regiment to Individuals Suffering from the New Disease of Libertomania.* No publication details, late 1905. An example of this postcard was confiscated from August Tsenter in April 1906.

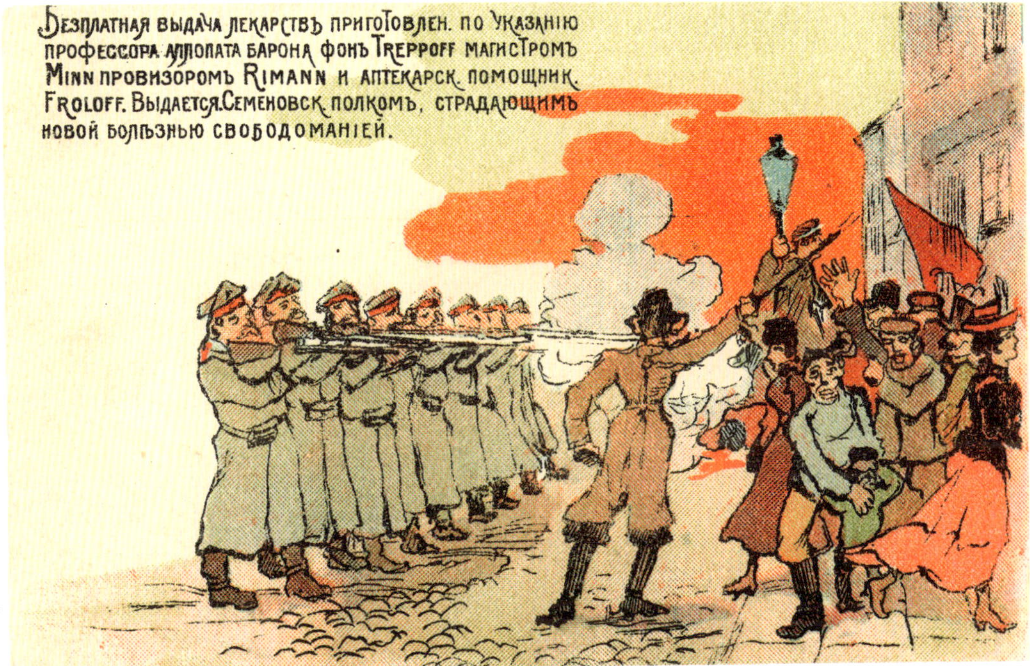

'under the counter', many anti-government postcards were openly displayed, particularly in the weeks after the Manifesto. In December 1905, for example, it was reported that opposition cards were, 'not only being sold in several shops in Riga, but even being exhibited in shop windows.'[44] This was not always a deliberate act of dissent. Booksellers were genuinely confused over what they were allowed to sell, with the view that the Manifesto had established complete freedom of the press still widespread.

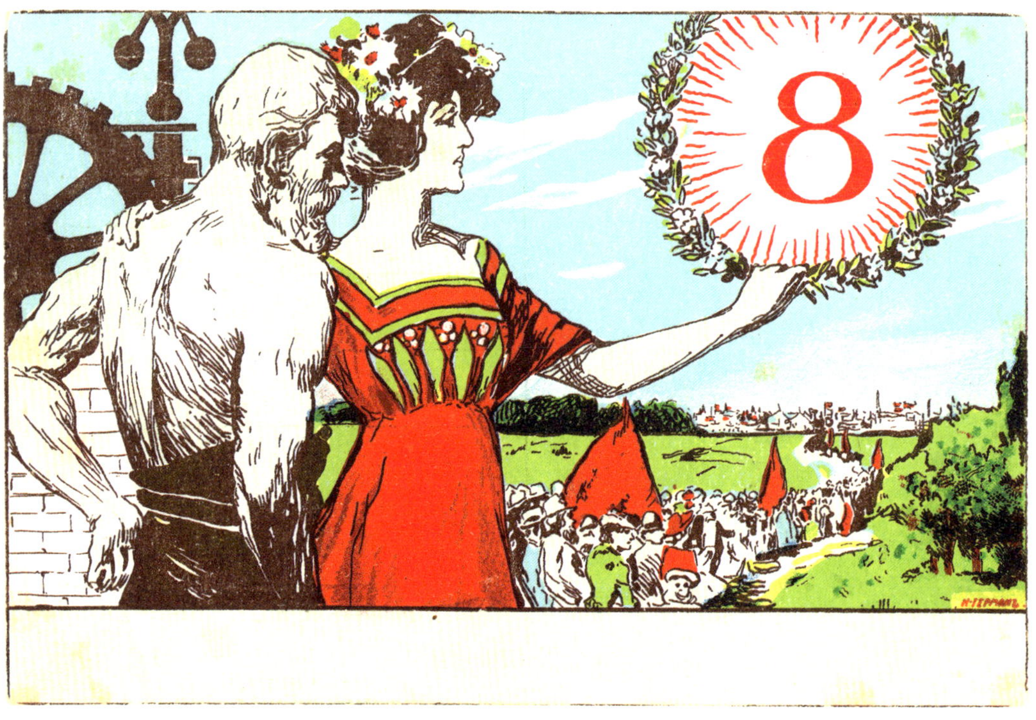

N. German. Untitled postcard promoting the cause of an 8-hour working day. Published by A. Freinkel, Saint Petersburg, 20 April 1906. This is a copy of a German postcard, originally published in 1902. One similar to it was arrested by the Press Administration in early 1908.

Even if booksellers were savvy enough to hide illegal material from the Inspectors, who only had time to make infrequent visits, the police provided invaluable back-up, sending daily reports to the Press Administration detailing their many discoveries of suspect works. Both government bodies were also helped by an extensive network of informants, as well as by anonymous denunciations. For instance, on 7 June 1906 the Administration received an unsigned postcard sent from Saint Petersburg, reading: 'I consider it my patriotic duty to point out to whomever it may concern that ... the Egorov bookshop in the Andreev Market on Vasilevskii Island is selling all kinds of revolutionary pictures and portraits, which are even being displayed in the shop windows.'[45]

Anti-government images were not the only menace officials faced. Disobedience and criminality had also given rise to a vibrant trade in pornography. In late 1906, Empress Alexandra's office warned that the market in obscene material 'has recently reached such proportions that it presents a serious danger to the student population.'[46] But even if officials were aware of the problem, there was little they could do about it. One journalist complained that while anti-government postcards were quickly removed, pornographic images were ignored because they did not malign the government.[47] Opposition postcards certainly may have been a priority; nonetheless, the authorities had their work cut out to stop any form of illegal imagery, whether immoral or seditious.

Booksellers found to be contravening regulations were liable to a fine of fifty roubles on the first offence, 100 on the second, and up to 200 on the third. Furthermore, the items in question would be confiscated, and the bookshop shut down until proper decorum had been restored. The financial risks of selling illegal works were therefore potentially ruinous, but in late 1905 and early 1906, it appears that members of the Inspectorate often took into account the difficult position that many booksellers found themselves in immediately after the October Manifesto. Although attitudes varied considerably, the evidence suggests that when Inspectors did come across legally registered traders selling subversive or uncensored postcards, the punishments were comparatively mild.

'Bringing sellers to book, and all the more so with such harsh measures such as shutting down bookstores, would on the one hand, at least in the provinces, hardly be fair, and on the other, impossible to achieve,' wrote the Senior Inspector for Vilnius, Collegiate Counsellor Vinogradov in February 1906.[48] During an inspection of booksellers that month, he reported having found many examples of uncensored works, including postcards with 'humourist images on current affairs.' In an effort to impose order without endangering the livelihood of booksellers, he did not bring charges, but instead confiscated the material, informed the sellers of the regulations, and warned them against selling similar items in future.[49]

While the Inspectorate achieved moderate success in removing illegal postcards from commercial establishments, it was far less effective in stopping unlicensed traders. Over the course of 1905, networks of revolutionaries and entrepreneurial middlemen had sprung up across the Empire to cater to the trade in seditious works.[50] Although regularly disrupted by the authorities, their sheer numbers ensured a near continuous supply of anti-government material. On the streets, behind closed doors, and at every conceivable revolutionary gathering, cheap photomechanical postcards were sold not only to young intellectuals and student firebrands but also to workers, many of whom could now both afford to buy the occasional postcard and moreover had the political inclination to do so.

Next spread

Anonymous artist. *Witte's Government*. Hand-drawn postcard, circa 1906.

ПРАВИТ

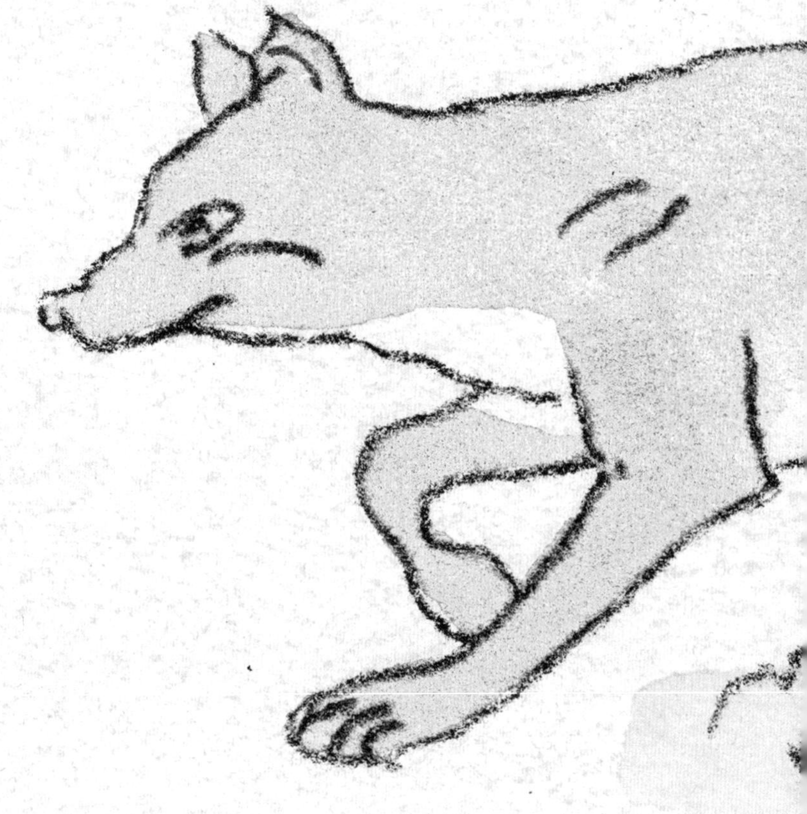

ьство Витте

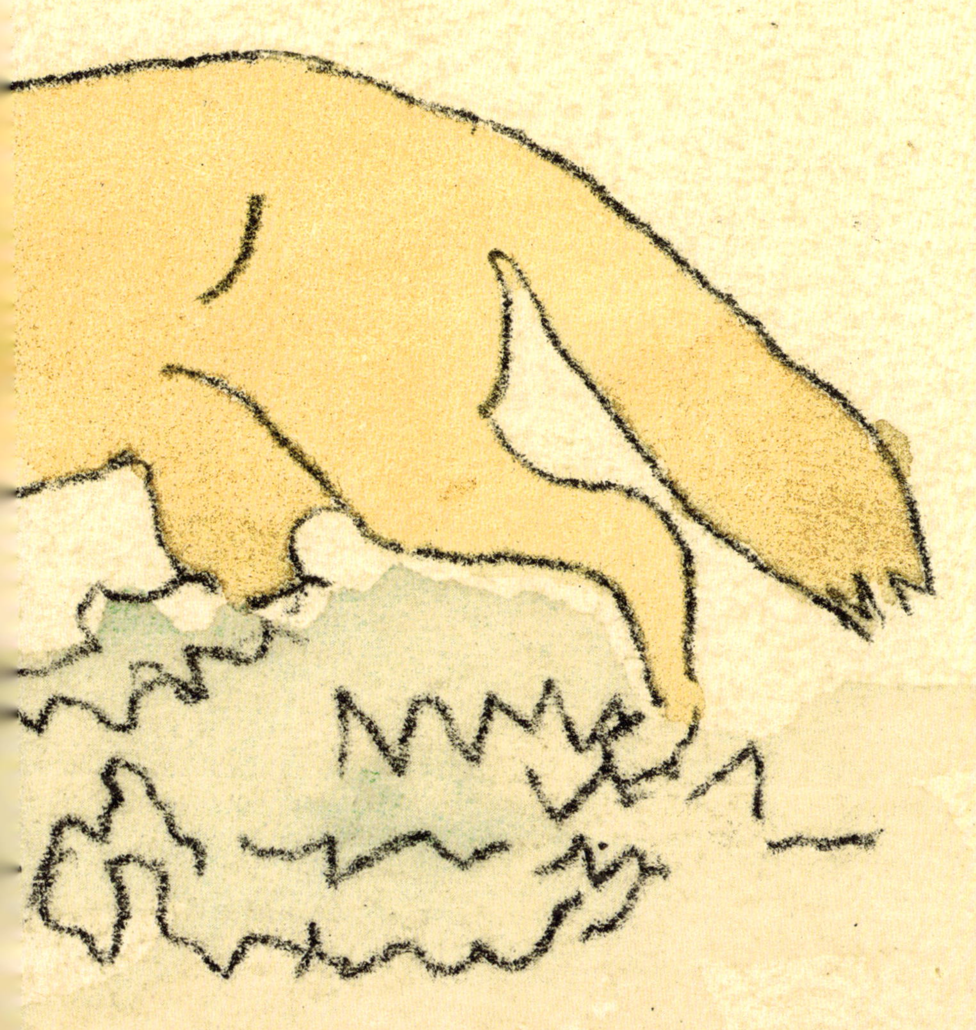

Collegiate Counsellor Vinogradov's attempt to find a workable compromise between legality and practicality illustrates the difficulties of implementing the new press regulations, and offers an indication of how the Press Administration's attitude towards anti-government material played out on the ground. His more amenable approach, however, was not shared by all inspectors, or by the other government organs of the Interior Ministry, who had little time for such nuanced distinctions, regularly confiscating any material they viewed as suspect, whether or not it had passed the censor.[51] The view of the Imperial police, which was shared by most governors, was that to a greater or lesser degree all leftist images promoted revolutionary feeling, and so all were undesirable.

The main legal tools used by the police to suppress opposition postcards were emergency regulations, which over the course of 1905 had been brought back into widespread use. On the basis of a law of 1881, the Interior Minister or regional governor could declare a situation of 'Enhanced Security' in any particular province, giving local organs the power to disband meetings, stop trade, shut down printers, make arrests and impose fines. More seriously, the Committee of Ministers could introduce a measure of 'Extraordinary Security', which placed all control in the hands of the governor. Under both, anti-government images, whether approved by the Administration or not, could be impounded without the need for judicial approval.

The police often came across anti-government postcards in the course of their day-to-day duties, particularly in relation to efforts to combat revolutionary activity, something that naturally influenced their negative view of the medium. Alongside books, pamphlets, leaflets, and other forms of printed propaganda, postcards regularly appear in the lists of items confiscated from revolutionaries during searches of their hideouts. In March 1906, for example, ten photographic cards of the December Uprising were found in the flat of Moscow University student Aleksei Shepel.[52] These images were nominally legal, but the police were still within their rights to appropriate them, either under the powers of the emergency regulations then in force, or as evidence of seditious intent.

The articles under which illegal production and distribution were prosecuted covered extensive ground. Transgressors were charged under Criminal Code Articles 104 (making, owning or reproducing an image insulting to the Imperial Family), 128 (showing disrespect to the monarch or autocratic system), 129 (publicly displaying or distributing an image that incites the overthrow of the system, or serious crime), and 132 (making an image punishable under Articles 128 or 129 that was not successfully distributed, or

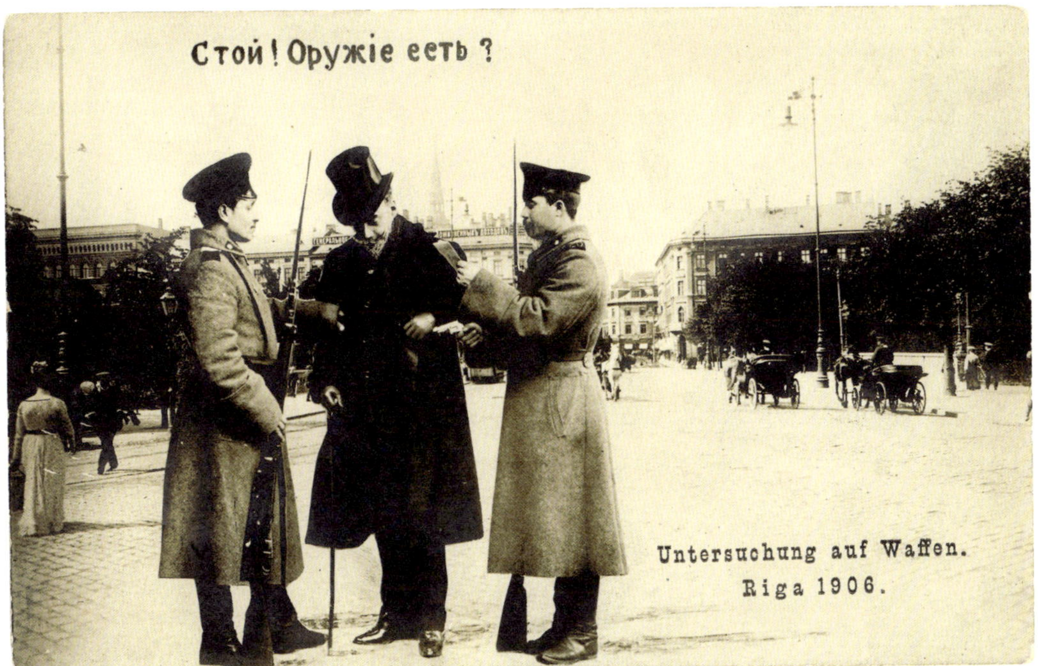

Anonymous designer.
Stop! Are You Armed?
No publication details,
Riga, 1906.

storing such images).[53] These were grave offences, the most serious of which was punishable by up to three years in a fortress prison. Only a handful of individuals, however, were tried for postcard offences alone, nearly all of them committed revolutionaries.

Underground publishing was often carried out in tandem with other revolutionary pursuits, and this greatly complicates any attempt to assess how successful the police were in suppressing the production of subversive postcards. Offences relating to illegal production and distribution were frequently listed under generic headings, amalgamated with other infractions, or superseded by more serious crimes. Many activists caught making or disseminating postcards were eventually sentenced under Criminal Code Article 126: 'Participating in an association that has intentionally set itself the goal of overthrowing the existing state and social system.'[54] In other words, they were punished for membership of a revolutionary group, not for their involvement in propagating illegal postcards.

While vast numbers of revolutionary cards were confiscated, it appears that the Interior Ministry did not achieve much success in stopping their manufacture and dissemination prior to summer 1906. Even then, the suppression of underground production largely came about as a result of the destruction of the liberation movement, as opposed to any specific efforts to combat revolutionary publishers. Given that the battle to impose Imperial authority on the street was still ongoing, postcards were not a priority: their discovery and removal was nothing more than a by-product of efforts to

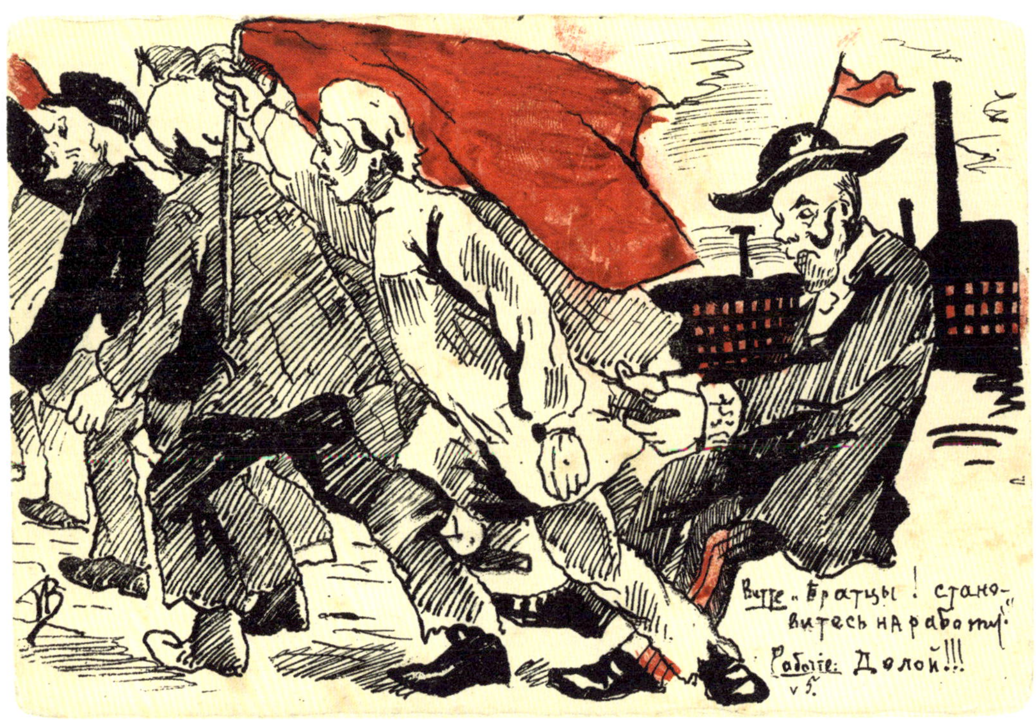

N.V. *Witte: 'Brothers Come Back to Work!' Workers: 'Be Gone with You!!!'*. No publication details, late 1905.

eradicate more egregious forms of revolutionary activity. For much of the period, therefore, the regime remained reliant on removing pernicious imagery at the point of circulation.

In terms of possession, the attention of the police was focused squarely on radical activists, rather than on the mass of intellectuals, professionals, students, and workers who also bought and owned anti-government cards. As Staff Captain Ivan Kosovich was no doubt relieved to discover, unless the images indicated membership of an illegal group or were deemed insulting to the Tsar, private ownership was neither particularly dangerous, nor of pressing concern to the authorities. Gendarmes stopped Kosovich in March 1907 while he was travelling by train in the Moscow Region. When searched, they discovered seventeen photographic cartoons 'on contemporary political subject matter.' The postcards were confiscated, and Kosovich was allowed to carry on his way.[55]

Since 1873, active efforts had been made to monitor postcards sent through the mail. Government perlustration during the 1905 Revolution was prolific, but there is no evidence to suggest that large quantities of anti-government images were removed from the postal system. The infrequency with which one finds cards that have travelled through the post may be due in part to the fact that fewer have survived, but it is chiefly because they were never intended to be sent as open letters: anti-government postcards were primarily designed and bought for private contemplation as opposed to written correspondence, not least because the potential for discovery was deterrent enough to make most think twice about mailing subversive pictures to their friends and family.

⁂

The six months that followed the Manifesto were a stalemate. As one journalist wrote: 'We have no censor, but we also have no press freedom.'[56] Repression was on the up, but neither the Administration's policy of divide and rule, nor the police's more sweeping approach to confiscation achieved any real success in stopping the spread of undesirable imagery prior to the First Duma. Production of contentious material was curtailed, but a shortage of resources, absence of uniform approach, and widespread anonymity meant that attempts to restrict distribution were largely dependent on chance. Just as the police were effective in combating individual revolutionaries but largely powerless to act against mass movements, so it was with anti-government postcards. They were overwhelmed by the sheer numbers.

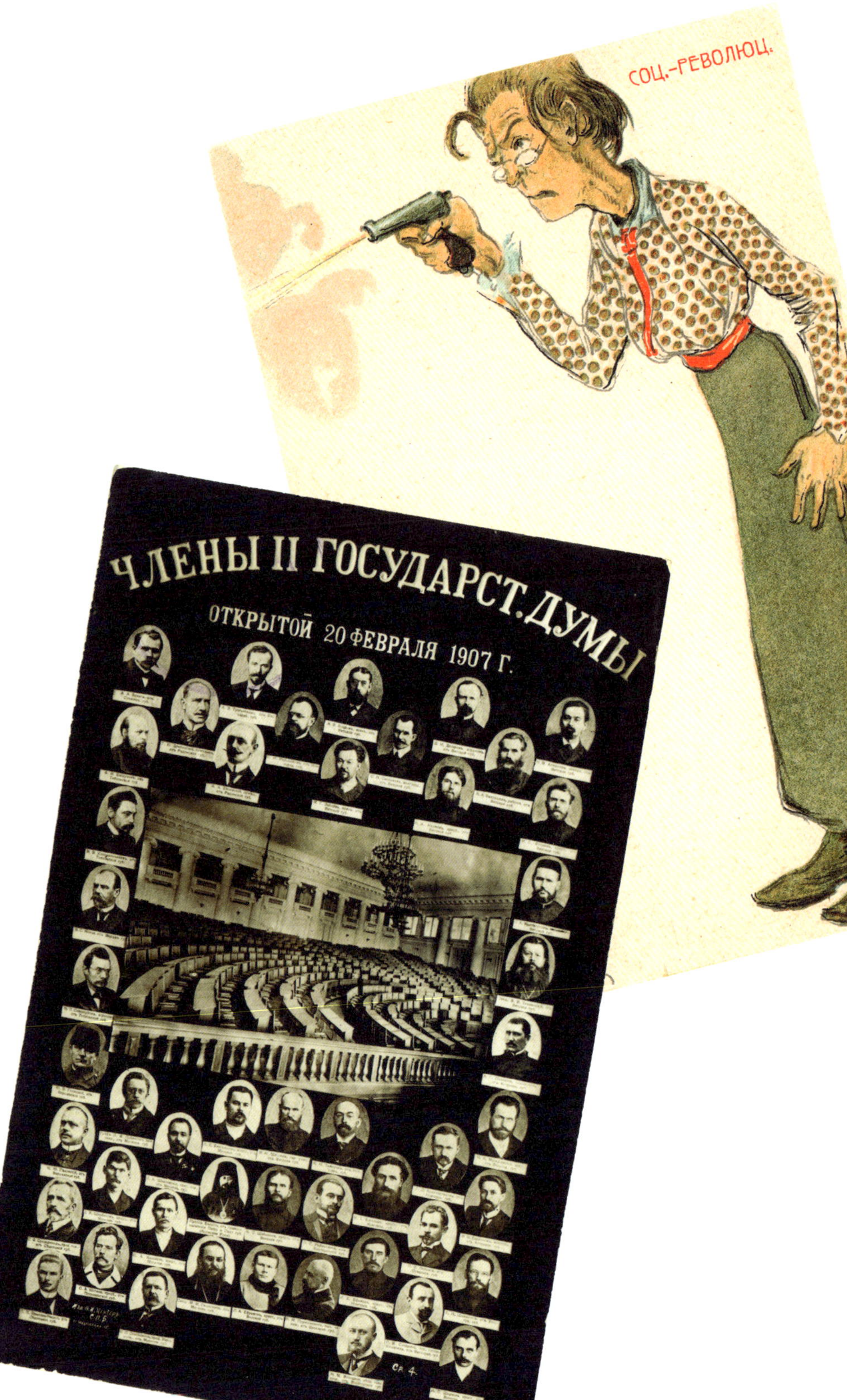
СОЦ.-РЕВОЛЮЦ.
ЧЛЕНЫ II ГОСУДАРСТ. ДУМЫ
ОТКРЫТОЙ 20 ФЕВРАЛЯ 1907 Г.

DUMA AND DEMISE

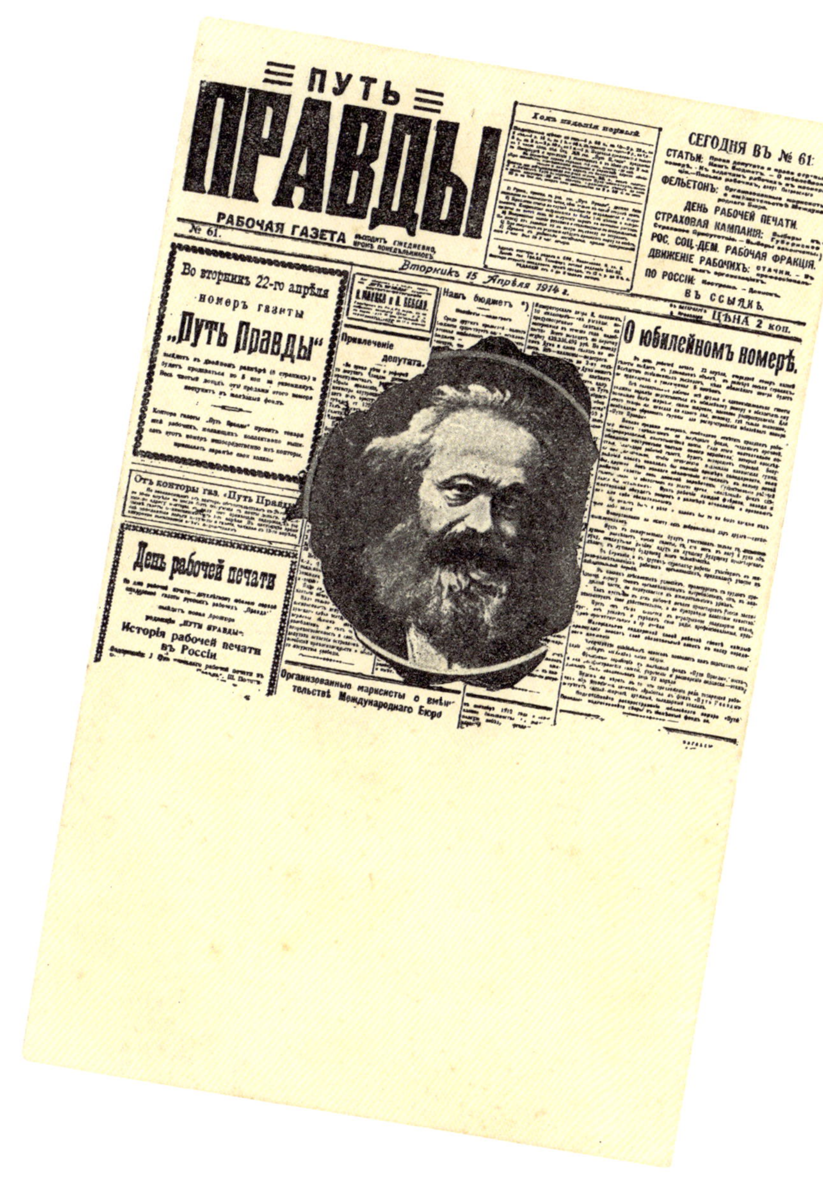

ПУТЬ ПРАВДЫ

РАБОЧАЯ ГАЗЕТА

№ 61.

Вторникъ 15 Апрѣля 1914 г.

СЕГОДНЯ ВЪ № 61:

ФЕЛЬЕТОНЪ:

ДЕНЬ РАБОЧЕЙ ПЕЧАТИ.

СТРАХОВАЯ КАМПАНІЯ:

РОС. СОЦ.-ДЕМ. РАБОЧАЯ ФРАКЦІЯ.

ДВИЖЕНІЕ РАБОЧИХЪ:

ПО РОССІИ:

ВЪ ССЫЛКѢ.

ЦѢНА 2 коп.

Во вторникъ 22-го апрѣля номеръ газеты „Путь Правды“

Отъ конторы газ. „Путь Правды“

День рабочей печати

Исторія рабочей печати въ Россіи

Привлечение депутата.

Нашъ бюджетъ

О юбилейномъ номерѣ.

Организованные марксисты о вмѣшательствѣ Международнаго Бюро

1906–1917

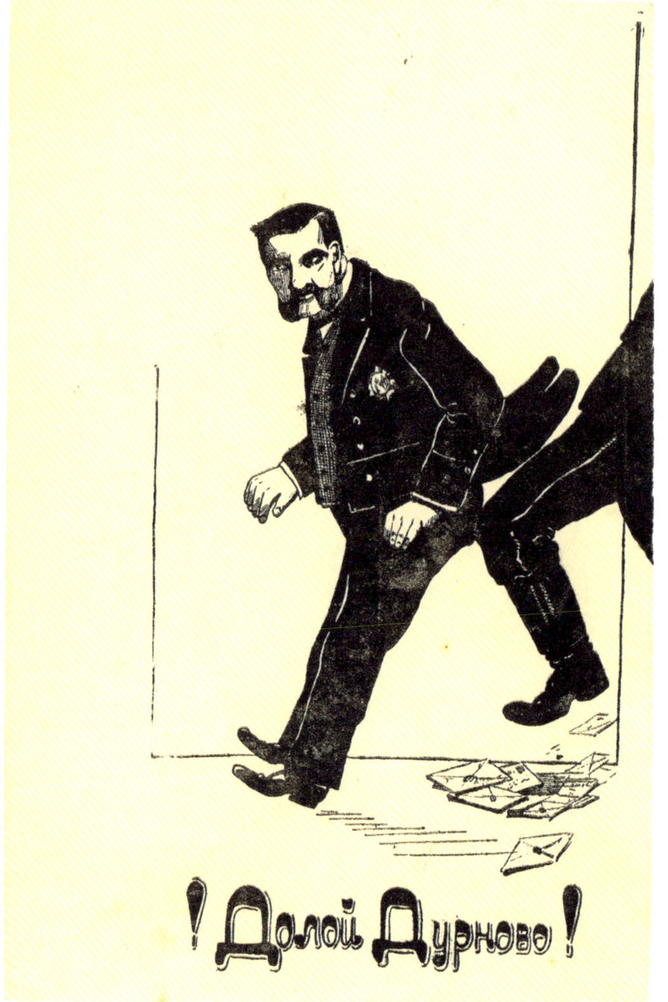
! Долой Дурново !

In the early hours of 1 May 1906, the police arrived at the Moscow residence of a twenty-five-year-old masseuse named Antonina Romanova.[1] A few weeks previously, postal workers had intercepted a letter sent to Romanova from Nizhnii Novgorod. The contents of the dispatch, which included a fake passport and an unsigned note, had led the Okhrana to believe that Romanova was sheltering a wanted revolutionary by the name of Aleksei Pavlov.

When the premises were searched, Pavlov was nowhere to be seen; instead, the police discovered a veritable bonanza of revolutionary propaganda. Alongside an abundance of pamphlets, leaflets, and newspapers, they also found eighteen packets of anti-government postcards, as well as another twenty-one loose images. Inside each of the packets was a receipt reading: 'Three roubles received in aid of political exiles and prisoners. M. M. Chemodanov.'[2]

Earlier in the year, Chemodanov had been introduced to Dmitrii Peschanskii, the owner of a photographic studio in central Moscow. With the encouragement of local Social Democratic activists, Peschanskii had consented to start reproducing Chemodanov's drawings in postcard form, at last providing an outlet for the more controversial satires that he had been making throughout the previous year. The resulting images were sold across the city by an organised network of revolutionary helpers.

At the time Romanova's flat was raided, Chemodanov's postcards had already been in circulation for a few months, but the evidence found there was the first to link him directly to the images. As a result, Romanova was arrested and the hunt for Chemodanov began.[3]

Eighteen days later, police officers searched the home of suspected revolutionary Nina Morozova, who shared a flat with three Moscow University students named Vasilii, Viacheslav, and Vladimir Kalashnikov. Morozova was found with various items of illegal literature, and twenty-four 'postcards that denigrate the person of the RULING EMPEROR,' all signed with Chemodanov's pseudonym 'Cherv.' Vladimir Kalashnikov, meanwhile, was caught with forty-seven pre-addressed packets, thirty-one of which contained postcards with 'revolutionary content.'[4]

Three distributors of Chemodanov's postcards had now been detained and a warrant was duly put out for his arrest.[5] Chemodanov himself, however, was nowhere to be seen. In fact, he was not even in Moscow, but in Yalta. Around a year and a half previously, he had developed chronic bronchitis, a legacy of his days as a country doctor. In a bid to improve his health, he had recently gone south for a few months to enjoy the warmer climate. Wisely, he had not informed anyone where he was going.

Previous spread from left to right

Anonymous designer. *Members of the Second State Duma. Opened on 20 February 1907.* Published by August Tsenter, Saint Petersburg, early 1907.

Evgenii Sokolov. *Socialist-Revoltutionary.* Printed by E. Kudinova and A. Lezina, Saint Petersburg, circa April 1906. This is a lightly-disguised caricature of Maria Spiridonova.

Anonymous designer. Postcard commemorating 'Proletarian Press Day'. No publication details, April 1914.

Opposite

Anonymous artist. *Down with Durnovo!* No publication details, circa late 1905.

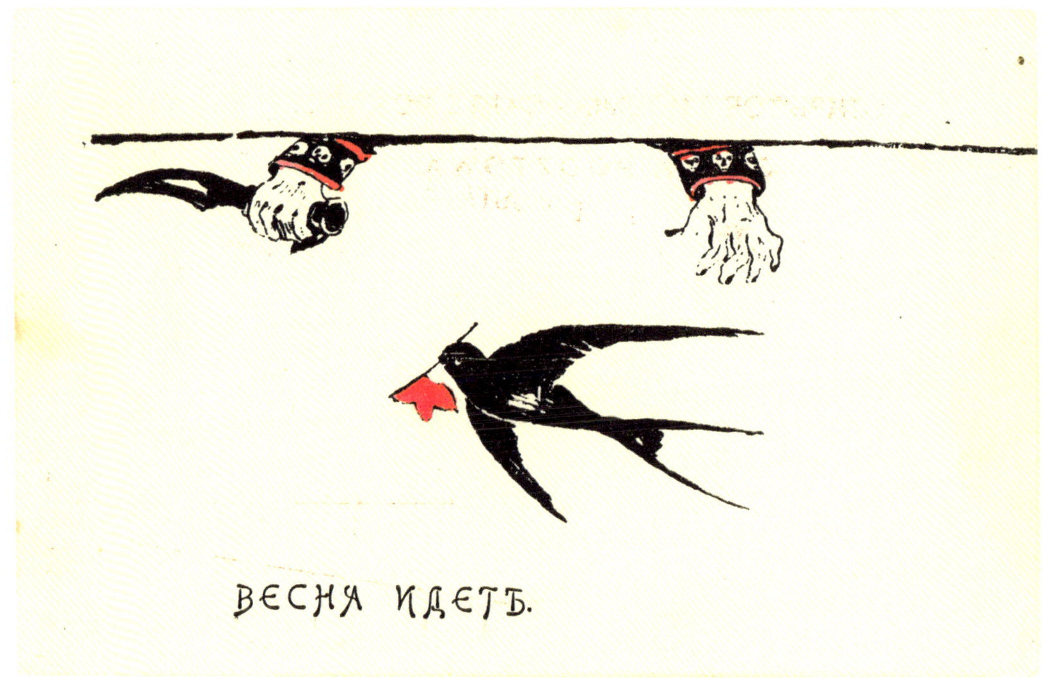

Anonymous artist. *Spring Is Coming.* Published by E.S.V. or E.C.B., Warsaw, early 1906.

Arrests and detentions were now occurring with greater intensity across the Empire, a sure sign that the autocratic state was beginning to resume its authority. Since December, the regime had shown itself determined to suppress all forms of dissent on the streets, and in early 1906 it started to reassert itself more fully in the political arena. The thought of an alternative system of government had provided sustenance to disillusioned liberals weary with revolt, but over the preceding months the atmosphere had become more and more polluted by reactionary politics. Many still looked to the upcoming Duma as a beacon of hope, but the government was working hard to ensure that its power would be largely symbolic.

In February, the State Council was transformed into a legislative assembly with powers equal to the Duma, weakening the role of the latter before it had even convened. Worse was to come in April with a revision of the country's Fundamental Laws, the legal framework that defined the parameters of monarchical authority. In what amounted to a new constitution, the principles of autocracy were reaffirmed and only nominal advances made towards safeguarding the promises of the October Manifesto. The Tsar reluctantly relinquished his right to 'unlimited power,' but few had any illusions about what this meant in practice. Promulgated just three days before the opening of the Duma, the Laws were characterised by leading liberal Pavel Miliukov as a fraud against the people.

Opposite

Anonymous artist. *Neither Ours nor Yours.* No publication details, circa 1906. Caricature of Sergei Witte being tossed back and forth between a worker and Petr Durnovo.

These changes, however, did little to loosen the hold of opposition sentiment over the people, and in the lead-up to the Duma, sales of anti-government

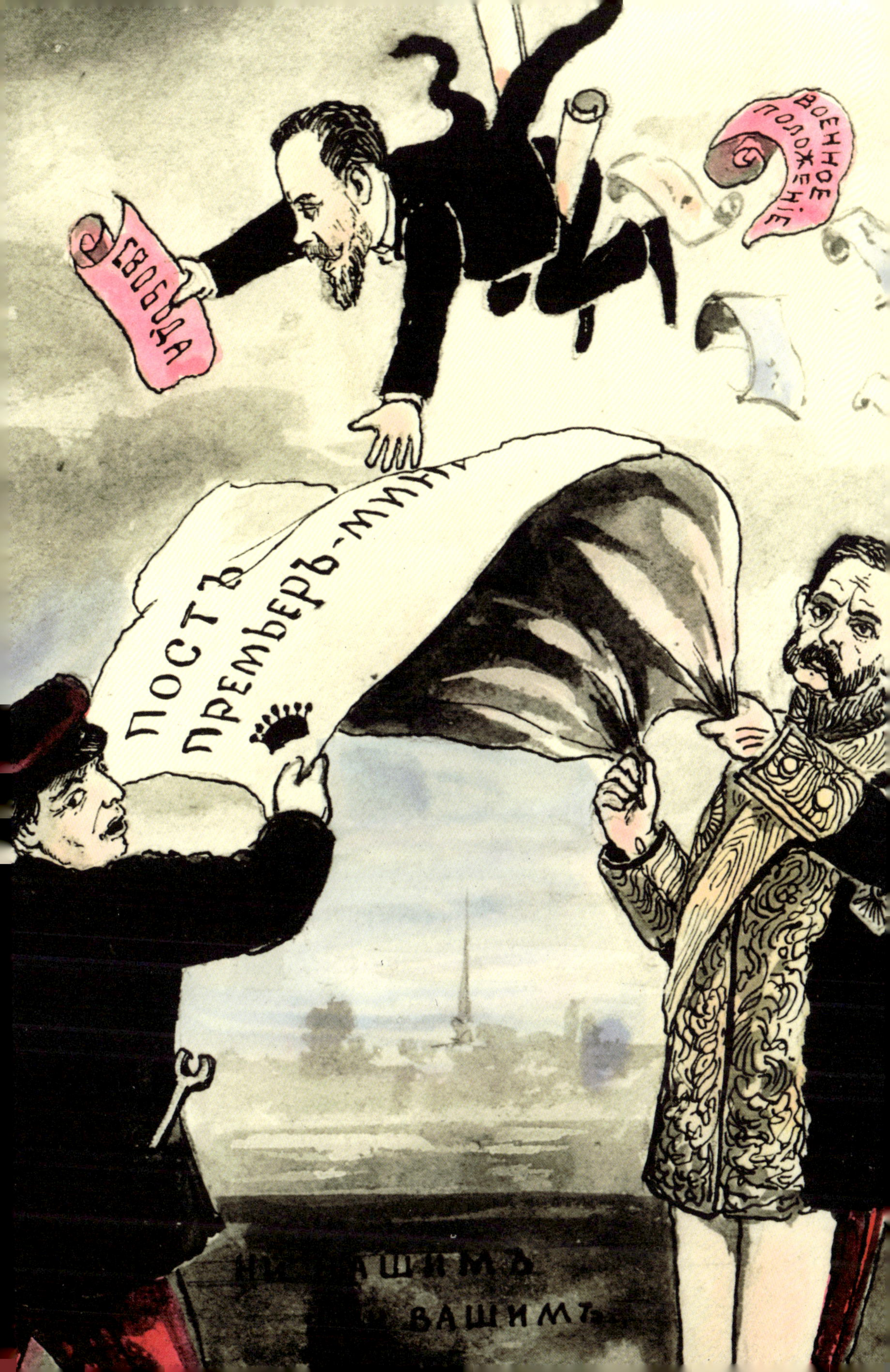
СВОБОДА
ВОЕННОЕ ПОЛОЖЕНІЕ
ПОСТЪ
ПРЕМЬЕРЪ-МИН
НИ
АШИМЪ
ВАШИМЪ...

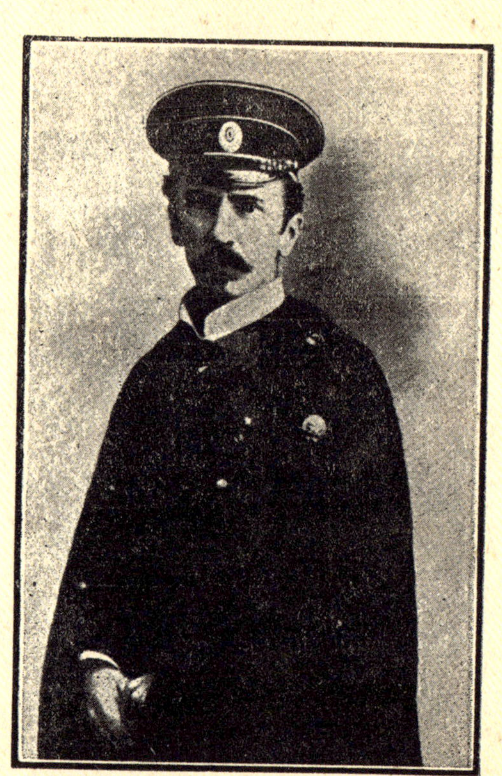

Не топчите мой прахъ... Я дома а вы въ гостяхъ...

Лейтенантъ П. Шмидтъ

imagery remained extensive. In early March, the execution of Lieutenant Schmidt provoked an outpouring of postcards that sought both to commemorate his accession to the pantheon of revolutionary martyrs and to stoke anger against the state. Realising the effect that they might have, officials responded with a heavy hand. Five days after his death, the Inspector of Printing Houses in Odessa reported the appearance of 'images and photographs of the final days and execution of Lieutenant Schmidt,' and suggested to the governor that the police remove them from circulation.[6]

Dimitrii Pudichev (photographer). *Do Not Trample on My Ashes… I Am Home and You Are Still a Guest. Lieutenant P. Schmidt.* Lopshits Printing House, Odessa, circa March 1906.

The First Duma

The opening of Russia's first elected parliament on 27 April 1906 presented a legitimate opportunity for postcard manufacturers to celebrate the major achievement of the Revolution. As one postcard enthusiast recalled: 'Pictures of the Tauride Palace and portraits of deputies quickly became popular, helped in no small way by their affordability.'[7] For the time being, the Duma represented the acceptable face of opposition politics, and having been awarded the Imperial stamp of approval, subject matter relating to the assembly not only attracted liberal firms, but also publishers closer to the throne. For instance, both the Society of Saint Eugenia and Imperial warrant holder Karl Bulla produced photographic postcards commemorating the inauguration of the Duma.

Chromolithographic postcard cartoons also went through a minor resurgence, although it is evident that repression had by this time severely blunted the sharpness of their satire. Whereas during the Days of Freedom, political cartoons had been directed outwards against the government, most now looked inwards to find their sources of mockery among the opposition and newly-elected deputies. These new works were less subversive than broadly humorous. A series on political parties by the artist Evgenii Sokolov, for example, caricatures the revolutionaries as fanatical and often violent zealots, but at the same also lampoons liberal activists, who are derided as bookish intellectuals.

Perhaps inevitably, the Tsar and his assembly were set against each other from the start.[8] The debates themselves were rowdy, and if the state was guilty of not taking the body seriously, then opposition deputies were at fault for trying to push matters too far. The main and most controversial topic of discussion in the chamber was the intractable 'agrarian question,' a subject driven forward by famine and ongoing waves of peasant unrest, which had re-emerged with a vengeance in May. This gave rise to a few cartoons – the majority comparing the fate of the poor with that of the rich – but as a general rule, the assembly's deliberations were not the focus of many postcards, a reflection of an overall decline in production.

Next spread

Vasil Gulak. *Sign up to the Party!/Ye Gads, How Many of You Are There?* Printed by I.N. Kushnerev, Moscow, 9 November 1905.

Запишите

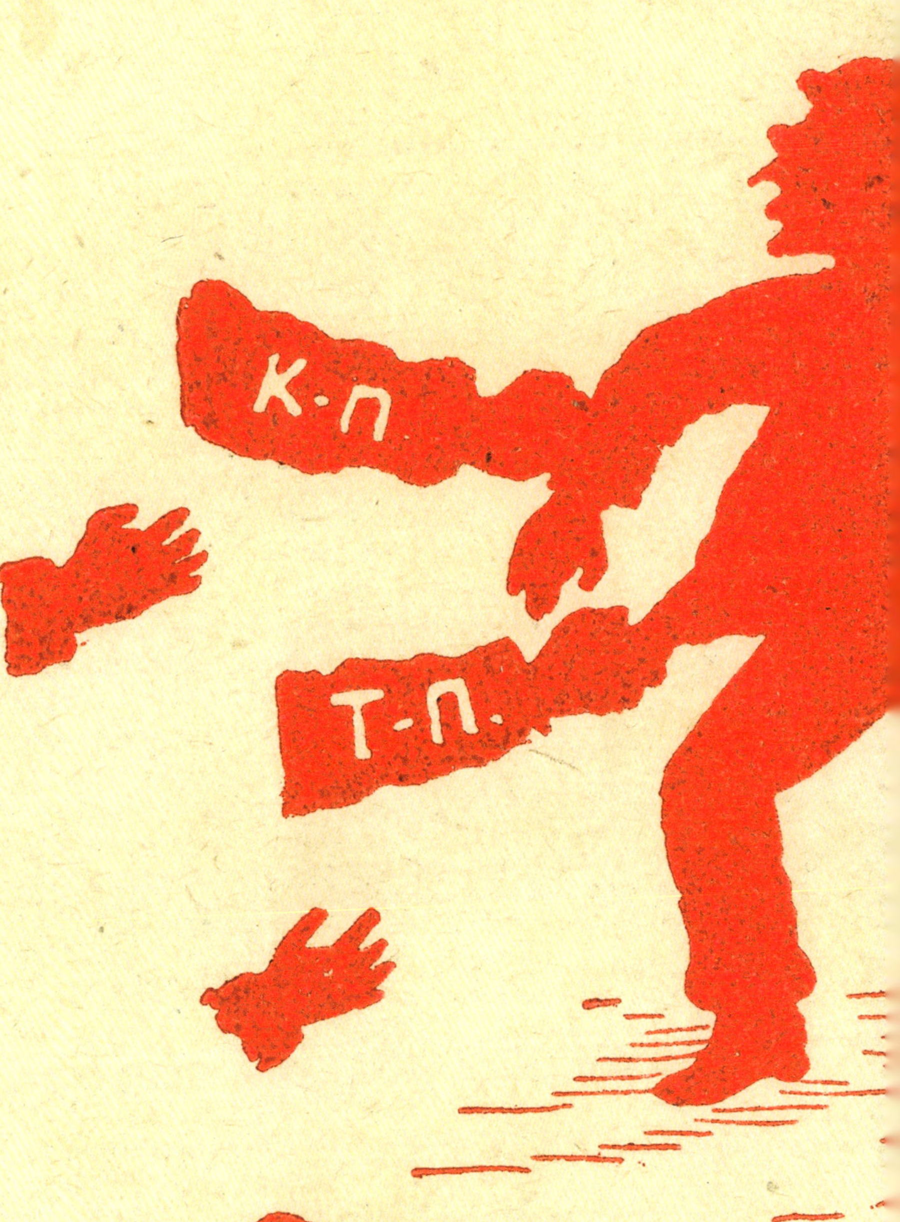

Батюшки,

ВЪ ПАРТІЮ!

СКОЛЬКО ВАСЪ!

After a lengthy period of indecision on the part of the Tsar, and heavy intrigue on the part of those who surrounded him, the decision was eventually made to prorogue the legislature. Deputies arriving for the morning session on 9 July found soldiers posted at the doors and their entry barred. The trigger for the dissolution was a dispute over redistribution of land, but the underlying issue was the government's belief that the Duma was interfering in matters that lay far outside its remit. For the Tsar, the assembly had become both a thorn and a threat, and given the intransigence of one and the blindness of the other, a collision had become all but inevitable.

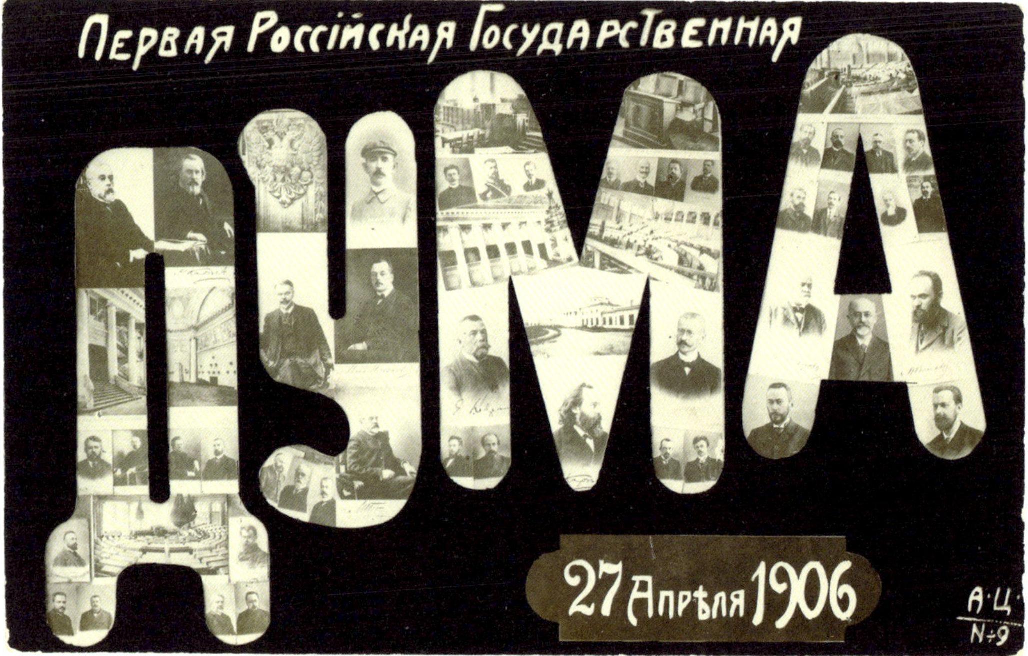

Anonymous designer. *The First Russian State Duma, 27 April 1906*. Published by August Tsenter, Saint Petersburg, April 1906.

Revolutionaries and liberals alike were counting on the nation to rise up in protest against the dissolution, but it was not to be. A call for public resistance issued by leftist deputies in Vyborg proved a damp squib. The text of their appeal spread with great rapidity nonetheless. On 19 July, gendarmes discovered eighteen postcards reproducing the so-called Vyborg Manifesto in a bookshop in Tambov Province. These had been sent, unprompted, by a wholesaler in Saint Petersburg a few days previously; thus, a mere week and a half had passed from the appeal being issued to the postcards appearing for sale in Umansk – a round trip of well over a thousand kilometres – true testament to the versatility of the medium and the strength of contemporary retail networks.[9]

In general, however, reactions were muted. Both Chemodanov and Karrik produced postcards condemning the closure of the Duma, but there was no outpouring of material to match its inauguration. Production, in common with the national mood, may still have been firmly against the government, but after months of repression it was beginning to cool.

Mutinies in Sveaborg and Kronstadt in July prompted a few more postcards, but these events gave little cause for celebration, proving only that the revolutionaries were too weak to mount a serious revolt. The ostensible purpose of such images was to spread news of discontent among the armed services, but they also reflected an opposition that was running out of ideas and a population that was growing tired of death and violence. While one postcard on the Sveaborg mutiny shows heroic sailors firing at government troops, another on the Kronstadt Uprising shows a sailor on a red flag flying off into the distance accompanied by an allegorical figure of death. It is hardly a ringing endorsement of revolution.

Stolypin, Repression and Falling Interest in Radical Imagery

On the day that the Duma was dissolved, Petr Stolypin took over as prime minister. In the days leading up to its closure, repression had been stepped up; now, the authorities moved decisively to re-establish full control. Thousands of revolutionaries were rounded up and a crackdown was initiated against members of the liberal opposition. Punishments were also augmented, culminating in the introduction of a system of field courts-martial serving summary justice with only the faintest veneer of due process. Over the eight months that they were in force over 1,000 people were allegedly executed, provoking widespread public outrage.[10]

At the same time, there was a further clampdown on the press: *Knizhnyi vestnik* compared the position of publishers during this period to hares being hunted by a pack of dogs.[11] Periodicals were the primary target of official ire, but repression affected all aspects of the print trade. There were now perceptibly fewer new political postcards being manufactured, not so much a reflection of contemporary events as of the deteriorating circumstances for their production. It was still in principle possible to print anti-government images, both in commercial printing houses and underground, but the factors that would bring about their eventual demise were already apparent.

The day before the Duma was prorogued, Saint Petersburg's Governor Vladimir Von der Launitz had written to the Press Administration to convey his incomprehension at the fact that anti-government postcards were still legally available. 'The Department of Police has forwarded me two examples of postcards with images of political criminals ... and asked for my instructions on removing them from circulation. Having requested that officials from the Inspectorate of Printing Houses carry out this order, we would both like to clarify to what extent the distribution of portraits of political criminals is generally advisable. It would appear that the Saint Petersburg Committee on Press Affairs does not see any legal basis to ban this type of publication.'[12]

Belgard replied a few days later confirming that such images were legal. He was tactful enough not to mention it, but the implication was that von der Launitz's actions were at odds with the Administration's own approach, further evidence that governors were inclined to act on their own initiative, taking a prohibitive approach to all forms of oppositionist material. Belgard, however, went on to provide a get-out clause, remarking that in regions where martial law or Extraordinary Security was in place, 'it appears that images of political criminals have been subject to confiscation on the orders of the authorities.'[13] Having paid lip service to the concessions, he was then suggesting that there might be a way around them.

This communiqué is the earliest known occasion that emergency regulations were cited by the Administration as a possible way of combating anti-government postcards. Belgard was still scrupulous about acting within the confines of the law, but he clearly recognised the regulations' potential for combating seditious works. In the months ahead, they would prove a fearsomely effective weapon. By the spring of 1906, nearly seventy percent of the territory of the Russian Empire was under some form of emergency governance, and in many provinces, emergency regulations remained in force for several years afterwards.[14] In these areas, no anti-government postcard of any hue could be offered without the risk of confiscation.[15]

The downward trajectory of opposition postcards, however, did not follow an entirely uniform path, and police reports from this period show that they were still being printed and sold in large numbers. Even in the summer of 1906, when the mood was notably more subdued, officials were regularly coming across subversive images. On 28 July, for example, the Department of Police sent a circular to governors in provinces along the Volga River, reporting that, 'postcards with images of state criminals are being traded in vast quantities on the quayside of the Volga Steamship Company.' Governors were requested to take measures to suppress the images – confirmation, as if any were needed, of the Administration's increasingly repressive approach.[16]

Perhaps the clearest illustration of the continuing appeal of opposition imagery comes courtesy of the Society of Saint Eugenia. In August 1906, Vladimir Kurbatov, an art historian and member of the Society's artistic committee, suggested that the charity should 'make an agreement with Shipovnik to sell their postcards in our kiosks on a semi-official basis.' Kurbatov was well aware that it was an unusual proposition for the establishment publisher par excellence to sell socialist postcards, albeit ones of such quality; however, the charity's need for income was pressing: 'It would

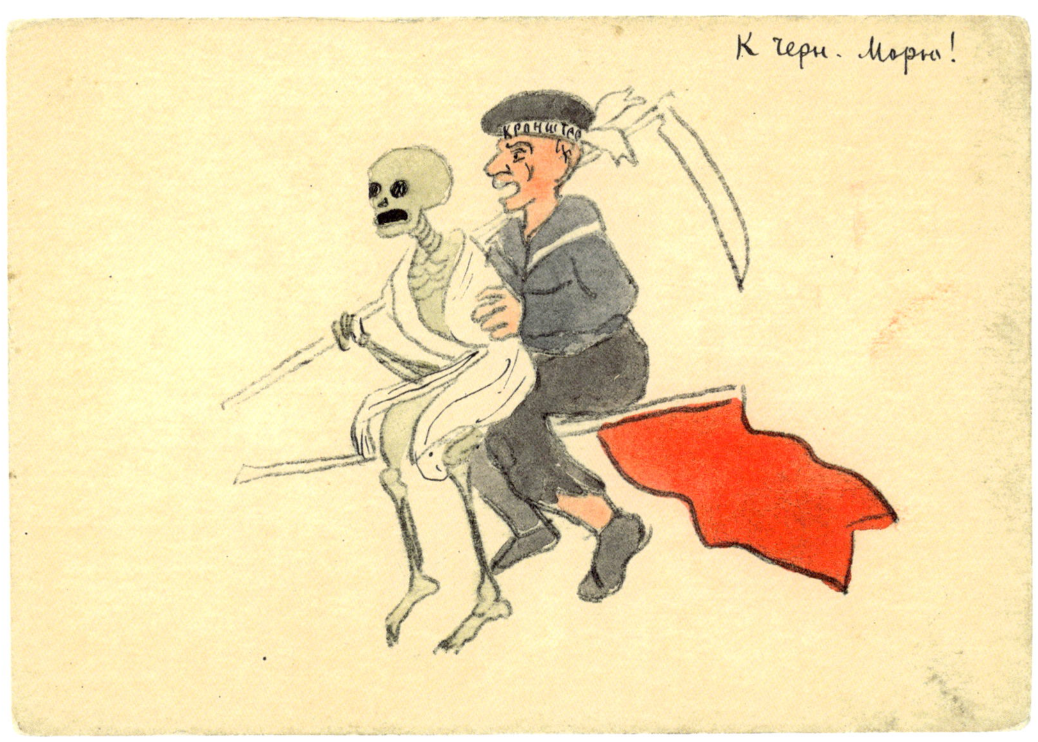

Anonymous artist.
To the Black Sea.
Hand-drawn postcard, July 1906. The sailor's cap band is marked 'Kronstadt'.

of course be awkward for us to issue political postcards ourselves, but at the moment it's hard to generate money without political subject matter.'[17]

Even as he was making the suggestion, Kurbatov appears to have understood that it was a non-starter, remarking that if the Society could not publish political subject matter, then it should at least print more 'zesty imagery.' His comments underline the degree to which popular taste had become politicised and by extension, anti-government imagery commercialised, factors that forced even mainstream publishers into commissioning their own political postcards or making up for it by coming up with new, exciting alternatives. It is evidence as well that although public displays of revolutionary dissent had largely been curbed by mid-1906, opposition thoughts and inclinations had not disappeared into thin air, but were still in need of an outlet.

Nonetheless, although the population as a whole was more politicised than at any previous time, appetite for the most seditious forms of imagery was beginning to diminish. 'By the autumn of 1906, Chemodanov's postcards had stopped arousing so much attention and interest as before,' reported Nikolai Druzhinin, an activist responsible for their distribution.[18] Members of the liberal bourgeoisie and democratic intelligentsia had begun to shrink away, taking fright at Chemodanov's uncompromisingly forthright images of the Tsar. Distributors regularly returned with their wares unsold, and as a result many ceased their involvement. This fall in fervour

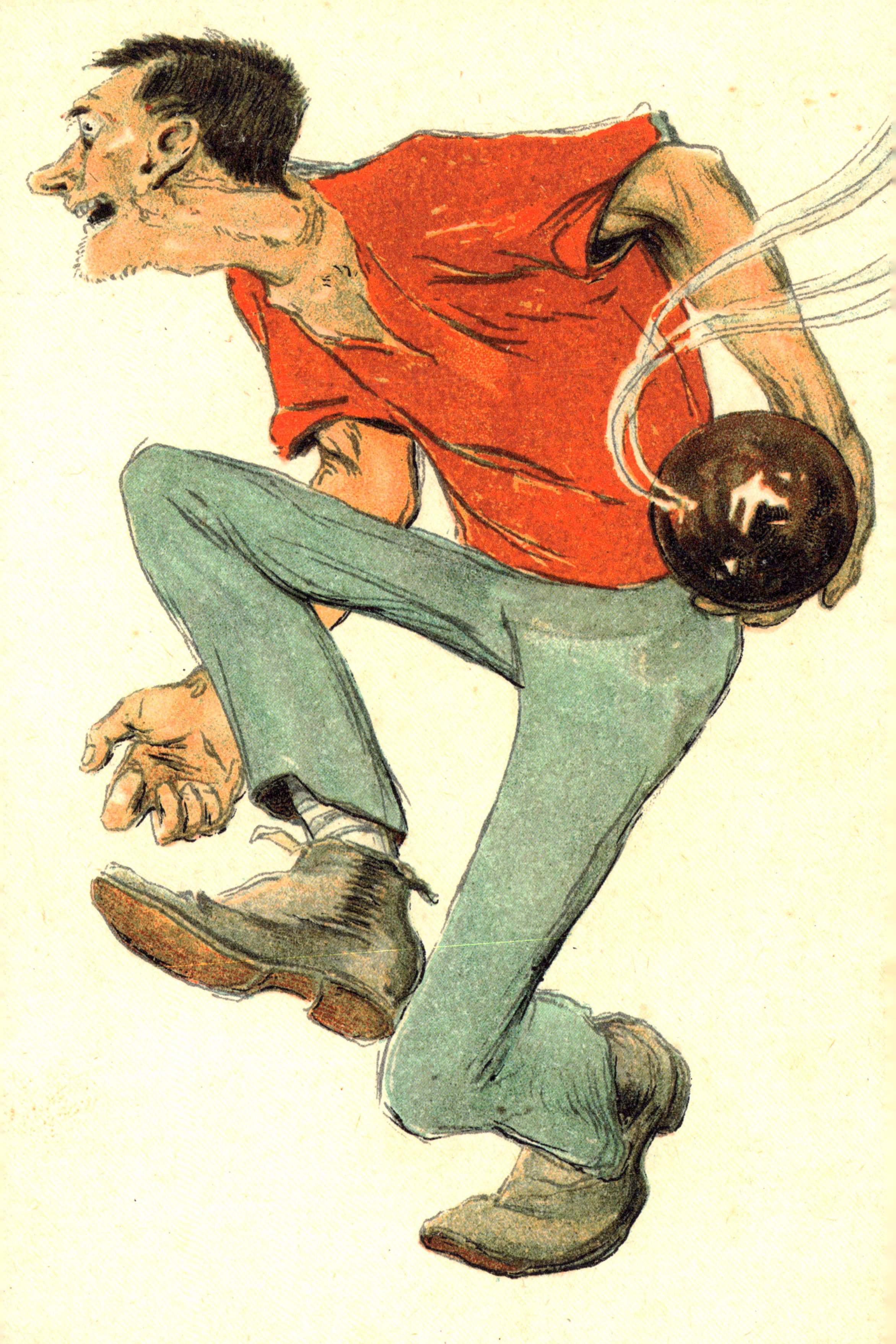

was mirrored by a sharp drop in the production of satirical journals, which by this time had largely lost their bite.[19]

Evgenii Sokolov. *Anarchist*. Printed by E. Kudinova and A. Lezina, Saint Petersburg, circa April 1906.

Government crackdowns had weakened public enthusiasm for revolution. Crushed by repression, the liberation movement exerted less of a pull than it had done even just a few months previously. While much of the population was no more reconciled to the government, a year and a half of unrest had exhausted them and by late summer 1906, this was affecting demand for more radical postcard imagery. The Revolution was no longer so novel, so exciting, or so full of possibilities. Violence had suppressed public demonstrations of dissent and with them the enthusiasm and belief that had once been felt. With the government's hand now fully revealed, it was no longer realistic to entertain any genuine hope for wholesale change.

The Demise of Mikhail Chemodanov

Chemodanov left Moscow again in the autumn, this time for the Caucasus.[20] On his return in October the atmosphere in the city had become significantly more stifled, and he now began to sound 'notes of alarm' in his conversations.

Earlier the previous month, Druzhinin had been caught attending a revolutionary meeting. The police had searched his flat and he was put under official surveillance.[21] Another of Chemodanov's distributors, a twenty-year-old hereditary noble named Boris Evreinov had also been detained. More ominously, he had been found with Social Democratic Party documents, several packets of postcards, and a letter addressed to Chemodanov containing compromising information.[22]

As the nights were drawing in, the noose was tightening, and Chemodanov was right to be nervous. A few days after his return, the Moscow Administration of Gendarmes had sent a secret communiqué to the Okhrana requesting confirmation of Chemodanov's identity, and asking for instructions on carrying out a search of his flat.[23]

On 31 October, the police visited Chemodanov's home on Prechistenka Boulevard, but despite an extensive search, they failed to uncover any incriminating evidence.[24] Chemodanov, however, was living on borrowed time. On 11 November, the Okhrana sent out an alert to all policemen in Moscow, warning them about the spread of his postcards, and demanding that they make 'the most strenuous efforts to detain the distributors.'[25] The police in turn gathered together the city's janitors and ordered them to keep a look out for anyone seen posting proclamations or carrying large bundles of letters.[26]

On 1 December, a janitor noticed a woman loitering suspiciously in the vicinity of a block of flats in the central south-west of the city. After seeing that she was carrying a small package, he called over a local policeman, and together they detained the woman, who was later identified as a twenty-five-year-old teacher and former peasant from Smolensk named Aleksandra Petrova. She was found to be carrying sixteen packets of postcards, all containing receipt slips signed by Chemodanov.[27] The police later discovered more postcards at Petrova's home, as well as a large quantity of revolutionary publications.[28] Armed with this new evidence, the police returned to Chemodanov's flat, and late on 3 December he was finally arrested.[29]

Other members of the network were soon rounded up. Apparently by coincidence, Irina Zelentsova, a seamstress from Kazan, and Anna Romanova, a home tutor, were captured that same day during an operation against a cell of Socialist-Revolutionaries.[30] Hidden inside a linen basket in their Moscow flat, the police found two envelopes containing postcards, and nineteen other bundles of cards, each wrapped with a signed receipt. In Zelentsova's bedroom were several items of revolutionary propaganda, a box of ten cartridges for a Browning revolver, and yet more postcards. Among the latter, the police made a particular note of *Two Perspectives*, Chemodanov's last and most subversive image, which predicted the Tsar's death at the hands of the people.[31]

Mikhail Chemodanov. Finished drawing for *Two Perspectives*. Moscow, October 1906. The caption reads: 'The triumph of battlefield autocracy (more than 300 executions in two months!!)' / 'It will all come to a bad end.'

It was January before the police realised that Zelentsova was a pseudonym. The woman they had arrested was none other than Antonina Romanova, Anna's sister, who had first been detained in connection with Chemodanov's postcards back in May 1906.[32] Perhaps the most extraordinary discovery, however, came with the re-arrest of activist Boris Evreinov. During a search of his home in early 1907, the police found: sixty envelopes containing postcards, 1,994 empty pre-addressed envelopes, 157 loose postcards, a packet of notes and letters, 196 business cards belonging to various individuals, and 819 receipts signed by Chemodanov.[33] The sheer amount of material bears witness to an enterprise carried out on a near industrial scale.

Following his arrest, the police questioned Chemodanov on charges of inciting the overthrow of the system and distributing a work denigratory to the Tsar. After a short interrogation, he was moved to the Pugachev tower of Butyrka Prison, where, placed in a damp cell with little to protect him from the cold, he became seriously ill with bronchitis.[34]

Next spread

Anonymous artist. *Goodness Me! What Has Happened to My Dun Horse?* Hand-drawn postcard, 1906. The jockey carries a flag marked 'Agrarian Reform'.

On 8 December 1906, Chemodanov wrote to Stolypin to proclaim his innocence and petition for his release on grounds of ill health. For good measure, he also included details of his various professional engagements with members of the prime minister's own family. 'If all my guilt is due to the fact that I did everything within my power and means to direct my endeavours towards relieving the suffering people (irrespective of their political convictions) and if my name, which is relatively well-known

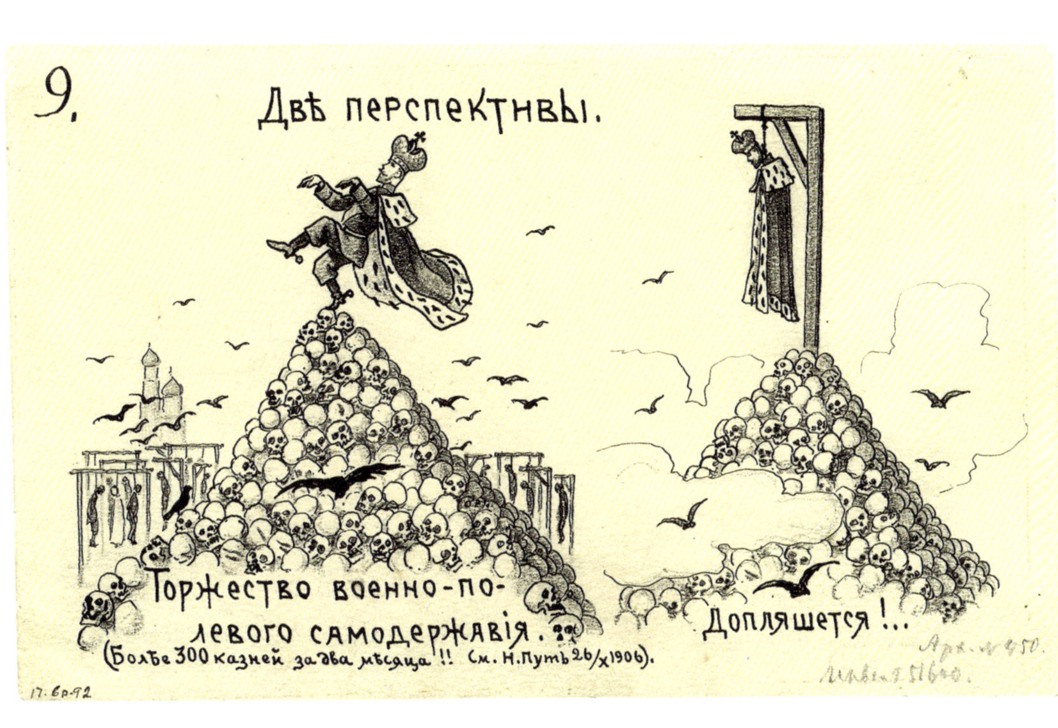
9.
Двѣ перспективы.
Торжество военно-по-
левого самодержавія.
(Болѣе 300 казней за два мѣсяца!! См. Н. Путь 26/x 1906).
Допляшется!...

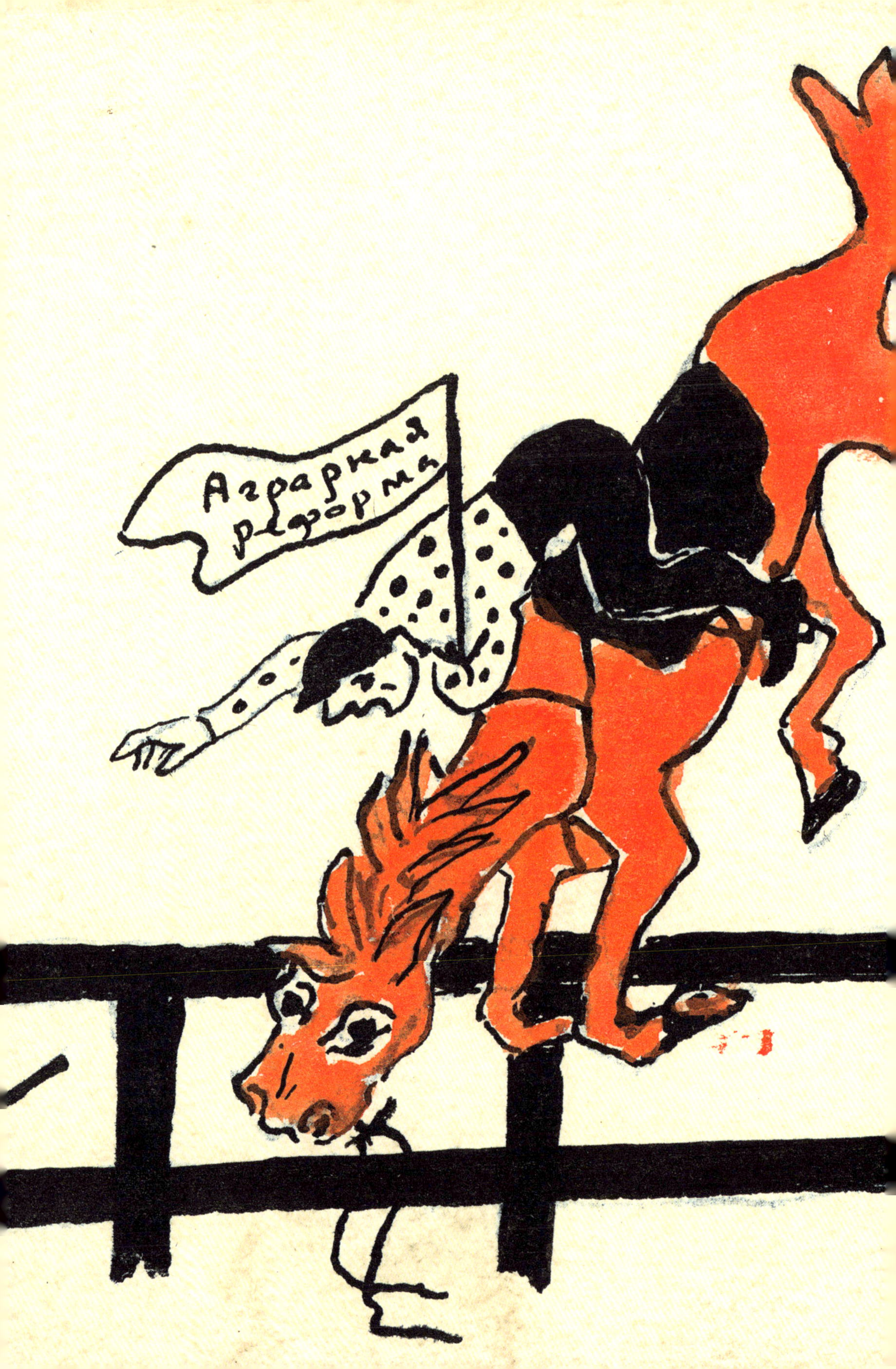
Аграркая реформа

Боже!
Что сталось
съ моимъ
Савраской?

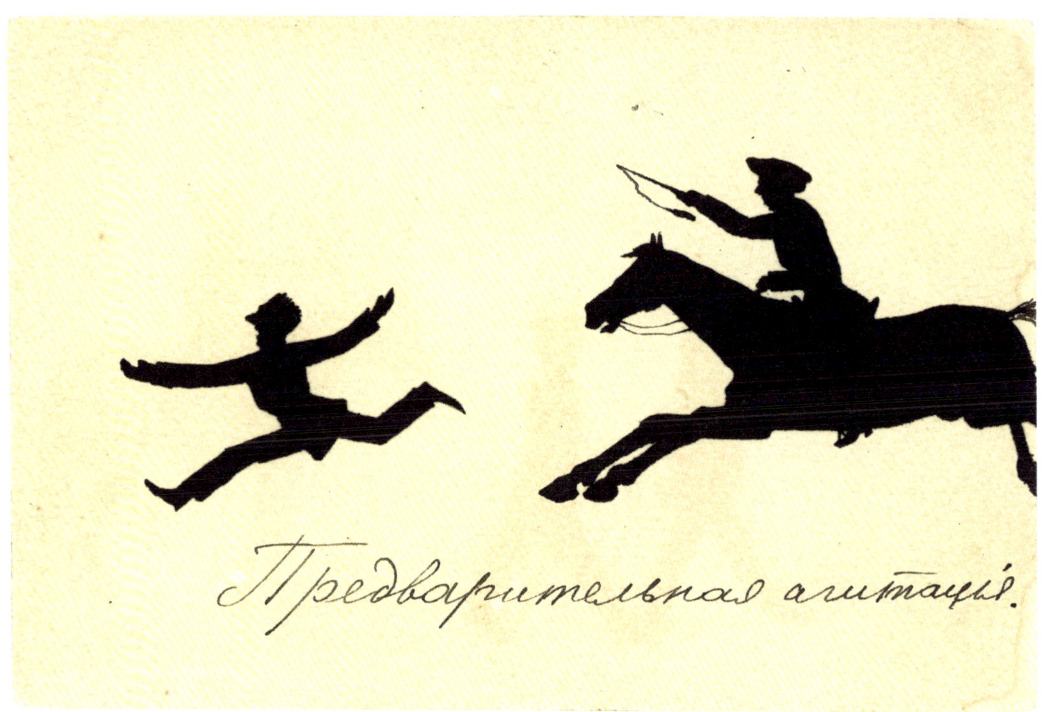

Anonymous artist. *Preliminary Agitation*. Hand-drawn postcard, 1906.

in various circles, somehow became mixed up with the whole political movement, then all the same, in view of my extremely bad health, I humbly ask Your Excellency to make arrangements for my immediate release from gaol.'[35]

Having received no reply, Chemodanov sent a follow-up telegram to report that he had developed pneumonia, and that his life was now in grave danger.[36] The recipient's copy bears a handwritten note from Stolypin's office reading: 'carry out immediately.'[37] Despite an attempt by the head of the Moscow Administration of Gendarmes to suggest that he was not as ill as he claimed, Chemodanov was eventually released under conditions of police supervision on 17 December.[38]

In a letter to his lawyer written shortly after he returned home, Chemodanov expressed regret that he had not been able to achieve more in life, particularly in the field of dentistry. 'The pity is not for myself, but for others and for other reasons. I still have much left to do in the branch of research to which I dedicated the second part of my life.'[39] He continued to practice medicine after his release, but his health had been fatally weakened, and he knew that he did not have long to live. In the final months of his life, Chemodanov dispassionately recorded the progress of his illness in a small notebook, noting down the regularity of his coughing, temperature and lack of sleep.[40] He died late in the evening of 16 January 1908.

Chemodanov was buried on a bright sunny day. True to his ideals, his coffin was decorated with red ribbons and red flowers, and in an unusual departure from tradition, the service was conducted (at his request) without the participation of a priest.[41] The focus of the eulogy was on the lasting significance of good deeds, and in all the reminiscences of his contemporaries, it is Chemodanov's great humanity that comes across most strongly. Druzhinin recalled a figure who was 'very human and kind-natured, an intellectual of the old school,' while an obituary in the newspaper *Russkoe slovo* [*The Russian Word*] reported simply that Chemodanov would be remembered 'as an extraordinarily sympathetic and good man.'[42]

The evidence against Chemodanov and his fellow activists was passed on to the Moscow's prosecutor's office in July 1907, but the case did not come to court for another two years.[43] By this time, Chemodanov and Evreinov were both dead, Morozova had been sent to prison for a different crime, and Kalashnikov had disappeared.[44] But on 19 May 1909, Antonina Romanova was sentenced to a year and a half in a fortress prison, and Aleksandra Petrova to a year.[45] Anna Romanova, meanwhile, was found not guilty.[46] Kalashnikov was finally caught in July 1909, but in April the following year he was reported as having been 'freed from detention with no further consequences.'[47] A lucky escape, it appears.

The arrest of Chemodanov and his co-conspirators concluded a momentous year. Between 17 October 1905 and 31 December 1906, 370 publishers were closed down, 430 publications confiscated, ninety-seven printing houses temporarily or permanently closed (sixty-nine in 1906), and 607 publishers and editors arrested.[48] The revolutionary movement was disintegrating all the while, losing support, income, and personnel. The successful destruction of Chemodanov's network is reflective of this precipitous decline in opposition activity, but conversely it also highlights the chronic inefficiency of the police. It is unlikely that he would have been caught had he not signed the receipts, and moreover the authorities never discovered where the postcards were made, nor made any apparent effort to do so.[49]

The Chemodanov investigation as a whole is characterised more by coincidence than by design, giving credence to the notion that most attempts to combat anti-government postcards were a spin-off from the wider struggle to crush the revolutionary movement. Repression naturally had a serious impact on production – as more and more radicals were arrested the opposition was left with fewer and fewer resources. But while the liberation movement remained alive there were still gaps in government power to be exploited, both legally and illegally. The regime was on the march, but it could not yet assert its power in the way that it might have wanted. For those willing to risk it, pockets of opportunity remained.

For some months the environment for manufacturing anti-government postcards had been steadily worsening, but legal production, while feeling the squeeze, had not yet been fully suppressed. In late 1906, Vasilii Metalnikov, a former peasant who ran a small publishing enterprise in Saint Petersburg, embarked on a new venture printing photomechanical cartoons. Between 28 November and 15 December, the censor approved nine of Metalnikov's postcards, all of which were strongly oppositional in tone.[50] Some satirised the Gurko-Lidval Affair, a government corruption scandal involving a stitched-up contract for famine relief, while others harshly condemned the government's use of capital punishment, and inaction in the face of widespread rural famine.[51]

Aleksandr De Paldo. *In Memory of 9 January*. Published by Vasilii Metalnikov, Saint Petersburg, January 1907.

Metalnikov, however, did not have to wait long to discover the censor's less obliging side. In early January 1907, he submitted a postcard to the Saint Petersburg Committee titled *In Memory of 9 January*. This commemorative image by the artist Aleksandr de Paldo depicts two allegorical female figures mourning the dead, which lie sprawled in a bloody heap near the Winter Palace. One day before the anniversary of the massacre, the Administration issued an order to arrest the postcard after it was found to contain 'evidence of an offence having been committed.' The Inspector of Printing Houses duly removed 103 copies of the image from Metalnikov's studio, along with the original negative and drawing.[52]

Just over a week later, Metalnikov again came up against the Administration, this time over a postcard titled *Crime and Punishment*. There is nothing in the censor's archives to indicate why the Saint Petersburg Committee took objection to the image, which compares the actions of a terrorist with his subsequent execution by the state, but it was likely seen as an impermissible critique of capital punishment. The Committee placed the postcard under arrest, but this time, when the Inspector went to Metalnikov's studio he found only one copy out of a proposed print run of 1,000. This, the negative, and the original drawing were confiscated, pending official confirmation by the courts.[53]

Both cases came before the Saint Petersburg Regional Court later in the year and on both occasions the judge confirmed the Press Administration's original decision to arrest the postcard. As a result, the original negatives and all surviving copies of the images were destroyed.[54] Metalnikov himself went unpunished, as in line with legal requirements he had ostensibly submitted the postcards to the Saint Petersburg Committee before they went on sale, and so had not committed a criminal offence. As for the artists who drew the images, their names do not appear in any of the official documents, and in common with other cases, no obvious attempt was made to involve them in the process.

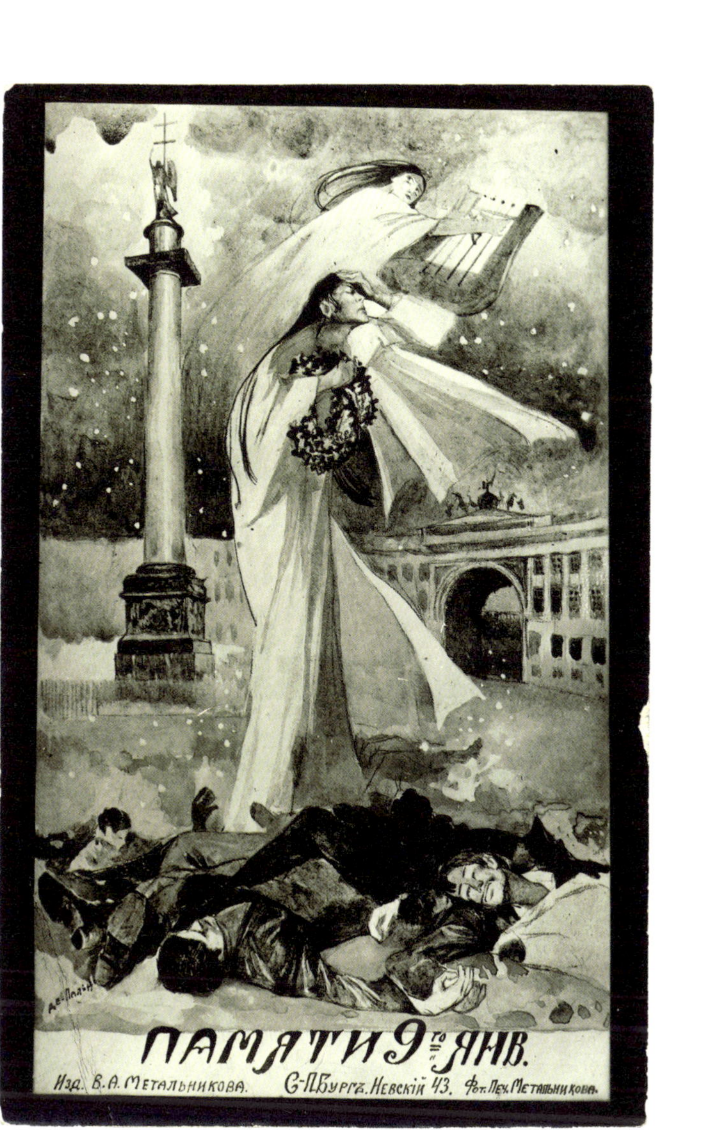
ПАМЯТИ 9ГО ЯНВ.
Изд. В. А. Метальникова. С-ПБургъ. Невскій 43. Фот. Печ. Метальникова.

In early 1907, a very similar series of opposition postcards were published by August Tsenter – the same Tsenter whom police had questioned the previous spring over sales of illegal cartoons. Between February and May, the censor passed seven of his images, all of which carry near identical subject matter to those published by Metalnikov.[55] Again, none pull their punches, showing the degree of censorial leeway that still remained. The production of original cartoons was, however, by this stage extremely uncommon. Metalnikov excepted, Tsenter was all but alone in trying to publish satirical images legally – the only other anti-government postcards listed in the censor's records at this time are a group of portraits depicting members of the Saint Petersburg Soviet.[56]

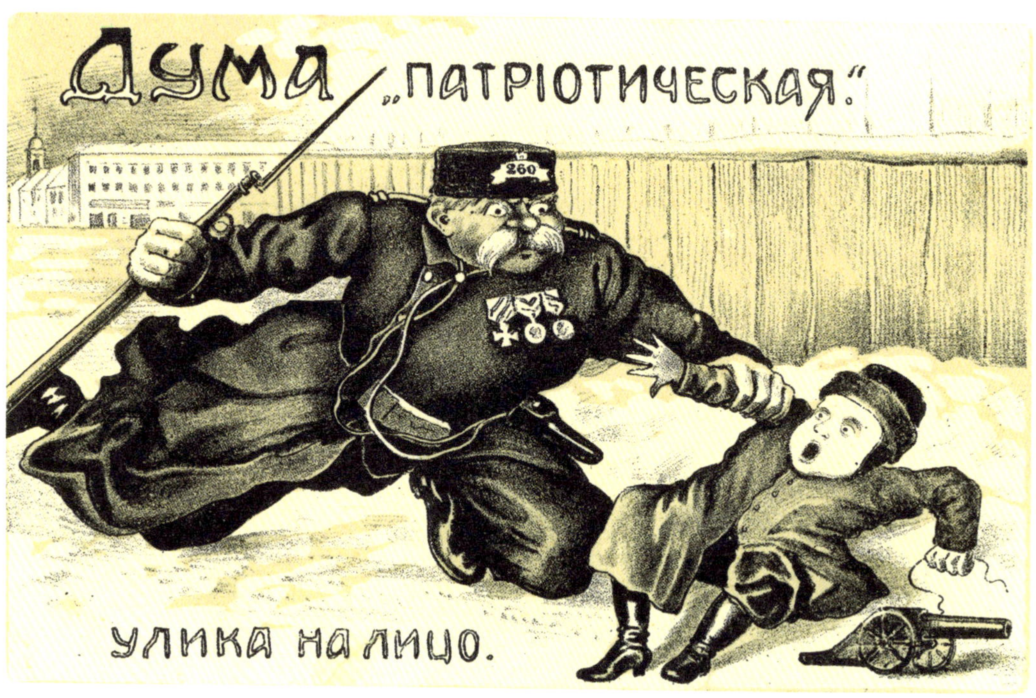

Anonymous artist. *'Patriotic' Duma/ Thought. Caught in the Act.* Printed by Robert Bakhman, Saint Petersburg, 1906.

In February that year, Merder advertised twenty-five photomechanical postcards on anti-government themes in *Domashnii muzei*. Most were reproductions of socialist paintings, still a staple of leftist production, but there were also postcards of the First Duma, along with the promise of forthcoming images of the Second Duma.[57] As this would suggest, the public at large maintained a vestige of trust in the Duma as an institution, and following the reopening of the legislature on 20 February, there was popular demand for images of the newly-elected deputies. Karrik, Tsenter and Metalnikov all produced examples, with the latter offering portraits 'of the most outstanding orators and leaders', as well as bespoke commissions of specific figures.[58]

Whatever Metalnikov may have claimed about 'outstanding orators', the Second Duma was filled with far less experienced politicians than the First. This was both a consequence of the Vyborg Manifesto, whose signatories had been banned from participating, and the recent volte-face of the revolutionary parties, who after seeing the popularity of the assembly, had changed their minds about participation. The liberally-orientated Kadets were still the dominant Party, albeit with a reduced majority, but the Second Duma took a more radical form than its predecessor. Naturally enough, the government, which had failed in its attempts to manipulate the electoral process, was no more inclined to be generous to this sitting than it had been to the previous.

Even at this stage, the Okhrana estimated that there were still nearly 200 enterprises 'speculating' in left-wing literature in Saint Petersburg alone, and in March the police took advantage of a lull in the unrest to launch another crackdown.[59] Much, however, still came down to chance. In Moscow, a booklet on Bloody Sunday was arrested, while in the capital postcards with identical subject matter were sold freely.[60] Generally speaking, though, repression achieved its aim. Few dared to print anything other than images relating to the Duma. The funeral of assassinated Kadet Grigorii Iollos that same month attracted huge crowds, but no photographic postcards were produced. Indeed, there had been no new images of opposition rallies since the Moscow Uprising.

In April, Metalnikov published two sets of political cartoons, the first looking at the relationship between the government and the Duma, and the other with an Easter theme.[61] The censor took objection to one of the latter postcards, contending that the image, which depicted soldiers preventing young chicks from hatching from an egg, insulted the army. This time, however, the courts disagreed and allowed publication to proceed.[62] The following month, Metalnikov submitted four more postcards, one of which (a satire of the agrarian question) was again deemed illegal. But before the case could go to court, he cut his losses, writing to the Administration to say that he was withdrawing the image, having submitted it in error.[63]

Dissolution of the Second Duma, and the End of Legal Manufacture

Postcard publishers did not cover the debates in the Second Duma in any detail, not least because of the increasing difficulty of printing opposition images. Nonetheless, the convocation provided a small fillip to producers, who were conscious that postcards still retained a financial and promotional power that few other media could match. During a discussion on capital punishment in March 1907, Duma deputy, Father Fedor Tikhvinskii made a speech harshly condemning what he referred to as the government's 'lack of conscience.' The English historian Bernard Pares reported that, 'in a day he was one of the most popular men in Saint Petersburg, and his picture was in all the shops.'[64]

Speeches by Tikhvinskii and others did little to enamour the Second Duma to the regime, and despite initial optimism, rumours soon circulated of its impending dissolution. The assembly was eventually disbanded under the pretext of a revolutionary conspiracy on 3 June. Differences of opinion on how the country should be reformed and governed were simply too great for either side to overcome.

Any hopes that the Duma might eventually lead the way towards a constitutional monarchy were now firmly dashed by a new electoral law designed to ensure that all future convocations would be more amenable to the government's will. According to Pares, there was barely a squeak of protest from the harried population, only 'complete prostration and disillusionment.'[65] Amid the despair, the government made further moves to restrict the print industry. Fresh measures were introduced limiting the freedom of the press, and a broad ban was brought in against anything that could be construed as advocating an anti-government position.[66]

The dissolution of the Second Duma marks the final chapter in the legal publication of anti-government postcards. Examples could still be bought, but production itself had almost completely dried up. Metalnikov and Tsenter both published their last cartoons on 26 May 1907.[67] Having put a stop to their manufacture, the government's task was now to remove all remaining opposition postcards from sale.

In April 1907, the Governor of Tver contacted the Department of Police to inquire about the legality of two of Metalnikov's postcards that were being sold in local kiosks.[68] The question was forwarded to Belgard, who answered in the affirmative. Clearly unhappy with this response, the Department of Police then wrote to the Saint Petersburg governor's office to ask how it was dealing with such images. The reply came back to say that irrespective of the censor's ruling on their legality, 'these and many of Metalnikov's other postcards on political themes that were previously judged by the [Saint Petersburg] Committee to be lawful, continue to be confiscated on the orders of the governor.'[69]

Now that he had got the answer he was after, the Director of the Department of Police wrote back to Belgard to apprise him of the situation. While acknowledging that the postcards were in principle legal, the Director maintained that in his view such images were 'unacceptable', and using the example of the Saint Petersburg Governor to support the case for confiscation, asked for guidance on how to proceed.[70]

In areas of political turbulence, governors, inspectors and the police had been impounding anti-government postcards without heed to censorial rulings for several months; now, in his reply to the Department of Police, Belgard brought the Administration into line with their more repressive approach. Although he was still careful to note that Metalnikov's postcards were technically legal and so could not be made subject to an official arrest order, he called their confiscation under Saint Petersburg's state of Extraordinary Security 'fully justified'. Whereas previously he had merely remarked on the practice, Belgard was now unequivocally authorising the removal of postcards in provinces subject to emergency regulations.

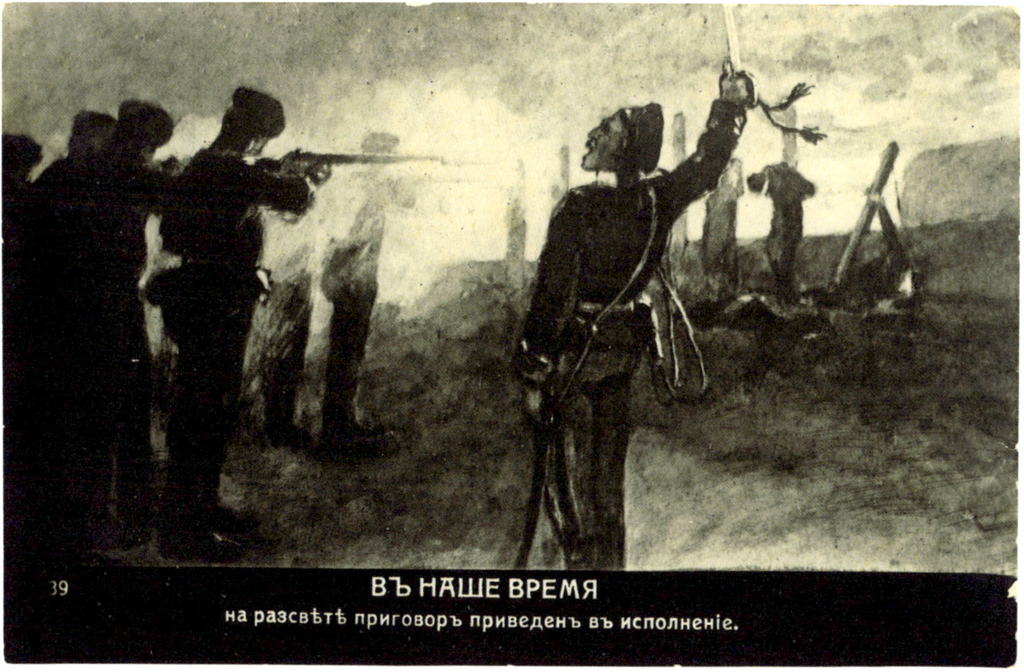

Anonymous artist. *In Our Time. The Sentence is Carried out at Dawn.* Published by Vasilii Metalnikov, Saint Petersburg, December 1906.

Belgard added that in order to stop the spread of anti-government material, the Saint Petersburg Committee had agreed to inform the governor if they came across any works contravening the regulations. Noting that this in itself might not be sufficient, Belgard reported that he had arranged for the city Inspector to sit in on the Committee's meetings in order to keep a close watch on the situation.[71] Just as the political freedoms granted in the October Manifesto had been rolled back, so too were the greater latitudes in postcard production. All remaining openings were now being closed off, and with anti-government images of all types vulnerable to appropriation, the political and financial returns were fast diminishing.

Booksellers who became caught up in these measures were shown little mercy. In July, Aleksandra Legasova, a peasant-turned-bookseller in Rostov-on-Don, was fined 300 roubles for 'displaying postcards in her shop windows that glamourised criminal activity' – that is to say, promoted revolutionary sentiment. Legasova complained that when she had bought the postcards, which were all published by Metalnikov, they were listed as having been approved by the censor. This was indeed true for all but two of the images (*Crime and Punishment* and *In Memory of 9 January*), but in accordance with emergency regulations then effective in the province, their sale could be deemed a criminal offence.[72]

The government now had the wind in its sails. In early 1908, a 'criminal prosecution' was launched against three comparatively anodyne May Day postcards that had been discovered in Grodno.[73] Two of them were produced by the Saint Petersburg publisher A. Freinkel, and the other carried no publication details.[74] Both of the former had censorial markings, but officials believed these to be spurious. The courts, however, later confirmed the legality of all three images.[75] Although the overall number of postcards 'arrested' during this period was pitiful, this case illustrates just how much had changed between April 1906, when the censor originally approved the cards, and January 1908 when any sort of leftist image aroused suspicion.

The menace posed by opposition postcards is clear. In official reports they are referred to as 'anti-government' images, and as such characterised as undermining the authority of the autocratic regime. Publishers could get away with this when state power was on the ebb, but the Tsar was now ready to rule again, and he was confident enough to proceed without due attention to the demands of the opposition. Attempting to publish anti-government postcards by legal means still engendered little personal risk, but it had now become a financially unviable activity. If it was access to commercial infrastructure that had allowed leftist postcard production to take off, then it was the closure of the markets that led to its collapse.

Falling demand and increased risk affected publishers and booksellers across the Empire. In 1906, Shipovnik's colour postcards were sold for ten kopecks, but the following year they were being advertised for just half that amount. Its black-and-white postcards, meanwhile, dropped from eight kopecks down to just three.[76] Those who persisted in producing anti-government postcards now had to be motivated by much more than mere financial gain.

In hindsight, it is easy to suppose that the government's promise of freedom of speech was issued in bad faith. This may be true on the part of the Tsar, who was only a reluctant signatory, but the Press Administration's actions in the aftermath of the October Manifesto demonstrate a genuine attempt to establish new legal parameters for the press, albeit ones weighted heavily in the government's favour. It may be that given a less contentious environment and more time, a less restrictive modus operandi might have evolved naturally in the wake of the reforms, but Belgard came under considerable pressure from reactionary forces, and he himself also grew exasperated at the refusal of radical publishers to toe the line.

The task he had been given, of allowing partial freedom of speech while at the same time reasserting Imperial authority, was Sisyphean in nature, and like many officials who were initially in favour of change, Belgard eventually came around to the view that wholesale suppression was the only viable way forward. Nonetheless, the reforms that he had overseen left a lasting legacy: leftist politics was now once again a restricted area, but the print industry retained both a vastly expanded playing field, and just as importantly, the regulatory improvements to enable its continued growth. Although weakened from its revolutionary peak, the public sphere remained a potent force.

Publishing Returns to Western Europe

The Bolshevik publishing house Vpered was closed down in the summer of 1907, largely bringing an end to the Party's experiments in legal postcard production. The Socialist-Revolutionaries meanwhile, split by internal division and woefully short of money, also came under serious pressure. In June, the entire Saint Petersburg Committee was captured, and in the months that followed many other regional cells were broken up. Revolutionary postcards were still being sold intermittently, but by late autumn production had been all but extinguished. The last Socialist-Revolutionary accounts to record postcard sales in Russia are from September 1908.[77]

With increasing numbers of revolutionaries leaving Russia, the focus of propaganda production shifted back to Western Europe. Activists abroad had continued to publish socialist material throughout the duration of the revolution, and, as in Russia, the money raised from postcard sales had grown to become a regular source of income for Socialist-Revolutionary cells in exile.[78] Regional accounts from Party groups in Bern, Geneva, Zurich, Baden-Baden, Darmstadt, Heidelberg, Karlsruhe, Lausanne, Liège, Montpellier, Nancy, Paris, Antwerp, Brussels, Italy, and London all record funds raised from postcard sales in the years leading up to 1917.[79]

As before Bloody Sunday, postcard output predominantly comprised portraits of martyred terrorists. But the Party's archives also offer an occasional glimpse of other images, such as photographs of female hard-labour convicts, printed by the Regional Foreign Committee in March 1907, and the following year, pictures of inmates at Akatui Prison in Siberia, where many prominent revolutionaries were imprisoned.[80] A mail-order list from around this time includes a postcard cartoon titled *The Tsar and the Peasant* as well as the more commonly found photographic portraits of 'Gershuni, Balmashev, Kaliaev, Lavrov, Spiridonova, Konopliannikova and others'.[81]

Deaths provided a further impetus for production. In March 1907, the passing of revolutionary mastermind Grigorii Gershuni gave cause for an edition of 1,000 postcards.[82] And in 1910, a similar-sized print run was commissioned to commemorate the life of terrorist Egor Sazonov.[83] It appears that most of the Party's postcards were produced and distributed under the aegis of the Regional Foreign Committee, which ordered the images from commercial establishments, before disseminating them to groups in other areas.[84] One letter sent by a cell in Bern, for example, requests that the Committee send several different Party publications, and 'as many photographic cards of Gershuni and others as you can spare.'[85]

After 1908, lack of money became an ever more serious issue for the Socialist-Revolutionaries, made worse by the necessity of supporting the large numbers of activists who had recently decamped to Western Europe.[86] The following year, the Party suffered its worst crisis to date with the discovery that the then head of the Combat Organisation, Ezno Azef, was an Okhrana double-agent. So far-reaching was this revelation that the very existence of the Party itself was placed in doubt.[87] Propaganda work and morale were badly affected, and from 1910 onwards evidence of postcard production abroad becomes much thinner on the ground.

Production and Distribution in the Twilight Years of the Regime

Back in Russia, leftist commercial publishing had been all but squeezed dry. One of the last successful attempts to publish anti-government postcards legally was made by a former revolutionary named Viktor Zheglinskii. Originally from Kiev, Zheglinskii, had been banished to Vologda in 1901.[88] He remained in the area after his term of exile was up, and in 1908 founded his own publishing house. Under the imprint Severnoe Izdatelstvo [Northern Publisher], he issued a large series of portraits, each of which came with a biographical pamphlet stapled to the card.[89] Although rare today, they were published in huge numbers. According to *Knizhnaia letopis* [*Chronicle of Books*], Zheglinskii printed 142,800 postcards, which sold for twenty kopecks each.[90]

Production on such a scale was bound to attract the attention of the authorities, and sure enough in June 1908, the governor of Vologda Province wrote to the Department of Police to complain. In a replay of earlier discussions about Metalnikov's postcards, he noted that although Zheglinskii's images were legal, 'public distribution of these biographical portraits is undesirable, because the publisher is undoubtedly trying to glorify the most serious criminals in Russia.'[91] The Department of Police agreed and informed the governor that a letter would be sent to the Press Administration to find out the 'general position on printing and selling [anti-government] postcards.'[92]

In October, Vologda's governor wrote again to the Department of Police to let them know that he himself had written to the Press Administration to formally apprise them of the situation, stressing 'the [restive] mood of the population and the undesirability of the further production of these images.'[93] His efforts to put a stop to publication were presumably successful, as out of a proposed series of forty-nine portraits, Zheglinskii only managed to print twenty-eight. This marks the last known occasion before the 1917 Revolution that a series of anti-government postcards was published legally. It is not, however, quite the end of the story. Although uncommon, there were still occasional attempts to push opposition images past the censor.

In 1909, the Press Administration ordered the arrest of a group of seven postcards, one of which – a reproduction of a painting by 'Kolen' titled *Revolution* (date unknown) – was eventually banned through the courts.[94] The following year, the Administration attempted to prohibit a postcard produced on the occasion of Tolstoy's death, claiming that the image was 'intended to encourage a negative attitude towards the government and to support a mood of protest among the public, particularly students.' The subsequent court ruling on the postcard, which commemorated the author's repudiation of the death penalty, eventually went in favour of the publishers, but the case shows just how stifled the discussion of public issues had become.[95]

'The revolutionary movement has ground to a halt, revolutionary organisations have been broken up. The forces of reaction are getting stronger and stronger every day, and the people and society are being pushed back to beyond the confines of 1905 and even 1904,'[96] reported one Socialist-Revolutionary leaflet in 1910. By now, Shipovnik had stopped advertising their political postcards completely, even at discounted prices. But however bad the situation may have appeared to the radical opposition, the regime's victory over the forces of revolution was largely superficial; beneath the surface a strong undercurrent of discontent boded ill for the long term.

None of the key political and social issues had been solved, and although severely curtailed, the revolutionary movement limped on, in spirit if not always in body. Underground propaganda production clung on in one form or another, and once a year or so anti-government images were still submitted to the censor.[97]

In April 1912, the brutal repression of strikers at the Lena Goldfields contributed to a sudden upsurge in revolutionary activity and gave rise to the first documentary postcards since the Moscow Uprising. Contemporary propaganda claimed that over 250 were killed and an equivalent number injured in a massacre that was immediately compared to Bloody Sunday.[98] Postcards depicting the incident all reproduce the same photograph, taken covertly a few hours after the killings, which shows a group of onlookers surrounding a dense mass of bodies.[99] Such images could only have been produced illegally, indicating that the revolutionaries still had the ability to print postcards in Russia when the opportunity arose.

The Tsar soon seized back full control over the country, but opposition images continued to emerge. In 1913, the year of the Romanov tercentenary, an attempt was made in Kherson Province to sell anti-government postcards in aid of a charity patronised by the Empress. It is not clear whether the move was prompted by naivety or politics, but the governor's office expressed deep concern that the postcards would prompt, 'all kinds of foolish talk, as well as serving as a visual guide for politically unreliable individuals to distribute false rumours about the measures taken to curtail the disorder in past years.'[100] None of the designs were new; testament to how little had changed over previous years.

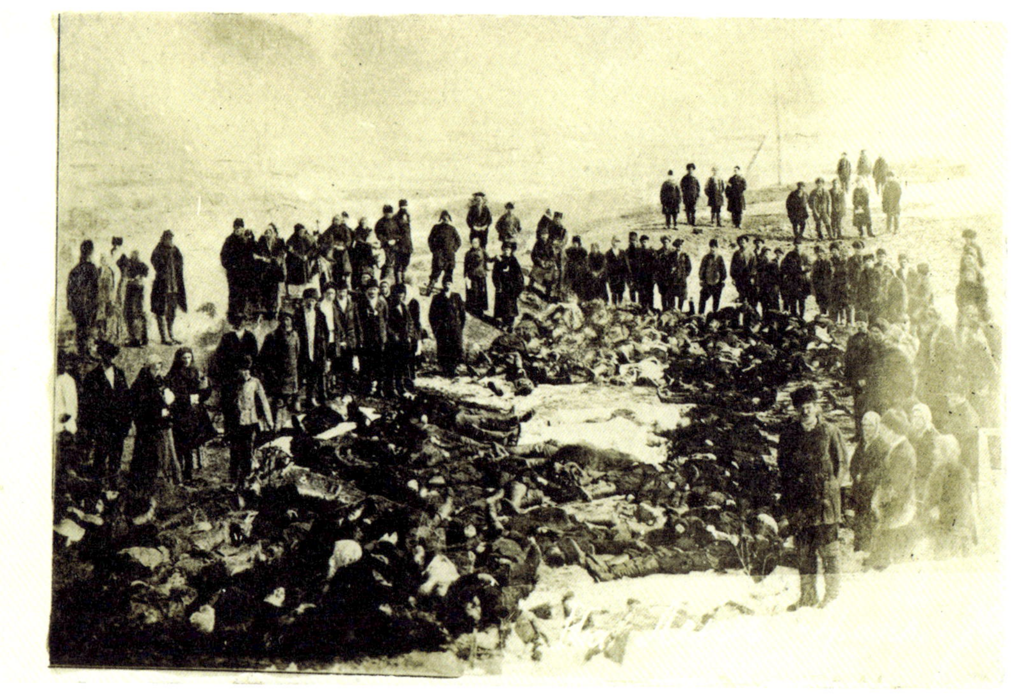

Anonymous photographer. *Lena*. No publication details, 1912.

Anti-government postcards were not the only type of political postcards to be banned at this time. In early 1912 Luka Zlotnikov, the artist and publisher of a virulently right-wing journal named *Pauk* [*Spider*], wrote to the Department of Police to complain that Saint Petersburg's governor had stopped him from advertising a set of 'anti-Jewish' postcards. As it turned out, the governor's ban had only been imposed on a technicality; nonetheless, the postcards were all deeply unsavoury slanders against the Jews, among them illustrations of 'ritual murders' in Hungary, Pontoise and Trent, stereotypical caricatures, and lampoons of prominent opposition politicians.[101]

Following Zlotnikov's complaint, the police weighed in with their own opinion of his works: 'The postcards are sharply satirical ... and their imagery will inevitably be seen as demonstrably offensive and tendentious in regards to the Jews ... Under no circumstances should these postcards be allowed to be sold, because their circulation among the masses could lead to extremely undesirable consequences.'[102] Further letters went back and forth between the police and governor's office before the Interior Minister himself made the decision to ban the illustrations of the ritual murders, but to allow the rest to pass.[103] It was, one supposes, a balance of sorts.

The outbreak of the First World War saw a revival of the political cartoon, now redirected outwards towards a common enemy. Professional artists who had mocked the autocratic regime in 1905 turned their attention instead to German sausages and Kaiser Wilhelm's moustache. But despite the surge in satire, the war had a damaging impact on the printing trade as a whole. Many foreign publishers were forced to close their offices in Russia, and paper imports fell dramatically. The quality of commercially manufactured items went down in tandem, and with paper scarce, postcards, popular prints and posters were all conscripted to help the war effort.

The introduction of military censorship in 1914 strengthened the government's hold over the industry, bringing in harsher punishments for transgressors and heralding the return of preliminary censorship for all illustrated works. Anything seen to be contrary to the country's interests was banned, to the extent that even food labels written in German were prohibited. Naturally, postcards with Teutonic symbols were considered a grave threat to Russian sovereignty, and many such images were confiscated from bookshops.[104] Under these conditions the chances of producing anti-government imagery legally were almost nil, and the censor's archives show no further attempts to publish leftist postcards before 1917.

The First World War, however, did bring about improvements of a different sort. Defeats abroad and economic difficulties at home buoyed the revolutionary movement, leading to the production of new anti-government postcards. In late 1914, five Bolshevik deputies in the Fourth Duma were exiled to Siberia for their opposition to the war. Portraits soon followed. 'I managed to get hold of a postcard with an image of our 'quintet', and organised for this to be reproduced and distributed en masse,' reported the Bolshevik Aleksandr Shliapnikov. 'I found the photograph on Stekliannyi Street ... and within a short time had managed to illegally manufacture a few thousand postcards, which sold out quickly.'[105]

In January 1915, Shliapnikov, then based in Stockholm, wrote to Lenin to ask that he arrange for an edition of the postcards to be printed in Bern for distribution among foreign workers.[106] Shliapnikov specified that the images should be 'well printed, and if possible with some type of ideologically-orientated Internationalist inscription in one or more European language.'[107] He added that they would be distributed across Scandinavia, and expressed the hope that they might be able to sell between 3,000 and 5,000 copies. Such postcards not only helped to spread an anti-war message among workers in Russia and Western Europe, but yet again, also provided valuable income for the Party.

That same year in London, the future Soviet foreign minister Georgii Chicherin wrote to the Hampstead branch of the Independent Labour Party to thank it for a recent donation: 'We are very gladly impressed by the splendid response … and by the expression of sympathy in its part for the suffering Russian comrades, realising thus Internationalism in act and deed. We shall have in some time for sale postcards with prison views and Siberian sceneries, and stamps at 1d., sold for the benefit of our own fund. If you are able to sell some, we shall then be very glad to send you the necessary supply.'[108] In Chicherin's telling, postcards were helping make the communist dream a reality.

Production had fallen to near-zero in Russia, but beyond its borders exiled radicals continued to keep the flame alive.[109] Even inside the country, however, seditious images, like thoughts of political change, were never entirely suppressed. In rooms, desk drawers, and private albums, anti-government postcards smouldered away like slow-burning fuses, hidden from view, but carrying no less accusatory power than when they had first been made.[110] In 1917, the long-standing social and political problems that they had so tenaciously documented once again coalesced in violence, and with the fall of the Tsar and the coming of a new age, postcards re-emerged to celebrate openly what could once only be contemplated in private.

Anonymous photographer. Untitled postcard depicting a toppled statue of Tsar Nicholas II. No publication details, 1917.

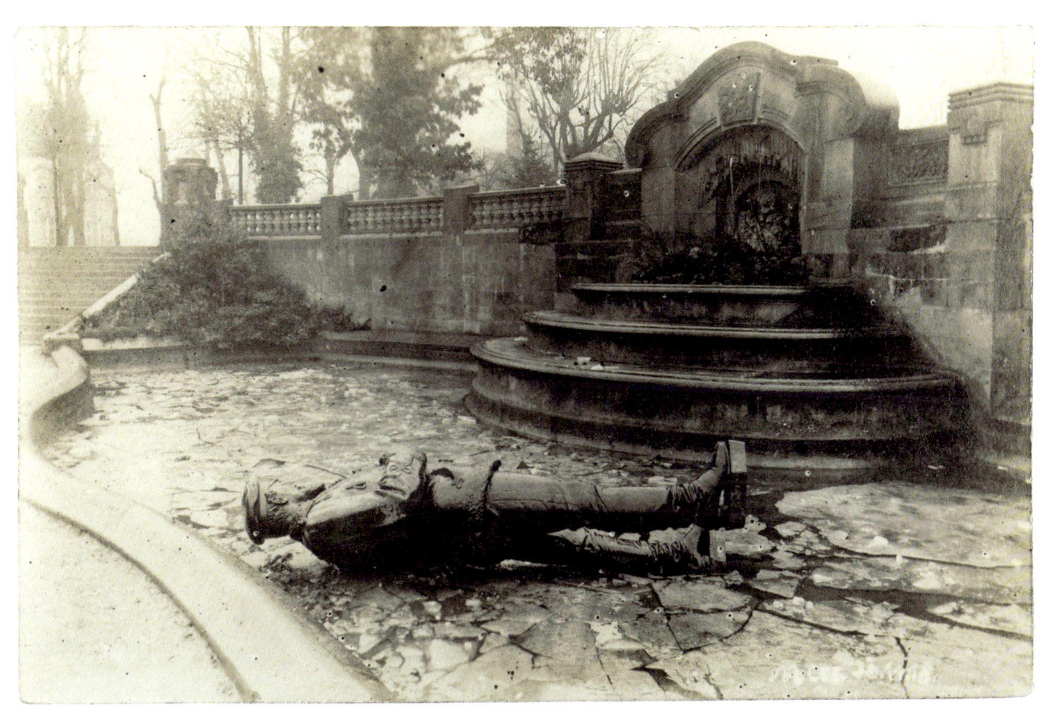

Арестованная Росс. Соц.-Дем. Раб. Фракція

La fraction ouvrière sociale-démocrate de la „Douma" arrêtée.

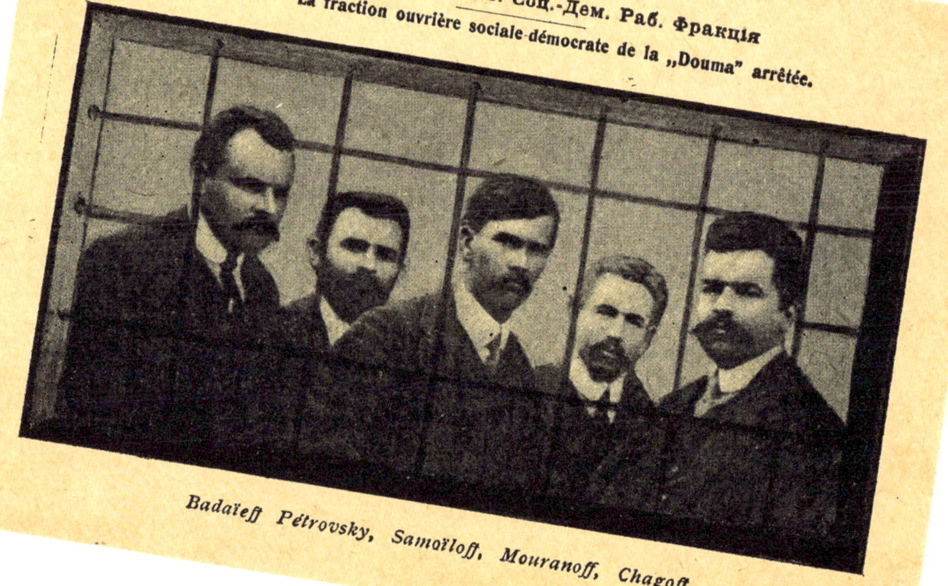

Badaïeff Pétrovsky, Samoïloff, Mouranoff, Chagoff.

THE SOCIAL DEMOCRATIC PARTY

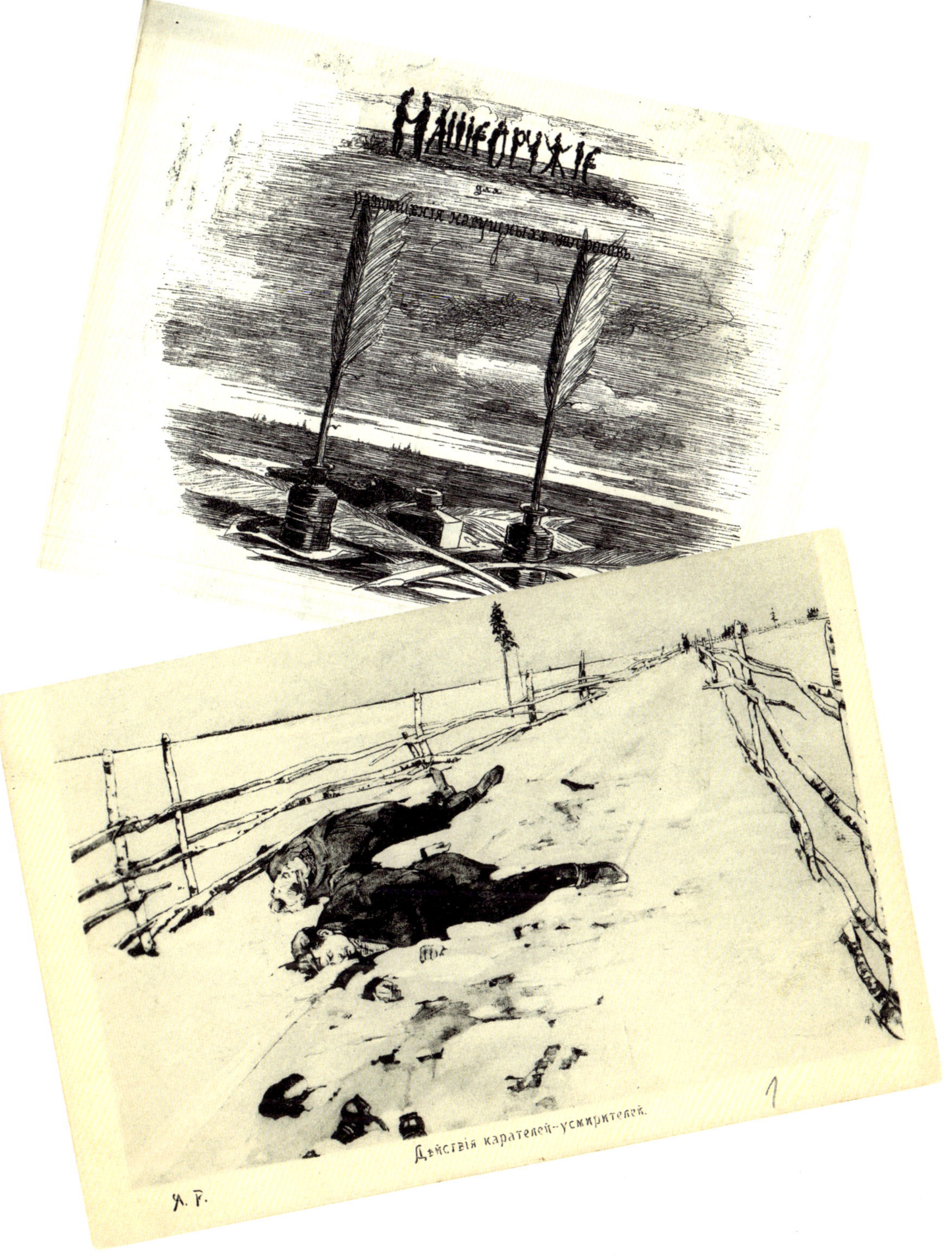

35

Старая басня на новый лад.

(Послѣ грандіозной, безпримѣрной въ исторіи міра, всероссійской 1-й всеобщей политической забастовки въ октябрѣ).

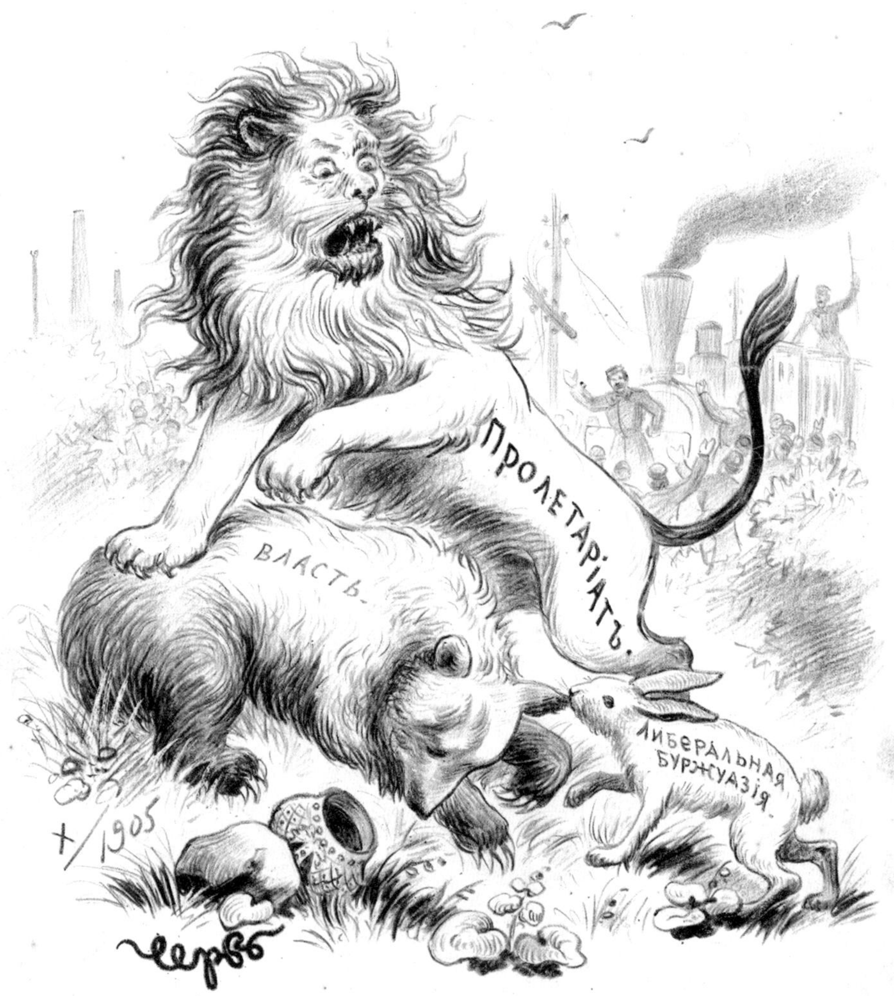

Заяц на ловлѣ.

—Ба! Ты, косой, пожаловал откелѣ?
Тебя никто на ловлѣ не видал!

п. вр. 92

Underground Production

Previous spread from left to right

Anonymous designer. *Arrested Members of the Russian Social-Democratic Workers' Party Faction*. Western Europe, early 1915.

Mikhail Chemodanov. *Our Weapon for Resolving Pressing Issues*. Published in *Svet i teni*, Moscow, March 1881.

A. R. *The Actions of the Punitive Repressors*. Published by Vpered, Saint Petersburg, 1906.

Opposite

Mikhail Chemodanov. Finished drawing for *An Old Song Played to a New Tune*. Moscow, October 1906.

On 3 June 1906, city police carried out a search of a residential building in central Kiev. Concealed inside one of the upstairs flats, they found a cell of student revolutionaries manufacturing illegal propaganda. Along with sundry printing equipment and over fifteen hundred anti-government works, officers also discovered a small bronze handstamp that had been hurriedly discarded inside a wastepaper basket. On it was engraved: 'The Kiev Committee of the Social Democratic Party.' Elsewhere in the flat, the police came across detailed Party accounts going back to October 1904. Thanks to a government spy, they had uncovered a secret printing facility belonging to one of the major revolutionary parties.

Three men were detained in the raid: tenant Vasilii Meznev, and his associates Isaak Berliner, and Leon Stambulov. Meznev was at the time enrolled in the agricultural department of the Kiev Polytechnic Institute, while Berliner, a twenty-year-old merchant's son, and Stambulov, a twenty-four-year-old townsman from Erevan, were both students at the nearby Saint Vladimir University. The police believed that Berliner's brother Efroim, who attended the latter institution, was also involved.[1] These four men made up the organisational nucleus of the group, a sleek set-up standard among Party cells that echoed Lenin's demand for a lean core, buttressed by a mass of sympathisers.

The cell operated under the cover of a university photography club, a pretence that provided the necessary excuse for purchase of materials and a regular meeting place. All four were party affiliates, but Meznev, a twenty-seven-year-old hereditary noble, was the senior figure – a member of the Kiev Committee and keeper of the revolutionary purse. His role as Committee treasurer is indicative of the key part played by money in all aspects of propaganda production. While the Party's technical bureaux obtained materials and equipment, overall responsibility always lay with the resident finance committee – a reflection of the cost of printing propaganda, as well as its importance as a source of revenue.

The long list of objects in the police charge sheet shows the extent, and simplicity of Meznev's operation, which involved the production of a hectographic journal, leaflets, and photomechanical postcards: 'Two tablets of hectographic mass, … a flask containing hectographic ink, two photographic apparatuses, phials and boxes with saline solutions and liquids for photographic processing, two lamps and four basins for the same purpose, five retouching pens and a guillotine for cutting card.'[2] The entire process, from composition to dissemination, was directed from a single room in a flat that was shared with two other people, neither of whom appear to have been directly involved.

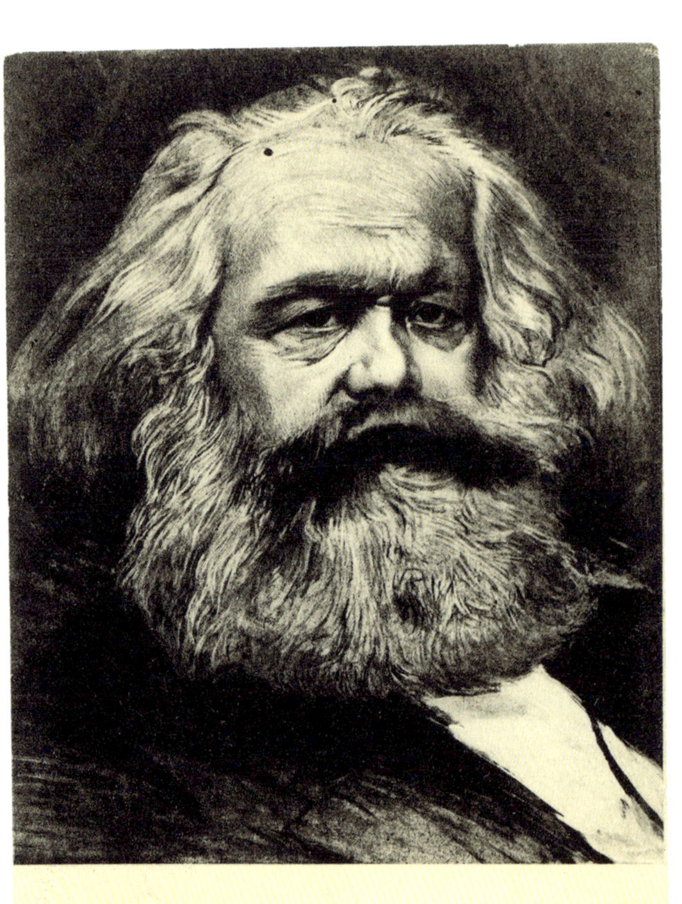

Karl Marx

The police characterised the postcards as 'views, scenes and portraits relating to the revolutionary movement.' They included: depictions of Bloody Sunday, pictures of Lieutenant Schmidt, a triple portrait of Zheliabov, Hryniewiecki and Perovskaia, photographs of a pogrom in Zhitomir, and an allegorical personification of Russia with the Imperial eagle cast down at her feet.[3] These images pushed a strong narrative of opposition, lauding revolutionary martyrs, and promoting awareness of government violence; however, none were unique to the group, and none show a particular party-political leaning. In common with most revolutionary postcards of the period, the choice of imagery was likely dictated largely by circumstance.

Anonymous artist. Untitled portrait of Karl Marx. Published by Utro and printed by Kordovskii and Dressler, Saint Petersburg, 1906.

Although the resources required meant that underground printing ventures could usually only be undertaken with the participation of the local party committee, the structural composition of groups involved was necessarily fluid, particularly where distribution was concerned. Meznev's output, which amounted to many thousands of postcards, was sold through a network of (paid) sympathisers. Most were disseminated locally, but notebooks found at the scene listed postcard sales in Mogilev-Podolsk to the south-east, Gomel to the north, and even as far away as the Caucasus.[4] Specific figures are not provided, but the police were in no doubt that the venture proved an effective way of 'strengthening the means of the Committee.'[5]

Meznev's enterprise is significant for illustrating the overlap of different types of propaganda production, but it is also notable for underlining the extent to which illegal publishing tied in with other forms of revolutionary activity, not only through the profit raised, but also through the people involved. When detained, Meznev was found to be carrying a Browning revolver, and hidden inside a tin of Montecristo cigars in the flat were several bullets and empty shell casings. Clearly, postcard manufacturing was not an endeavour carried out in isolation from the violence of the streets; those involved were committed activists who could turn their hand to everything from accountancy to murder.[6]

Legal Revolutionary Publishing

Underground printing always remained an important component of revolutionary propaganda production, but Party leaders recognised that the only way to achieve critical mass was by using the commercial infrastructure of the print industry. As finance director Leonid Krasin pointed out at the Third Party Congress in April 1905: 'Publishing, distribution and networking cannot be carried out satisfactorily using illegal forms of activity. We do not now need tens, or hundreds of thousands of leaflets, but millions. We do not need half a dozen printing offices, three-quarters of which use ratchety homemade presses, but scores of rotation printers so that we can bombard any regional point with our agitational literature.'[7]

Prior to 1905, only a handful of socialist publications had been printed legally, but Bloody Sunday marked the beginning of an ambitious new phase of revolutionary publishing in Russia. The discontent and disarray that flowed from the massacre offered the radical opposition an unprecedented opportunity to press their case, and at the Congress in April, the Party resolved to broaden both its conspiratorial and public propaganda apparatus.[8] Establishing commercial publishing operations, however, was a precarious process, requiring a lot of time, funds, and personnel; consequently, much of the Party's initial activity in the sphere of legal publishing was focused on cooperation with pre-existing private publishers and printing houses.[9]

In around mid-1905, the first legal Bolshevik publishing house was established in Odessa.[10] Named Vpered [Forward], it was founded by an activist named Iosif Belopolskii in cooperation with the local Party Committee. The aim was to 'publish literature propagandising Marxist ideas at the cheapest possible prices,' and in just over seven months, around twelve books were issued.[11] The majority were translations of books by foreign socialists, such as August Bebel, Jean Jaurès, Karl Kautsky and Paul Lafargue – a cheaper and easier alternative to commissioning original texts. These works were distributed in partnership with the bookshop Obrazovanie [Education], a good early example of collaboration between private and revolutionary enterprise.

The establishment of their own commercial publishing house allowed the Social Democrats to reap all the benefits of legal production – that is to say the ability to print vast quantities of literature without the risk of confiscation – while at the same time retain control over price, content, and profit. The Party's key concern here was for the numbers: the more propaganda produced, the more money raised, and the more people exposed to revolutionary ideology. Accordingly, considerable value was placed on legal ventures, and Belopolskii later recalled that Lenin had rebuked him and the Odessa Committee for having jeopardised the entire enterprise by disseminating Vpered wares among illegal workers' circles.[12]

The police arrested Belopolskii in August 1905 and Vpered was closed down shortly afterwards. He was kept in solitary confinement in Odessa prison for several weeks, whereupon he was administratively exiled to Kostroma Province for three years. Two months in, however, the political amnesty that followed the October Manifesto led to his early release. From Kostroma, Belopolskii made his way first to Moscow and then on to Saint Petersburg, where an old comrade made the suggestion that he might like

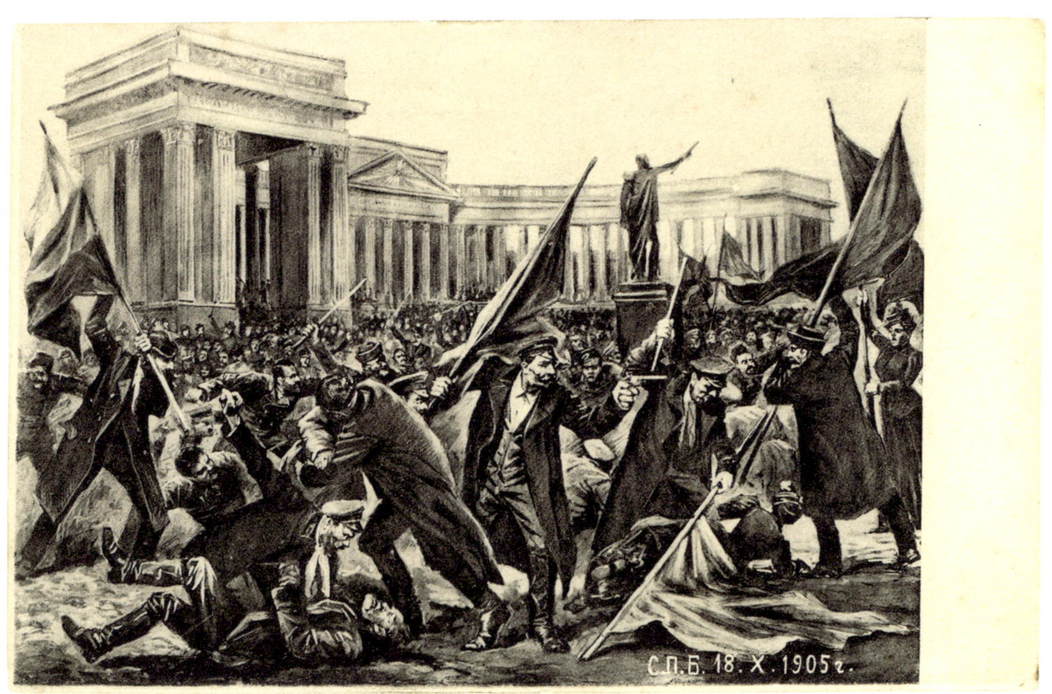

Anonymous artist. *Saint Petersburg. 18 October 1905*. Published by Vpered, Saint Petersburg, 1906.

to resume his revolutionary activities. A meeting of senior Party figures was arranged for late December, and there the decision was taken to set up a new legal publishing house named Utro [Morning].

As the Party had no money to spare, Belopolskii was forced to bankroll the new firm himself. His initial efforts to raise funds through donations fell far short of the amount he needed, but the chance sight of a lottery ticket in the window of a small printing house inspired him to try a similar scheme, the prize for which, he determined, would be a set of Marxist classics. Belopolskii immediately put in an order for ten thousand tickets, and these were subsequently sold to the public through a network of student activists. Meanwhile, he obtained a fake passport and submitted an official application to the authorities for permission to open a new publishing house.[13]

By the time all the money was in, the lottery had raised 2,700 roubles, a sum far in excess of expectations. A meeting was again convened, and during the discussions, Lenin's wife, Nadezhda Krupskaia, suggested that an existing Social Democratic print and postcard publisher named Petukh [Cockerel] be appended to Utro, so as to provide the new firm with a picture department.[14] Krasin's approval for this was sought and promptly given. Thus, Utro's visual inventory, far from being a casual afterthought, was the result of a carefully calibrated plan put together at the highest levels.[15] This demonstrates both the regard in which postcards were held and the importance given to uniting Party output.[16]

The collapse of government authority presented pitfalls as well as opportunities, and as the market in socialist wares expanded, the Party had become concerned that their propaganda was getting corrupted and lost amid fierce commercial competition. In November, Lenin responded to these worries with a seminal article calling for all ideologically-consonant publishing to be integrated within the Party system. The creation of literature, he insisted, could never be a private enterprise, independent of the 'common cause of the proletariat.' This he summed up with the statement: 'All Social Democratic literature must become Party literature.'[17] In essence, Lenin was arguing for a cultural world wholly subservient to the needs of the Party.

After the October Manifesto, clandestine printing continued to serve as an important way of propagating revolutionary material, but Lenin's push for greater consolidation gave a boost to the Party's efforts to establish large-scale commercial publishing enterprises. Such enterprises not only enabled more works to be manufactured, but also for output to be concentrated in, and supervised from, a single location. Although Lenin did not mention visual propaganda specifically, these efforts naturally had had a knock-on effect on all aspects of production. In the major cities therefore, the revolutionaries now resolved to channel the main thrust of their postcard propaganda through centralised legal facilities. Utro was among the first significant steps taken in this direction.

In early 1906, Utro issued a small series of prints, phototype pictures, and postcards.[18] These, Belopolskii wrote, marked 'the beginnings of our work as a publisher.'[19] The images chosen for reproduction, all of which were copied from published sources, were necessarily mild in content, comprising portraits of socialist theoreticians and revolutionary heroes, and copies of socialist paintings. Although all these works were in principle legal to produce, as an official party enterprise, Vpered did, nonetheless, follow a broadly Marxist orientation, deploying portraits of leading socialist ideologues, pictures of workers, and images of significant political events to portray the emergence of a new proletarian power, from initial strike action to eventual revolution.[20]

Distribution was again largely achieved through non-revolutionary enterprise. While some postcards were sold individually, many were sold in bulk to commercial firms.[21] 'They were bought in significant quantities by the largest shops, such as Datsiaro, Felten and others,' recalled Belopolskii.[22] After only a month of trading, the firm was able to hand over 700 roubles to the Party's finance committee, and by March enough profit had been made to roll out the production of books and pamphlets. Even though he still had several unpublished manuscripts left over from Odessa, Belopolskii noted that these works took far longer to publish than postcards, a good illustration of why the latter made for such effective propaganda.[23]

Sales techniques did not depend solely on the political inclinations of the masses, but also included marketing strategies still recognisable today. Shortly after production commenced, Utro launched a public competition to find the best drawing 'encompassing the idea of the workers' struggle for a better future.'[24] The idea of a design competition was not original, but it shows the revolutionaries' willingness to adopt commercial practice in order to promote their wares.[25] The considerable prize money of fifty roubles was awarded to Petr Buchkin, a student at the Academy of Arts, who went on to become a celebrated Socialist Realist painter.[26] Buchkin's image, titled *The Death of a Worker* was subsequently published in both print and postcard form.

One month after the publication of Lenin's article, Vladimir Bonch-Bruevich returned to Russia, where soon afterwards he was joined by the man himself. Bonch-Bruevich's first role was to sit on the editorial board of the Social Democratic newspaper *Novaia zhizn* [*New Life*], a reflection of Lenin's obsession with maintaining influence over the ideological direction of the movement. From here, his thoughts turned to the need to establish a Bolshevik newspaper and publishing house in the capital. Although there were already a large number of enterprises printing Social Democratic material, commercial operations were becoming increasingly wary, making the requirement for a publishing house of their own ever more acute.[27]

Bonch-Bruevich's initial step was to establish a small legal printing facility. With this in place he was able to gain the Party's approval for the creation of a new magazine.[28] *Nasha mysl* [*Our Thought*] was launched as a weekly illustrated 'scientific and literary journal' in January 1906. It was shut down by the censor within weeks, but not before five instalments (in three issues) had been printed, each in editions of up to 50,000 copies.[29] A little over two months after the closure of *Nasha mysl*, Bonch-Bruevich was up and running again with a new publication named *Biblioteka nashikh chitatelei* [*Our Readers' Library*]. However, this time, he only succeeded in printing two issues, in April and May.

At the final board meeting, a resolution was approved to create a 'new Party centre for book publishing and distribution.'[30] Called Vpered, like its Odessa predecessor, the resulting enterprise amalgamated the resources of three smaller Social Democratic publishers: Utro, which had recently been compromised after a police raid, Marksist [Marxist], and what was left of *Nasha mysl*. The first publications of this new endeavour appeared in late April, and a few weeks after that a new shop and bookstore was opened in the capital.[31] Founded just as the reactionary right was on the up, Vpered would become a key hub for Social Democratic propaganda and an important conspiratorial centre for the Party itself.

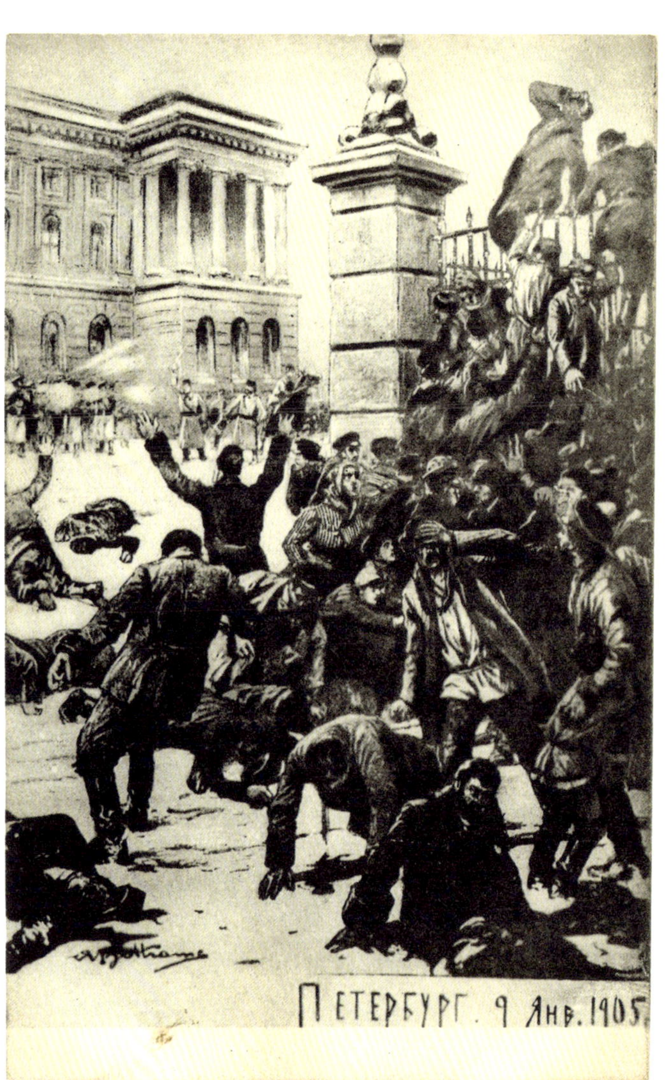
ПЕТЕРБУРГ. 9 Янв. 1905.

Back in February 1906, while still working on *Nasha mysl*, Bonch-Bruevich had started selling socialist-themed prints.[32] Again, none of the designs were original because, as he explained: 'We had not yet established sufficient contacts among artists, and moreover we could not yet pay for the illustrations.'[33] The pictures were instead taken from whatever material came to hand. Some came from books on the French Revolutions and Paris Commune that Bonch-Bruevich had brought with him from exile, and others from works issued by the fellow-travelling Social Democrat publishers Georgii Kuklin, in Geneva, and Johann Dietz, in Stuttgart.[34] Despite their lack of originality, these reproductions reportedly generated 'huge demand among the toiling masses.'[35]

Achille Beltrame. *Petersburg. 9 January 1905*. Published by Vpered, Saint Petersburg, 1906.

Bonch-Bruevich evidently had a good understanding of the importance of pictorial propaganda, but his output does not at this stage appear to have included postcards. The merger with Utro in May 1906, however, provided him with a ready-made production programme. The transition between the two ventures was seamless. Once the new business was underway, all output was simply rebranded – from around 23 May advertisements for Utro ceased and thereafter its wares reappeared under the Vpered imprint. The only difference between Utro and Vpered postcards is that the latter were printed at the Party's own facilities (a mark of ongoing efforts to consolidate production) and perhaps as a consequence, carry no publishing details.[36]

Soon after launching Vpered, Bonch-Bruevich moved to expand the firm's visual repertoire beyond the initial lines that he had inherited from Utro and *Nasha mysl*. In the final issue of *Biblioteka nashikh chitatelei*, there is an advertisement for Vpered listing prints of socialist paintings and revolutionaries, as well as a statement declaring that a further 'series of pictures and portraits' was in preparation.[37] A Vpered pamphlet on the French Revolution published later in the year contains an advertisement for twenty-five postcard reproductions of paintings, and fifty portraits, and an announcement reporting that another series of postcards had just been published.[38] Uncontroversial content gave these images wide appeal, and all were printed in considerable quantities.

Vpered's main focus was on written propaganda, which Lenin supervised personally, but the firm's visual inventory was always considered a significant part of its output, featuring prominently in its publicity material. In mid-to-late 1906, Vpered issued a series of stamps decorated with portraits of revolutionary heroes. Although postally invalid, these designs were a bold attempt to displace autocratic power in the philatelic sphere.[39] No other form of pictorial propaganda, however, ever exceeded postcards in the numbers manufactured. The steady expansion of their production during the year shows that even after the dissolution of the First Duma, the state was still not strong enough to deter a committed revolutionary organisation from printing leftist imagery.

Throughout much of Vpered's existence, postcards reproducing socialist portraits and paintings were still nominally legal to publish.[40] Activists continued to push seditious postcards through underground channels, but in 1906 secrecy was no longer an absolute prerequisite for the dissemination of anti-government wares, thus ensuring that it came to assume a commercial character. In Saint Petersburg alone there were hundreds of bookshops selling opposition material, places like Glagolev's, a Menshevik store that prided itself on 'being able get around confiscation orders,' and Znanie [Knowledge], a Bolshevik firm, which according to the Okhrana, had in stock 'two to four million agitational pamphlets.'[41] Such places were also major outlets for anti-government postcards.

Vpered publications were available both through the firm's own premises and through other bookstores. Much of the firm's output was sold wholesale, but Bonch-Bruevich also regularly swapped Vpered wares with those of other enterprises, thereby distributing his own material effectively and enabling new stock to be acquired at low cost.[42] To the casual observer, Vpered's shop on Karavannaia Street was a well-established legitimate enterprise; however, illicit material was also offered 'under the counter'. Bonch-Bruevich recalled that government spies used regularly to drop by, asking: 'Do you perhaps have anything a little bit spicy?'[43] He claims to have been able to spot these provocateurs with ease, but no doubt other booksellers were not so practised.

Like many of the larger bookstores in Saint Petersburg and Moscow, Vpered also operated a mail-order system, with payment due on delivery. Using the state-run railways and postal service to distribute anti-government propaganda was just one of the many advantages and ironies of running a quasi-legal operation at this time. Orders came in 'from all corners of the Russian Empire,' recalled Bonch-Bruevich. 'We dispatched a colossal quantity of books ... primarily to all our party organisations, but huge quantities were also sent to bookshops and bookselling cooperatives, who then themselves distributed these books through newspaper sellers, across cities, factories, mills and along the railways.'[44] This was propaganda distribution on an industrial scale.

Disseminating propaganda in this manner was hugely profitable, but commercial sales resulted in the severance of any real connection between the revolutionaries and their clientele.[45] Postcards had always been sold to the highest bidder, but because of the illegal nature of the imagery, distribution before the October Manifesto was less widespread and as a consequence more targeted. Now, as production increased, and the consumer pool grew, links between publishers, distributors and buyers continued to loosen. Low prices and uncomplicated content ensured that many postcards did end up with workers, and to a lesser extent, peasants. But unrestricted sales meant that the Party had little say in who bought their images, or in how they were used.

This did not, however, greatly concern the Party; after all, the main purpose of legal publishing was to maximise production, and in this the Social Democrats were undoubtedly successful. Indeed, the Party's graduation from small underground printing operations to large commercial enterprises offers proof of its becoming a mass organisation. In this respect, technology and commerce were integral to the emergence of popular opposition parties in Russia, for without access to printing presses and distribution facilities, the revolutionaries would never have been able to muster the activists to convince even a modicum of the population to back their political views. Party work was no longer so personal, but it was now a great deal more powerful.

Following the dispersal of the Second Duma, the Press Administration started to pay closer attention to Vpered, and consequently several works by Lenin and others were made subject to court-ordered bans. In July 1907, a raid on the shop led to Bonch-Bruevich's arrest, and by the autumn, Vpered had closed. During the eighteen months that it was in operation, the firm published fifty-eight books, and around one hundred and twenty-five postcards.[46] It has been widely assumed that the latter were routinely confiscated, and no doubt many were under emergency regulations, but despite their revolutionary origins, none were ever officially arrested and none were mentioned in connection with the criminal case that eventually forced Vpered to close.[47]

Through portraiture and painting, Vpered conveyed the basics of Marxism to an audience that stretched from the workers to the intelligentsia. But the power of its postcards lay less in their content, which showed no real individuality, than in how they were produced and disseminated. Years of experience had fostered an awareness of the need for organisation and discipline, as well as for consolidation and compromise – in Vpered's case, managing its own printing and distribution facilities, while at the same time extending its reach through commercial enterprise. These attributes allowed the Party to exploit the system to an extraordinary degree, creating a potent propaganda machine at a time when repression was on the rise.

Utro and Vpered were among the earliest legal publishers in Russia to create a pictorial repertoire adhering to a socialist ideology.[48] Their use of fine art as propaganda has an obvious antecedent in the artist-drawn postcards produced by the Society of Saint Eugenia, but in ideological terms, the firms' output provides a clear departure point for later developments.

During the 1905 Revolution, art and literature became an inseparable part of the Party's activities, or as Lenin put it, the 'cog and screw' of one great machine.[49] Postcard production formed an essential part of this unitary endeavour, and in its ambition, scale and content, foreshadowed what was later to become the Soviet propaganda state.

Mikhail Chemodanov and Dmitrii Peschanskii

E. Chekhovskaia Photographic Studio. Portrait of Mikhail Chemodanov. Moscow, early 1900s.

Despite their grand plans, the Social Democrats could never hope to bring together all their propaganda under one roof: to have done so would have required far greater resources, and exposed them to a markedly increased risk. For practical purposes therefore, Bolshevik collaboration with private firms was extensive.[50] Legal publishers, printers, and photographic studios not only had the experience and the equipment to make large runs of anti-government postcards, they also provided a legitimate cover for revolutionary production of leftist material, and by extension for revolutionary fundraising. Outsourcing printing and publishing thus provided the radicals with a temporary alternative or an additional resource to setting up a publishing house of their own.

Some private firms were merely contracted to manufacture postcards, but there were other businesses more obviously sympathetic to the revolutionary movement that were prepared to run greater risks, as well as to donate a part of their profits to revolutionary causes. These firms operated under the authority or guidance of Party members, but had no official status. In Bonch-Bruevich's words, there were 'a large number of small publishers that did not completely belong to the Party, but which our Party influenced, and even controlled in part, frequently channelling our own people onto their staff.'[51] The extent to which they became approved Party facilities, or at least placed ideology above commerce, is open to debate.

Connections with artists and illustrators were established in much the same ad hoc way. Not all were commissioned directly by one or other of the revolutionary parties; many also contributed to party propaganda by working for ideologically-linked publications or publishing houses. Today, few of their names are known, and in the rare circumstances that their identities have been passed down, finding information on them or their work is nigh-on impossible. It is for this reason that Chemodanov's well-documented activities constitute such an important resource. In his case, not only do we know the name of the individual who designed the images, where they were printed, and how much they cost, but also how they were distributed and to whom.

Chemodanov was born in October 1856 in Viatka Province in a 'small, far-off, little village, surrounded by woods.'[52] He was the eldest in a large family,

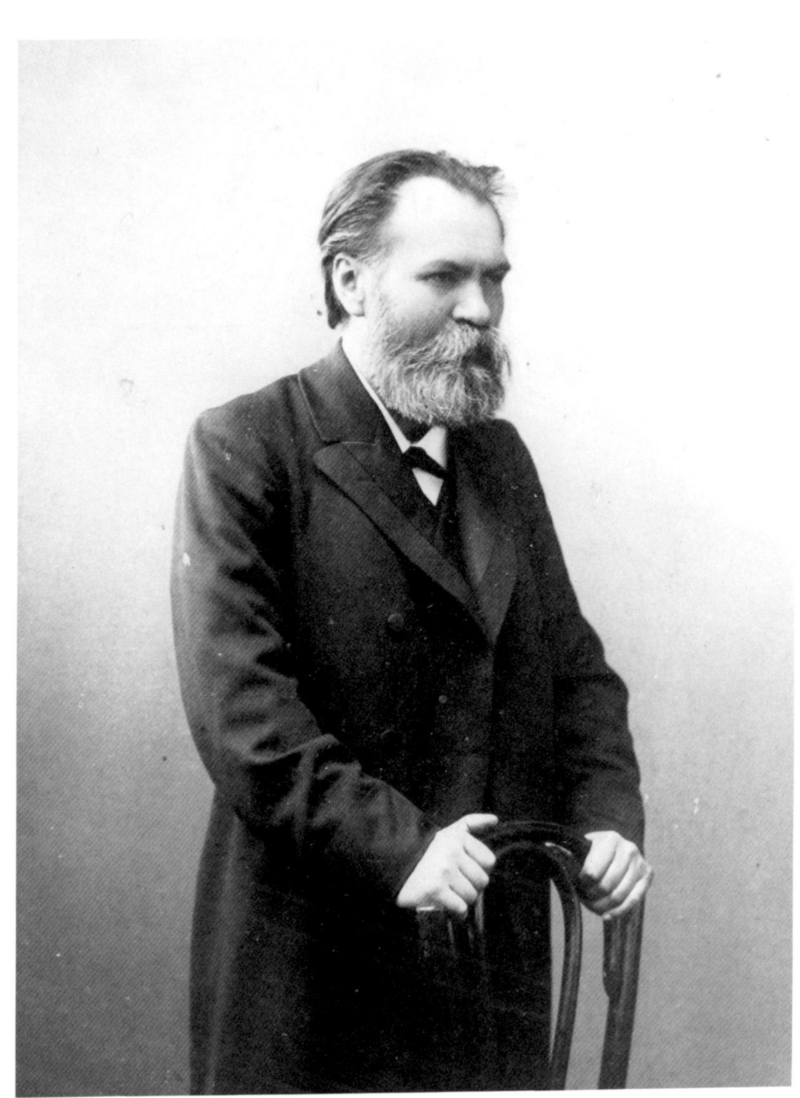

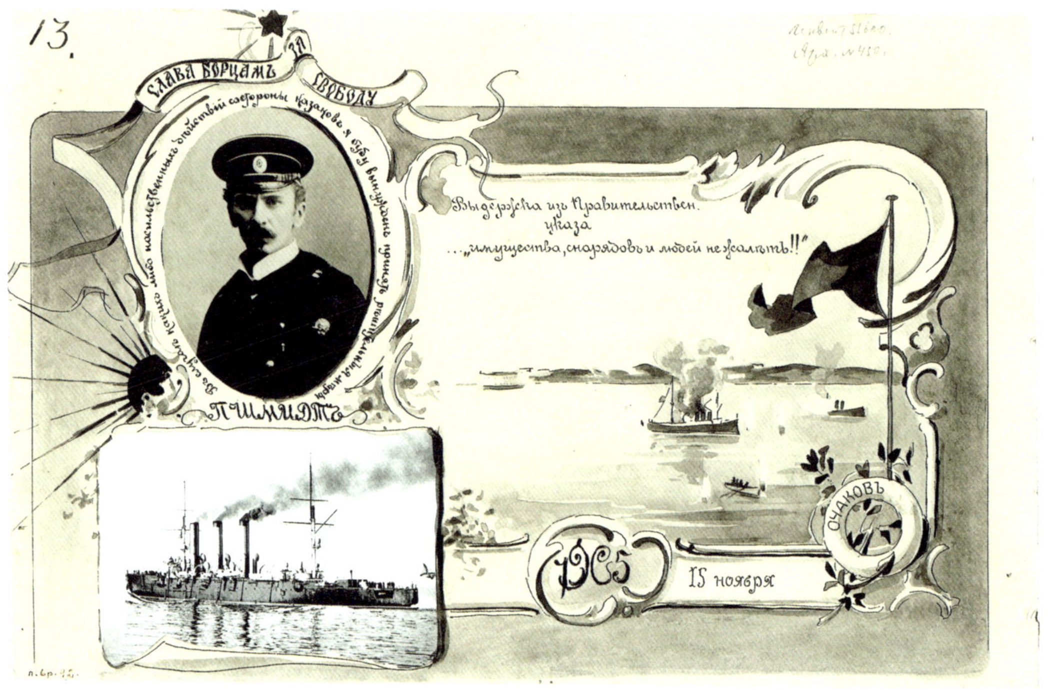

Anonymous artist. Maquette for postcard commemorating Lieutenant Schmidt's mutiny on the Black Sea Fleet. Moscow, 1906. The caption reads: 'Glory to Freedom Fighters. P. Schmidt. In the event of the Cossacks carrying out any kind of violent reprisals against members of the local population, I will be forced to take decisive measures. Extract from Government Decree: "Have no regard for property, shells or people".' From the archive of Dmitrii Peschanskii.

sustained by the meagre income of his clergyman father. According to his nephew, the future diplomat Ivan Maiskii, Chemodanov's overriding personality traits were kindness, charisma, and enthusiasm. Maiskii fondly recalled 'Uncle Misha' as 'the personification of vitality, energy and movement.' 'He was a short, stocky man with shining brown eyes, an unkempt beard and a mane of black hair that stuck out in all directions ... He had a loud infectious laugh, and loved everyone around him to laugh. He was always full of incredibly interesting thoughts, proposals, plans and projects.'[53]

Drawing was Chemodanov's first love. He claimed to have 'amazed everyone with a portrait of a local peasant aged nine, and had made skilled copies of magazine illustrations by the age of ten.'[54] After leaving school, he gained a place to read medicine at Moscow University, and it was while a student there that he published his first cartoons. In the 1870s, Russian satire was still deeply conservative, humorous rather than political, and rarely straying far on to the home front. Chemodanov, however, nurtured a keen sense of social injustice, and as the decade wore on he began to look to caricature as 'a serious tool of satire' that might permit the realities of life under Tsarism to be exposed.[55]

Shortly after the assassination of Alexander II, this ambition brought him into conflict with the authorities. In March 1881, the journal *Svet i teni* [*Light and Shadows*] published a cartoon of Chemodanov's titled *Our Weapon for Resolving Pressing Issues*.[56] After submitting a draft for official inspection, he had secretly amended the illustration, transforming it from a dig at the censor into a bold attack on government repression.[57] He proudly recalled that it, 'caused a furore among a public that was unused to seeing such provocative anti-government cartoons.'[58] The censor was fired, and the new Tsar approved a recommendation to close the journal for six months.[59] Chemodanov himself fled south to Georgia, where undaunted, he went on producing satirical cartoons.

Chemodanov returned to Moscow to finish his degree in 1882. He remained under police supervision for another four years, but continued to publish regularly.[60] However, although he became adept at balancing his own needs with those of the censor, this became an increasingly difficult act to maintain.[61] In late 1890, he wrote in his journal: 'I wanted to be a doctor, but thought to cure social ills rather than individuals, and the tool I chose for the cure was not the scalpel but the pen and brush ... The weapon of satire once held an allure for me ... but the merciless censor has clipped my wings and I am convinced of the futility, or at least the little use of my cartoons in the current censorial environment, so I will put away my favourite tool, and exchange the pen and the pencil for the scalpel and the stethoscope.'[62]

Soon after this, Chemodanov gave up drawing to concentrate on his medical career.[63] A few years previously, he had started training under the surgeon Nikolai Sklifosovskii, who had suggested that he would do well to take an interest in stomatology and orthodontics. The area at first held little appeal for him, but in time Chemodanov became attracted to the idea of making a name for himself in what was then a neglected branch of the sciences. Over the next ten years he wrote a book illustrated with his own drawings, gave lectures, edited a specialist magazine, and was involved in organising the first school of dentistry in Russia.[64] By the time of the Russo-Japanese War, he had become the 'most famous dental specialist in Moscow.'[65]

In around 1904, unhappiness at the state of Russia pushed Chemodanov into resuming his fight against autocracy. Medicine was a major part of his life, but it never quite eclipsed his fervour for satire. As he once said, 'there are many good doctors, but few caricaturists.'[66] Chemodanov's decision to remount the barricades, however, cannot be credited solely to his beliefs. Aleksandr Smirnov, a university friend, recalled that one of the main reasons why Chemodanov had originally given up drawing was to find more stable employment so as to better support his family. Similarly, Chemodanov told Smirnov that he felt inclined to pick up his pen again, not only for reasons of political expediency, but also because he was now financially secure.[67]

Chemodanov's first cartoons of the new era were printed in the newspaper *Novosti dnia* [*News of the Day*] in early 1905.[68] Later that year, however, the mass of satirical journals that sprung up after the October Manifesto

Next spread from left to right

Mikhail Chemodanov. Sketch for postcard captioned: *Illustration of the Mood After the Dispersal of the Second State Duma – La Douma est morte! Vive la Douma! (Campbell-Bannerman)*. Moscow, July 1906.

Mikhail Chemodanov. *Illustration of the Mood After the Dispersal of the Second State Duma – La Douma est morte! Vive la Douma! (Campbell-Bannerman)*. Printed by Dmitrii Peschanskii, Moscow, July 1906.

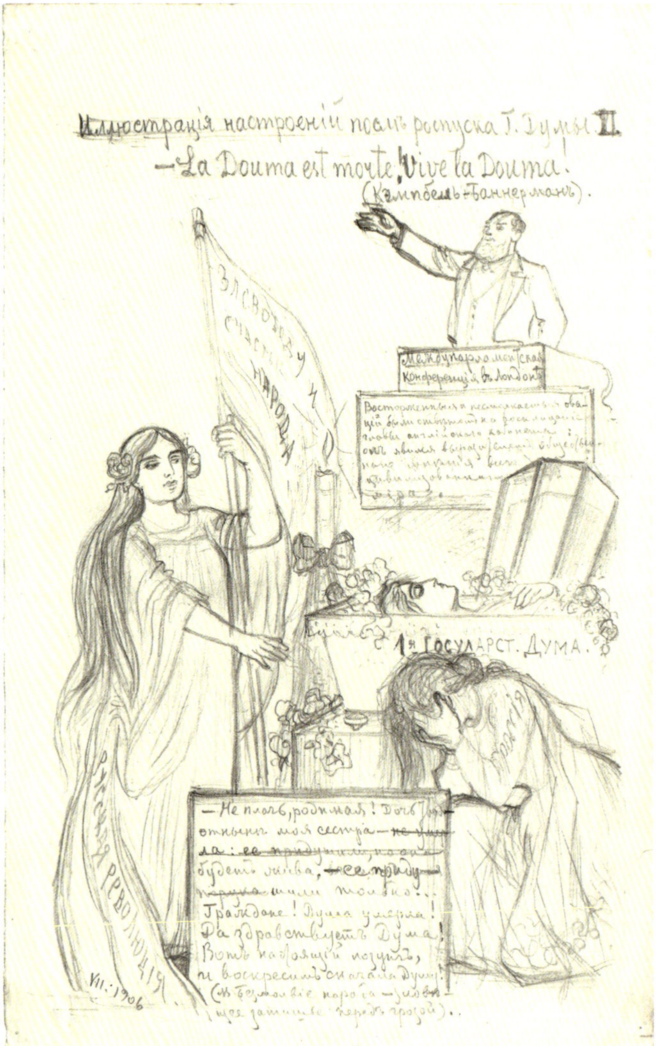

Иллюстрація настроеній послѣ роспуска Г. Думы. II.

— La Douma est morte, Vive la Douma!
(Кэмпбель-Баннерманъ).

За свободу и счастье народа

Междупарламентская конференція въ Лондонѣ

Восторженныя и нескончаемыя оваціи были отвѣтомъ на восклицаніе главы англійскаго кабинета: онъ явился выразителемъ общественнаго мнѣнія всего цивилизованнаго міра.

1я Государст. Дума.

Россія

Русская Революція

VII. 1906

— Не плачь, родимая! Дочь твоя отнынѣ моя сестра — ~~не умерла: ее придушили~~, но она будетъ жива, ~~ее придушили~~ только...
Граждане! Дума умерла!
Да здравствуетъ Дума!
Вотъ настоящій лозунгъ,
и воскресимъ сначала Думу!
(Въ безмолвіе народа — зловѣщее затишье передъ грозой)..

28. Иллюстрація настроеній послѣ роспуска Г. Думы. 2.
— La Douma est morte! Vive la Douma!
(Кэмпбелль-Баннерманъ).

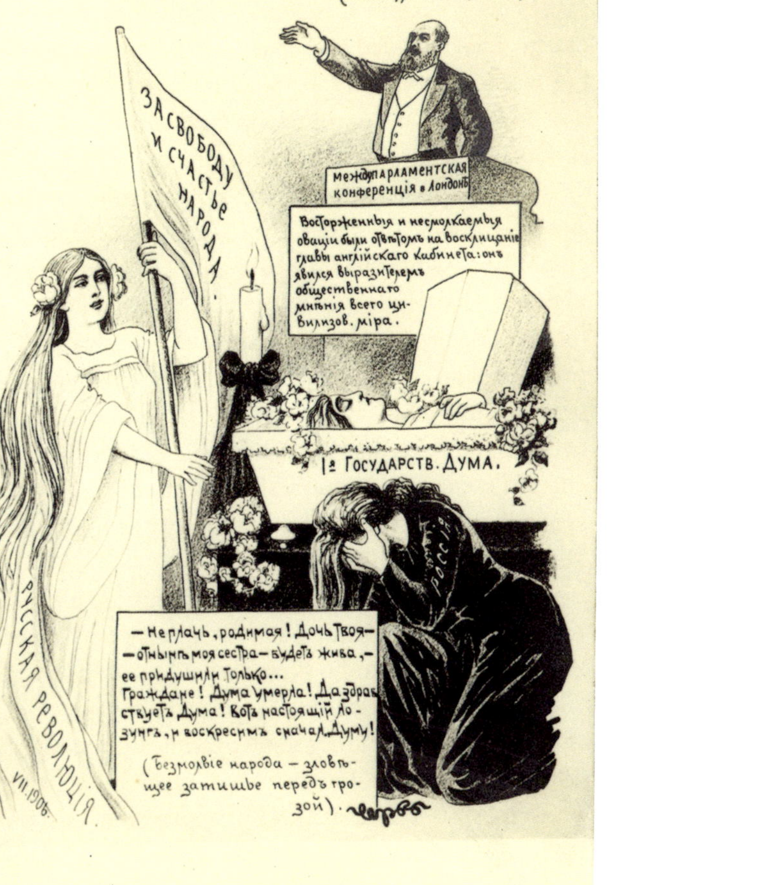

allowed for a return to more familiar territory. In November, Chemodanov's *An Old Song Played to a New Tune*, which lauded the proletariat's role in the October General Strike, appeared in the Bolshevik journal *Zhalo* [*The Sting*].[69] And the same month, his take on the government's repudiation of the Zemstvo Congress was published in *Kramola* [*Sedition*], a shortlived news-sheet also linked to the Social Democrats.[70] Chemodanov's most extensive collaboration, however, was with the liberal journal *Na rasputi* [*At the Crossroads*].

In February 1906, fourteen of Chemodanov's illustrations appeared in the first issue of the periodical – most of them sharp but uncontroversial satires on government repression, rural poverty and pettifogging bureaucrats.[71] This heralded an impassioned return to previous form, and yet it all but marked the end of Chemodanov's activities in the journal medium. He was advertised as a future contributor to *Na rasputi* (alongside Bakst and Bilibin), but only one further drawing of his appeared.[72]

At some point the previous year, Chemodanov had been introduced to Boris Grinberg, a member of the Social Democratic Party's Moscow finance committee.[73] Through Grinberg an arrangement had been made with a local photographic studio to reproduce Chemodanov's cartoons in postcard form.[74] The owner of the studio, Dmitrii Peschanskii, was a Bolshevik sympathiser, who in 1905 had started allowing the revolutionaries to use his premises for illegal activities. 'The studio was well set up for conspiratorial matters and served as a place for secret meetings, gatherings and conferences,' Peschanskii wrote, adding, 'we also hid literature, weapons (after the December Uprising) and other items belonging to the military-technical bureau there.'[75]

Peschanskii was an experienced photographer specialising in images relating to the performing arts. His wares were printed on site and offered for sale through a studio shop, located next door to the Bolshoi Theatre. In addition to his own output, Peschanskii also stocked postcards from other manufacturers, including some relating to the revolutionary unrest.[76]

Production of Chemodanov's cartoons started in around late 1905 or early 1906.[77] The method of replication was simple. His original ink drawings, measuring approximately 22 × 35 centimetres, were photographed and then reproduced as required on plain-backed photographic paper.[78] The finished postcards carry several different pseudonyms, but all are easily identifiable on stylistic grounds.[79]

The majority of Chemodanov's satires were closely related to specific events, particularly political developments and incidents of government oppression. All the images are dated, sometimes to the day, and this shows that several were made prior to Chemodanov's first meeting with Peschanskii, suggesting that he had been in need of an alternative publishing

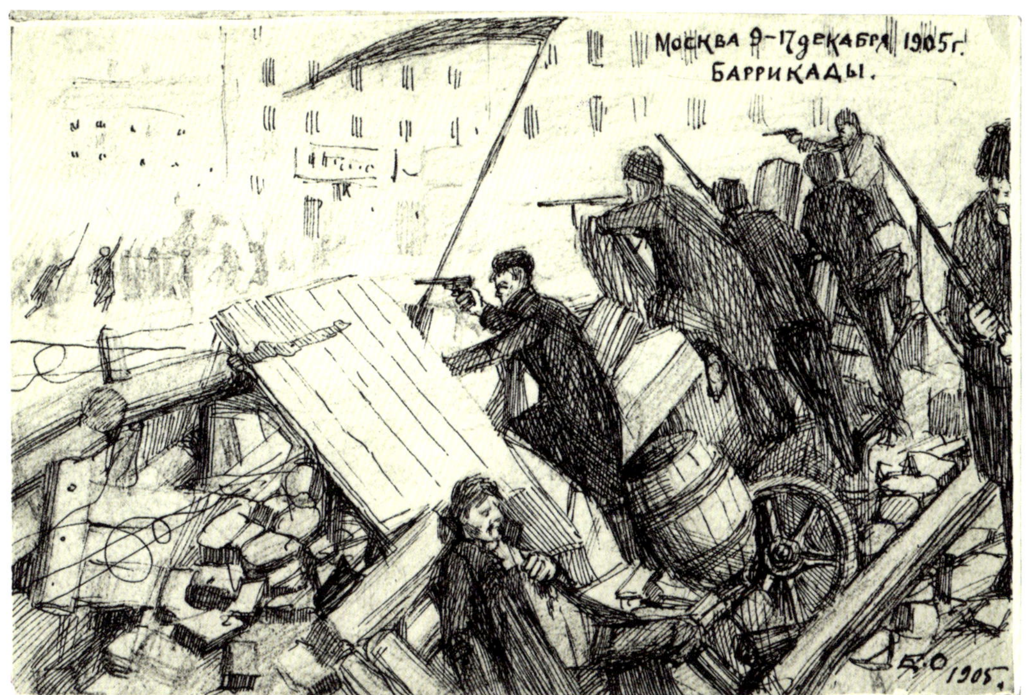

Evgenii Orlovskii. *Moscow 9–17 December 1905. Barricades.* Printed by Dmitrii Peschanskii, Moscow, circa early 1906.

outlet for some months. Peschanskii provided a more reliable, if dangerous, way of propagating his work, which eliminated the need to kow-tow to the censor. It is no coincidence that his satirical journal work ceased at around the same time that he found such a convenient and profitable way to circulate his drawings.

Without the need to placate officialdom, Chemodanov's work became increasingly bold. 'The cartoons provided a release for all his pent-up political energy,' recalled Druzhinin, adding that, 'through the power of pen and pencil he became a part of the great movement of his times.'[80] Chemodanov continued to produce new cartoons right up to a few weeks before he was caught, but following the break-up of his network, production and distribution of his works was soon wound up.[81] In total, Peschanskii reproduced around thirty-five of Chemodanov's cartoons, each of which was printed in multiple editions.[82] Only four of these of works had previously appeared in other formats.[83]

Peschanskii also printed works by other artists, including Evgenii Orlovskii, and Mikhail and S. Komenko.[84] The work of the Komenko brothers, who studied at the Stroganov School of Art and Industry, has never been identified, but that of Orlovskii is better known.[85] In common with Chemodanov, he contributed illustrations to *Kramola*, and separately made pen-and-ink drawings of the Moscow Uprising, several of which were reproduced as postcards.[86] These small sketches are closely-observed and drawn with great fluidity, suggesting that Orlovskii was a witness to the events he depicted.[87] One, illustrating a clash of arms, includes a vignette of a Social Democratic flag, locating his sympathies firmly within the Party camp.

Peschanskii's influence stretched far further than has previously been acknowledged. In 1924, he sold a collection of just under a hundred drawings, designs and postcards to what was then the Museum of the Revolution in Moscow. This appears to be Peschanskii's working archive for his underground postcard work.[88] One of the distinguishing features of this collection is the great variety of postcard images that it contains, which range from anti-government cartoons and caricatures to real photographs of popular demonstrations. There are also several prototype works included in the assemblage, some of which are original designs, and others which have been photographically reproduced, or copied by hand from Russian and foreign satirical journals.[89]

With the exception of drawings by Orlovskii, and to some extent Chemodanov, few of the postcards in Peschanskii's archive display any obvious political allegiances. While some might broadly be termed Social Democratic, others are more liberal in orientation, and others still, such as portraits of Maria Spiridonova, ostensibly Socialist-Revolutionary. This was not unusual. Peschanskii's actions may have been politically motivated, but like most, he was still open to compromise, especially where money was concerned.

Despite regular attempts to reign in Social Democratic propaganda production, the Party did not at any stage exert full control over all the material from which it derived its income. While Vpered output was tightly monitored, the images in the Peschanskii collection indicate that the organisation did little to regulate the editorial line of non-official publishers, with the inevitable result that their output often traversed ideological borders. It appears that as long as propaganda was not being issued in the Party name, the revolutionaries were disinclined or, more likely, unable to monitor production, even when profiting directly from the result. In order to achieve the larger aims of politicising the population and the financing the party, sacrifices had to be made.

Control over artists was equally loose. Although Chemodanov was dependent on Social Democratic contacts, he did not use Party money (likely because none was forthcoming), paying for everything, including the activists who disseminated his postcards, out of his own pocket. In practice, this meant that Chemodanov had complete authority over the content, production, and distribution of his images. The principal role played by the Party was to receive the profits. His postcards, although closely affiliated, are therefore best described as 'fellow-travelling.' They broadly subscribed to Social Democratic ideals, but were produced without an official imprimatur. This was a political union, but one in which the terms of engagement were never clearly delineated.

Underground Distribution

Revolutionary publishers relied heavily on middlemen to distribute their wares. For precautionary reasons, few works stayed long at the printers, so an established distribution network was a vital part of any enterprise printing anti-government works. In all the major cities, there were unlicensed representatives, activists and shady individuals managing the trade in legal and illegal publications. In the capital, they were a common sight: 'On practically every corner of Nevskii Prospect, there were types from Gorky's novels hanging around near the newspaper vendors. They carried briefcases containing a copy of [the right-wing newspaper] *Russkoe znamia* [*Russian Banner*] in order to deflect the watchful eyes of the police, but hidden from view they had bundles of 'other' wares on offer.'[90]

Some were persuaded by politics, others by money. Two offenders caught by the Inspector of the Printing Houses in Vilnius offer an example of the mixture of different people who were drawn into the trade in opposition wares. The first, Esfir Gringauz, a midwife and mother of two children, was the local representative of Molot [Hammer], a commercial publishing house specialising in socialist works, which cooperated closely with the Social Democratic Party.[91] She became involved after her brother, who was already working for the firm, suggested that she become a regional agent, receiving a twenty to twenty-five percent cut on sales. Gringauz readily agreed, apparently unaware that a license was required to sell any type of printed material.

Her counterpart, Doctor I. Romm, was the Vilnius representative of the Saint Petersburg publisher E. M. Alekseeva.[92] Both he and Gringauz stored their books in large stores, from which runners (in Romm's case 'Jewish boys') sold the works directly to the public. According to Collegiate Counsellor Vinogradov, Romm was a very different character from Gringauz – politically unreliable and well-known to the police. He reported: 'Romm is not a simple trading agent like Gringauz, but a person who acted in full awareness of what he was doing.'[93] Gringauz was a rank amateur compared to a man such as Romm, but between them they show the complicated patchwork of political and financial incentives that drove the trade in illegal works.

Another useful conduit through which to funnel opposition material was the Political Red Cross, which also received a generous percentage of the profits, but the mainstay of revolutionary distribution channels were local students, many of whom were members of university political groups.[94] All

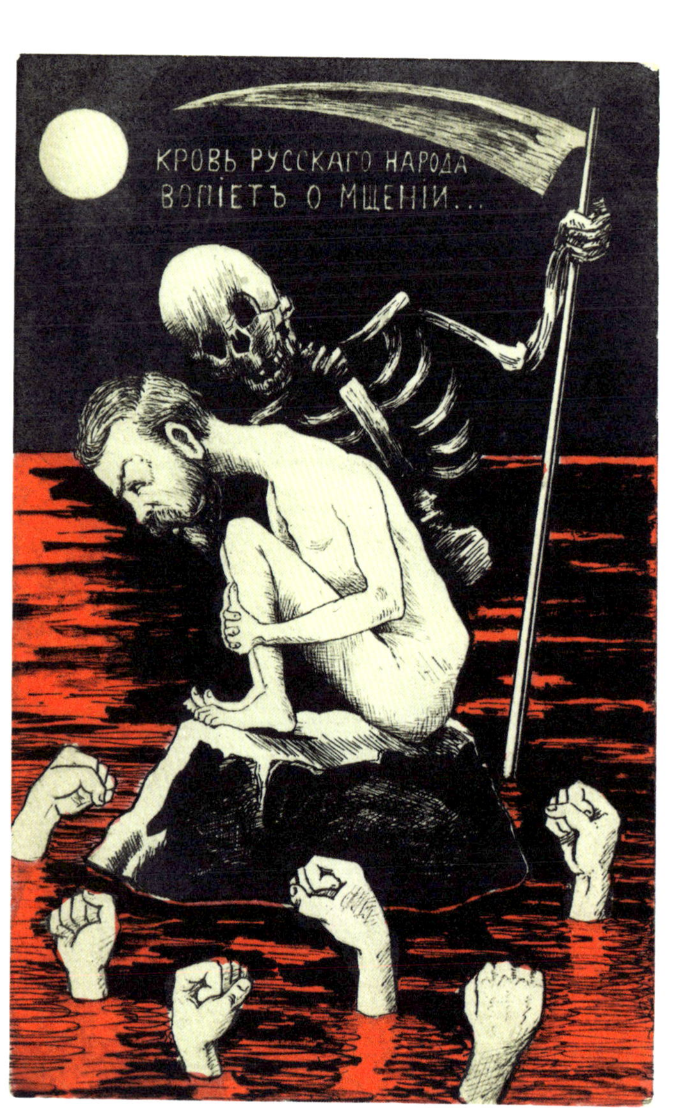
КРОВЬ РУССКАГО НАРОДА
ВОПІЕТЪ О МЩЕНІИ...

provided youthful enthusiasm and easy access to classmates, and, just as importantly, few were burdened with the need to support a family. There were cells of activists in all the larger institutions of higher education in Saint Petersburg and Moscow, each with their own student committees, finance departments, and propaganda circles. These groups could be called upon at any moment to help the Party find meeting places, store goods, and distribute anti-government material.[95]

After August 1905, when a law granting immunity to universities was temporarily reintroduced, the halls and auditoria of the Empire's educational facilities were regularly used for speech-making and demonstrations, attracting crowds of up to ten thousand people. This provided an excellent opportunity for publishers to sell their wares – even those that had access to commercial distribution facilities.[96] Utro, for instance, sold its postcards both through the capital's bookshops, and through the Party's extensive network of student agitators.[97] Propaganda was also sold in the streets, at meetings, around the work place, and door-to-door. In short, wherever discontent was heard, young radicals were on hand to offer the public a material expression of their anger against the regime.

After Félix-Antoine Marmonier. *The Blood of the Russian People Cries out for Revenge...* No publication details, 1906.

Chemodanov was unusual in being closely involved in every aspect of the postcard-making process, from design to finished product, but in respect of dissemination he followed regular practice, employing a large and ever-changing rostrum of students and revolutionary activists to circulate the cards. At any one time, there were between twenty and thirty young men and women involved in selling his works, presided over by a group secretary who coordinated the day-to-day distribution plans. In the summer of 1906, this role was taken on by Nikolai Druzhinin, an agitator and member of the Social Democratic Party's Moscow Committee, after the previous incumbent – a Socialist-Revolutionary – was killed in a failed expropriation attempt.

Druzhinin's first task was to collect the postcards from Chemodanov's workplace. Then after a secret meeting place had been arranged, the distributors would come by and pick up a bundle of around ten to fifteen envelopes. Inside the envelopes were twenty postcards and a handwritten receipt, signed by Chemodanov.[98] Each distributor was also given a list, compiled from a directory, containing the names and addresses of various 'liberal activists and representatives of the 'free professions' – lawyers, artists, doctors and teachers.' These were the type of people thought most likely and most able to buy expensive anti-government postcards. However, given the abundance of police spies in the city, such a speculative approach carried serious risks.

Druzhinin recalled that before commencing distribution, he would always make a careful note of the layout of the building that he was about to

Next spread

Evgenii Orlovskii. *Moscow 9–17 December 1905. The Revolutionary Red Cross.* Printed by Dmitrii Peschanskii, Moscow, circa late 1905.

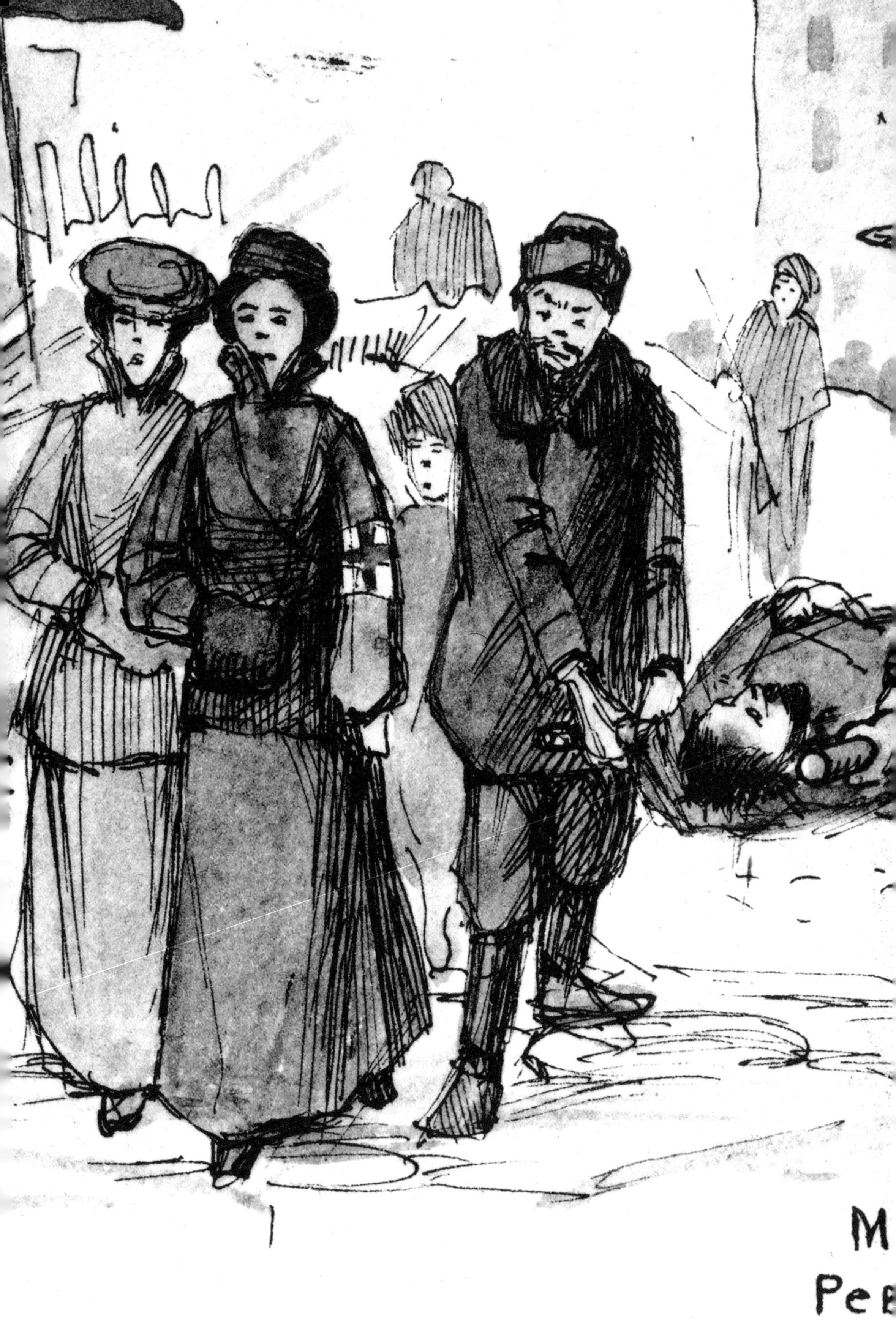

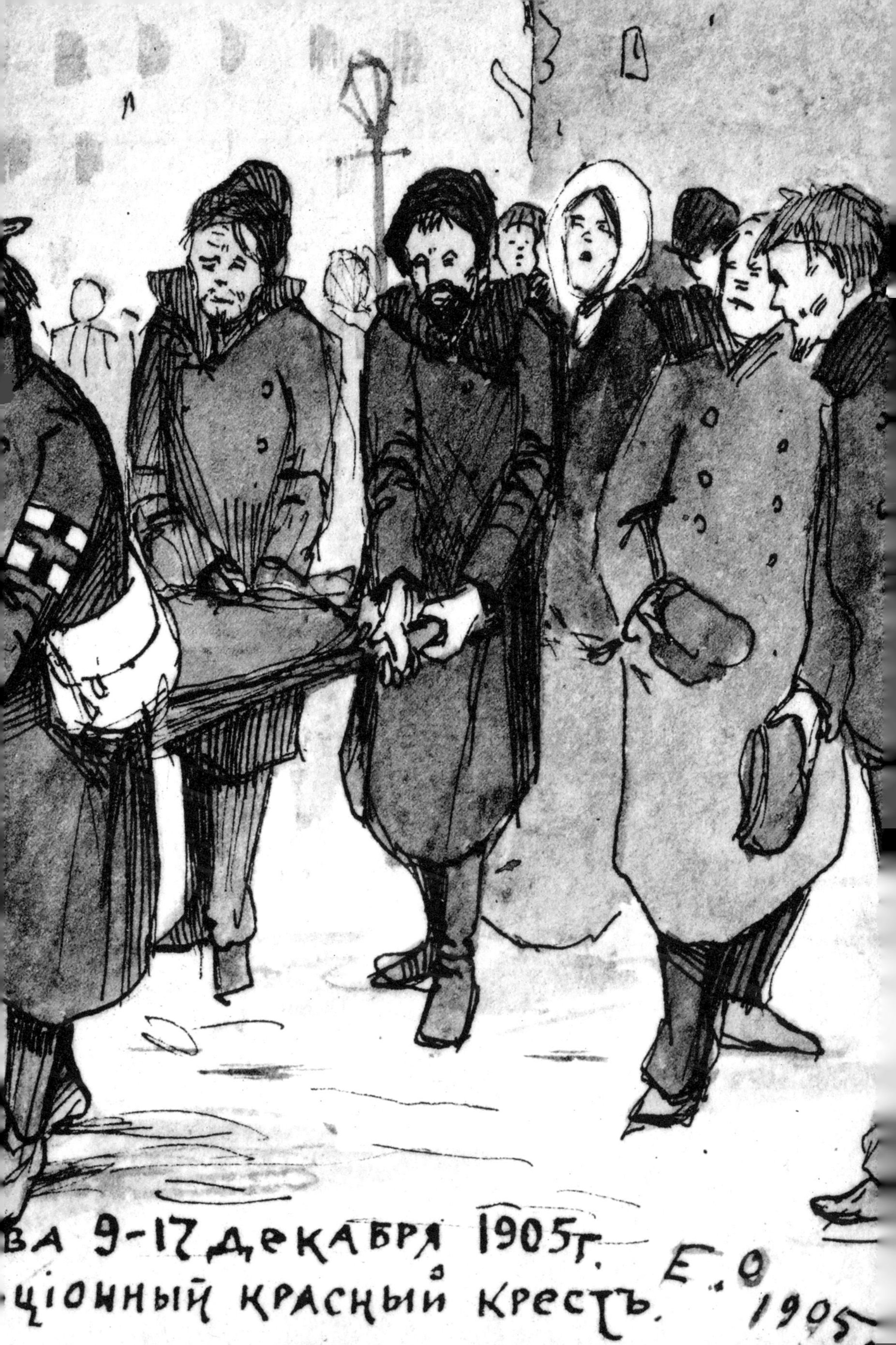
ва 9-17 декабря 1905г.
ціонный красный крестъ.
Е. О
1905

enter, just in case. 'Carrying a briefcase rammed with envelopes ... I rang the doorbell and asked the housekeeper to speak to the owner. I then handed the addressee the ready-prepared envelope and suggested that they might like to make a donation in aid of suffering freedom fighters.'[99] More often than not money would be given. Some, Druzhinin said, were not keen but felt obliged to cough up, but occasionally people refused, and sometimes the police were called, in which case a speedy exit was the only thing that could save the distributor from arrest.

Having completed their rounds, the students would regroup and hand over the money they had raised. The margins on Chemodanov's postcards exceeded those of all other comparable images, and even at conservative estimates, the network could distribute thousands of images every week, generating significant income for the Party.[100] In return, the distributors received a percentage of the profits – around twenty kopecks an envelope. For some, such as Druzhinin, this income was critical. He had become involved after the newspaper he worked for was shut down by the authorities; the money from postcard distribution enabled him to survive while he continued to work (unpaid) for the Party – another illustration of the crossover between practical necessity, commerce, and ideology.[101]

Chemodanov's postcards spread across the Russian Empire, copied and distributed by the revolutionary parties, like-minded sympathisers, and opportunists. Organised distribution only took place in Moscow, but examples of his cartoons travelled as far as Siberia. In July 1906, a police raid on the Ekaterinburg newspaper *Uralskaia zhizn* [*Urals Life*] uncovered several 'blasphemous images of the Sovereign Emperor,' which had recently been sent to the editor by a colleague in Saint Petersburg. Among them were two postcards illustrated by Chemodanov, as well as several others reproducing French and German satirical journal illustrations.[102] Some of Chemodanov's works even ended up in Japan, where the Socialist-Revolutionary publisher Volia [Will/Liberty] reprinted at least two of them in postcard form.

The October Manifesto prompted a rush of political and commercial entrepreneurship that pushed even the most dogmatic of revolutionaries to compromise on doctrine in order to take advantage of the opportunities, and keep financial pace with the market. Lenin characterised the period as one of 'unnatural alliances and strange bedfellows,' but as Bonch-Bruevich makes clear, the work done by these 'ideological companions' was critical.[103] Cooperation with both private enterprise and rival revolutionaries extended the Party's tentacles far beyond their own small bands of full-time members, enabling Social Democratic propaganda to penetrate deep into Russian society. However unnatural these alliances may have seemed, short-term compromises were in the revolutionaries' long-term interests.

The Party's relationship with Peschanskii and Chemodanov is a prime example of the way in which the revolutionaries accommodated dissonant elements within their activities. Neither was formally a member of the Social Democratic Party; indeed, Chemodanov was nominally a Populist, yet both met through Party contacts, used Party networks to disseminate their wares, and donated their profits to Party organisations. The Party's role was one of facilitator – it provided introductions and manpower, and reaped a financial and political reward in return. Even when the Party leadership was more closely involved, such as with Utro and Vpered, production and distribution still relied on a similarly loose range of alliances between revolutionaries, sympathisers, and opportunists.

⁎

Any attempt to judge the effectiveness of Social Democratic postcard production must bear in mind the multiplicity of factions and enterprises involved.[104] Chemodanov's occasional use of Socialist-Revolutionaries to distribute his works is an excellent example of the complications. And yet, it is precisely this ability to mobilise different elements for their own ends that marks the Social Democrats out as such an effective force. Their deployment of small, highly resourceful groups of activists, fluid use of legal and illegal practices, and skilful management of private-revolutionary partnerships enabled Party leaders to establish a means through which to produce and distribute their wares effectively and profitably, thereby ensuring that the organisation remained both competitive and solvent in a crowded marketplace.

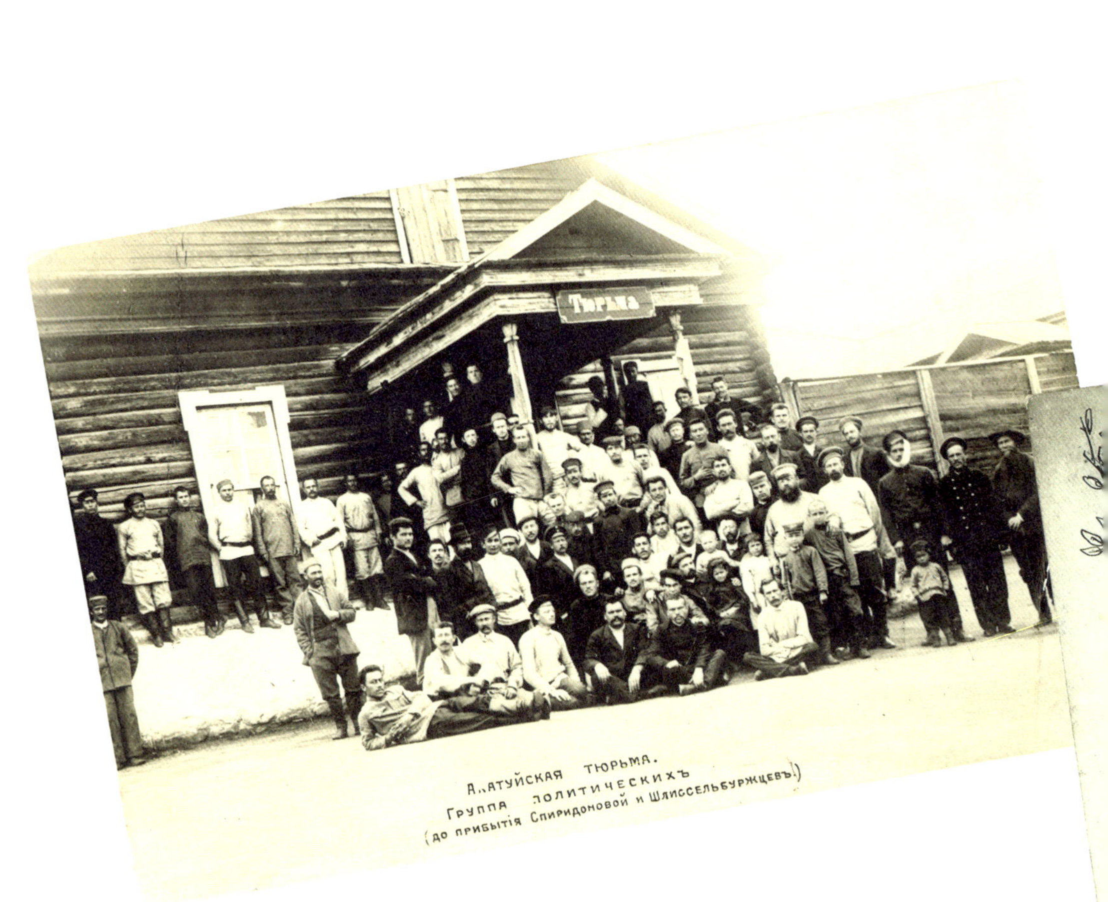
Тюрьма
А..атуйская тюрьма.
Группа политическихъ
(до прибытія Спиридоновой и Шлиссельбуржцевъ!)

THE SOCIALIST-REVOLUTIONARY PARTY

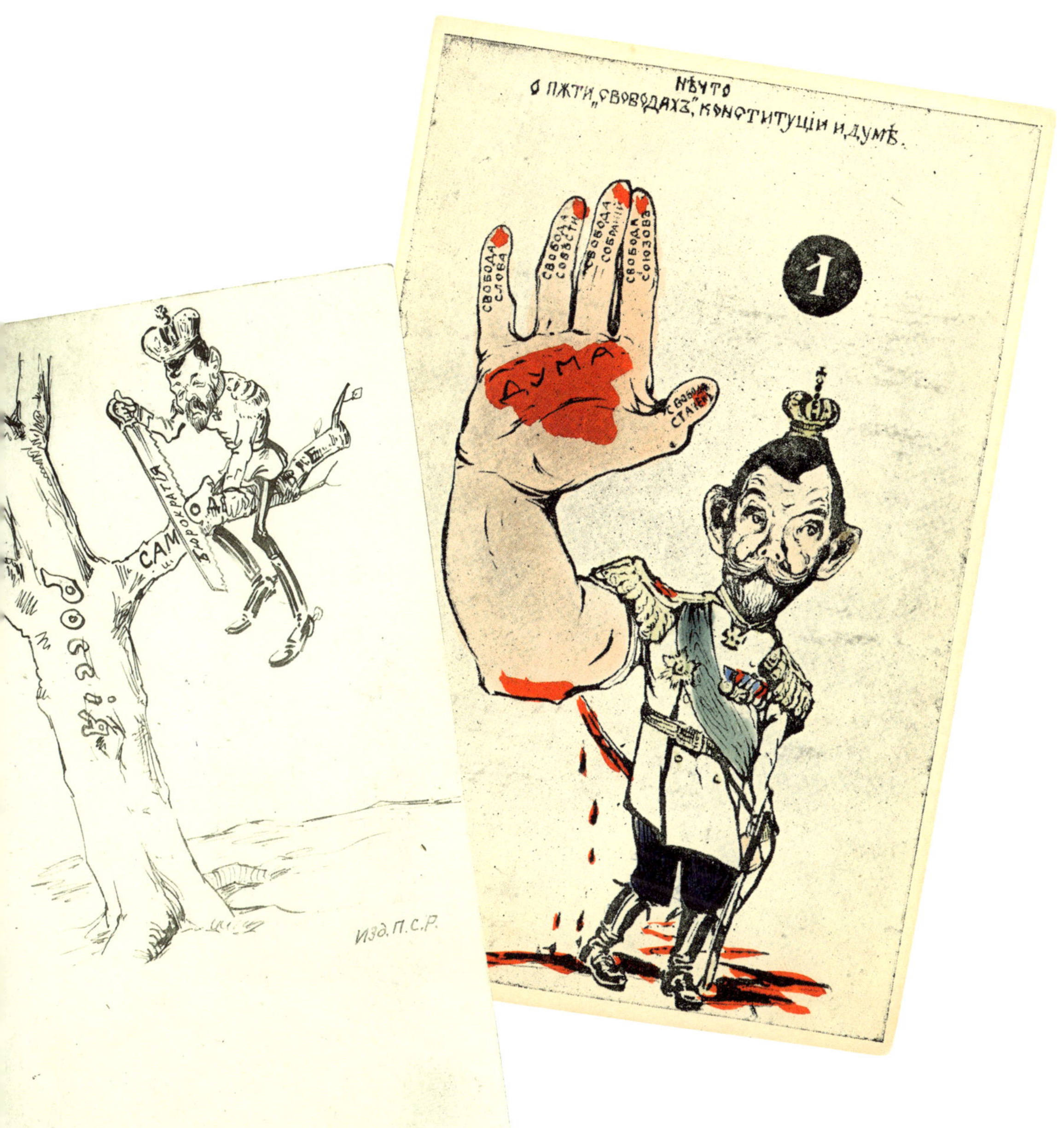

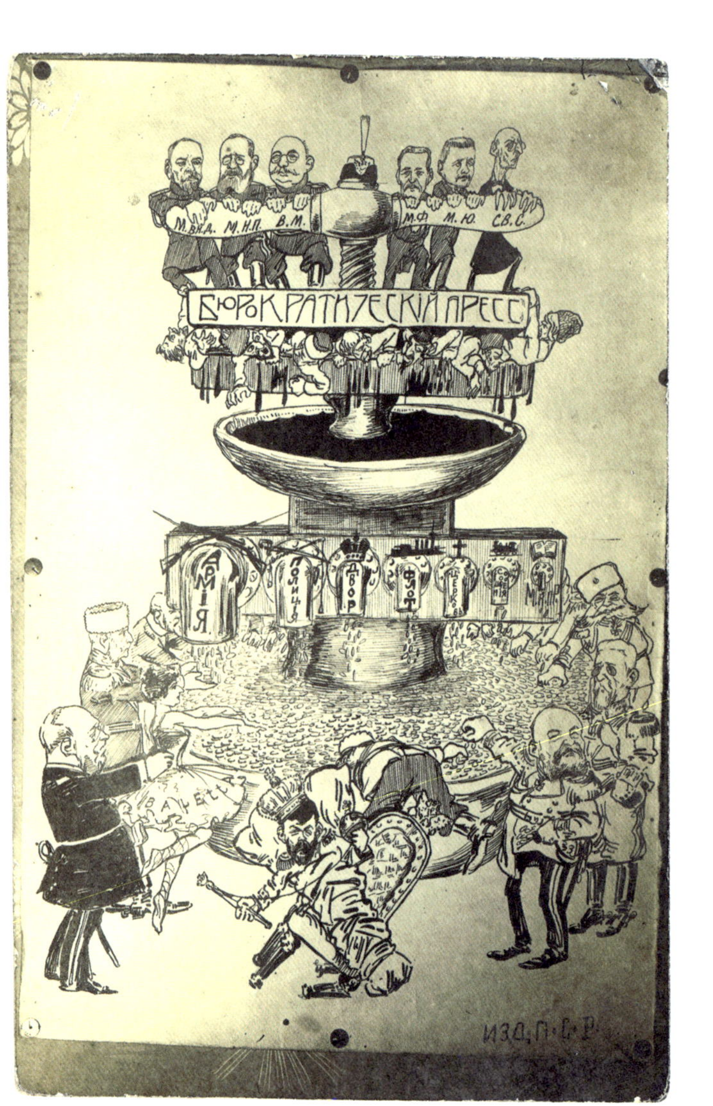

М.ВН.Д.
М.Н.П.
В.М.
М.Ф.
М.Ю.
СВ.С.
БЮРОКРАТИЧЕСКІЙ ПРЕСС
АРМІЯ.
ПОЛИЦІЯ
ДВОР
ФЛОТ
ЦЕРКОВЬ
М.Н.П.
ИЗД.П.С.Р.

Underground Production

On 16 March 1907, the police conducted a search of a dormitory at a university hostel in Moscow. On a table beside the bed of Konstantin Mikhailov, a student at the School of Painting, Sculpture and Architecture, they found: 'fourteen photographic negatives carrying explicitly revolutionary content (political cartoons and portraits of state criminals), all inscribed with the initials O. S. R. [believed to stand for the Socialist-Revolutionary Organisation], three photographic postcards of [the martyred revolutionary] Volodia Mazurin, and one other carrying an illustration in the form of an icon depicting Father John of Kronstadt and SOVEREIGN EMPEROR NICHOLAS II.' On a shelf above his bed, the police also discovered a camera.[1]

A few weeks after the raid, a friend of Mikhailov's named Nikolai Vinogradov turned up at the local police station to claim possession of the camera. He denied all knowledge of the negatives, but a follow-up search of his classroom desk revealed a trove of incriminating evidence: 'Eight ink cartoons, exactly matching the negatives confiscated from Mikhailov, two sheets of pornographic pencil drawings; an ink cartoon with revolutionary subject matter, nine song sheets, ... nine printed Socialist-Revolutionary proclamations, four lithographed proclamations, a printed Party leaflet titled 'training courses for propagandists', along with the original ink draft, 11 pamphlets, and 17 colour postcards satirising the main political parties.'[2]

Vinogradov, who was enrolled at the same art school as Mikhailov, appears to have spent rather less of his time on life drawing than he did on trying to subvert government power. In December 1905, he had taken part in the Fidler House siege that presaged the Moscow Uprising, and now, he was evidently involved in creating agitational material and training propagandists on behalf of the Socialist-Revolutionary Party.[3] Given the fact that propaganda production and dissemination came under the remit of the local finance committee, the additional discovery of a small notebook listing sales of 'tendentious literature' makes it seem likely that Vinogradov served as the treasurer of the Art School's student Party committee.[4]

The scope of Vinogradov's activities extended well beyond the precincts of his school. Shortly after he was arrested, Moscow Committee member Maria Volkova was found in possession of: '25 shocking drawings, comprising an obscene caricature of the Sovereign Emperor, evidently intended for reproduction.' The police subsequently linked Volkova to a workshop belonging to Vladimir Kuzis, a 'townsman' from Sergiev Posad, where the police uncovered another large cache of revolutionary material. This included twenty-seven zinc printing blocks, and seven 'blatantly criminal' caricatures

Previous spread from left to right

Russian photographer. *Akatui Prison. Group of Politicals (Before the Arrival of Spiridonova and the Shlisselberg Prisoners).* No publication details, circa 1906.

Anonymous artist. Caricature of Nicholas II sitting in a tree sawing off a branch labelled autocracy. Published by the Socialist-Revolutionary Party, circa 1905.

Anonymous artist. *Something Apropos the Five 'Freedoms', Constitution and Duma.* Published by Volia, Nagasaki, circa 1906.

Opposite

Anonymous artist. *The Bureaucratic Press.* Published by the Socialist-Revolutionary Party, circa late 1904.

of the Tsar.[5] The original drawings for these caricatures, which the police attributed to Vinogradov, were later found at the home of workshop manager Boris Meston.

This was plainly an established and wide-ranging Party-run operation involving the mass production and sale of photographic postcards and letterpress prints. In its make-up and modus operandi, Vinogradov's enterprise bears close comparison to that of Social Democrat Vasilii Meznev, indicating that the underground activities of both the main revolutionary parties followed very similar practice. The production of obscene drawings may not have been quite such common custom, but it is a good example of the moral and political compromises that the revolutionary parties were prepared to make in their quest for funds. For their crimes against the state, Vinogradov was sentenced to a year in a fortress prison, and Mikhailov to eight months.[6]

Legal Publishing

In common with their Social Democratic rivals, the Socialist-Revolutionaries continued to invest heavily in underground production throughout the 1905 era, generating vast numbers of illegal postcards. But, for all revolutionary organisations the October Manifesto and the rampant commercialisation of socialist material that ensued fundamentally shifted the goalposts of propaganda manufacture. For those enterprising enough to grasp the opportunity, commercial production not only became a viable option, it became the only option. Amid intense competition from private firms, the revolutionary parties could not hope to stay financially or politically competitive without establishing a way of publishing their wares legally, an undertaking that required great organisational discipline and extensive monetary resources.

Both the leading revolutionary parties faced similar challenges in establishing legal publishing houses, and both initially looked to collaborate with pre-existing firms. The main conduit for Socialist-Revolutionary publishing and distribution was Shkolnoe i bibliotechnoe delo [Academic and Library Supplies], a Saint Petersburg bookstore founded in 1903. This business, which was owned by Z. N. Bobyleva, had been set up with the aim of spreading radical thought through legal means, and in its early years became well-known for its cheap pamphlets on history and the natural sciences. During the 1905 Revolution, the firm became a key publisher and commercial outlet for Party propaganda, as well as an important meeting place and conspiratorial centre.[7]

In early 1906, the Party leadership looked to expand their control over legal propaganda production with the formation of a secret alliance of fellow-travelling publishing houses, named the Union of Socialist-Revolutionary

Publishers. Under the direction of two Party-controlled enterprises, Novoe tovarishchestvo [New Cooperative] and Molodaia Rossiia [Young Russia], the Union brought together around thirty-five different firms, predominantly based in Saint Petersburg and Moscow.[8] Its aim, according to the police, was to 'spread revolutionary ideas on a legal footing, using the cover of popularising general knowledge among the less well-educated.' A Party-run editorial committee oversaw a unified publishing programme, and was remunerated with an unspecified percentage of the profits.[9]

The police did not latch onto the Union until 1907, meaning that for over a year publishers were able to turn out huge quantities of Socialist-Revolutionary-linked material largely unnoticed. An idea of the scale of Party activities at this time can be ascertained from a report in the organ *Trud* [*Labour*] from December 1906, which claimed that there were some three hundred activists working in thirty different firms in Saint Petersburg alone.[10] Publishers in the Union had extensive sales networks, and much of the resulting propaganda was sold commercially. Some was also sent to provincial groups, which were perennially short of propaganda. The alliance thus not only helped to secure production, but also to manage distribution.

So far, there is little to distinguish the Party's activities from those of its rivals. Bonch-Bruevich, for example, claimed that the Social Democrats collaborated with nearly sixty different commercial publishing houses during the 1905 period.[11] However, it appears that the Party's hard work in the centre was let down by poor infrastructure in the periphery. Socialist-Revolutionary cells intent only on conspiratorial propaganda work had long treated commercial publishing and bookselling as a petit-bourgeois activity of little import, not realising that over the previous year propaganda production had essentially become a mercantile activity that required a well-managed operations base and a wide range of delivery channels in outlying areas. By late 1906, provincial indifference had led to huge financial losses.[12]

In a long report, *Partiinye izvestiia* spelled out the situation:

> With the obvious exception of agitational leaflets, charitable distribution for the purposes of propaganda and agitation has lost its meaning and practical sense ... the producer who does not tailor his organisation to the demands of the market ... will be forced to endure the unpleasant experience of having to watch as others take over his business ... Where he with his amateur methods distributed tens of works, they produce thousands ... private owners have funds, capital and a complete commercial distribution chain, while the Party has an empty trough – decimated publishing houses, no capital, an outsider meddling in its business, and hundreds of unemployed workers.[13]

In short, provincial over-reliance on underground production and dissemination had led to empty coffers.[14] The blame for this, however, cannot be placed entirely on the regions. Although the Socialist-Revolutionary leadership achieved much by way of propaganda production, the Party's failure 'to adapt to a market-orientated system of distribution' is indicative of the issues faced by the organisation as a whole. At the heart of the problem was a lack of unity, both ideological and structural. The Party's centralised, undemocratic administration and loose criteria for membership had led to a politically diffuse organisation, with weak links between headquarters and the regions, factors that served to undermine its propaganda endeavours and, more significantly for its long-term future, its finances.

Although the Party was initially well-off, it had long avoided implementing reforms that might have put its fundraising activities, and the organisation as a whole, in a better position to cope with the vast influx of new members who had joined after Bloody Sunday. As it was, ideological and geographical distance, indolence, and the absence of a clear financial relationship between the leadership and its regional supporters, meant that provincial cells were lax about raising money, and often reliant on handouts and other highly fickle sources of income; donations and armed robbery in particular. The result was a Party membership that had insufficient inclination or practical ability to support the propaganda activities of the central leadership.[15]

The solution advanced in autumn 1906 was to introduce membership fees and impose a ten percent tithe on all Party groups. In a further effort to reduce dependency, it was stipulated that cells should become more involved in the production and dissemination of legal propaganda.[16] But without wholesale restructuring, and with repression already in the ascendant, this proved an unrealistic demand. By the year's end, the Party was in a fix, aware that neither its finances nor its publishing were on a sustainable footing. These failings, however, while carrying grave implications, did not end up registering as much as they might have done, for within months both the revolutionary movement and legal publishing had been suppressed across the board.[17]

Legal Postcard Publishing

It is clear from reports in *Trud* that postcard production was taken seriously by the Party hierarchy.[18] Nevertheless, because of its use of proxies, the extent of Socialist-Revolutionary activities is very hard to ascertain. There were undoubtedly others, but the only legal Party-linked publisher that I have identified is Vera Vodovozova, who set up an eponymous company issuing prints and postcards in Kiev in around 1905. Vodovozova, whose

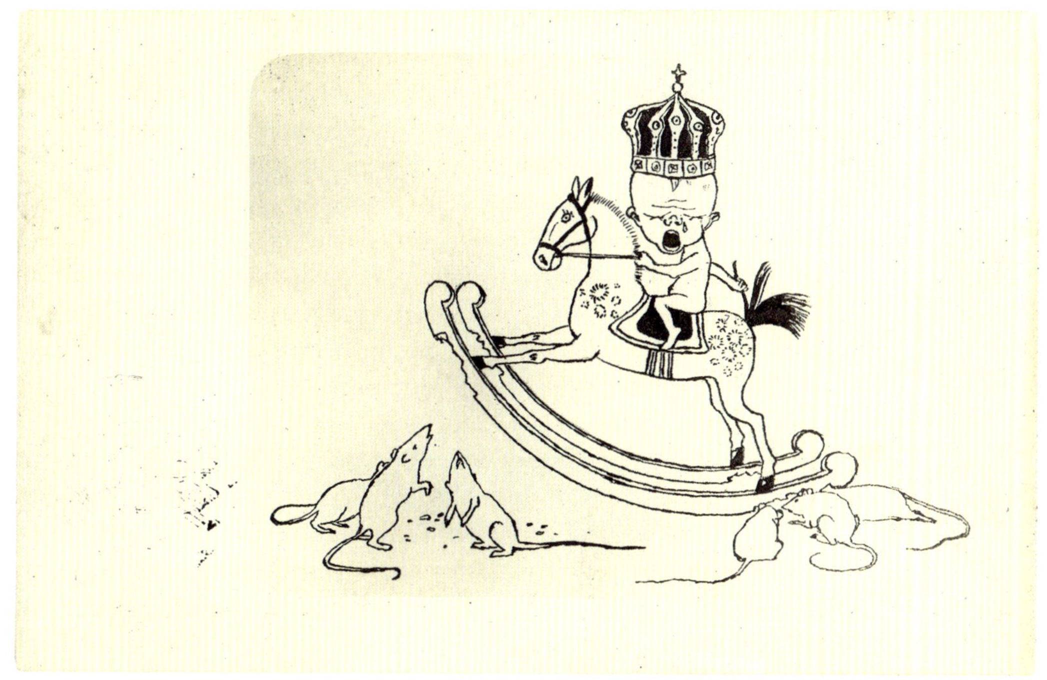

Anonymous artist. Caricature of Nicholas II as a crying baby. Published by the Socialist-Revolutionary Party, circa 1905.

husband was the publicist Vasilii Vodovozov, was a committed revolutionary with an extensive police record. Although already known to the authorities before this time, the Okhrana identified her in April that year as a member of the Socialist-Revolutionary Party's Kiev Committee, operating under the codename 'Shelkovistaia' ['Silky'].[19]

One month after her unmasking, Vodovozova applied to the Saint Petersburg censor for permission to produce a series of prints depicting Russian writers. The censorship committee, apparently unaware of her revolutionary credentials, allowed all except one to pass (a portrait of the theorist Petr Lavrov).[20] In March 1906, following the partial relaxation in postcard regulations, Vodovozova received permission to print images of the revolutionaries Ivan Kaliaev and Petr Polivanov, and shortly afterwards, successfully submitted a request for a far more extensive group of anti-government portraits, each to be printed in editions of five hundred copies.[21] Many of her works were commissioned from S. V. Kulzhenko, one of the largest commercial printing houses in Kiev.[22]

In mid-1906, Vodovozova either moved or expanded her publishing activities to Saint Petersburg, where her husband was now living. Over the summer, she placed advertisements in *Byloe* [*The Past*] offering a portrait album and separate prints of activists formerly imprisoned in Shlisselburg Fortress.[23] These were marketed under the trade name 'V. P. Vodovozova – publisher of portraits and pictures', and the address provided was for

Nasha zhizn [Our Life], a socialist-orientated bookshop in the city centre.[24] Nothing else is known about Vodovozova until January 1907, when the governor of Kiev ordered the confiscation of two photographic postcards of revolutionaries. Vodovozova's name is not mentioned, but as Kulzhenko was the printer, it seems likely she was the publisher.[25]

A letter from the following year survives in which Vodovozova asks Boris Orzhikh, a Socialist-Revolutionary publisher based in Japan, to send her a selection of revolutionary portraits for possible publication. It is clear, however, that by this time government repression had put an end to her endeavours to propagate anti-government postcards. 'At the moment I am only collecting portraits like these,' Vodovozova wrote, 'but as far as printing them is concerned, we must wait for better times; I'll get them into print at the first available opportunity.'[26] The evidence suggests that this opportunity never came, and apart from a single, tantalising mention of her in 1918, nothing else is known of Vodovozova's further activities and ultimate fate.[27]

Anonymous photographer. *Vera Nikolaevna Figner*. Published by Vera Vodovozova and retailed by P. N. Chelli, Kiev, circa 1906.

Orzhikh was an old revolutionary hand and an experienced printer, who had at one time run an underground press for Narodnaia Volia in the south of Russia.[28] In April 1906, he helped to set up, and later became the editor of a twice-weekly Russian-language newspaper intended for distribution in the Russian Far East. The *Volia* newspaper and publishing house, which were based in Nagasaki, were not initially affiliated to any political group, but the Socialist-Revolutionary Party provided much of the start-up capital, and there were many sympathisers among the staff, not least Orzhikh himself. As a consequence, Socialist-Revolutionary ideology exerted a heavy influence from the outset, and in March 1907 Volia was officially appended to the Party's Far Eastern Group.[29]

After the newspaper was fully established, propaganda production expanded to include other forms of anti-government material, including books, pamphlets, illustrated albums, and postcards. Output of all these items was extensive, and as the business continued to grow, Volia was required to take on five Japanese employees to help with the increasing workload. Between April 1906 and March 1907, the firm reportedly published up to 20,000 postcards, mainly comprising portraits of revolutionary activists and anti-government cartoons, the majority of which were lifted directly from Russian and European satirical journals.[30] The postcards were printed on both card and thin paper, and in a reference to the recent Russo-Japanese War, many carry an emblem of soldiers on the reverse.

Russian prisoners of war offered a good local market, but as Vodovozova's letter implies, the firm's reach extended far beyond the country's borders.[31] Much of its printed output was dispatched from Nagasaki and the Russian post office in Shanghai to buyers and Party activists in the Far East, but Volia's accounts testify to a remarkably widespread customer

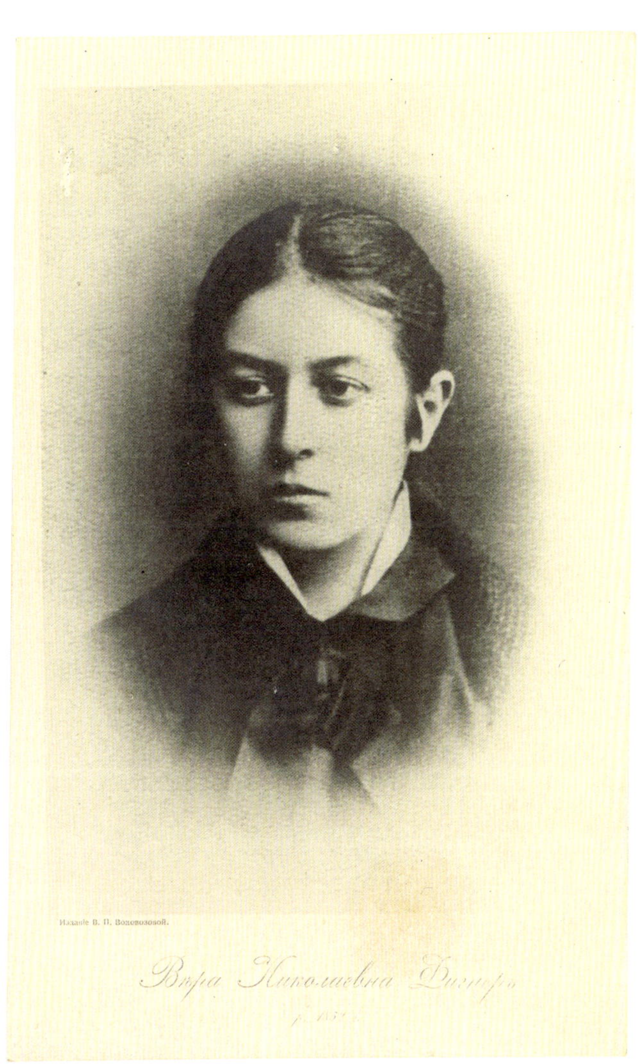

Изданіе В. П. Водовозовой.

Вѣра Николаевна Фигнеръ

р. 185[illegible] г.

pool that stretched from Vladivostok to San Francisco.[32] In March 1907, Volia's operations were transferred to Siberia, where affiliates had been heavily involved in organising revolutionary activity, and that same month the newspaper was closed.[33] Publishing work continued in Nagasaki until 1910, and Orzhikh emigrated to Chile the following year. He died in Santiago in 1947.

Postcards in the Provinces

In comparison to the Social Democrats, all-too little is known about Socialist-Revolutionary postcard manufacturing and distribution, largely a result of the absence of any first-hand accounts of their activities in this sphere. The names of most of the front companies they used, the individuals involved, the printers commissioned, even much of the content of their postcards remains obscure. However, what does exist is a wide-ranging record of its economic aspects in the provinces. The financial records of provincial Socialist-Revolutionary groups, now held in the Party archives in Amsterdam, provide a unique insight into propaganda production and dissemination in cities beyond Saint Petersburg and Moscow, enabling a much more detailed examination of the publishing difficulties that the Party faced.

The Central Committee required all smaller cells to submit regular financial reports, many of which were subsequently published in the official Party organs. Openness served to highlight monetary support, as well as to expose Socialist-Revolutionary activities to public scrutiny, thereby hinting at the secrecy of government finances, which were kept entirely hidden from the people. These statements of income and expenditure vary in the periods they cover and in the information they impart, but together they offer a comprehensive guide to how the Party earned and spent its money. As with their publishing efforts, many cells were lax about sending in reports, but the situation improved after autumn 1906.[34] Most examples are from this later period.

The statements are not infallible. In order to reduce mandatory contributions to the Party centre, few Socialist-Revolutionary groups declared all their income, particularly in respect of expropriations. Where postcards are mentioned, the subject matter is never revealed, and it is rarely clear whether the cards themselves were bought, received from central party structures, or printed by the revolutionaries themselves. Furthermore, runs of accounts are usually incomplete – many were either lost, destroyed during police raids, or not compiled.[35] The opportunities for comparing production and sales across regions and time periods are therefore limited. But these difficulties notwithstanding, the accounts remain one of the only available sources of information on postcard manufacturing and distribution outside the capital.[36]

Postcards are more commonly found in provincial accounts not because sales were more prevalent outside Moscow and Saint Petersburg, but because the statements submitted by regional groups deal with smaller sums and therefore usually contain greater detail. Of the approximately fifty-eight locations from which financial records survive, over a third of them list income derived from selling postcards.[37] Given the deficiencies of the records, this is a remarkable figure, which yet further underlines their importance as a propaganda medium.[38] Moreover, it is evident that the Party's postcards had an extraordinary reach, with sales recorded over vast tracts of the Empire, from the northwest of Russia to the Caspian Sea, from the Pale of Settlement to Siberia.

Sales were strongest in Western European Russia, particularly in the so-called 'Central Region', which had Moscow as its hub. This was the industrial heartland of the country, and the majority of the Party's support in this area came from the proletariat. Groups reporting profits here include Kostroma, which had a large textile industry, Tula, Elets, and Nizhnii Novgorod, similarly, towns densely populated with factories. Trade was also widespread in the 'Northern Region', the name given by the Party to the wider area radiating out from Saint Petersburg. Sales are registered in Novgorod, Pskov, and Vologda, all of which had good links to the capital and a reliable consumer base, chiefly workers, students and white-collar professionals.

Unsurprisingly, sales reflect the areas in which the revolutionaries themselves were most active. In the Volga region, where much of the Party's core membership was to be found, committees in Saratov, Tsaritsyn, and Astrakhan sold postcards. Although a largely rural area, these towns were located in the more developed west, where the Party enjoyed modest support among workers. This was a predominantly urban market; sales in agricultural areas, such as western Ukraine, southern Russia and the north Caucasus, were meagre. The heavily industrialised Urals region, by contrast, is well represented. Zlatoust and Votkinsk, which had sizable armament factories nearby, as well as the larger cities of Viatka, Perm, and Ekaterinburg, all list income from postcards.

Evidence of provincial production is almost entirely absent. Printing costs were often listed under generic titles such as 'publishing', 'printing house' and 'technical equipment', and it may well be that related expenditure was subsumed under these headings. Nonetheless, accounts that explicitly mention postcard manufacturing are extremely rare. Of all the groups, only Viatka refers to printing expenses, while in their accounts for February through March 1907, Tula has a one-off entry marked 'postcards'.[39]

Publishing was one of the few ways in which provincial affiliates could generate a regular income, but these accounts confirm the conclusions of *Partiinye izvestiia* that most groups were either unable or unwilling to do much more than print off a few hectographic leaflets.

It is difficult to tell to what extent the Party administration in Saint Petersburg acted as a production facility for smaller groups, but the sparsity of expenses relating to provincial manufacturing suggests that the centre played a significant role in commissioning and disseminating postcards. Most of these would likely have been channelled to the regions through the Organisation Bureau, the leadership's primary mechanism for exerting control over the wider network. From the start of the Bureau's operations in early 1906, its role was to bring increased rigour to Socialist-Revolutionary activities by: maintaining financial and ideological links between the centre and outlying groups, communicating ideological directives, and overseeing the circulation of printed material.[40]

However, neither the publishers printing ideologically-consonant literature in the bigger cities, nor the Bureau itself could keep up with the huge demand for revolutionary material, and in the absence of any other readily available options, many provincial cells resorted to buying propaganda from commercial firms. The above-mentioned entry for Tula might refer to the cost of buying postcards as opposed to the cost of their production, but either way, accounts for Ekaterinburg and Pskov include specific references to 'buying postcards'.[41] This practice was less onerous for activists, but it resulted in far less profit for the Party. *Partiinye izvestiia*, deeply exercised over the phenomenon, thundered: 'This is how the capitalist accumulates his plunder!'[42]

While official and unofficial Party structures ensured that postcards were distributed across a wide geographical area, sales were erratic. In localities where postcards are mentioned, they will often be present in only one set of accounts, and very rarely in more than two or three. The revenue they generated was equally insubstantial. Good money was to be made in the larger cities, but in the provinces it was uncommon for postcard income to rise above a few tens of roubles a month. The market may have been broad, but the sporadic nature of sales and the scarcity of manufacturing outside the capital indicate that postcards were not exempt from the problems suffered by Party publishing as a whole.

Viatka Province

Viatka Province, now modern-day Kirov, is a predominantly rural area, located to the west of the Ural Mountains. I have chosen it for a more detailed look at regional Socialist-Revolutionary propaganda and agitation, not because the accounts of the groups operating there are the most representative, but because they are among the most complete. Furthermore, the Party Committee in Viatka is the only regional organisation to include both postcard production costs and sales figures in its records.[43] This automatically indicates a capability beyond that of many of its counterparts; nevertheless, the information conveyed in the Committee's reports, questionnaires and statements is broadly indicative of the ways in which the Party looked to spread its message in the regions.

The Province consisted of eleven administrative districts, governed from Viatka town. The latter had a population of around 25,000 and was the location of over fifty small industrial enterprises – mostly tanneries, chandleries, and distilleries.[44] Socialist-Revolutionary presence in the region dated back to the early part of the century, but the disorder in 1905 allowed for a marked expansion of Party activities. According to one report, the Viatka Committee operated openly after the October Manifesto, holding huge demonstrations, and even conducting talks with the local administration. 'Then the repression started, with mass deportations and arrests. There were Black Hundred pogroms and clashes.' Armed struggle was quickly suppressed and soon afterwards a state of enhanced security was imposed.[45]

Government crackdowns wreaked havoc with the Committee's activities, and it was some months before the group could get back on its feet. In June 1906, the date from which the accounts start, Socialist-Revolutionary operations in the area were divided between two Committees, based in Viatka and Sarapul.[46] Numbers fluctuated, but in early 1907 the main cadre in Viatka, which included a local branch of the Organisation Bureau, consisted of around forty people. The Viatka Committee presided over smaller Party groups in the nine administrative districts for which it was responsible, each made up of between five and thirteen activists.[47] It in turn formed part of the Urals Regional Committee, which reported back to the Central Committee.[48]

The official role of local Party committees was to: 'carry out propaganda, agitational and organisational work, issue proclamations, pamphlets, periodicals … and organise strikes, demonstrations and protests.'[49] In the latter half of 1906, the Viatka Committee succeeded in coordinating a few small workers' rallies, but no strikes. There were occasional clashes between peasants and officials, but the Committee had no armed groups under its control.[50] The failure of violent resistance late the previous year had shown that the local population was not yet sufficiently politicised to rise up en masse, and with no prospect of defeating the regime militarily, the Party's energies were primarily focused on propaganda, particularly in regard to upcoming elections to the Second Duma.

The long-term aim of the Viatka revolutionaries was to mobilise and agitate the local population in preparation for what they hoped would be an eventual showdown. This undertaking fell into two overlapping strands of activity. The first was organisational: creating political bodies through which to control and educate the masses, primarily consisting of peasant committees, workers' circles, brotherhoods, and unions. The second was ideological: producing and distributing anti-government propaganda in order to rouse and expand the political instincts of the local population. Both were complicated and expensive endeavours, and as the accounts show, they absorbed the vast majority of the time and the resources of the Socialist-Revolutionary groups in Viatka Province.

Between 1 June 1906 and 26 June 1907, the Viatka Committee devoted approximately forty-two percent of its total expenditure to propaganda activities, a sum slightly above average for provincial groups in Russia during this period.[51] Other regular outlays included paying off unspecified debts, regional travel, and so-called 'conspiratorial expenses,' but the only area that competes with propaganda in these, or any other Socialist-Revolutionary accounts, is that of charitable giving, principally supporting fellow Party members (including imprisoned activists) and making donations to the Political Red Cross. The Viatka Committee's accounts are unusual in not containing any entries for money given in support of local workers and peasants; in most areas this was a regular occurrence.[52]

Propaganda dissemination and agitation came under the auspices of the Viatka Organisation, which was described in one Party report as the largest and most established branch of the Organisation Bureau operating in the Urals.[53] In early 1907, there were around thirty activists from the Organisation based in Viatka itself (three quarters of the total number of revolutionaries operating there), as well as independent groups in four smaller districts: Glazov, Kotelnich, Slobodskoi and Nolinsk.[54] Activists carried out work across the Province, using study circles, classes, and propaganda to spread the Party's message among five key target audiences: the peasants, the workers, soldiers, students, and the intelligentsia. Together, they ministered to a population of just over three million people.[55]

In October 1906, the Viatka Committee was running eleven workers' circles and had influence over a small number of factories and workshops. However, unlike most other groups in the Urals, its operations were predominantly aimed at the peasantry. In each district of the Province there were mobile agitators who travelled through the countryside delivering literature, holding meetings, and giving lessons on the revolutionary cause. As of early 1907, the main Party cell in Viatka District had four or five itinerant activists, who between them were able to cover around fifty percent of the locality. Supporting them were sympathetic local teachers, enlightened

After Carl Hassmann. *The Russian Crown.* Published by Volia, Nagasaki, circa 1906. Based on an illustration done for the cover of *Puck*, New York, 17 December 1905.

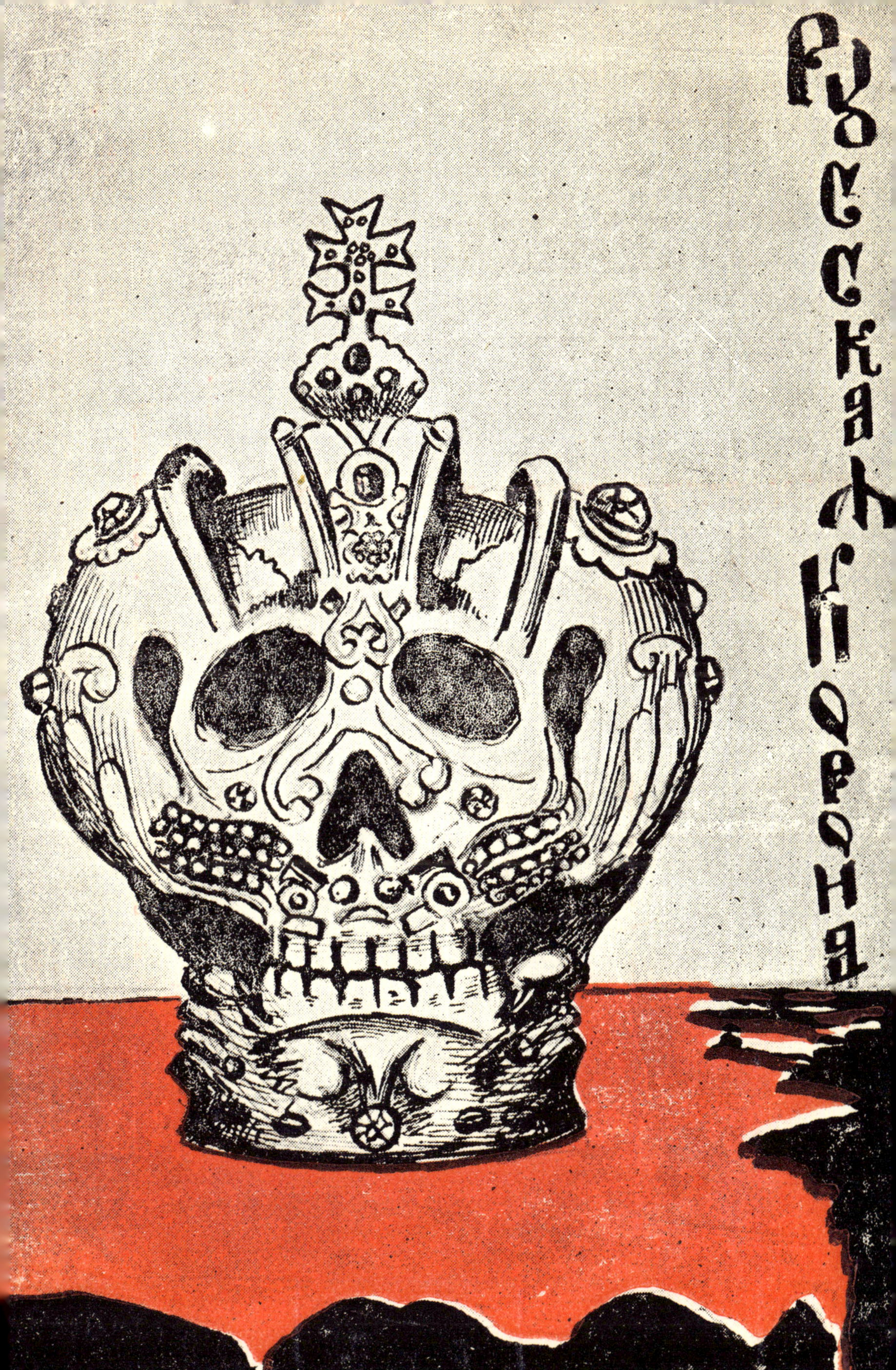
Русская Корона

members of the Zemstvo and the intelligentsia, and a few class-conscious workers and peasants.[56]

The task of these revolutionaries was never easy. Although much of the population was unhappy with the status quo, agitators regularly came up against hostile reactions in rural areas. One Party communiqué reported that many peasants were still determined supporters of the Tsar, and that some agitators had been beaten up during the course of their work.[57] The gulf between the masses and the revolutionaries was still great. Quite apart from the trouble posed by both the authorities and the locals, the Viatka Committee still had to contend with a range of practical difficulties, the most serious of which were reported to be: 'lack of party literature, shortage of personnel, financial difficulties, and the wide dispersion of the villages.'[58]

Propaganda Production and Dissemination in Viatka Province

The Party's efforts to boost legal publishing in autumn 1906 had little tangible effect in the provinces, where commercial production remained uncommon. Viatka followed the prevailing trend towards conspiratorial enterprise, but its publishing achievements were still better than most. In mid-1906, the Committee had its own print works, as well as a hectographic and mimeographic press. Over the previous circa eight months, it had manged to print around 123,000 proclamations and pamphlets. The average run of the former was 3,000 copies, but on occasion, such as with the Vyborg Manifesto, it went up to 16,000. Nonetheless, despite a gradual increase in activity over this period, these quantities were reported as being insufficient for all except a few areas.[59]

In the second half of the year, the Committee continued to issue a few items of propaganda every month. However, their main publishing activities during this period were focused on the complicated and expensive task of producing a newspaper, aimed at the rural population. *Krestianskii listok* [*The Peasant News-sheet*] was launched in late spring 1906, and thereafter came out roughly every six weeks, initially in a run of 1,000 copies, but later rising to five times that amount.[60] Its content was not extensive, consisting only of a few rousing articles spread across a single folded sheet, but carrying out such a project was a serious achievement, requiring organisation and initiative, as well as writers well-versed in Socialist-Revolutionary ideology.[61]

According to Party regulations, regional committees were required to disseminate literature among smaller organisations without the facilities to print their own.[62] As few provincial cells managed to produce more than a handful of hectographic leaflets and pamphlets, most were heavily reliant on material from larger groups. In Viatka Province, the Viatka and Sarapul Committees both received propaganda from the Urals Regional

Committee, and they in turn printed and distributed propaganda among smaller cells in their own province. One district cell in Viatka also reported being sent literature from as far away as Moscow and Saint Petersburg.[63] But as another was swift to point out, deliveries of literature came all too infrequently and were often woefully inadequate in quantity.[64]

Topping up supplies in this manner helped to make up for regional deficiencies in technical and organisational capacity and gave a vital boost to the stocks available for agitational purposes. Much of the literature was also sold on, another way in which the leadership propped up its less efficient members. Propaganda distribution can thus be seen as a unifying tool within the Party itself, establishing an ideological and financial link between headquarters, regional committees and provincial cells. Delivery failures and shortages therefore speak not only to the disorganisation of the centre, but also to the inadequacy of its relationship with the periphery, a problem that greatly affected the Party's efforts to project a uniform political message.

The consequence of regional negligence and deficient trading networks can be seen in the widespread practice of buying literature from private firms, a phenomenon repeatedly criticised by *Partiinye izvestiia*, which described it as a sad indictment of the contemporary state of Party publishing.[65] This expensive custom was a regular habit for almost every Socialist-Revolutionary group. Provincial accounts from Novgorod to Tsarinsk, and Pskov to Krasnoiarsk, all contain entries for purchasing books and pamphlets. Even in areas where local committees were resourceful enough to print their own propaganda, the literature they disseminated was still a combination of self-produced, commissioned, and bought. All except one of the Viatka accounts include an entry for the 'purchase of books'.[66]

Postcard Production in Viatka

The Viatka Committee's statement for July 1906 records an expense of forty-two roubles for 'postcard work'.[67] In terms of expenditure, the sum is noteworthy, amounting to just under nine percent of the group's total outlay for the month. Although the phrasing is unclear, the entry probably refers to the price of commissioning postcards from a commercial printer, as opposed to the cost of design work. We are in the dark as to what the images depicted, but if the previous supposition is correct, it is unlikely that the works were unique to the Viatka Committee. Although the Party did produce some original political cartoons, most Socialist-Revolutionary postcards consisted of revolutionary portraits and generic reproductions of socialist-themed paintings.

Even in the regions, where the population was less well-off, less politicised and less heavily concentrated, postcards were still sold rather than

Next spread

Anonymous artist. *How Money Is Obtained Nowadays.* No publication details, circa 1906.

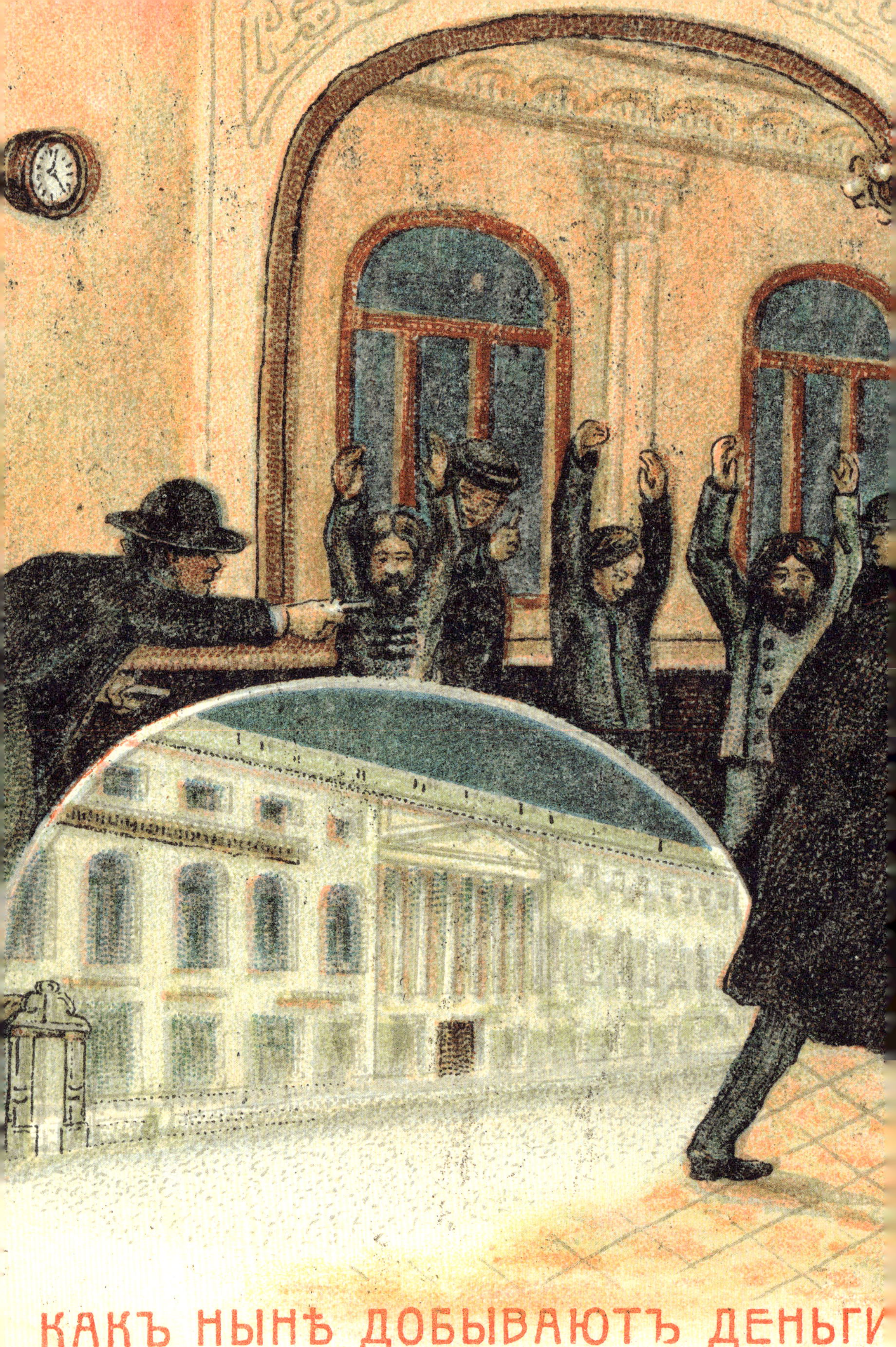

КАКЪ НЫНѢ ДОБЫВАЮТЪ ДЕНЬГИ

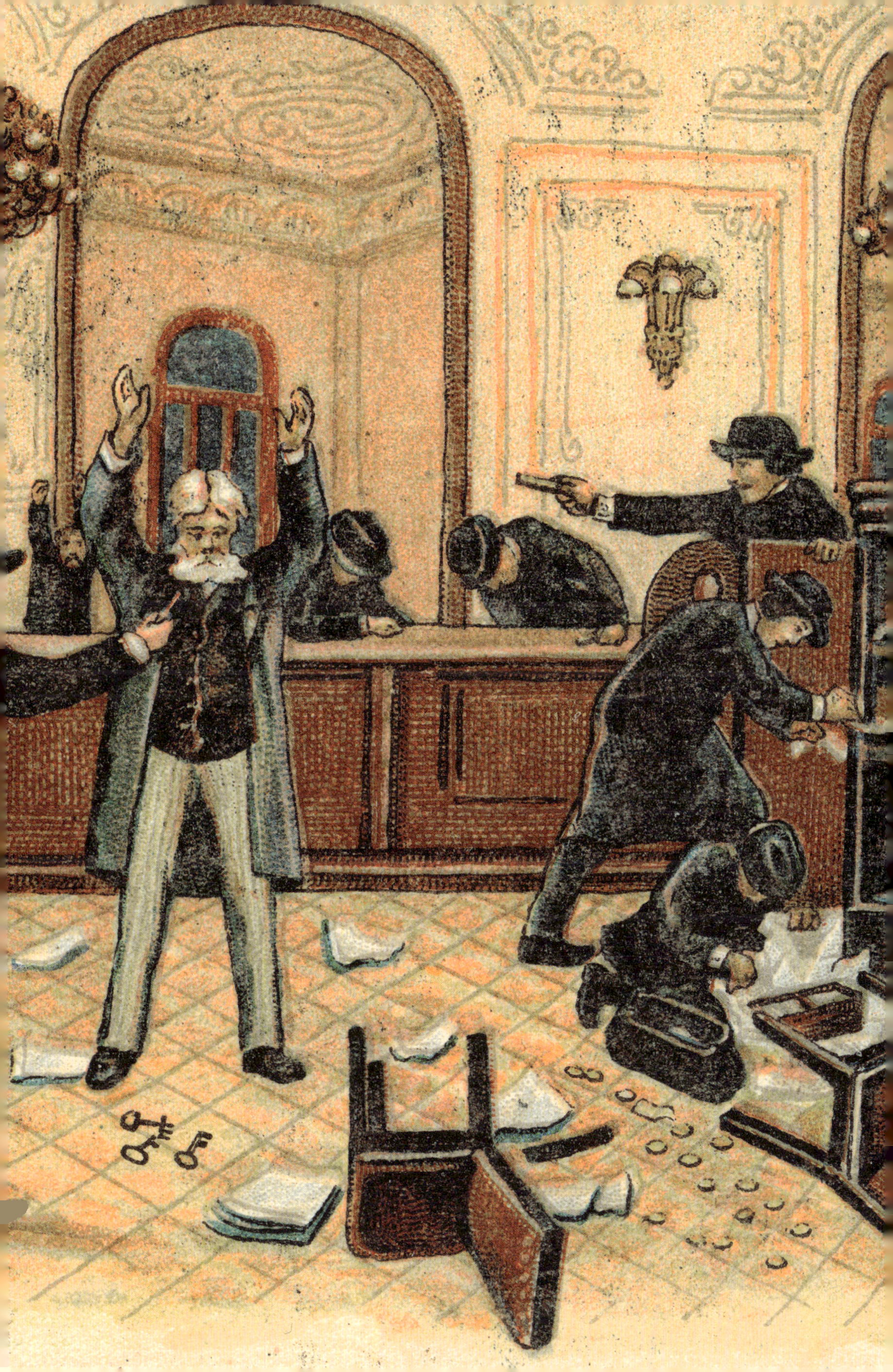

given away. In the month they were printed, the postcards generated fifty-two roubles, or around ten percent of the Committee's income, and over the next four months they raised a further fourteen roubles twenty-five kopecks. But despite this modest profit, the venture was not immediately repeated.[68] The Committee's only other postcard-related expense came in January 1907, when one rouble forty was spent on 'books and postcards'. It is clear, therefore, that selling postcards never became a game-changing activity. Between June 1906 and June 1907, they comprised under two percent of the Committee's total revenue.

Both the occasional nature of the Committee's postcard endeavours and the comparatively small amount of income that they generated are common to other provincial accounts, which indicate that profits from postcard sales rarely exceeded five percent of a group's total monthly income. More seriously, these unremarkable earnings are also replicated in the far more widespread practice of selling written propaganda. Between June 1906 and June 1907, literature sales contributed approximately seven percent of the Committee's earnings, less than was raised from a single concert in July. Any addition to its funds was a help, but as it stood the Party's hope that publishing and selling propaganda might enable provincial groups to cover all their operating costs was wholly unrealistic.

The Viatka Committee's only regular source of income came from membership dues, which contributed just one and a half percent to their overall income. Three times that amount was generated from selling lottery tickets. No wonder then that the leadership was so concerned about establishing reliable sources of income. Viatka received support from the centre only latterly, but it still depended for over a third of its funds on public donations. When opposition support dropped away in 1907, the Committee's income fell away dramatically, as it did across the revolutionary divide.[69] The consequences were nearly terminal – lack of structural unity, discipline, and loyalty meant that when the Tsarist authorities came knocking, the Party collapsed with great rapidity.

⁎

The combination of a commercially-run publishers' union and the dedicated work of a concentrated cadre of Party activists enabled the Socialist-Revolutionaries to print and disseminate enormous quantities of material in what were often highly challenging circumstances. Nonetheless, the Party's failure to institute wholesale organisational and financial reform after Bloody Sunday led over the long term to increasing problems in maintaining propaganda production, distribution lines, and income. It is unlikely that the Socialist-Revolutionaries were unique in suffering from such difficulties; however, it is evident that the Party's lack of a solid structural and ideological core severely weakened its efforts to produce anti-government propaganda in the circumstances of greater freedom that followed the October Manifesto.[70]

But regardless of the issues that the Socialist-Revolutionaries faced in publishing and distributing their propaganda, the Party's activities in the postcard sphere offer emphatic confirmation of the importance of the medium as a tool of mass propaganda, providing clear evidence of its spread among groups across the length and breadth of the Empire. By late 1905, opposition to the regime had extended far beyond the narrow layer of the urban population who had once dominated the revolutionary movement; the tentacles of dissent now reached deep into the provinces. Postcards, as an accessible and popular medium, proved instrumental in conveying and representing opposition politics throughout Russia as the nation at large slowly progressed towards the modern age.

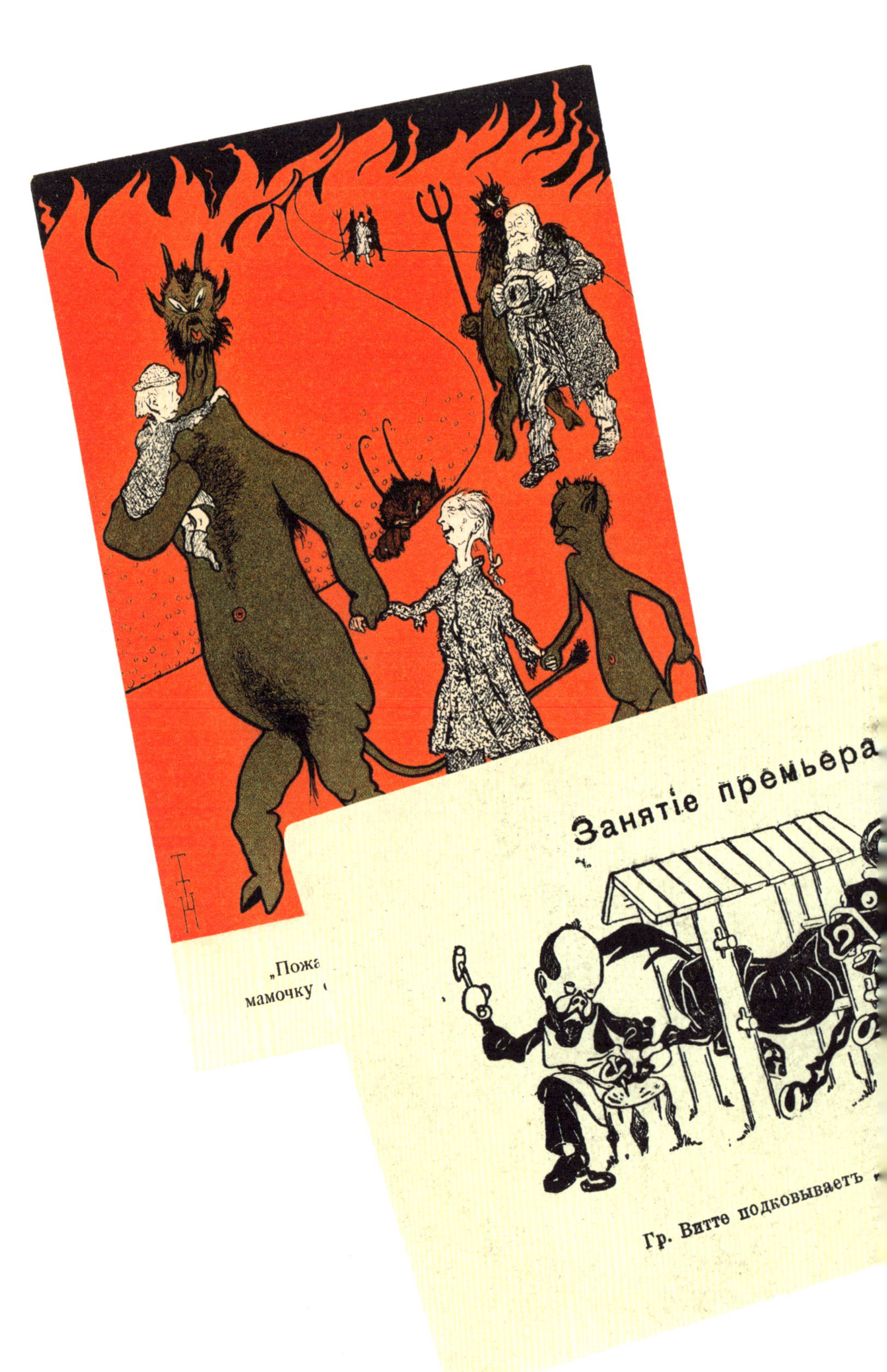
„Пожа
мамочку
Занятiе премьера
Гр. Витте подковываетъ

PRIVATE PUBLISHERS, PRINTERS, AND ARTISTS

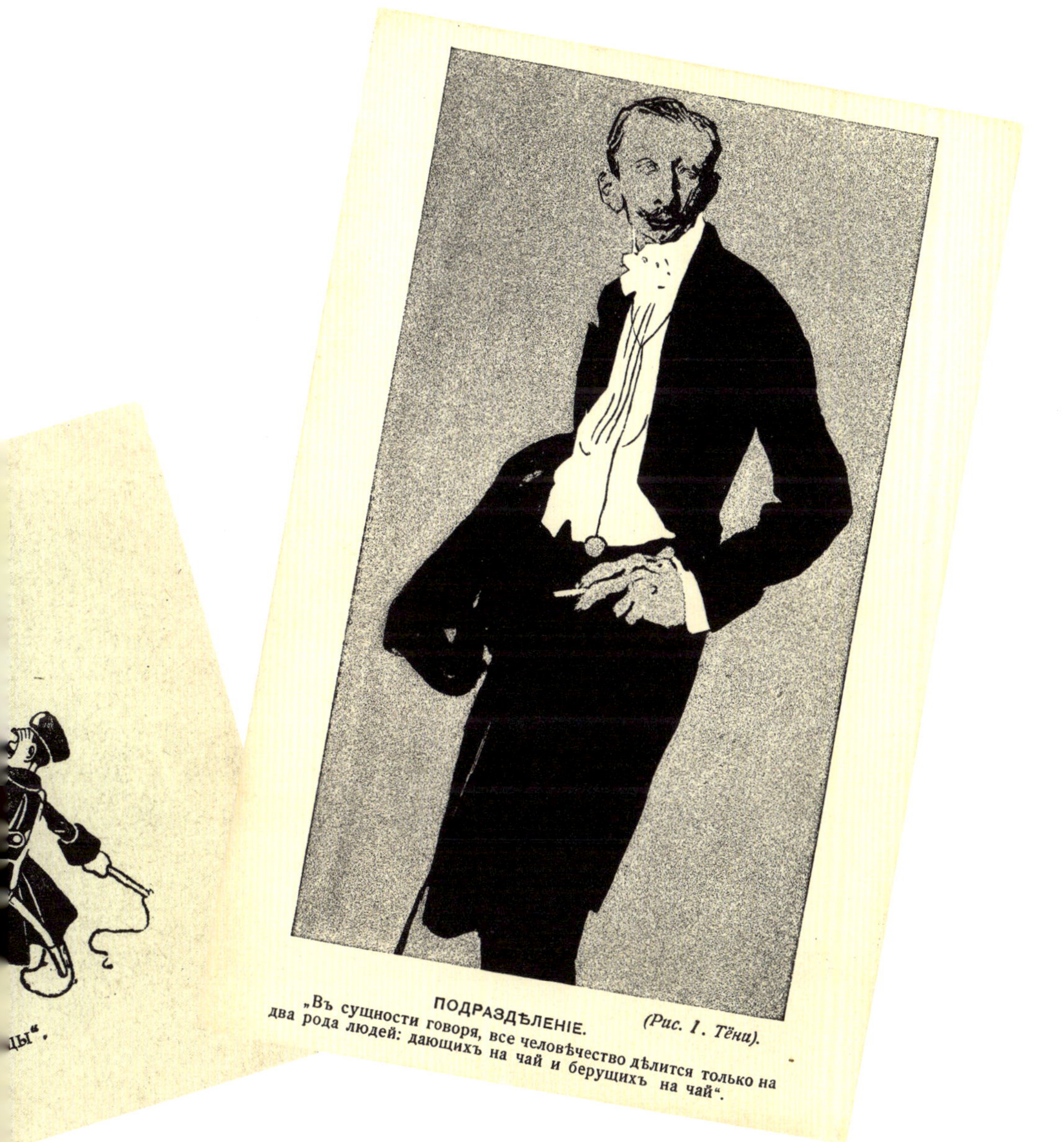

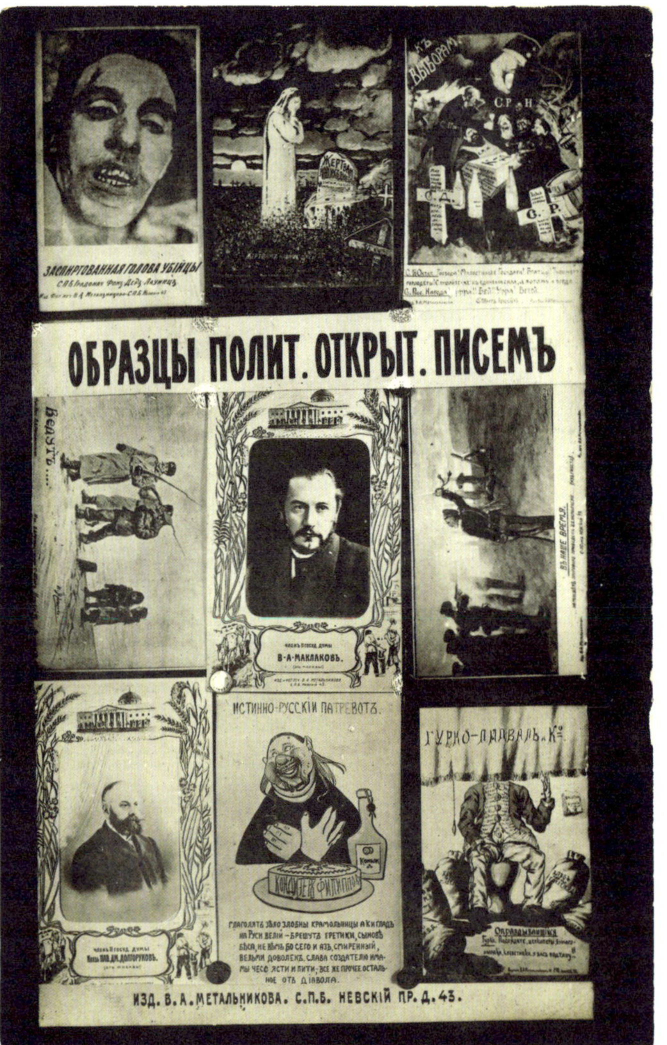
ОБРАЗЦЫ ПОЛИТ. ОТКРЫТ. ПИСЕМЪ
В-А-МАКЛАКОВЪ
ИСТИННО-РУССКIЙ ПАТРЕВОТЪ
ГЛАГОЛЯТЪ ЗѢЛО ЗЛОБНЫ КРАМОЛЬНИЦЫ АКИ ГЛАДЪ НА РУСИ ВЕЛИЙ – БРЕШУТЪ ЕРЕТИКИ, СЫНОВѢ БѢСА, НЕ ВѢМЪ БО СЕГО И АЗЪ, СМИРЕННЫЙ, ВЕЛЬМИ ДОВОЛЕНЪ. СЛАВА СОЗДАТЕЛЮ ИМАМЫ ЧЕСО ЯСТИ И ПИТИ; ВСЕ ЖЕ ПРОЧЕЕ ОСТАЛЬНОЕ ОТЪ ДIАВОЛА.
ИЗД. В. А. МЕТАЛЬНИКОВА. С.П.Б. НЕВСКIЙ ПР. Д. 43.

Private Publishers

Before 1905, the production of anti-government postcards was the near-exclusive preserve of the revolutionary parties. This changed after the October Manifesto, when many of the barriers that had previously barred the way to commercial publishers were lowered and the way was opened to anyone with a degree of enterprise, money, or artistic skill. Those who became involved covered the gamut of the print trade; some were artists, illustrators, or photographers, others were publishers, owners of printing houses, photographic studios or bookshops. Their experience and commitment varied greatly – among them were novices and professionals, activists and capitalists. What united them was the scent of opportunity, whether for money, art or rebellion.

Most private publishers were bona fide opponents of the regime, but the parameters of their engagement ran the breadth of the political spectrum. Among them were liberals who believed in the possibility of changing the bathwater without throwing out the baby, and revolutionary hardliners, who rejected all prospect of reform while the Tsar remained in power. This great diversity of outlook resulted in a broad range of postcards, both in respect of their content and also their quality. Whereas at the top end of the market, many original chromolithographic cartoons were produced, at the bottom end, much of the imagery was identical to that being printed by the revolutionary parties.

Given the overlap of imagery, ideology, and infrastructure, any attempt to divide private and revolutionary publishers into two distinct categories is problematic. Indeed, there is no easy separation to be made, along either practical or political lines. In broad terms, however, a difference can be established in their respective economic aims: while revolutionary publishers used publishing revenue to help fund the Party, private publishers used it to help fund themselves. This does not mean that the impetus for private production was purely commercial in character, or that it was always at ideological odds with the revolutionaries; only that not all the profit raised from the postcards was ultimately directed at fomenting violent insurrection.

Chromolithographic Satire: Shipovnik

During the first flush of private production in autumn 1905, the market was awash with uncensored chromolithographic postcard caricatures and narrative cartoons. The majority were printed anonymously or at most carry only the initials of the artist, printer or publisher. The freedoms of the October Manifesto were still fragile, and at this stage few were prepared to take the risk of acting openly. Despite repeated attempts to discover their names,

Previous spread from left to right

Thomas Theodor Heine. *Please, Kind Devil, Can My Mother Also Come Here, Your Place is so Warm.* Published by Shipovnik and printed by Golike and Vilborg, 1906.

Evlampii Kosvintsev. *The Prime Minister at Work. Count Witte Nails on the Four Freedoms.* No publication details, circa February 1906.

Eduard Thöny. *Categorisation: In Essence, All Humanity Is Divided up into Two Categories of People: Those Who Serve Tea, and Those Who Drink it.* Published by Shipovnik and printed by Golike and Vilborg, 1906.

Opposite

Vasilii Metalnikov. *Samples of Political Postcards.* Saint Petersburg, 1907.

Next spread

Anonymous artist. *Now You Can See for Yourself that Heartfelt Relations Cost Me a Great Deal More Than Violence.* No publication details, circa late 1905. Caricature of Dmitrii Trepov.

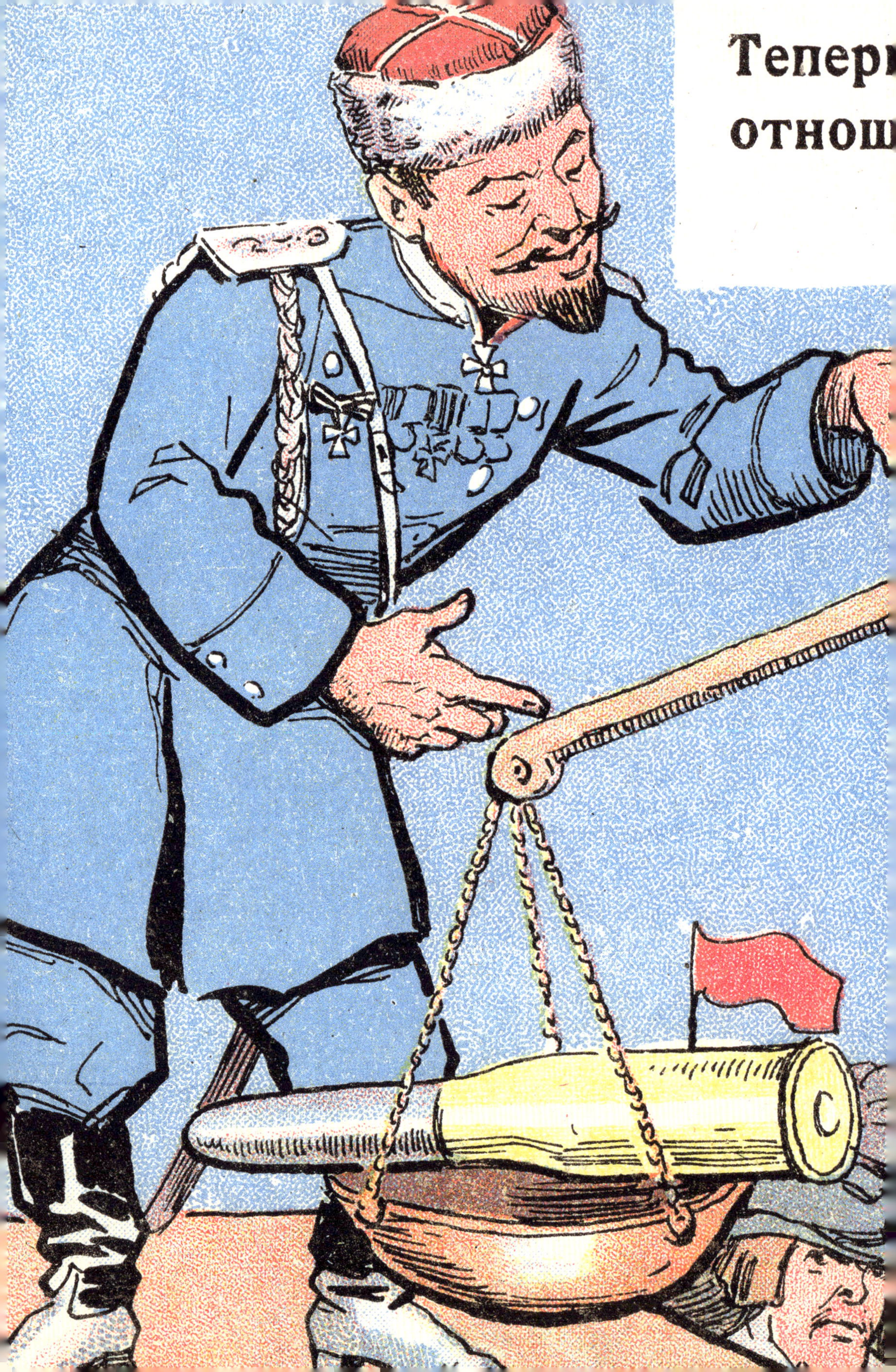
Тепер
отнош

ы видите сами, что сердечныя
я для меня стоятъ гораздо выше
насилія.

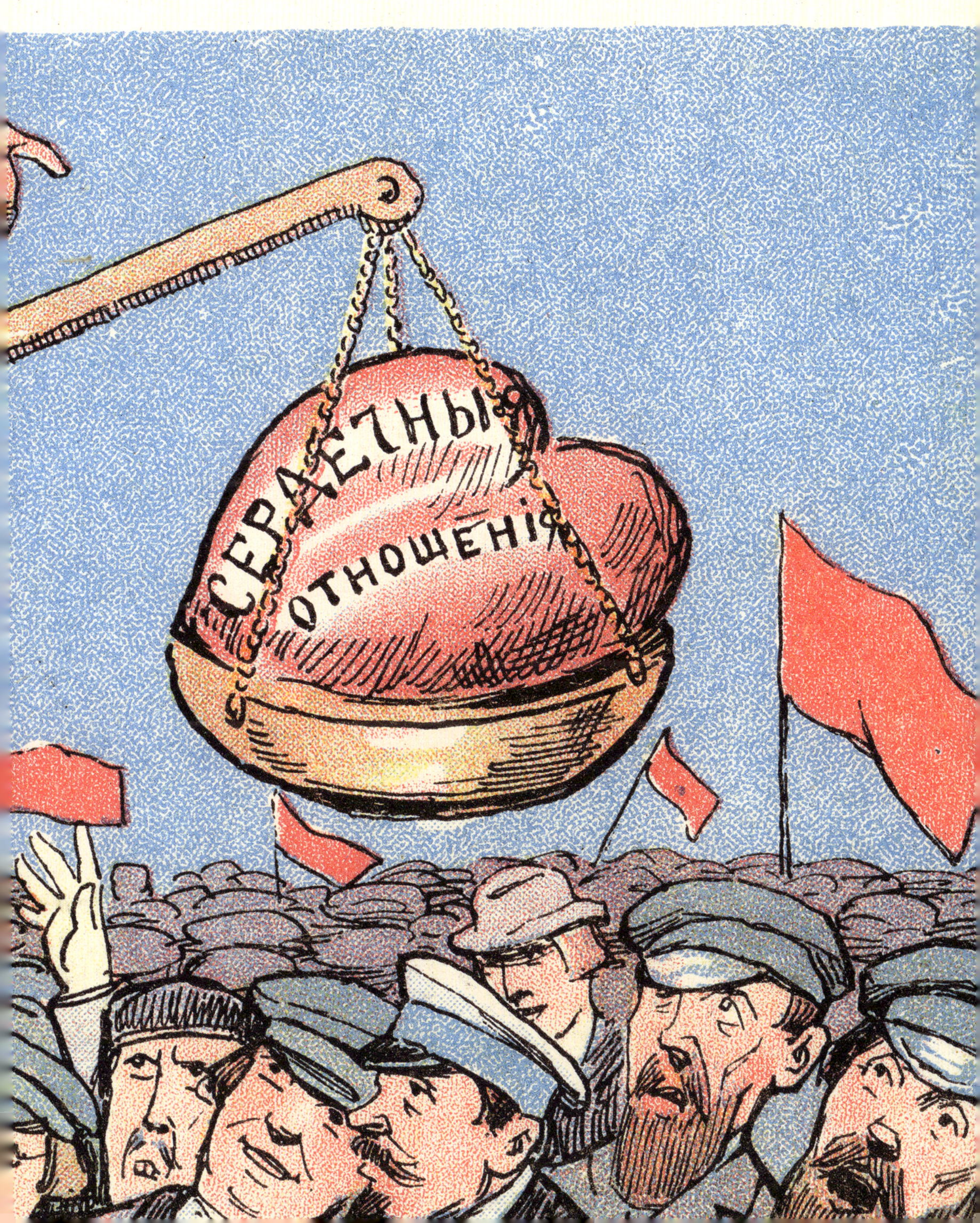

there is still not a single publisher of original colour satires from the Days of Freedom who I have managed to positively identify. In this, however, I am in illustrious company – the Imperial police proved equally unsuccessful in tracking down those responsible at the time they were produced.

Although the revolutionary parties were involved in printing photomechanical cartoons, they do not appear to have had much (or any) involvement in the production of original, higher quality images. In postcard terms, chromolithographic satires were luxury items – expensive to commission, print and buy – and thus very different from the cheap photomechanical or typographic images that the revolutionary parties are known to have made up to this point. Improvements to their political and economic circumstances after Bloody Sunday may have afforded the radicals greater opportunity, but money was still tight. For organisations intent on spreading their message as widely as possible, affordability of production and ease of acquisition always took priority over quality.[1]

Chromolithographic cartoons and revolutionary photomechanical postcards shared the same basic objective of conveying a political message in pictorial form, but the quality of their production and originality of their imagery suggests that publishers of the former were also concerned with propagating 'fine art' in the manner espoused by the Society of Saint Eugenia. This takes them yet further away from the revolutionaries, for whom the dividing line between good and bad art was grounded in politics not aesthetics, and instead brings them closer into line with the illustrated

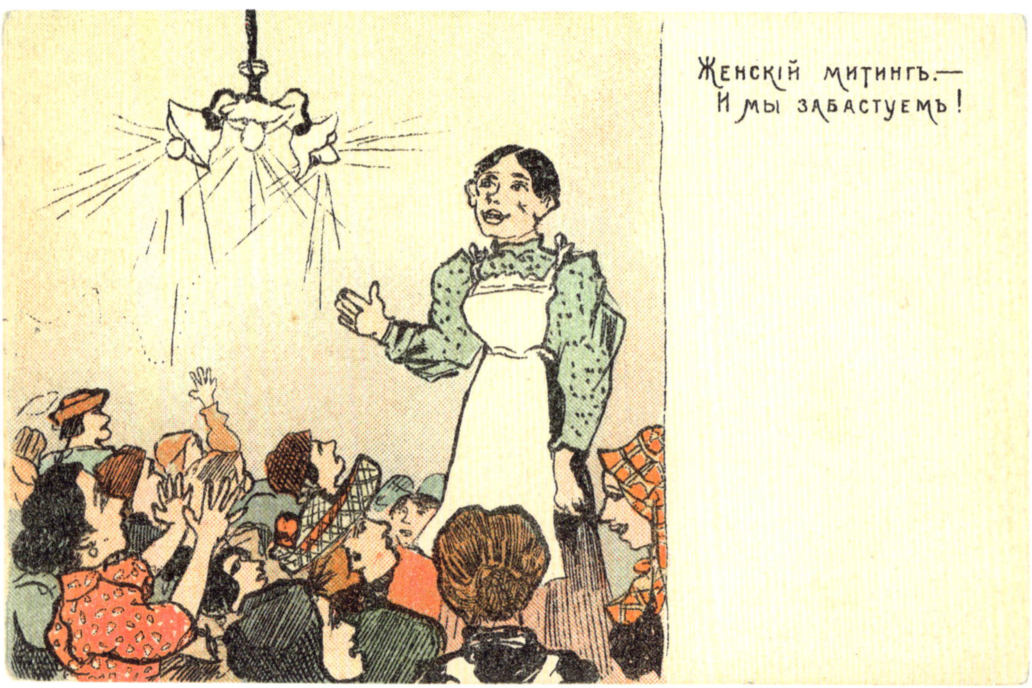

Anonymous artist. *Women's Political Meeting. We're Going on Strike!* No publication details, circa late 1905.

journals of the period, which at their very best were self-consciously high-end literary and artistic productions. Links between the two, however, are not easy to find.

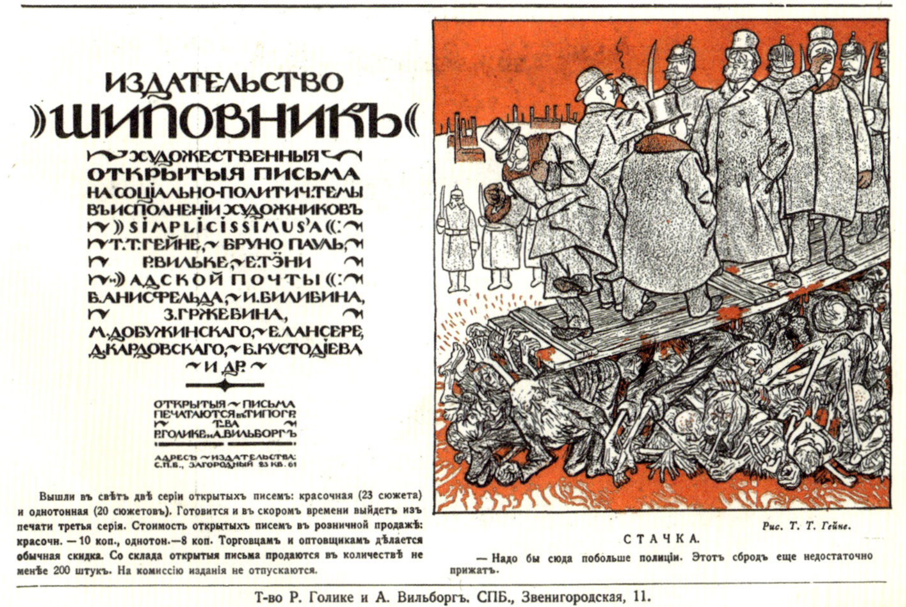

Advertisement for Shipovnik Postcards in *Adskaia pochta*, No. 3, Saint Petersburg, 1906.

In May 1906, the short-lived satirical journal *Adskaia pochta* [*Hellish Post*] carried an advertisement for two series of legally printed 'picture postcards on socio-political themes.'[2] These were the first publications of Shipovnik, a publishing house set up by the artist and editor of the journal Zinovii Grzhebin, and his partner Solomon Kopelman. Grzhebin was a man of firm anti-autocratic views, but is perhaps best characterised as a left-leaning liberal as opposed to a socialist. Kopelman, however, was more radical. He had originally trained as a lawyer, but had only recently been able to return to Russia after having fled the country while on bail, in order to escape a charge of distributing illegal literature.

While at art school in Munich in the early 1900s, Grzhebin had become friendly with a group of illustrators from the German journal *Simplicissimus*.[3] This publication was a pioneer of European satire, characterised by its daring political content. Although banned in Russia, it was still well-known there and much admired. 'I remember the interest and enjoyment we felt on those rare occasions we were able to get hold of a copy,' recalled artist Evgenii Lansere, adding, 'no one read the articles but the illustrations were very popular.'[4] These illustrations went far beyond anything that could appear in Russia, attacking not only government policies, but also the very societies over which they presided.

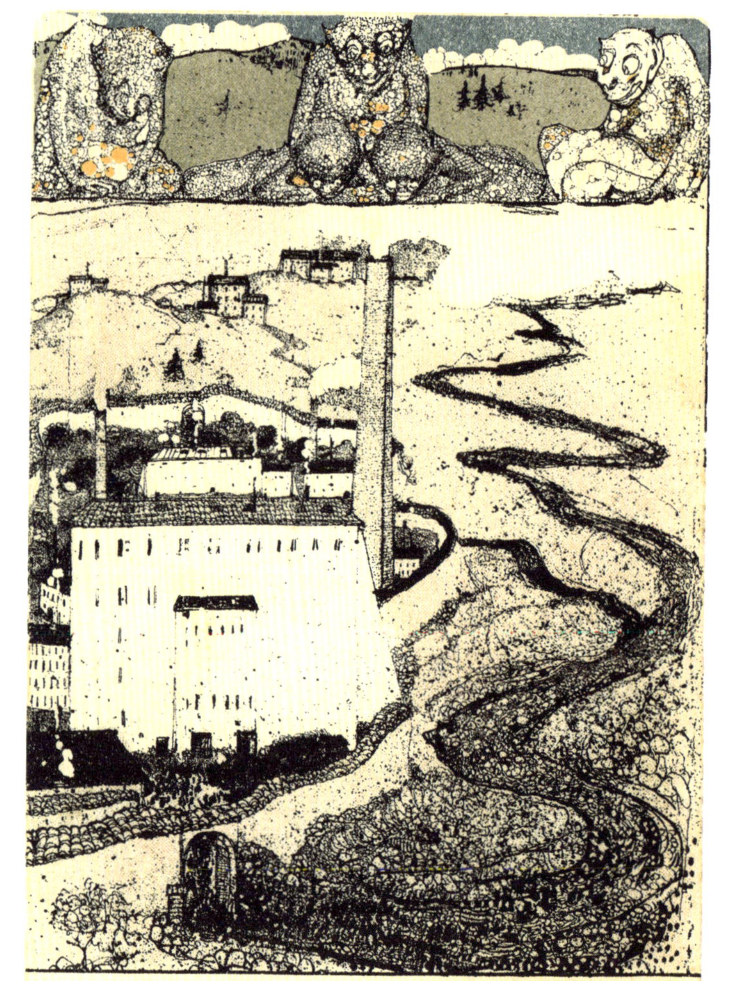

(Рис. Б. Анисфельда).

Кошмаръ капитализма.

On his return home in 1905, Grzhebin was inspired to create his own illustrated magazine based on *Simplicissimus*. This came to fruition later in the year as *Zhupel* [*Bugbear*], a boldly anti-government publication that brought together many of the leading lights of Russian modernism. The first number appeared in November, but it was shut down after only three issues. Undeterred by an imminent court appearance, Grzhebin co-founded *Adskaia pochta*. By the time the advertisement for Shipovnik appeared, he had already been sentenced to six months in jail and had further charges pending. His punishment also included a five-year ban on publishing or editing a periodical, but this did little to curtail his activities.

Boris Anisfeld. *The Nightmare of Capitalism*. Published by Shipovnik and printed by Golike and Vilborg, Saint Petersburg, 1906.

The initial plan was to publish twenty-three colour and twenty black-and-white satirical postcards.[5] The designs for these works were, with one exception, all drawn by foreign artists working for *Simplicissimus*, where many of them had previously been published.[6] The cartoons range in content from political lampoons of world leaders to satires denouncing the capitalist exploitation of workers. Noticeably absent, however, are any relating to Russia. The only image made by a Russian artist, Boris Anisfeld's *The Nightmare of Capitalism*, shows three squalid demons counting coins, while below them a factory billows smoke into a deadened landscape. Although resolutely socialist, the image is generic, as opposed to Russia-specific.

Cartoons on Russian subjects regularly appeared in *Simplicissimus*.[7] Most, however, featured the Tsar and as such were unconscionable subject matter for a legal publisher such as Shipovnik, all the more so given that Grzhebin had recently been up before the courts. In his place, individuals as diverse as Kaiser Wilhelm II, Franklin D. Roosevelt and the Ethiopian Negus serve as stand-ins. These all-powerful rulers appear alongside caricatures of their countries' administrative officials, soldiers, and ordinary subjects in what amounts to a near-total excoriation of worldly authority. Russia's own internal political situation may not be clearly visible, but the condemnation of the morally bankrupt ideals upon which it rested is plain enough.

Despite Grzhebin's avoidance of any overtly controversial subject matter in these two sets of postcards, it appears that he always did intend to publish a group of Russia-themed images. The original advertisement in *Adskaia pochta* includes an announcement for a third series of postcards, this time reproducing the work of the journal's Russian artists, including Ivan Bilibin, Mstislav Dobuzhinskii, Dmitrii Kardovskii, Evgenii Lansere, Boris Kustodiev, and Grzhebin himself. None were ever printed.

In July 1906, the fourth issue of *Adskaia pochta* was arrested and the journal closed down. Four months later, Grzhebin was still declaring his intention to publish the cards, but by this stage the atmosphere had turned.[8] The government was beginning to regain control over the wayward press, and publishers were no longer able to push the boundaries of acceptability

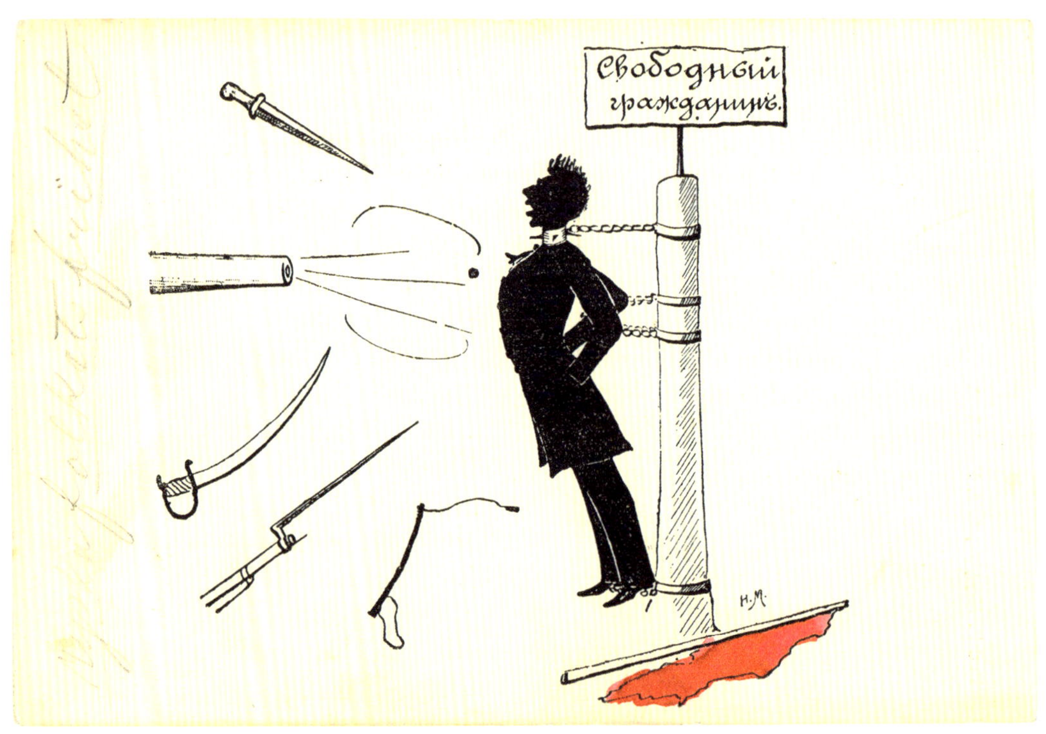

N. M. *Free Citizen.* Published by Nikolai Merder, Saint Petersburg, late 1905.

quite so freely as they had once done. Postcards by foreign artists on socialist themes were one thing, but political cartoons satirising Russian subjects were another matter altogether. Concerns about potential punitive measures, as well as the prospect of financial loss in the event of confiscation, likely dissuaded Grzhebin and Kopelman from going ahead with their plans.

In terms of anti-government postcard production, Shipovnik was exceptional. The existence of a legal publishing company, branded output, and a clear link to satirical journals, all mark it out. Nevertheless, the aesthetic rationale for its postcards formed part of a broader effort by liberal publishers and artists to introduce high art into the realms of opposition politics. In a letter to Maxim Gorky, sent in November 1906, Grzhebin described Shipovnik's ultimate purpose as being, 'to pursue two strands of life – socialism and beauty.'[9] This fusion of critical realism and fine artistry is reflected in the journals he edited, but it is significant that the medium chosen for Shipovnik was the postcard, long valued as a method of spreading good taste.

'We want to break into every sphere with proper art,' wrote Grzhebin. 'The average member of the public has developed a liking for decorative postcards. It turns out that when an illustration is reproduced on a postcard, it gets remarkable exposure, much more than in a special album, and all the more so than in a museum.'[10] Grzhebin had come to realise, like many other publishers before him, that the postcard's form and popularity made it an extraordinarily effective vehicle for disseminating ideas. As he rightly understood, the medium was now so much more than a mere correspondence card; it had become an object of desire, beauty, and social aspiration.

Shipovnik's use of celebrated illustrators and insistence on high production standards was a conscious attempt to emulate the Society of Saint Eugenia, still the gold standard of Russian postcard publishing. Advertisements all highlight the fact that Shipovnik postcards were printed on 'good quality paper' and manufactured by Golike and Vilborg, one of the best printing firms in the country, and one employed on many occasions by the Society itself. At ten kopecks for colour card and eight for black-and-white, Shipovnik's postcard output was aimed at a similarly discriminating audience. In fact, the only real difference between the two publishers was in the message that they were seeking to impart – whereas one was social, the other was socialist.

In February 1907, Shipovnik produced the first of its literary almanacs, the undertaking for which it is now best known. Sales of its *Simplicissimus* postcards (the only images it ever published) continued until at least 1909, far longer than almost all other anti-government images.[11] The firm was eventually shut down by the Bolsheviks in 1922.

Shipovnik was not the first publishing house to marry ideas about the communal role of postcards to an age of revolution, nor was it unique in its use of the medium to convey a politico-aesthetic message, but it was one of the largest and most sophisticated. Its images were the only socialist caricatures and cartoons to be advertised in the contemporary press, and it was the only newly established publisher of leftist postcards to have had its own trademark. Shipovnik means 'wild rose' in Russian, and for its emblem the firm used a stylised flower head framed by leaves and thorned stems. It was an appropriate choice for a company whose output was intended to represent the symbolic union of artistic beauty and political suffering.

Commercial Enterprise: Nikolai Merder

Other publishers shared Shipovnik's concern with disseminating 'good' political art, but in 1905 topicality came to compete with aesthetics as a way for publishers to make their products stand out from the crowd. Sophisticated design was in itself no match for revolutionary spectacle, as the Society of Saint Eugenia was made to realise.[12] This move towards current affairs was not new. Greater awareness and quicker delivery of information had prompted demand for images that reflected the wider world in which consumers lived, and as the postcard's focus shifted from word to image, it ceased to function only as a record of individual lives but also came to serve as a way of engaging in communal or national experience.

Next spread

Anonymous artist. *The Sun of Russian Freedom Has Been Smeared with Blood.* Published by Nikolai Merder, Saint Petersburg, late 1905.

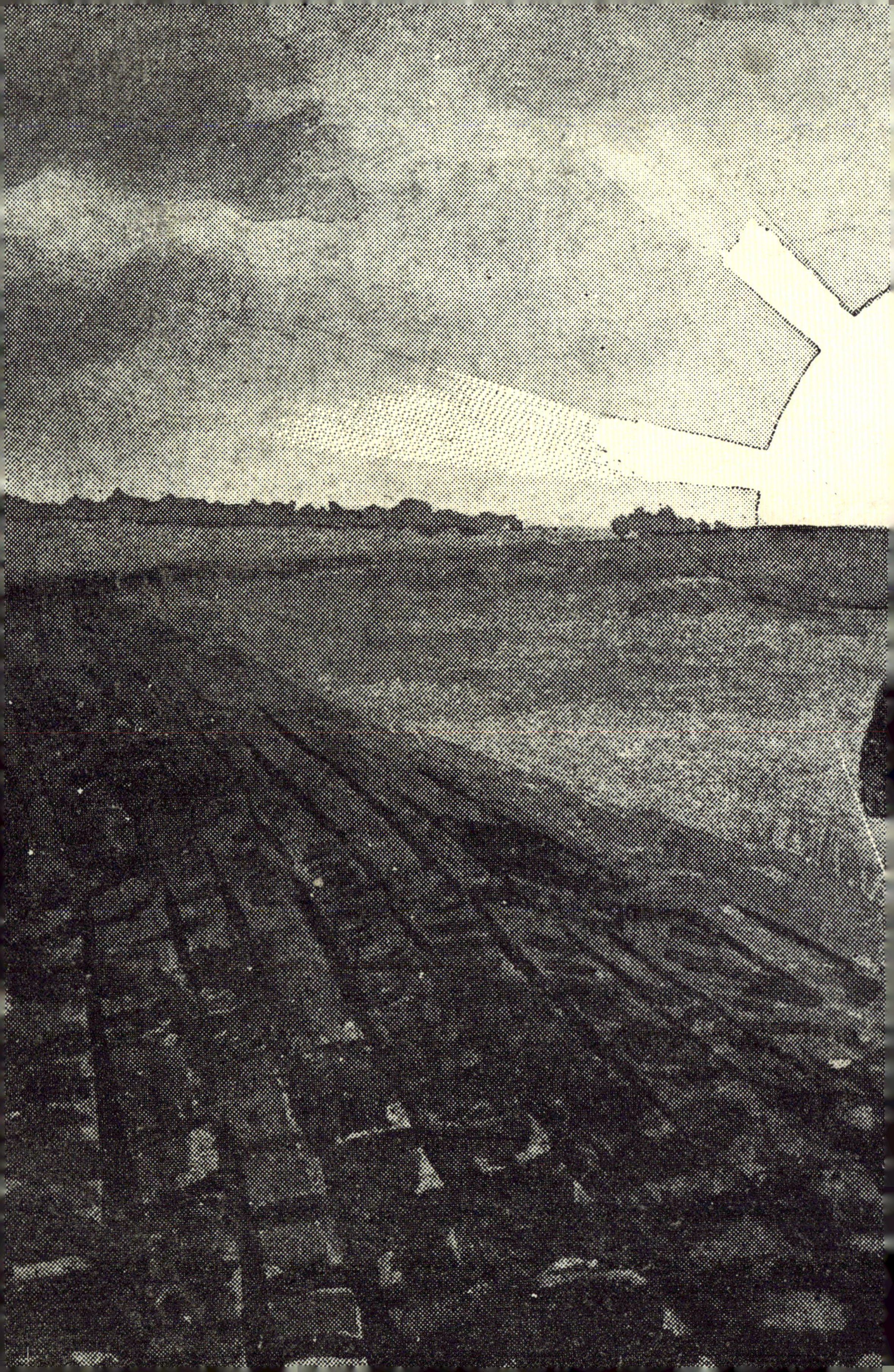

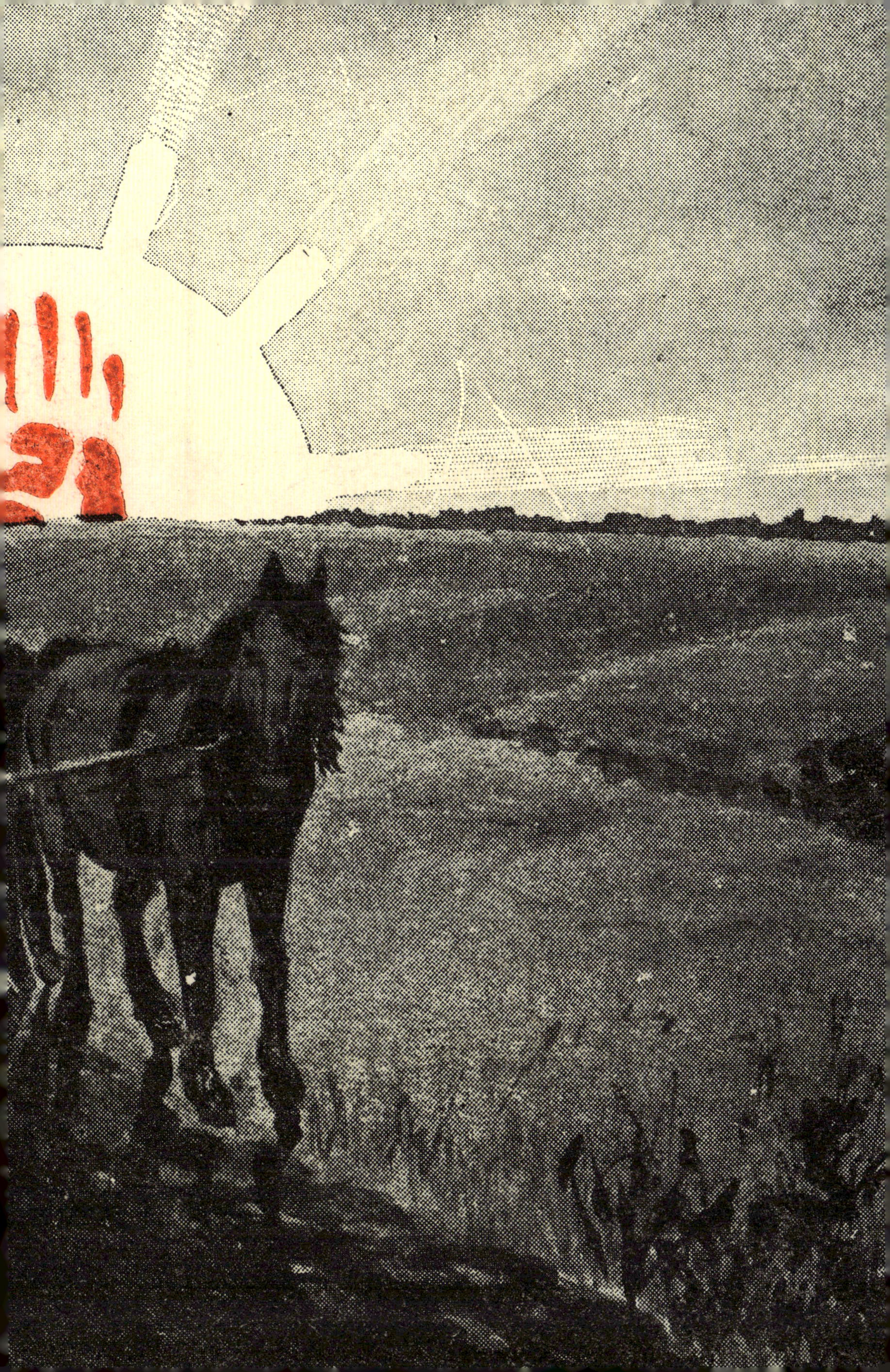

As befits such a resolutely commercial publisher, Nikolai Merder hedged his bets by promoting concerns about both art and topicality. This former French teacher-turned-magazine-editor was a strong proponent of the postcard as a force for cultural improvement, but he also claimed an important role for the medium in documenting public events, and by extension in instilling civic identity.[13] 'The main aim of our publishing activities is to promote the most outstanding Russian and foreign works of art among the colossal mass of the Russian public,' he explained. 'But alongside this key endeavour, we also intend to provide instant postcard reproductions of all the heroes and principal events in the life of the capital and the country.'[14]

The speed with which they could react to events and their broadly ephemeral nature made postcards the ideal medium through which to reflect the relentless pace and disjointed nature of modern life. Merder pointedly trumpeted his ability to print a postcard on 'any sensational new subject' within one or two days, further asserting that his firm 'tries to move with the times.'[15] By late 1905, the times had indeed moved, and where once the country's heroes had been the soldiers of the Russo-Japanese War, they were now the opponents of the Tsar. 'Life in our age moves fast,' Merder once remarked, 'what grabs one's interest today, is tomorrow already forgotten and replaced by something else.'[16]

Between late-1905 and mid-1906, Merder published three series of anti-government cartoons, the most commonly found of which are a set of monochrome silhouettes satirising the October Manifesto. While none show great individuality or sophistication (many are strongly influenced by the artist Vasil Gulak), they are still all well-construed, appealing images that excoriate the regime for its failure to deliver on promised reforms and uncompromisingly condemn government brutality. At least three different artists appear to have contributed designs, but none have been identified. A few of the silhouettes, however, are signed with the initials 'N. M.', suggesting that Merder himself may have been responsible for some of the images. In all, he published more than twenty original works.

The postcards were likely retailed through Merder's shop in central Saint Petersburg.[17] All of the cards include his name on the reverse, a strong indication that they were legally published.[18] This effort to adhere to censorial regulations suggests that Merder was not solely interested in turning a quick profit, but was also intent on enhancing the reputation for topical subject matter that he had won over previous years. These ambitions, however, were stymied by repression. Sometime in 1906, Merder stopped publishing opposition cartoons, and turned instead to less controversial portraits and realist narrative scenes.[19] This, however, only postponed the inevitable, and around 1907, he ceased printing anti-government images altogether.

Merder's writings in *Domashnii muzei* suggest a broad confluence with Shipovnik's high-flown aesthetic aims, but his ideological ambitions appear to have been of a very different order. He may have claimed a social purpose for his publishing, but there is much about it that smacks of political opportunism. During the Russo-Japanese War, he not only made appeals for patriotic unity, but also published postcards of the Imperial Family, images that he continued to advertise in the months after Bloody Sunday.[20] Then in 1905, when it became propitious to do so, he turned his attention to the opposition. The unrest undoubtedly nudged Merder's views to the left, but his main allegiance seems to have been to profit rather than to politics.

Merder was far from unique in taking advantage. With political subject matter of all flavours in great demand, commercial publishers were quick to come aboard. The revolutionaries, who deeply resented the competition, saw this as capitalist expediency in its purest form. Bonch-Bruevich complained vociferously about firms printing socialist works for commercial gain, dismissing them in his memoirs as unscrupulous 'money-grubbers.'[21] Opportunistic forms of political engagement were by no means limited to the print industry. It is hard not to express cynicism, for example, about an advertisement in the Bolshevik newspaper *Novaia zhizn* [*New Life*], which assured readers that Kneipp's 'nutritious' malt coffee was the drink of choice for German workers.[22]

Business and revolutionary practices became thoroughly intermingled during this period, and as private publishers became more politicised, revolutionary publishers became more commercialised. Even nominally socialist establishments were prepared to overlook the ideological content of their wares. The Saint Petersburg bookshop Nasha zhizn [Our Life], for instance, placed advertisements in the Bolshevik newspaper *Volna* [*The Wave*] offering: 'portraits of Shlisselburg prisoners, writers, civic activists, reproductions by [Arnold] Böcklin, [Lionello] Balestrieri, [Gustav] Marx and others.'[23] The images of Shlisselburg prisoners were on message, but Böcklin, Bellestieri and Marx were popular European painters whose works had nothing to do with the liberation movement.

Photographic Studios: August Tsenter and Vasilii Metalnikov

Photographic studios, which were among the most prolific of early postcard publishers, provided a rich source of opposition imagery during the Revolution. Here, as well, the catalysts for engagement were as many as the individuals involved. The greatest documenters of the revolutionary unrest were professional photographers working for the periodical press. Foremost among them was the pioneer of Russian photo-reportage Karl Bulla, who owned a prestigious studio in Saint Petersburg carrying an Imperial warrant.

His earliest images of the political turmoil could initially only be printed abroad, but after the October Manifesto, they were published inside Russia itself. There were also several other, smaller studios contributing pictures to Russian illustrated newspapers during the latter period, both in Moscow and in the capital.

Like many in his line of work, Bulla's involvement was primarily of a professional, rather than a political nature, and in this regard, it is notable that despite publishing many postcards on other subjects, his firm does not appear to have printed anti-government images in this less contextualised, and thus more contentious medium.[24] But while the more established studios avoided reproducing anti-government images in postcard form, smaller enterprises were only too happy to take their place, printing both their own photographs and those of larger firms. Whether Bulla's photographs of opposition demonstrations were licensed to other publishers or simply pirated is not clear, but one of those who became involved was August Tsenter, the owner of a small photographic studio in the capital.[25]

Between late-1905 and mid-1906, Tsenter published several photomechanical postcards relating to the October Manifesto and the First Duma. Among them is a photograph by Bulla captioned: *Demonstration on the Banks of the Neva. 18.XI.05.*[26] At the same time as he was printing these images, Tsenter was also selling illegal chromolithographic postcards produced by other publishers. Although he was detained for the latter practice in 1906, it evidently proved a worthwhile venture, as in February 1907, he started issuing his own (photomechanical) satirical postcards, which he continued to publish until May.[27] Although there are no clear links between the two, their content and design bear a remarkable similarity to the images printed by his fellow Saint Petersburg publisher, Vasilii Metalnikov.

Metalnikov was born in Voronezh in 1878. He, like Tsenter, was of peasant origin, another indication of the many opportunities engendered by increased literacy and dramatic social change.[28] After graduating from his local school around the age of seventeen, he moved to Saint Petersburg and there fell in with a group of Tolstoyans presided over by the writer's foremost disciple, Vladimir Chertkov. The two developed a close relationship, and in the spring of 1896, Metalnikov started working for Chertkov on a monthly retainer.[29] His real wish, however, was to become an actor. 'I think I could be useful to you,' he wrote to Chertkov, 'but not as much as I might like, because my yearning for the theatre has only grown … and a slave cannot serve two masters.'[30]

Here the plot thickens. At some point Metalnikov ended up in Rzhevsk, where he had an argument with a fellow Tolstoyan over a woman he had been courting.[31] Metalnikov then returned for a period to Voronezh, and in the spring of 1897, was approached by the head of the local Administration of

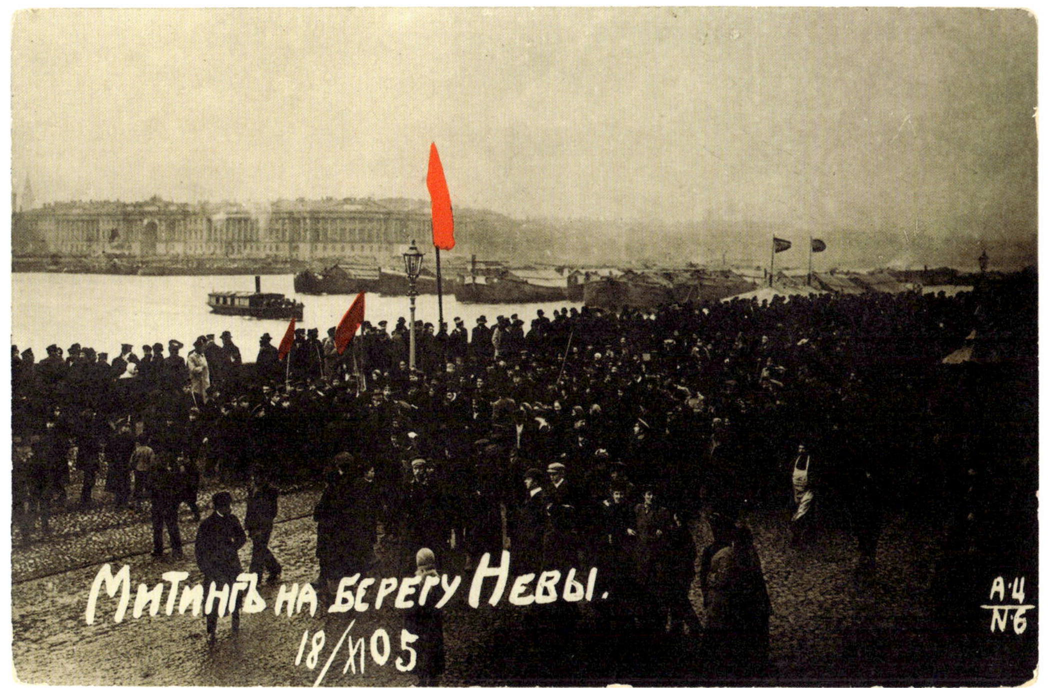

Karl Bulla. *Demonstration on the Banks of the Neva. 18.XI.05*. Published by August Tsenter, Saint Petersburg, late 1905.

Gendarmes with an offer to spy on his comrades. It is not at all clear why he agreed. Metalnikov himself said that he had been inspired by religious orthodoxy, telling the police: 'I truly hate Tolstoy, Chertkov, and their friends for their preaching, which drags down a mass of people who are attracted by the whimsy and vagueness of the doctrine that these gentlemen promote.'[32] But in reality his betrayal appears to have been sparked either by resentment or the need for money.[33]

He was seemingly of little use to the authorities, and after a few months, serious doubt was cast on his character: 'Metalnikov has never and will likely never be an agent and should definitely not be given any serious assignments in view of his extremely ambiguous behaviour,' reported Colonel Nikolai Vasilev, adding, 'I do not believe it is possible for him to discover a single name of any of the people I am monitoring.'[34] By now, he was also viewed with suspicion in revolutionary circles, where rumours were beginning to circulate. Following a dispute over payment, which prompted Metalnikov to write a vituperous letter of complaint to the Department of Police, the two sides parted ways, and he does not appear to have had any further contact with Vasilev.

This is a very murky episode, but, perhaps concerned that talk of his actions had already got out, Metalnikov wrote to Chertkov to tell him about it. 'The Colonel called me in to see him … I was asked what I was doing with you, how I lived, and how you interacted with me … It was suggested that I work for the Department of Police … I refused everything.'[35] Metalnikov

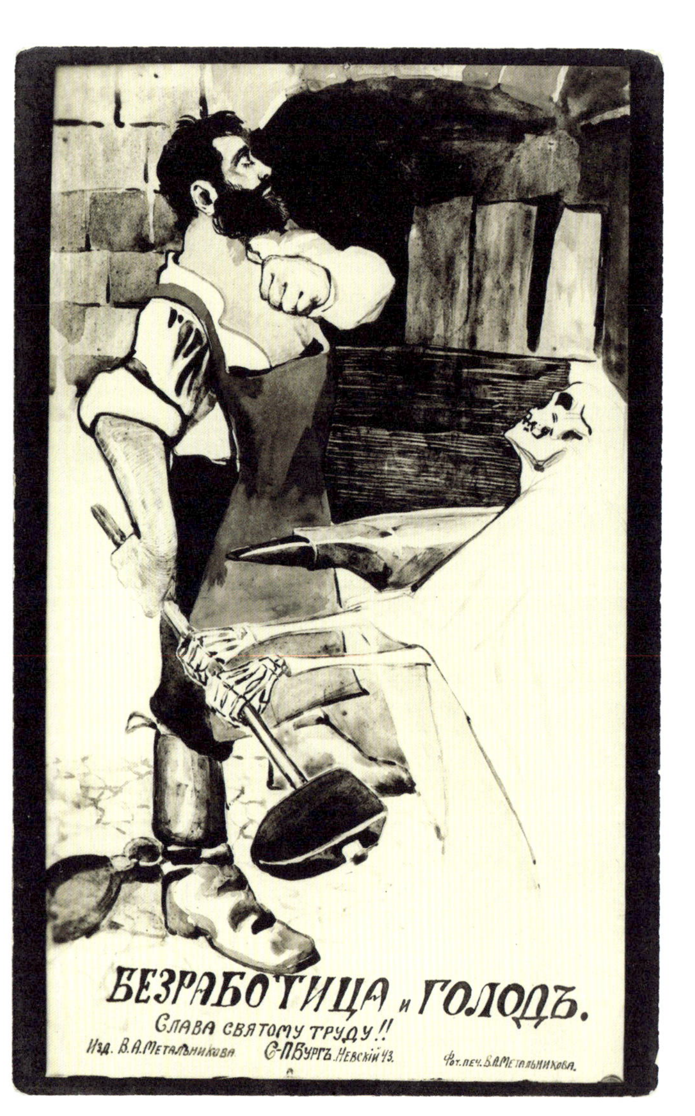
БЕЗРАБОТИЦА и ГОЛОДЪ.
Слава святому труду!!
Изд. В.А.Метальникова
С-ПБургъ. Невскій 43.
Фот. печ. В.А.Метальникова.

is clearly lying, but any attempt to determine where his true loyalties lay is further complicated by the fact that in July 1901, he was caught sending Tolstoyan literature to a priest-friend in Kazan.[36] No other evidence against him was found, but this suggests that he was indeed a true Tolstoyan, and that his earlier behaviour was opportunistic, as opposed to idealistic.

Metalnikov emerges from this incident as a mercurial character, thin-skinned and impetuous. However, his letters to Chertkov and his wife Anna also suggest someone who was deeply sensitive, both to the pain of others, and to the wider world around him. An awareness and understanding of the difficulties of human existence comes through strongly in his later postcards, which show profound concern for the suffering peasantry, and in line with his Tolstoyan beliefs, a distaste for violence and all forms of government excess. He seems to have retained a strong affection for Chertkov, fondly recalling their time together in a letter from 1907, and this is further confirmation that his earlier collaboration was prompted by youthful rashness, rather than by distaste for the man and the movement he espoused.[37]

Anonymous artist. *Unemployment and Famine. Glory to Sacred Labour!!* Published by Vasilii Metalnikov. Saint Petersburg, circa 1906.

By the spring of 1903, Metalnikov was back in the capital, where he had started attending a business course, making ends meet through teaching and editing.[38] Later the following year, he wrote to the Saint Petersburg governor's office to apply for permission to open an editing, translation and design business operating under the trade name 'Trud' [Labour]. At the same time, he also requested a license to manage a bookstore, and in line with procedure, this application was referred to the Interior Ministry. The police, who were still investigating his alleged dissemination of Tolstoyan literature, did not raise any objections, remarking only that Metalnikov had undertaken not to leave the city while proceedings were ongoing.[39] The case against him was eventually dropped in September 1904.[40]

Nothing is known about Metalnikov until May the following year, when he is recorded as working for the Fuchs Publishing House alongside his eighteen-year-old brother Arkadii.[41] Then, in late 1906, having kept his head down throughout the revolutionary period, he applied to the censor for permission to publish two postcard cartoons satirising a recent cash-for-contracts scandal. Over the months that followed, he submitted numerous other anti-government designs.[42] These covered a broad range of political subject matter, from state repression to rural famine. Although all were published under Metalnikov's name, the address 43 Nevskii Prospect, given on the postcards, is the same as that recorded by the police for the Fuchs Publishing House. The nature of their relationship, however, remains opaque.[43]

Metalnikov employed at least eleven different artists to design his photomechanical postcards, among them Pavel Martens and Mikhail Stoliarov, both of whom were also prolific contributors to satirical journals.[44] The images were initially printed in runs of a thousand copies, but many later went through multiple reprints.[45] Indeed, his postcards proved so popular that by 1907 they were being issued in editions of 5,000: an almost unprecedented number for this time and subject matter.[46] Although the firm always remained something of a studio enterprise, Metalnikov almost certainly comprised the most prolific legal publisher of anti-government postcards in Imperial Russia. An advertising list from 1907 includes over fifty different original cartoons and narrative images, as well as thirteen portraits of Duma deputies.[47]

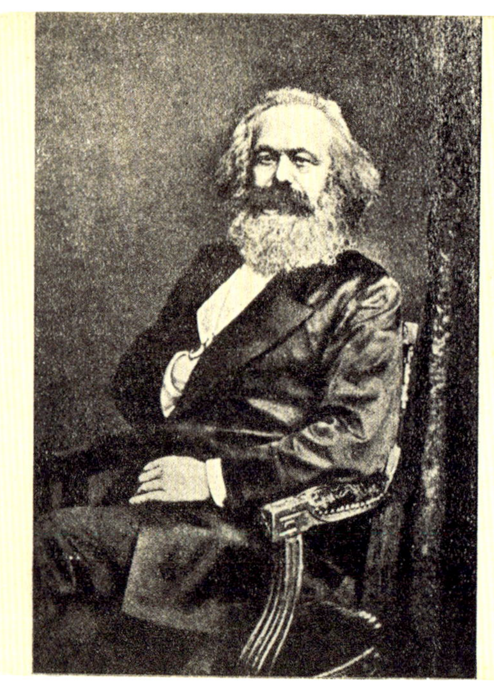

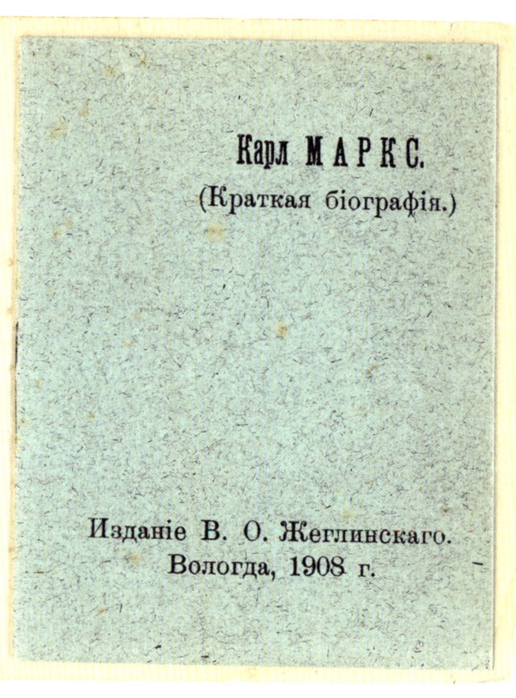
Карл МАРКС.
(Краткая біографія.)
Изданіе В. О. Жеглинскаго.
Вологда, 1908 г.

John Mayall (photographer). *Karl Marx*. Published by V.O. Zheglinskii, Vologda, 1908.

In the interests of protecting his financial outlay, Metalnikov was always careful to stay on the right side of the law, on occasion writing to the Press Administration to check whether the censor had approved certain images for publication.[48] Furthermore, he made a particular point of declaring in his advertisements that: 'All postcards have been passed by the Main Administration for Press Affairs.'[49] But like so many publishers, he was not squeaky clean. Despite notifying customers that *Crime and Punishment* and *In Memory of 9 January* had been 'confiscated', at least some copies of these postcards were still sold – examples of both survive in the Russian State Library.[50] Some risks were evidently worth taking in the pursuit of profit.

Irrespective of Metalnikov's past as a police informer, it is evident that the anti-government sentiment expressed in his postcards was heartfelt. Whatever the explanation for his previous conduct, by the time of the 1905

Revolution he was opposed to the existing system of government, but as an advocate of reform not of revolution, a position that is underscored by his unalloyed support for the First and Second Dumas.[51] Metalnikov's route into opposition postcard publishing was unquestionably a convoluted one, but this was a tumultuous period that gave rise, not only to changes of opinion, but also of status, and occupation. His career is therefore best seen as the product of a complex merger of political, personal, and practical circumstance.

Metalnikov and Tsenter both ceased publishing anti-government postcards in May 1907. The only other images that Metalnikov is known to have produced are a group of photographic cards depicting nude sculptures by contemporary European artists, some published in conjunction with a certain I. I. Seferiadis. Tsenter, by contrast, has left posterity with a clearer trail to follow. He continued to print postcards throughout the late Imperial era, issuing a large number of patriotic designs during the First World War. Following the overthrow of the Tsar, he became a prominent publisher of real photograph postcards showcasing the revolutionary disorder and delight. Tsenter's firm was nationalised in 1919, but he continued to work in photography until the mid-1930s.[52]

Former Revolutionaries: Viktor Zheglinskii

One of the most significant ramifications of the October Manifesto was to have made it possible for socialist-orientated publishers to advance an oppositionist ideology without the need for a relationship with a political organisation. Not only were there now many more views that an opponent of the Tsar could hold, there were also (temporarily at least) many more ways in which those views could be expressed, of which membership of a revolutionary party was only one. This led to a period of entrepreneurship in publishing and politics, as activists of all stripes went it alone, happy, as circumstance dictated, to swap and change between the commercial infrastructure of the print industry and that of the revolutionary parties.

Viktor Zheglinskii is a good example of a revolutionary for whom political profit and financial gain were mutually beneficial activities. In March 1898, Zheglinskii, a hereditary noble from Kiev, had been arrested for membership of an underground Marxist organisation, named the Union of Struggle for the Liberation of the Working Class. After languishing in prison for just over a year, he was forcibly conscripted into the army, serving in the ranks until August 1901. Shortly before demobilisation, he was sentenced for his earlier revolutionary activity to two years in exile. After working at a sugar factory in Olshansk in Voronezh Province, he moved to Vologda in north-west Russia, where having served out his punishment he chose to remain.[53]

In Vologda, Zheglinskii worked for the regional Zemstvo, managing warehouses for local craftsmen.[54] In 1908 – late in terms of political postcards – he launched a legal publishing business printing portraits of prominent socialists and revolutionary theorists under the name Severnoe Izdatelstvo [Northern Publisher].[55] These postcards soon came to the attention of the police and local governor, who especially objected to the biographical booklets that came stapled to the images. The cards were eventually banned, but not before Zheglinskii had turned a healthy profit, which as far as can be ascertained, he kept for himself. Although opposition-minded, Zheglinskii does not appear to have collaborated with underground groups; while his views were revolutionary, his aims were also commercial.

Postcard Artists

There are barely more than a handful of anti-government postcard artists working for commercial firms whose names have survived.[56] While it is possible that there are better-known individuals hiding beneath the cloak of anonymity, both private and revolutionary publishers tended to employ unsung art-school students because they were cheaper, content to be nameless, more open to taking risks, and occasionally, prepared to work for ideological reasons alone. When established professional illustrators drew postcards on contemporary themes, their images were often published legally, and were of correspondingly mild content, perhaps because they had more to lose.[57] As with publishers, the nature of an artist's output was a trade-off between ideological intent and practical concerns.

Nonetheless, the lack of any postcard cartoons or caricatures by leading adherents of the World of Art movement is surprising. Not all of them favoured freely mixing art and politics, but Sergei Chekhonin, Boris Kustodiev, Mstislav Dobuzhinskii and Ivan Bilibin, all of whom had experience of postcard illustration through their work for the Society of Saint Eugenia, did contribute cartoons to satirical journals and were therefore, one presumes, ready to apply their talent to the work of political reform. The machinations of the authorities may have acted as a barrier to Grzhebin's postcard plans in mid-1906, but this need not have stopped other publishers from commissioning or reproducing examples of their work before this date.

After Georgii Erastov. *Engrossed in Reading.* Hand-drawn postcard, circa 1905. This caricature of Tsar Nicholas II was first printed in *Burelom*, No.1, Saint Petersburg, November 1905.

The explanation for their absence may in fact be straightforward. Although their work for satirical journals was more often than not aligned with personal belief, it remained at heart a commercial transaction: these were professional artists, whose self appointed role in life was to promote art, not revolution. The absence of any anti-government postcards by World of Art affiliates might therefore simply come down to a lack of commissions,

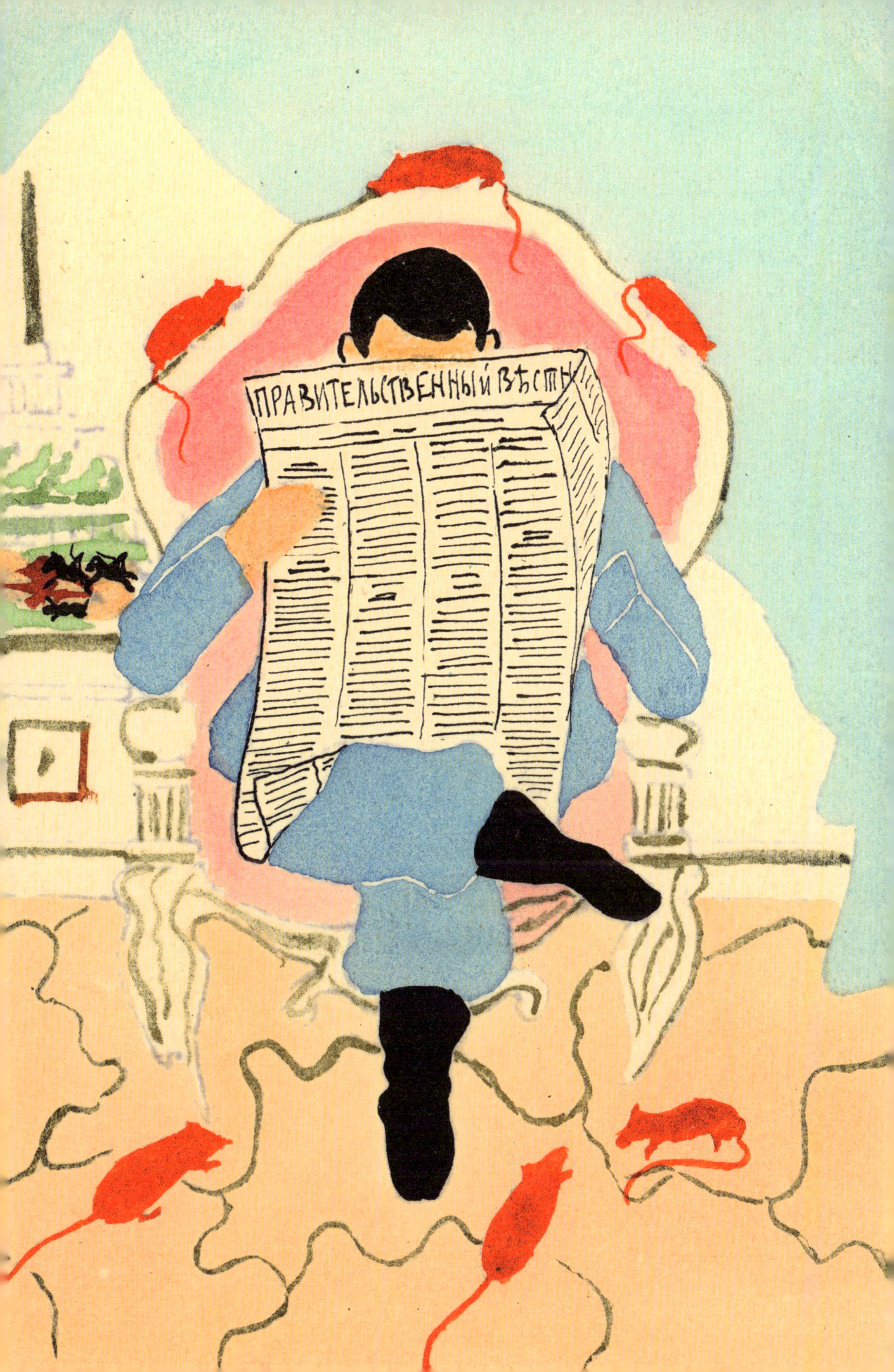
ПРАВИТЕЛЬСТВЕННЫЙ ВѢСТН

ОРЕЛЪ-ОБОРОТЕНЬ

ИЛИ

ПОЛИТИКА ВНѢШНЯЯ И ВНУТРЕННЯЯ

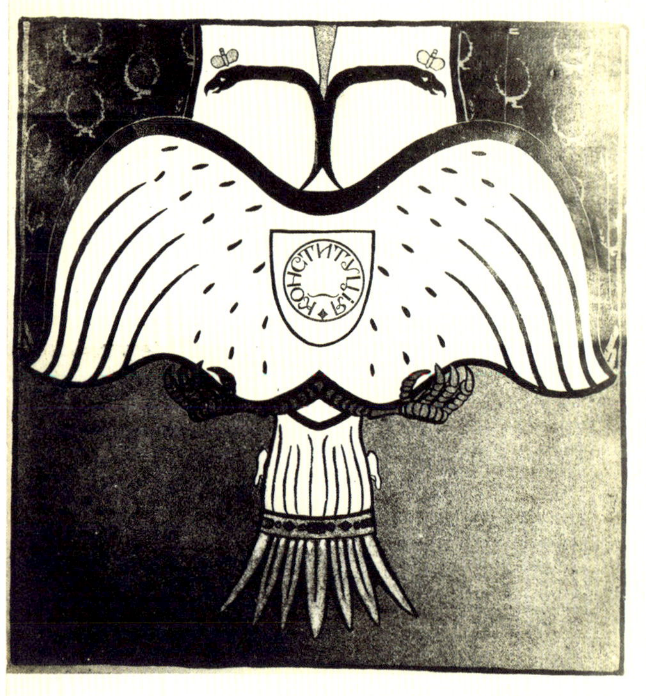

likely because for publishers the risk of confiscation was too great to balance out the expense of production. Creating a product at the level of Shipovnik, *Zhupel* or *Adskaia pochta* required considerable vision, contacts, time, and financial support, none of which were in ready supply.

The proliferation of anti-government material in late 1905 created many openings for illustrators, and for the more talented among them, the money-making opportunities were legion. In place of well-known professionals, amateur artists and students flocked to take advantage of the regime's temporary incapacity. Few stuck to a single medium, and fewer still to a single publication or publisher. Pavel Martens, who studied at the Stieglitz School of Art, worked for Metalnikov and Tsenter, while Mikhail Stoliarov, who published his artwork in at least fourteen different journals, was employed by Metalnikov and the Bolshevik publisher Vpered. He was at that point a full-time student in the legal faculty of Saint Petersburg University.[58]

Zinovii Grzhebin. *Werewolf-Eagle, or Internal and External Politics*. No publication details, 1906. This caricature was originally published in *Zhupel*, No. 1, Saint Petersburg, December 1905.

Over half the illustrators who are known to have produced anti-government postcard designs also submitted work to satirical journals.[59] But despite the considerable similarity in their subject matter and circumstances of production, the relationship between periodicals and postcards does not appear to have been especially fluid, particularly in regard to publishing and design. Grzhebin is the only journal editor who is also known to have published a set of anti-government postcards, but notably, he did not reproduce works from his own magazines. Straightforward copies of journal illustrations are uncommon – photomechanical reproductions were occasionally made in underground facilities (such as that of Peschanskii), but better-quality lithographic works are rare.[60]

The absence of extensive interchange between satirical journals and postcards may in part be due to publishers' lack of experience with the latter, but it more likely comes down to the fact that postcards were seen by publishers and artists alike as a separate art form. This would also explain why, despite the obvious connections between the two, the vast majority of anti-government postcard illustrations were unique to the medium. Mere repetitions would not do, particularly given that they were competing for the attention of much the same politicised, urban audience. Thus, while each fed off the same political and artistic environment, postcards and journals should be understood as two distinct media with their own symbiotic relationship.

Handmade Postcards: Valerii Karrik

With postcard blanks widely available, handmade cards had long been popular among the leisure classes, but as far back as the nineteenth century, revolutionaries had also used the medium to disseminate seditious messages and drawings. This custom expanded exponentially in 1905, when it served

ВЫСОЧАЙШІЙ МАНИФЕСТЪ.

Божіею милостію,

МЫ, НИКОЛАЙ ВТОРЫЙ,

ИМПЕРАТОРЪ И САМОДЕРЖЕЦЪ ВСЕРОССІЙСКІЙ,
царь польскій, великій князь финляндскій,
и прочая, и прочая, и прочая.

Смуты и волненія въ столицахъ и во многихъ мѣстностяхъ Имперіи Нашей великою и тяжкою скорбью преисполняютъ сердце Наше. Благо Россійскаго Государя неразрывно съ благомъ народнымъ, и печаль народная—Его печаль. Отъ волненій, нынѣ возникшихъ, можетъ явиться глубокое нестроеніе народное и угроза цѣлости и единству Державы Нашей.

Великій обѣтъ Царскаго служенія повелѣваетъ Намъ всѣми силами разума и власти Нашей стремиться къ скорѣйшему прекращенію столь опасной для Государства смуты. Повелѣвъ подлежащимъ властямъ принять мѣры къ устраненію прямыхъ проявленій безпорядка, безчинствъ и насилій, въ охрану людей мирныхъ, стремящихся къ спокойному выполненію лежащаго на каждомъ долга, Мы, для успѣшнѣйшаго выполненія общихъ преднамѣчаемыхъ Нами къ умиротворенію государственной жизни мѣръ, признали необходимымъ объединить дѣятельность высшаго Правительства.

На обязанность Правительства возлагаемъ Мы выполненіе непреклонной Нашей воли:

1. Даровать населенію незыблемыя основы гражданской свободы на началахъ дѣйствительной неприкосновенности личности, свободы совѣсти, слова, собраній и союзовъ.

2. Не останавливая предназначенныхъ выборовъ въ Государственную Думу, привлечь теперь же къ участію въ Думѣ, въ мѣрѣ возможности, соотвѣтствующей краткости остающагося до созыва Думы срока, тѣ классы населенія, которые нынѣ совсѣмъ лишены избирательныхъ правъ, предоставивъ, засимъ, дальнѣйшее развитіе начала общаго избирательнаго права вновь установленному законодательному порядку,

и 3. Установить, какъ незыблемое правило, чтобы никакой законъ не могъ воспріять силу безъ одобренія Государственной Думы и чтобы выборнымъ отъ народа обезпечена была возможность дѣйствительнаго участія въ надзорѣ за закономѣрностью дѣйствій поставленныхъ отъ Насъ властей.

Призываемъ всѣхъ вѣрныхъ сыновъ Россіи исполнить долгъ свой передъ Родиною, помочь прекращенію сей неслыханной смуты и вмѣстѣ съ Нами напрячь всѣ силы къ возстановленію тишины и мира на родной землѣ.

Данъ въ Петергофѣ, въ 17-й день октября въ лѣто отъ Рождества Христова тысяча девятьсотъ пятое, Царствованія же Нашего одиннадцатое. На подлинномъ Собственною Его Императорскаго Величества рукою подписано:

„НИКОЛАЙ".

Къ сему листу Свиты Его Величества Генералъ-Маіоръ Треповъ руку приложилъ.

Nikolai Shebuev. *Major-General Trepov of His Majesty's Retinue Had a Hand in This Document.* No publication details, 1906. This caricature was originally published in *Pulemet*, No. 1, 1905.

as both a highly convenient and highly profitable way for artists and activists to release uncensored images into the public domain. Although the majority of the designs were original artworks, few were one-off productions. Unlike their domestic counterparts, most of which were individual works reflecting the personal experiences of their creators, homemade political postcards were often mass produced, with the outlines of the illustration printed by mimeograph, and the rest filled in by hand.

The artist Valerii Karrik was perhaps the most popular and certainly the most famous illustrator of hand-drawn postcards in Tsarist Russia. By the time of the 1905 Revolution, he was a well-known figure in intellectual circles, where he was often to be found quietly sketching his fellow guests:

> At every literary gathering in Saint Petersburg, at every literary evening, lunch, in every circle where Petersburg literary types gather, you will always see a tall man with brown hair, a small, elongated, hemmed beard, and a cheerful face. Taking his place somewhere to the side, where he will try to get the best view of those present, he takes out of his pocket a small booklet and without anyone noticing, stealthily begins to draw.[61]

Karrik was born in Saint Petersburg in 1869. He was raised bilingual but always considered himself Russian, despite never becoming a citizen of his adopted country.[62] Both of his parents held enlightened views. His father William Carrick, a Scot descended from timber merchants, was a pioneering photographer celebrated for his sympathetic and eminently human images of Russian types and tradespeople.[63] And his mother, Aleksandra Markelova, a translator and writer, was one of the first female journalists in Russia and a passionate believer in sexual equality. She had a reputation among her contemporaries for being both 'godless and a nihilist,' beliefs that no doubt proved a strong influence on the political opinions of her children.[64]

Even while still at school, Karrik was already aware of a difference between the people and the gentry, a social awareness fostered in part by his parents, but also by the domestic environment in which he was raised. As a child he developed a close relationship with his nanny and family servants, whom he would often overhear in the kitchen complaining about their masters. Karrik credited his full political awakening, however, to Herzen, who 'opened my eyes to the nineteenth-century sources of Populism, the Populism of my mother, and to my own Populism.' From 1886 onwards, he spent successive summers teaching peasants in a village in Novgorod Province, an experience he later characterised as 'going to the people.'[65]

Karrik's older brother Dmitrii carried out his own, far more serious act of rebellion in 1888. One afternoon in March, a plainclothes gendarmes officer started following him after he was seen acting in a suspicious manner near the home of the Interior Minister. Realising that he was being tailed, Dmitrii first tried to evade the officer, then challenged him, saying: 'You're a spy, and if you don't leave me alone, I'll put a bullet through your head.' When the police were summoned to arrest him, he indeed pulled out a revolver, but soon thought better of it, and after a brief escape bid, was apprehended. As punishment for his gross 'political unreliability,' the hotheaded Dmitrii was exiled for three years to Orenburg Province.[66]

The Karriks were devastated. While in police custody, Dmitrii received a letter from his uncle reporting that the family was in disbelief that this should have happened to their 'Mitia' [Dmitrii]. He commented that, 'Valerii is very down, although as usual he stays silent.'[67] Valerii and his mother were both pulled in for questioning over the incident (his father had died ten years previously), and such a difficult event cannot but have helped bolster whatever negative views of the regime he already had. Far from discouraging him in his political pursuits, this brush with the authorities seems to have been a defining experience, and over the next decade he would be drawn ever closer into the revolutionary sphere.

After leaving school, Karrik attended a teaching college in Saint Petersburg, graduating in 1890. His report card shows an unexceptional, if satisfactory record, with strong marks in physical education and drawing.[68] He appears, however, to have decided against pursuing a teaching career,

Next spread from left to right

Evlampii Kosvintsev. *The First Activists of the Russian Revolution. Gen. Stessel, Adm. Alekseev, Gen. Kuropatkin.* No publication details, circa February 1906. Stessel, Alekseev, and Kuropatkin were the key military leaders during the Russo-Japanese War.

Anonymous artist. *Don't Spare the Bullets.* Hand-drawn postcard, circa 1905. Caricature of Dmitrii Trepov.

Первые дѣятели русской революціи

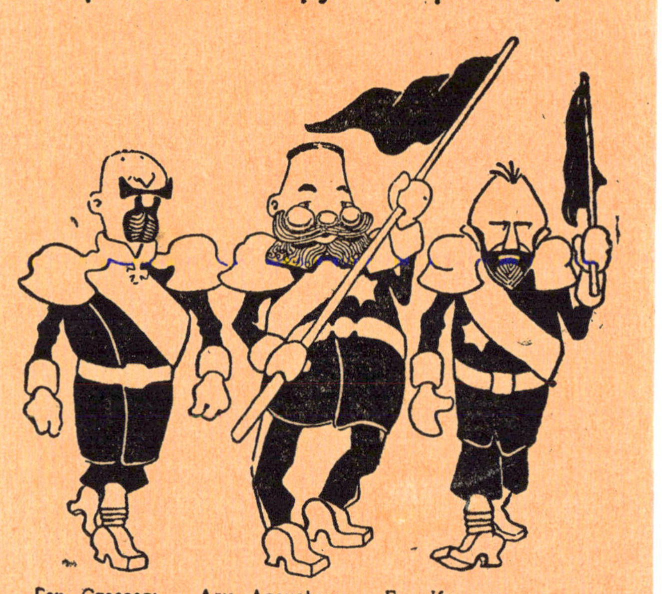

Ген. Стессель. Адм. Алексѣевъ. Ген. Куропаткинъ.

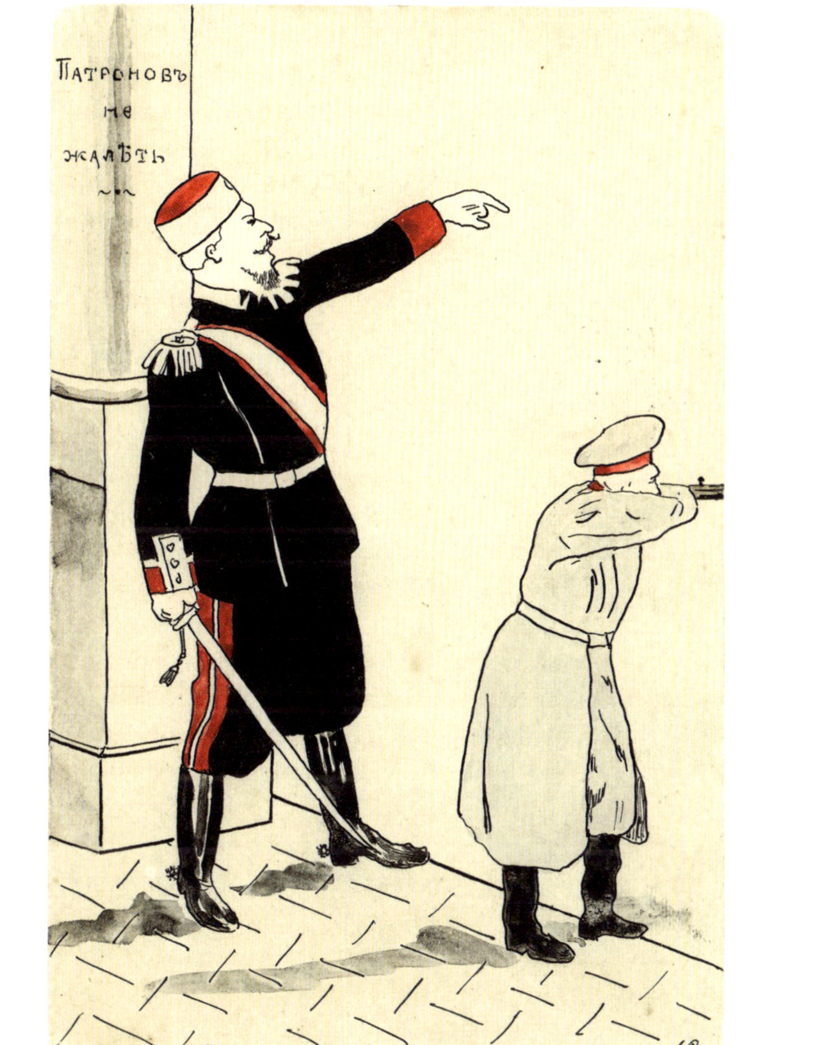
Патроновъ
не
жалѣть

and in around 1894, he began freelancing for the editorial department of the *Finance Ministry Journal*.[69] Over previous years, Karrik had become close to radical circles abroad, and based on his newly privileged access to government data, he started sending illegal political reports and satirical poems to the Free Russian Press in England.[70] Not for nothing did the police later describe him, just like his brother, as 'extremely politically unreliable.'[71]

Towards the end of the century, Karrik was made secretary of the Imperial Free Economic Society, a bulwark of liberalism that freely encouraged the discussion of political ideas. Here he met many prominent politicians and reform-minded luminaries, including Maxim Gorky, who once recommended him to fellow writer Leonid Andreev as an 'interesting Englishman (sic) and a good man.'[72] Gorky was far from alone in admiring Karrik, who was characterised by family members as a gentle and playful figure, much liked by his contemporaries. One long-time friend in exile wrote after his death: 'For me he was the ideal human being – the most excellent of men … I shall never meet anyone who has the half of his goodness and wealth of mind.'[73]

Anonymous photographer. Portrait of Valerii Karrik. Norway, circa 1930s.

In April 1898, Karrik travelled to England and Scotland, a trip that sparked the keen interest of the Imperial police. The exact purpose of his journey is unknown, but he carried with him a letter from Tolstoy to Vladimir Chertkov, and passed much of his time in London meeting Tolstoyans and revolutionaries. While in the capital, an Imperial spy tracked his every move. It was reported that he spent two hours wandering through the galleries of the British Museum in the company of the anarchist Petr Kropotkin, and later met the leaders of the Free Russian Press. The informant related that the latter: 'showed him great respect and were very pleased with his work as an agent for the Society of Friends of Russian Freedom'.[74]

These activities eventually caught up with Karrik, and in March 1904 he was detained on suspicion of collaborating with revolutionary organisations abroad.[75] A letter to Paris containing information pertaining to a secret government order had been intercepted, and Karrik had been fingered as the prime suspect. His flat was searched and there, in open view, the police found 'a significant quantity of tendentious writings, anti-government proclamations, and cartoons, the latter, which he claimed to have drawn himself.' Officials, who suspected that he had been sending examples of his cartoons abroad for publication, po-facedly described them as, 'done with the clear intention of mocking the existing system of government.' Karrik, however, claimed to have made them for his own amusement.[76]

On examining their haul, the police accused Karrik of being a member of the Socialist-Revolutionary Party. He denied this, and after further investigation, the authorities concluded that he had not after all been responsible for sending the intercepted letter. Nevertheless, having arrested him they

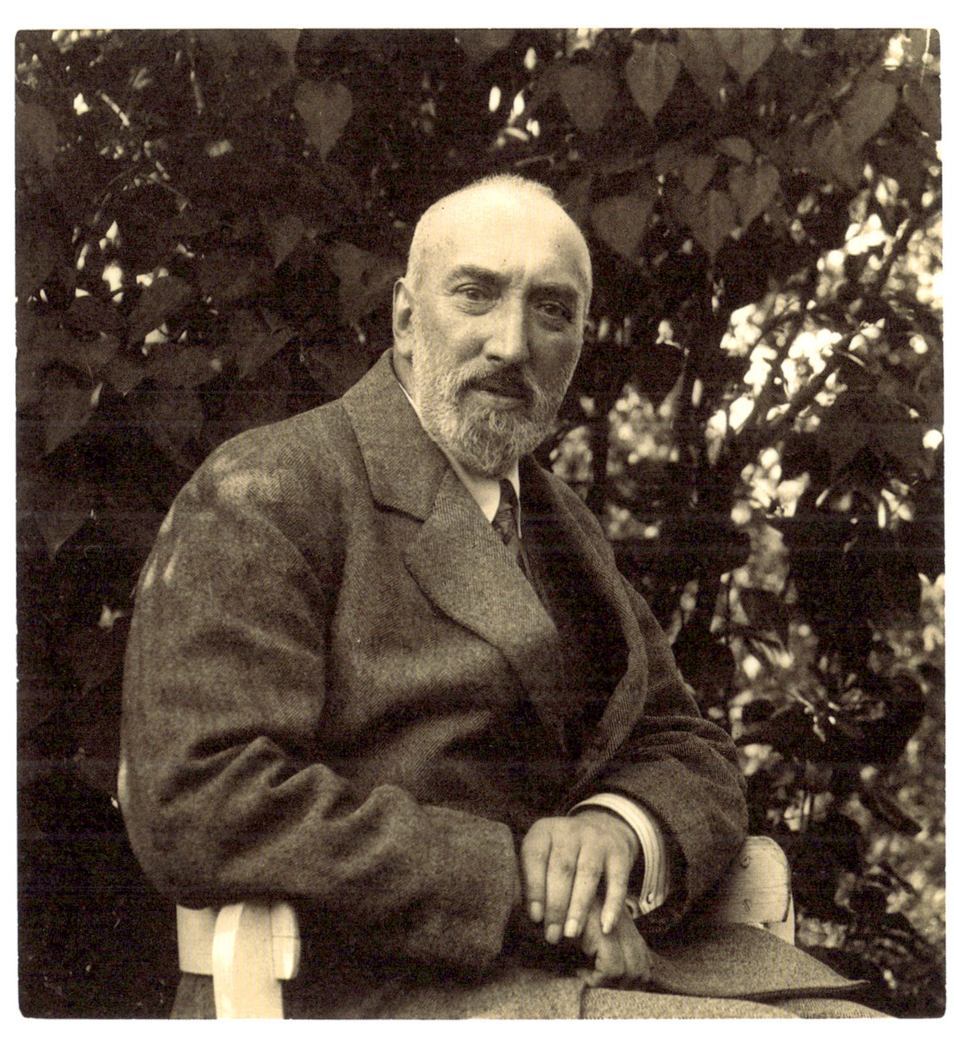

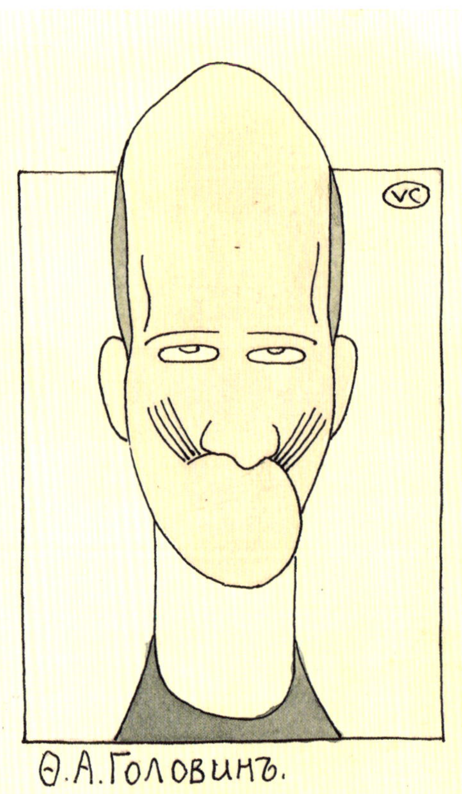
VC
Ѳ.А.Головинъ.

were now very reluctant to let him go. Claiming that if nothing else, his political guilt had been sufficiently established, the foreign ministry issued an order to have Karrik expelled as an undesirable alien. Only an appeal to the British Ambassador saved him from this ignominious fate. Thanks to his prompt intervention, the case was dropped a few months later, and Karrik was eventually given permanent leave to remain in Russia.[77]

He stopped working for the *Finance Ministry Journal* in the spring of 1904, presumably as a result of his arrest.[78] Sometime after this, just as the political situation was starting to hot up, he started drawing and disseminating anti-government postcards in earnest.[79] Karrik's revolutionary sympathies were already reason enough for him to create opposition propaganda, but it is surely no coincidence that he started making postcards just at the moment that his main source of income dried up.[80] Here was a viable commercial activity that might supplement his other artistic and journalistic work. Sales appear to have been restricted initially to his immediate circle of acquaintances, but they increased markedly after Bloody Sunday, reaching a peak in mid-1906.[81]

Opposite

Valerii Karrik. *F. A. Golovin.* Hand-drawn postcard, Saint Petersburg, 1906. Fedor Golovin was the chairman of the Second Duma.

Karrik's largest body of work relates to the First and Second Dumas. Between 1906 and 1907, he produced around 150 caricatures of deputies, journalists, writers, and activists, not only from the opposition, but also from the State Council and the reactionary right.[82] Karrik's beliefs may have been immutable, but he was not partisan in his artistic attentions – further evidence of the role played by money in spurring on the production of his postcards. Despite their comparative expense, Karrik's portraits found great favour with the public, who praised his skill in capturing likenesses using just a few carefully applied penstrokes.[83] Their sharply observed details and strong linearity bear stylistic comparison to the work of Max Beerbohm.[84]

Karrik's most political images came in the form of zoomorphic cartoons. These works feature a range of different birds and animals, each of which posits a variation of the question: 'How can the government be sincere in its promises to reform when repression goes on unabated?' His aim in these cartoons is to expose the fallacy of liberal trust in the regime, and this he does in a whimsical but unforgiving manner. Like the portraits, many are signed with his Latin initials 'V. C.'. Whether Karrik had any assistance in producing the postcards is unclear, but all were produced in considerable quantities. Eight of his zoomorphic cartoons were also printed in chromolithographic editions (likely in Finland), with captions in Russian, Finnish and Swedish.[85]

Next spread

Valerii Karrik. *We're Here by Virtue of the Decree… / And I'm Here by Virtue of the Government Circular.* Hand-drawn postcard, Saint Petersburg, 1906.

In later life, Karrik claimed an ideological affinity with the Popular Socialist Party, a Socialist-Revolutionary offshoot rooted in nineteenth-century Populism. 'My moral, if not my political sympathies were always with them,' he wrote.[86] As far as socialism was concerned, Karrik said that

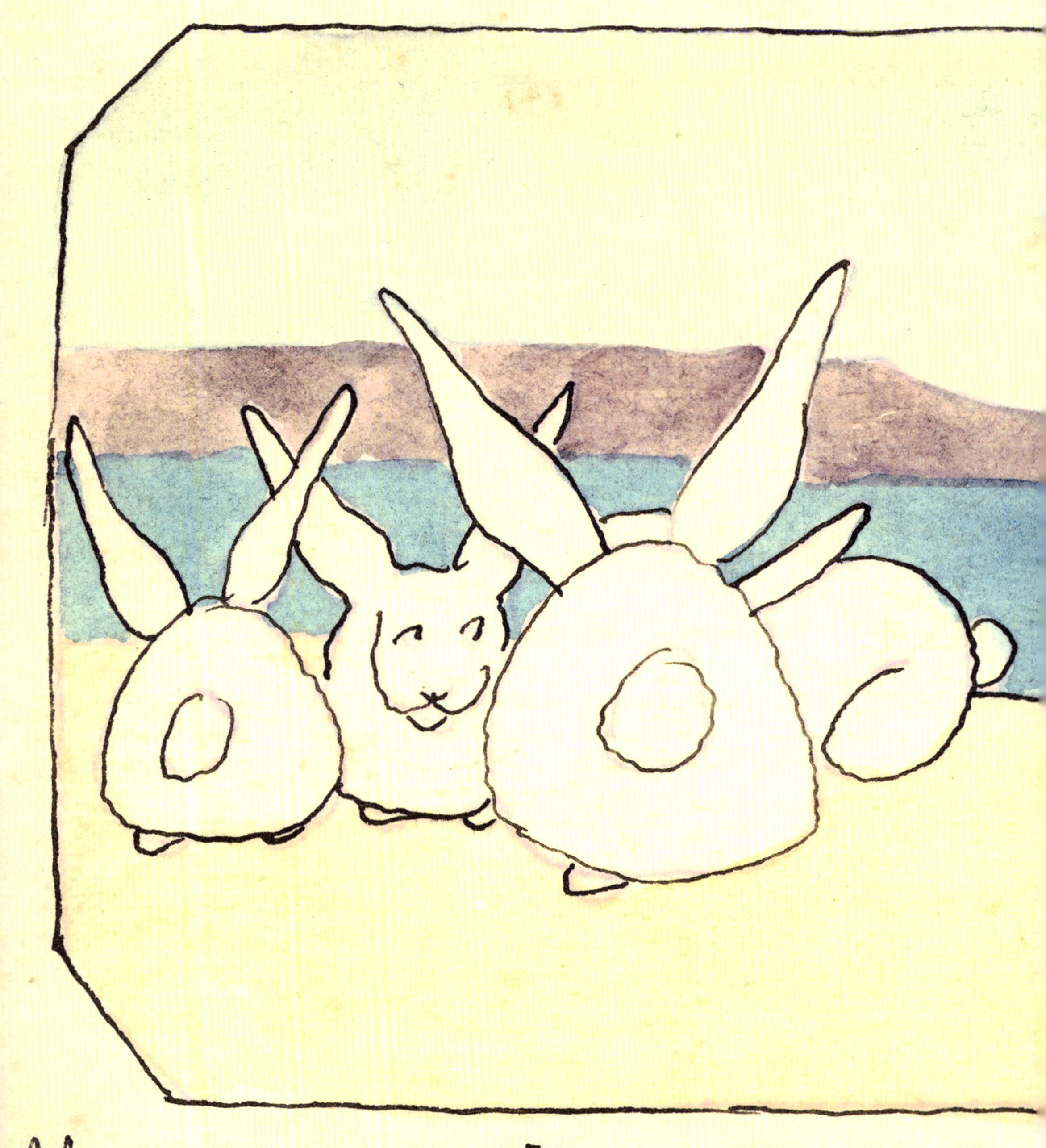

Мы на основаніи указа....

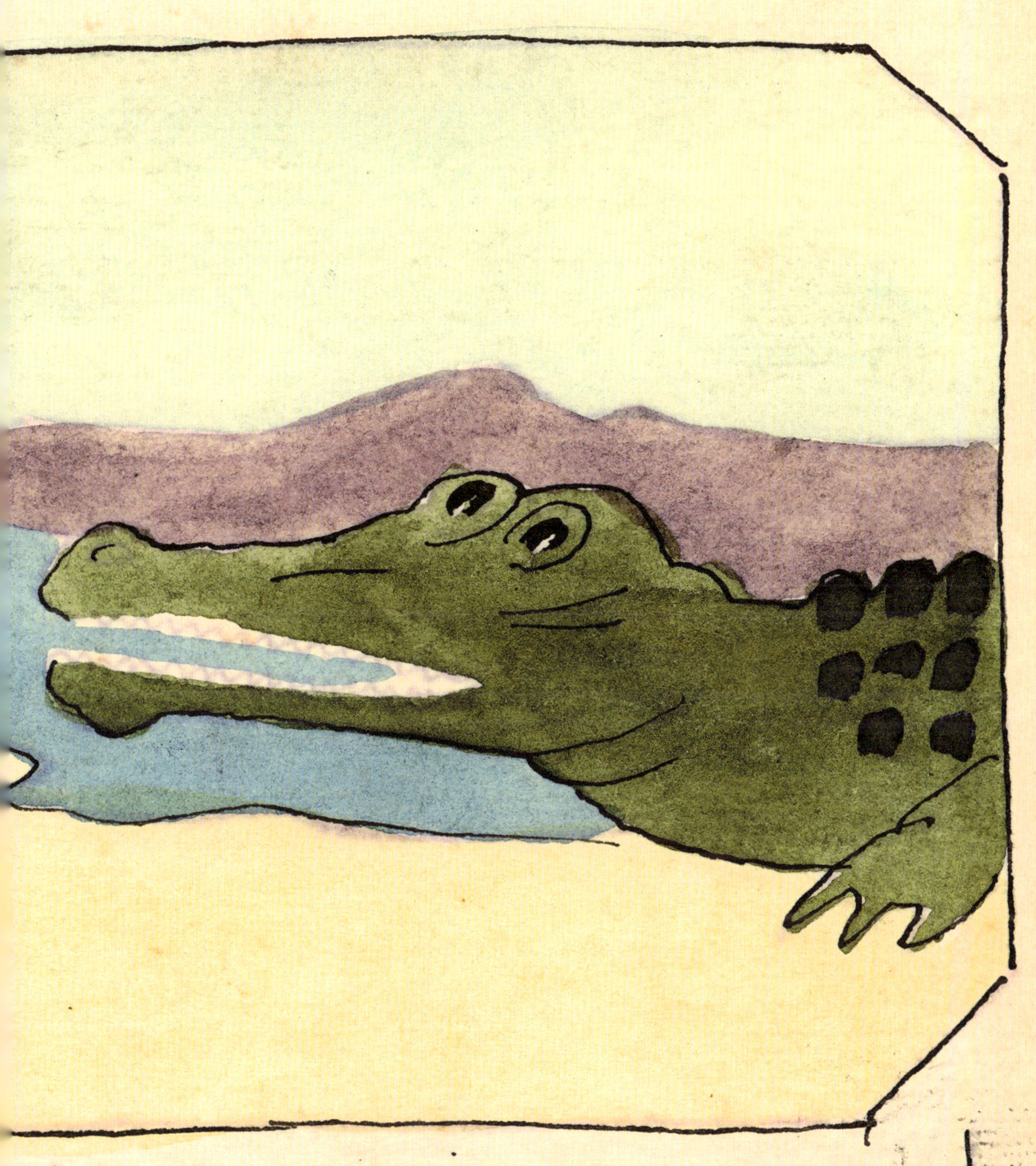

А я на основанії циркуляра!...

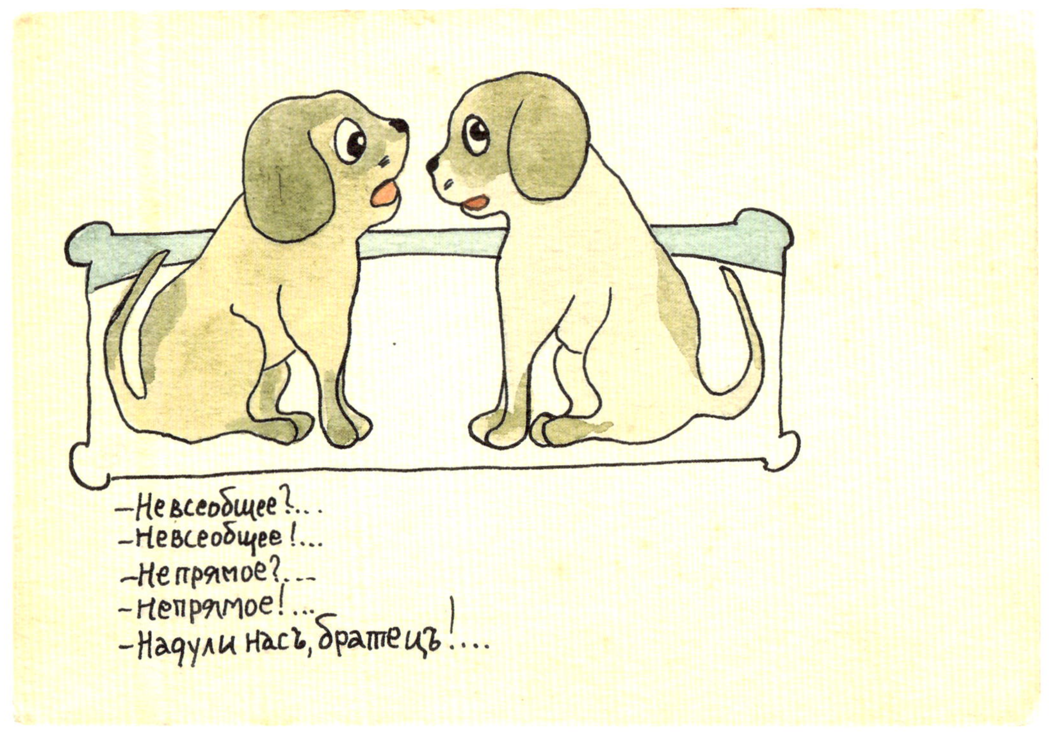

Valerii Karrik.
– Not Universal?...
– Not Universal!...
– Not Direct?...
– Not Direct!...
– My Friend, We've Been Had!...
A satire on Duma suffrage. Hand-drawn postcard, Saint Petersburg, 1906.

it had never attracted him, but that he was drawn to socialists themselves, the majority of whom were 'good people.'[87] This in many ways sums him up. Karrik was first and foremost a humanitarian, whose interest lay more in people than in politics.[88] The aim of his postcards was not so much to advance an ideological cause, as to highlight a social one. To Karrik, the system of government was less important than the quality of its rule.

Repression forced Karrik to stop producing anti-government cartoons in around 1907.[89] An article on him in the *Manchester Guardian* the following year reported that political satire was 'in abeyance in Russia at present' and that all topical work had been suppressed.[90] Despite this, he went on producing postcard portraits of writers, intellectuals, artists, and civic activists.[91] According to a feature piece from 1910, these works continued to enthral the public:

> There are specialist collectors, who assiduously collect all of Karrik's work; they diligently buy up each new work by this talented caricaturist, and moreover become concerned in the first few days after its appearance on the market that in a week or two it will already have become a rarity.[92]

Karrik started writing and illustrating a series of children's booklets on Russian folk tales in 1909, and in old age he considered these to have been his greatest achievement. In 1917, he greeted the overthrow of the Tsar with joy, but being already ambivalent about socialism, he was left disillusioned by the Bolshevik takeover later in the year. Within a month of this change he and his wife had decided to leave the country. In a letter to the historian Sergei Melgunov, sent on 25 December, Karrik wrote: 'Olga and I are going away for an unknown length of time, at any rate, not less than two months.'[93] Karrik went no further than Norway, where he remained until his death in 1943. He never returned to Russia.[94]

⁂

The multiplicity of different publishers involved in anti-government postcard production during the 1905 Revolution speaks to the development of a consumer economy, in which every aspect of society, even political thought, was becoming subordinated to the desire or need to make a profit. As the country entered the modern age, the public had begun to demand, and been given, greater choice in both the political and commercial spheres. Now, whatever their personal beliefs may have been, no artist, printer, or publisher was entirely spared the need to adapt their activities to the market. This resulted in a rich and complicated range of motivations, which spread from the heavily politicised through to the largely mercenary.

The diversity of those involved gives credence to a broadly liberal interpretation of the Revolution, 'not as an event that made any one path of development inevitable, but rather as a critical juncture that opened up several paths.'[95] To characterise the turmoil as a few high points set against a backdrop of Tsarist perfidy and liberal acquiescence is to miss its central importance, which was that for the first time all of Russia was beginning to play a part in the political and social life of the country. Herein lay its power. The noisy chatter of different aims and objectives was the kernel of a developing civil society that might in time have helped reform the system.

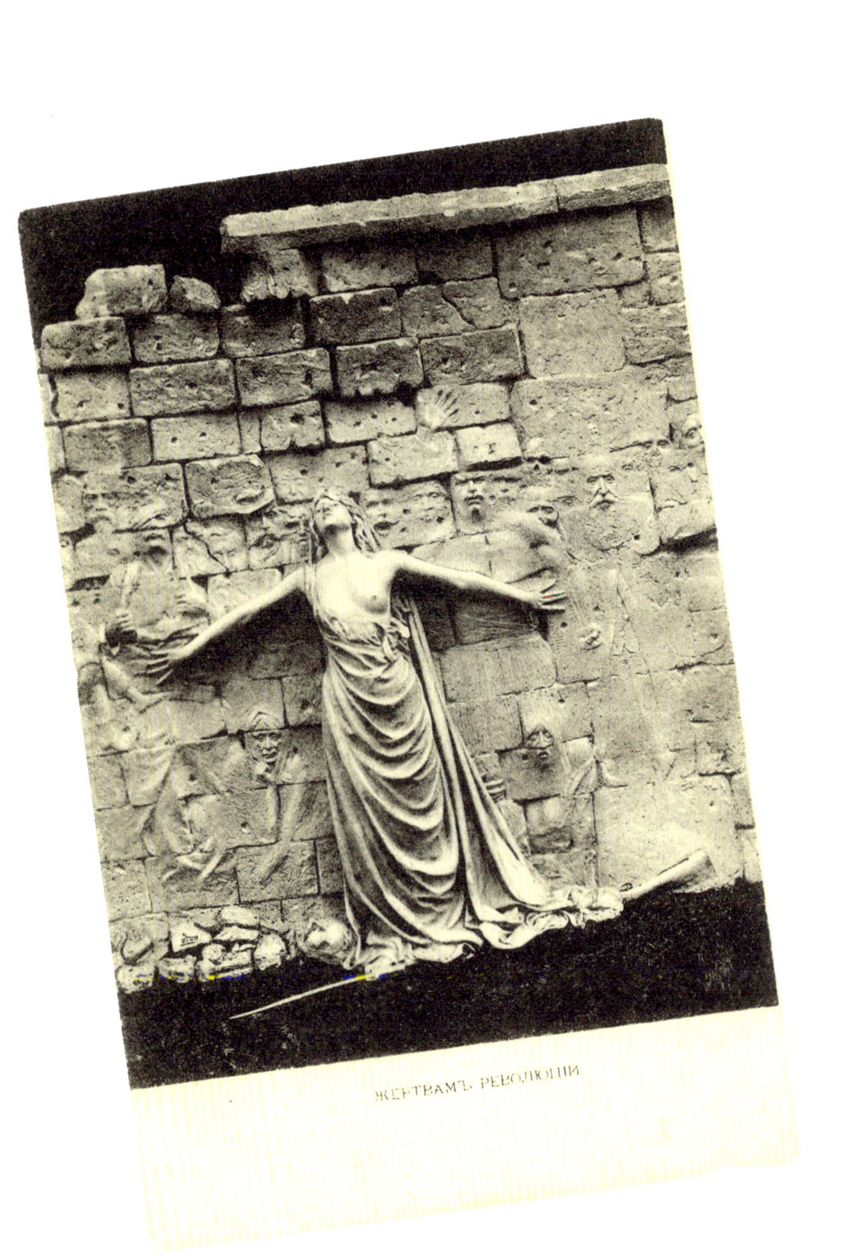

ЖЕРТВАМЪ РЕВОЛЮЦІИ

NARRATING EVENTS

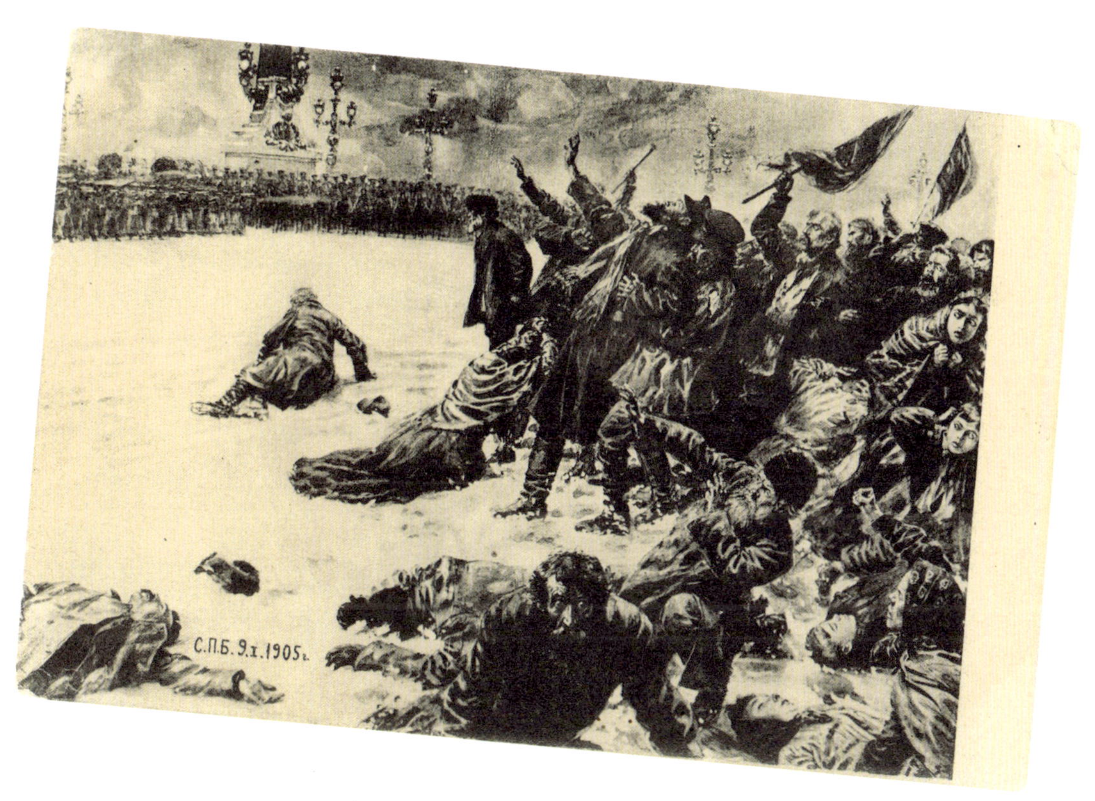

PAINTINGS AND PHOTOGRAPHS

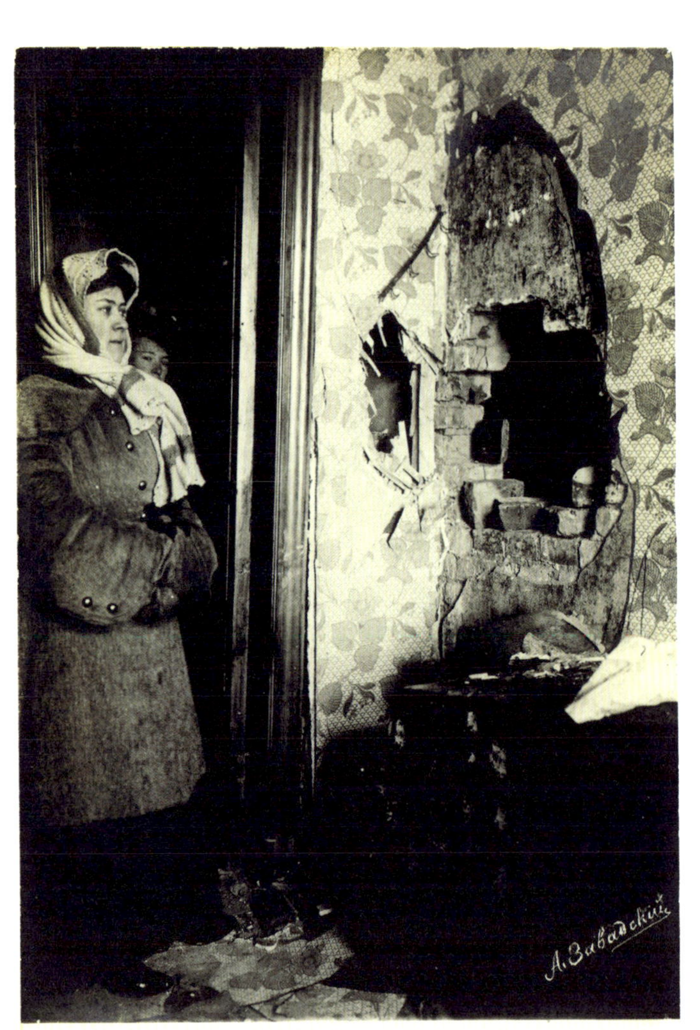

РЕВОЛЮЦІЯ ВЪ МОСКВѢ съ 7 по 19 ДЕК.

The Role of Art

In February 1905, the painters Valentin Serov and Vasilii Polenov sent a short statement to the board of the Imperial Academy of Arts condemning the government's role in bringing about Bloody Sunday and pushing for the replacement of the military governor of Saint Petersburg Grand Duke Vladimir Alexandrovich as the Academy's president: 'We artists deeply regret the fact that the person in ultimate command of the troops who spilt the blood of our brothers, should at the same time preside over the Academy of Arts, an establishment whose purpose is to bring to life humanist ideas and higher ideals.'[1] The head of the board immediately suppressed the letter and both artists resigned in protest shortly afterwards.

On the face of it, the statement was an expression of disgust at government repression, but the principles at stake here were as much about art as they were about politics. Although there were few outright supporters of the regime's repressive actions, there was considerable disagreement in the art world over how, and indeed whether, to respond to Bloody Sunday. Some maintained that all artists had a moral duty to engage with the key social issues of the day, while others firmly rejected all such temporal considerations. As Sergei Diaghilev asked: 'Does an artist, this true servant of the arts ... the creator of all true and lasting values, have anything in common with all of these ephemeral, everyday concerns?'[2]

In this struggle to define the role of art in society, the art for art's sake mentality was primarily espoused by a younger generation linked to the World of Art Group, a loose affiliation of artists who had adopted a doctrine of aestheticism in opposition to the utilitarian approach of their realist forebears. Beauty and decorative precepts always remained integral to their work, but the increase in revolutionary tempo after Bloody Sunday pushed many towards greater engagement with the contemporary world. 'Our recent work was far from politics, but our sympathies were drawn towards the liberal left,' recalled Evgenii Lansere.[3] Their political art largely comprised narrative cartoons, the majority of which were published in satirical journals.

Leftist postcard imagery, by contrast, was dominated by the work of their realist rivals. Artists adhering to this school, called the Peredvizhniki or Wanderers, believed passionately in the social function of art, and put everyday scenes at the forefront of their imagery. By the time of Bloody Sunday, the critical realist movement was already some four decades old, and although still prominent exhibitors, the Wanderers were no longer considered avant-garde. The massacre, however, brought their imagery rushing back into focus, placing them at the forefront of the push for an art that reflected the ongoing political turmoil. Largely through postcards, their work would come to pictorialize the 1905 Revolution in the popular imagination.

Previous spread from left to right

Jean-Paul Moreau-Vauthier. *To the Victims of the Revolution.* Published by Vpered, Saint Petersburg, 1906.

Samuel Begg. *Martyrs in the Cause of Freedom: The Massacre of Strikers at the End of the Troitzky Bridge.* Published by Vpered, Saint Petersburg, 1906. Originally published in *The Illustrated London News* on 4 February 1905.

Opposite

Aleksei Zavadskii. *The Revolution in Moscow 1–19 December.* No publication details, Moscow, late 1905.

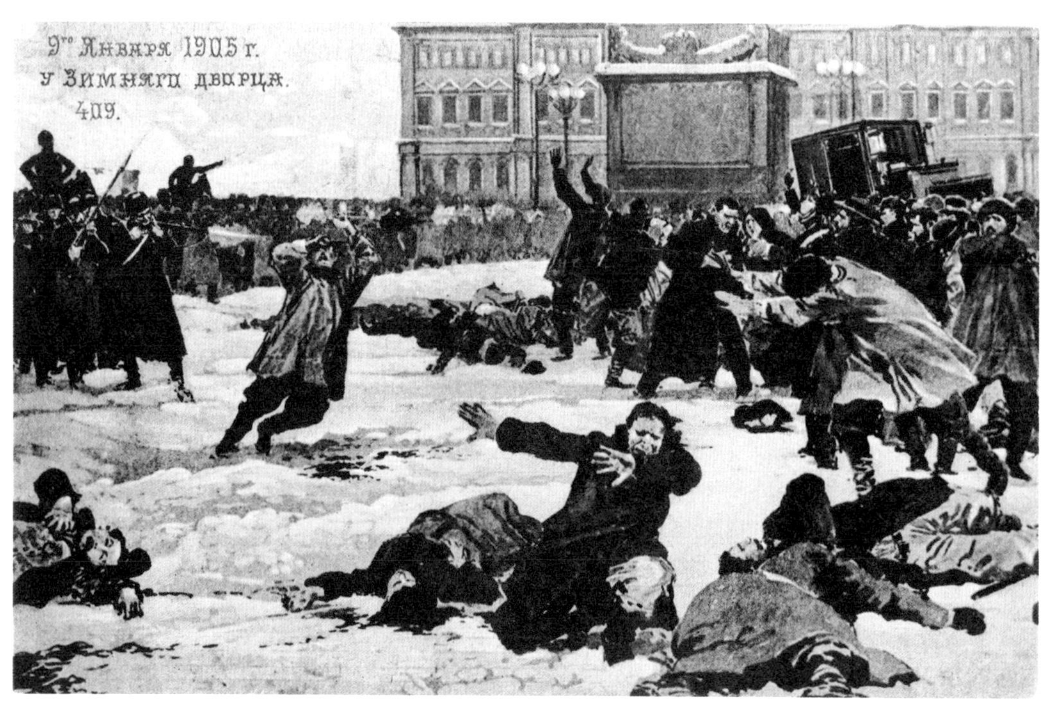
9го Января 1905 г.
у Зимняго дворца.
409.

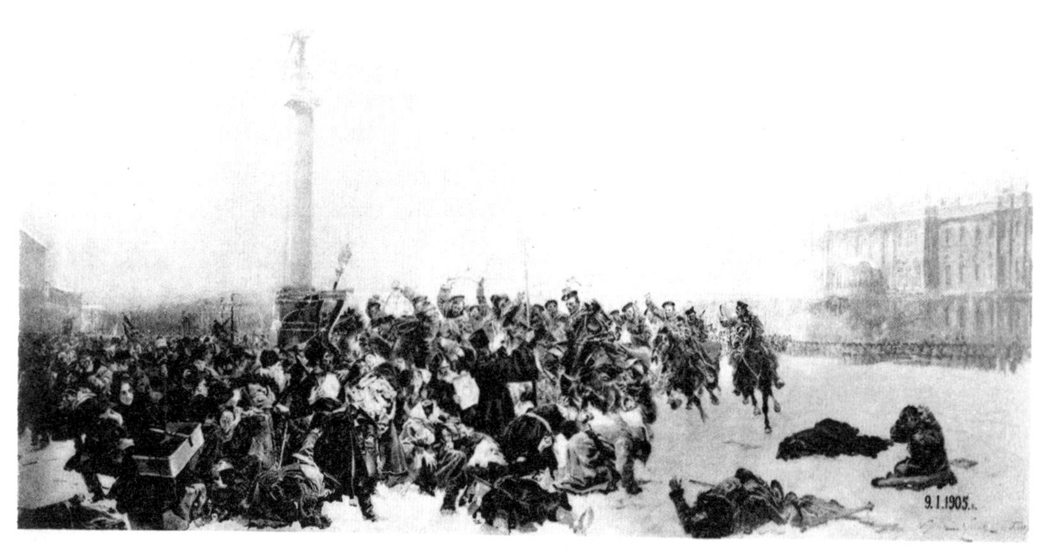
9.1.1905.

Several artists made sketches of the 9 January massacre, but very few, if any, were exhibited or published prior to the October Manifesto.[4] Angering the regime still carried penalties, and for most the political and financial risks of showing such work in public were disincentive enough. The issue, however, was not only a lack of legal outlets, but also the want of any links to revolutionary organisations that might have provided alternative methods of reproduction and dissemination.[5] Largely for this reason, none of the postcard depictions printed in the immediate aftermath of Bloody Sunday were made by Russian artists. Instead, most reproduce illustrations taken from Western European periodicals, which were easily obtained and smuggled into Russia by the revolutionaries abroad.[6]

Fortunino Matania. *9 January 1905. By the Winter Palace.* No publication details, circa 1905.

None of the artists who made these illustrations were present at the events they depicted, instead basing their finished works on sketches provided by eyewitnesses. All, however, offered an uncompromisingly stark image of Tsarist brutality. *9 January 1905*, a drawing by the French illustrator Georges Scott, shows mounted cavalry slashing their way through a tide of panic-stricken demonstrators. To the forefront a worker runs towards the viewer, his face gripped with fear, while behind them, silhouetted against the snow, lie the bodies of a woman and a small child. The caption to the image in *The Illustrated London News* reads: 'The deeds that were done in Saint Petersburg … will one day bear the bitter fruit of revolt.'[7]

Paintings by the British-born artist Samuel Begg and the Italian Fortunino Matania show similar scenes of horror, in which the violence is disproportionate and the victims often women and young children. While it is intriguing to think that the Russian population's initial impressions of the killings were informed by foreign fantasy, their benefit to the radical opposition is not hard to see. Irrespective of the original intentions of their illustrators, in the eyes of the revolutionaries these images advanced the cause of violent insurrection, showing that the state would meet even peaceful protesters with blades and bullets. The only message that could be drawn from this was that in the future more extreme methods of protest would be needed.[8]

Wojciech Kossak. *Bloody Sunday.* Published by Vpered, Saint Petersburg, 1906.

Such unambiguous depictions of Bloody Sunday helped to push forward the revolutionary cause by creating an easily comprehensible narrative of events. They instructed viewers in the story of an oppressive state killing its own citizens and they established the dead as martyrs to the cause of liberation, martyrs whose deaths would by implication need to be justified and avenged through further action. The political complexities of early twentieth century Russia were thus reduced to a simple fight between good and evil – for freedom and against tyranny – and in clearly defining the heroes

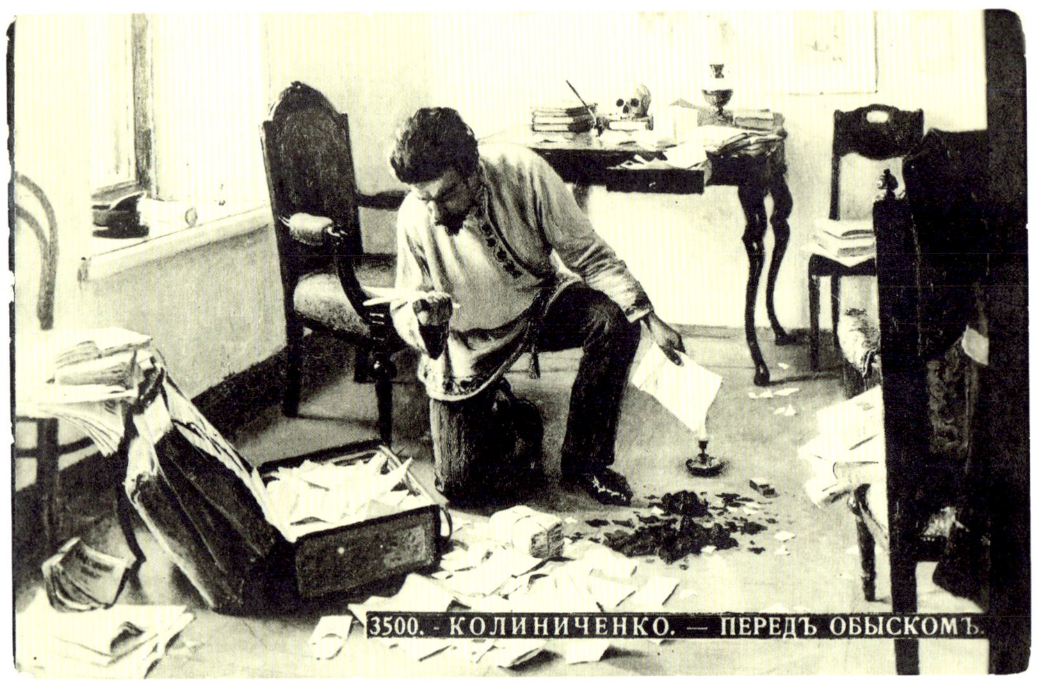

Iakob Kalinichenko. *Before the Search.* No publication details, circa 1906.

and villains that represented the two sides, they provided a template for interpreting this, and future revolutionary events.

Postcards were the only images of Bloody Sunday that received widespread distribution in Russia in early 1905 and, in the absence of other visual documentation, their version of the 'truth' won out. The idea that the state had brutally suppressed a popular demonstration without care for human life became common currency not only among revolutionaries, but also among the population at large.

Imperial officials, who understood the dangers of these images all too well, made various attempts to curtail their dissemination. In June 1905, the Press Administration sent a circular to all censorship committees forbidding the reproduction of two paintings of Bloody Sunday, then being exhibited in Vienna. So concerned was the Administration about the paintings, which were by the artists Wojciech Kossak and Hans Temple, that it also forbade any mention of them in the press.[9] This, however, did little to prevent revolutionary groups from printing postcards underground, and irrespective of government efforts, images of Bloody Sunday were widely disseminated.

For the regime, which wanted nothing more than to forget that the event had ever happened, opposition postcards showcasing regime violence were a menace that would not go away. In December 1906, Major General Bendorf sent a telegram from the Saint Petersburg Central Military Precinct reporting that there were 'photographs and cards displayed in the windows of many shops carrying completely unacceptable imagery relating to current events.' These postcards, he added, 'undoubtedly serve to keep the [revolutionary] unrest in the minds of people.'[10]

Bendorf's concerns were fully justified. From 9 January onwards, government repression was a major catalyst for the ongoing upheaval in Russia. Postcards commemorating the killing of innocents fed the appetite for revolution, providing memories of the sacrifices that had been made, and giving the public an ever-present reminder of the day the state turned the guns on its own people.

Paintings on Political Themes

By the spring of 1905, the range of postcards being printed by the revolutionaries had widened to include reproductions of paintings on subject matter other than Bloody Sunday. Contemporary artists in Russia, however, still had their hands tied. One critic, discussing the latest artistic trends, noted the disappointment of visitors to that season's exhibitions who had hoped to find some resonance of recent political developments in the paintings on display: 'Even the Wanderers, who if previous years were anything to go by, gave the public full reason to expect pictures on contemporary subject matter, did nothing to justify their hopes.'[11] In the absence of any new works to reproduce, postcard publishers turned their attention to earlier paintings.

Two of the most popular images were Iakob Kalinichenko's *Before the Search* (1895) and Nikolai Iaroshenko's *Prisoner* (1878).[12] Both are narrative scenes that transmit a story of defiance against current circumstance. In the former, a revolutionary hurriedly sets light to a pile of compromising papers, while in the latter an imprisoned radical is shown gazing through the window of his cell. The prisoner looks not only to the world outside but also to the future, which radiates light back into the darkened confines of the present day. As with images of Bloody Sunday, these pictures were intended to guide the population towards political action. But in this case, rather than fostering resentment against the state, they inspire the viewer to believe that through revolutionary dedication a better world would one day be achieved.

With the promulgation of the October Manifesto, realist painting on contemporary subject matter started to emerge into the public sphere. It took time for larger oils to be completed and shown, but at the 1906 spring salons, the authorities granted permission for a group of openly political images to be exhibited. Scenes dealing with contemporary social issues were now placed on an equal footing with grand history painting of the past, strengthening the notion that the fate of the people was somehow fundamental to the future of the nation. The popular press was quick to pick up on these changing winds – in March the illustrated supplement *Iskry* ran a large picture feature, titled 'New Motifs in Russian Art'.[13]

Nikolai Feshin. *An Accidental Victim*. No publication details, circa 1906.

The ostensible purpose of the article was to acquaint the public with recent artistic developments, but its aims were political as well as cultural. The paintings chosen were all strongly anti-government in tone, with a heavy emphasis on images of state violence. Furthermore, at least two of them, including Viktor Mazurovskii's *Clearing the Square* (1906) (depicting Cossacks dispersing a demonstration), and Petr Geller's *After the Pogrom* (1905), had been banned from public exhibit, yet again showing the role of the print industry in disseminating imagery that might otherwise not have found an audience. Both these works, as well as many others illustrated in *Iskry*, were also distributed in postcard form, further extending their public reach.[14]

Among the paintings to appear in the feature were Ivan Vladimirov's *In Presnia* (1906), depicting troops confronting civilians amid a scene of urban devastation, and Nikolai Feshin's *Pacified* (1906), showing the death of a young man during the Moscow Uprising. Unlike earlier representations of depredation and poverty, which allude only vaguely to the entity responsible, the presence of government soldiers in both these pictures serves to point the finger of blame directly at the regime. In *Pacified*, the more forceful of the two, the viewer's focus is drawn first to the feet of a dead body near the front of the image then guided back through the tip of a bayonet to a line of troops: sympathy for the victim is thus channelled into anger against the state.

Moisei Maimon. *Back Home*. Published by Vpered, Saint Petersburg, 1906.

Feshin's painting is also known by the title *An Accidental Victim*. Innocent protagonists are common to almost all representations of government repression – the characters who inhabit them are rarely armed revolutionaries dying heroic deaths, but guiltless martyrs killed by a despotic system. Moisei Maimon's *Back Home* (1906), which was also reproduced in *Iskry*, marks a highpoint of the genre. It depicts an injured Jewish soldier returning home from the Russo-Japanese War to find that his wife and child have been murdered during a recent pogrom. He has the thanks of an ungrateful nation. Nationalistic and anti-Semitic violence aroused widespread revulsion and the effect of pictures such as this was not only to turn public opinion against the regime, but also to radicalise it.

The inevitable upshot of repression can be seen in Vladimirov's *Don't Go* (1906), the archetypal image of a revolutionary from the 1905 period, as well as one of the most widely reproduced of all anti-government postcards. The painting, which depicts an armed worker resisting the entreaties of his beloved not to fight on the barricades, was based on a sketch that Vladimirov made from life during the Moscow Uprising. As the man's wife pleads with

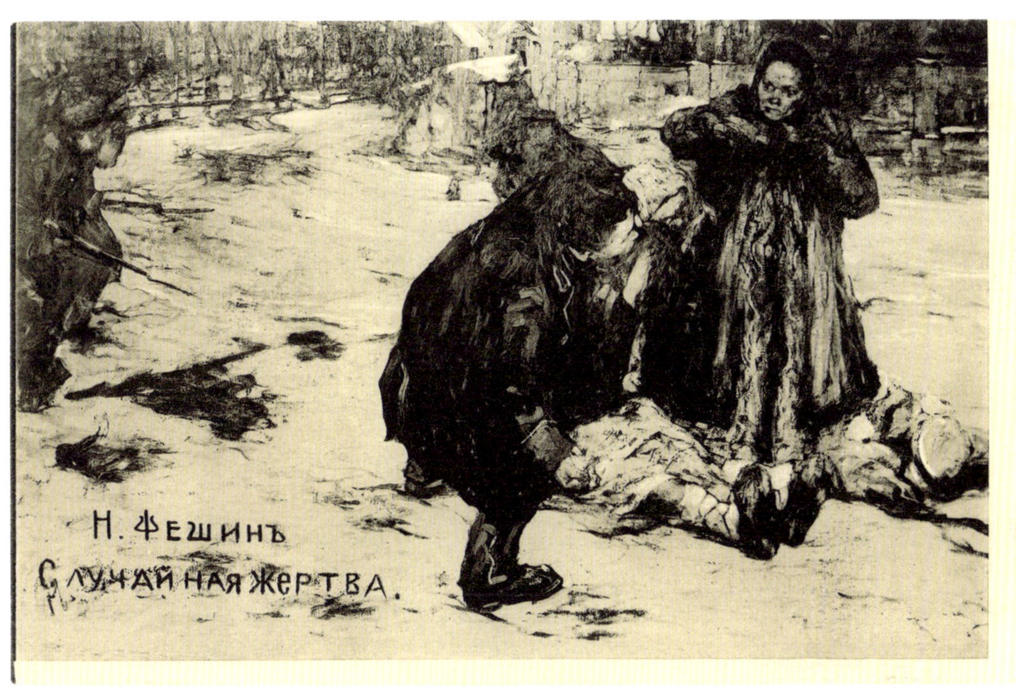

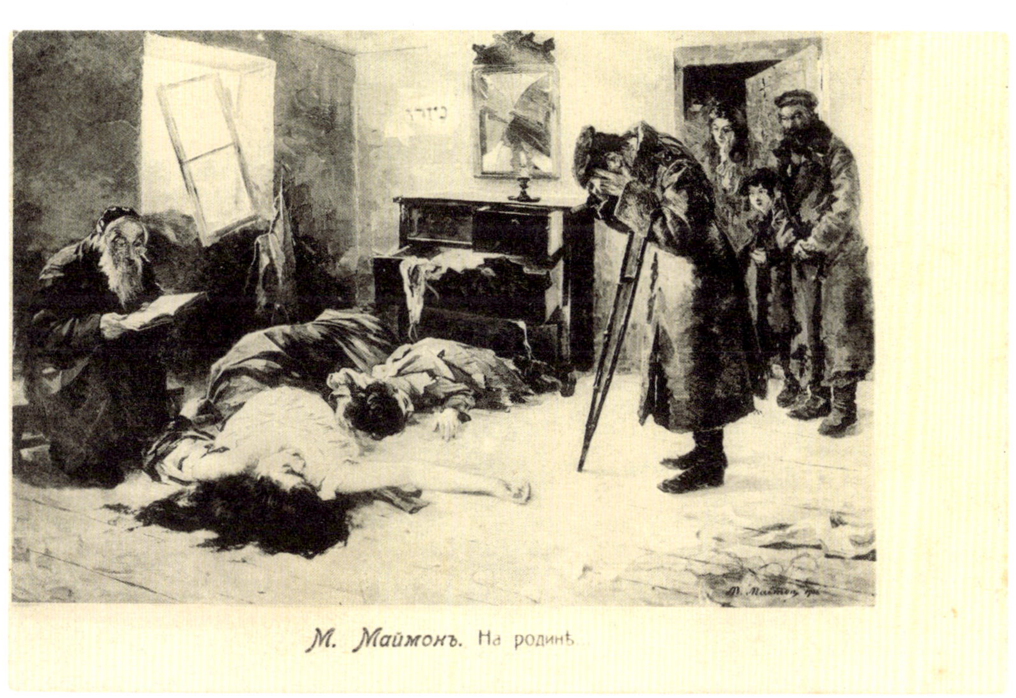

М. Маймонъ. На родинѣ

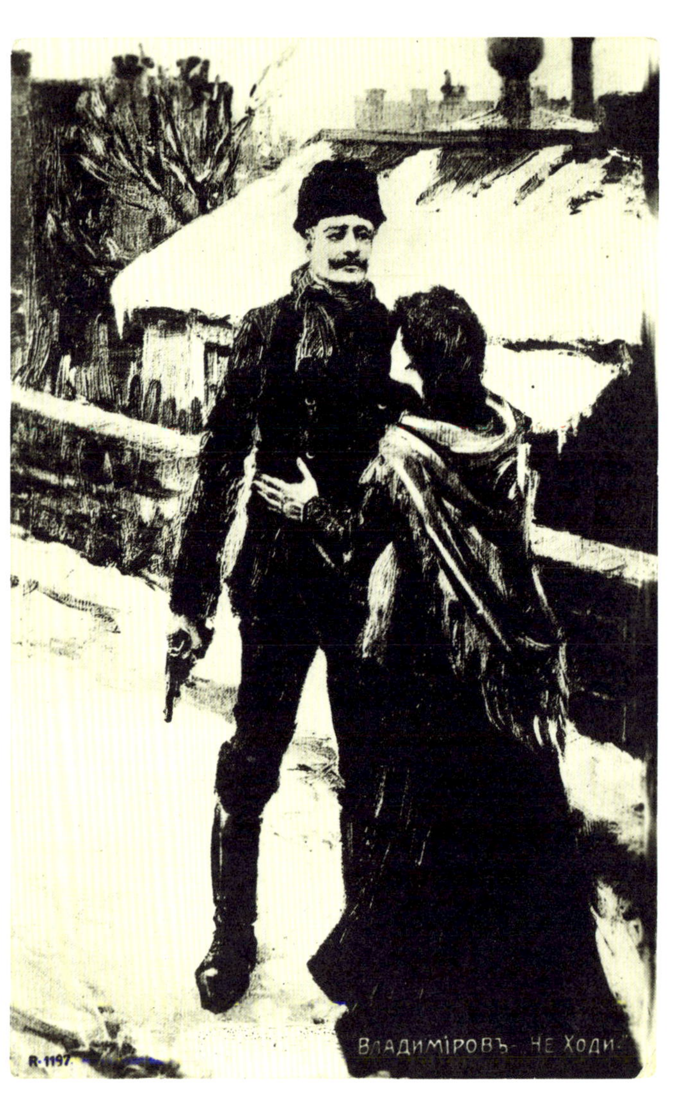
ВЛАДИМIРОВЪ - „НЕ ХОДИ“
R·1197

him not to leave her, he stands firm, a drawn pistol by his side. His look is broadly sympathetic, but while she speaks, his attention is fixed on the middle-distance, where we imagine the barricades to be located. He knows where his duty lies.

It is a heroic image, but the heroism is as much about personal sacrifice as it is about bravery; this dispute between husband and wife contrasts a weak-willed woman, guided by her emotions, and a stout-hearted revolutionary, who understands the importance of overcoming individual feelings in the fight for freedom. Everything, even love, must be renounced, if liberty is to be gained.[15] For those inclined to revolutionary action, or even for those who simply resented the government, Vladimirov's picture offered a source of inspiration, serving as a counterpoint to images of repression by presenting an alternative to simply knuckling under in the face of ongoing government repression.

Ivan Vladimirov.
Don't Go.
No publication details, circa 1906.

The Art of Historical Appropriation

The 1905 Revolution saw a boom in printed pamphlets relating to international socialism and political rebellion. These have a direct analogue in postcards reproducing scenes from the French Revolutions and 1848 uprisings in Europe. At their most basic, the aim of these works was to promote images of insurrection to an embittered public. Fighters on the barricades, flag-waving maidens, and heroic martyr revolutionaries all served to propagandise opposition to the status quo. Celebrated paintings such as Delacroix's *Liberty Leading the People* (1830), and Doré's *The Marseillaise* (1870) also provided a veneer of historical legitimacy, as well as a touch of glamour to the idea of revolution, chiming with contemporary myth-making about events in Russia.

For many commercial firms, postcards on historical subject matter simply offered another way to profit from anti-government sentiment, but for a concentrated nucleus of revolutionary publishers they also had a compelling theoretical dimension. While more liberal firms were intent on publicising past revolutions to foment opposition to the regime and so gain support for democratic reform, the revolutionaries, and in particular the Social Democrats, were set on using historical imagery in order to educate a dedicated cadre of socialist activists, whom they hoped might one day stand in the vanguard of violent revolt. Their postcards were essentially instruction manuals, designed to advance a long-term programme of ideological indoctrination.

The postcards produced by Utro and Vpered can be divided into four distinct categories: portraits of Marxist theorists, depictions of striking workers, images of the unrest in Russia, and pictures of historical revolutions.

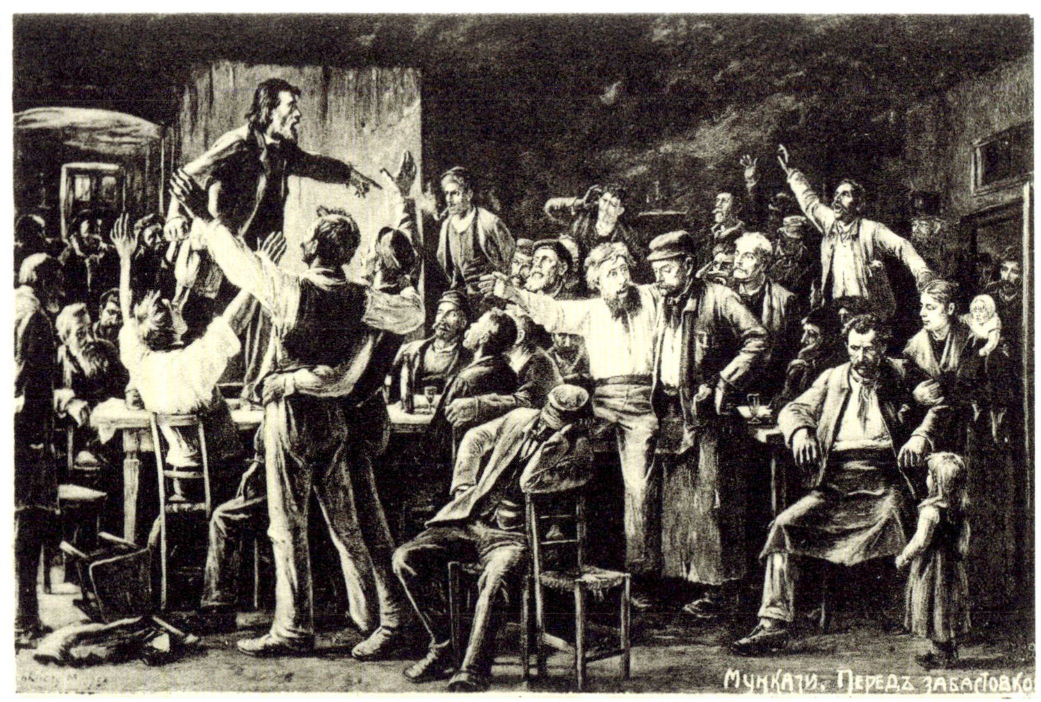

Mihály Munkácsy. *Strike*. Published by Vpered, Saint Petersburg, 1906.

These works had three overlapping aims: propagandising revolutionary belief, instructing the people in Marxist thought, and establishing Russia in general and the Social Democratic Party specifically as the inheritors of the European revolutionary tradition. Broadly speaking, they can be read as a sequence: the theorists interpret historical developments to show that industrial progress creates class conflict, which in turn leads to clashes with the regime, and eventually to a popular uprising and change of government.

The Social Democrats therefore used postcards on historical themes as a way of grounding political and economic developments in Russia within the Marxist dialectic. Their role was to offer visual evidence of the emergence of new social forces in Europe over the previous 120 years, and to link these changes to the situation in Russia. This ideological conceit was neatly summarised by Bonch-Bruevich in *Nasha mysl*: 'Just as happened there [Europe], so in Russia the development of the country's production forces created new social relationships and brought forth new social classes, which in turn also became new political forces, thus forcing the old powers to give way to them, and hand over power.'[16]

The first stage in this historical process is illustrated by postcards parading the miseries of an exploited labour force, such as Petr Buchkin's *Death of a Worker*. This pitiful image was not solely an expression of sympathy with the working classes but also an attempt to stir opposition to capitalism, and so to speed along the economic and political timeline.

The belief was that once the workers had become aware of their downtrodden position in society, they would immediately assume an active stance in response. This much-hoped-for next step can be seen in pictures such as Mihály Munkácsy's *Strike*, which according to a Marxist worldview, were intended to illustrate the creation of a new political force.

Such images helped to reinforce the politicisation of strike action, giving a sense of progressive unity to what were more often than not uncoordinated acts of protest, stimulated by economic, as opposed to political constraints. Their commemoration at the expense of images celebrating the ongoing political process in the Duma, where liberal reformers were pushing for change in their own, very different way, reflects efforts by the Social Democrats to highlight the purported role of the proletariat in driving forward events. In a determinist recasting of the mechanisms at work in 1905, the Party's postcards present the workers as a united, class-conscious force, capable of their own political organisation.

Apart from theorists who were valued for their ideas, not their actions, there are no individual heroes here, just the collective force of the proletariat. Bringing about its political unification was the Party's primary task – only once this had been achieved could coordinated strike action begin, and from here, revolt against the regime itself would inexorably follow. Claims that this stage was already underway in Russia were validated by images of Bloody Sunday and the December Uprising, which in the Social Democratic worldview illustrated the early stirrings of class warfare against the capitalist classes.

The denouement to this teleological narrative is provided by depictions of past revolutions in Europe, which were meant to offer proof of the historical inevitability of popular rebellion. Russia, these images all imply, was next in line.

Within the context in which they were produced, Social Democratic postcards constitute little more than ideology masquerading as reality, and in this, they bear a strong affinity to Soviet-era Socialist Realism. Indeed, together, the images provide an ideological model for what was to follow: projection of the future through manipulation of past and present.

Photographic Postcards

Amateur snapshots of the revolutionary upheaval are rare, and as far as can be ascertained, there were no specialist photographers among the revolutionary groups. Instead, most of the pictures used for anti-government postcards were taken by professionals, often on behalf of foreign and, later, Russian illustrated journals.[17] This explains the great rarity of photographic postcards depicting revolutionary events before autumn 1905. Until this

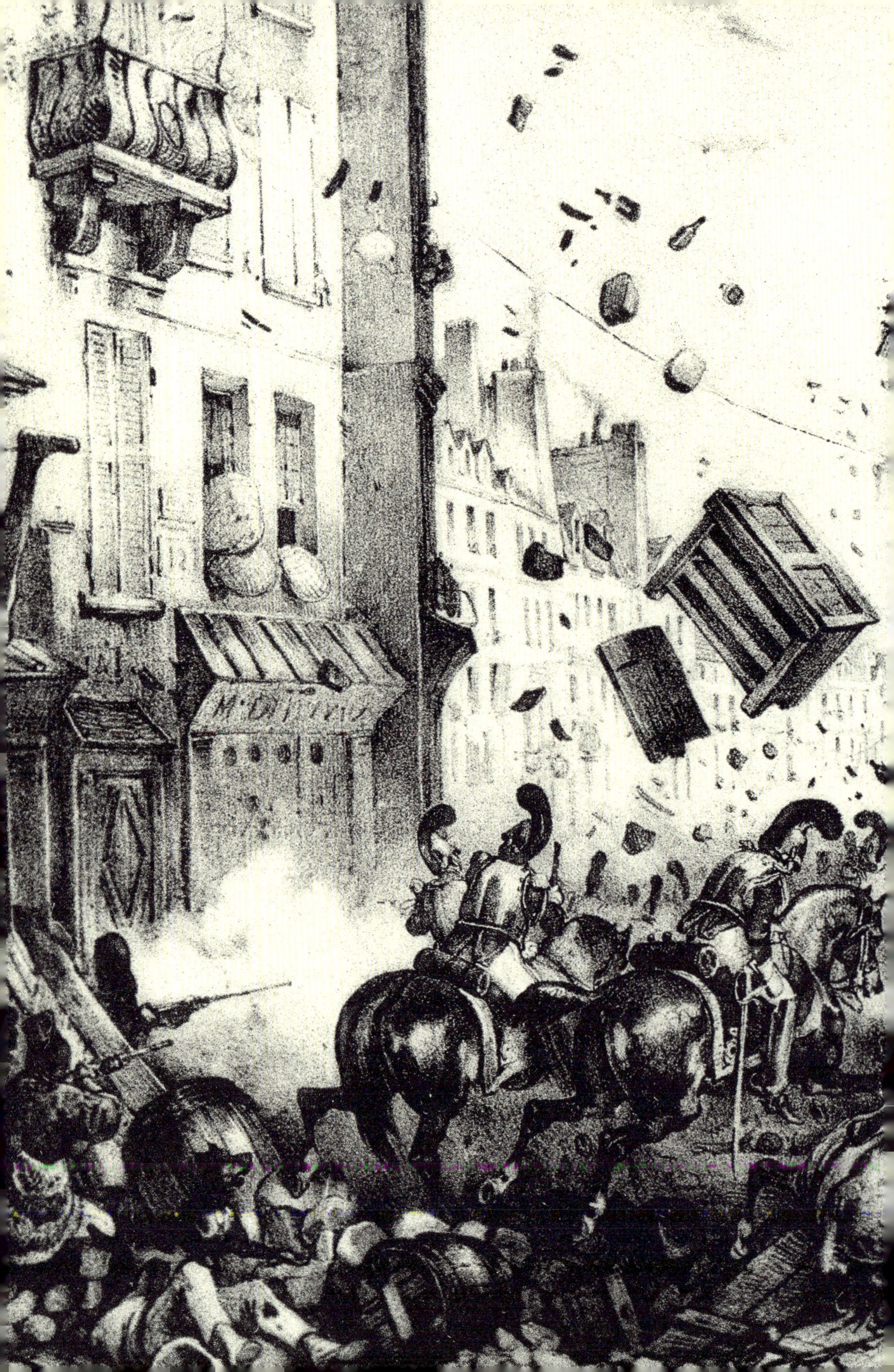

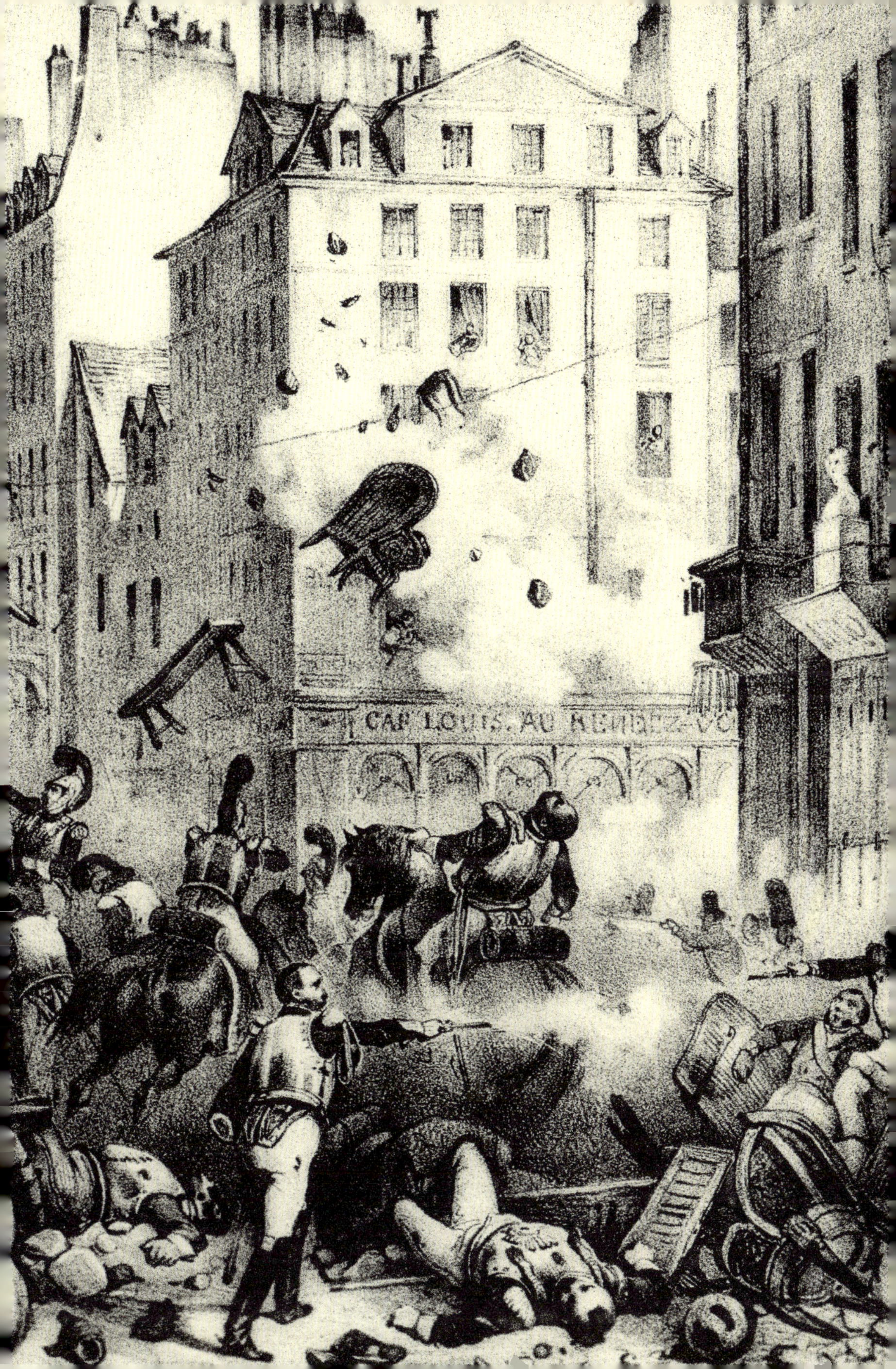
CAF LOUIS. AU

Previous spread

Victor Adam. *Saint-Antoine Street. 1830*. Published by Vpered, Saint Petersburg, 1906.

time, the only legal outlet for such imagery was in Western Europe; therefore, unless a particular political event or incident constituted serious unrest or terrorism, there was limited incentive or, for that matter, opportunity for photographers to document instances of popular protest in Russia.

The predominantly commercial nature of revolutionary photography meant that ideology played little part in governing what was recorded. Choice of subject matter was instead based on what the censor would permit. These were therefore images that, initially at least, sought to record political developments rather than to define them. Coverage was largely restricted to the major revolutionary spectacles, in particular, the popular demonstrations that took place after the October Manifesto and the December Uprising in Moscow. Despite ubiquitous violence, the dead are rarely shown – this was a view of revolution that had been strained through the censor's sieve, and as a result, it was largely unbloodied by reality.

Photographs relating to pogroms are a curious exception to this tendency towards sanitised imagery. In August 1905, the Kiev censor had banned images of anti-Semitic rampages in Zhitomir, but by November *Iskry* was openly printing images of violent attacks in Ekaterinoslav and Mikhailovsk, and later the same month in Sebastopol and Kaluga.[18] Graphic pictures of the aftermath of these pogroms circulated as postcards, many of them depicting long lines of brutally disfigured corpses. Like all images of death, they are voyeuristic. But if interest in them was at least partly prurient, they also played an important political role, revealing the depths to which regime supporters were now stooping.

The loosening of restrictions that had for so long constrained the political sphere, and the markedly increased possibilities for publication after October 1905, generated a strong commercial incentive for professional photographers to go into the streets and start documenting the revolutionary action. On 18 October, when crowds gathered in the capital to celebrate the passing of the Manifesto, Bulla was on hand to capture the scenes. His photographs of the street demonstrations appeared the following month in the illustrated journal *Niva*.[19] Two were later reprinted in postcard form: one of crowds outside Saint Petersburg University, and the other of a political rally on the banks of the River Neva.[20]

Violence soon cut festivities short. Among the victims that day was the thirty-two-year-old Bolshevik and veterinarian Nikolai Bauman. His funeral in Moscow on 20 October was the occasion for a mass outpouring of collective grief. Funerals often assumed political dimensions in Tsarist Russia because they were one of the few occasions when large crowds were permitted to gather on the streets, and as such had long served as a focus for displays of opposition sentiment. Earlier that month, liberal opponents of autocracy had congregated to mourn the reformer Prince Sergei Trubetskoi;

now, Bauman's untimely death provided the opportunity for another display of popular might.

The authorities allowed a public funeral to take place but did not bargain for its size. The funeral procession was attended by tens of thousands of people and went on for most of the day. As the crowds marched through the streets of Moscow, the atmosphere of resistance was enlivened by songs, flags, and banners, some of which called openly for the downfall of autocracy. Bauman's laying to rest thus became both a public synthesis of anti-government anger and an expression of sorrow at the loss of political freedom that his death portended. In Gorky's opinion, the funeral's 'beauty, grandeur, and sense of order' was without compare.[21]

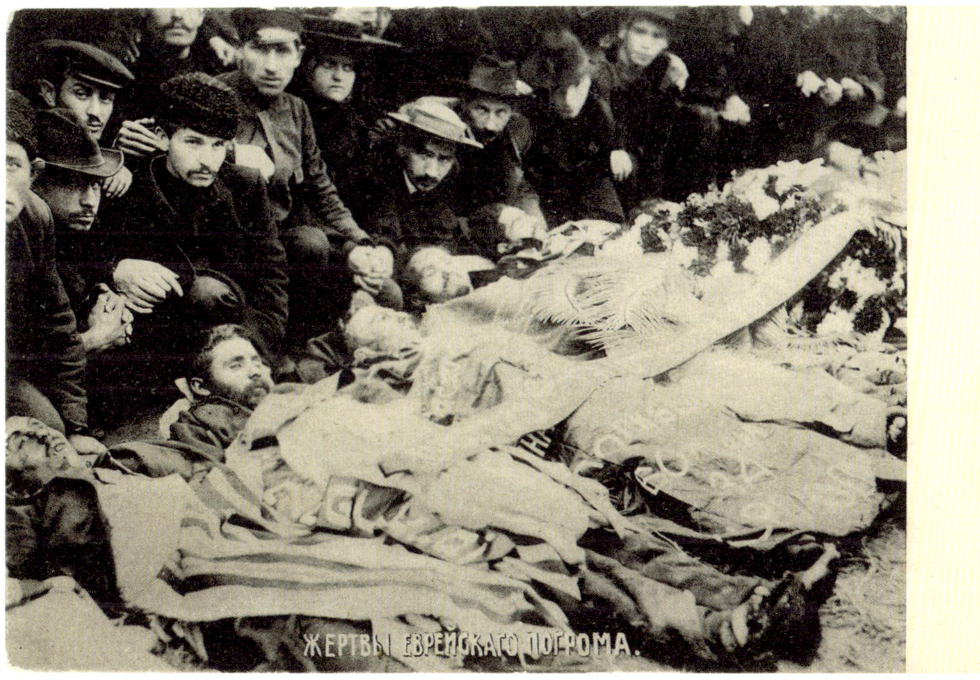

Anonymous photographer. *Victims of a Jewish Pogrom.* Published by A. Freinkel, Saint Petersburg, 1906.

At least five different firms published photographic postcards of the procession, of which there are around seven different images known.[22] Some of these enterprises, such as the Moscow printing house LUMO, were small photographic studios working largely for commercial gain. Others were underground facilities run by individuals closely connected to the revolutionaries, such as Dmitrii Peschanskii. It is not known who was responsible for taking the original photographs, but irrespective of their identity and ideological orientation, the process of mass reproduction transformed what was essentially a medium for documenting an occasion into a device for propagandising it.

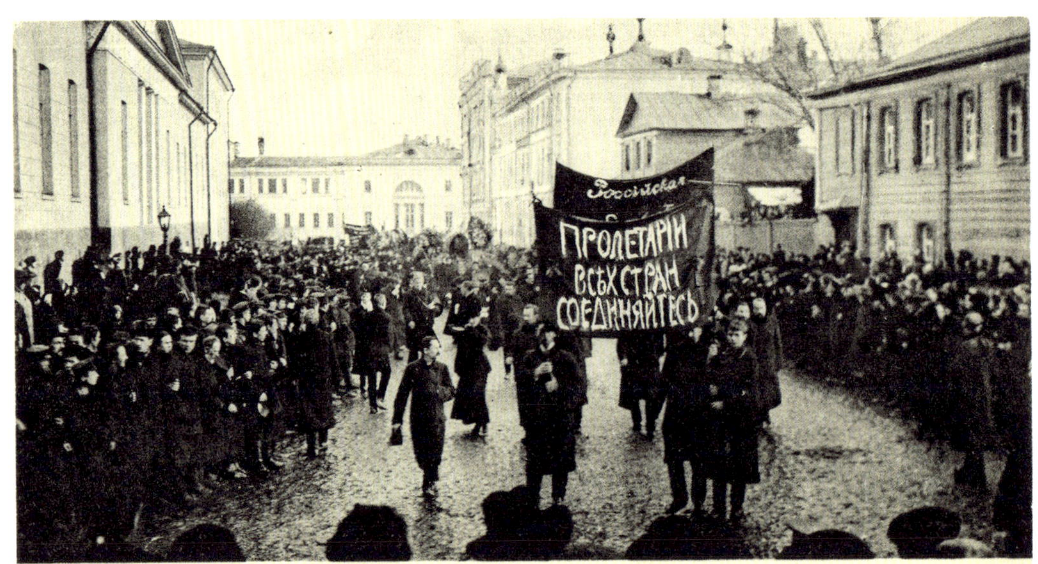

Похороны Н. Е. Баумана 20 окт. 1905 г.

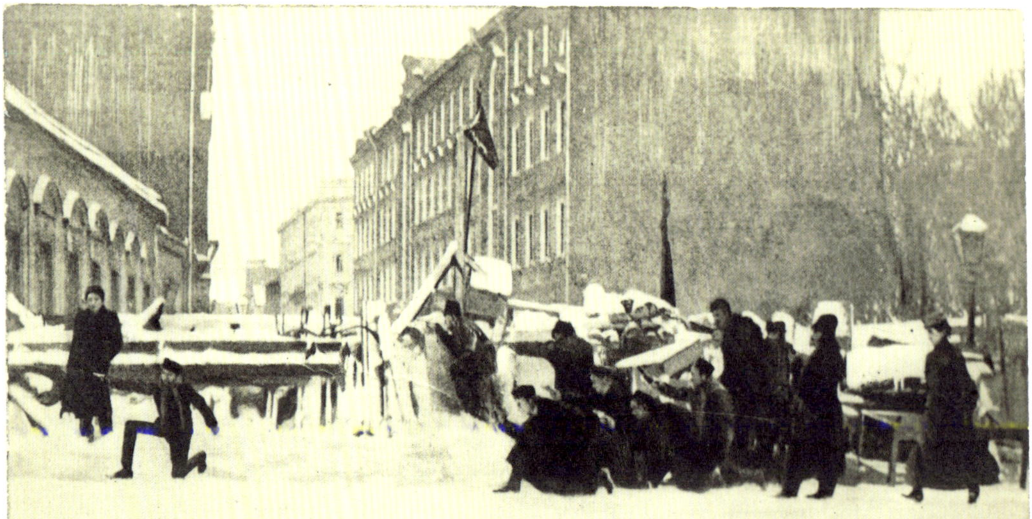

For the first time in history, the Russian people were portrayed in photographic form as driving forward events. Artists had looked to achieve something similar in painting, but there was a difference between a picture that reproduced an idea and a photograph that conveyed an unvarnished visual truth. The reality it presented, however, was all soft focus. Revolutions are uncertain times and crowds are unpredictable entities, but these images presented a completely settled view of the liberation movement and the cause for which it was fighting. Held fast by photographic fixer, the pictures imposed a sense of order on the contemporary chaos and offered a unified vision of opposition to the Tsar, around which all could coalesce.

Anonymous photographer. *The Funeral of N. E. Bauman 20 October 1905*. No publication details, late 1905.

Pictures of large political meetings were intended by the revolutionaries to reinforce the notion of popular hostility towards the autocratic regime and so to provide encouragement to the movement at large as it headed towards what was always portrayed as an unavoidable confrontation with the state. In the official report of the Social Democrats' Second Congress, demonstrations were described as being 'one of the most important means to educate the masses politically and to strengthen our influence.'[23] The bigger they got, the Party claimed, the more likely it was that they would end up in armed clashes. Such images were thus intended both to inspire and provoke.

Photographic postcards of anti-government demonstrations laid permanent claim to the civic spaces of Russia's two greatest cities. The streets of Saint Petersburg and Moscow had only been the property of the Revolution for a few days, but photography fixed these moments in time forever. Anyone wanting to know about the revolutionary situation in late 1905 now had material proof of what had happened, showing these people demonstrating, in this location, on that day, in those numbers. Just as regimes erect monuments in towns and cities to remind the population of their political dominance over the surrounding area, so too postcards immortalised the 1905 Revolution in the minds and homes of their owners.

Anonymous photographer. Photograph of revolutionaries on the barricades during the Moscow Uprising. No publication details, late 1905.

The Moscow Uprising

In December 1905, armed confrontation with government forces brought forth a final rush of photographic postcards, most of which reproduce images published in Moscow and Saint Petersburg illustrated journals between late 1905 and early 1906.[24] These can be divided into two categories, named for the titles of the commonly found postcard series: 'Moscow under the Barricades' and 'The Aftermath of the Uprising in Moscow'. The first group of images, which show the extensive network of barriers erected before the fighting broke out, date to 10–15 December. Pictures in the second group, which detail the destruction caused by light artillery on buildings in the Presnia District, were taken around 19 December.[25]

Unlike Bloody Sunday, the Moscow Uprising resulted in serious damage to the material fabric of the city. Once the blood had been washed away from Palace Square, there was little left to show that a massacre had taken place, but in Presnia the smoking stumps of buildings stood testament to the revolt and its barbarous suppression for months to come. The obvious physical impact of the Uprising meant that, on a superficial level, depictions of the aftermath could transcend their immediate revolutionary subject matter to serve as straightforward souvenirs. In this sense, they fed into the popular genre of 'disaster postcards,' which specialised in showing urban landscapes disrupted by phenomena, both natural and human.

Postcards of the familiar brutalised had a ready appeal, and purchasing works relating to the revolt need not have reflected strongly-held opposition beliefs. Their allure was to anyone who was interested in Russia, inside and outside the country. Many, including cards published by LUMO and D.P. Efimov, had captions in French and Russian, and these proved popular among foreign residents. A typical message on one postcard sent from Russia to France reads: 'My dear Marcel, I am sending you this souvenir of the uprising in Moscow last December, and I'll send you another card soon, Yours,

Booklet of postcards titled: *Moscow in December/Barricades.* Russkoe tovarishchestvo pechatnogo i izdatelskogo dela, Moscow, 1906.

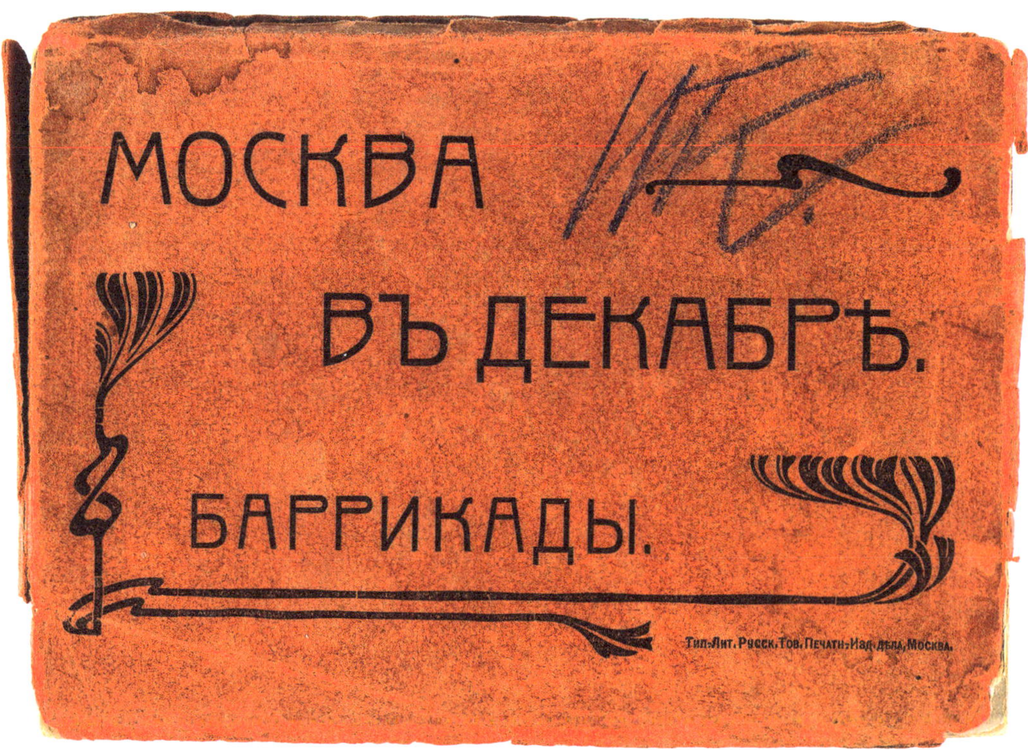

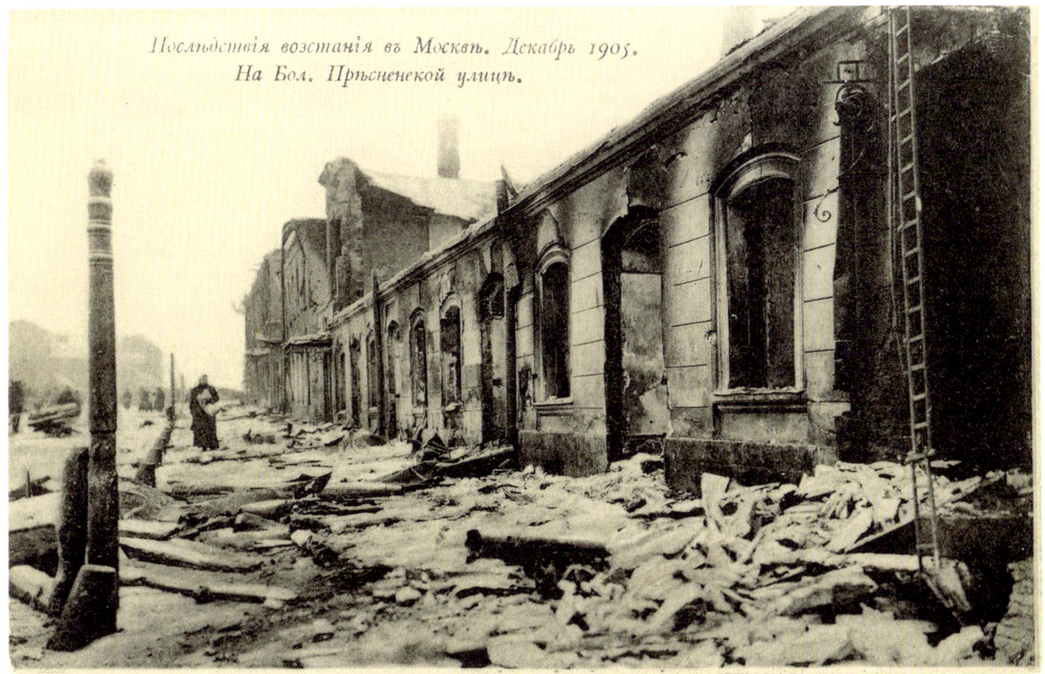

Anonymous photographer.
The Aftermath of the Uprising in Moscow. December 1905. On Bolshaia Presnenskaia Street.
No publication details, circa early 1906.

L. Lecomter.'[26] It was not quite 'wish you were here,' but it still represented a light-hearted look at contemporary affairs from a non-partisan observer.

The propaganda function of these postcards is self-evident. Pictures of militants standing atop the barricades celebrated opposition to the regime and established a visual link to images of their Western European predecessors. Furthermore, the contrast between photographs of the heroic insurgents and those of the smouldering buildings that were left in their wake clearly conveys a narrative of brave rebellion against a ruthless state. Even for non-revolutionary consumers, images of the destruction fed into widespread disapproval at the way in which the rebellion had been put down, without care for private dwellings or factories, giving credence to accusations that the government had used excessive force against the rebels.

However, none of these postcards can be proven to be revolutionary publications. Although the episode would later assume mythic status, it was seen at the time as a painful disappointment, seeming only to represent a deficiency of tactics and organisation. While photographs of the devastation are anti-government in spirit, the destruction that they document is not only to parts of Moscow, but also to hopes of a successful rebellion. Defeat marked the end of any immediate possibility of overthrowing the state, and as a result many revolutionaries may have felt that other events were more worthy of celebration. Only once victory has been assured can past failure be commemorated with confidence.

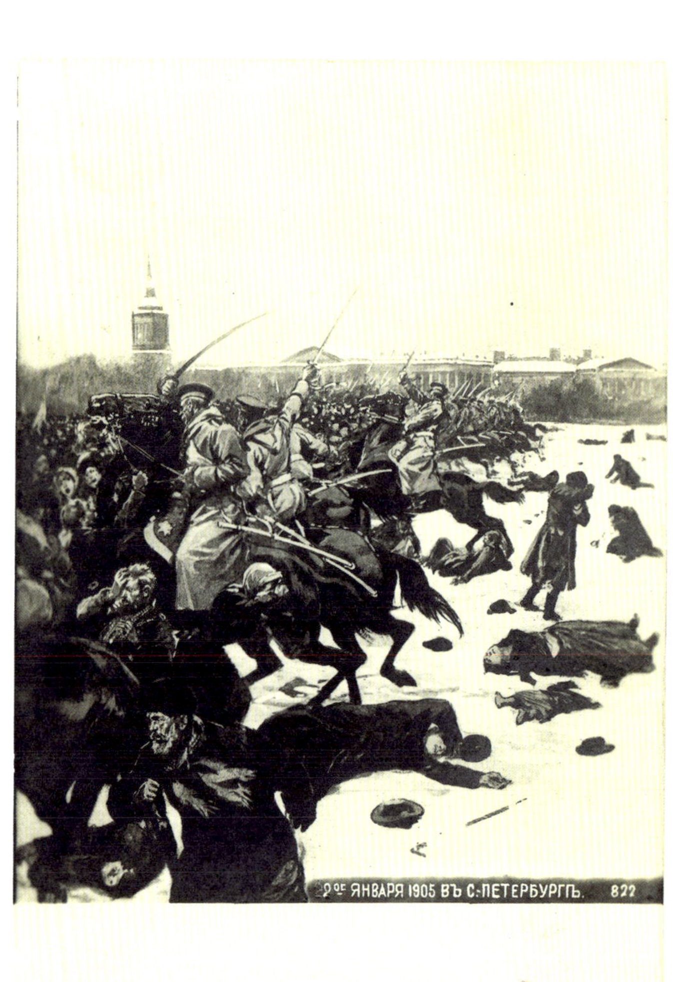
9ое ЯНВАРЯ 1905 ВЪ С.-ПЕТЕРБУРГѢ. 822

⁜

Realist images of political events helped to forge a parallel reality during the 1905 Revolution, one that existed alongside the Imperial version, but that allowed the nation to see and experience an alternative rendition of history from that presented by the autocratic regime. Anti-government postcards thus constructed a simulacrum of opposition power and moral superiority, which served on the one hand to establish a pictorial space in which both revolutionary hardliners and liberal reformers could affirm, explore, and live out their seditious beliefs, and on the other, to provide the population at large with a compelling political vision of the Tsarist state as an illegitimate entity intent on clinging onto power whatever the cost.

Georges Scott. *The Cossacks' Onslaught*. Here captioned: '9 January 1905 in Saint Petersburg'. No publication details, 1905.

In presenting the public with a narrative of revolution, past and present, that required neither great literacy nor knowledge to understand, realist imagery brought the overwhelming need for political change into sharp focus. Clarity of content, paucity of words, and pictorial vibrancy made these postcards both accessible and appealing, and through them the notion that the regime was a heartless tyranny, and the opposition a heroic resistance force, spread throughout the Empire. Overwhelmingly focused on repression, their imagery was like salt on a suppurating wound, exacerbating feelings of hurt and anger against the state, which were then used to justify current actions and encourage future ones.

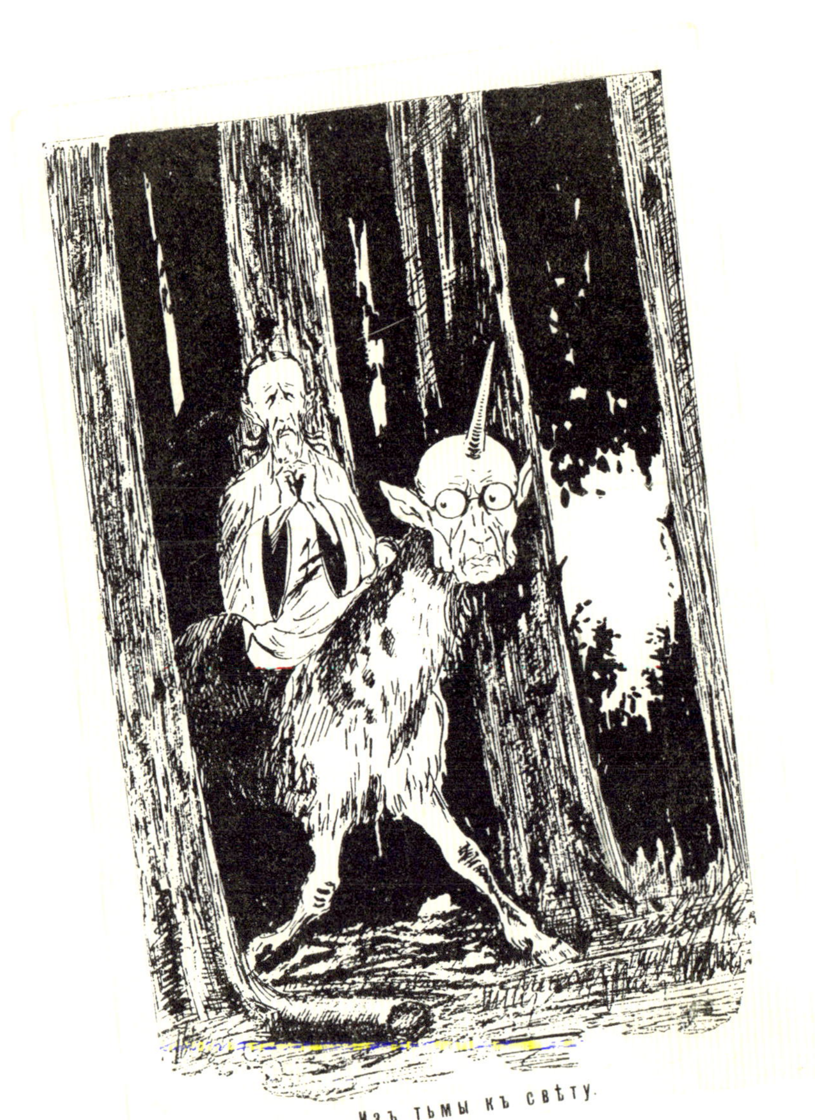

Изъ тьмы къ свѣту.

PLAYING POLITICS

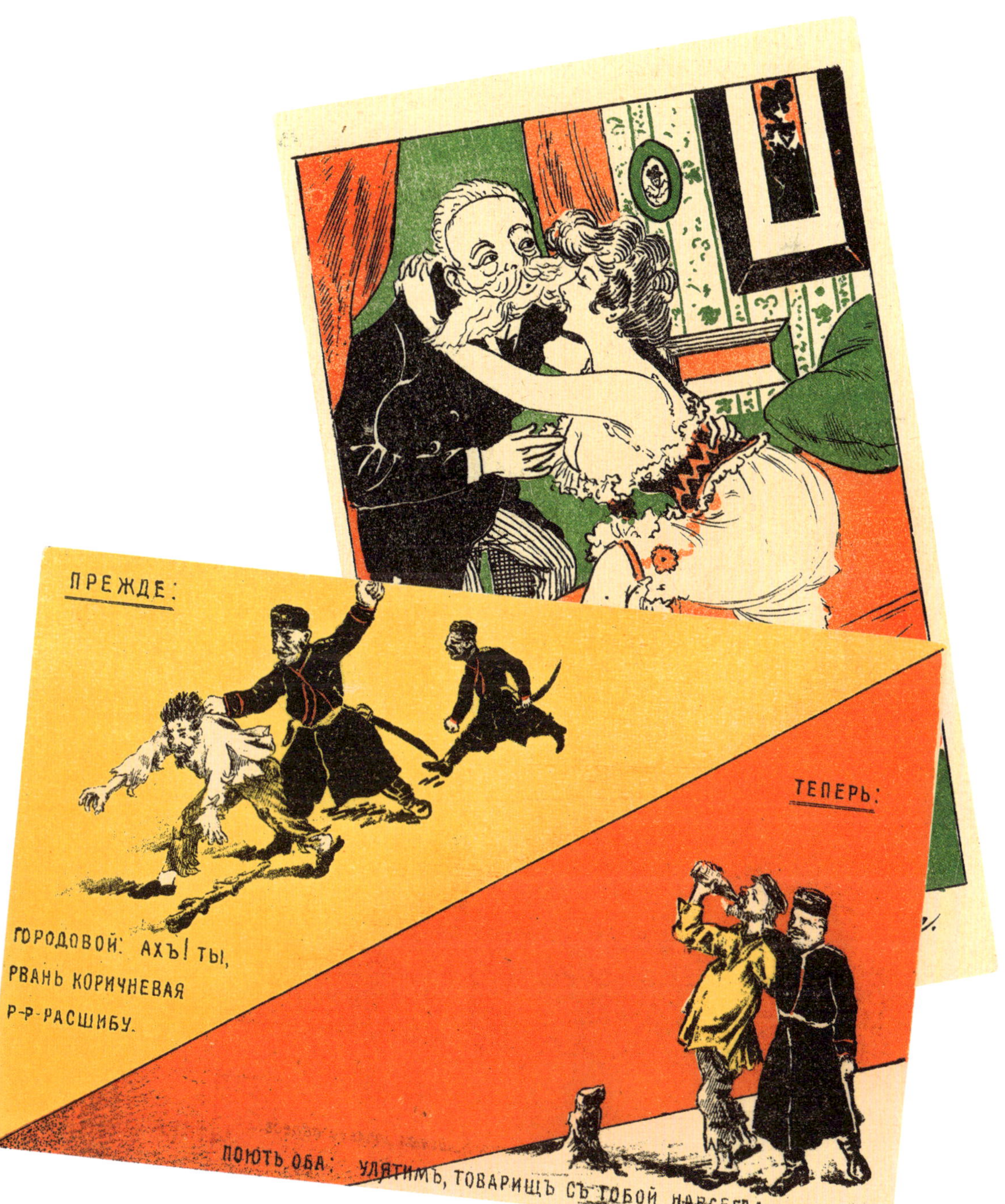

SATIRE AND PARTISAN REPRESENTATION

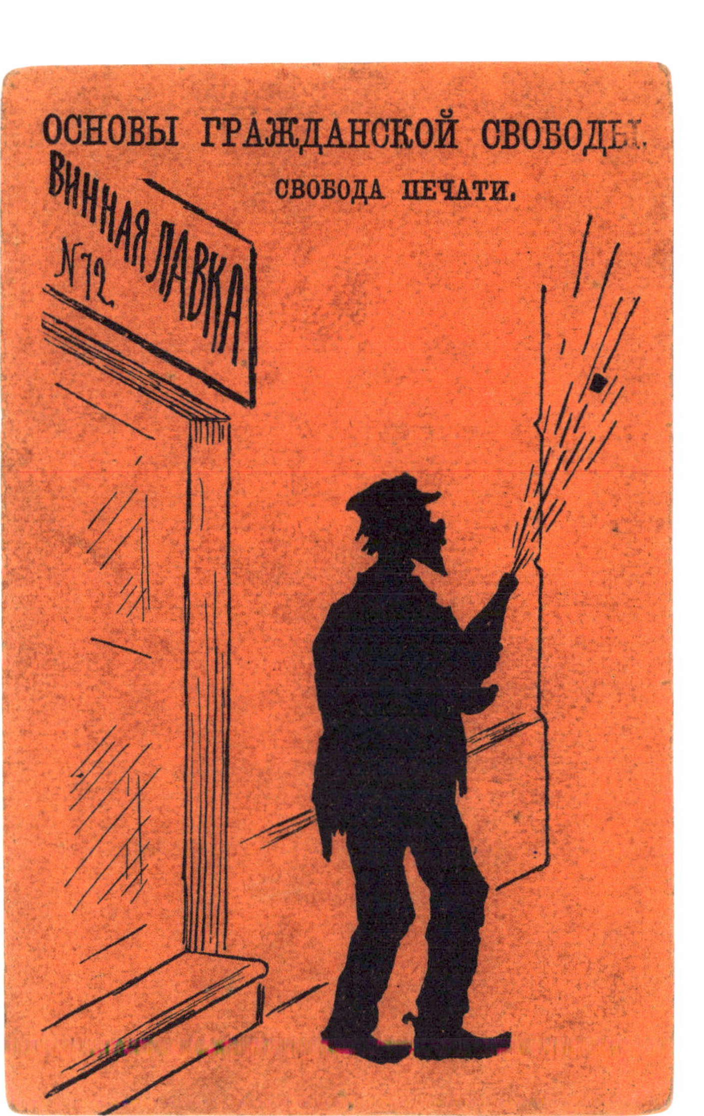
ОСНОВЫ ГРАЖДАНСКОЙ СВОБОДЫ.
СВОБОДА ПЕЧАТИ.
ВИННАЯ ЛАВКА
№ 12.

Government Deception

The period that followed the October Manifesto was a time of hopes raised and hopes dashed. Within days of its promulgation, the joy with which the proclamation had been greeted morphed into angry reproach as belief in its veracity was buried beneath a wave of shootings, pogroms and executions. State-sponsored violence made a mockery of the Manifesto's promises of personal inviolability, freedom of assembly and freedom of association. And delays, meanwhile, in introducing new press laws indicated that the government was no more prepared to allow freedom of speech and freedom of conscience. To the reform-minded opposition it seemed as though the concessions that had been won at such a price were being retracted before they had even been realised.

The revolutionaries had long been sceptical about the government's readiness to reform, but the Kadet Party and its liberal bourgeois supporters, who were looking for political compromise rather than radical change, initially consented to work within the legal framework of the Manifesto. It rapidly became apparent, however, that the regime was either unwilling or unable to keep its word. Liberal members of the intelligentsia were left bitterly disappointed by what they saw as the state's brazen betrayal of its political promises, and many lost faith in the government's ability to instigate meaningful reform. It is their profound disillusionment, and the heartfelt anger that this brutal awakening caused, that informs the majority of commercially-printed anti-government postcard cartoons.

Several of the earliest images to satirise government duplicity were by the Ukrainian artist Vasil Gulak. His popular series of silhouettes, titled *The Principles of Civil Freedom*, uses visual puns to parody the intended aims of the Manifesto. *Freedom of the Press*, for example, which depicts a man cracking open a bottle of champagne, plays on the different meanings of the word 'pechat' – commonly used to refer to the periodical press, but here denoting the seal on a bottle. In Gulak's topsy-turvy world, freedom of speech is the freedom to be shouted at by one's wife, freedom of assembly only applies in public conveniences, and freedom of conscience and association mean nothing more than the freedom to be beaten up by right-wing thugs.

The use of wordplay and veiled meanings was a time-honoured feature of humorous postcards, but in anti-government cartoons, the duality of the imagery was clearly also intended to reflect the political double-dealing and deception of the world outside. For instance, an image by 'R' titled *Long Live Freedom* does not, as one might expect, commemorate the advent of popular liberty; it instead shows soldiers violently dispersing a peaceful demonstration of striking workers. Freedom was a deeply contested notion in Russia,

Previous spread from left to right

Anonymous artist. *From Darkness into Light.* No publication details, late 1905. Caricature of Konstantin Pobedonostsev and John of Kronstadt.

Anonymous artist. *Before/Now.* No publication details, late 1905.

Iosif Ridiger. *Papa, I'll Trust You.* No publication details, late 1905. Caricature of Minister of the Imperial Court Baron Frederiks.

Opposite

Vasil Gulak. *The Principles of Civil Freedom. Freedom of the Press.* Printed by I. N. Kushnerev, Moscow, 9 November 1905.

Next spread

Anonymous artist. *Long Live Freedom.* No publication details, late 1905.

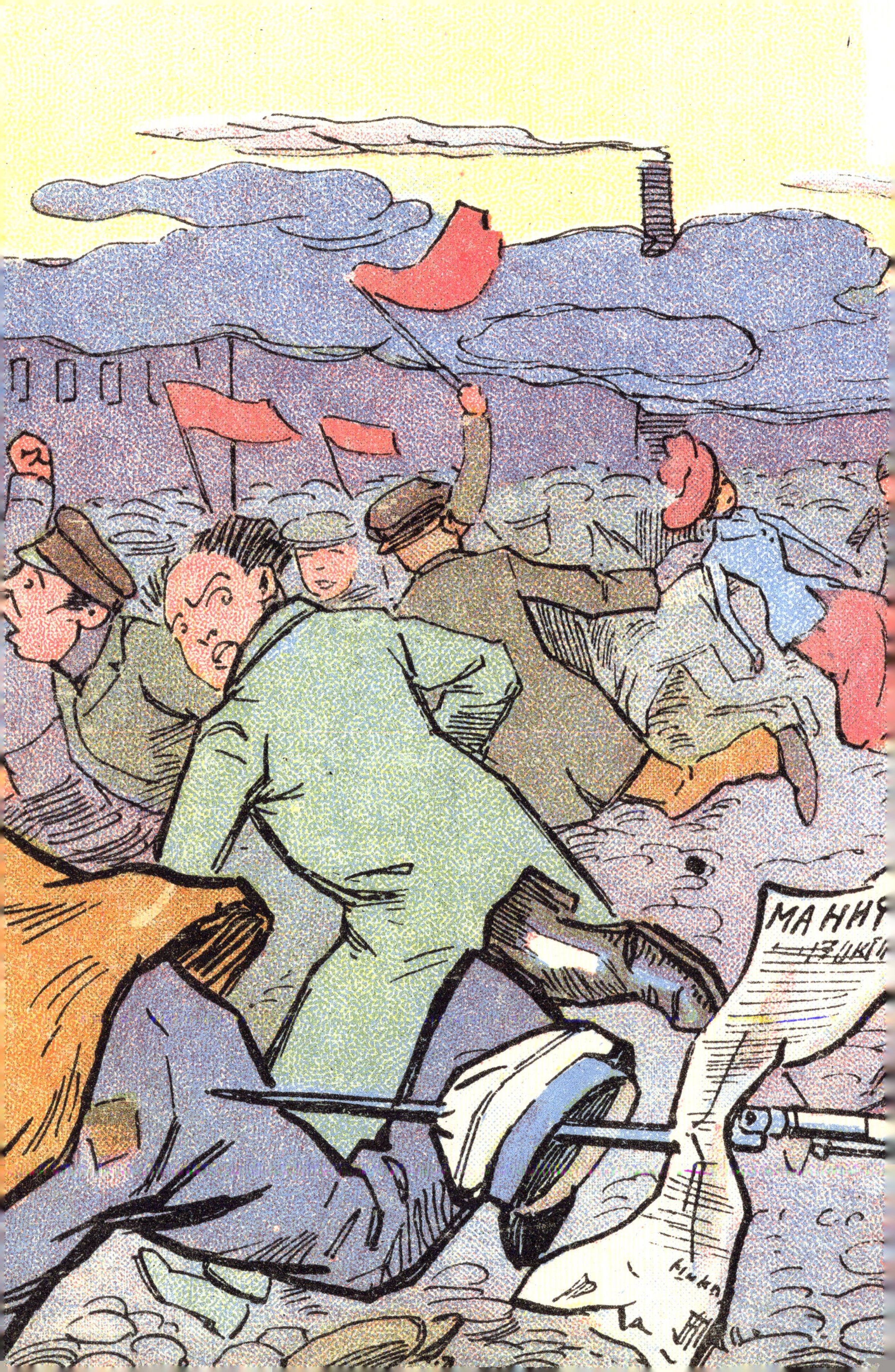
МАНИ

Да здравствуетъ свобода!!

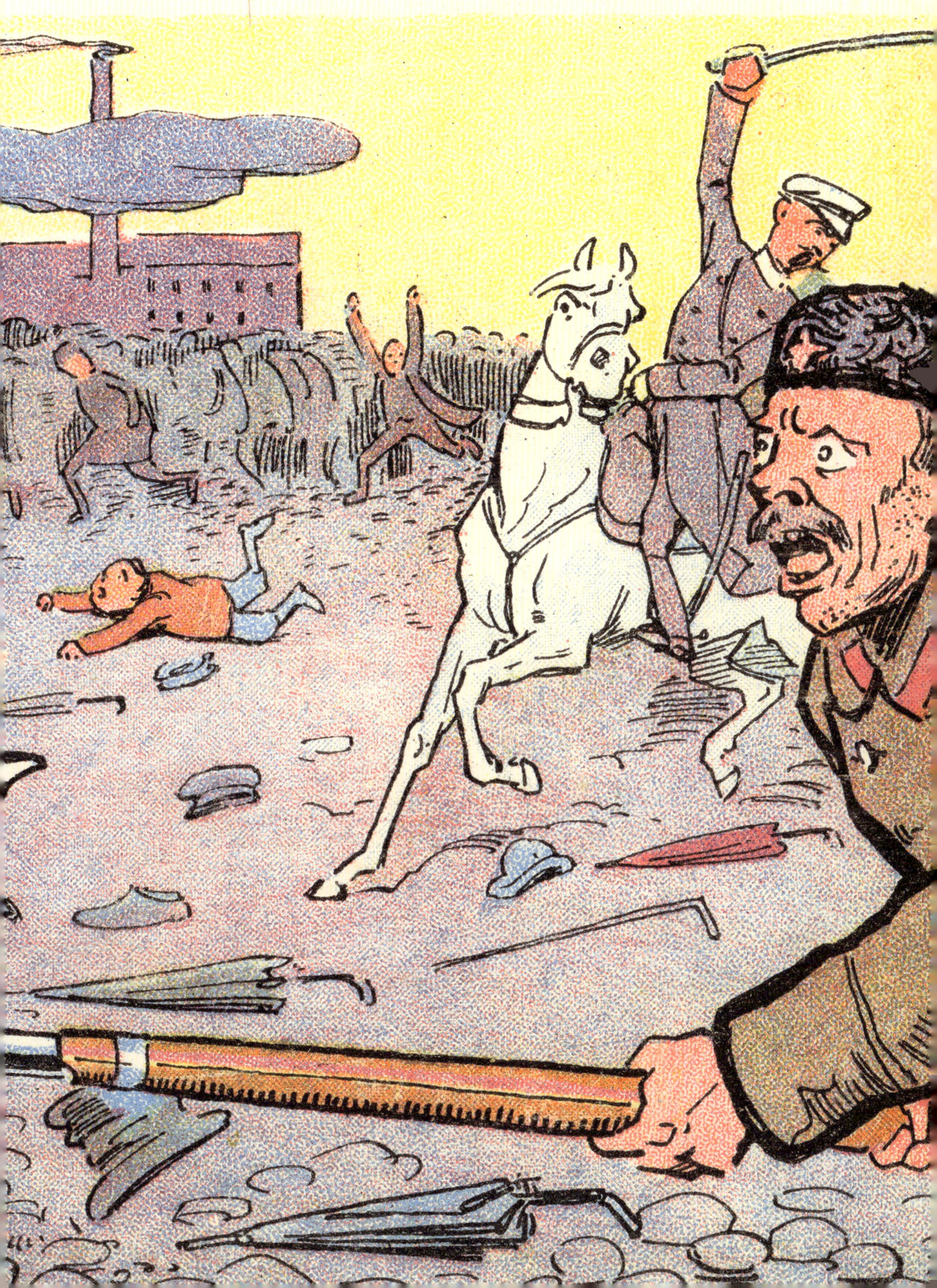

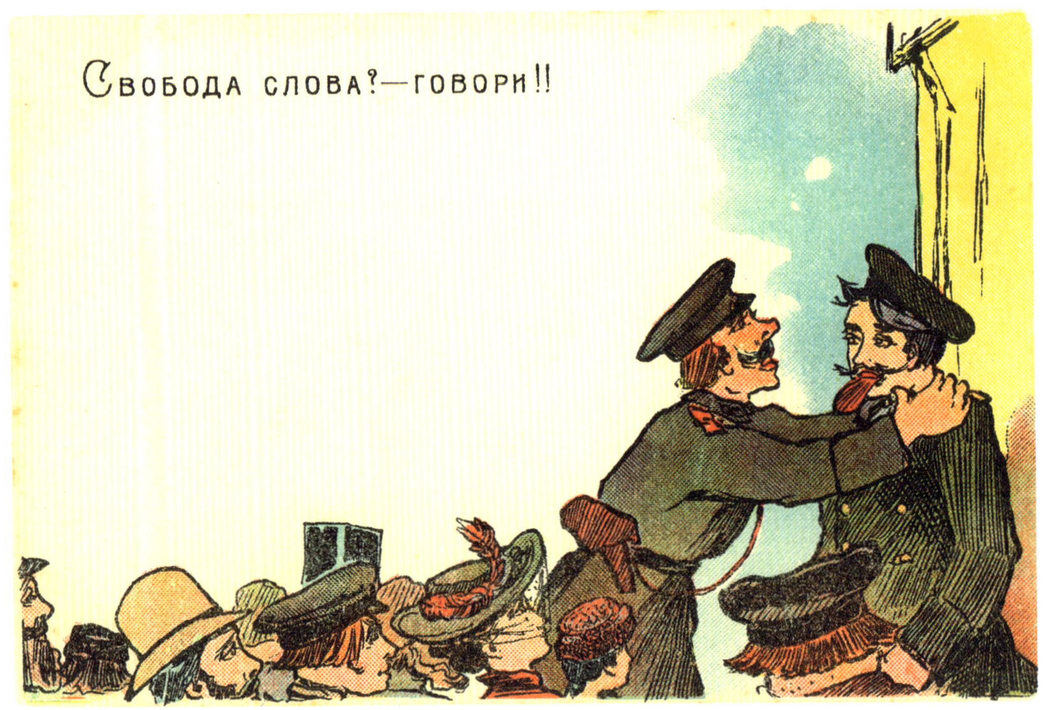

Anonymous artist.
Freedom of Speech? – Well, Go On, Speak!!
No publication details, late 1905.

but the artist's subversion of the literal meaning of the caption serves to make the viewer aware of the ever-widening gap between their expectations of the Manifesto and the reality of what was being delivered.

The regime's ability to govern effectively depended on it being able to exert ideological sovereignty over the written word. The danger for the government in late 1905 was not only that it had lost control over what the opposition was saying, but that it could no longer even regulate the reception and meaning of its own announcements. The right to interpret words meant being the arbiter of truth and justice, and in postcard image after postcard image the opposition turned the government's statements against it, revealing them to be the perfidious falsehoods of a brutal regime. Through their worldview, the Manifesto became little more than a paper promise, and the government an unruly instrument of authoritarian power.

Repression and the Regime

Anti-government cartoons are overwhelmingly focused on the iniquities of government repression. As one artist put it, 'the chemical components of Russian freedom' were Cossack whips, bayonets, bullets, blood, and death. Red is the prevailing colour in many of the postcards published in the wake of the October Manifesto, splashed freely across the paper to symbolise opposition to the regime and the blood that was being shed in its name. This widespread preoccupation with gore both made for a provocative political statement and helped to increase the commercial appeal of all forms of opposition material. In the words of one writer: 'The worth of a [satirical] journal and the size of its print run was determined by the amount of red ink it contained.'[1]

Postcards place all the blame for the bloodshed squarely on the shoulders of the regime, starting with its most low-ranking representatives. At street level, it was widely believed that officials had not only failed to rein in the excesses of the Black Hundreds, but in many cases actively colluded with them. 'Beat the rebels, beat those intellectuals,' a policeman orders a rightist vigilante in one card. Another interactive postcard cartoon, featuring a policeman and hooligan, instructs viewers to focus on a dot in the middle of the image and then to bring it slowly towards their face. As it draws nearer, the two figures come together in a warm embrace. 'See the reality for yourself,' the caption urges, 'it's right before your eyes.'

After the street hoodlums came the army, whose leading role in suppressing opposition protesters was characterised as being devoid of all honour, patriotism, and bravery. Particularly devastating in this regard are images that compare the readiness of soldiers to shoot down women and children with their inability to see off the Japanese. The army's recent drubbing in the Russo-Japanese War had inflicted enormous damage on its prestige and morale, and this was exploited to great effect by artists such as Iosif Ridiger, who produced two series of postcards mocking the prowess and behaviour

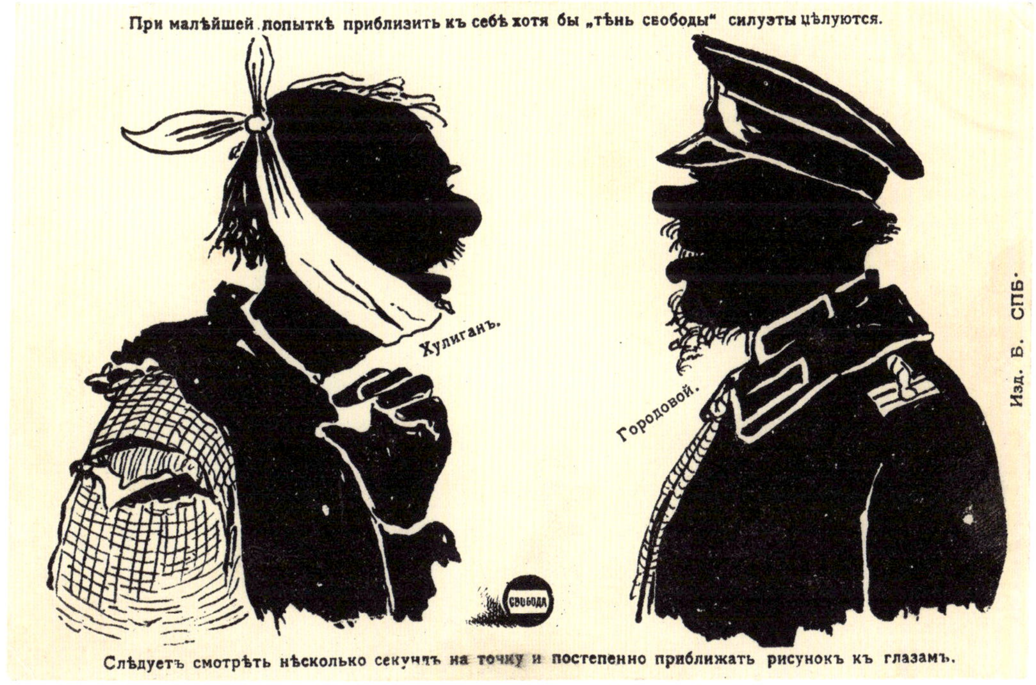

Anonymous artist. *Look for a Few Seconds at the Black Spot and Then Bring it Slowly Towards Your Face. Even the Slightest Attempt to Come Close to the 'Shadow of Freedom' Will Make the Silhouettes Embrace.* Published by 'B', Saint Petersburg, late 1905.

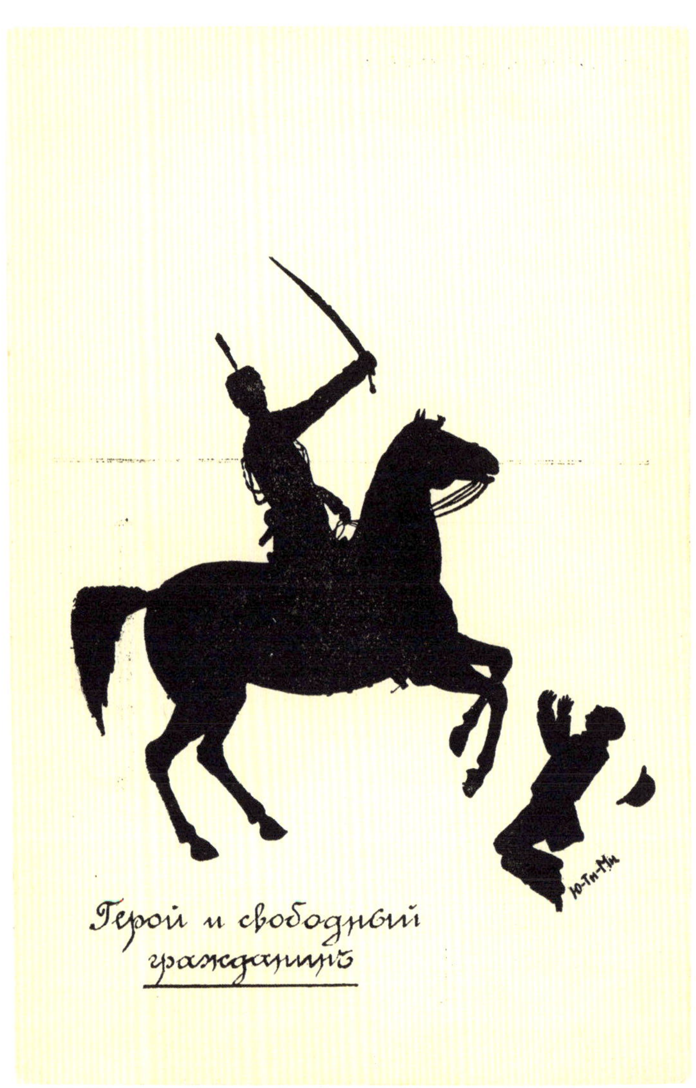
Ю-Ти-Ми
Герой и свободный
гражданинъ

of the military elite. In his works, ministers and senior officers are good for little more than fooling around with harlots and murdering innocents.

Nikolai Merder's postcard *The Hero and the Free Citizen* shows how the public role of the armed forces, as well as notions of good and bad, had been turned on their heads. It depicts a mounted Cossack in the traditional throes of heroic action, sword raised, hat feather standing proud; only, his intended target is not an enemy soldier but a defenceless civilian. Here is the reality of 1905: the Cossack is not a hero, and the citizen is not free. In this upside-down world, the old certainties no longer applied. The moral and social structure of the country had been upended, and in this literal revolution, the army had ceased to be the defender of the nation and had instead become its oppressor.

Opposite

Iu-Ti-Mi. *The Hero and the Free Citizen.* Published by Nikolai Merder, Saint Petersburg, late 1905.

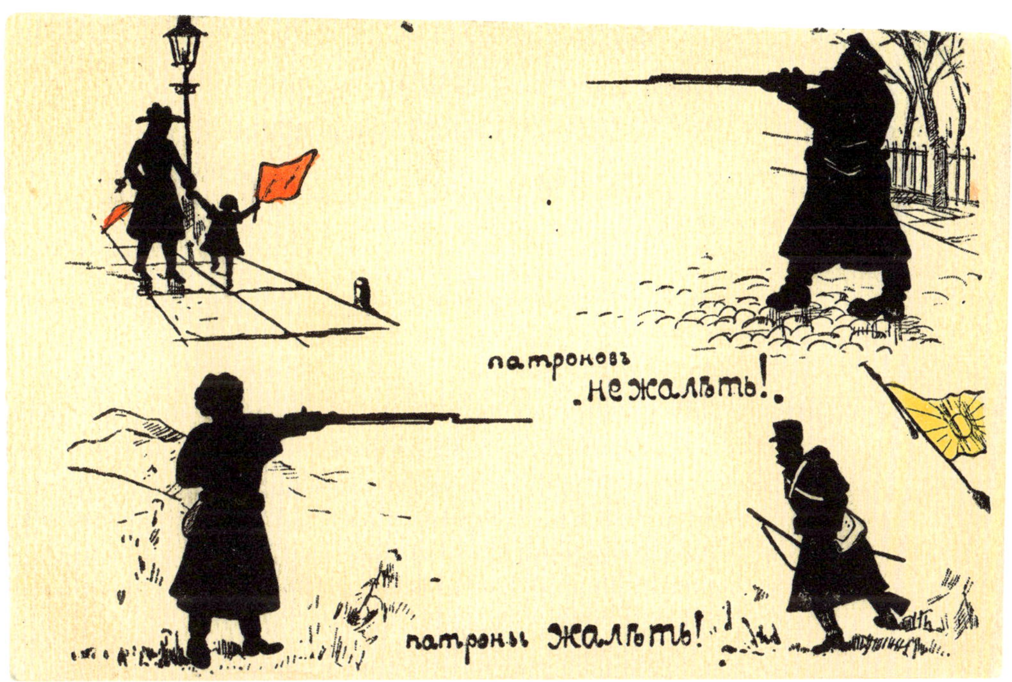

Anonymous artist. *Don't Spare the Bullets/Spare the Bullets.* No publication details, late 1905.

If the army, the police and the Black Hundreds were the blunt instruments with which violence was meted out, then Saint Petersburg Governor Dmitrii Trepov was the man most often seen to be directing it. Trepov wielded great power during this period, both as a key regime official and as one of Tsar's most trusted advisers. Widely regarded by revolutionaries and reformers alike as a repressive reactionary, he was infamous for the order he gave to troops during the October General Strike: 'Don't spare the bullets and don't use blanks.' This command, aimed at ending work stoppages and curtailing demonstrations, was used repeatedly in postcard imagery as shorthand for the state brutality that Trepov was seen to represent.

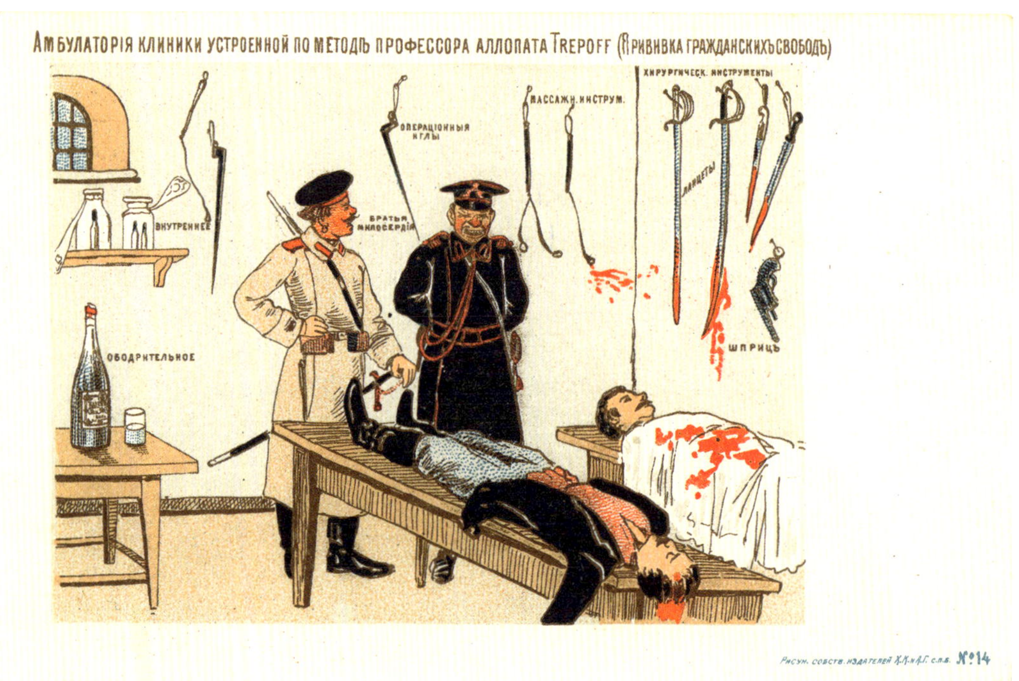

Anonymous artist. *Clinic Built According to the Designs of Physician Professor Trepov. (Inoculation Against Civil Freedoms)*. Published by Kh. K. and A. G., Saint Petersburg, late 1905.

Trepov was satirised in one postcard as a quack doling out medicine to counteract the revolutionary disease. *Clinic Built According to the Designs of Physician Professor Trepov* shows two dead protesters laid out in a room adorned with the instruments of state repression. Standing over them, a soldier and a red-faced policeman chat away, while on a table nearby an open bottle of vodka stands ready to encourage them in their work. Another image from the same series, captioned *Free Medicine Distributed by State Chemists According to the Prescription of Physician Professor Trepov*, depicts two pharmaceutical receptacles, one containing bullets and the other Cossack whips – the former to be ingested and the latter to be applied externally. Liberty was contagious, and the only known cure was violence.

Trepov's hapless foil in government was Sergei Witte, the man who had persuaded the Tsar of the need for reform and the author of the October Manifesto itself. In *Witte and Trepov*, the pair are caricatured as a timid cat and a snarling dog, with the former attempting to protect the decree, while the latter, blood dripping from his jaws, tries to snatch it away. In all such images, Witte is shown as powerless to fight against reactionary elements within the regime.

Opposite

Anonymous artist. *Witte and Trepov*. Hand-drawn postcard, circa 1905. The document is labelled 'constitution'.

Witte had an equal lack of influence with the left. *Brothers, Come Back to Work*, depicts him hanging onto the coat tails of a striking worker, who marches on unawares, red flag in hand. This image refers to an appeal he made in November 1905 for his 'brother workers' to return to the factories

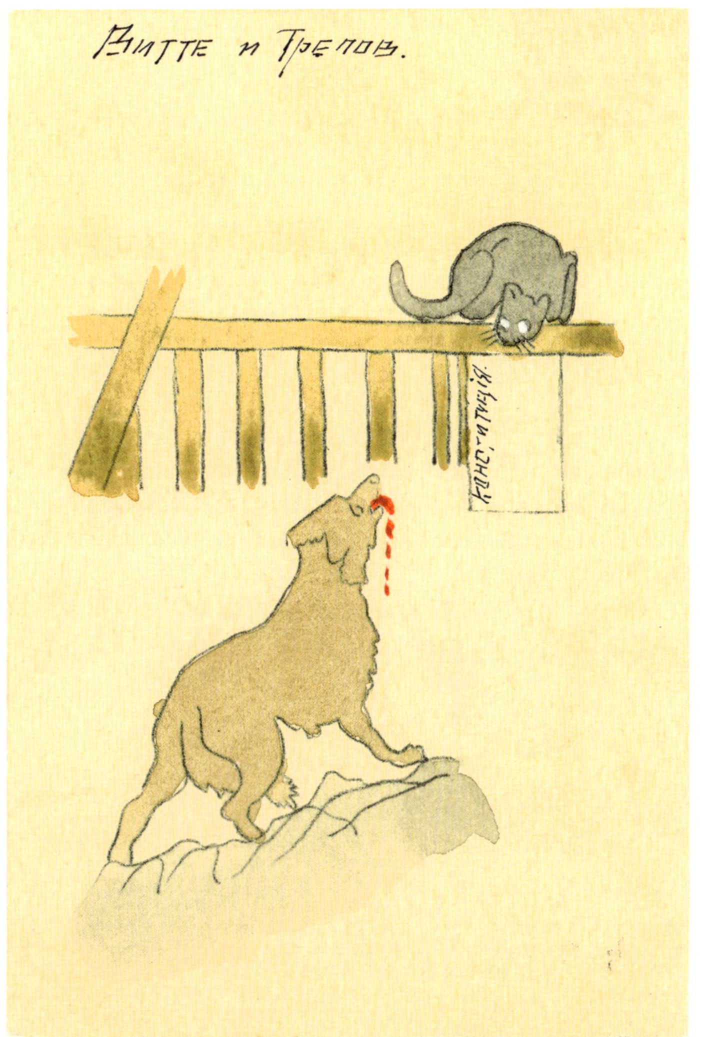
Витте и Треповъ.
Конституція

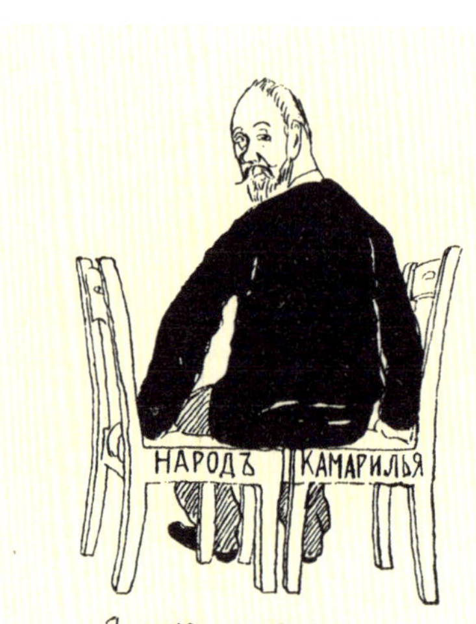

– Я и на двухъ стульяхъ усижу!

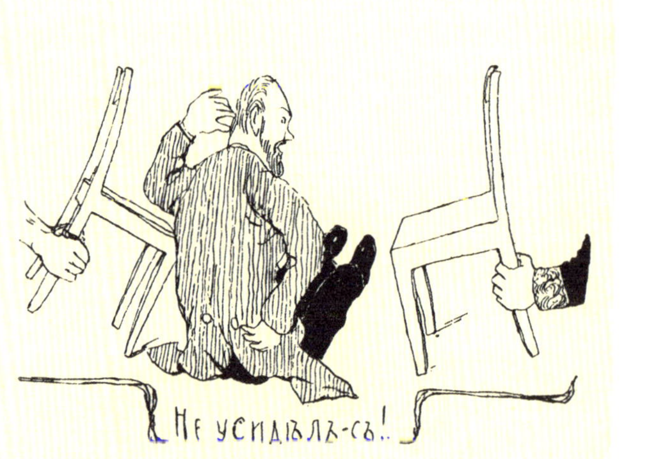

Не усидѣлъ-съ!

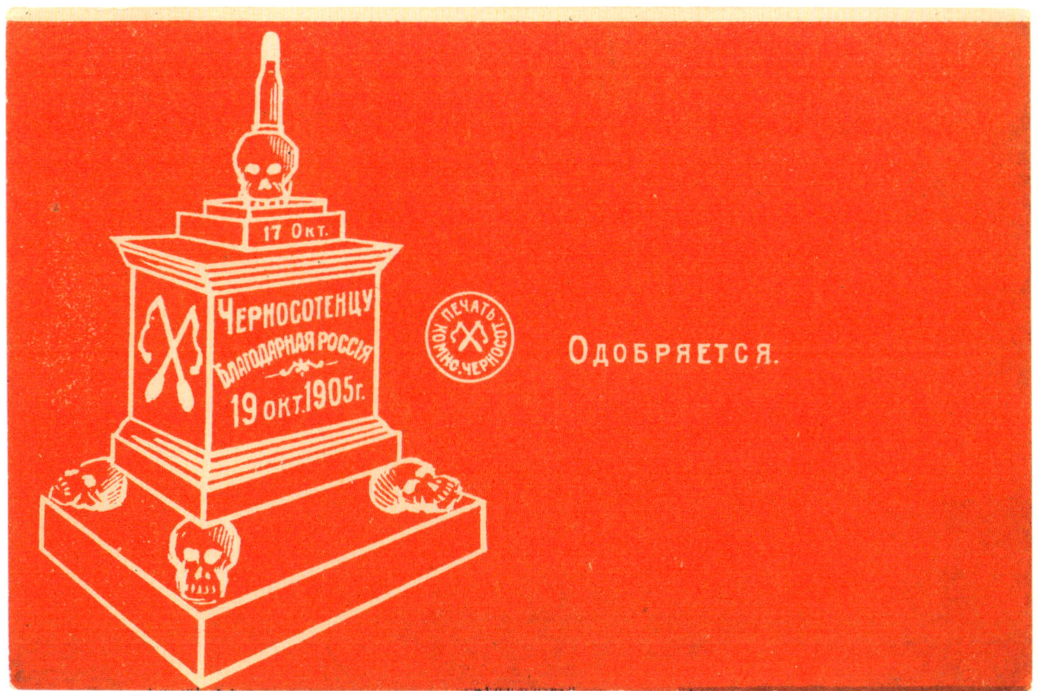

following the cancellation of redemption dues in the countryside. Their two-fingered response can be seen in another postcard titled *A Worker's Reply to His Brother*, which shows Witte with his tongue being nailed to a table. Failure to stop the revolutionary movement eventually led Witte to reassess his political position, and in late 1905, he abandoned reformist views and became an ideologue for violence.

Anonymous artist. *Approved.* No publication details, late 1905. This satirical postcard depicts a fictional monument dedicated 'to the Black Hundreds from a grateful Russia'.

Witte's original aim had been to use the reforms of the October Manifesto to drive a wedge between the revolutionaries and the more moderate opposition, but at every step of the way he had found himself stymied by extremist elements on the right and the left. Indiscriminate government repression against the population fatally undermined his attempts to attract more liberal members of the opposition to the government, and all that ended up happening was that Witte was seen by the reactionaries as a friend of the revolutionaries, and by the revolutionaries as a friend of the reactionaries. His was an impossible position to be in, and he is shown in one postcard literally falling between two stools.[2]

Opposite

L. Ch. *I'll Sit Down on These Two Stools!* [one labelled 'the people', the other 'the cabal'] *Oof, I Didn't Manage to Sit on Either*! No publication details, late 1905. Caricature of Sergei Witte.

Other officials were no more able or willing to stop the unrest. The former Interior Minister Aleksandr Bulygin, on whose earlier work the Manifesto was based, is depicted blowing up a giant balloon labelled 'Constitution', only for it to burst in his face. As for the reactionary right and the Orthodox Church, they had nothing to offer in the place of reform except violence. The Procurator of the Holy Synod, Konstantin Pobedonostsev is shown in a cartoon from late 1905 flicking through a tome on jurisprudence, the devil

Next spread

Anonymous artist. *A Worker's Reply to His Brother.* No publication details, late 1905. Caricature of Sergei Witte.

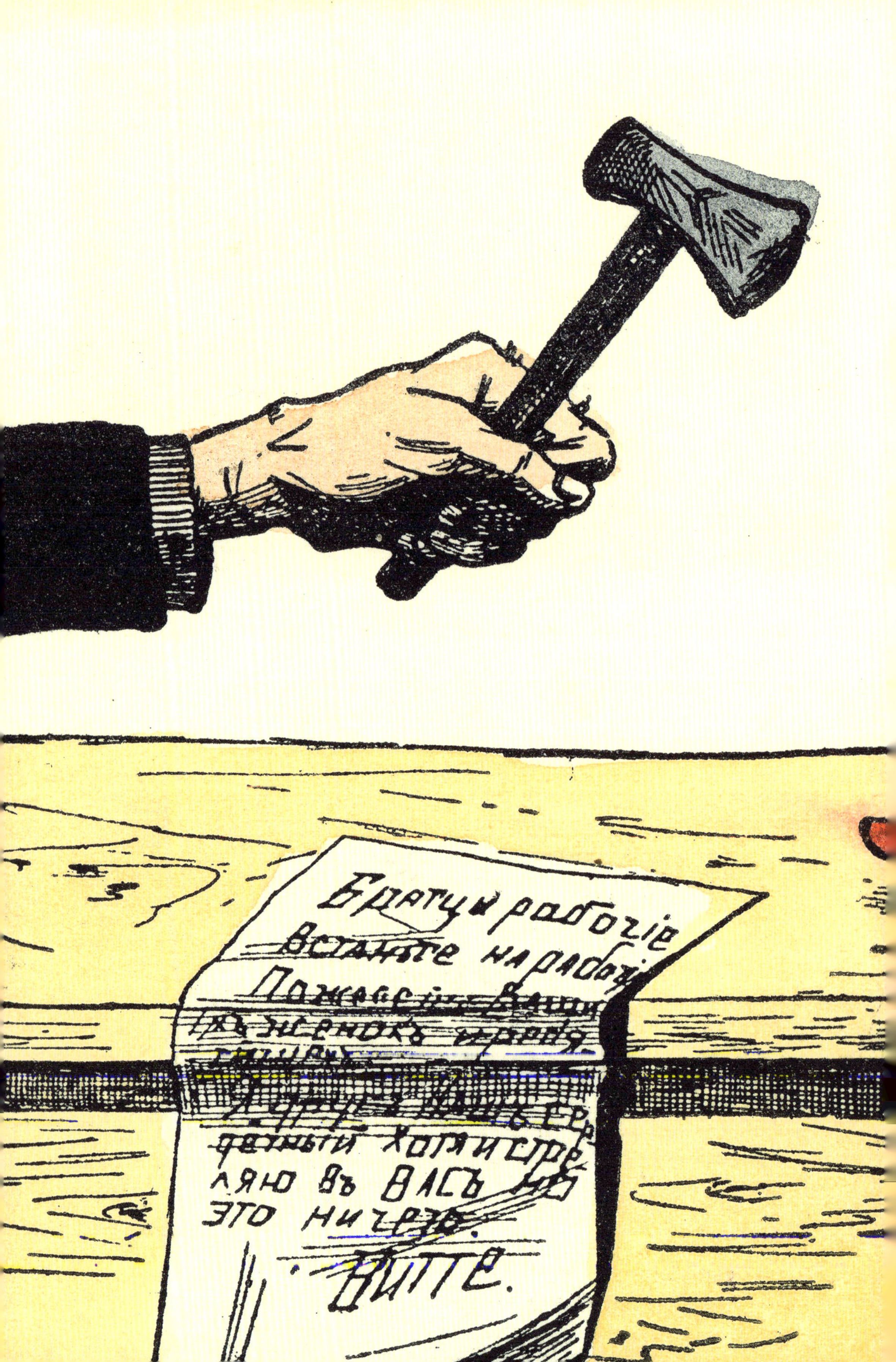

Братцы рабочіе
Встаньте на работ
ляю въ ВАСЪ но
это ничего
Витте.

Отвѣтъ братцу отъ —
работяго.

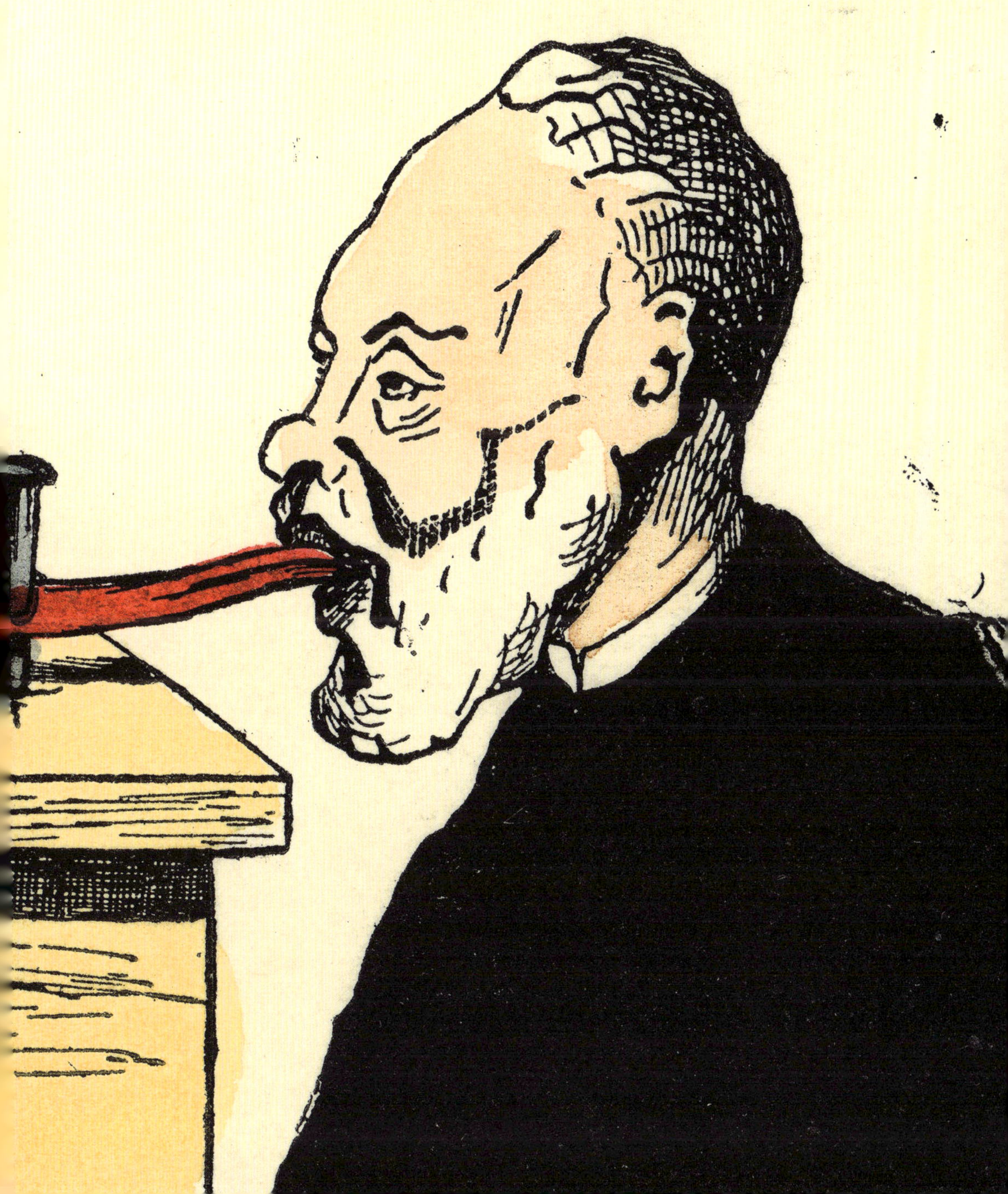

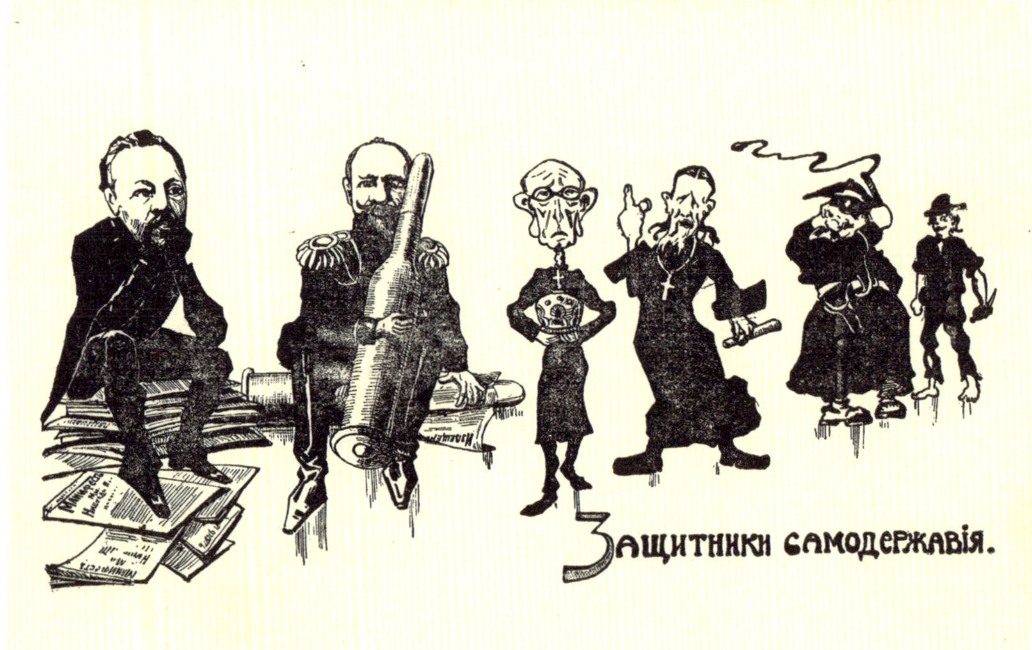

Anonymous artist. *The Defenders of Autocracy*. No publication details, circa late 1905. From left to right: Sergei Witte, Dmitrii Trepov, Konstantin Pobedonostsev, John of Kronstadt, Policeman, Black Hundred Supporter.

at his shoulder, and skulls around his feet. 'Hmmm,' he ponders, 'how can we turn Rus back to Christianity?' The answer was 'by force' – the only method in which the government truly believed.

This whole sorry structure is encapsulated in *The Defenders of Autocracy*. At the bottom of the pile are the Black Hundreds, and above them the police; next comes the church in the form of the Tsar's confessor John of Kronstadt, and then Pobedonostsev. At the top are Trepov, who clutches an artillery shell, and Witte, who sits astride a pile of manifestos. The point being made is that state violence is not a temporary aberration, but the key mechanism through which the regime holds onto power. *The Three Pillars*, depicting a mounted thug, whip at the ready, following behind a guardsman and a bureaucrat, makes this explicit: reform will never happen because if the repression stops, the edifice of autocracy will collapse.

The Politics of Violence

Opposite

Anonymous artist. *The Chemical Components of Russian Freedom*. No publication details, late 1905.

Chromolithographic satirical cartoons exude raw indignation at the injustices of life in Imperial Russia, but they make very few clear political demands in response. They do not obviously seek to advance the interests of any particular organisation, nor to press the case for fairer distribution of government power. Instead, they are primarily concerned with social justice. Promises of inviolability are made and not kept, innocents are shot

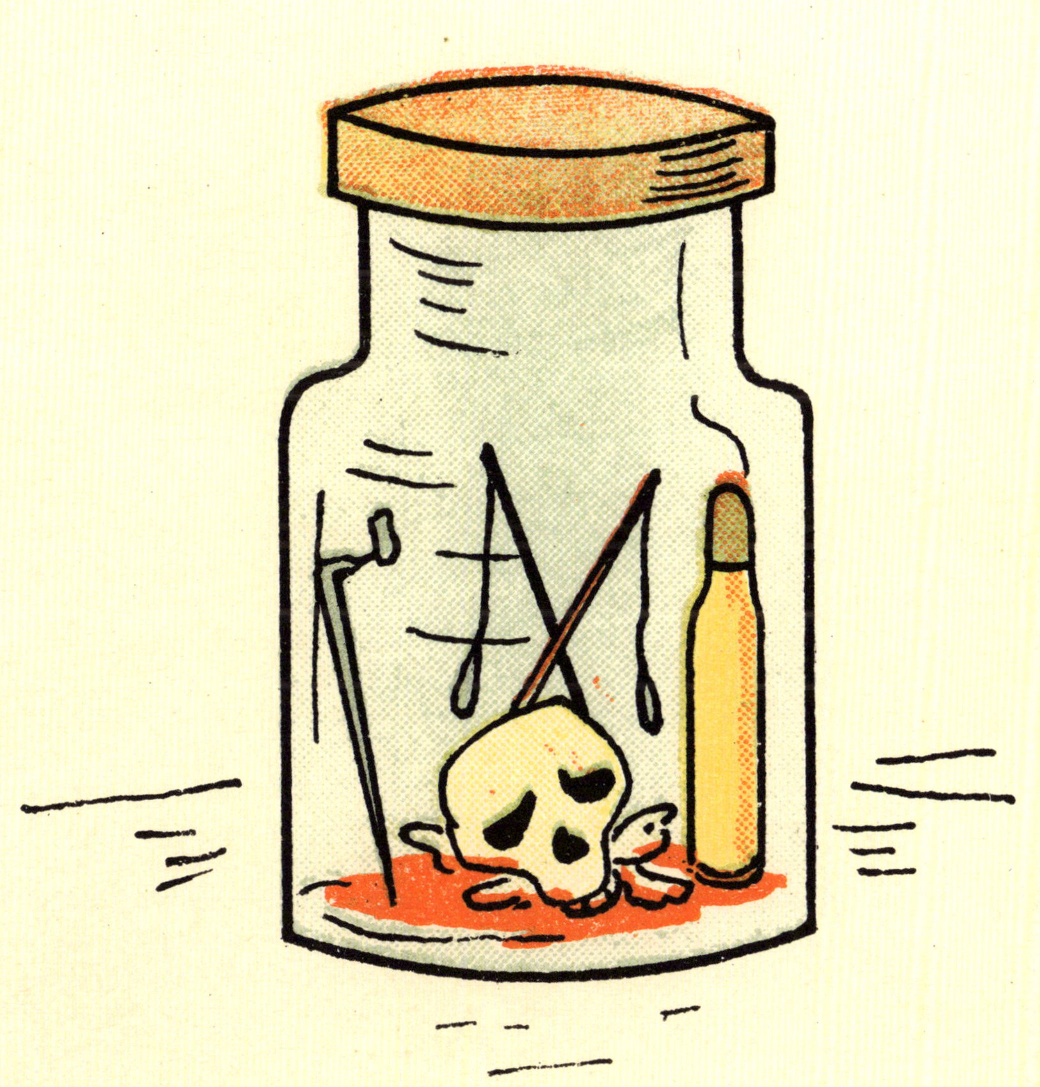

down, free talkers jailed, Jews killed and revolutionaries murdered. These images are not about achieving political liberty for the masses, but about establishing civil freedom for the individual, pushing the simple notion that people should be able to express themselves without fear of reprisal.

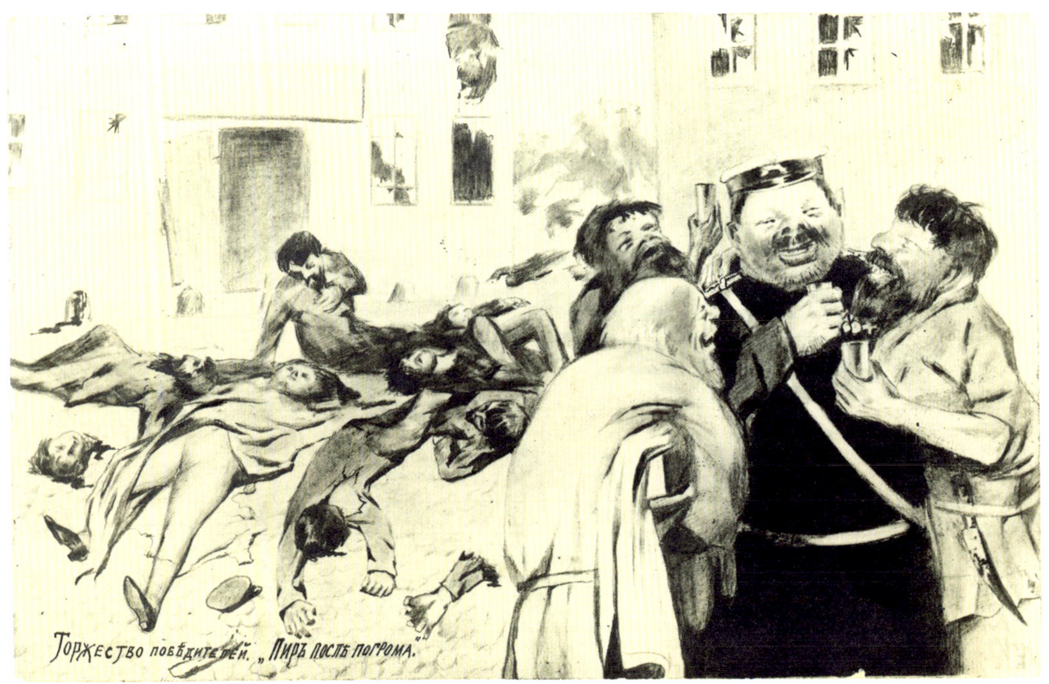

Anonymous artist. *The Exultation of the Victors. The Feast after the Pogrom.* No publication details, circa 1905.

In this respect, they represent the core concerns of the liberal movement. What they want is not a new system, but reform of the old, that is to say proper adherence to the October Manifesto. However, the cartoons clearly warn that the government's refusal to grant the people their promised rights will not only lead to it being seen as cruel and inept, but also take it perilously close to bringing about its own destruction.

Uncompromisingly direct imagery of state violence and, by extension, the non-implementation of reforms, forced the public to examine their attitudes towards the regime. Demands for civil freedom had only ended in death and disappointment, leading many to ask: 'Are you happy with a government that treats its people in this way, and if not, what are you going to do about it?' With a bitter laugh, postcards made the liberal opposition confront the reality of what their hoped-for change had become. The Duma still gave some grounds for optimism, but widespread repression had fundamentally undermined public trust in the government, and with it the expectation that the legislative assembly would serve as a true mechanism for reform.

Opposite

Anonymous artist. *King of Spades, Bullets and the Lash.* No publication details, late 1905. Caricature of Dmitrii Trepov.

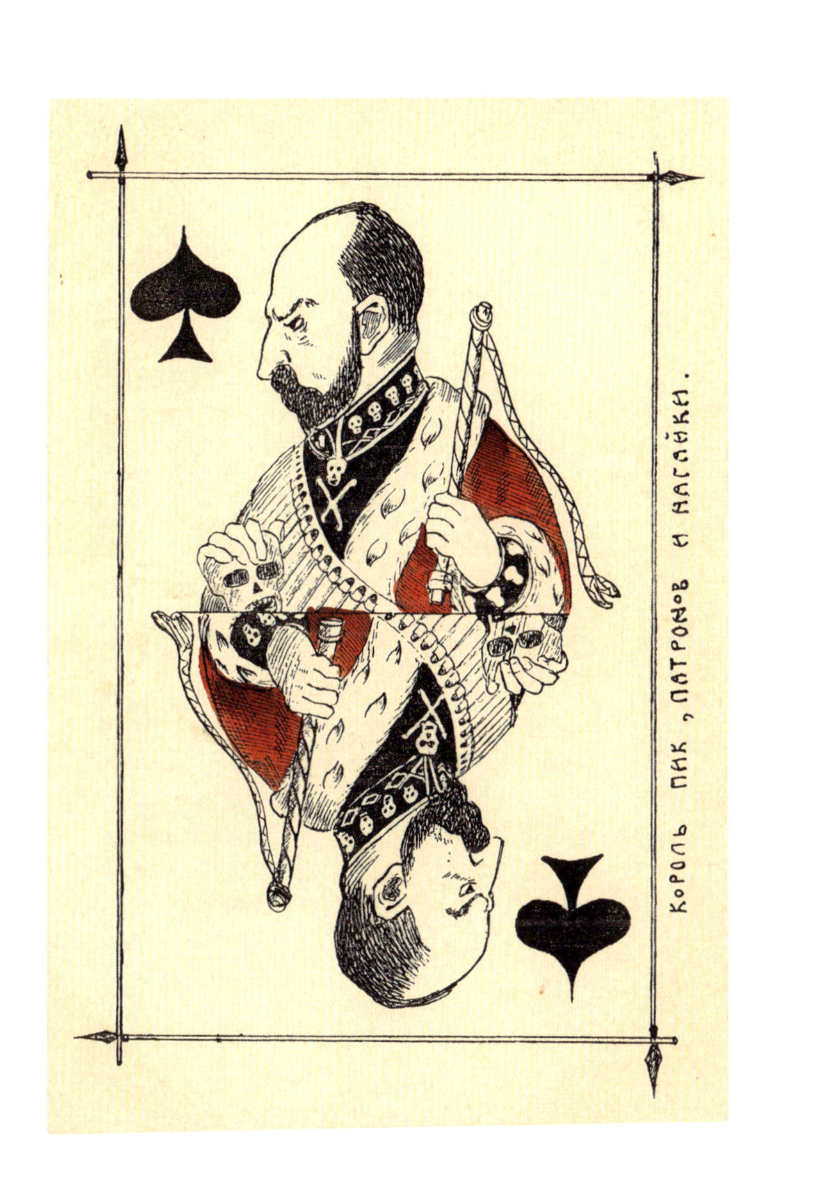
Король пик, патронов и нагайки.

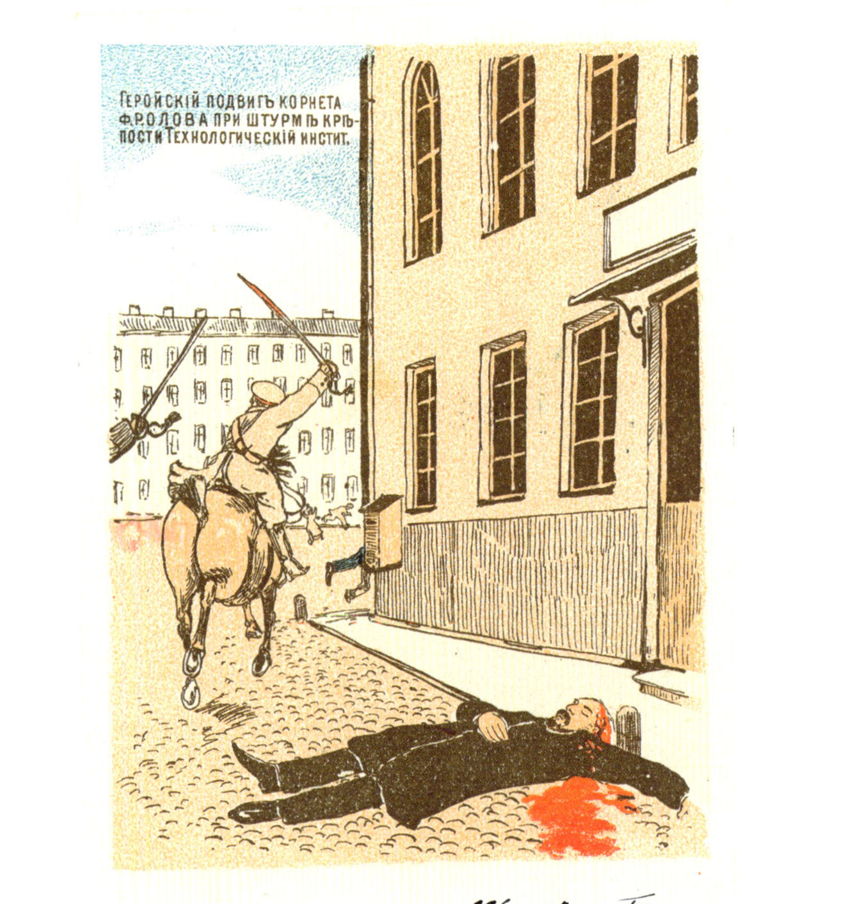

Paris. 30/7 1907

№12

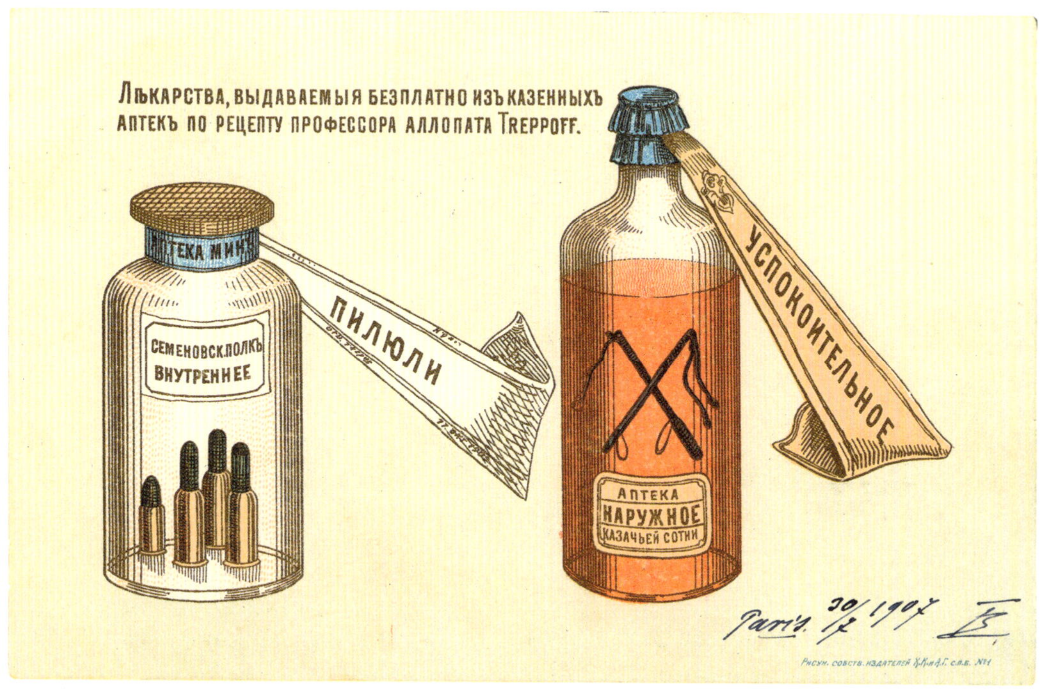

Anonymous artist. *Free Medicine Distributed by State Chemists According to the Prescription of Physician Professor Trepov*. Published by Kh. K. and A. G., Saint Petersburg, late 1905.

The longer violence gripped the streets the more it energised the Revolution. 'Even those who were decisively against politics have been forced by experience to change their minds,' wrote the Printers' Council in September 1905.[3] Brutality was an excellent recruiting sergeant, radicalising many sectors of the opposition, including workers, students and members of the intelligentsia, all of whom became more strident in their demands for change. Postcards reflect the fine line trodden by much of the liberal community which, outraged by the government's actions, flirted with the possibilities of violence, their views oscillating back and forth between the need to wait for change to come from above and the desire to force it from below. But while they warn of the impending possibility of revolution, most stop short of actually demanding it.

The word 'revolution' occurs only occasionally in postcard imagery, but where it does, it is most often used as a collective term for the events of the 1905 period, rather than in reference to the future overthrow of the regime. Where the latter is invoked as a definite possibility, it is almost always cast as the consequence of government actions, with a clear connection made between the blood being shed by the regime and the prospect of its forthcoming destruction. In *Bowling Alley*, for instance, a red ball marked 'revolution' is shown hurtling towards a group of skittles, personified as the Tsar's leading ministers and advisers. Long shards of blood-red lines mark the ball's path towards the representatives of the autocratic state. Repression is thus shown to be easing the path towards revolution.

Opposite

Anonymous artist. *The Heroic Deed Carried out by Cornet Frolov during the Storming of the Technological Institute Fortress*. Published by Kh. K. and A. G., Saint Petersburg, late 1905. While suppressing crowds near the Institute on 18 October 1905, Cornet Frolov struck and badly wounded the history professor Evgenii Tarle.

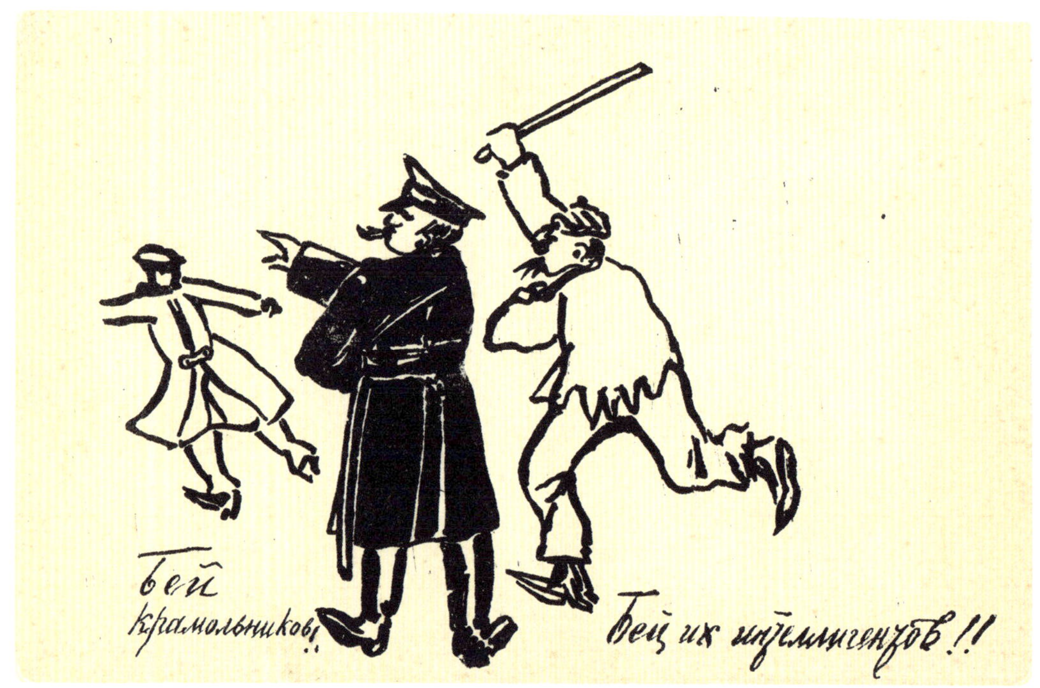

Anonymous artist. *Beat the Rebels! Beat Those Intellectuals!* No publication details, late 1905.

In all such cartoons, rebellion is not a popular choice but an Imperial one, directly brought about by the abominations of the regime. The Marxist view of revolution as the inevitable consequence of capitalist development is rarely portrayed. Even Chemodanov's works show revolution to be a consequence of Imperial policy, and therefore by implication suggest that it could be avoided if the proper reforms were implemented. His cartoon *True Russian Anarchists* has Trepov, representing the police, Bulygin, the Interior Ministry, and Vladimir Gringmut, the reactionary right. Together they add fuel to a fire that is heating a giant cooking pot labelled 'revolution'. Perched on top, with only his back visible, is the Tsar. Chemodanov's message is simple: carry on like this and the lid will blow.

Opposite

Mikhail Chemodanov. *'True Russian' Anarchists. The Disservice of Those Who Seek to Defend Autocracy. They Know Not What They Do.* Printed by Dmitrii Peschanskii, Moscow, May 1905. Caricature of Nicholas II, Dmitrii Trepov, Alexander Bulygin, and Vladimir Gringmut.

Many on the reform-minded left may not have wanted to abolish the monarchy, but as these postcards reveal, they became increasingly frustrated at the country's lack of political progress. If the government eliminated all other options, then it left the liberal opposition with little choice other than to support a revolution. The regime was thus always cast as the agent of its own political misfortune, and the catalyst for its future downfall invariably shown to be repression. The last postcard that Chemodanov drew before his arrest contains two vignettes, one showing the Tsar balancing on a pile of skulls against a gibbet-strewn backdrop, and the other of him dangling from a noose. The caption beneath reads: 'It will all come to a bad end.'[4]

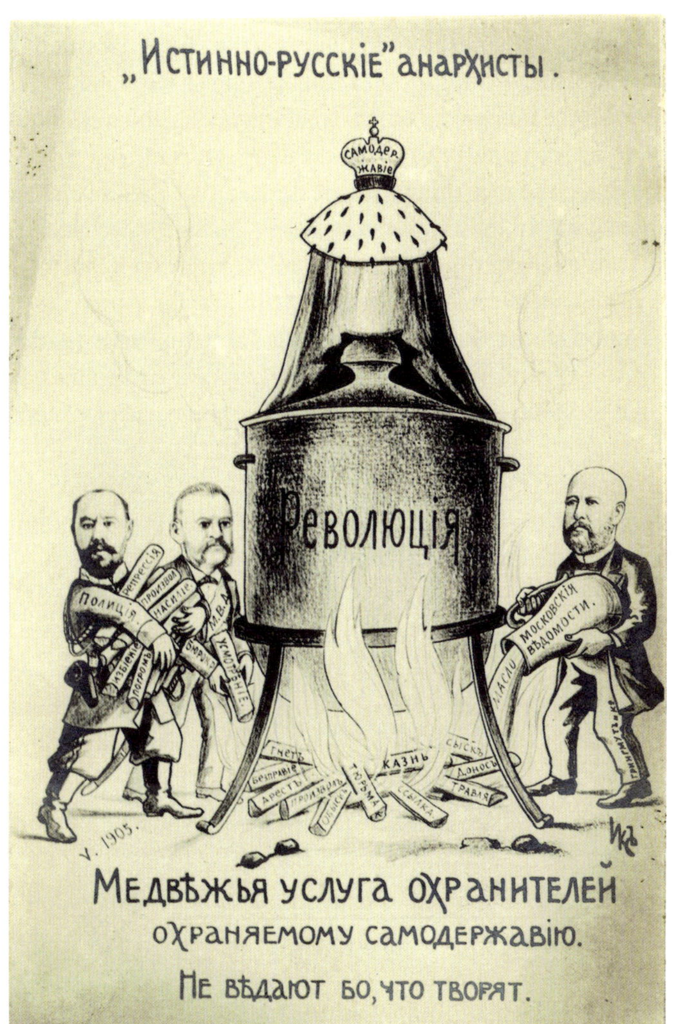
„Истинно-русскiе" анархисты.
Самодер-
жавiе
Революцiя
Полицiя
Репрессiя
Произволъ
Насилiе
Погромъ
М.В.Д.
Усмотрѣнiе
Гнетъ
Безправiе
Арестъ
Обыскъ
Тюрьма
Казнь
Сыскъ
Доносъ
Травля
Ссылка
Масло
Московскiя вѣдомости.
V. 1905.
Медвѣжья услуга охранителей
охраняемому самодержавiю.
Не вѣдают бо, что творят.

Although Nicholas's presence hovers over all these images, he himself is often missing. Caricaturing the Tsar was a dangerous activity, punishable by up to eight years' penal servitude; a risk that few but the most committed considered worth taking. His absence, however, should also be considered within the context of production. After the Manifesto, private firms became the leading publishers of anti-government cartoons, and they differed from the revolutionaries both in their practical objectives, and in their ideology: despite the shifting political planes, most were still agitating for reform within the framework of the existing system, and would therefore have considered it counterproductive to call openly for the overthrow of the Tsar.

Even the revolutionaries recognised that anti-Tsarist agitation could be damaging to the cause. Support for Nicholas declined throughout 1905, but it is telling that the Socialist-Revolutionary Combat Division specifically avoided trying to assassinate the Tsar until after the dissolution of the Second Duma, because to have killed him might have had a negative impact on their popularity.[5] The Party newspaper *Trud* acknowledged in 1906 that in Russia 'there are still millions of people, especially among the peasantry, who continue to believe and trust in the decency and good intentions of Nicholas II.'[6] For revolutionaries and liberals, therefore, the decision not to print caricatures of the Tsar was underpinned by both political and commercial considerations.

Anonymous artist. *It Burst, Your Excellency*. No publication details, late 1905. Caricature of Alexander Bulygin – the balloon is labelled 'Constitution'.

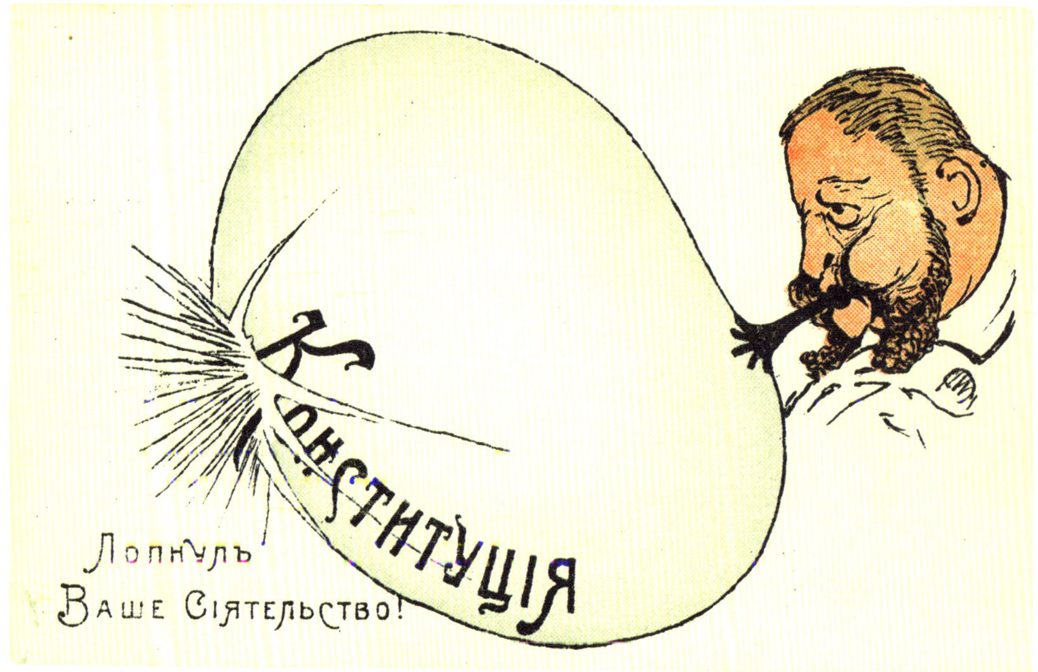

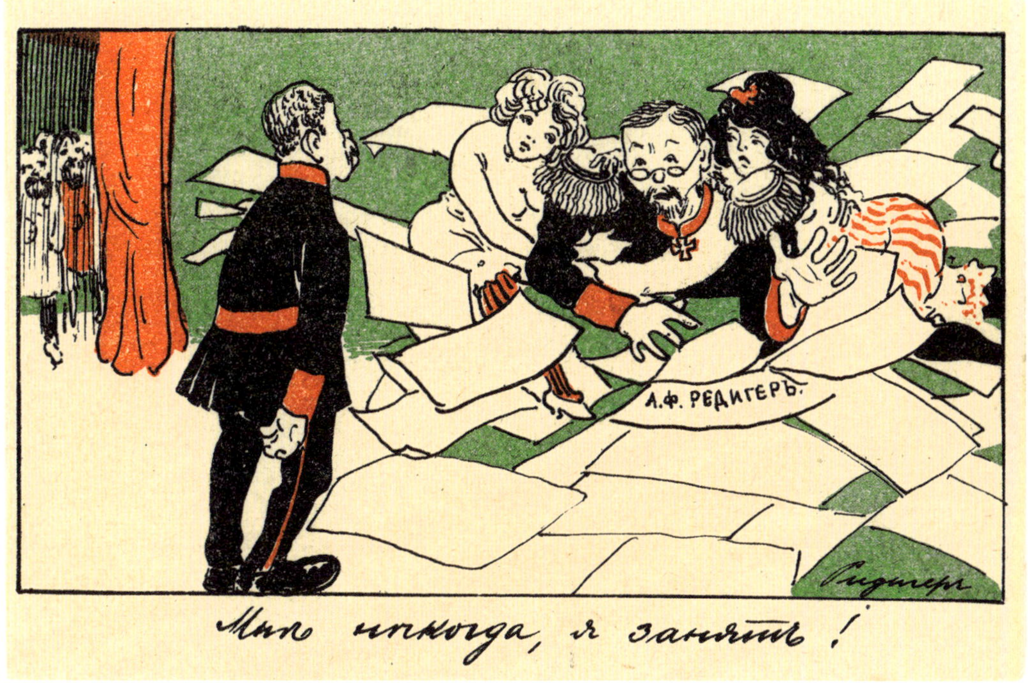

Iosif Ridiger.
I Haven't Got the Time, I'm Busy! No publication details, late 1905. Caricature of War Minister Alexander Rediger.

In liberal satire condemnation of Nicholas comes by proxy. Government servants, particularly Trepov, Durnovo and latterly Stolypin, are always cast as the main instigators of repression. No one could be under any illusion as to whom they were ultimately serving – these were the executors of the Imperial will and their every action reflected back on the Tsar – but there remained an important difference between criticising state employees and criticising the man at the top: with the former it is the system that is seen to be at fault and not the monarch himself. So while Nicholas was indirectly damaged by liberal caricatures, the broader message they conveyed was that the regime needed wholesale reform, not wholesale eradication.

Most postcard caricatures of the Tsar were revolutionary publications, often direct copies of European works, duplicated photomechanically or reproduced by hand with translated captions. In these images, Nicholas is rarely shown in relation to specific political events, but instead cast as the symbolic representative of a despotic tyranny that will soon be overthrown. An image by Félix-Antoine Marmonier (Mille), published in the journal *L'Arc en Ciel* [*The Rainbow*] and later reproduced as a postcard in both France and Russia, pictures the Tsar perching naked on a small rock. Beside him stands the Grim Reaper, while all around clenched fists rise up through a sea of red. The caption reads: 'The Blood of the Russian People Cries Out for Revenge.'

Next spread

Anonymous artist. *Bowling Alley*. No publication details, late 1905. Among those depicted are: Aleksandr Bulygin, Dmitrii Trepov, Aleksei Ignatiev, Sergei Witte, and Konstantin Pobedonostsev.

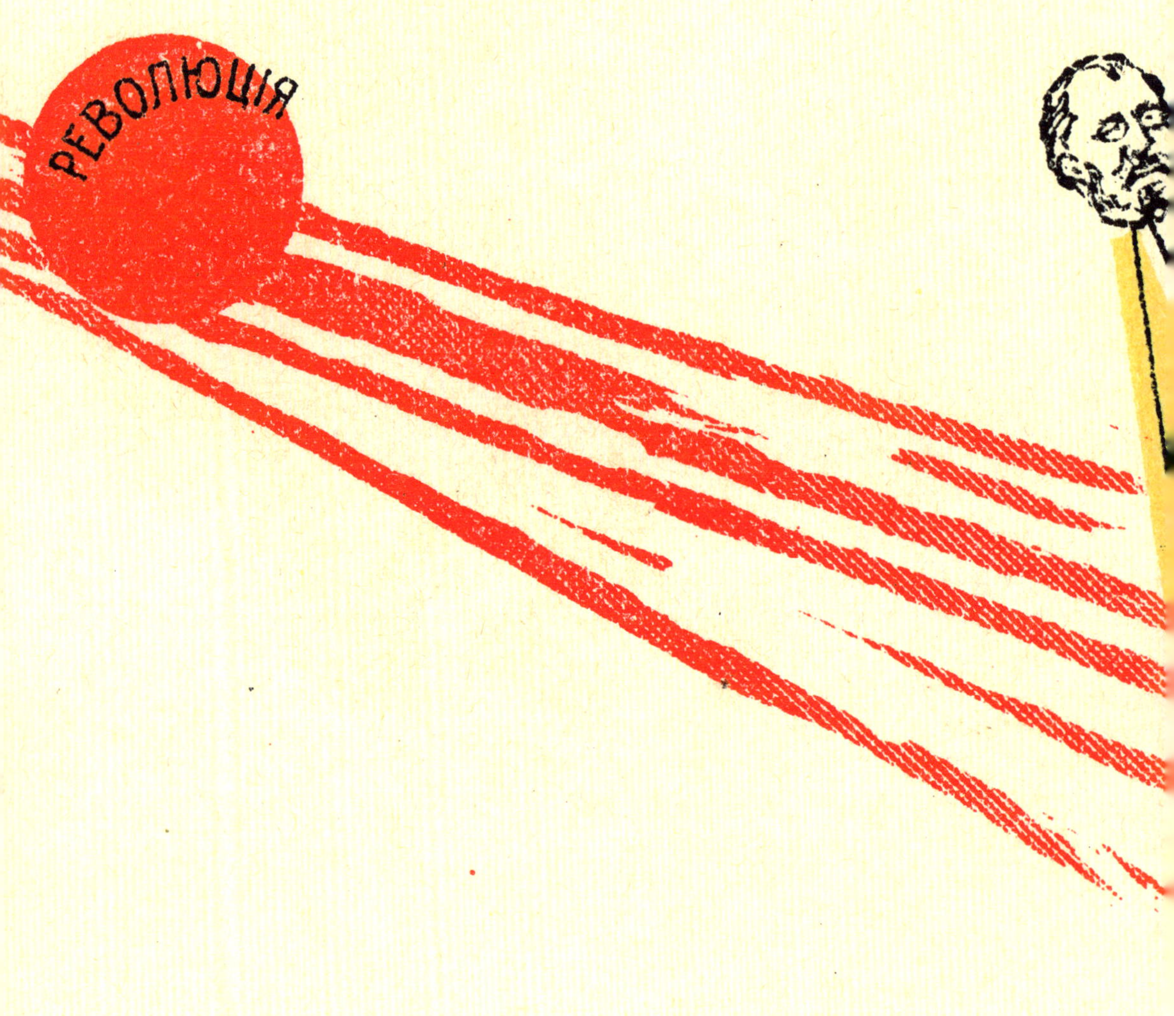

Кегель-бан

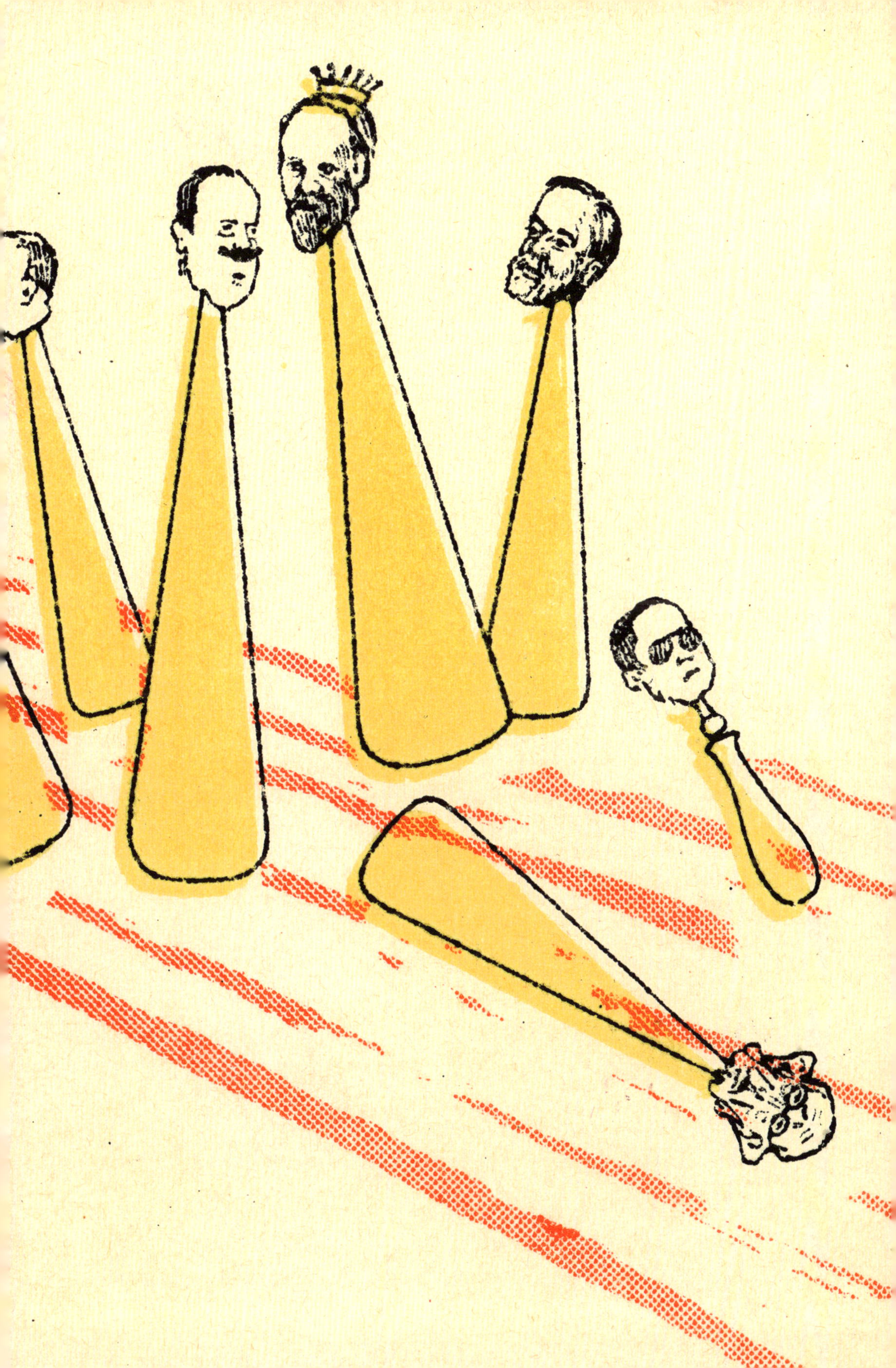

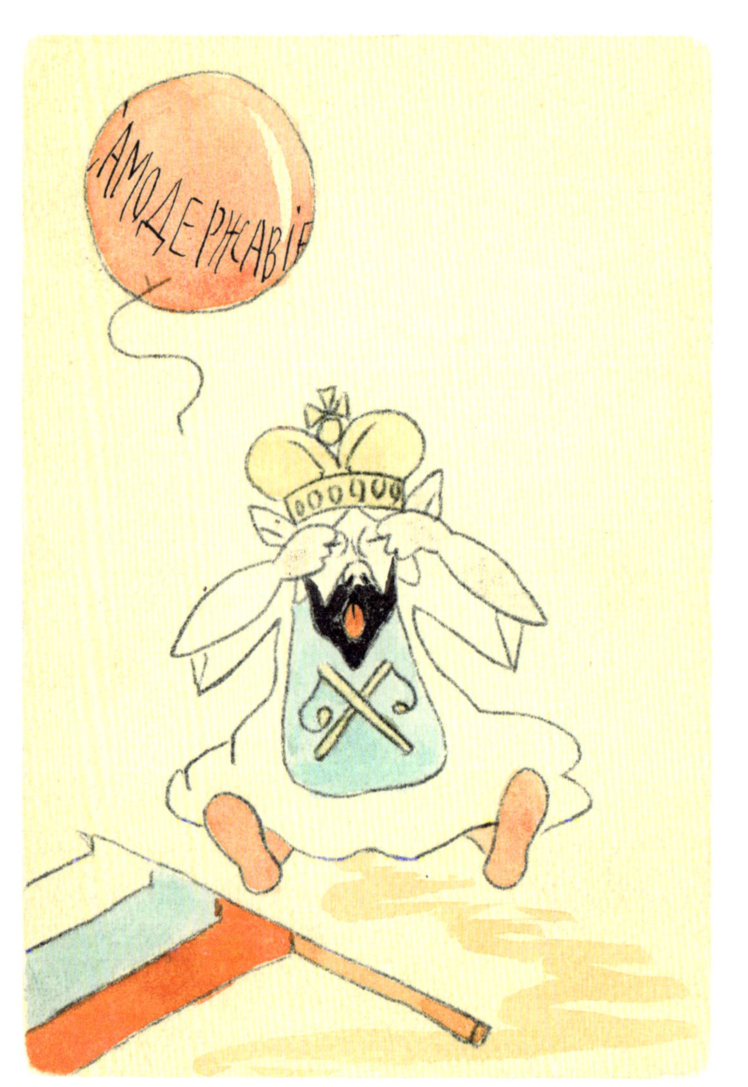
АМОДЕРЖАВІЕ

Many of the foreign caricatures circulating in Russia during this period emphasise the near inevitability of the Tsar's eventual demise. An image taken from *Der Wahre Jacob*, and republished as a postcard by Volia, has Nicholas juggling swords while a succession of bombs go off all around him. 'Will he be able to keep it up for long?' the caption asks.[7] French artists, no great fans of the Russian state, delighted in creating parallels between the Tsar and Louis XVI. One postcard titled *The Premonition* has Nicholas dreaming of a bomb-carrying revolutionary assassin, King Louis, and the guillotine.[8] Another shows him praying before a 'gallery of executed kings,' including Louis and Charles I of England.

Unlike satirical journal imagery of Nicholas, which often used indirect or 'Aesopian' language, postcards did not resort to allegory in their depictions of the Tsar, and as such, they were among the only caricatures to lampoon the head of state openly.[9] Original Russian works depicting Nicholas are, however, uncommon. Like their European counterparts, the majority were photomechanical reproductions printed underground by revolutionary organisations. Hand-drawn satires were also made, but there do not appear to have been many, or indeed any, chromolithographic caricatures of the Tsar, both because of the dangers involved and because the expense of their production was likely not worth the risk of confiscation.

Anonymous artist. Untitled caricature of Tsar Nicholas II. Hand-drawn postcard, circa 1905. The balloon is labelled 'autocracy'.

Russian caricatures of the Tsar maintain the tendency towards non-event-specific imagery but incline towards more personal attacks. Nicholas is frequently portrayed as a small child, his slight physical build and inexperience used to ape his diminished political stature. In one image, he is shown having his bottom spanked by a Japanese soldier, and in another, hand-drawn card, he is depicted as a bawling toddler who has been deprived of his toys. On the floor beside him is a small Russian flag, while a balloon above, labelled 'autocracy', floats off into the sky beyond. The aim was to belittle the Tsar, both literally and metaphorically, thereby fostering the notion that he was neither physically nor politically strong enough to rule.

In common with their European counterparts, Russian satirists routinely painted the Tsar as a bloodthirsty tyrant. Death tells 'Nicholas the Last' in one photo-caricature: 'Be gone, Bloody one! There has been much work during your reign and now I am tired. Even I cannot put up with this depravity any longer.' Not only was government repression characterised as wicked, it was also shown to be pointless. Chemodanov, one of few artists who dared to draw images of the Tsar with any regularity, portrayed Nicholas wielding a sword, labelled 'repression', to ward off a many-headed hydra intended to symbolise the revolutionary movement. It is titled *A Fight to the Death*, and the caption reads: 'If a head is cut off, dozens will take its place.'

The traditional role of a strong Tsar was to guard against chaos by balancing the different interest groups that surrounded the throne. Nicholas,

Next spread from left to right

Anonymous artist. *Death to Nicholas the Last. 'Be Gone, Bloody One! There Has Been Much Work during Your Reign and Now I Am Tired. Even I Cannot Put up with This Foulness Any More.'* No publication details, circa late 1905.

Anonymous artist. *We need Bread! We're Starving. Brothers, Help Those Who Have to Provide for Their Family.* Published by Vasilii Metalnikov, Saint Petersburg, circa late 1906.

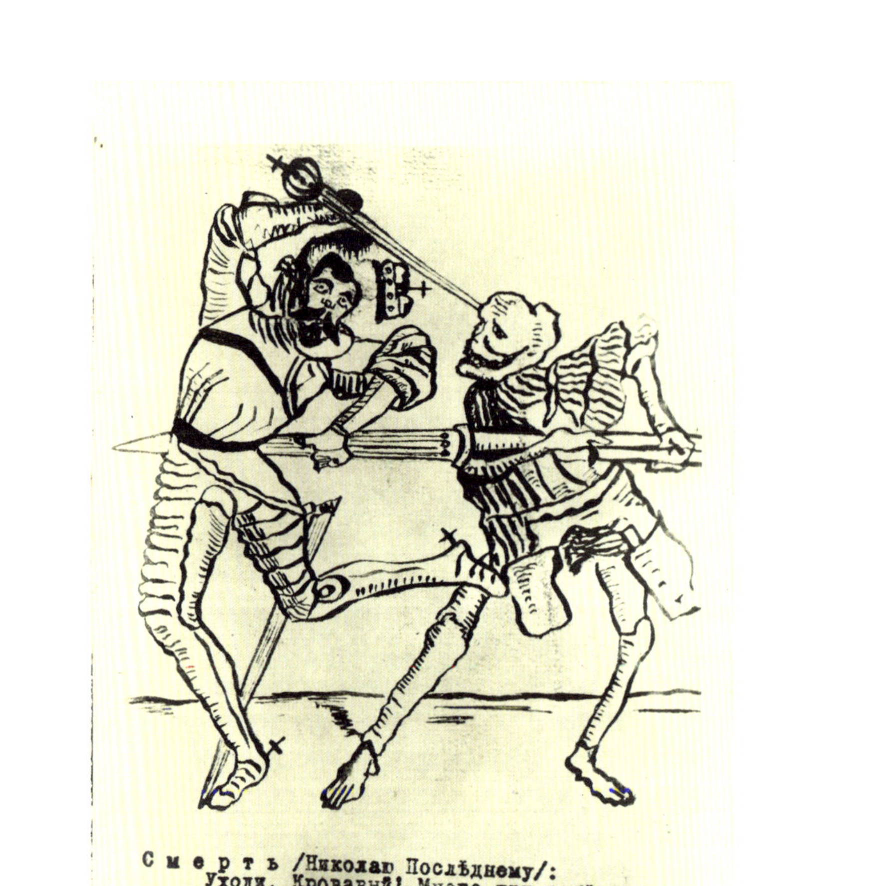

С м е р т ь /Николаю Послѣднему/:
Уходи, Кровавый! Много при тебѣ работы было,- устала я. Даже и мнѣ, постылой, не в терпеж.

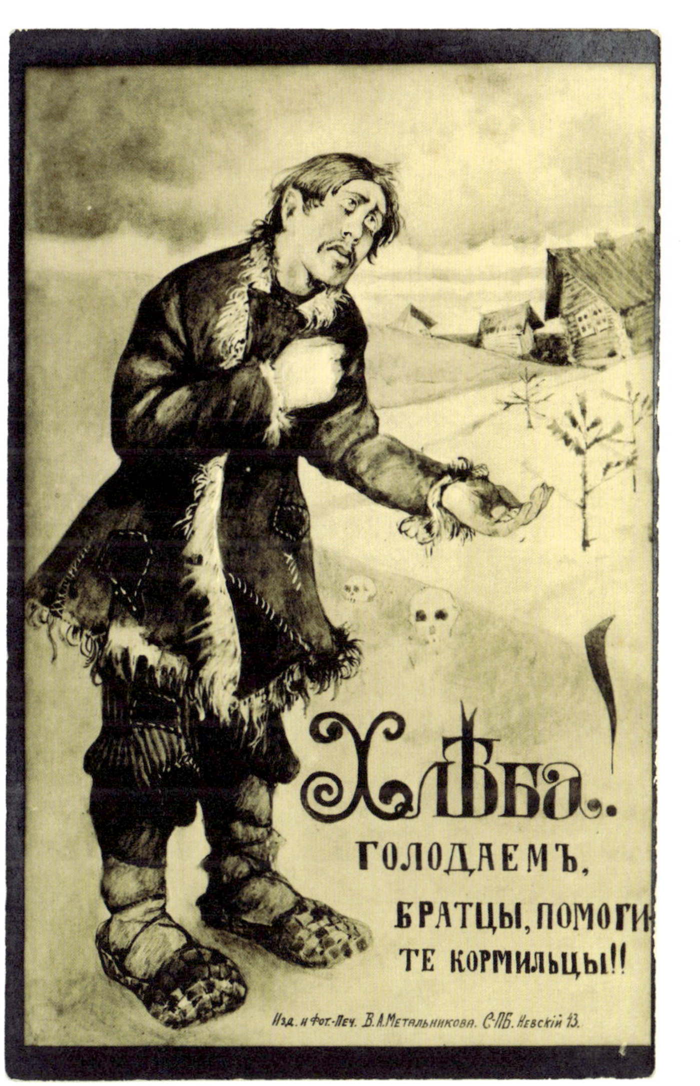
Хлѣба!..
ГОЛОДАЕМЪ,
БРАТЦЫ, ПОМОГИ-
ТЕ КОРМИЛЬЦЫ!!
Изд. и Фот.-Печ. В. А. Метальникова. С-ПБ. Невскій 43.

however, had not only failed to do this, but in condoning state violence, he had broken the compact between an absolutist state and its people – that in exchange for loyalty the ruler keeps the peace. The Tsar was thus seen to have abandoned his fundamental purpose, and so forfeited his right to rule.

The Exploitative State

Repression was not the only downside to life under the Tsars; it was merely the most visible symptom of a diseased state. Autocracy had evolved as a patrimonial system, at every level of which power was used as a way of keeping the masses in their place. Social conditions in Imperial Russia were thus fundamentally weighted against the common people. Officials were not there to help the population, but to stop any individual from attempting to rise above their station, and this they did through widespread corruption and repression. The Tsar led by example, but in order for the system to work, it required all officialdom to sign up to a system of government extortion, collectively known as the bureaucracy.

As the mechanism through which the state exercised its power, the bureaucracy provided rich pickings for postcard artists. *The Bureaucratic Press*, a Socialist-Revolutionary image from late 1904, shows a group of government ministers crushing the Russian nation to death between the jaws of an enormous wringer. The blood of the people drips out from their bodies

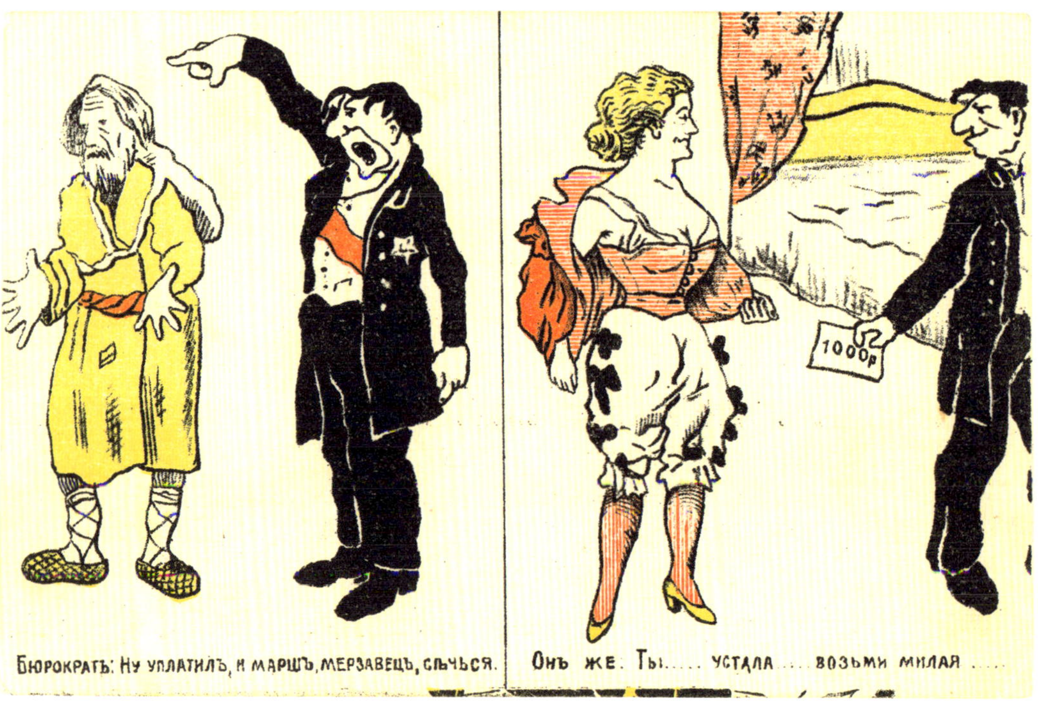

Anonymous artist. *Bureaucrat: 'I've Paid You, so Take a Hike, Scum. Be Off With You.'/The Same Man: 'You… Are Tired… Take This, My Dear'.* No publication details, circa late 1905.

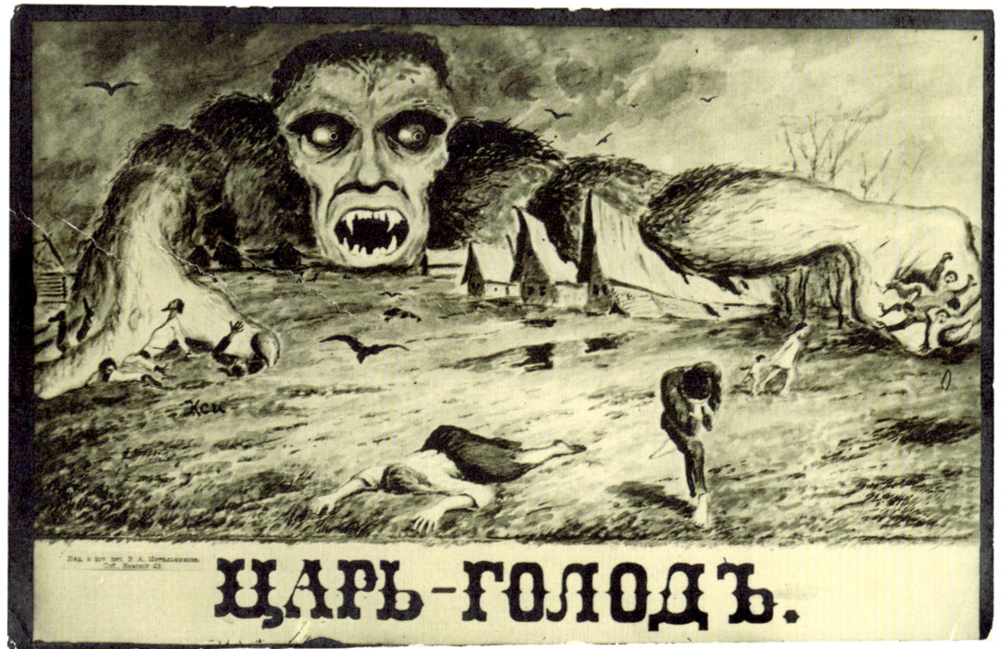

Sasha Kosoi. *Tsar Famine.* Published by Vasilii Metalnikov, Saint Petersburg, 1906.

and into the key institutions of the state, including the police, the armed forces, the church, and the court, which in turn pour out money into a large collecting trough, from which members of the Imperial elite are liberally lining their pockets. For those who subscribed to an opposition worldview, Tsarist Russia was a parasitic state par excellence.

Among the biggest losers in the autocratic system were the peasants. Their onerous existence was a particular focus of the publisher Vasilii Metalnikov, who grew up in the predominantly agricultural region of Voronezh. Many of his works deal with starvation, an issue then affecting much of south-eastern Russia. 'Tsar-Famine', a title that plainly hints at Imperial culpability, portrays hunger as a giant ogre stalking the countryside, scattering terrified villagers in every direction.[10] Other images take a more literal approach. 'We want bread! We're starving,' says an emaciated peasant in a postcard from 1906. Another, captioned *Famine in the Countryside* shows four young children begging their mother for food, as their father slumps dejectedly behind them.

Metalnikov's postcards not only illustrate the poverty of rural existence, but also contrast it with the prosperous world of the ruling classes. In *Famine is Coming* a wretchedly-dressed peasant family loiter outside a local manor house. Through a window behind them, a man in white tie can be seen tossing back a glass of champagne. The pressures on the countryside, however, were as much social as they were political. Sergei Zhivotovskii's *One with a Plough and Seven with a Spoon* shows a peasant being assailed by figures representing Russia's different social estates, all of whom demand that their bellies be filled. This widely reproduced image lays bare the enormous strain that farmers were under to provide food for a rapidly expanding population.[11]

Any attempt to generate sympathy for rural multitudes had an obvious propaganda objective, but Metalnikov's postcards were also intended to elicit a practical response. 'Citizens of Russia, remember that there is famine in Russia, and you can help,' reads the caption to one. This plea indicates Metalnikov's deep sympathy for the suffering peasantry, but it also reveals a profoundly liberal agenda. He is telling more enlightened members of society that in the absence of a compassionate state they have a social responsibility to help the poor. Far from informing the peasants of their downtrodden position in order to foment revolt from below, Metalnikov's paternalistic images were about gaining liberal support to bring about reform from above.

The grand narrative of Imperial exploitation continues in postcards dealing with the labour question. *Labour and Capital*, Metalnikov's depiction of profiteering at the expense of the working classes, borrows from Wilhelm Liebknecht to show capital as a giant spider trapping workers in its web of sin.[12] Likewise, *The Nightmare of Capitalism*, Boris Anisfeld's contribution to Shipovnik, characterises factory owners as grotesque money-hoarders who turn workers' sweat into capitalists' gold. No doubt propagandists and consumers interpreted these postcards in accordance with their own beliefs, but like many cartoons, the emphasis of both images is on exposing

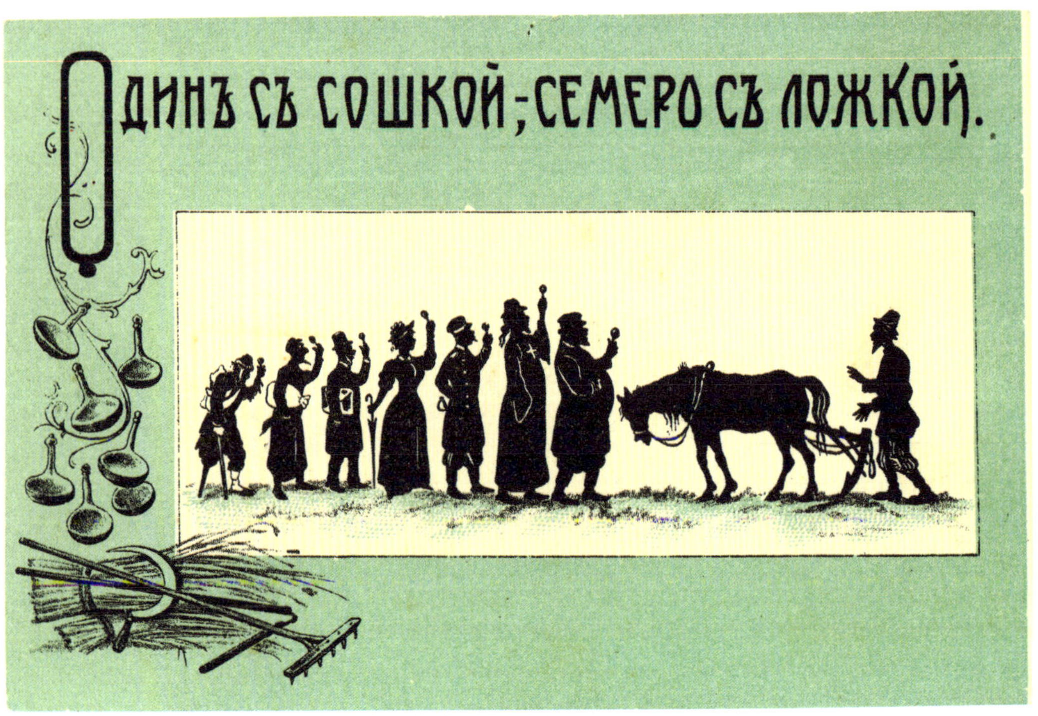

Sergei Zhivotovskii. *One with a Plough and Seven with a Spoon.* No publication details, circa 1906.

the conditions of the working classes in order to generate momentum for reform, not on exploiting class disparity for purely revolutionary ends.

The works discussed up to this point have cast the people of Russia as objects of pity and the Imperial government as the agents of their fate. Far less prevalent are postcard works that depict the toiling masses as a politicised workforce. The most common of these are images of workers going on strike, but there are also a small number of postcards that explicitly characterise the proletariat as assuming the status of a new social power. For example, one nominally Social Democratic postcard of two workers turning a mill wheel carries the exhortation: 'The Labour Question – Forward!' Other images are more confrontational: *The Proletariat and the Bourgeoisie* shows a disembodied fist being brandished at a small lapdog.

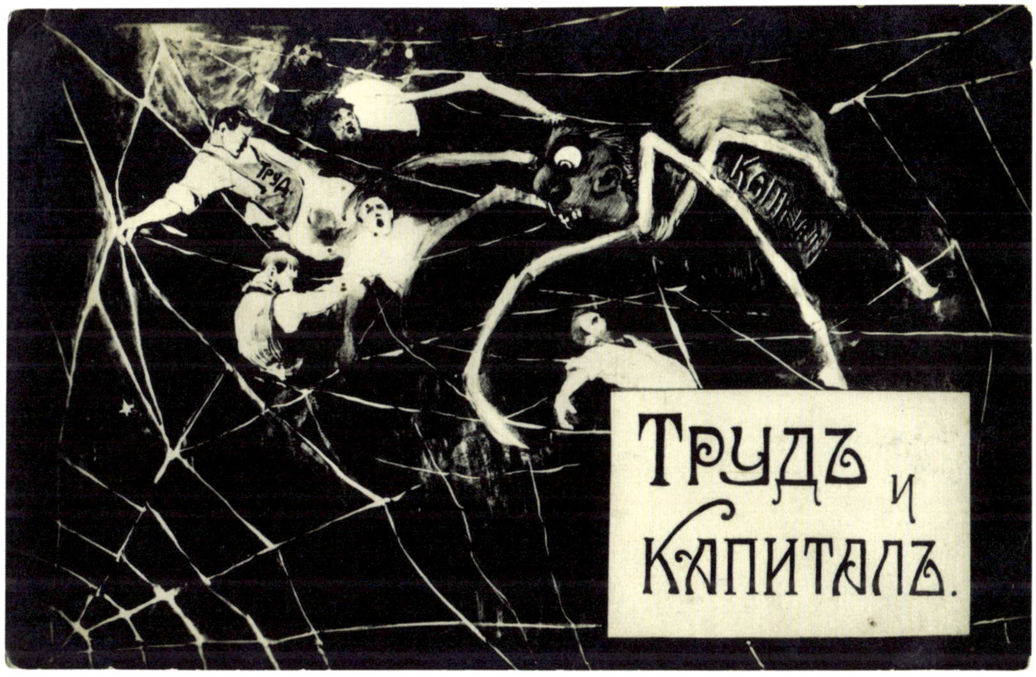

Anonymous artist. *Labour and Capital.* Published by Vasilii Metalnikov. Saint Petersburg, circa early 1907.

The proletariat was often represented symbolically through a single individual whose defiant stance signalled eventual victory over oppression. *The Russian Proletarian*, a tribute to the rebels of the Moscow Uprising, imagines a statue of an armed worker, sword in one hand and flaming torch in the other, standing on a plinth above a pile of dead bodies. Against a backdrop of destroyed buildings, the monument both commemorates the revolutionary sacrifices that have been made by the working classes and keeps alive the flame of their continuing struggle against the regime. Boldly asserting his political presence and power over the pictorial landscape, the figure of the proletarian proclaims on paper what cannot yet be achieved in practice.

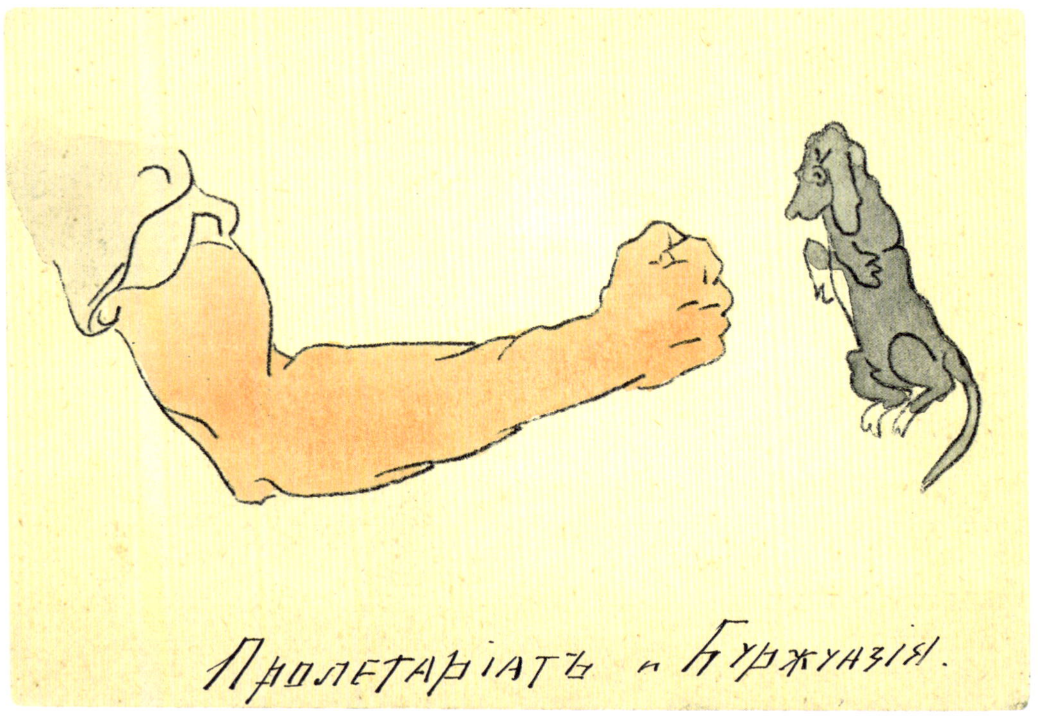

Anonymous artist. *The Proletariat and the Bourgeoisie.* Hand-drawn postcard, circa 1905.

The Social Democrat's belief in the decisive role played by the working classes in 1905 can also be seen in Chemodanov's *An Old Song Played to a New Tune.* This celebration of the October General Strike depicts the 'proletarian' lion standing triumphantly atop the 'government' bear. All the 'liberal' hare can do, meanwhile, is nibble at the bear's ear. But even in Chemodanov's work orthodox Marxist depictions of the 1905 Revolution are rare. Like most artists, he took a top-down approach, satirising individual officials as opposed to glorifying the masses who seethed beneath them. Soviet commentators later criticised him for speaking of a 'popular consciousness,' not the 'consciousness of the proletariat,' and for rarely having singled out workers as a class.[13]

While strongly coloured by revolutionary sentiment, Chemodanov's politics were essentially humanist as opposed to Marxist. He was concerned to improve the lot of all social classes in Russia, not one in particular.[14] The overall paucity of references to the concerns of the urban and rural masses in anti-government postcard cartoons reflects the domination of the medium by the moderate left-wing opposition, whose political anxieties and target audience were not to be found among the lower orders. Their primary aim was to trumpet the regime's betrayal of the October Manifesto, not to foment popular revolution; consequently, their postcards were always focused more on denigrating the government than they were on extolling the masses.

Opposite

N. V. *To the Russian Proletariat.* No publication details, late 1905.

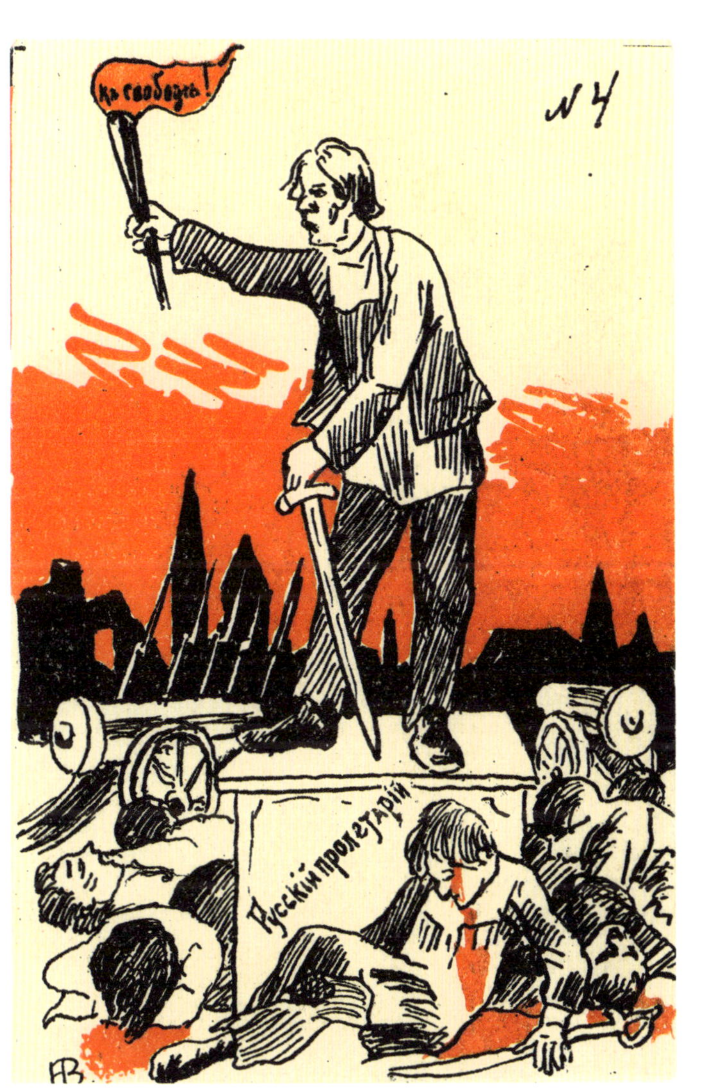
къ свободѣ!
№ 4
Русскій пролетарій

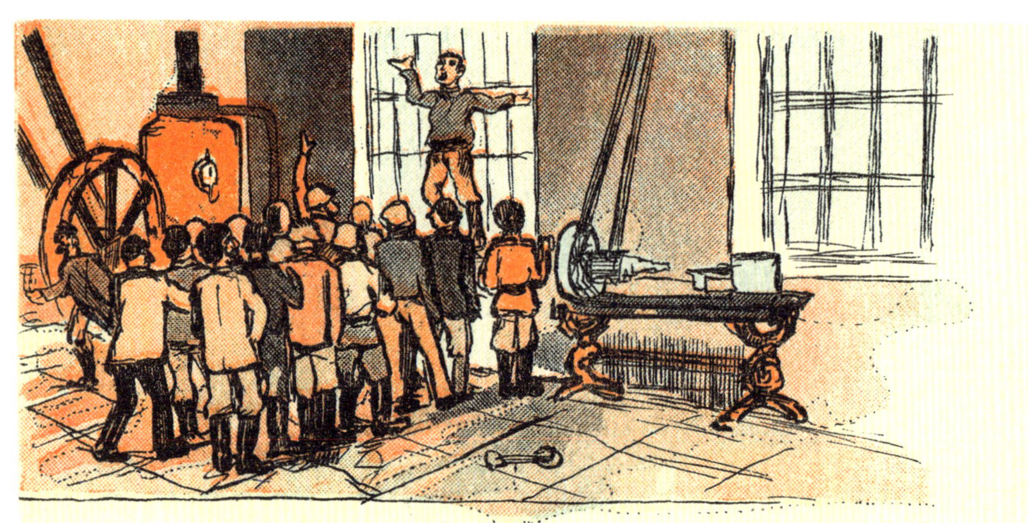

Товарищи! Забастуемъ !!!

Postcards on political themes were not entirely one-sided. On a broad level, portraits of the Tsar acted as a counterpoint to anti-government pictures by helping to propagate imagery of the Imperial power that Nicholas embodied. More subtly, postcards of Romanov palaces and possessions established an inextricable link between Russia's national patrimony and the ruling dynasty, thereby anchoring the Romanovs to the land and making all those who sought to uproot them appear traitorous by comparison. Purchase of such postcards did not necessarily signal allegiance to the throne, but any image linked to the Imperial Family served to disseminate a traditional view of Russia that was sharply at odds with that of the anti-government opposition.

Portrait postcards of Nicholas's ministers are uncommon, as are images of the commanders of his armed forces. Production of the latter increased during the Russo-Japanese War, but there was never any great tradition of portraying officialdom in postcard form. The main reason for their paucity during the revolutionary period, however, was the unpopularity of the government itself. A handful of postcards depicting Witte and Stolypin were printed, but as far as can be ascertained, there were none of Durnovo, Trepov, or other key officials. As the government was often made a scapegoat for the excesses of the regime, the commercial prospect of such portraits was poor, and as a result few were produced.

Anonymous artist. *Comrades! Let's Strike!!!* No publication details, circa late 1905.

In late 1905, several right-wing monarchist groups were formed in an attempt to combat the prevailing mood of opposition in Russia. Propaganda publications soon followed, but although they attracted large state subsidies and a degree of popular support, financial and organisational mismanagement meant that the printed output of the reactionary right never came close to the levels achieved by their opponents.[15] While examples of anti-revolutionary satirical journals and satirical postcards have survived in Russian archives and museum collections, they are excessively rare in today's collecting market, a result of the small numbers printed, lack of sales, and the inherent danger of owning such material during the Soviet period.[16]

Black Hundred postcards can be divided into two interlinked groups: those that seek to smear the revolutionaries as foreign interlopers, and those that portray reform as a Jewish conspiracy directed against Orthodox Russia. The revolutionary unrest in 1905 posited an acute threat to the Imperial status quo, a political emergency that forced even committed supporters of the Tsar to accept that the regime could not continue to exist in its present absolutist form. But rather than face up to the reality that the autocratic state was somehow imperfect, the easiest way for most monarchists to comprehend the political upheaval was to explain it away as something alien to Russia, an infectious plague spread by external enemies bent on destroying the country.

Because Russia had no great revolutionary culture of its own, the liberation movement took much of its inspiration from abroad. Both the notion of individual freedom and its iconography were imported – red flags, Phrygian bonnets, and female personifications of liberty all came from Western Europe. Even the language of political resistance had foreign origins: revolitsiia, reforma, politika, manifest, miting, etc. Black Hundred propaganda turned this reliance on a European revolutionary tradition against the opposition, using it to unify the nation against 'outsiders,' who were purportedly attempting to corrupt the country with foreign ideas. As one postcard entreated: 'Awake Russian People, the time for action is upon us, we must all close ranks, to save our Tsar and Father.'[17]

Taking their cue from the Tsar, who in early 1905 had blamed the political turmoil on 'foreign elements,' the Black Hundreds sought to cast all opposition beliefs and institutions as alien to Russia.[18] Whereas the forces of revolution looked outwards, stressing their internationalism, right-wing propagandists looked to a home-grown, jingoistic ideology to shore up support. *Hymn for the Tsar*, one of a series of postcards reproducing nationalist verses, reads in part: 'Our enemies sing in French, Republics they want to see, and we reply in Russian, Republics will never be.' By suggesting that the idea of political change was contrary to Russia and Russian values, right-wingers hoped to convince the population of the futility of reform.

The principal rallying cry of these postcards is that of 'Orthodoxy, Autocracy, Nationality,' the rigid framework of Imperial nationhood first initiated under Nicholas I. In such a rapidly changing political environment, it was hoped that these core values might act as a bulwark against all types of democratic and revolutionary belief. Any attempt to undermine these ideological pillars of state was taken to constitute an attack on Russia itself. Proponents of a constitutional monarchy, let alone a republic, were 'traitors,' who only wanted power for themselves. Calling their cause 'a masonic heresy,' one postcard asks: 'Why do you subject God-given Tsarist Power to such ridicule ... is it because you want to steal the crown!?'[19]

In rousing the masses to the defence of Russia, many postcards invoke examples of individuals who had defended the country from foreign incursions in ages past. Some recall how the folk hero Ivan Susanin 'defeated evil plots to defend the Tsar and Rus,' while others celebrate the feats of Kuzma Minin and Dmitrii Pozharskii, who in 1613 helped to expel Polish invaders from the Kremlin. The postcards reproducing nationalist verse all carry a small vignette of the monument to Minin and Pozharskii in Red Square, and underneath it, the slogan 'Russia for the Russians'. To this day, the event still has a special place in the hearts of nationalists, both as the dawn of the Romanov dynasty and as a symbol of Russian independence.

The October Manifesto forced all elements of society to engage with the notion of political reform. Loyalists who could not stomach the dilution of Tsarist power – or more to the point the transfer of power to people unlike them – looked for someone to blame, and this they found in any person who did not belong to their own religious and ethnic grouping. Individuals perceived as trying to force Russia from its historic path were besmirched as foreign agents – fifth columnists who were aiming to subvert Russia from within. In one postcard verse, titled 'Two Counts,' Witte is labelled a Jew and the nineteenth-century reformist statesman Mikhail Loris-Melikov, an Armenian: 'the sons of two homeless nations, two superfluous and foreign tribes.'

The most common way of implying that reform was extraneous to Russia was by caricaturing it as a Jewish plot. Anti-Semitism was well established long before 1905, but concerns about change and loss of identity came together at this time in the hate figure of the Jewish revolutionary. The success of the reformist Kadet Party, and the corresponding failure of the monarchist parties in the First Duma elections, attracted the wrath of right-wing artists, who stereotyped the Kadets as money-grubbing Jews who were demanding 'shmeedom' [shvaboda] at the point of a gun. In transposing Jewish attributes onto the liberal parties, the opposition as a whole was cast out, their ideology and intents shown to be anathema to the Russian nation.

The concept of revolution as a Jewish conspiracy aimed at world domination is explored more fully in a postcard published by the monarchist Union of the Archangel Michael. *The Yid Onslaught on Europe* casts the Jews as being intent on undermining Christian values and seizing control of key European institutions, including its 'stock exchanges, banks, newspapers, magazines, pharmacies, bakeries, and forestry and grain trades.' The caption reads: 'The worldwide Jewish qahal is doing everything in its power and will not shrink from using any method, including bombs, to try to snatch away two letters from "Evropeiskie" [European] states: "O" (otechestvo) [fatherland] and "P" (patriotizm) [patriotism], and so transform Europe into a group of "Evreiskie" [Jewish] states.'

Many Tsarist officials believed that the Jews were responsible for the upheaval in 1905 and repeatedly said so in public. *The Protocols of the Elders of Zion* had been published just two years earlier and for those who wished to believe it, widespread Jewish support for the revolutionary movement appeared to confirm their veracity. Judeo-Masonic conspiracies were an expression of deep fear on the part of those who felt that reform and revolution were putting everything they held dear under mortal threat. Confused and under attack, the Black Hundreds tried to counteract this peril by drawing on the myth of Russian exceptionalism, deriving strength from their history and religion as they prepared to do battle for 'the sacred identity of Rus.'

In order to fight against the calumnies of the Right, the opposition created its own symbolic vision of contemporary Russia. If supporters of the Tsar depicted the country as a strong, patriarchal state, guided by religion and inspired by brave heroes from the past, the left portrayed Russia as a defenceless maiden, under assault from the very people tasked with protecting her. In one postcard on the Moscow Uprising, 'Holy Rus' is shown as a naked woman being repeatedly stabbed by Black Hundred thugs; in another, Durnovo, watched on by Witte, strangles a female nude who lies supine on a red flag. In bringing together Liberty and Russia in a single figure, attacks on reform are equated with attacks on Mother Russia herself.

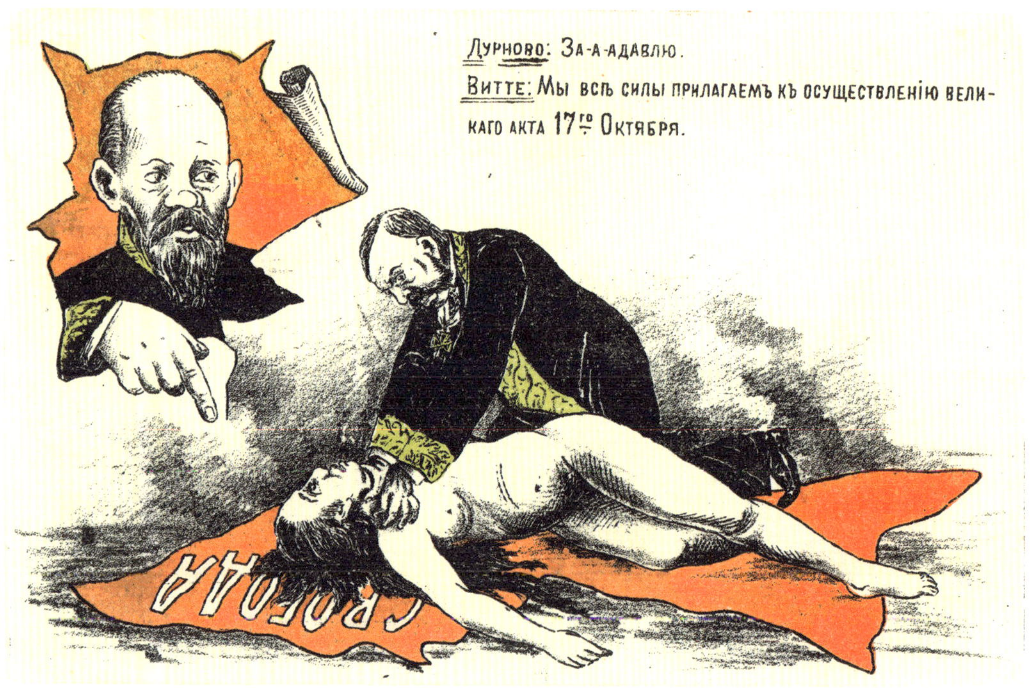

Anonymous artist. *Durnovo: 'I'm Sque-ee-eezing!' Witte: 'We are Doing Everything in Our Power to Realise the Great Decree of 17 October'.* No publication details, late 1905.

In common with their nationalistic counterparts, anti-government postcards define the actions of their enemies in opposition to the values that they claim to represent. Both sides needed to convince the population that they were acting in the best interests of the country, and the easiest way to do this was not by trying to legitimise their own aims, but by trying to delegitimise those of their opponents. Left and right went about doing this in a very similar manner, each portraying their political rivals as alien beings in order to show that their actions and objectives were unsuited to the country that they wanted to maintain or create. This was a struggle to define the very identity of the Russian state.

Opposite

Anonymous artist. *Poisonous Toadstool.* Hand-drawn postcard, circa 1905. Caricature of Konstantin Pobedonostsev.

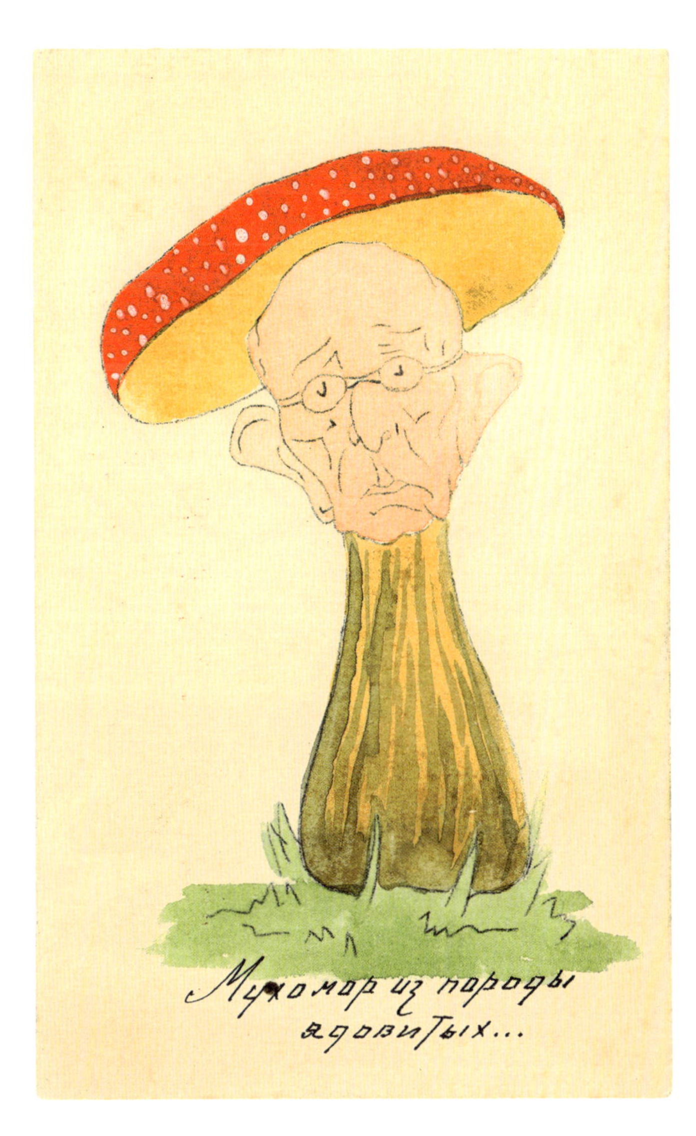
Мухомор из породы
ядовитых...

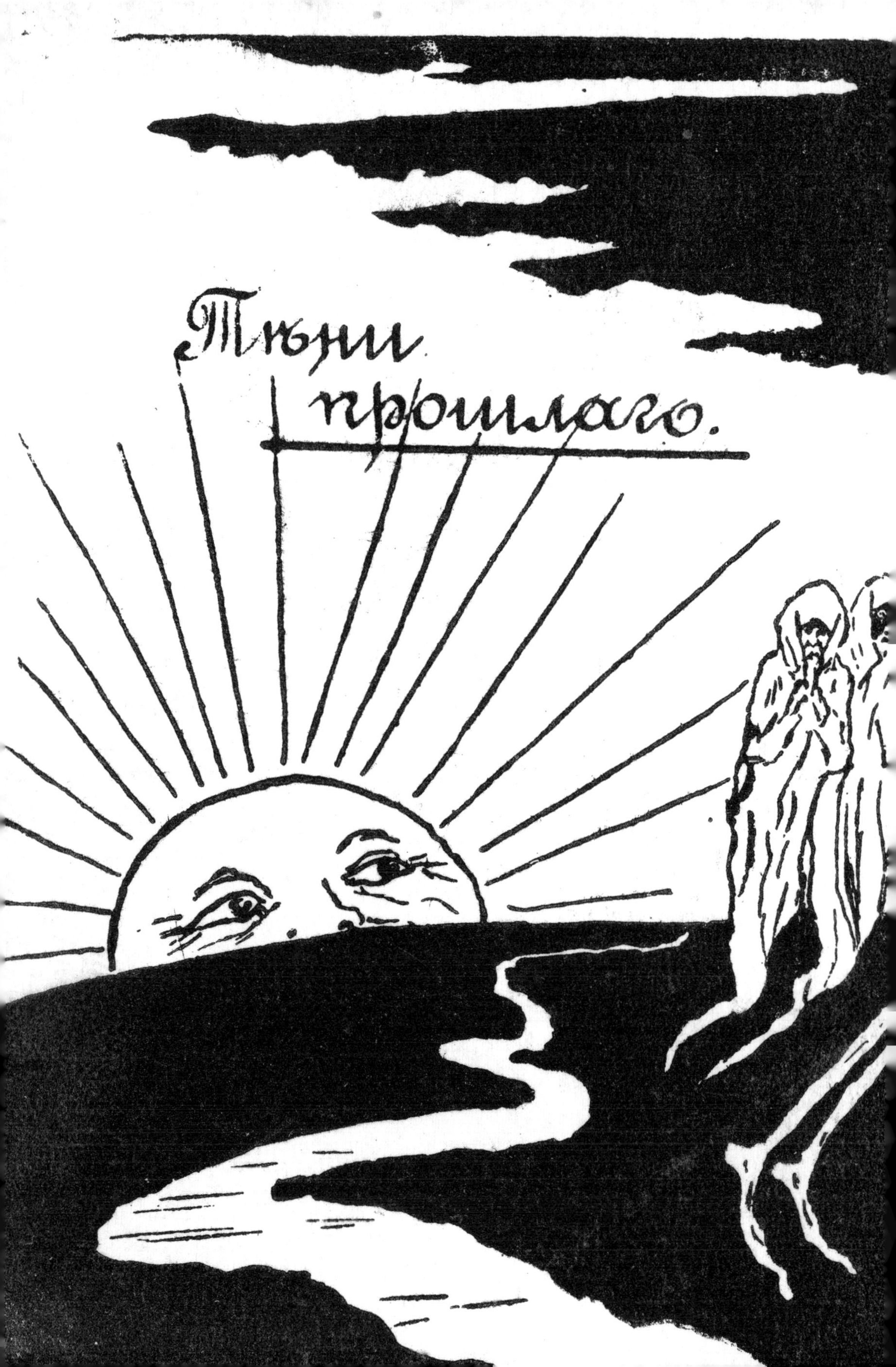
Тѣни
прошлаго.

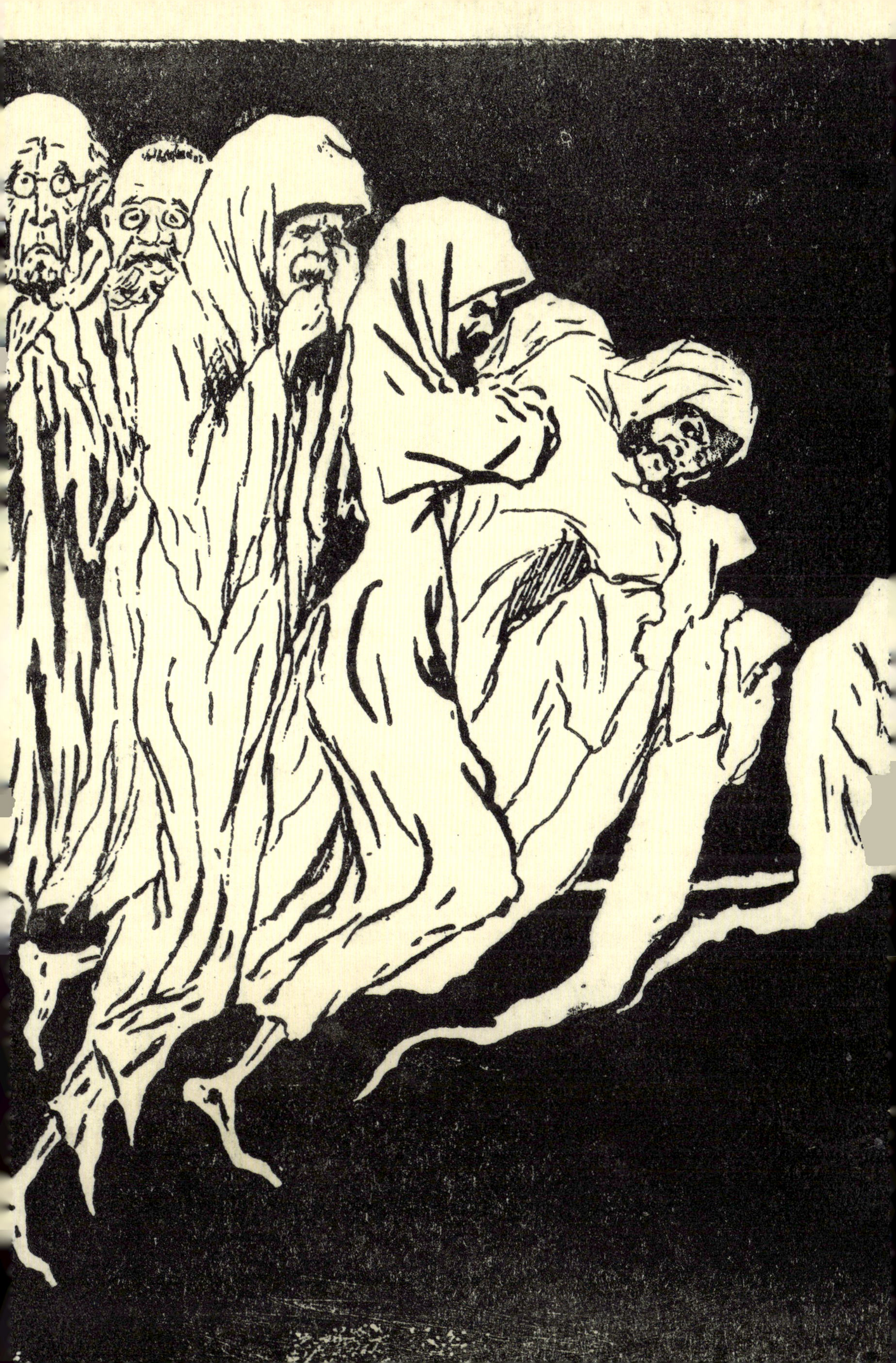

Previous spread

Anonymous artist. *Ghosts of the Past.* Published by Nikolai Merder, Saint Petersburg, late 1905. From left to right: Konstantin Pobedonostsev, Vladimir Glazov, Petr Durnovo, Dmitrii Trepov, and Alexander Bulygin.

In anti-government imagery, the Imperial hierarchy often belongs to another world, removed from contemporary Russia in time and body. Merder's postcard *Ghosts of the Past* portrays the Tsar's chief ministers as ethereal forms, gently floating off into the night sky as a watchful sun rises up behind them. The ministers (who include Bulygin, Durnovo, Minister of Enlightenment Vladimir Glazov, Pobedonostsev, and Trepov), have been cast in folkloric tradition as demons, malevolent spirits who are intent on keeping Russia submerged in the murky depths of the past. Political and social change, symbolised by the sun, is shown as an illuminating force for good, chasing off an evil power into the darkness beyond.

The concept of the regime as a sinister entity is particularly prevalent in images of Pobedonostsev. As the lay supervisor of the Orthodox Church, he wielded great power, right down to determining what books could be issued by the church presses. He had been a tutor and was now a counsellor to Nicholas II, and to his father before that. Pobedonostsev viewed all political reform as a sign of weakness, and throughout his long career waged a fierce battle against any attenuation of autocratic power. The October Manifesto, which he had advised against, represented a significant defeat, and he was forced into retirement shortly afterwards. Nonetheless, he remained one of the most widely depicted bogeymen of the period.

Pobedonostsev, a skinny man with ears too large to ignore, was regularly shown in zoomorphic guise. He appears in different postcard caricatures as a poisonous toadstool, a snake, a centaur and a werewolf. As the latter, he wears a monk's cowl and grasps a rosary. While his top half is human, his bottom half is wolf. The caption reads: 'Time to go, it's getting light.' He may appear to be religious, the image suggests, but really, he is a demon. Pobedonostsev was the key intermediary between the autocratic state and the Orthodox Church (the divine authority through which the Tsar exercised his earthly power), and in impugning him, the liberal opposition was looking to question the moral and religious prerogative of Imperial rule.

As the ideological backbone of the regime, the Church presented a prominent target, but more for its connections to the throne than for the actions of its clergy. Caricatures of gluttonous priests living off the fat of the land do exist, but this was always more about anti-Tsarism than anti-clericalism. It is no coincidence that Nicholas's own priest, John of Kronstadt was another key figure of opposition opprobrium. Ridiger depicted him consorting with scantily clad female devotees, while in the anonymous cartoon *He Departed from Evil and Did Good*, he is shown running from the scene of a pogrom.[20] By inverting traditional notions of Good and Evil, the Church's integrity was undermined, and with it the probity of the regime as a whole.

Opposite

Anonymous artist. *Time to Go, It's Getting Light!...* No publication details, late 1905. Caricature of Konstantin Pobedonostsev.

Most scathing of all are representations of the regime's keenest supporters, the Black Hundreds. Affiliates of the movement are parodied as thickset

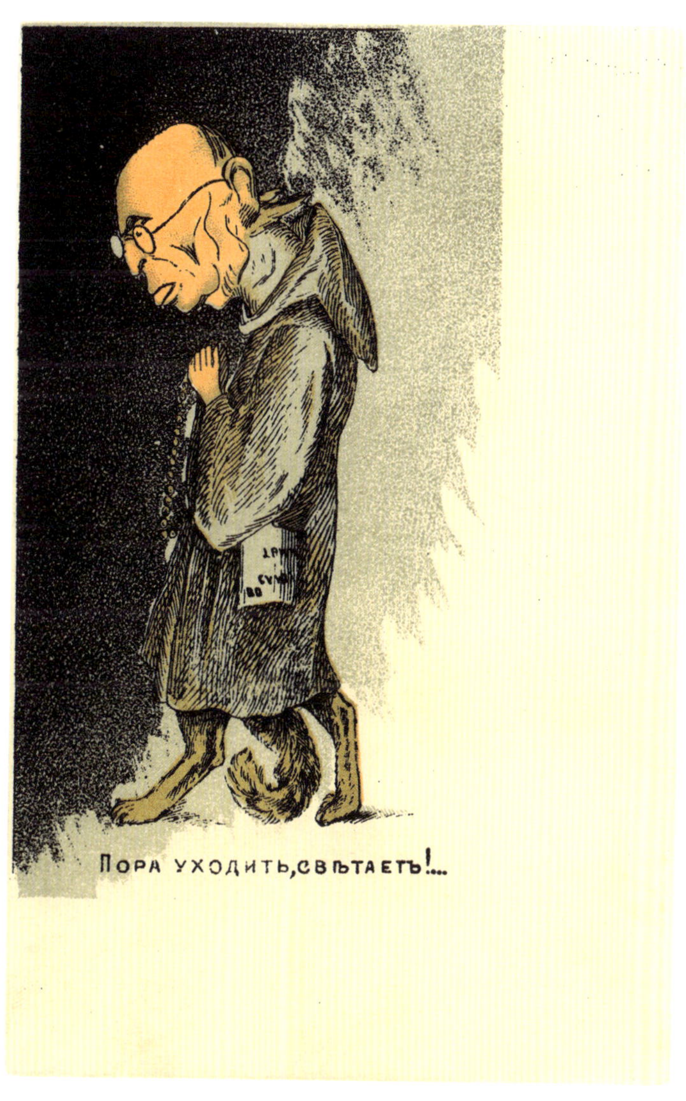

Пора уходить,свѣтаетъ!...

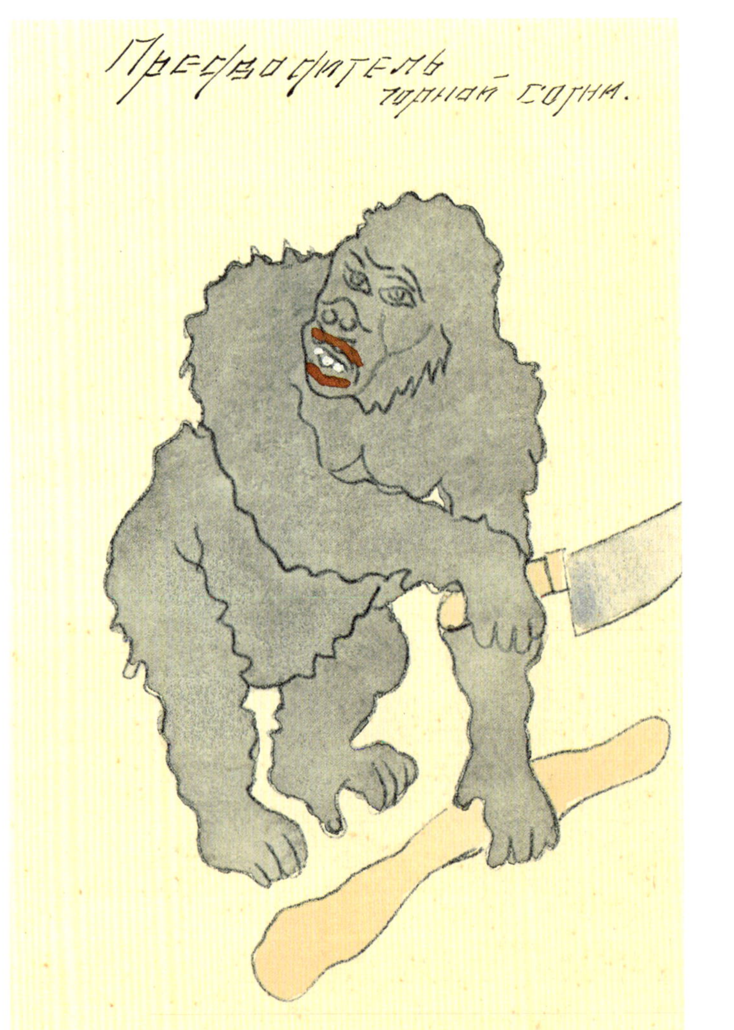
Предводитель
чорнай сотни.

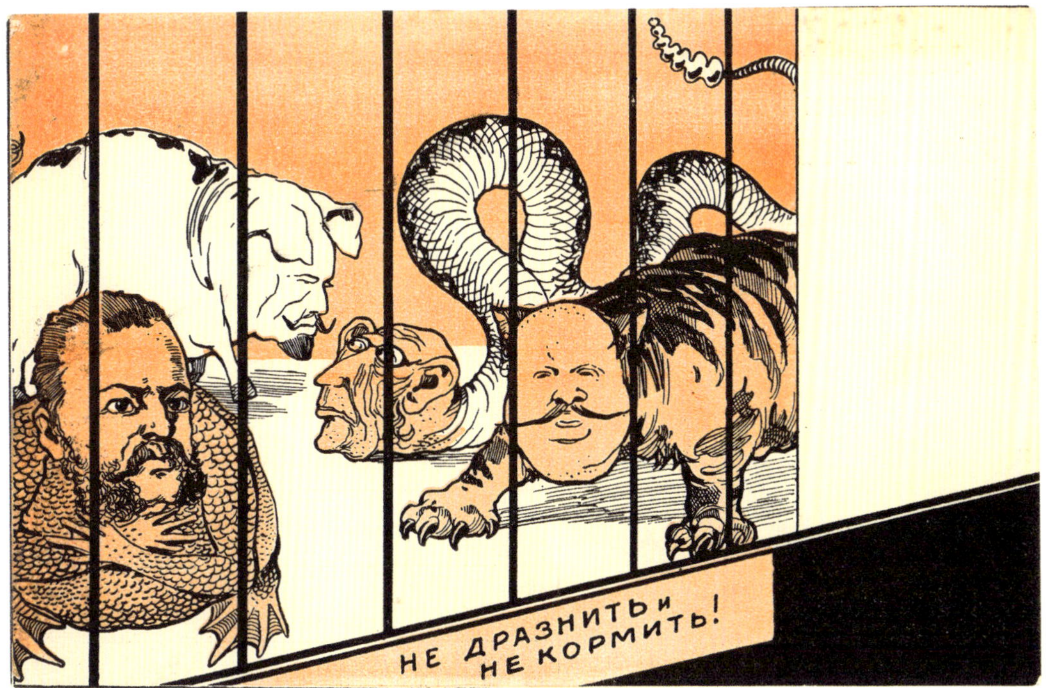

Anonymous artist. *Do Not Feed or Provoke.* No publication details, late 1905. From left to right: Alexander Bulygin, Dmitrii Trepov, Konstantin Pobedonostsev, and Aleksei Ignatiev.

hoodlums closer to beast than man. With a craving for violence whetted by alcohol, they are seen to indulge in animal-like ravages against what one cartoon satirises as the 'yids and the entelijentsia in generull.' Deliberate misspellings make out defenders of the monarchy to be idiotic savages who are driven by an unholy cocktail of stupidity, religion and nationalistic fervour. These delinquents are not even worthy of the title of human beings. A hand-drawn caricature titled *Black Hundred Ringleader* shows a bipedal gorilla with a club in one hand and a meat cleaver in the other.

In more than one postcard, Trepov is portrayed as a man-eater. Indeed, *The European Cannibal* has him literally stuffing people into his mouth. This both conveys his great appetite for violence and brands him a 'primitive' – a man who cannot behave according to the 'civilised' norms of the West. In this distorted realm, the Imperial government is run by monsters and supported by individuals who are little more than wild animals. Autocracy is thus shown to stand in opposition to the modern and, indeed, the human world, wallowing in a state of pre-Enlightenment savagery. As such, it can have no place in contemporary European society: reform is progressive and rational, while resistance to it is little more than demonic barbarism.

Opposite

Anonymous artist. *Black Hundred Ringleader.* Hand-drawn postcard, circa 1905.

The Duma

On 27 April 1906, the streets of Saint Petersburg were filled with people, closely watched by large numbers of troops, recently brought in from the

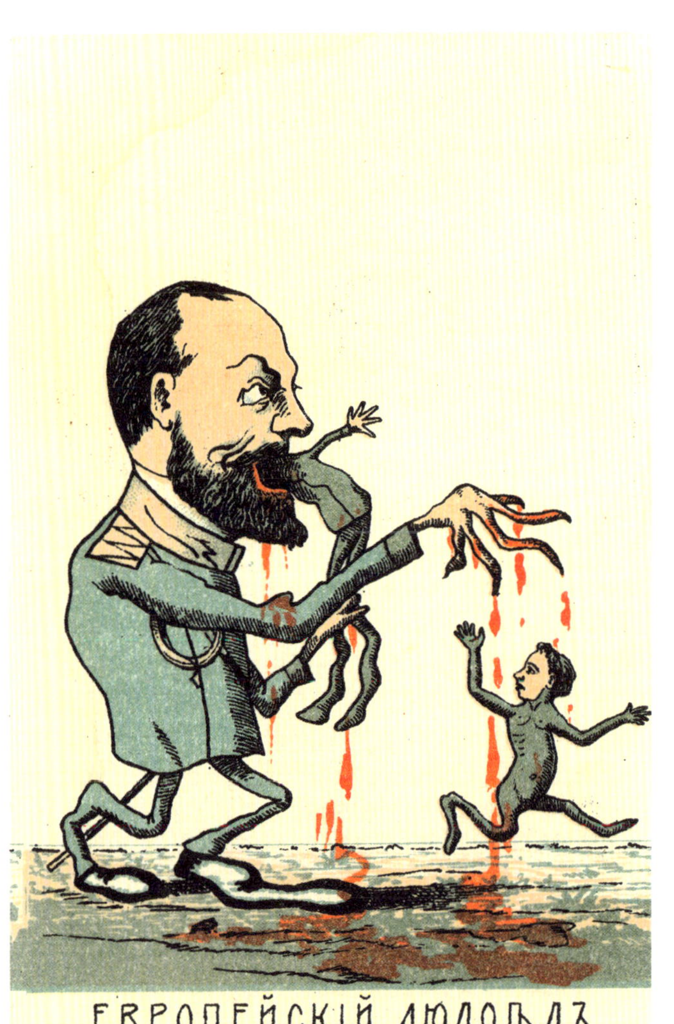
ЕВРОПЕЙСКІЙ ЛЮДОѢДЪ.

surrounding districts. The State Duma, inaugurated that morning, was the legacy of both popular revolution and Imperial fiat. On the one hand, opposition unrest had forced Nicholas into making the concessions that had brought about its convocation, and on the other, the assembly had been established solely through personal decree of the Tsar, and as such could not be entirely disregarded by his supporters. Consequently, the role of the institution was highly contested, and as in the chamber itself, postcards became an arena for both left and right to assert rival interpretations.

Anonymous artist. *The European Cannibal.* No publication details, late 1905. Caricature of Dmitrii Trepov.

For liberals who trusted in political reform, the Duma was the apex of a long and acrimonious struggle. Postcards subscribing to their worldview celebrate this achievement and commemorate the cost. One photomontage image depicts two groups of deputies arranged above a pile of skulls. Between them a female figure wearing a Phrygian bonnet carries a flag inscribed with the date of the October Manifesto. 'Citizens,' the caption reads: 'Never Forget that the Path to Freedom was Paved with the Corpses of Your Brothers.' The Manifesto was not merely a step on the way to civil liberty, but the culmination of the fight. Now, in their moment of triumph, the public could reflect on what it had taken to get there.

The outlook of loyalist publishers was rather different. For them, the weakening of Imperial power was a bitter pill to swallow; nevertheless, they had a duty to believe that Nicholas had his people's best interests at heart. In an article accompanying the publication of a commemorative postcard by Dobuzhinskii, the journal of the Society of Saint Eugenia expressed its hope that the assembly would 'provide the strength that we so desperately need for the future achievements, success, and revival of our tormented and exhausted fatherland.'[21] Given his satirical work for *Zhupel* late the previous year, the Society's choice of artist, and Dobuzhinskii's agreement, is surprising, but such transactions appear to have been primarily commercial in nature.

Dobuzhinskii's design features a line drawing of the Tauride Palace, framed by decorative swags and buttressed by two fasces, which in turn support the wings of a large double-headed eagle. The prominent placing of the Imperial crest, which entirely dwarfs the grand classical building, leaves the viewer in no doubt as to where the Duma lies in relation to the throne. This is a depiction of the Assembly, not as a legislative body won through lengthy struggle, but as a piece of political cake gifted to the people through Imperial benevolence. Its origins in the 1905 Revolution, so heavily emphasised in anti-government postcards, are here totally obscured; the legislature has simply been recast as another arm of the autocratic state.

Even those with only a modicum of political capital invested in the Duma looked to it with cautious optimism. In the telling of artist Elizaveta Bem, it was now up to the deputies to ensure that these aspirations were fulfilled. Bem produced six postcards depicting young children acting out Russian

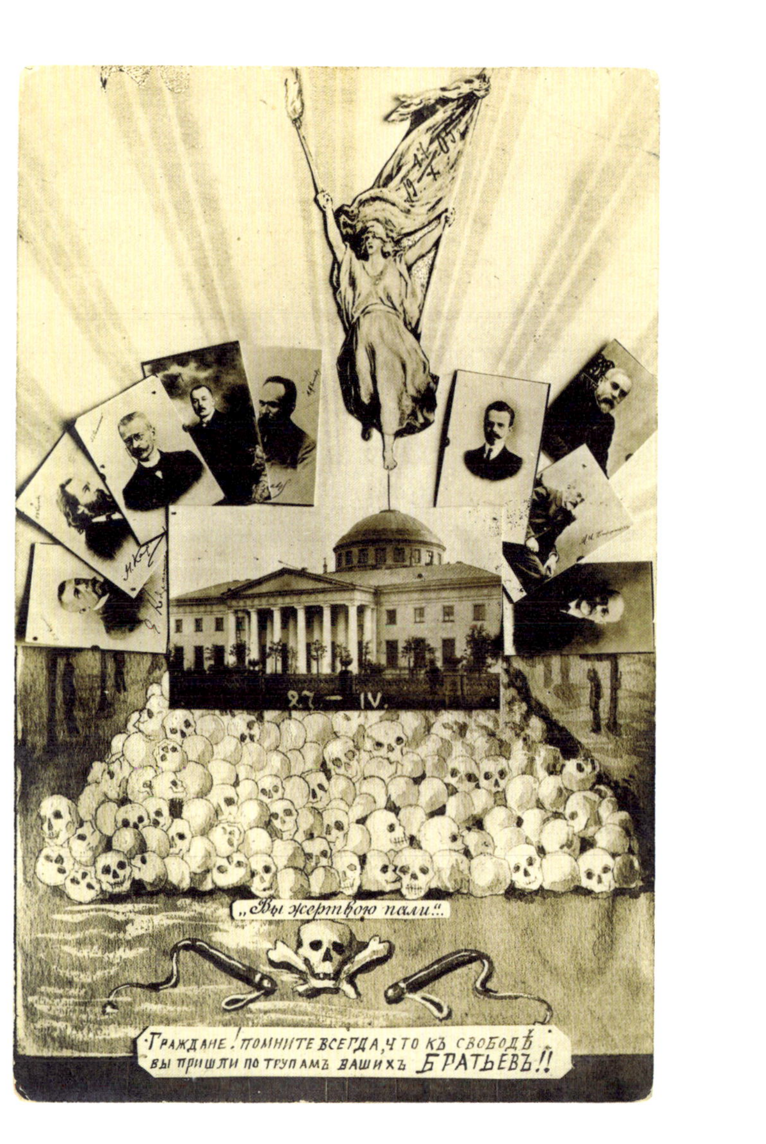

27 — IV.
„Вы жертвою пали!"
Граждане! помните всегда, что къ свободѣ вы пришли по трупамъ вашихъ БРАТЬЕВЪ!!

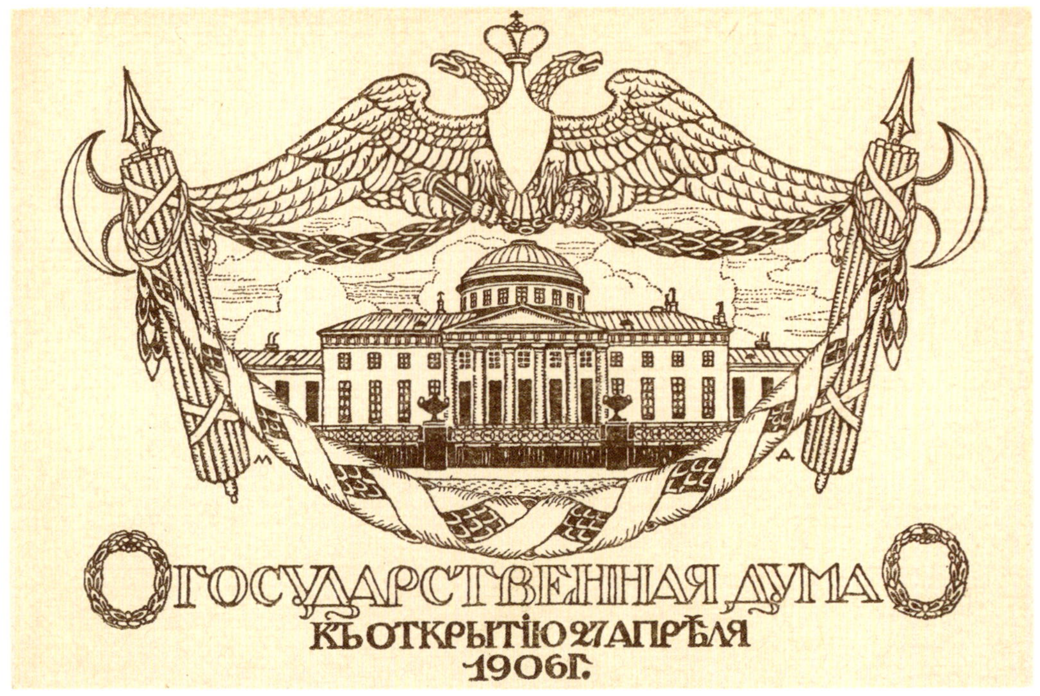

Mstislav Dobuzhinskii. *The State Duma. In Commemoration of the Inauguration: 27 April 1906.* Published by the Society of Saint Eugenia, Saint Petersburg, April 1906.

sayings, all of which play on the root word 'Duma,' meaning 'thought.' For example, one image of a ponderous child is captioned: 'Duma kuma, ne lishi nas uma.' ['Good Lady Duma/Thought, please don't befuddle, and leave our minds a muddle.'] The point that Bem is making in her postcards – and this is a lesson for all sides – is that the Duma should not be used as a talking shop, but as a place for doing business.[22]

There was, however, another way to think about the Duma, and that was as a dangerous waste of time. For the extreme left, the assembly represented neither a victory nor a loss, but a government trap. Both the main revolutionary parties officially boycotted the first sitting, seeing it only as a diversionary tactic designed to split the opposition. According to one Social Democratic cartoon, the Manifesto was a bait and switch – the Duma was a bone that the liberals (shown as slavering dogs) had accepted from the Tsar in exchange for his crown.[23]

There are few Duma-related postcards firmly attributable to the revolutionary parties, but a number closely reflect their political viewpoint, sharply criticising the willingness of reform-minded liberals to compromise with the government. The most prominent advocate of this position was Valerii Karrik. His postcards reject any possibility of working with the regime and decry all those who continue to believe in its sincerity as at best naïve and at worst stupid. One cartoon shows a wide-eyed mouse heading towards a baited trap. The caption reads: 'Am I foolish to have believed in

Opposite

Anonymous artist. *'You Fell a Victim…' Citizens! Never Forget that the Path to Freedom was Paved with the Corpses of Your Brothers!!* No publication details, April 1906.

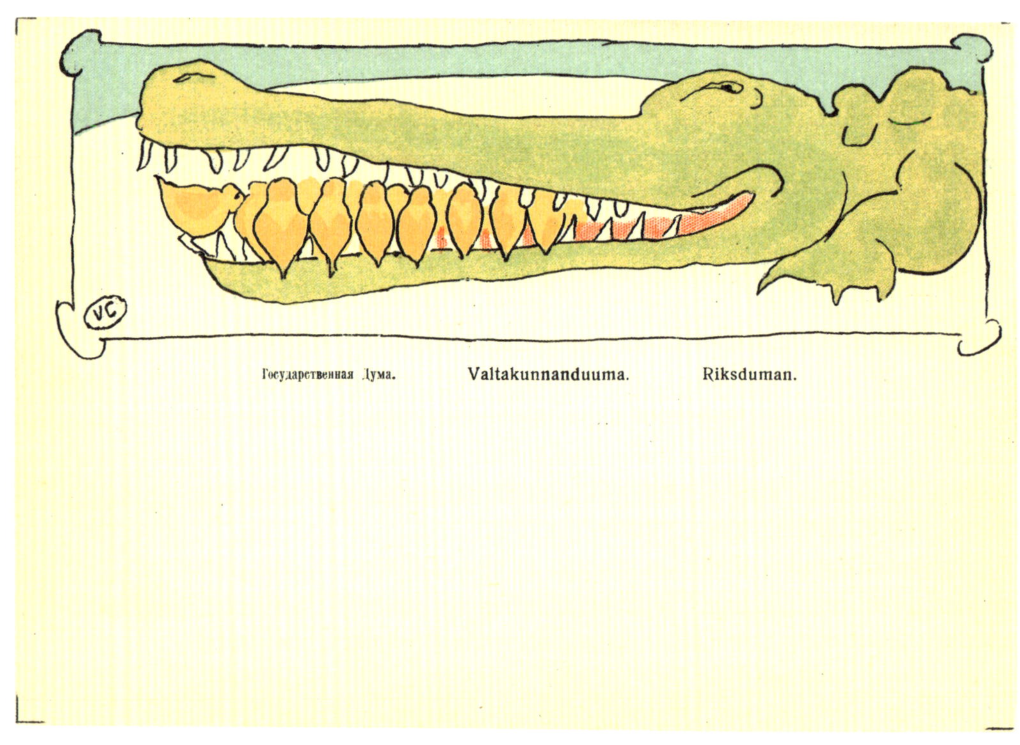
VC
Государственная Дума.
Valtakunnanduuma.
Riksduman.

the Manifesto?' In another, a crocodile advances on a group of rabbits, who squeak in terror, 'We're here by virtue of the decree.'

For Karrik, the Duma was a ploy to buy the regime time before it could wrest back full control. The first of a two-part cartoon on the assembly depicts the liberal opposition as small chicks rushing to find their places between the open jaws of a crocodile. Its partner image, *The State Duma*, shows the chicks chirping away unawares in the jaws of the smiling croc. The innocence of Karrik's images belies the seriousness of their message – the Duma will only end in failure, and anyone who trusts the government is liable to get badly hurt. Liberals, who are often characterised by Karrik as rabbits, are merely the playthings of far more powerful creatures, the willing dupes of a vicious regime.

Not all Duma postcards carried such a strong political line. This was one of the first modern political events to become lodged in the Russian collective consciousness, and as such it provided a rich source of inspiration for commercial publishers, who churned out a wide range of light-hearted cartoons. In humour there is also truth, and puns again served to express the uncertainty of the times. One series printed by Robert Bakhman plays on the word 'vybrat,' meaning to elect, choose, or pick-out.[24] The postcards, titled *Vybory* [*Choices/Elections*], show individuals carrying out various activities involving the need for selection, from a woman picking nits out of a child's hair, to a man chatting up a lady on the street.

Valerii Karrik.
The State Duma.
No publication details, circa mid-1906.

Bakhman's postcards look at the decisions people make and why. A man about to commit suicide does so because 'there is no other way out,' a vagrant rummages through rubbish bins 'out of necessity,' and so on. These are all entertaining images, but they underline the bewildering array of choices faced by the population in 1906. Having never before had to select their own political representatives, the public was now required to decide whom they thought might best serve their long-term interests. The choice to which all the postcards allude is notably absent, but by its very absence, it prompts the question on everybody's lips: 'Whom will you vote for and why?'

By 1906, the revolutionaries, like other political groups, were fair game for satire. They had become a permanent fixture on the political landscape, and for commercial manufacturers they were as much objects of amusement as opinionated mothers-in-law and inveterate drunkards. In a popular series by Evgenii Sokolov, the Social Democrats are cast as haranguing pamphleteers, the Socialist-Revolutionaries as gun-waving terrorists, and the monarchists as bloody butchers. When viewed together, these caricatures convey a sense of cynicism, or at the very least amused weariness, at the fierce ideological battles that had consumed Russia. In his even-handed treatment, Sokolov implies that all political extremes are bad, no matter their ideological orientation.

The significance with which the public endowed the Duma is reflected in the popularity of postcard portraits of its deputies. But alas, these high hopes

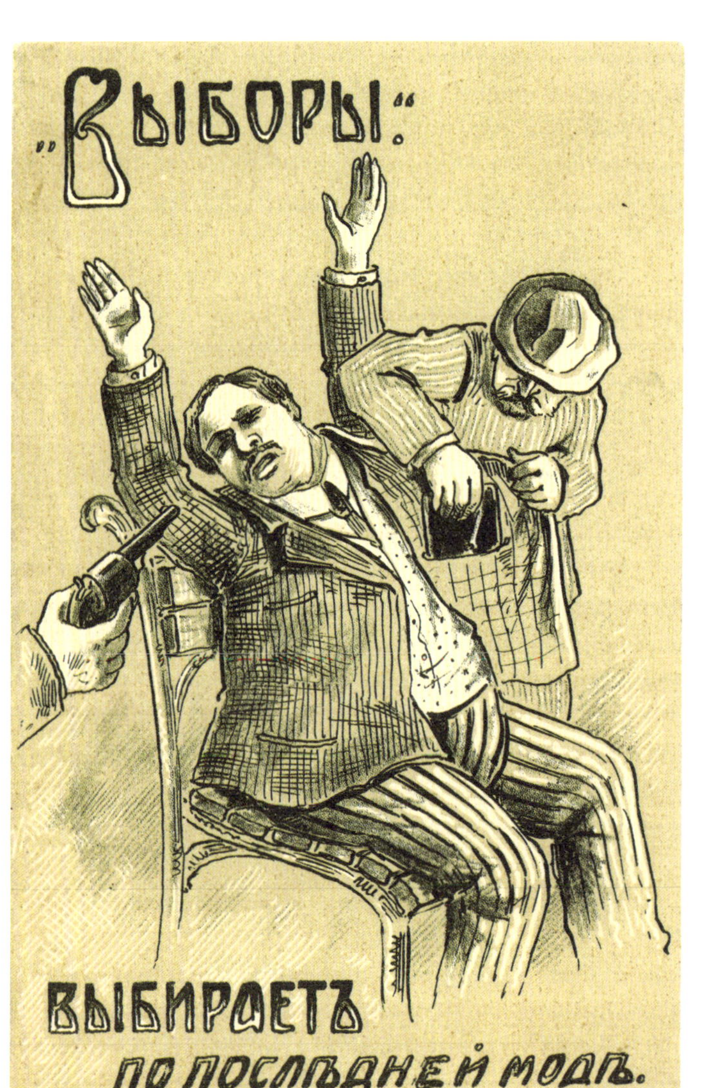
„Выборы“
Выбираетъ
по послѣдней модѣ.

were not fulfilled. Soon after the assembly commenced work, Duma-related subject matter quickly dropped off. This was partly a result of increased repression, but it was also a consequence of fractious debates that produced no viable solutions. The problem of how to achieve fairer allocation of land dominated the deliberations, but tellingly few images deal directly with the substance of the discussions. In short, the Duma disappointed, and when it was eventually prorogued, few publishers responded, realising that as a political failure the institution held little commercial appeal.

Anonymous artist. *Elections/Choices. Picking in Line with the Latest Fashion.* Printed by R. Bakhman, Saint Petersburg, 1906.

Following its dissolution, the revolutionaries attempted to push a militant line, but plans for an uprising proved woefully optimistic. Chemodanov was one of the few artists to reflect these bellicose hopes in print. *For Popular Freedom*, drawn in July 1906, shows a mounted bogatyr, symbolising the 'revolutionary people,' spearing a devil labelled the 'criminal government.' It is captioned: 'Boldly into battle, the hour of victory has come.' Karrik, for his part, simply expressed knowing resignation. A postcard of a raven staring mournfully into a pool of blood carries the caption: 'I told you so!.. I told you so!..' As he had feared all along, the dissolution of the First Duma marked the end of reform and the beginning of yet another round of repression.

⁂

In 1905, Russia's body politic was still inextricably and indistinguishably bound to the autocratic regime. Liberal cartoons can therefore essentially be seen as an attempt to reforge the country's national and political identity by dismantling the visual tropes of nationhood that had stood fast since the Napoleonic Wars. The army, once symbolised by the brave Cossack, is shown to be cowardly; the Orthodox Church, once the country's spiritual backbone, is shown to be immoral; and finally the Tsar himself, the father of the nation, is shown to be a despotic tyrant who cares nothing for his people. The stalwarts of Imperial visual culture were thus cut down to size, and in their place an alternative value system was advanced, one based on modern European notions of equality before the law, and respect for human rights.

The revolutionaries were also intent on breaking the Tsarist grip. But naturally, liberal values, particularly individual rights, find no place in their postcards, which instead concern themselves chiefly with the inevitability of popular rebellion. Despite their differences liberals and revolutionaries did, nonetheless, agree that the regime could not continue in its current state. What should be done was another problem altogether. The emphasis on social justice suggests that many would have been satisfied with an enlightened despot who allowed his subjects to live in nominal peace. The Tsar's refusal to listen led, however, to his displacement as the moral guardian of the land, and in view of the lack of alternatives, to increasing calls for his violent overthrow.

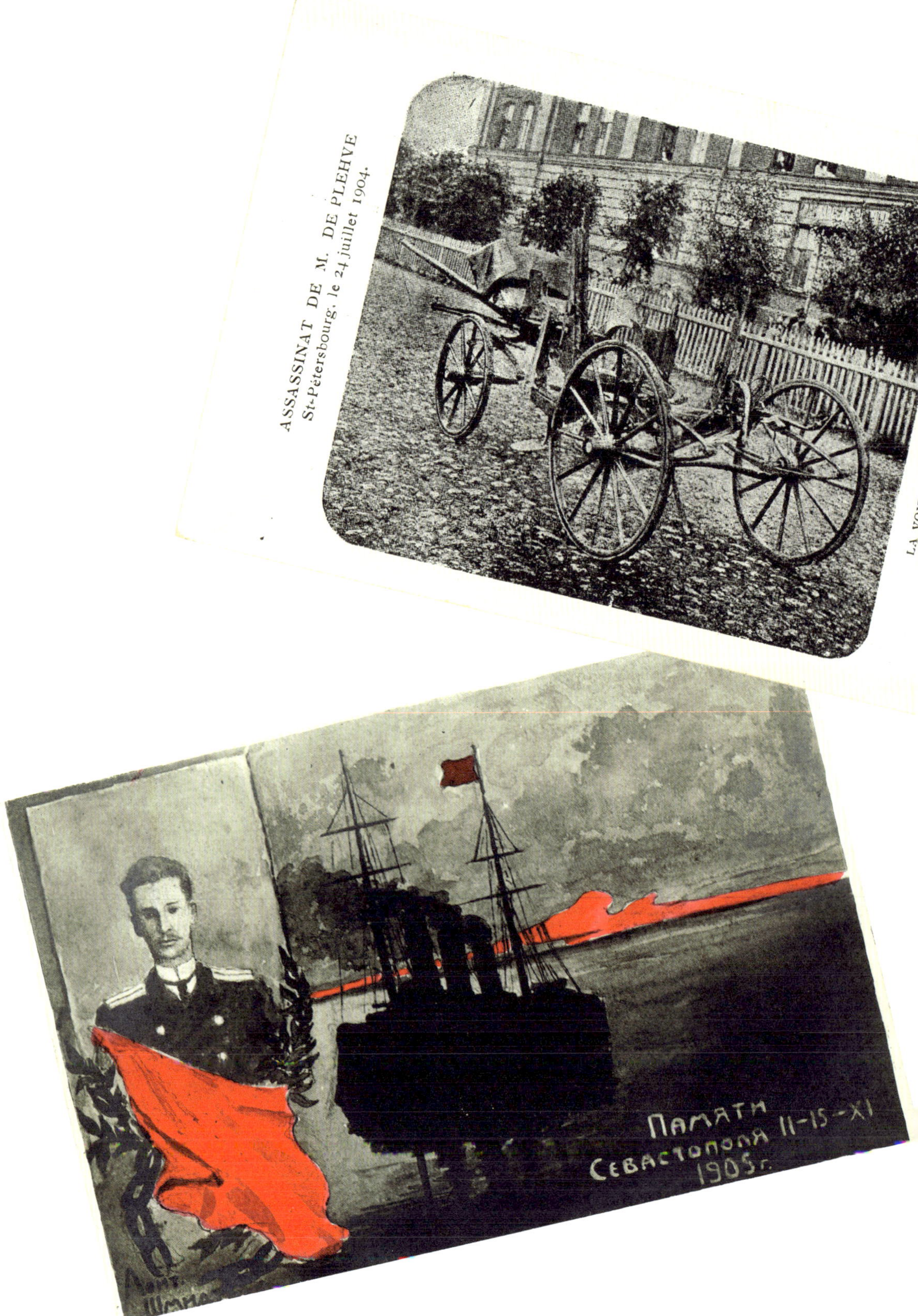
ASSASSINAT DE M. DE PLEHVE
St-Pétersbourg, le 24 juillet 1904.
ПАМЯТИ 11-15-XI
СЕВАСТОПОЛЯ
1905г.

POPULAR HEROES

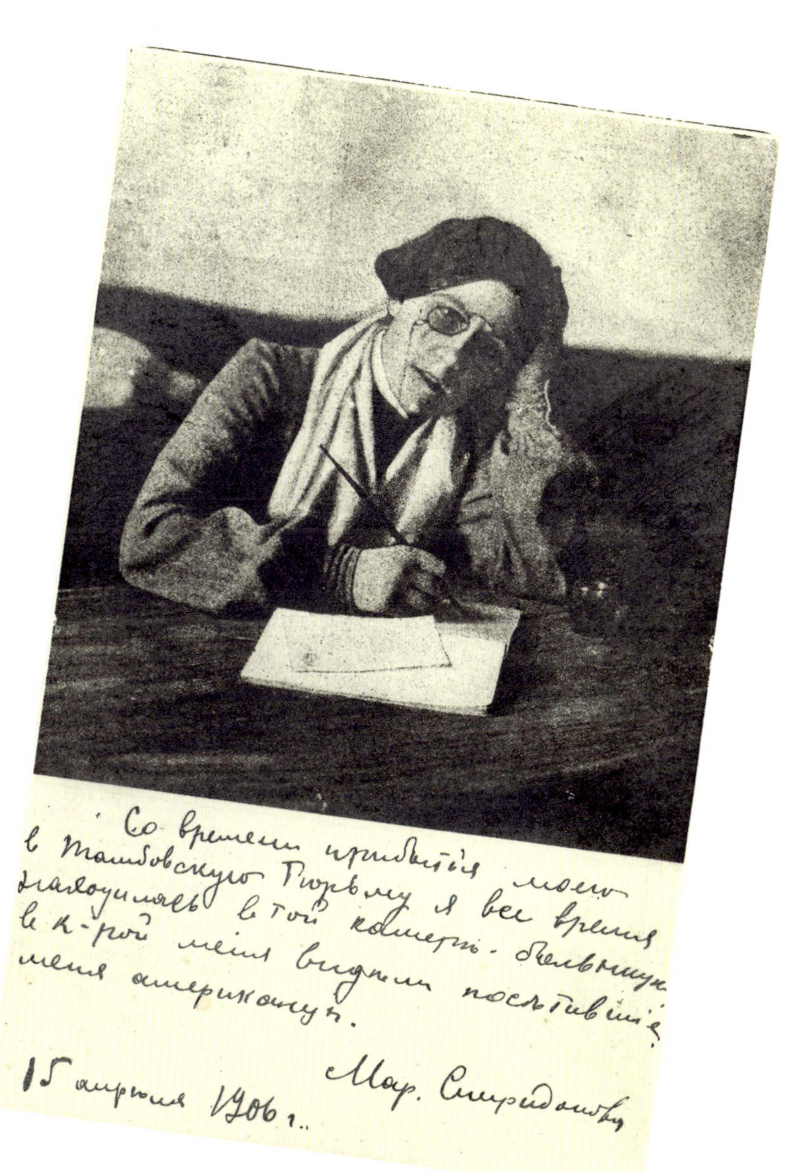

REVOLUTIONARIES AND TERRORISTS

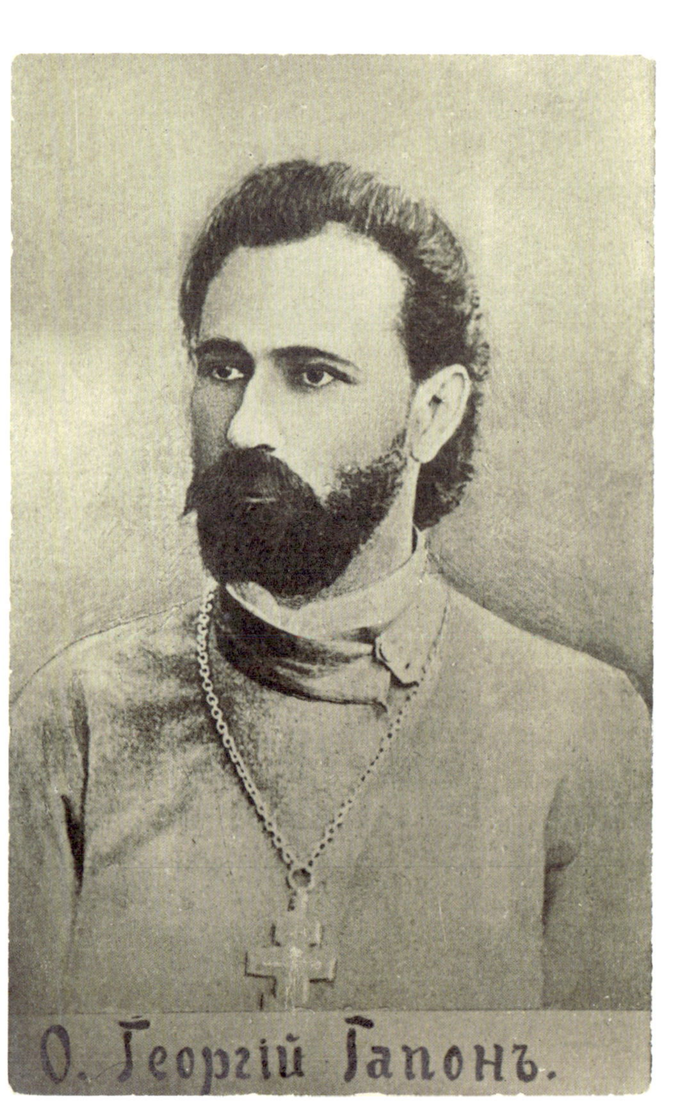

О. Георгій Гапонъ.

New Heroes

In November 1905, an anonymous piece titled 'On Heroes' was printed in the satirical journal *Pulemet* [*The Machine Gun*]. It reads in part:

> Up to this point we have had no political heroes about whom it was possible to talk aloud … for a long time we have only had heroes that have been approved by the censor. Now the censor has fallen. Heroes will appear without permission. Heroes will be chosen by the people, not imposed from above or created by dint of their years of service. Hero-slaves, hero-scoundrels, hero-slugs and hero-parasites will all disappear. Look how many were created in the last war alone. Free, popular heroes will appear and are already appearing.[1]

As the author implies, national heroes are rarely made during the natural course of events, but instead arise to fulfil a certain requirement or function of the state. In 1905, the autocratic government needed political role models more than ever, but as power slipped from its grasp so too did its ability to create and maintain a positive image of its own political heroes, including of Nicolas II. The opposition stepped into the breach, and amid a clatter of anti-government cartoons, portraits, and images of the unrest, Tsarist voices were temporarily muffled. In their place a new narrative arose, dominated by individuals who consciously defined themselves, both politically and morally, in opposition to the Imperial throne.

Until the October Manifesto, pictures of opposition figures were strictly forbidden, but soon after its promulgation they started appearing legally in mainstream newspapers and satirical journals.[2] The mass distribution of these portraits, however, was largely achieved through postcards. From autumn 1905 onwards, both revolutionary and commercial publishers printed a wide range of photomechanical portraits depicting well-known adherents of the liberation movement. Writers, journalists, philosophers, and theorists were among them, but the most popular portrayed terrorists; that is to say, radicals who employed violence to achieve their political aims. Most were either members, or close adherents of the Socialist-Revolutionary Party.

The promotion of terrorism achieved two key party objectives: it enabled the Socialist-Revolutionaries to show that they were playing an effective role in countering Tsarist repression, and at the same time it offered a convenient mask for their lack of political unity. Revolutionary assassinations were therefore used to project a coherent image of the organisation as a party of action, the political embodiment of its slogan 'in battle you acquire your rights.' Terrorist portraits were among the very first postcards printed by

Previous spread from left to right

Anonymous artist. *Lieutenant Schmidt. In Memory of Sebastopol 11–15–XI 1905*. No publication details, 1906.

Karl Bulla. *The Assassination of M. de Plehve. Saint Petersburg 24 July 1904. The Carriage after the Explosion.* No publication details, France, 1904.

Attributed to Nahum Luboshitz (photographer). Untitled postcard depicting Maria Spiridonova at her desk in Tambov Prison. No publication details, 1906.

Opposite

Anonymous photographer. *Father Georgii Gapon.* No publication details, early 1905.

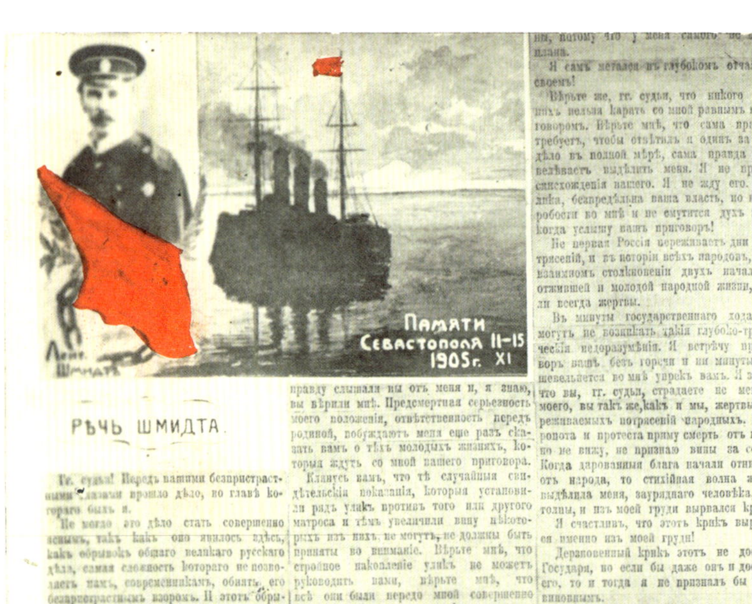

Anonymous designer. *Lieutenant Schmidt. In Memory of Sebastopol 15 November 1905. Schmidt's Speech.* No publication details, circa March 1906.

the Party, and throughout the 1905 Revolution they played a significant part in furthering this message, the shockwaves of each attack reverberating endlessly through images of their perpetrators.

The Party's belief in terrorism continued a Populist legacy, central to which was the idea that free will had a role to play in the historical process. A very different approach was taken by the Social Democrats, who were united by doctrine and driven by the ideological imperative of industrial development. Little is known of their early postcard production besides a few images of Marx, but with the creation of Utro and then Vpered, portraiture became an established part of Social Democratic propaganda output.[3] These publishers largely avoided images of activists, instead focusing on foreign theorists, whose portraits were intended to promote the Party's determinist belief in the eventual victory of the proletariat.[4]

Following the Manifesto, there was a huge increase in the range of anti-government postcard publishers and the diversity of their wares. Portraits of political activists, which were legalised by the Press Administration in early 1906, became an extremely popular subject matter for commercial publishers, who produced countless images of opposition figures from a wide variety of political groupings. The general population purchased these cards in vast numbers; the demand for anti-government portraits was such that in late 1905 the popular weekly *Vokrug sveta* [*Around the World*] offered a free album as a sweetner for new subscribers depicting 'activists of the Russian liberation movement.'[5]

Alongside contemporary activists, publishers also printed postcards of opposition figures from Russia's more distant past. Many featured Populists from the 1870s and 1880s, in particular the assassins of Alexander II. The revolutionary timeline, however, was regularly pushed back as far as the Decembrists. The heroes of the 1825 revolt usually appeared in group portraits – photomontage compositions containing depictions of the most prominent activists and revolutionaries. These tightly ordered displays served to impose a uniform narrative on the liberation movement, characterising its contemporary incarnation as heirs to a grand tradition, and thus conferring historical legitimacy on the actions of their modern-day counterparts.

Few private firms paid much attention to the political allegiances of the individuals they were commemorating. One of the largest portrait series, published anonymously circa late 1905, includes images of Social Democrats and Socialist-Revolutionaries, perhaps to provide a balanced overview of the movement, but more plausibly to attract the widest possible audience.[6] Similarly, while both the main revolutionary parties used portraiture to exert political ownership over events, they shared with private publishers a keen understanding that some personalities sold better than others.[7] The market may have been broad, but it was dominated by two particular activists, whose commercial draw transcended the ideological divide.

The idolisation of Maria Spiridonova and Petr Schmidt was partly a result of timing. Their nearest rivals in terms of postcard numbers were Stepan Balmashev and Ivan Kaliaev, who carried out their acts of terror in 1902 and 1905 respectively – before the legalisation of anti-government portraiture and at a time when revolutionary sentiment was only just beginning to achieve mass support. By contrast, Spiridonova shot to death Police Inspector Gavril Luzhenovskii in January 1906, and was put on trial and sentenced in March, the same month that Schmidt was executed for his part in the Black Sea Mutiny. By this stage, both the opposition movement and revolutionary propaganda production were in full swing.

But there was also something about the activists themselves. Schmidt's revolt offered a tale of opposition and sacrifice that went beyond party allegiances. Furthermore, he was one of the few revolutionaries to come from the armed services, and crucially, had no firm links to either of the main political parties. As a female murderess and a Socialist-Revolutionary, Spiridonova was a more complicated, and beguiling, character – young, pretty, unmarried, and from a noble, ethnically Russian background.[8] Her harsh treatment and alleged rape, which was heavily publicised in the liberal press, made her an object of great sympathy – a victim of tyranny, as opposed to a violent killer.[9]

Portraits of Schmidt and Spiridonova proved hugely appealing to publishers and population alike – they gave commercial enterprises the

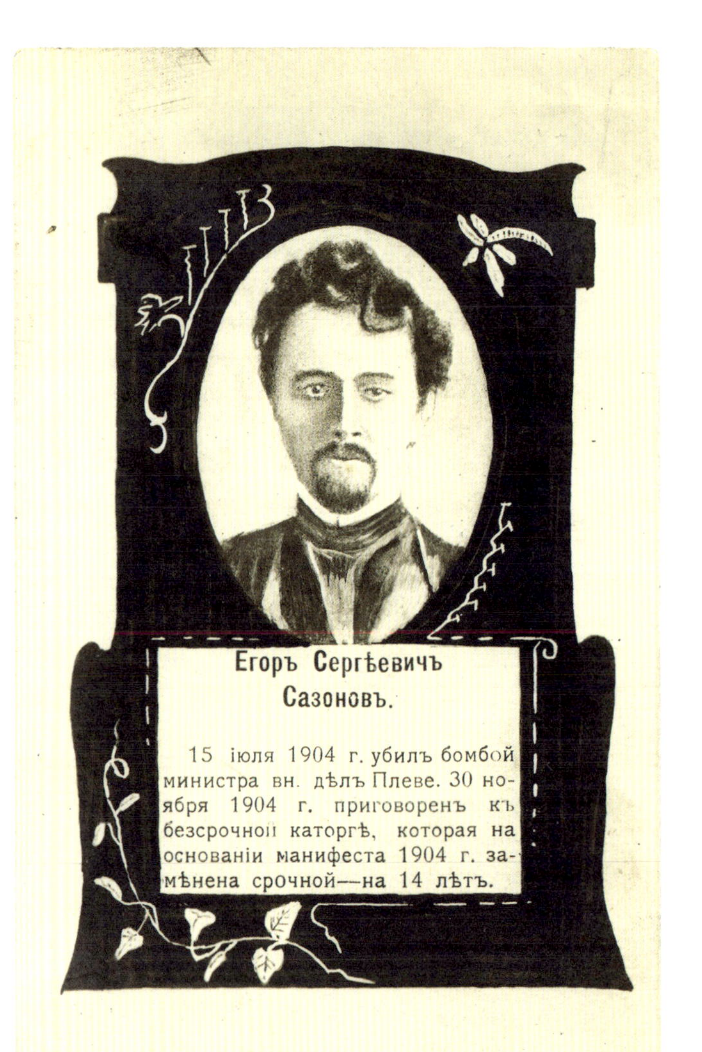
Егоръ Сергѣевичъ
Сазоновъ.
15 іюля 1904 г. убилъ бомбой министра вн. дѣлъ Плеве. 30 ноября 1904 г. приговоренъ къ безсрочной каторгѣ, которая на основаніи манифеста 1904 г. замѣнена срочной—на 14 лѣтъ.

possibility of flirting with revolution, and the revolutionaries a popular hero whom they could co-opt for their own ideological and financial ends. Even those who did not support all the ideals of the liberation movement could see in Schmidt and Spiridonova virtuous characters made to suffer by the regime. The sheer quantity of postcards that were printed – well over thirty different photographic portraits and compositions – testifies to the way in which opposition politics became a mainstream concern in 1906, the allure of revolutionary action pulling in both hardened believers and fashion-conscious sympathisers.[10]

Anonymous photographer. *Egor Sergeevich Sazonov.* No publication details, circa 1906.

Appearances: Power and Modesty

The first postcards of revolutionary activists, which date from the early 1900s, closely replicate the format of late nineteenth-century cartes de visite. Decoration was kept to a minimum and little information was included on the image beyond the name of the individual. The plainness of these portraits originally came down to practicalities. In many cases, studio photographs were the only type of image available, and these required little effort and expense to reproduce in postcard form using a photographic enlarger. The simplicity of their design, however, also corresponded to revolutionary notions of asceticism, and they would come to set the standard for the depiction of opposition activists until the 1917 Revolution and beyond.

In 1906, as opposition postcard production expanded, more elaborate portraits started appearing – depictions of Schmidt, for example, can often be found with inset illustrations of the Black Sea Fleet Mutiny. Nonetheless, the majority of postcard portrayals remained comparatively simple, often communicating little more than their subject's physical appearance and, occasionally, a little background information on their revolutionary deeds. One portrait of Sazonov, for example, simply informs the viewer: 'Killed Minister of Interior Affairs Plehve with a bomb on 15 July 1904. 30 November 1904 sentenced to life in penal servitude, later amended to fourteen years on the basis of the 1904 Manifesto.'

This concentrated focus on the perpetrator is significant. Illustrated periodicals in Western Europe were filled with dramatic renderings of the revolutionary attacks in Russia, and these images were regularly reproduced there in postcard form. For instance, alongside a multitude of cartoons illustrating the explosive demise of Grand Duke Sergei, French firms also published photographic postcards showing the remains of Viacheslav von Plehve's bomb-devastated carriage.[11] But while foreign publishers and artists avidly exploited the visual possibilities offered by revolutionary assassinations, narrative illustrations and cartoons depicting terrorist outrages were not widely reproduced on Russian postcards, either legally or illegally.

Police photographer. *I. P. Kaliaev. Last Letter to His Mother, Written Half an Hour Before He Died.* No publication details, circa 1906.

Russian images dealing with the subject of political violence tend toward implicit, as opposed to explicit celebrations of terrorism. The force of the attack and its significance to the movement are represented not through the event itself but through depictions of the individual responsible. If Western European illustrators were primarily concerned with the effect of violence, then Russian postcard publishers were concerned with its cause. Their aim was to personify terrorism, making the viewer identify first and foremost with the attacker, who through their single-minded devotion and great personal sacrifice could provide a point of inspiration and ideological orientation for the masses.

One of the most compelling of all revolutionary portraits reproduces the police mug shot of Kaliaev, taken shortly after his arrest. In this image he glowers at the camera, his determined gaze unsettling. It is a look suggestive of death and profound experience, the stare of a man who has just killed another and narrowly avoided inflicting the same fate upon himself. Beneath his steely glare, Kaliaev's garments are heavily disordered; shrapnel has carved open the front panels of his thick winter coat, the white stuffing of its inner recesses barely covering three gaping holes. It is an extraordinarily powerful, awe-inspiring image that, like a portrait of an all-powerful monarch, seems to demand the viewer's respect.

Revolutionary portraits may have followed a very different ideology from their royal counterparts, but both were fundamentally concerned with establishing the right to rule. These were not accurate depictions of individuals, but symbolic vessels used to convey an idea of the movement and its values. Kaliaev is depicted here in his own particular clothes of state. Instead of orb and sceptre, the symbols of monarchical authority, he wears ripped rags, burnt from the blast and sprinkled with slivers of debris. If their disarray bears testament to his power, then their simplicity reflects its source. The very ordinariness of his dress heralds a new type of leader, one whose prerogative comes not from God, but from the people.

Simplicity of dress is common to all revolutionary portraits. Photographic postcards of the revolutionary heroine Sofia Perovskaia, for example, show her in three-quarter profile, wearing a plain black smock, adorned only with a square white collar. Her youth is immediately apparent, and in keeping with her craft she wears an intently serious, almost doleful expression. Despite her noble origins, there is nothing in her appearance to suggest status or wealth. This is not an unapproachable monarch bedecked in splendour and draped in the robes of office, but a dignified woman who has placed herself at the service of the nation. In her very normality, she becomes a figure of admiration to whom the public can relate.

The seriousness of the revolutionaries' demeanour and the restraint of their attire, unencumbered as it was by the accoutrements of worldly power,

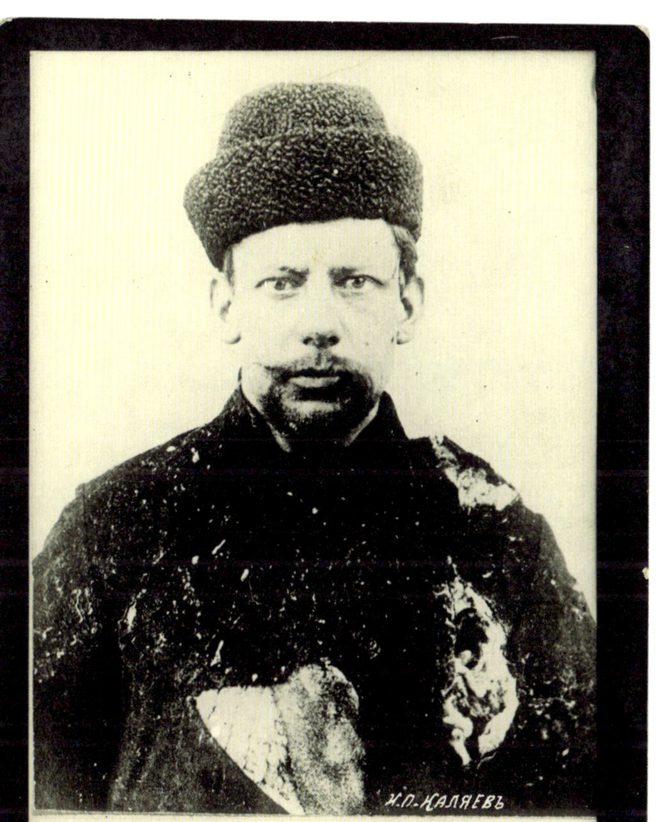

ПОСЛѢДНЕЕ ПИСМО КЪ МАТЕРИ ЗА 1/2 ЧАСА ДО СМЕРТИ

Дорогая, незабвенная моя мать!

Итакъ, я умираю. Я счастливъ за себя, что съ полнымъ самообладаніемъ могу отнестись къ моему концу. Пусть же ваше горе, дорогіе мои,—вы всѣ, мать, братья и сестры,—потонетъ въ лучахъ того сіянія, которымъ свѣтитъ торжество моего духа.

Прощайте. Привѣтъ всѣмъ, кто меня зналъ и помнитъ.

Завѣщаю вамъ: храните въ чистотѣ имя нашего отца.

Не горюйте, не плачьте. Еще разъ прощайте. Я всегда съ вами.

Вашъ И. Каляевъ.

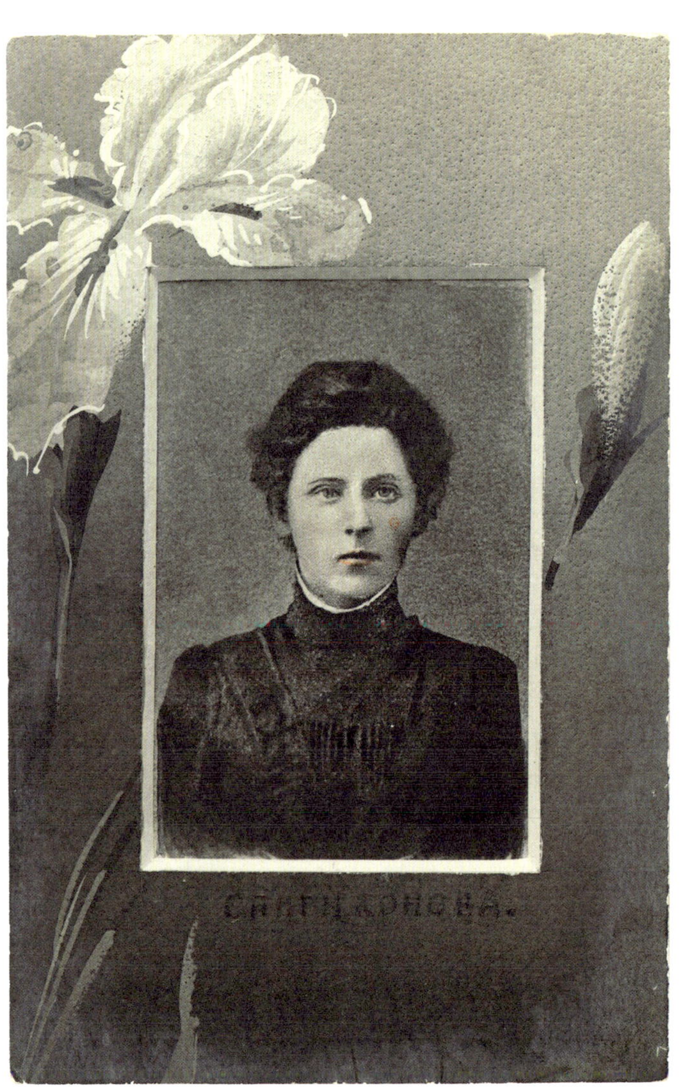
СПИРИДОНОВА.

served to present the revolutionary opposition as uncorrupted beings, untainted by the material wealth and venality of autocratic rule. This not only implied that their souls were pure, it suggested that their motives were as well. The effect of their unpretentious appearance was therefore to establish a clear contrast between the authority of the revolutionaries and that of the Tsar, both in its origin and in the manner in which it was wielded. Anti-government portraiture was thus intended both to project the power of the revolutionaries and to assert their moral supremacy.

Anonymous designer. *Spiridonova.* No publication details, circa March 1906. Lilies, which surround Spiridonova, traditionally symbolise the purity and virginity of the Virgin Mary. Note also, her rouged cheek and lips.

Beyond its political implications, lack of ostentation also ensured that the face of the sitter became the main focal point of the image, thereby underscoring their humanity and allowing for a more intimate relationship to develop with the viewer. In her memoirs, the Populist Vera Figner offers an indication of the emotive power and sense of familiarity that such imagery evoked. 'This is the only portrait that moves me every time I see it,' she wrote about a picture of Perovskaia. 'This portrait fully conveys her youthful features, in which there was something childlike, and also shows a barely noticeable crinkle around her mouth, which to me seems like an expression of determination and stubbornness, and perhaps also childish caprice.'[12]

Female activists were a notable component of the revolutionary movement, and the youthfulness and aura of innocence that Figner highlights in this extract was a particular feature of their portraits. Spiridonova was presented to the public in a similar manner, as a pure, virginal figure – the polar opposite of the state functionaries who allegedly desecrated her. Most postcards reproduce the same photograph, which shows a beautiful woman, aged around twenty, dressed in a demure black dress. Posed in three-quarter profile, Spiridonova stares intently into the distance, her hair tied back, with only a few loose strands hinting at the unruly ardour that may lie beneath. It is an image of enormous serenity that wholly belies the reality of her actions.

Portraits of female terrorists demonstrated the progressive attitude of the revolutionary parties, who provided an equal opportunity for both sexes to sacrifice themselves for the cause. But their appeal, while fundamentally ideological, went beyond the merely political. For male, and no doubt also female consumers, there was a strong element of physical attraction in the allure of terrorist heroes. These paradigms of revolutionary virtue were the pin-ups of their age, and as such they became objects of sexual as well as ideological consumption. One sixteen-year-old schoolboy in Kiev, for instance, became so obsessed with Spiridonova that on hearing of her death sentence drowned himself, unable to bear the thought of their eternal 'separation.'[13]

The aesthetic of revolutionary portraiture was entirely geared towards establishing political identity; precious little is conveyed about the true nature of the sitter and even less about their actions. But in many ways this is the whole point. Too much personal information muddies the ideological waters. These were representative symbols; their modesty, purity and beauty everything that Tsarist power was not. The myriad of pathological impulses that pushed a particular individual into committing an act of terrorism have been entirely subjugated. Guilt, social isolation, or instability of mind, all of which were known, are nowhere to be seen. Instead, there is only a virtuous character onto whom to project ideals, allegiances, and personal desires.

Anonymous artist. *No More Parasites. The Most Reliable Way to Get Rid of Harmful Insects. Request It Everywhere. Watch out for Fakes.* No publication details, circa late 1905.

Justifying Terrorism: The Ethics of Violence

Terrorists were the celebrities of their day, and portrait postcards of the revolutionary greats were avidly bought and collected by a dedicated fan base. Their extraordinary prevalence in today's marketplace is proof that large numbers of the population, deprived of legal forms of redress against ongoing Tsarist oppression, came to see violence as the only way forward. Support for the terrorists was extraordinarily widespread, sustained by romanticised accounts, the thrill of seeing the regime attacked, and opposition politicians who refused to condemn their actions. Yet murder was still murder, and so the question arises: how did the revolutionaries succeed in convincing their supporters to accept the validity of political violence?

Despite the best efforts of Party ideologues to present terrorism as a controlled enterprise underpinned by political theory, this rarely translated either into individual actions on the ground or into related propaganda. Spiridonova's own account of Luzhenovskii's murder, which was widely reproduced in postcard form alongside her portrait, shows a typical disparity between the Party's theoretical stance and the deeds of its members. Luzhenovskii, she claims, was killed for his 'criminal interference and excessive torment of the peasantry during the agrarian and political disorder, and … for the organisation of Black Hundreds in Tambov, and in response to the imposition of martial law and a state of enhanced and extraordinary security.'[14]

In other words, the killing was not so much a political stimulant, as a way of getting even. Similarly, Vladimir Vladimirov, an investigative reporter who interviewed Spiridonova, wrote: 'This woman did not want to, and could not live, if life was going to be nothing more than a festival of tyranny … she'd seen men who'd been driven mad by the brutality, and an old mother who had gone out of her mind after her fifteen-year-old daughter was left in a clearing after being assaulted by Cossacks. These victims commanded her to carry out this act of revenge.'[15] Vladimirov's characterisation of the killing as an act of retribution became the dominant public narrative, not only in regards to this event, but to revolutionary violence in general.

Like their Populist predecessors, the Socialist-Revolutionaries viewed socialism in moral terms, not as the inevitable outcome of capitalism, but

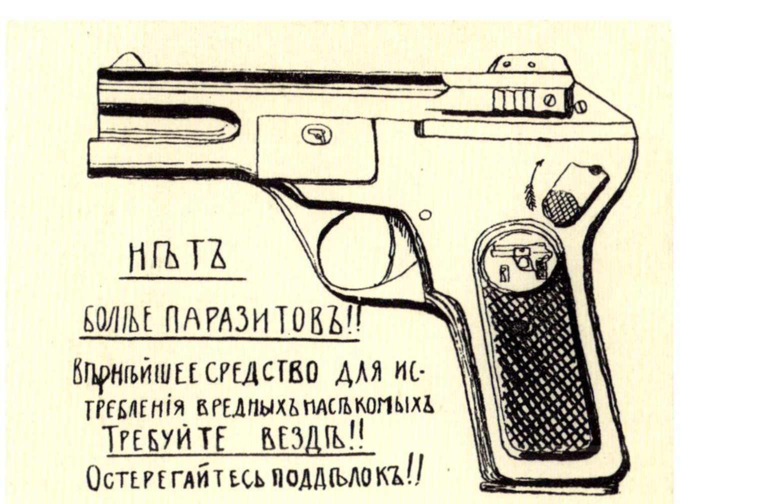
НѢТЪ
БОЛѢЕ ПАРАЗИТОВЪ!!
ВѢРНѢЙШЕЕ СРЕДСТВО ДЛЯ ИС-
ТРЕБЛЕНІЯ ВРЕДНЫХЪ НАСѢКОМЫХЪ
ТРЕБУЙТЕ ВЕЗДѢ!!
ОСТЕРЕГАЙТЕСЬ ПОДДѢЛОКЪ!!

as an ethical choice, and here Spiridonova's actions are shown to have been motivated primarily by her own highly-attuned sense of social morality. Irrespective of the theoretical complications to which this gave rise, if a terrorist act could be presented in public as both a human and humane response to a despotic regime, it allowed the assassin and their deeds to be seen as rational, and moreover confirmed the revolutionaries in their self-appointed role as popular representatives. These were not cold-hearted murderers, but avenging angels compelled into taking a stance against Tsarist brutality.

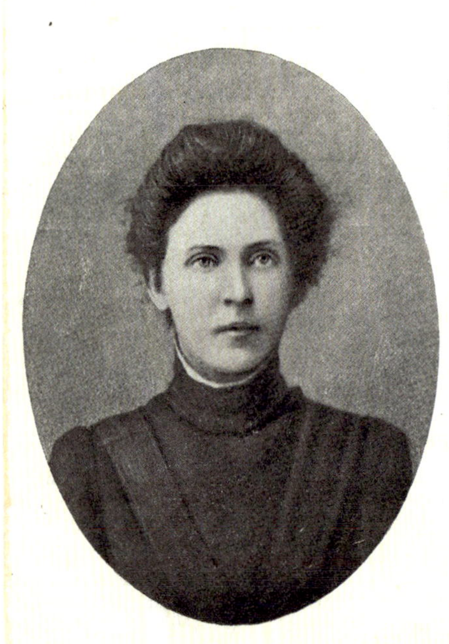

Выдержки изъ письма Спиридоновой.

. . . . Я вошла въ вагонъ и на разстояніи 12—13 шаговъ, съ площадки вагона, сдѣлала выстрѣлъ въ Луженовскаго. . . . .

. . . . . Руками я закрывала лицо; прикладами руки снимались съ него. Потомъ казачій офицеръ, высоко поднявъ меня за закрученную на руку косу, сильнымъ взмахомъ бросилъ на платформу . . . . Потомъ за ногу потащили внизъ по лѣстницѣ. Голова билась о ступеньки, за косу внесена на извозчика. . . . .

. . . . Ударомъ ноги Ждановъ перебрасывалъ меня въ уголъ камеры, гдѣ ждалъ меня казачій офицеръ, наступалъ мнѣ на спину и опять перебрасывалъ Жданову, который становился на шею. . . Раздѣтую, страшно ругаясь, они били нагайками (Ждановъ) и говорили: „Ну, барышня (ругань), скажи зажигательную рѣчь!“ Одинъ глазъ ничего не видѣлъ и правая часть лица была страшно разбита. Они нажимали на нее и лукаво спрашивали: „Больно, дорогая? Ну, скажи, кто твои товарищи?“ . . . . выдергивали по одному волосу изъ головы и спрашивали, гдѣ другіе революціонеры. Тушили горящую папиросу о тѣло и говорили: „кричи же, сволочь!“

Показанія слѣдующія: 1) Да, хотѣла убить Луженовскаго по предварительному соглашенію и т. д. 2) По постановленію тамбовскаго комитета партіи соціалистовъ-революціонеровъ за преступное засѣканіе и безмѣрное истязаніе крестьянъ во время аграрныхъ и политическихъ безпорядковъ и послѣ нихъ въ тѣхъ уѣздахъ гдѣ былъ Луженовскій, за разбойничьи похожденія Луженовскаго въ Борисоглѣбскѣ въ качествѣ начальника охраны, за организацію черной сотни въ Тамбовѣ и какъ отвѣтъ на введеніе военнаго положенія и чрезвычайной и усиленной охраны въ Тамбовѣ и другихъ уѣздахъ. Тамбовскимъ комитетомъ партіи соціалистовъ-революціонеровъ былъ вынесенъ приговоръ Луженовскому; въ полномъ согласіи съ этимъ приговоромъ и въ полномъ сознаніи своего поступка, я взялась за исполненіе этого приговора.

Слѣдствіе кончено, до сихъ поръ сильно больна, часто брежу. Если убьютъ, умру спокойно и съ хорошимъ чувствомъ въ душѣ.

Спиридонова.

Anymous photographer. *Excerpts from Spiridonova's Letter*. No publication details, circa March 1906.

Opposite

Anonymous artist. *M. A. Spiridonova*. No publication details, circa March 1906. Spiridonova is shown here being haunted by the memory of her Cossack gaolers.

The conviction that Spiridonova was carrying out just redress against a despicable regime was powerfully reinforced by reports of her alleged abuse at the hands of her gaolers. The liberal newspaper *Rus*, where Spiridonova's account was first published, printed several letters from female readers expressing indignation at what had taken place. 'On reading about the suffering that Spiridonova experienced my heart drained … she is such a young girl, almost a child,' reads one.[16] Another wrote: 'I read Spiridonova's most shocking letter and the horror of it all torments me like a nightmare … what was done to her, is a crime completely in and of itself so beastly and so shocking that her act pales into insignificance beside it.'[17]

Few directly condoned Spiridonova's actions. The latter writer made sure to highlight the fact that her crime was 'clearly and firmly proscribed by law.' The underlying implication of the letter, however, was that terror was

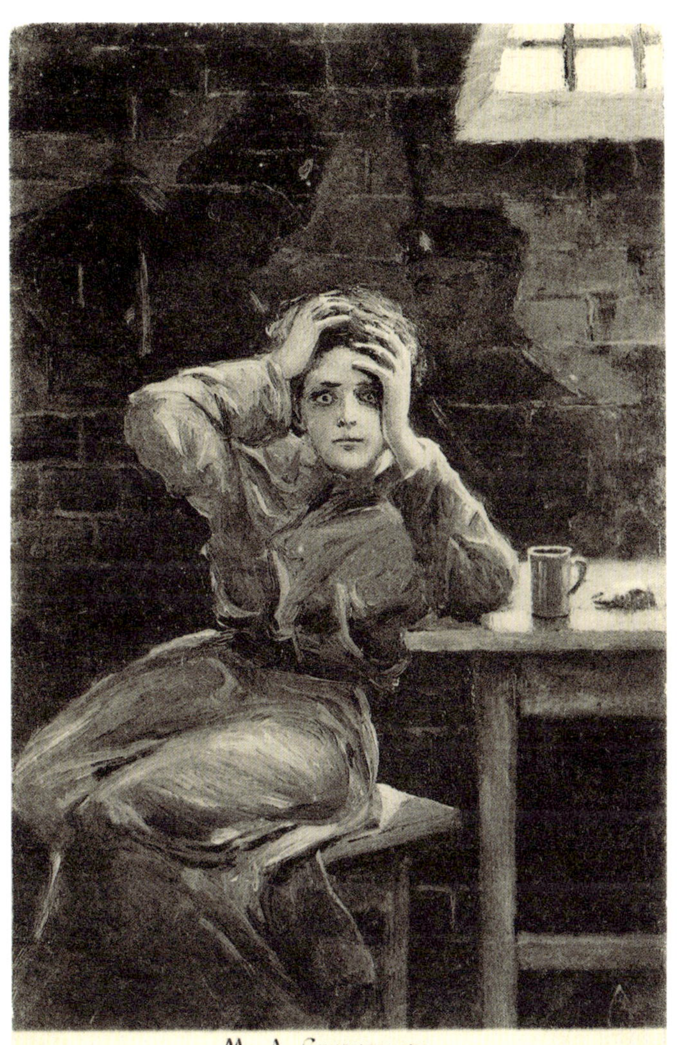

М. А. Спиридонова.

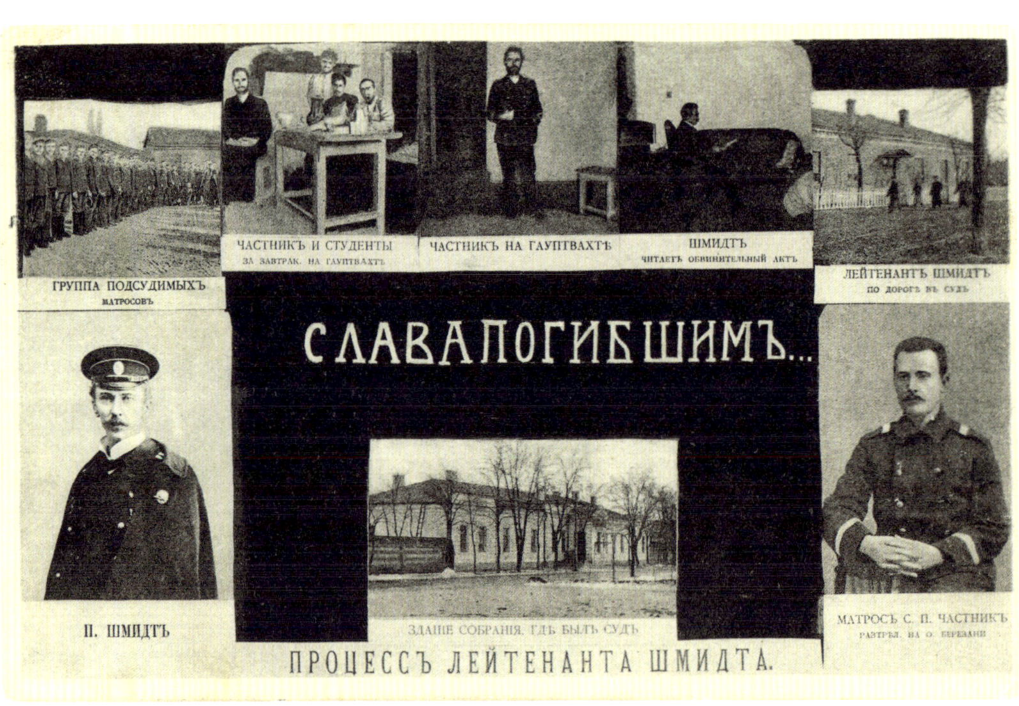

ГРУППА ПОДСУДИМЫХЪ
МАТРОСОВЪ
ЧАСТНИКЪ И СТУДЕНТЫ
ЗА ЗАВТРАК. НА ГАУПТВАХТѢ
ЧАСТНИКЪ НА ГАУПТВАХТѢ
ШМИДТЪ
ЧИТАЕТЪ ОБВИНИТЕЛЬНЫЙ АКТЪ
ЛЕЙТЕНАНТЪ ШМИДТЪ
ПО ДОРОГѢ ВЪ СУДЪ
СЛАВА ПОГИБШИМЪ...
П. ШМИДТЪ
ЗДАНIЕ СОБРАНIЯ, ГДѢ БЫЛЪ СУДЪ
МАТРОСЪ С. П. ЧАСТНИКЪ
РАЗТРѢЛ. НА О. БЕРЕЗАНИ
ПРОЦЕССЪ ЛЕЙТЕНАНТА ШМИДТА.

not only justifiable but also socially necessary.[18] In the eyes of many readers, Imperial tyranny constituted a far greater existential threat to society than revolutionary violence. 'Mothers,' the letter continues, 'think about it and understand that whatever your social position at the current time, you never know what might happen to your children.'[19] In such ways was terrorism equivocated: even if someone did not agree with Spiridonova's deed, they could still deem it morally acceptable, because it served the greater good.

Understanding of Spiridonova's actions was thus inextricably linked to a public image of her as an immaculate presence despoiled by a villainous government. When seen through the prism of her post-arrest trauma, it became far easier to view her crime as an admissible retort to despotism. But as well as providing a frame of reference through which to comprehend her actions, the legend that arose around Spiridonova also served to transfer political responsibility for the killing onto the regime. As Vladimirov suggests in his book, the real culprit here was the state, whose savagery had corrupted a young innocent into murder, and when the case came to court it was not Spiridonova who was seen to be on trial, but the regime.

Anonymous designer. *Glory to the Dead... The Trial of Lieutenant Schmidt*. Published by Vpered, Saint Petersburg, circa March 1906.

Spiridonova was not alone in being presented to the public as a beacon of humanity. It was widely reported, for example, that Kaliaev had called off a previous attempt to kill Sergei, so as to avoid harming the Grand Duke's wife and children. This action was described in one Socialist-Revolutionary pamphlet as, 'illustrating better than could ever be expressed on paper the poignant emotional sensitivity and innate nobility of soul of an individual subsequently condemned as a killer.'[20] Kaliaev's compassion was often highlighted in postcards through the reproduction of his loving, final letter to his mother. The expressions of duty and care therein offer a sharp contrast to the regime's own conduct, not least in permanently separating a mother from her son.

The leitmotif of revolutionary humanity versus Tsarist inhumanity can also be found in depictions of Schmidt. One postcard from around March 1906 sets a portrait of the sailor against a depiction of the aftermath of his rebellion. The overwhelming focus of the image is not on the mutiny itself but on the regime's excessively harsh response towards those who took part. The accompanying caption cites a government order instructing the army to 'have no regard for property, shells or people,' and this is followed by the exhortation: 'Glory to freedom fighters.' A clear distinction is thus established between the unjustifiable violence used by the state to suppress political freedom and the justifiable violence used by the revolutionaries to fight for it.

Schmidt is quoted on the same postcard as saying: 'In the event of the Cossacks carrying out any kind of violent reprisals against members of the local population, I will be forced to take decisive measures.' As with

Next spread

Anonymous artist. *Favourite Food of the Russians*. No publication details, circa late 1905. From left to right: Sergei Witte, Dmitrii Trepov, Konstantin Pobedonostsev, and Aleksei Ignatiev.

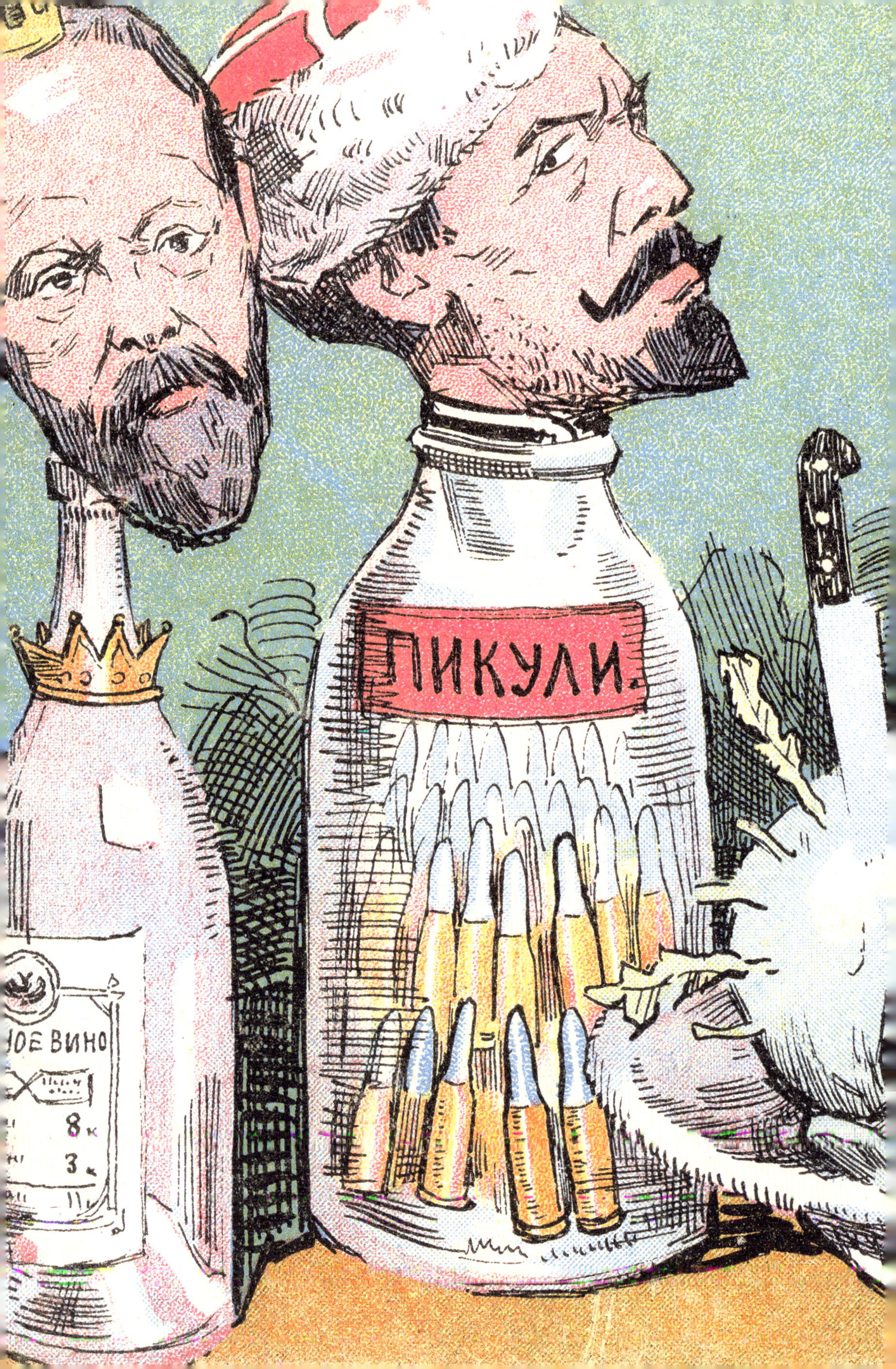

ПИКУЛИ.
НОЕ ВИНО
8 к
3 к

Любимыя кушанья русскихъ.

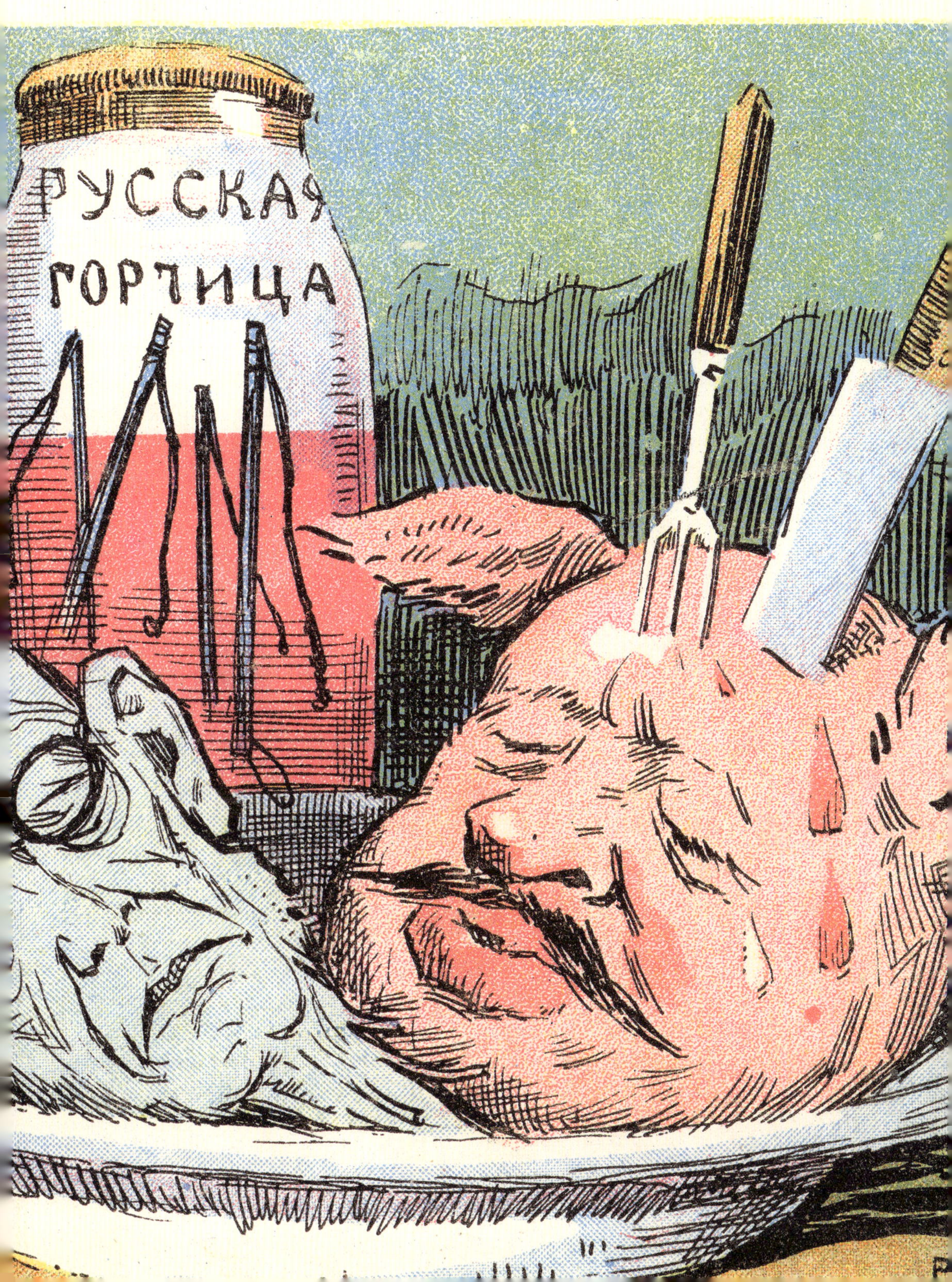

Spiridonova, it is the regime that is to be held responsible for any bloodshed, no matter who pulls the trigger. Repression was the government's original sin. In the eyes of the revolutionaries, Imperial despotism had severed the social contract between the ruler and the ruled. The population was now neither free nor safe, and any action, including violence, could be justified as atonement for the regime's repeated misuse of power. When tyranny is law, revolution is order.

Anonymous artist. *Victims of Tyranny, You Fell Victim in the Fateful Struggle.* No publication details, circa 1906.

Martyrdom: Sacrifice and Victimhood

Portraits of terrorists make almost no attempt to explain what the perpetrator's attack was intended to achieve, beyond the removal of a hated figure. Instead, where captions are present, their essential aim is to convey the individual's readiness to martyr themselves on behalf of the people. One postcard of Balmashev quotes him as saying: 'I offer my life as a sacrifice to the great cause of alleviating the fortunes of the toiling masses and the downtrodden.' His killing of Interior Minister Sipiagin goes unmentioned, making it appear all but irrelevant in comparison to his eagerness to die for the cause. Postcards of Konopliannikova carry a similar message: 'Forgive me, my people! There was so little that I could give you – only my life.'

In revolutionary portraiture, it is not the act of killing that is seen to advance the movement, but the act of sacrifice. In Konopliannikova's telling, giving up her life was all that she could do. No clarification of exactly how her death might help advance the cause of freedom is offered; the caption merely suggests that the achievement of dying in the people's name will in and of itself accelerate the overthrow of autocracy. For the revolutionaries, martyrdom was an end per se, a validation of the individual's life and beliefs, and a confirmation of the political import of their final act. As Spiridonova wrote: 'I want them to kill me ... death will have a tremendous revolutionary significance'.[21]

Key to this cult of martyrdom was the willing nature of the sacrifice. Kaliaev's letter to his mother reads in part: 'I am happy for myself that I can look upon my death with complete composure. Let your grief, my dearest ones ... be drowned out by the bright rays that shine forth from the exultation of my soul.' Spiridonova, meanwhile, is quoted as saying: 'If they kill me, I will die peacefully and with a good feeling in my soul.'[22] This emphasis on death as a conscious choice both highlights the extraordinary commitment of the activists, and underscores their agency; in taking control of their own destiny, the revolutionaries are able to influence that of the world outside.

The power of revolutionary sacrifice therefore revolved around ability and intent. Anyone prepared to give up their life so freely held immense power as a physical threat to the government and as an inspirational force

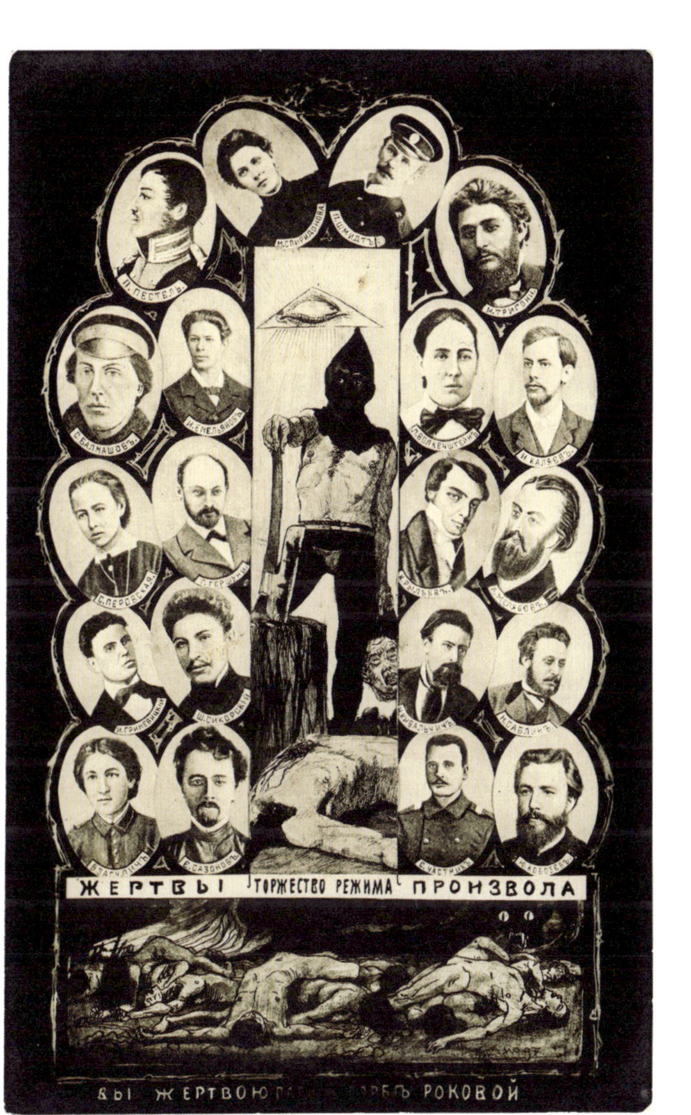
ЖЕРТВЫ
ТОРЖЕСТВО РЕЖИМА
ПРОНЗВОЛА
ВЫ ЖЕРТВОЮ
РОКОВОЙ

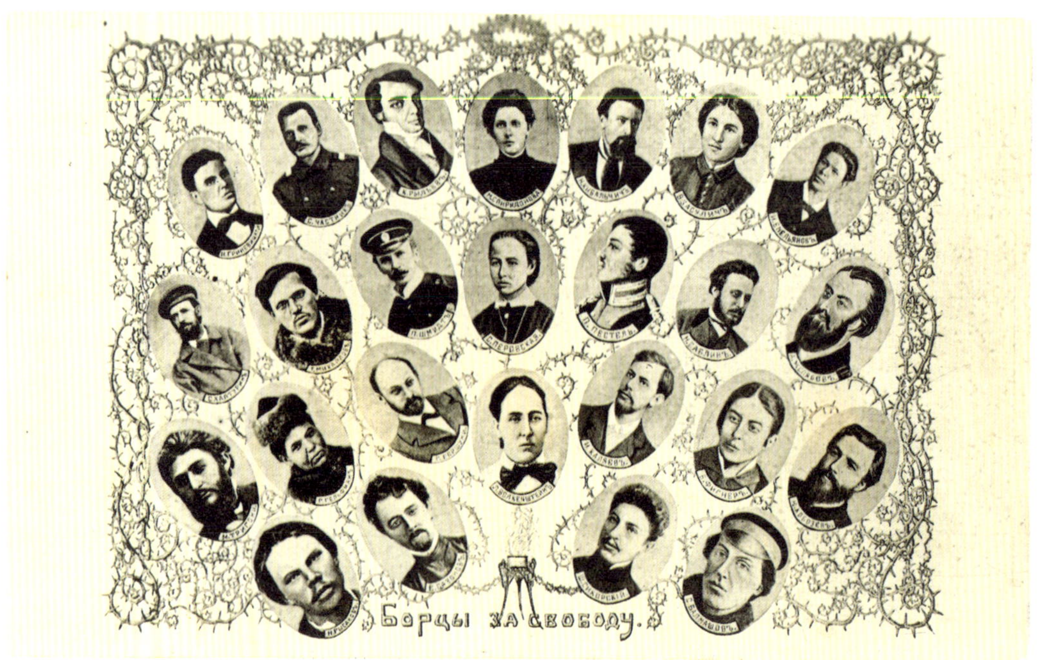

Anonymous designer. *Freedom Fighters.* No publication details, 1906.

to its opponents. Revolutionary promotion of terrorism relied first and foremost on these two aspects: on the one hand, its significance to the Party lay in the act itself – assassinations were used to project the capacity of the revolutionaries to wreak vengeance on the Imperial regime. And on the other, irrespective of whether anything concrete was achieved, they served as visible proof of the extraordinary lengths to which revolutionary activists would go to realise a better future for the people.

But although depictions of revolutionaries who had sacrificed themselves for the 'common good' were clear declarations of opposition capability, the assassins themselves were rarely cast as militant heroes. In this respect the Kaliaev portrait card is an exception; most terrorists were instead portrayed as victims, moreover ones who had been doubly punished. First, moral duty compelled them to fight against the iniquities of repression, then they were executed or imprisoned for the very crime of having followed their conscience. Thus, in accentuating victimhood, revolutionary portraits both underline the sacrifices that the activists had made, and also highlight the government's actions in repressing them, and by extension the population at large.

An explicit characterisation of revolutionary terrorists as victims can be seen in *Victims of Tyrrany, You Fell Victim in the Fateful Struggle*. This group portrait, titled after the revolutionary song, shows twenty political activists positioned on either side of a masked axeman. Beneath the opposition figures, the caption reads: 'Victims of Tyranny,' and beneath the executioner:

'The Exultation of the Regime.' The word 'zhertva,' used twice in the image, can be taken to mean either 'victim' or 'sacrifice,' and here the revolutionaries are both the victims of government misrule and the sacrifices that will help overcome it. In death, they are emblematic casualties of Imperial repression, but their demise also carries hopes for a brighter future.

That revolutionary portraits were intended to elicit popular sympathy is particularly evident in depictions of Perovskaia, which rarely allude openly to her participation in the assassination of Alexander II. One representative postcard from 1901, which reproduces a photograph of Perovskaia framed in black, includes only her name and the date of her execution. In leaving out any reference to her crime, focus shifts away from her actions and onto the state's role in bringing about the death of an apparently irreproachable young woman. It is no coincidence that postcards of the actual bomb-throwers Nikolai Rysakov and Ignacy Hryniewiecki are far rarer than those of Perovskaia, not least because they are far less sympathetic-looking figures.

The theoretical purpose of terrorism was to start a blood vendetta – to goad the state into responding to the revolutionaries and the people en masse in a wholly disproportionate manner, prompting them in turn to enact further revenge against the regime. Casting radicals as victims of the autocratic system, as opposed to active aggressors played an important part in pushing the population towards demanding reparation for revolutionary deaths and popular suffering. As one reader wrote in response to Spiridonova's ordeal: 'Surely this cannot go without challenge or protest?'[23] This particular comment was not a call to arms, but for less moderate individuals, terrorism was a vicious circle – the punishment became the justification for the crime.

It is possible on one level to see terrorist outrages as signs of weakness, the desperate acts of groups without any real power to challenge the status quo. This observation holds true for Russia before and during the 1905 Revolution, but it should not lead us to underestimate the fear that terrorism aroused among officials, nor to ignore the power of this fear to influence the political environment. For the purposes of revolutionary propaganda, the reaction of the government was just as important, if not more important than the attacks themselves. In abusing Spiridonova or executing Schmidt, officials arguably did far more to advance the cause of the revolutionaries than either of them could ever have done by themselves.

Terrorism may have been little effective in achieving tangible political gains, but postcard images of revolutionary activists helped to construct a broader narrative about the respective roles of the government and the radical opposition in late Imperial Russia. The principal achievement of revolutionary portraiture was to have cast terrorist actions against the state as an ethical imperative, thus shifting the blame for the revolutionaries' own

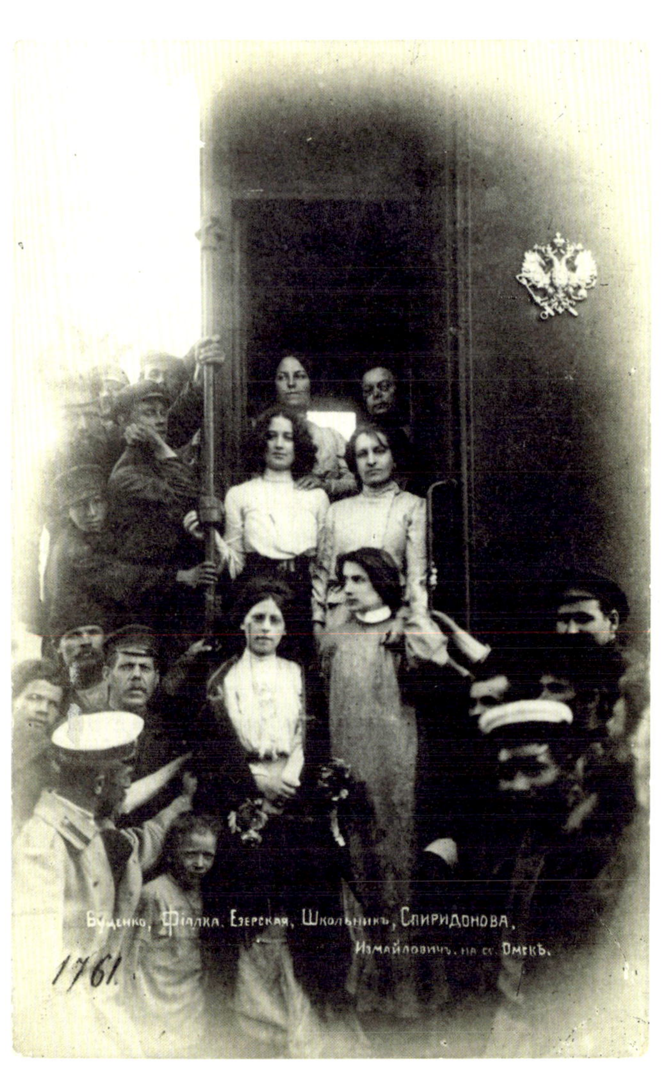
Буценко, Фіалка, Езерская, Школьникъ, Спиридонова,
Измайловичъ. на ст. Омскъ.
1761.

use of violence onto the autocratic regime. Regardless of the population's views on terrorism, for those in favour of change it was hard not to see the situation in Manichean terms, with noble sacrifice on one side and cruel despotism on the other.

Religious Iconography

We know that postcard portraits characterised the revolutionaries as humane, modest individuals who were giving their all to deliver the people from Tsarist despotism. But we are still no closer to understanding what their sacrifice was really intended to signify, beyond the power of the act itself. This is because the meaning of revolutionary terrorism in postcard imagery cannot be fully understood without reference to a Christian world-view. It is not only that terrorist portraiture borrowed extensively from Orthodox iconography in order to convey ideas of martyrdom, but that the images themselves were specifically meant to be read as icons of messianic figures, who served as the ideological prophets of a millenarian cult.

Anonymous photographer. *Bitsenko, Fialka, Ezerskaia, Shkolnik, Spiridonova, and Izmailovich at Omsk Station.* No publication details, 1906.

The sense of crisis in turn-of-the-century Russia led many to seek alternative routes of fulfilment, ones that deviated strongly from the traditional values of the Orthodox Church. The various routes of youthful experimentation encompassed drugs, sex, and death, as well as revolution, which had the advantage of promising both emotional excitement and spiritual satisfaction. Progressive individuals, including terrorists, saw revolution, or at least socialism, as presenting a viable alternative to old-world Orthodoxy as a way of solving the ills of contemporary society. This is not to suggest that all revolutionaries were atheists – far from it – but that revolution became a guiding principle and an end in itself.[24]

Religious language was used to elucidate revolutionary terrorism from its inception, a tendency that only deepened as the century drew to a disillusioned close, harried on all sides by unanswered questions of nationhood, politics and spirituality. It is associated particularly with the Socialist-Revolutionary Combat Organisation, which has been described by historians as resembling something close to a sect.[25] Members were placed above the ordinary Party rank and file, and their deeds regularly framed within a lexicon of deliverance from evil. Gershuni himself often invoked Old Testament terms of punishment to justify acts of terrorism, claiming that revolutionaries had a 'holy duty … to answer violence with violence.'[26]

The deployment of religious terminology attests to the lack of an alternative language to convey ideas of martyrdom, but it also reveals the elision of these two very different systems of belief. The revolutionary movement was a modern path to enlightenment, and in the repressive world of Imperial Russia its adherents came to see themselves as heirs to the Christian tradition. 'My Socialist-Revolutionary beliefs merged with my religion,' wrote Sazonov to his parents. 'We, the socialists, continue the work of Christ, who preached brotherly love … and died for the people as a political criminal … Christ's demands are clear. Who follows them? We, the socialists … want the kingdom of Christ to come to earth.'[27]

In compositional terms, the restrained aesthetic of many revolutionary portraits is broadly cognate with depictions of Orthodox saints, which were often set against plain backgrounds, entirely removed from time and space. The absence of any elements from the material world in postcard depictions of terrorist martyrs projects a similar sense of otherworldliness, advancing the notion that their acts had somehow set them above the rest of humanity. Balmashev is shown in one postcard sitting in a chair that seems to be floating, miraculously, in a sea of white. Whether deliberate or not, the image that we see is not of an earth-bound mortal, but of a martyr transfigured through his revolutionary deeds to attain socialist glory.

Anonymous photographer. *Balmashev*. No publication details, circa 1905.

The aim of anti-government postcards was not only to convey partisan interpretations of events, but also to create an environment in which the consumer could interact with the cause on a devotional level. By consciously cleansing the image of all except the figure, the obstacles for direct communion between the viewer and subject were removed, and the way was left open for the beholder to gain spiritual knowledge of the individual and the political church that they represented. Indeed, postcard images were often venerated by opposition supporters in unapologetically religious fashion. The aforementioned devotee of Spiridonova said that he worshipped her portrait, while one sailor, describing the revolutionary as a saint, confessed: 'I pray to her.'[28]

Postcards of all subject matter played a role in transporting the viewer from a place of reality into a world of fantasy. An article on penpals written in 1907 gives an example of the shift in perception that they could bring about: 'You see in your correspondent an all but idealised person, because all their faults are hidden from you … Sitting in front of this postcard that you intend to send to one of your abstract friends, you cut yourself off from the real world for a while, letting go of all its petty troubles and worries, and shift to an idealised, otherworldly sphere, to live, even for just a few minutes, a life of exalted thoughts, high-minded ideas; a life that I would call 'the life of the postcard'.'[29]

In many ways this encapsulates the experience that anti-government portraits offered; they presented a revolutionary figure, whom one would never know, who enabled the viewer to commune with a higher purpose and to dream, if only for a moment, about a better life. In common with the icon, which provided a bridge between heaven and earth, postcards were intercessors. They created a link from one political world to the next, only rather

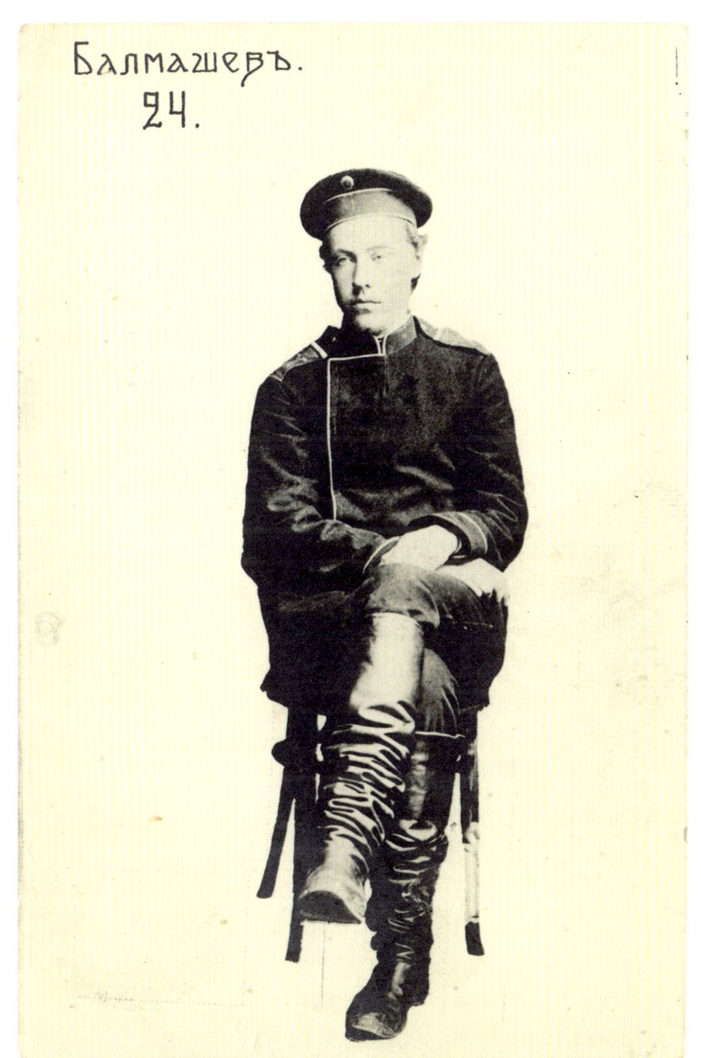
Балмашевъ.
24.

than guiding prayers between the faithful and God, portraits of activists created an ideological connection between party supporters and the otherworldly panoply of revolutionary martyrs who were working to bring about the political deliverance of the people.

Traditional modes of composition are replicated more fully in group images of revolutionary activists, which gathered together a range of individuals from different historical periods in rows of oval portrait medallions. These photomechanical compositions strongly echo pictorial throngs of Orthodox saints known as collective icons, of which the most prevalent type followed the menology, a liturgical work chronicling the *Lives of the Saints*. The placing of particular individuals was less rigidly structured in revolutionary portraiture than in comparable religious images, but their shared intention was to link the principal activists of the movement through the unity of their cause and affliction.

Attributed to Nahum Luboshitz (photographer). Untitled postcard depicting Maria Spiridonova in Tambov Prison. No publication details, 1906.

Narrative works are less common, but postcards recounting the deeds of the revolutionaries were meant to serve as visual hagiographies, guiding supporters towards a fuller appreciation of their life and fate. Two postcards of Spiridonova, for instance, depict her in Tambov prison, while another shows her travelling into exile.[30] These are secular versions of the Lives of the Saints – they invite the faithful to contemplate the torment endured by the revolutionaries on the way towards their eventual fate, be it execution or imprisonment.[31] As such, they formed part of a wider effort to construct a new culture of revolutionary martyrdom, which presented leading political activists as contemporary saints, epitomised, like their predecessors, by their dedication and suffering.

In the first of the Tambov postcards, Spiridonova stands by the window of her cell. No material possessions are visible apart from a small table. In the second, she is writing, a process that brings to mind her letter to *Rus*, and by extension her alleged rape. In concert with other portraits, the plainness of the imagery conveys the ascetic nature of revolutionary life, which in turn signifies the purity of the subject's commitment to the cause. Asceticism aligns Spiridonova both with the saints and with the revolutionary ideal epitomised by Rakhmetov, the self-denying hero of Chernyshevskii's *What Is to Be Done?* Her hardship is thus both a badge of martyrdom, and a mark of her being a proper revolutionary.

In Orthodox Christianity suffering and self-denial are closely linked to kenosis – the idea that through deliberate privation, the body will be emptied of the detritus of the material world and so made open to receiving God's holy will. The Tambov postcards invoke sympathy by highlighting the adversity that Spiridonova is undergoing, and at the same time, promote her as an exemplar, by showing her in the process of fulfilling her revolutionary destiny. As with the Christian saints, the punishing ordeals imposed upon

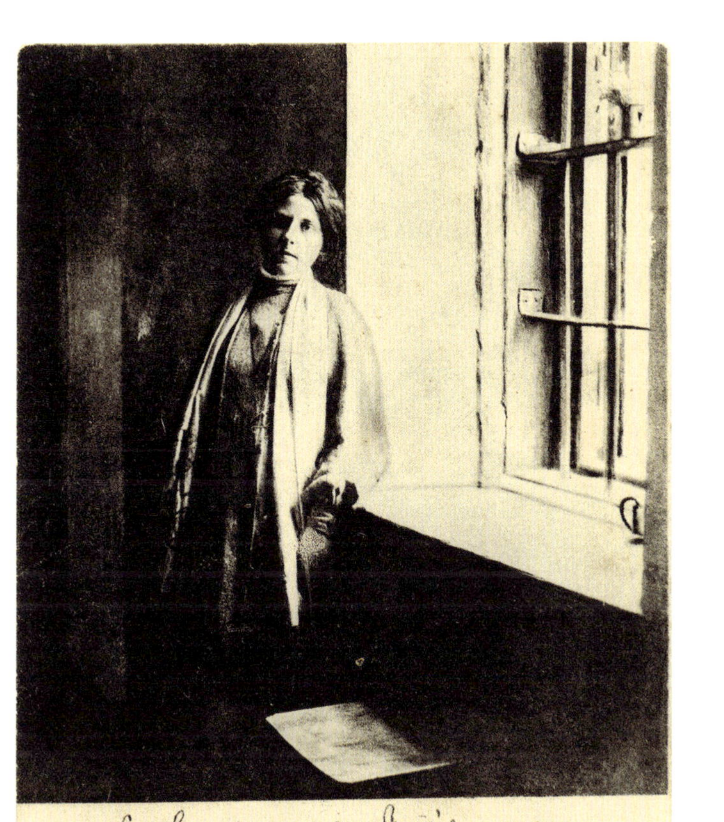

Со времени прибытія моего в Тамбовскую тюрьму я все время находилась в той камере-больнице, в к-рой меня видели, посетившие меня американцы.

Мар. Спиридонова

15 апреля 1906 г.

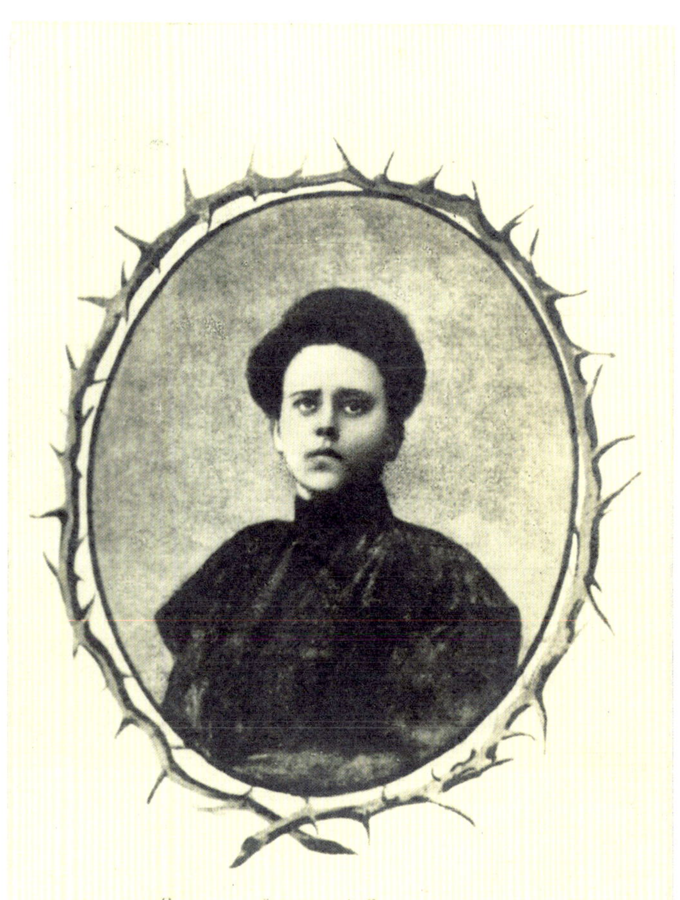

„Прости, мой народъ! Я такъ мало могла тебѣ дать—только одну свою жизнь".

Зинаида Васильевна Коноплянникова.

172

the martyr-terrorists helped them to acquire (political) grace, so enabling them to come closer to the ideals of the movement. Postcards of Spiridonova in prison are thus akin to paintings of Saint Jerome in the desert.

In 1906, a group of four leading terrorists, including Gershuni and Sazonov, wrote an open letter to Spiridonova, hailing her act in unashamedly religious terms. It reads in part:

> Like a conscientious Socialist-Revolutionary, taking on yourself all the torment of the working people, burning with hatred for the insults, humiliation and scorn of their oppressors, you took it upon yourself as a member of the Party to carry out the death sentence against this savage butcher of the Tambov peasantry, and in doing so gave up your life for the good of the people – you do not put your suffering above the suffering of those for whom you gave all of yourself to carry out this holy deed.[32]

Anonymous photographer. *Forgive Me, My People! There Was so Little That I Could Give You – Only My Life. Zinaida Vasilievna Konopliannikova.* No publication details, 1906.

Spiridonova is deliberately portrayed in this letter as a modern-day Christ. Her self-appointed role on earth was to atone for the iniquities of the regime, and this was evidently how both revolutionary adherents and sympathetic members of the public saw her actions. As one reader of *Rus* remarked: 'After all, didn't she pray when she fired the shots, as if she was bestowing a blessing?'[33]

The conceit that terrorists were Christ-like redeemers was often made explicit in revolutionary portraiture through the use of symbols associated with the Passion. *Freedom Fighters*, for example, links together twenty-five activists through a network of thorns, surmounted by a small crown. Postcards were also made of both Konopliannikova and Spiridonova showing them encircled by a crown of thorns.[34] Religious iconography was being used here not simply as a way of popularising or contextualising terrorist deeds, but as an ideological frame of reference through which to understand the entirety of the revolutionary struggle. As Sazonov had said, the revolutionaries were assuming the mantle of Christ's successors, and thus, in sacrificing themselves they were delivering the nation from Tsarist sin.

The common purpose of icons and anti-government postcards was to give pictorial expression to the written teachings of a particular belief system. Their role was not to reflect daily life but to explain it. In the words of the expert Leonid Ouspensky, icon painting uses 'images drawn from the material world in order to transmit the revelation of the divine world.'[35] Opposition postcards follow an analogous path, using real incidents and events from the lives of prominent revolutionary martyrs in order to impart knowledge of the coming transformation, and so convey the promise of the earthly paradise that activists were striving to create on man's behalf. To borrow Ouspensky's phrase, they 'prefigure the coming sanctification of the world.'[36]

Belief in the coming revolution gave meaning to all the death and disruption that Russia had for so long been forced to endure. The borrowing of religious symbology therefore not only allowed the revolutionaries to show the moral rectitude of their cause, but crucially to cast all aspects of it as being part of a struggle towards eventual victory over oppression. Thus, when reference is made to Kaliaev's execution in one Party leaflet, his death is described as bringing 'an impending happy life ever closer to realisation.'[37] As with icons, postcards channelled human existence towards a single ideological proposition, providing spiritual comfort in a disordered world by serving as the departure point from which to imagine a glorious future.

⁂

Revolutionary terrorism broke the state's centuries-old monopoly on the use of violence as a legitimate means of social regulation. Consciously emulating the Christian tradition of martyr saints, the radical opposition used sacrificial acts of terror to promote its members as righteous exemplars, extolling their public-minded deeds in order both to inspire and provoke change. Portraits of prominent revolutionaries were fundamentally designed to exert their moral superiority over the regime, thereby usurping the monarchical authority of the Tsar and establishing the revolutionary opposition as the legitimate embodiment of the nation. Claims to virtue were claims to power; they enabled the revolutionaries to distinguish right from wrong, and in doing so to advance the notion that they alone were the true representatives of the people.

The danger of these images to the regime was widely understood, as one governmental report makes clear:

> Accounts of the lives and deeds of individuals who in their time carried out anti-government agitation and waged an open, criminal struggle against the government are without doubt ultimately aimed at championing these figures as fighters for freedom, truth, and the interests of the people in the widest and most accessible way. Moreover, they will not only be distributed in Vologda Province but across the whole of the Russian Empire … Public dissemination … is undesirable because the publisher is undoubtedly trying to glorify the most serious criminals in Russia, people who have taken an active role in fighting against the government.[38]

This report, compiled in response to Viktor Zheglinskii's postcards, underscores the threat that revolutionary portraits presented to such a morally compromised government. Not only did they propagandise ideas that could be construed as damaging to the status quo, they also 'championed' activists as upholding the rights of the people.[39] Postcard portraits showed the revolutionaries assuming the traditional roles of the state, propagating the belief that it was not the government that best reflected the interests of the people, but the revolutionaries, not the state that offered freedom, but the revolutionaries, not autocracy that was the arbiter of truth, but the revolutionaries. In short, the portraits were a direct and deadly challenge to the authority of the Tsar himself.

Novotcherkassk
9/22 Avril

Зо Францію

Открытое письмо.—Carte Postale.

ВСЕМІРНЫЙ ПОЧТОВЫЙ СОЮЗЪ. РОССІЯ.

Мѣсто для корреспонденціи.

Mon cher Marcel,
Je t'envoie ce souvenir de
l'insurrection de décembre dernier
et j'y joins une autre carte
(Maison des orphelins)
tout à toi
L Lecomte

Адресъ.

Госпо M. Marcel Bricongne
Gannes
par Ansauvillers
(Oise)
France

ИЗДАНІЕ «UMO» МОСКВА.

6

CONSUMPTION AND DISPLAY

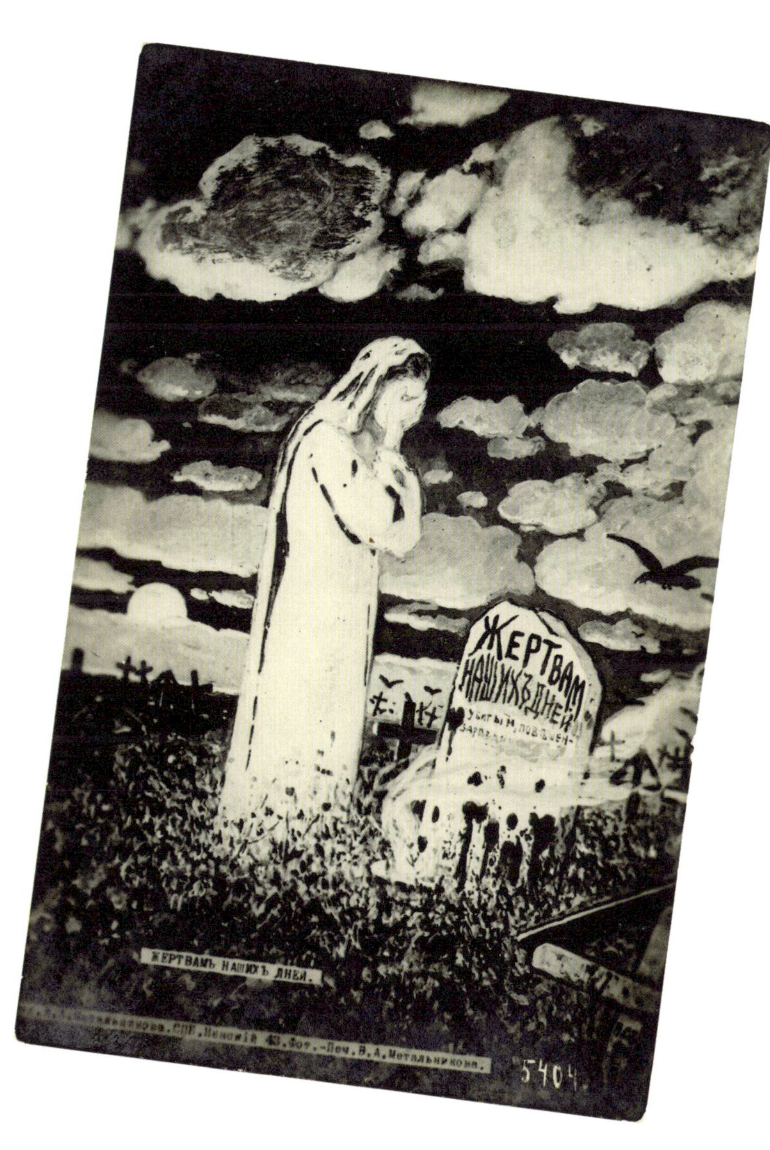

Я очень ловкій операторъ
И съ честью званіе ношу,
Я, господа, „экспропріаторъ"
И уважать меня прошу.
Васъ не спасетъ стѣна и крыша
Могу я всюду васъ сыскать.
Крикъ „руки вверхъ" едва услыша
Мнѣ деньги всѣ должны отдать
Вѣдь я не вредный агитаторъ,
Не воръ я и не хулиганъ,
Я, господа, „экспропріаторъ",-
Судьбой мнѣ жребій высшій данъ.

П.М.

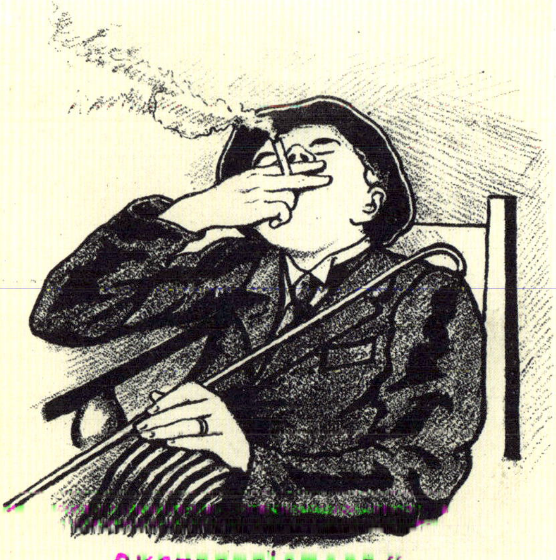

„Экспропріаторъ"
рисунокъ Ив. Горѣлова.

Cost and Audience

By late 1905, the only real barrier to acquiring anti-government postcards was cost. At the top end of the market were hand-drawn works. Karrik, for example, sold his portraits for twenty kopecks each. Next came high-end legal firms such as Shipovnik, which charged ten kopecks for colour images (and eight for black-and-white).[1] Most chromolithographic cartoons, however, cost slightly less – around eight kopecks, the same price as silver bromide picture reproductions.[2] Cheapest of all were typographic postcards. D. P. Efimov's pictures of the Moscow Uprising, for instance, sold for five kopecks. These amounts were all in line with market prices – the Society of Saint Eugenia's postcards cost between five and twenty-five kopecks each, averaging ten for colour images and five for black-and-white.[3]

Revolutionary postcards were naturally positioned at the cheaper end of the market. Utro's typographic cards initially cost eight kopecks, but their price dropped to six kopecks when the firm became a part of Vpered, and later to five, the fall no doubt reflecting an increase in production.[4] By comparison, Vpered's large photomechanical prints cost between ten and thirty kopecks, roughly the same price as its pamphlets.[5] As for illegally-produced postcards, there is little information available; all we have to go on is the case of Petr Iakovlev, who in mid-1905 paid five kopecks for a photomechanical portrait of Balmashev.[6] Although hardly conclusive, this suggests that there was no great premium attached to run-of-the-mill underground imagery.

Chemodanov's output presents something of an anomaly in regards to pricing. Unlike other revolutionary enterprises, which made an effort to keep their wares affordable for the masses, his cards were sold for between two roubles fifty and three roubles for a packet of twenty, nearly twice the going rate for photomechanical images. The aim of Chemodanov's works, however, was not to convert those whom the radicals hoped might bring about the overthrow of the regime, but to fundraise among the 'intelligentsia and liberal bourgeoisie.' These groups were also propaganda targets for the revolutionaries, but Chemodanov, as an independent operative, clearly made the decision to prioritise generating income, over and above converting the wider population.

As Chemodanov's sales practices would suggest, the liberal bourgeoisie were enthusiastic consumers of anti-government images. The purchase of such inessential goods as opposition postcards required both a disposable income and a degree of familiarity with current events, and individuals from this social milieu, which included members of the so-called free professions, such as lawyers, doctors, teachers, and artists, as well as better-off sections of the intelligentsia and student population, had both the ability and the political inclination to become regular purchasers of anti-government material.

Previous spread from left to right

Postcard depicting the Moscow Uprising sent by L. Lecomter to Marcel Bricogne in April 1906.

Mikhail Stoliarov. *To the Victims of Our Days*. Published by Vasilii Metalnikov, Saint Petersburg, December 1906.

Opposite

I. V. Gorelov. *Expropriator*. No publication details, circa October 1906. This postcard was sent to a collector of politcal images.

Moreover, many were already seasoned postcard collectors, practiced in using the medium to express their own personal tastes and interests.

Nonetheless, by the mid-1900s, postcards at the cheaper end of the market were both affordable for and bought and used by many of the poorer members of society, including workers and better-educated peasants.[7] The commercial trade in anti-government images was no different; indeed, the whole point of opposition parties and publishers using postcards as propaganda devices was not only that they were simple to produce and disseminate, but also that they were comprehensible and within financial reach of large swathes of the population. Therefore, while picture postcards may initially have been the focus of social aspirations among the middle classes, in 1905 they became the focus of political aspirations among the country at large.[8]

Ernest Meissonier. *Barricades*. Published by Vpered, Saint Petersburg, 1906. This example carries a handwritten excerpt from a poem by Petr Iakubovich.

Political Engagement

The role that postcards played as vehicles for opposition propaganda bears little relation to their original function as items of postal stationery; the revolutionaries utilised the medium primarily for the ease with which it could be manufactured and distributed, not for the ease with which it could be written on and sent through the post.[9] Tellingly, many photomechanical postcards, such as Chemodanov's cartoons, have plain backs – clear evidence that they were never designed to be sent as open letters. There were of course practical difficulties and dangers associated with mailing anti-government cards, but today it is uncommon even to find legal opposition images that have been sent through the post, indicating that most were bought by end users for their own personal consumption.

The primary purpose of anti-government postcards was to act as pictorial catalysts for ideological reflection. The notion that postcards offered a space in which different interests and enthusiasms could be pursued was already long established. Almost since their inception, critics had looked upon the medium as an instrument of learning that could complement the cultural and social outlook of their owners. To enlightened collectors, postcards were objects of secular contemplation, occasionally displayed in public, but often the totems of a private artistic, intellectual, or ideological interest. It follows that while some anti-government images passed between close acquaintances, most were the focus of private belief, offering a spur to political thought, and a mechanism for its further exploration.

To committed activists, postcards with socialist content were akin to devotional items. The artist Ivan Pavlov recalled how 'the revolutionary youth ... would carefully cherish postcard reproductions of [Iakob Kalinichenko's] *Before the Search*, which they hung on the walls of their

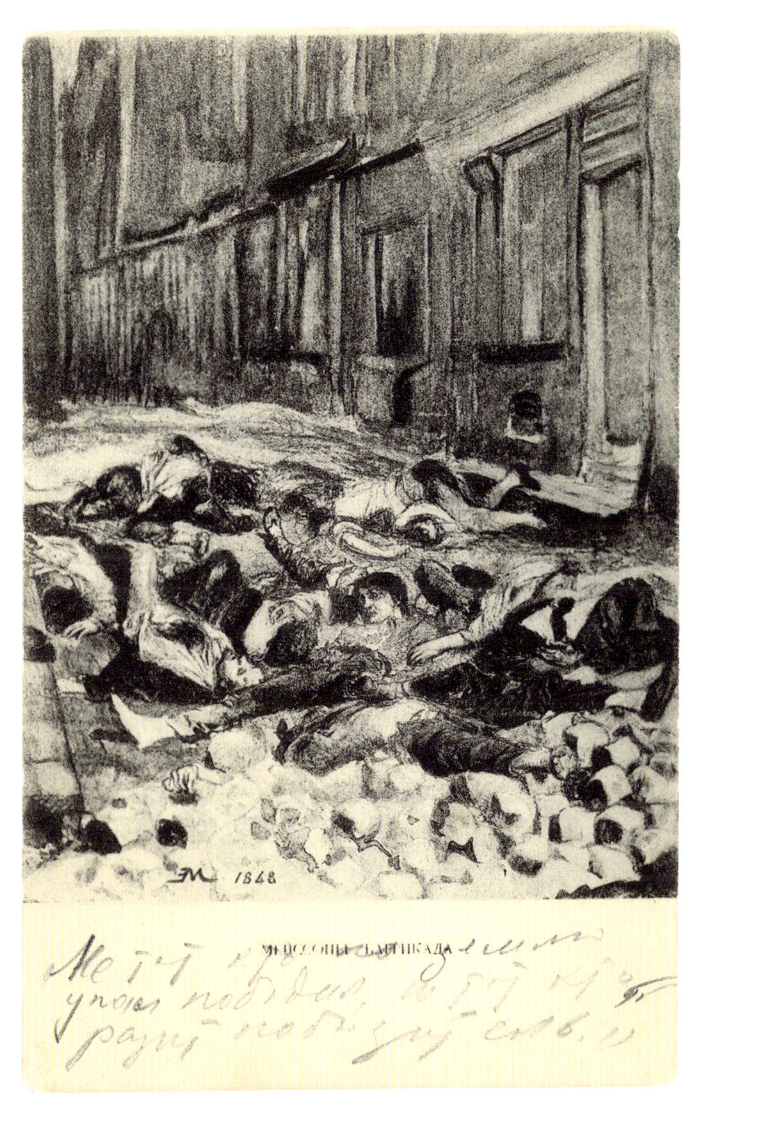
1848
МЕЙССОНЬЕ. БАРРИКАДА

poor student flats alongside images by [the painters] Repin, Surikov, Vereshchagin and Levitan.'[10] In such an environment, postcards were aids to piety, conveying political gospels through visual narrative, much as an icon might do the teachings of the Bible. This strongly didactic nature of their imagery often induced a deep political engagement, and while seeking greater understanding of the movement, the revolutionary faithful would occasionally make notes on the backs of the postcards themselves.

One Vpered postcard in my collection carries a handwritten quotation paraphrasing Lenin: 'Until autocracy falls, i.e. until the establishment of a democratic republic, every decent man should be a revolutionary. But you, the proletariat, will remain revolutionaries until the fall of capitalism.'[11] The image on the front, depicting the victims of government repression at Golutvino, provides a revenge-laden incentive to rise up against the regime, while the statement on the back emphasises the nobility of the cause and instils a sense of historical certainty in its outcome.[12] The owner can take comfort in the moral rectitude of their struggle, and find security in a shared sense of belonging. This was the membership card of an exclusive club of right-thinking individuals.

Another Vpered postcard, this time depicting a scene from the 1848 French Revolution, includes a handwritten excerpt from a poem by the Populist revolutionary Petr Iakubovich, reading: 'He who falls is not defeated, nor he who strikes, a conqueror.'[13] In common with the above-mentioned counterpart, the quotation and image serve as a portable guide to the movement; they remind the committed why the battle is being waged, and urge them to stay the course through good times and bad.

Politically-orientated inscriptions of this type are signs of meaningful engagement with the process of revolution, and as such they offer first-hand evidence of the rapid politicisation of the Russian population during the 1905 era. The owners of these two postcards have not merely swallowed the content of the postcards verbatim, but thought about their meaning, related it to their own experiences, and then formulated a response based on the theoretical knowledge that they have acquired. For the faithful, therefore, postcards were not just the physical expression of a personal interest, but a way to receive and understand political truths that might enable them to make sense of a disordered world.

This was a period of chaos, full of competing political developments and random acts of violence. Freedoms were promised then snatched away, the Duma was created and then dispersed. Hopes were raised then dashed, and throughout this time, all sides continued to blame each other for causing the ongoing upheaval. What was an individual to think? Even if one did oppose autocracy, how were opposition thoughts to be sustained when so much was still unresolved? For revolutionary adherents, postcards offered a sense of certainty in a deeply uncertain world by enacting rituals of worship and mourning that reinforced opposition to the regime, and gave the surrounding death and disarray a meaning that it did not otherwise possess.

In the absence of any opportunities to lament the deaths of revolutionary heroes in public, postcard portraits became a focus of opposition grief and political resolve.[14] A typographic postcard depicting the mutineer Lieutenant Schmidt carries the inscription:

> On Monday 6 March at 3.38 am, Lieutenant Schmidt, Chastnik, Antonenko, and Gladkov were executed ... [Shortly before his death, Schmidt said] 'Remember my people that you are giving your life for the noble cause of freedom! Christ dies for faith and we for truth ...' When the priest offered him the sacraments, Schmidt said: 'We will take Holy Communion only when the [Tsar] batiushka sits down and shows us where it says in the Gospels that killing people is allowed.'[15]

This account is intended to convey a broadly similar message of purpose and steadfast allegiance as the aforementioned Iakubovich postcard. It casts the executions of Schmidt and his comrades as necessary and heroic acts of martyrdom that will ease the path to liberation, thereby offering a political rationalisation of revolutionary sacrifice, and by extension a justification of the movement as a whole. In repeating Schmidt's suggestion that the soul should have no rest until the repression ceases, the writer doubles down on their commitment to the cause, reinforcing the moral superiority of its aims. Thus, revolutionary heartache at the loss of an activist and despair at the mutiny's defeat is channelled into reinvigorated opposition to a tyrannical Tsar.

The liberation movement was a surrogate family, and postcards enabled the population to mourn the symbolic representatives of the revolution, as if they were a friend or family member whom they had known and loved, and for this process of bereavement to be played out within the confines of the home. The function of anti-government postcards was therefore to a great extent cathartic. Much of their imagery, realist and satirical, was concerned with unmasking the government's violent suppression of both the population and the liberation movement; postcards supplied a template for coming to terms with these calamities, as well as a way to process them emotionally, by transforming private grief into political intent.

As the revolutionary tempo subsided, postcards came to provide a permanent record of events for future generations. A card given by Vilnius resident 'Isaak K.' to 'Tanechka' in April 1908 carries the message: 'When you're grown up, you'll remember these past days and all the many incidents that have taken place.' The postcard that he used, which was published by

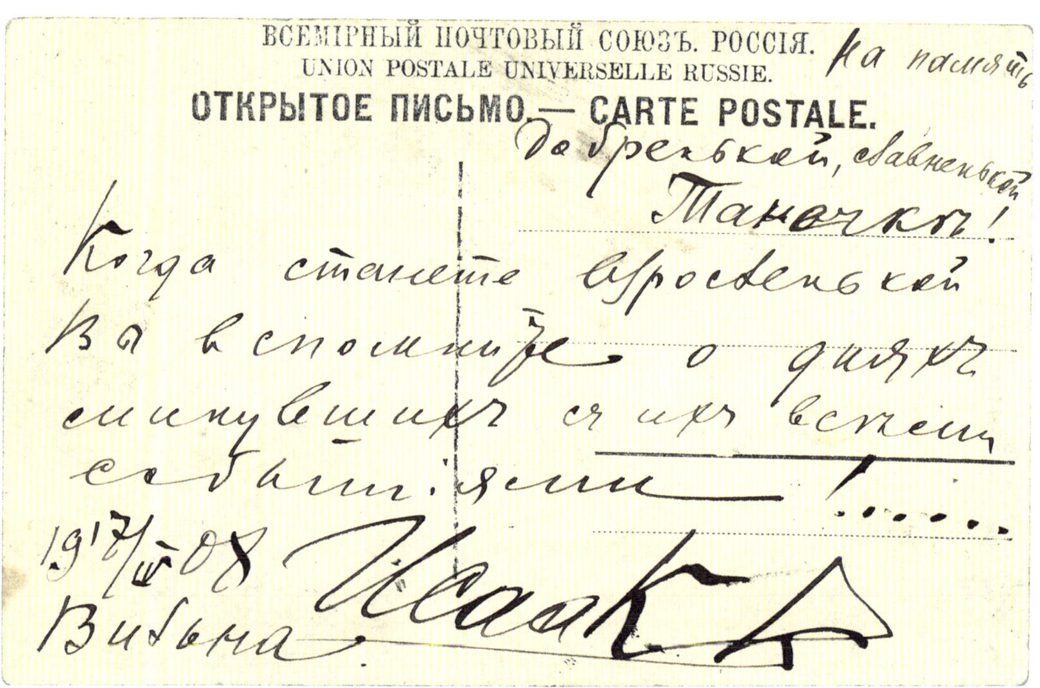
ВСЕМІРНЫЙ ПОЧТОВЫЙ СОЮЗЪ. РОССІЯ.
UNION POSTALE UNIVERSELLE RUSSIE.
ОТКРЫТОЕ ПИСЬМО — CARTE POSTALE.

На память добренькой, славненькой Таночке!
Когда станете взрослой вы вспомните о днях минувших с их вечными событиями!.....
19/IV 08
Исаак К.
Вильна

Message written by Isaak K. on the back of *To the Victims of Our Days*. Vilnius, April 1908.

Metalnikov, depicts an allegorical figure of Russia weeping over a grave inscribed with the words: 'To the victims of our days.'[16] By the time Isaak K. wrote this message the opposition movement had been largely destroyed. Through word and image, he sought to create a compact, easily accessible memorial to the Revolution, so as to ensure that its victims would never be forgotten.

Postcards enabled political events and seditious acts to resonate long after their immediate impact had passed. The substance of what they were conveying was ideological, and committed opposition to the Tsar was not a position that was likely to change overnight. Their permanence was far greater than that of either newspapers or satirical journals. To the politically minded, these were not temporary transmitters of news or fashion, but objects of long-term admiration that would remain relevant, either until the regime enacted wholesale reform, or was overthrown. Postcards such as the one used by Isaak K. helped to keep political beliefs alive for years, their content still relevant to a situation that remained fundamentally unchanged.

The Political Made Personal

There is no single, defining story of the 1905 Revolution. The reasons that lay behind the profound social and political changes, and their implication for Russia's future, were a matter of dispute, then as now. Organisations of every hue attempted to shape public understanding of the Revolution in their own image, and these diverse interpretations of events fractured yet further as they filtered down through the population. The degree of political engagement among postcard producers ranged from revolutionary to commercial, but at the point of sale, both artists and publishers surrendered control over how their images would be interpreted, and in the process of popular consumption a different, more subjective set of values came to be applied.

As the Imperial government itself discovered, political meanings could be elusive and the right to convey them easily lost. Anti-government postcards were bought in significant quantities by committed supporters of the liberation movement, and in these circumstances use of the medium dovetailed closely with the intentions of opposition publishers to deploy them as propaganda. For activists committed to bringing about reform or wholesale change, postcards provided a partisan way of interpreting, and gaining succour from the historical developments of the era in which they were living. But just as these images were not always published for political reasons alone, so, too, the motivation for buying them was not always exclusively ideological.

In contrast to other forms of propaganda, the interactive nature of the postcard medium left far greater scope for individual usage and interpretation. Although the majority never travelled, opposition images were still occasionally sent inside envelopes or conveyed from hand to hand. The messages they carry demonstrate the extent to which day-to-day reality came to overlap with ideological belief. 'I send you heartfelt greetings from Mother Moscow,' wrote Captain Ivan Borodin to his sweetheart on the back of a reproduction of Vladimirov's *Don't Go*. 'Take a look at this postcard and see how admirable it is. I am desperate to receive a message from you, I haven't yet managed to leave and I already miss… you. Yours Vanka.'[17]

The extent of Borodin's ideological admiration for the revolutionary fighter in the picture is not clear, but by taking the aspects of the scene that most applied to his own situation – that is to say separation, duty, and geographical location – he has sought to recast Vladimirov's hero in his own image, using his prerogative as a postcard correspondent to transfigure a portrayal of revolutionary commitment into one of romantic longing. Irrespective of Borodin's political beliefs, the strength of his emotional torment has ensured that the political intent of both the artist and the publisher has been almost entirely obscured, or at the very least been made to play second fiddle to the consumer's own personal experiences.

Opposition postcards thus had both a social and a political dimension, used to cement emotional bonds as well as to assert ideological belief. Where the two converged, the medium's basic function as a message bearer was retained and its role became that of greetings card for the socially conscious.

Another instructive example of the interplay between the personal and the political can be seen in a message written on a postcard of Moisei Maimon's *Back Home*: 'I send you my warmest congratulations, dear Elizaveta Nikolaevna, on your upcoming name day, and I hope with all my heart that your soul's desires are soon fulfilled. Surely you see now that, 'the pleasures of the mighty are the tears of the poor'. Kindest regards, N.'[18]

It is hard for the modern viewer to see how a painting of the aftermath of a pogrom could ever be considered an appropriate image to send a friend on their name day. But by conflating private concerns and ideological belief in this manner, the anonymous sender shows how present politics had become in the minds and everyday experiences of the population. Indeed, there can be few more vivid proofs of the population's familiarity with violence than the decision to use a postcard of a dead Jewish woman to send a personal message of congratulations.

The most clear-cut political tidings and responses tend to be found on revolutionary portraits and picture reproductions, likely because they were comparatively cheap and therefore affordable to impoverished activists, and also because their content presented such a straightforwardly inspiring depiction of the struggle. By contrast there are few similar messages on the back of cartoon postcards. The genre of satire was dominated by liberal-minded artists and publishers, and by its very nature presented a more complicated, and at times ambivalent, view of the Revolution.

Satirical postcards grappled with many of the same themes as their counterparts, but in place of realism, the iniquities of Imperial life were exposed through farce, allusion and distortion. Their power was rarely diminished by this approach; in fact, it was often amplified, but the broadly humorous nature of cartoon postcards enabled them to be treated by consumers as entertaining commentaries on current events, as much as objects of ideological allegiance. This made their use in non-political exchanges a less troubling affair. For example, in November 1906, the suitor of a young woman named T. A. Varkovskaia sent her a caricature of a 'monarchist' butcher, dressed in a bloodied apron and carrying two large carving knives. The note on the back reads: 'Tickets bought for Friday's performance of Carmen.'[19]

The use of an anti-government satire to confirm an opera booking does not automatically indicate contempt for, or a lack of affiliation with the liberation movement, only that there was more than one way to engage with images that were nominally oppositional. This was particularly true in respect of those who could afford to adopt a more casual attitude towards their acquisitions, such as the liberal bourgeoisie, who by dint of wealth and political outlook comprised the main audience for chromolithographic cartoons. But lest it be assumed that all such imagery was treated in a similarly superficial manner, it is worth pointing out that postcards from the

Evgenii Sokolov. *Monarchist*. Printed by E. Kudinova and A. Lezina, Saint Petersburg, circa April 1906. This postcard was used to invite a young lady to the opera.

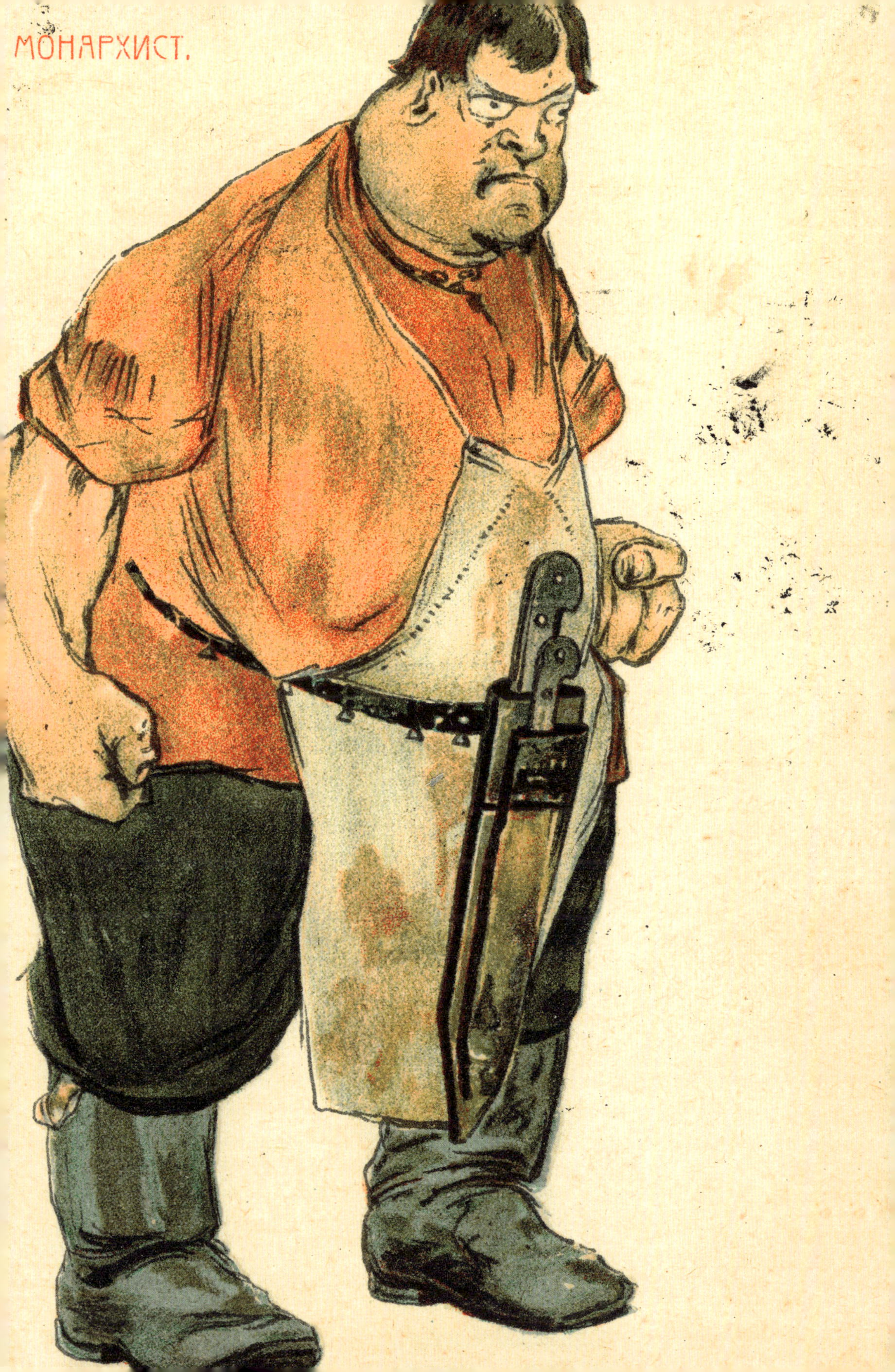
МОНАРХИСТ.

same series (by Evgenii Sokolov) were also bought and sold by revolutionary activists.[20]

The point is that postcard consumption was idiosyncratic. No matter what the subject matter, the medium was so popular and the politics so pervasive that it can never be assumed that the purchase of an anti-government image constituted a clear articulation of opposition belief. By late 1905, leftist postcards had become objects of mainstream consumption that could be acquired by anyone with the merest flickering of interest in the contemporary situation in Russia, the acquisition perhaps motivated in the first instance by political views or a particular connection to specific events, but beyond this, by an emotional response to the image itself, whether prompted by amusement, aesthetic appreciation, or individual experience.

Opposition to the regime was a nuanced and multi-layered phenomenon; consequently, ownership of anti-government postcards stretched far beyond the narrow sphere of committed activists who led the struggle against autocracy. At one end of the spectrum was a man like Mikhail Protopopov, an engineer arrested in 1906 during a raid on his Moscow flat. Along with bomb-making paraphernalia, the police also found: 'several uncensored pamphlets of assorted content, two cards with images of Lieutenant Schmidt and Spiridonova, and a collection of revolutionary songs.'[21] And at the other end was a man like Stepan Beletskii, a senior official working for the Governor of Vilnius, who also happened to be one of the founder members of the monarchist political group, The Russian Assembly.

'I'm sending you Schmidt,' reads a postcard mailed to Beletskii, 'but I imagine you've already got him, and T. also wants to send you one of Spiridonova.'[22] It is unlikely that Beletskii harboured any revolutionary sympathies, not least because he was a career servant of the regime who later became head of the Department of Police, but the message, nonetheless, plainly indicates an interest in collecting anti-government images. The underlying reason for this interest remains altogether unclear, but Beletskii's activities offer incontrovertible evidence that not only were the reasons for acquiring anti-government images subjective, they did not even have to depend on anti-Tsarist belief. Postcards could be all things to all people.

For some collectors, postcards simply fed an urge to acquire, irrespective of whether or not they subscribed to the values represented in the imagery. A 1907 article on 'How to Collect Postcards' specifically mentions political cartoons as a possible collecting theme for enthusiasts.[23] One card of a revolutionary expropriator in my collection contains a note on the reverse, reading: 'A new character type from our extraordinary revolution. This will make a good addition to your political album.'[24] Anti-government images even found their way into otherwise conventional compilations. An album of Russian views, types, and artist-signed postcards belonging to Nevill Forbes, a cousin of Valerii Karrik, includes two pictures commemorating the Duma, one of a political prisoner, and another promoting female emancipation.[25]

We will never know what prompted the vast majority of purchases, but if revolution was a 'fashionable disease,' then its material manifestations also became objects of vogue and desire. The appeal of the forbidden is well documented, and both legal and illegal anti-government images attracted collectors of all persuasions. However, for leftist sympathisers, anti-government postcards became items of great cultural and social cachet. Just as collecting them could be seen as a sign of good taste among the elite, owning opposition works also denoted clubability among the liberal intelligentsia. Possession was a badge of honour, marking out the individual who collected anti-government imagery as an enlightened soul, in step with the mood of the nation.

Boris Perott

The postcard collection of Russian medical student Boris Perott is the only contemporary grouping of anti-government images that I know to have survived intact.[26] It consists of just over three-hundred different postcards, ranging in date from 1904 to 1907, which are still preserved in Perott's original German-made album, bound in gilt-decorated red buckram. Without comparable examples, it is difficult to say with any certainty whether the collection is representative of other opposition compilations, but from a distance of over a hundred years, this is about the closest that it is possible to come to understanding the anti-government postcard acquisition patterns of the well-educated liberal members of society who were among their most regular purchasers.

In January 1905, Perott was a twenty-three-year-old student at the Imperial Military Medical Academy in Saint Petersburg.[27] His motivation for creating the collection must remain a matter of conjecture, but it is instructive to note that the first sixteen pages of the album contain postcards relating to the Imperial Fleet and the Russo-Japanese War. Scattered among the collection, there are also two portraits of the Tsar, and one each of the Tsarina and Tsarevich, Witte, and Stolypin. Their presence amid a mass of anti-government postcards is incongruous, and suggests both a development in Perott's political views, and a collecting interest centred as much on current events and postcards themselves as on the liberation movement.

The rest of the album, comprising some 250 postcards, is made up of anti-government images. These start with Bloody Sunday, run through the October Manifesto and the Moscow Uprising, and end with the Second

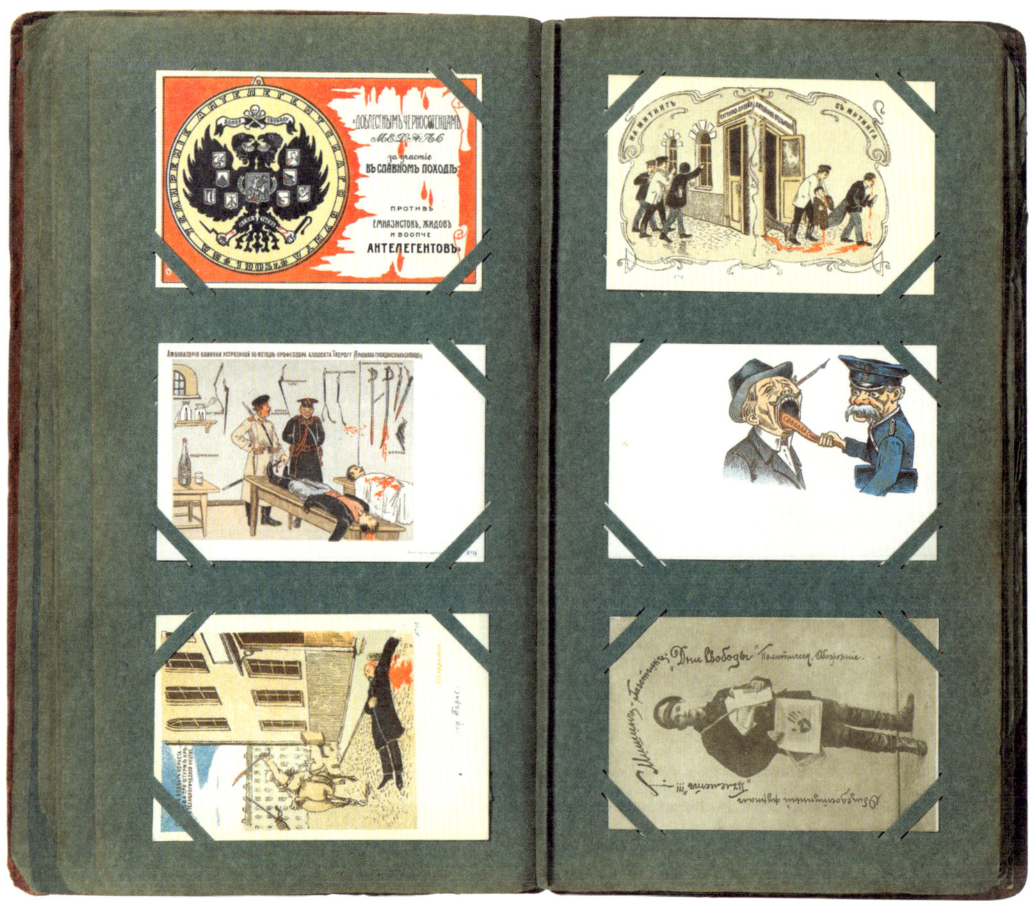

Postcard album belonging to Boris Perott, compiled circa 1904–1907 in Saint Petersburg.

Duma. The subject matter within this timeframe is very diverse. Alongside major events and portraits of leading revolutionaries, there is also less commonly found material, such as images of satirical journal sellers, the aftermath of Jewish pogroms, and, very unusually, dead protesters. Viewed in its entirety, Perott's collection immerses the viewer in every aspect of the Revolution, from questions of popular representation, to violent repression. The imagery is strongly oppositional in tone, but Perott's engagement appears to have been more experiential than ideological.

The variety of postcards in the album demonstrates what was possible to collect at the time. Most were still technically illegal, either due to their content, publisher, or lack of censorial imprimatur, but the majority would, nonetheless, still have been sold more or less openly, and therefore could have been bought by anyone with the money to spare. There were, however, grades of illegality, and postcards that dared to satirise the Tsar directly were far less easily acquired. Perott's collection has only three – likely more an indication of their scarcity than the dangers of purchase.[28] Indeed, the album attests to the fact that it was feasible to put together a large collection of anti-government postcards, seemingly without incurring any great risk.

The majority of Perott's postcards are photomechanical reproductions, but the album also contains some thirty chromolithographic cartoons. Their comparative prevalence indicates that he could afford to buy more expensive cards, and thus it can be presumed that his selection of images was not primarily dependent on financial considerations. Surprisingly, there is only one hand-drawn postcard, a caricature of Witte – their paucity perhaps reflecting personal preference. Cheaper typographical cards also find a place here alongside more expensive colour productions, suggesting that if collectors could afford to be, they were catholic in their tastes, and that at the upper end of the consumer range, price did not determine the type of postcards that were bought.

Postcards were sold individually, but many publishers printed sets in order to lure customers into making further acquisitions. Perott's album contains works from a number of different series, but none are complete. The possibility that this came down to a lack of availability or funds cannot be disregarded, but it ties into a more general pattern of Perott's collecting habits, which can reasonably be described as undisciplined. It is clear that he bought only the postcards that he liked, paying little attention to either artist or publisher. Several different firms are represented, including Merder, Freinkel, Metalnikov, Mysl, Peschanskii, Shipovnik, and Vpered. Just in this short list there are revolutionary, liberal, and commercial enterprises.

Perott's lack of discrimination highlights the generic nature of realist imagery and portraiture, little of which was unique, as well as the consequences of using commercial distribution practices to disseminate unmarked postcards. The latter enabled the revolutionaries to sell postcards en masse through shops and mail order without attracting undue attention from the authorities, but it meant that the organisation responsible lost any specific propaganda benefit. In the hands of consumers, anti-government postcards landed a blow against Tsarism, not a precision strike on behalf of a particular party. For consumers such as Perott therefore, anti-government postcards stood for a collective opposition to autocracy, no matter who produced them, or what the image was designed to represent.

Even where portraits of party activists were concerned, the personal appeal of a given figure often took precedence over their political attributes. Perott's collection contains several images of Socialist-Revolutionaries, including Balmashev, Kaliaev, Gershuni, and Spiridonova, but they compete for prominence with portraits of individuals as diverse as Father Gapon, Marx, and Duma Chairman Sergei Muromtsev, not to mention Witte, Stolypin and the Imperial Family. Perott was likely non-aligned, but a lack of doctrinal constraint in postcard buying holds true even the faithful.

For example, Elizaveta Schmidt, sister of the industrialist and revolutionary Nikolai Schmidt, balanced membership of the Social Democratic Party with owning postcards of Gershuni, Kaliaev, Spiridonova and Sazonov.[29]

The cards in Perott's collection therefore offer nothing on the specifics of his ideological beliefs, only a broad indication of his engagement with the notion of opposition. The extent of this engagement can only be guessed at, but given the presence of more loyalist imagery in the album, it would appear that Perott's decision to collect was at least in part a product of contemporary fashion and political circumstance. His postcards should therefore be seen, not so much as talismans of revolutionary allegiance, as political commodities that served to compliment his interests, character, and life experiences. The resulting collection was an object of contemplation and display, that in reflecting thoughts of opposition, also served to divert and entertain.

The postcards in Perott's album are in excellent condition and have evidently been little handled. The similarly pristine condition of many of the postcards found in today's collecting market indicates that storing them in this manner was common practice. Postcards that have been protected in albums are more likely to have survived, but their prevalence is further evidence that a sizable proportion of those who bought anti-government images were from a social milieu with sufficient income to buy and fill such albums. It also provides additional confirmation that most opposition postcards were not sent through the post, kept about the person, or used in the field, but instead enjoyed in the home, at their owner's discretion.

The use of anti-government postcards as objects of private display was very much in keeping with contemporary collecting practice.[30] As one enthusiast wrote: 'I collect foremost for myself, not to show off to others.' This does not, however, mean to say that their propaganda role was corrupted, or that they ended their lives as dead objects embalmed in cardboard mausoleums. Revolutionary material had in any case long been confined to the private sphere, but the fact is that postcards never had a solely ideological function. Their first task was to compete for custom in a crowded marketplace. Few publishers involved themselves with what happened next, trusting that where propaganda was concerned there was no such thing as bad publicity.

*

For revolutionary sympathisers, anti-government postcards played three main roles: they were a stimulus to thought and devotion, a guide to processing the political chaos, and a way of commemorating victims and preserving memories. By channelling the whirlwind of events into a partisan story of good triumphing over evil, opposition postcards answered a very human need to impose a rational narrative on the drama of revolution, while at the same time, serving to propagate anti-regime propaganda and create networks of individuals linked through common cause. However, as the messages that they carry show there were many different ways to engage with the unrest, and, even among particular social or political groups, there was no uniform response to the 1905 Revolution.

As the material expression of an individual mindset, opposition postcard consumption inevitably assumed a personal character. Neither the ideological orientation of the publisher nor the image itself predicated who bought particular images, or the way in which they were treated. Postcards intended for propaganda purposes could just as easily end up on the wall of a student dormitory, as they could be stored in the desk drawer of a private home. A picture on a revolutionary theme might serve as an object of temporary amusement, or one of fervent belief. When refracted through the lens of human experience, anti-government postcards came to be defined not only by their political dimension, but also by the lives of the people who bought them.

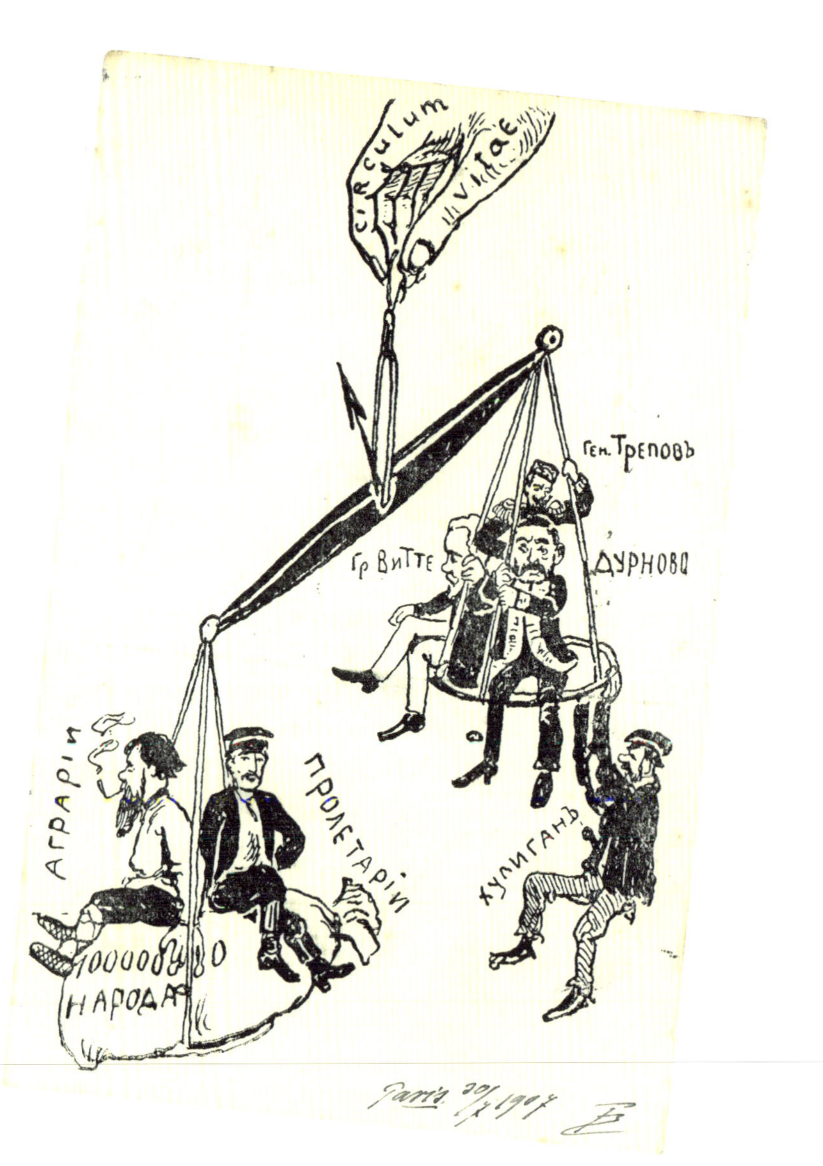
circulum vitae
ген. Треповъ
Гр Витте
Дурново
Аграріи
Пролетаріи
Хулиганъ
НАРОДА
Paris 20/X 1907

EPILOGUE

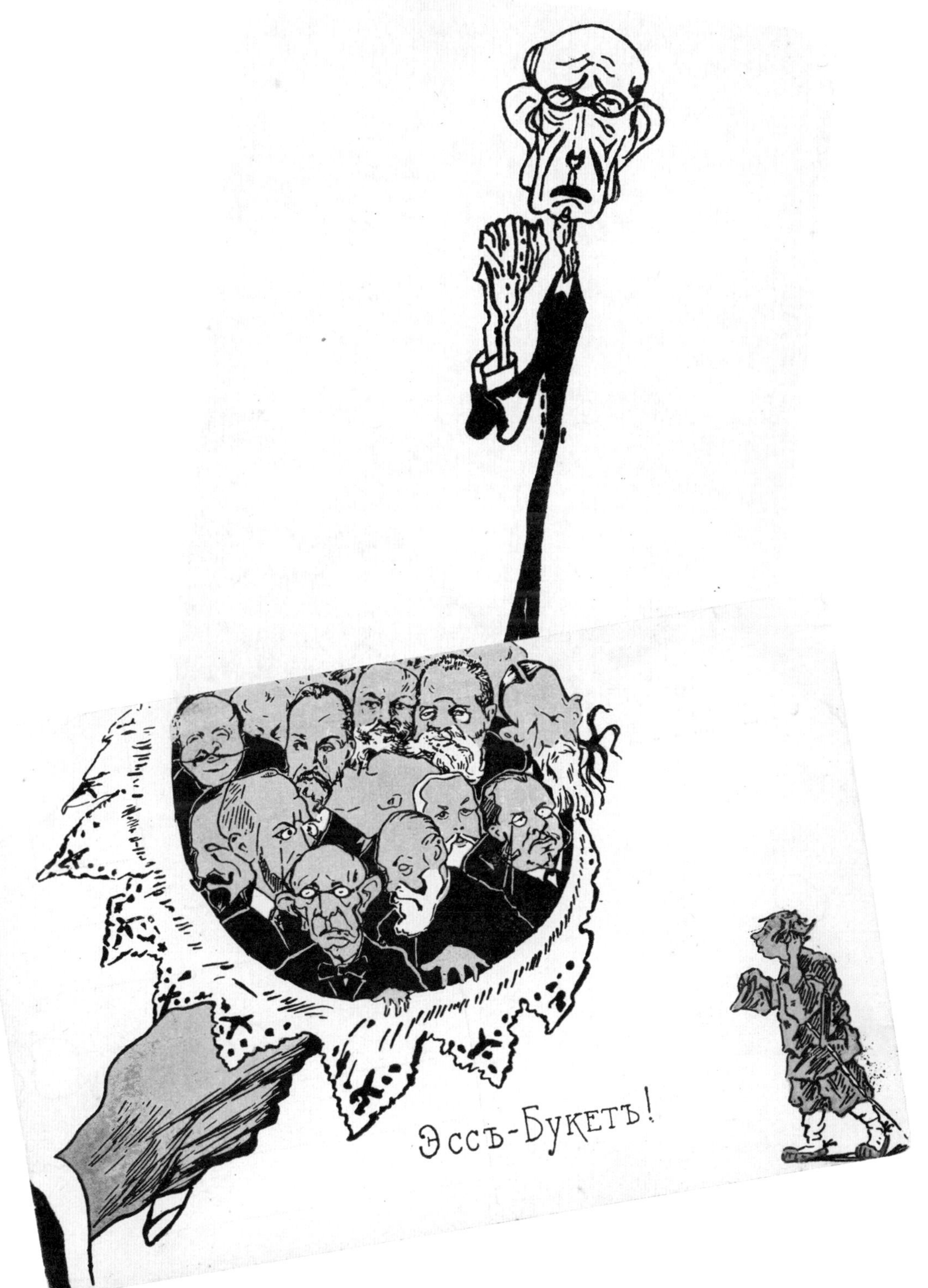

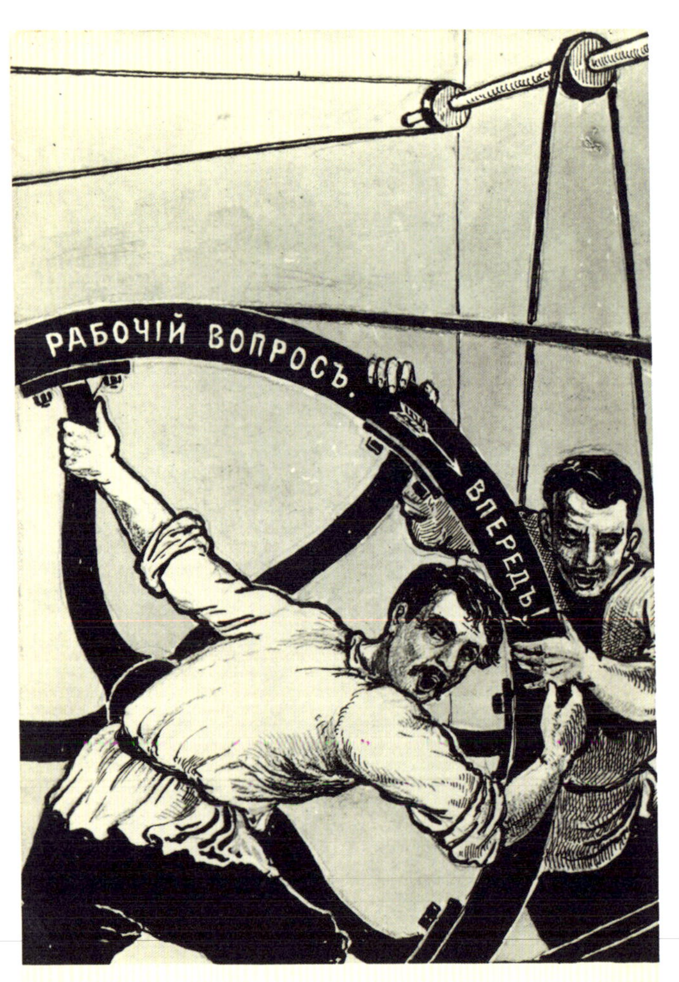

Впередъ!!!

Overview

In the early twentieth century, postcards gave people the opportunity to peer inside palaces, pin masterpieces on their wall, and travel to far-off lands. They were the great levellers of the age, a popular medium among rich and poor alike, granting the masses cheap access to the world's treasures, and thereby suggesting that they might have both an interest in and a right to the culture and history that had for so long been the preserve of the few. But as the new century marched on, and popular unrest in Russia grew, the people remained as far removed from the objects, and by extension the wealth and political privilege of the elite, as ever before. Picture postcards were just a glance through the window of an aristocrat's palace.

From the time of their introduction until the October Manifesto, the Tsarist regime succeeded in keeping postcard imagery largely untouched by opposition sentiment. But all the while other forces were in motion. As the censors toiled away, the print industry continued to expand, leading over the long term to the establishment of common spaces that lay beyond the immediate control of the regime. Even if few printed works referred to political events directly, the very existence of a non-governmental sphere of influence forced the state into competing with private enterprise for the attention of the masses. As in the factories, industrial development bolstered the mechanisms for resisting autocracy.

Open political subversion remained uncommon, but the growth of literacy and labour unrest led to ever-larger pools of potential recruits. In the early 1900s, revolutionary membership grew rapidly, and this in turn forced activists to come up with new ways of sustaining their embryonic groups, from imposing new bureaucratic structures, to diversifying propaganda output. Postcards had originally been conceived as a way of surmounting geographical boundaries, aiding cheap communication over distance. But the great popularity of the medium offered radicals the possibility of bridging a different gap, connecting the leaders who drove the theoretical side of the movement with the masses who thronged the streets.

Bloody Sunday was a transformative event, channelling widespread social discontent into concentrated political endeavour. With the vast increase in money and personnel that came their way, the revolutionaries set about taking advantage of a disordered government and restive population. Propaganda production and sales took off inside Russia itself, bringing in vital additional income and ideological influence. Throughout the year, opposition publishers of all persuasions pushed hard against the censor, but it was only after a general strike forced the Tsar to concede political ground that popular dissatisfaction received an official imprimatur. In principle, if not in practice, the Russian people were given their freedom.

Previous spread from left to right

Anonymous artist. *Circulum Vitae.* No publication details, late 1905. Captions on the left read: 'Agrarian', 'Proletarian' and '100,000,000 population', and on the right: 'Ct. Witte', 'Gen. Trepov', 'Durnovo', and 'Hooligan'.

Anonymous artist. Untitled caricature of Konstantin Pobedonostsev. No publication details, circa late 1905.

Anonymous artist. *Ess Bouquet.* No publication details, circa late 1905. Satire of chief government officials, among them: Aleksei Ignatiev, Vladimir Kokovtsov, Vladimir Gringmut, Vladimir Glazov, John of Kronstadt, Dmitrii Trepov, Konstantin Pobedonostsev, and Sergei Witte.

Opposite

Anonymous artist. *Forward!!!* No publication details, circa 1906. The wheel is marked 'The Labour Question → Forward!'

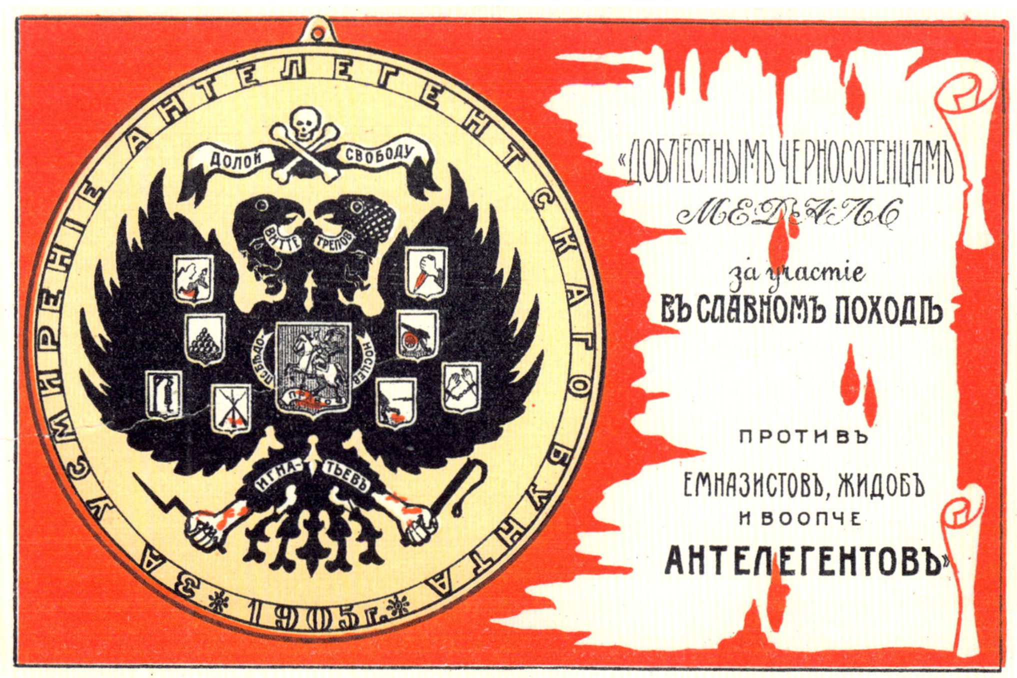

Anonymous artist. *Medal Awarded to the Valiant Black Hundreds for Participation in the Glorious Campaign against the Students, Yids and Intelligentsia in General.* No publication details, circa 1905. This satirical postcard depicts a fictional Black Hundreds award.

The deterioration in Imperial power that followed the October Manifesto opened up the commercial infrastructure of the print industry to the revolutionaries, enabling them to print and sell anti-government postcards in unprecedented numbers. Reduced risks of production and increased public appetite for politics proved an equal boon to private firms, who became enthusiastic participants in what one contemporary described as a publishing bacchanalia. Having been constrained for so long, the industry was now off the leash. Although intended as a moderate compromise, the Manifesto proved to be the release mechanism that allowed popular discontent to catch up with the social, technological, and commercial developments of the preceding fifty years.

The narrative of history is characterised by constant opportunism, whether for public or private gain, and this is particularly true for times of revolution, when uncertainty is easily exploited. The Tsar's decree legitimised the new public sphere, offering groups on all sides of the political divide the chance to publish their views openly, and at the same time to earn a healthy profit. It has long been assumed that the motivation to produce anti-government postcards was primarily ideological, but there can be no doubt that money also played a critical role. The effect of relaxing industry regulations was to create a vibrant trade in leftist wares, and as opposition belief became commodified, the dividing line between politics and commerce grew increasingly indistinct.

The government may once have been able to restrict revolutionary propaganda, but it struggled to stem the tide after private enterprise came aboard. There were simply too many individuals involved and too many opposition postcards being produced. The force of the industry-wide assault and the speed with which it took hold can be explained by the fact that the regime's political collapse had been preceded by the steady erosion of state dominance over the social arena, meaning that when the Revolution came, the government no longer had the power to shape popular understanding, either of its own actions or those of its opponents. With systems of production and delivery already in place, what the Manifesto provided was political and commercial expediency.

If private enterprise reacted to capitalist competition by diversifying postcard content and improving quality, then the radicals responded by endeavouring to enhance their methods of production. Both the main revolutionary parties continued to print anti-government postcards underground, but in late 1905 they redoubled efforts to create their own semi-legal publishing houses. Only through efficient organisation could the revolutionaries fund, produce and disseminate their propaganda in bulk, and only by taking advantage of the existing infrastructure of the legal publishing industry could they ever hope to achieve critical mass. For a party to be truly effective at this time, it not only needed a well-developed conspiratorial network, but also a sophisticated commercial one.

The commercialisation of revolutionary output after the October Manifesto was not so much a choice as a necessity. The greatest achievement of the 1905 Revolution was to have transformed politics from a minority interest, subject to the designs of the few, into a mass public activity. Similarly, following the Manifesto, anti-government postcard production expanded beyond the domain of the revolutionaries and into the ambit of the print industry at large, and as a result, was made subject to far larger commercial forces, outside their immediate control. As *Partiinye izvestiia* warned in 1906: 'The producer who does not tailor his organisation to the demands of the market will be left trailing in the wind, and risking bankruptcy.'[1]

It is ironic that the Marxist-inspired opposition was forced to engage with one of the key agencies of capitalism in order to realise their socialist ambitions, but the subordination of revolutionary propaganda to the consumer economy clearly proves the influence of the liberal-commercial sphere on revolutionary practices during this period.[2] A small market in anti-government wares already existed prior to the involvement of private publishing houses, but their participation brought a far greater degree of professionalism and pluralism to opposition production, a development that caused great concern to the regime. Just as during the October General Strike, the government was not imperilled by the force of one, but by the force of all.

For a short time, postcards became the ultimate visual representatives of the era, charged with bringing down the old and building up the new. In their imagery, the welfare of the nation was placed at centre stage, the lives and rights of the people made a crucial matter, just as relevant to the historical record as art and autocracy. The past may have been all about tsars and tsarinas, courtiers and generals, but in this new age, students, workers, and revolutionaries assumed their rightful place within the social hierarchy. Their dead and dying were commemorated, rather than crushed underfoot and swiftly forgotten. It truly was a revolutionary notion. For the first time, the people were told that they, too, had the right to demand more.

Ideological Impact

Postcards were an international phenomenon, but nowhere was their power to attract put to more concerted use than in Russia. Their popularity, size, and the comparative ease with which they could be printed and distributed, helped the medium to become the most widespread form of visual propaganda produced during the reign of the last Tsar. No other printed works can compete, either in the length of time that they were produced, or in the quantities that were manufactured.[3] This alone establishes the historical significance of anti-government postcards, making their longstanding obscurity all the more remarkable. Even so, the question must still be asked: Did postcard imagery have a tangible influence on the political beliefs of the Russian population during the 1905 Revolution?

Anti-government postcards are first and foremost compendiums of repression. State-sponsored violence is the unifying theme that runs through all the images of the period, from reproductions of paintings, through liberal cartoons, to revolutionary portraiture. Imperial oppression was universally despised and easily conveyed, but more than this, it was taken to represent the apex of autocratic injustice and abuse of power, and as such constituted a damning indictment of the system as whole. For all the reams of revolutionary political theory, in 1905, tyranny not only became the justification for continuing the struggle, but also the justification for the struggle itself. Tsarist despotism was the sine qua non of the liberation movement.

For the revolutionaries, autocratic oppression was like a wound that needed to be picked at regularly to remind the people of their pain and anger. Postcards acted as visual repositories of this emotional hurt, aiding the radicalisation of individuals inclined towards revolutionary action through a combination of partisan imagery and distressing subject matter. As Spiridonova showed, violence was a brutalising force that could turn young enthusiasts into cold-hearted killers. But even for those of a more liberal disposition, the widespread distribution of images showcasing government lawlessness served as a constant

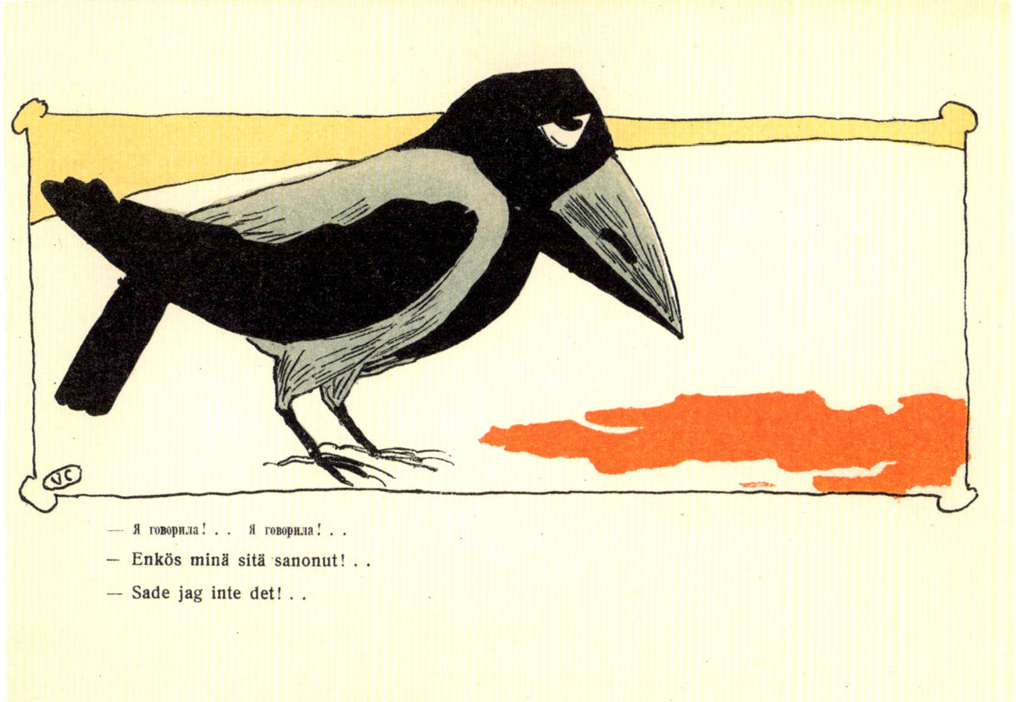

Valerii Karrik. *I Told You So!.. I Told You So!..* No publication details, circa mid-1906.

reiteration of the Tsar's preference for repression over reform, a blocked political pathway that pushed many into adopting more extreme positions.

The immorality of the regime was therefore the key premise on which the Tsar's enemies sought to delegitimise the autocratic state and legitimise their own opposition to it. If postcards had previously been used as a way of improving aesthetic taste among the masses, 'enabling even a peasant who receives only a couple of cards a year to choose between the fairer of the two,' then during the 1905 Revolution images of government brutality served as a way of educating the population on the rights and wrongs of Imperial politics.[4] In this way, postcards made commonplace the notion that the autocratic state was a murderous entity that cared nothing for its people, and in so doing helped deprive the Tsar of his moral authority to rule.

The first Russian postcard-collecting journal was named *The Home Museum*, a title that accurately captures the aim of the hobby itself, which was to create a small-scale conceptual arena in which an individual could curate, explore, and expound upon personal interests and ideas. Collecting anti-government postcard imagery was no different; it served to construct a pictorial world through which an alternative reality could be lived, one that allowed revolutionary sympathisers and the nation at large to live out a political fantasy of opposition power and authority. This political paradigm not only gave wings to a new vision of how the country should be ruled, but also critically undercut the official narrative of Imperial rule.

However, while postcards played a significant part in propagandising government repression and justifying revolutionary responses, their political influence largely remained non-specific. Irrespective of the original aims of their publishers, most cards did not serve as vehicles for party-political ideology. This was primarily due to the difficulties of identifying producers – the result of widespread crossover of imagery and lack of identifying marks – but it was also because consumer allegiances were so often fluid. Revolutionary portraiture was more obviously partisan, but as a rule, postcards played only a minimal part in increasing support for specific groups, instead occupying a more generic position in pushing for change among the nation at large.[5]

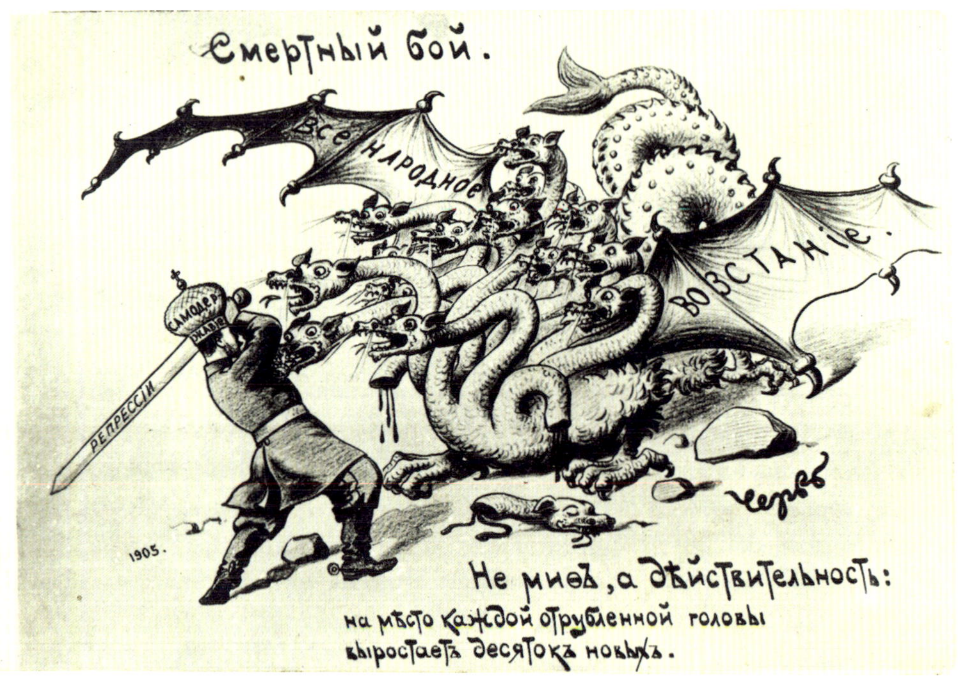

Mikhail Chemodanov. *Fight to the Death. Not Myth but Reality. For Each Head That Is Cut Off, Nine New Ones Will Grow in its Place.* Printed by Dmitrii Peschanskii, Moscow, drawn in 1905, but published circa 1906.

Among buyers, postcard consumption assumed many different forms. Seditious content naturally ensured that many images ended up in the hands of committed activists, but by early 1906 the discourse of political opposition had seeped so far into the fabric of everyday life that the purchase of subversive wares had become a wholly mainstream activity. Messages on the reverse of anti-government postcards bear testament to the ubiquity of their appeal, and the subjectivity of their usage. Within the domestic setting that characterised contemporary postcard consumption, everyday concerns were woven into the larger political narrative, with opposition ideology often being made subordinate to the emotions and experiences of the owner.

The extraordinary quantity of postcards produced during the 1905 Revolution shows how widespread opposition imagery and ideas became in Imperial Russia. But while their content did unquestionably influence popular opinion, political belief was always a complicated and at times amorphous concept. Opposition to the regime was rarely binary. Indeed, anti-government postcards show both the range of different views that were held at this time, and the subtlety of the ways in which they could be expressed, from full-blown rebellion to gentle mockery. Postcards should therefore also be understood as a form of popular release, constituting a significant public space in which political views could be voiced, without the need for firm commitment.

But, on a national level, postcards helped to shape the story of the Revolution, documenting and publicising the demonstrations, violence, and betrayals that so polluted the political landscape. They brought to life events for those who had only read or heard about them, and through mass production and circulation introduced opposition imagery into everyday currency. If dissatisfaction with the status quo acquired a more robust political form in 1905, then postcards channelled the emerging social consciousness, guiding partisan interpretations of different episodes in the revolutionary struggle, and ensuring that a version of events sharply at odds with government statements would find a place in homes across Russia for years to come.[6]

Not Quite the End

Any attempt to evaluate the importance and worth of anti-government postcards to the opposition must also consider their success in generating income. Despite the paucity of detailed sales figures, the Socialist-Revolutionary Party's financial statements show that under the right political and administrative circumstances, postcards made a small but notable contribution to Party funds. Concrete evidence of their financial value can also be found in the memoirs of Bonch-Bruevich and Belopolskii, who each separately highlight the importance of production in raising funds for the Social Democratic Party. Significantly, both also state that the money generated from postcard sales proved crucial in getting their own respective publishing ventures off the ground.[7]

Among private publishers, the rationale for manufacturing anti-government material varied widely, but the one constant was money, and here again, evidence of their economic importance is not hard to find. Vladimir Kurbatov's unlikely suggestion that the Society of Saint Eugenia sell socialist-themed postcards in order to boost its wavering revenues offers firm proof of their financial draw during the turbulent period after the October Manifesto. But the best indication of their economic appeal can be found in the sheer number of opposition postcards that were printed. If the propaganda effect of a particular image was impossible for a publisher to quantify, then its ability to generate money was far more easily and quickly ascertained.

Partial deregulation resulted in greatly increased political and economic opportunity for publishers, but the commercial viability of anti-government material always remained at the mercy of the regime. Imperial fiat had turned on the taps, and so, too, could it turn them off. In mid-1906, as repression was ratcheted up, regional governors started imposing martial law with ever greater frequency. Under emergency regulations, governors had the right to confiscate any opposition material that they deemed a threat to public order, whether or not it had been passed fit for publication. Coming at a time when the wider population was losing its appetite for the fight, the laws proved a powerful impediment to production.

For all their efforts to muzzle publishers and sellers using punitive deterrents, it was only by threatening profits – effectively by outlawing the sale of all leftist postcards – that the regime finally eradicated subversive imagery. Shops continued to stock less contentious images until mid-1907, but notice had been served long before. Production thereafter continued underground, but with diminished resources and no access to the commercial trade, the revolutionaries found themselves back in the same situation they had been in prior to Bloody Sunday. And with that the experiment was over. Despite genuine efforts to institute a new modus operandi, the pace of change had been too fast and too furious for the tastes of a reactionary Tsar.

By 1908, the visual traces of revolution had been effaced, but for the regime and the country as a whole, this could never be a simple return to business as usual. Opposition institutions had been severely weakened, but they had not been entirely destroyed. In the political sphere the Duma still stood. However emasculated it may have become after the promulgation of new electoral laws in June 1907, a legislative assembly filled with representatives of legal political parties served by its very existence to dilute autocratic power. And in respect of the print industry as a whole, the Revolution left a significant legacy of wider readership, increased periodical titles, stronger political content, and bigger print runs.

Beyond this, the popular mindset had evolved. The Tsar retained power because the army held fast in the face of a divided opposition and, equally importantly, he himself did not lose heart. Nevertheless, one of the most significant attainments of the Revolution was to have briefly pushed a broad swathe of the public into opposing the regime. Repression proved an effective deterrent to sedition, but while the nation may have been pacified, it was not at peace. Thoughts of change rose and fell over the following decade, boosted after the Lena Goldfields massacre, distracted by nationalism during the First World War, but they never entirely disappeared. The 1905 Revolution had planted the seeds of change, both in the system itself and in people's attitudes towards it.[8]

In common with other expressions of popular revolt, anti-government postcards were not only political phenomena occasioned by specific events, but also products of social and economic development, inextricably linked to Russia's advance towards modernity – in their case, increases in literacy, growth of the print industry, and establishment of a commercial class. And therein lies the rub: while the more obvious symptoms of revolution were readily cured, the underlying causes required a far stronger and more prolonged course of treatment. In 1905, a Pandora's box of opposition politics had been momentarily opened, and then just as quickly slammed shut. The government survived a critical test, but the long path towards modernity was still paved with potential pitfalls.

This does not mean, however, that the regime's problems were intractable, or that 1917 was inevitable. The political plurality and growth of civil society to which the turmoil had given rise opened up several possible routes forward, of which bloody revolution was by no means the most likely. While there was a concentrated period of retrenchment after 1905, the era as a whole can in fact be seen as one of gradual modernisation. Although erratic and troubled by severe birth pains, the Russian state and nation at large were slowly shedding their absolutist past and progressing towards a different, less despotic age. Moreover, the Imperial regime had shown that it was sufficiently robust to effect moderate change without succumbing to its internal foes.

But if not fatal, the 1905 Revolution and its printed offshoots still inflicted a deep wound on the autocratic state – a wound that needed time and care to heal. However, the government's continued suppression of the population, and the ongoing concentration of political power in the hands of one man left the regime far less able to weather the challenges that inevitably arise during the natural course of governance, something that an estranged public sphere did little to help. Russia's entry into the First World War and the economic and military collapse that ensued exposed the brittleness of the system, and as the popular mood turned against the Tsar, all the unresolved issues of the recent past came bubbling back to the surface.

Next spread

Anonymous artist. *One More Blow and They Will All Fall.* No publication details, late 1905. The ball is inscribed 'General Political Strike'. Among the officials depicted are Dmitrii Trepov, Baron Frederiks, Sergei Witte, and Konstantin Pobedonostsev.

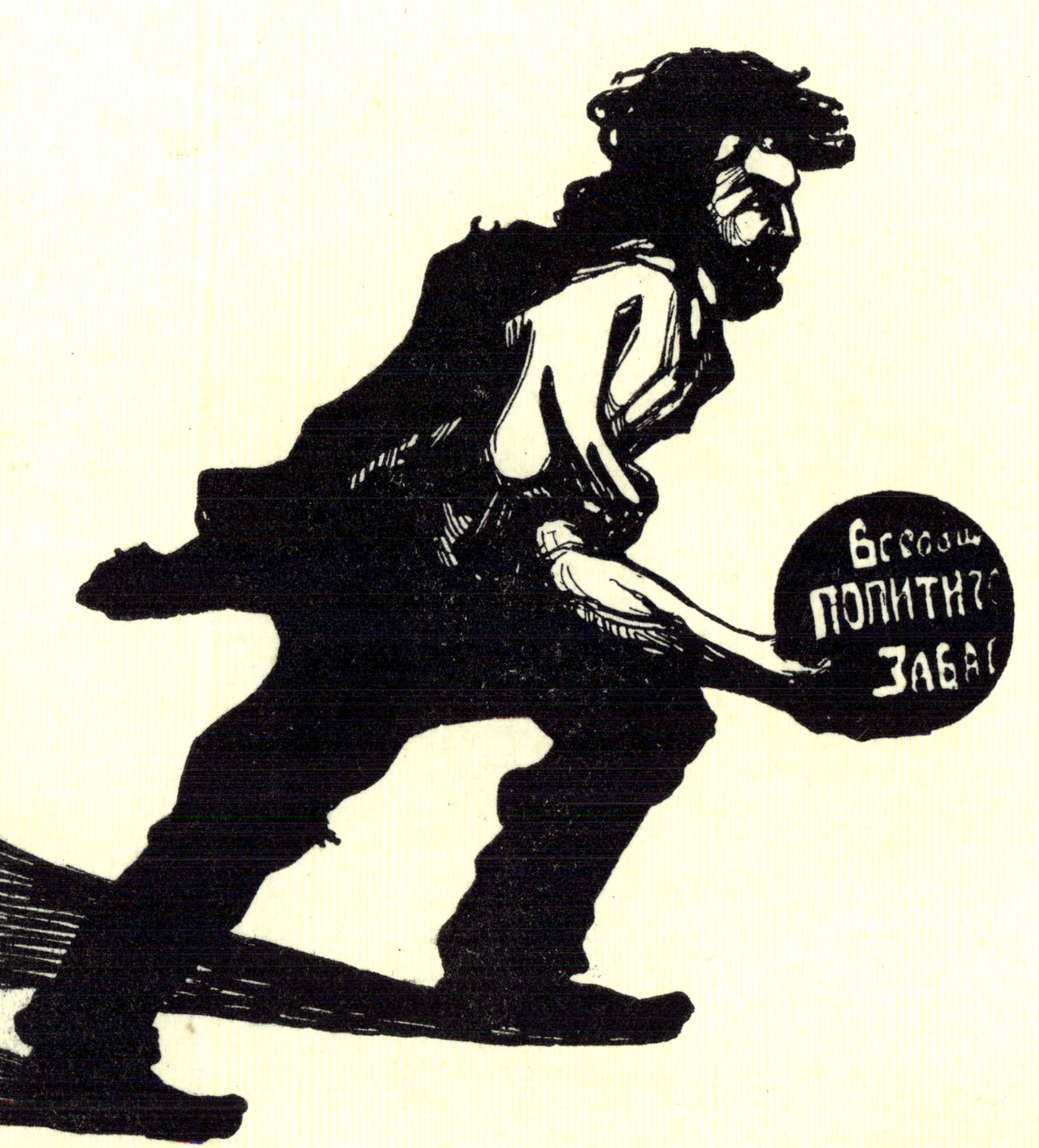

– Еш

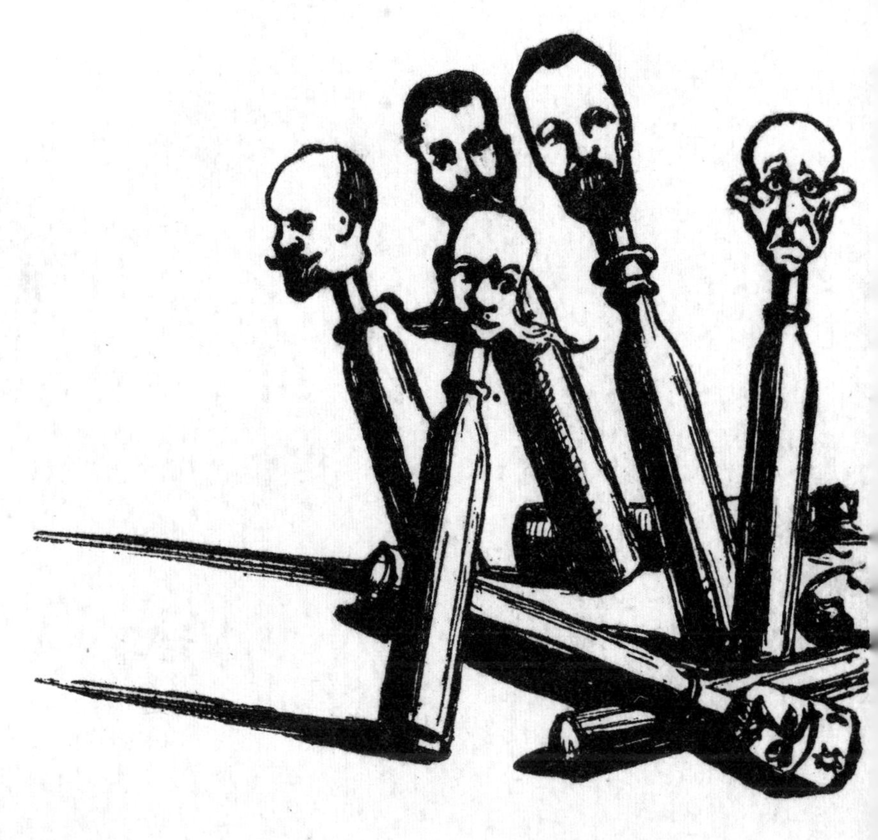

ДАРЪИ ВСЕ ПАДЕТЪ —

Abbreviations used for Archives and Museum Collections

GARF
State Archive of the Russian Federation, Moscow, Russia

GRM OR
State Russian Museum, Saint Petersburg, Russia: Manuscripts Department [Otdel rukopisei]

HIWRP BNC/OA
Hoover Institution on War, Revolution, and Peace, Stanford, United States: Boris Nikolaevsky Collection/Okhrana Archive

IISG PSR
International Institute of Social History, Amsterdam, Holland: Socialist Revolutionary Party Archives

LRA FA
Leeds University Library, Leeds Russian, Archive, Leeds, United Kingdom: Felicity Ashbee Papers (Carrick Family)

MM FC
Museum of Moscow, Moscow, Russia: Chemodanov Family Papers [Fond Chemodanovykh]

MSI KF/FG
Museum of Contemporary History, Moscow, Russia: Postcard Collection [Kollektsiia filokartii]/Graphic Art Department [Fond Grafiki]

RGALI
Russian State Archive of Literature and Art, Moscow, Russia

RGASPI
Russian State Archive of Socio-Political History, Moscow, Russia

RGB OR/KF
Russian State Library, Moscow, Russia: Manuscripts Department [Otdel rukopisei]/Fond IZO, Postcard Collection [Kollektsiia filokartii]

RGIA
Russian State Historical Archive, Saint Petersburg, Russia

RNB OE
Russian National Library, Saint Petersburg, Russia: Print Department [Otdel estampov]

TsGIA SPB
Central State Historical Archive of Saint Petersburg, Saint Petersburg, Russia

TsDIAK
Central State Historical Archive of Ukraine in Kyiv, Kyiv, Ukraine

Selected Bibliography

PERIODICALS

Adskaia pochta. Saint Petersburg, 1906
Biblioteka nashikh chitatelei. Saint Petersburg, 1906
Byloe. Saint Petersburg, 1906–1907
Domashnii muzei. Saint Petersburg, 1904–1907
Iskra. Leipzig, Munich, London, Geneva 1900–1905
Iskry (Illustrated supplement to *Russkoe slovo*). Moscow, 1905–1906
Knizhnyi vestnik. Saint Petersburg, 1905–1906
Kramola. Moscow, 1905
Krestianskii listok. Viatka: Izdanie krest'ianskoi komissii pri Viatskom komitete P. S-R., 1905–1906
Leshii. Saint Petersburg, 1906
Literaturno-khudozhestvennye al'manakhi izdatel'stva Shipovnik. Saint Petersburg, 1907–1909
L'Illustration. Paris, 1905
Manchester Guardian. Manchester, 1908
Na rasput'i. Moscow 1906
Nasha mysl'. Saint Petersburg, 1906
Niva. Saint Petersburg, 1905–1906
Novaia mysl'. Moscow, 1906
Novaia zhizn'. Saint Petersburg, 1905
Novosti dnia. Moscow, 1904–1905
Otkrytka. Kaluga, 1907–1909
Otkrytoe pis'mo. Saint Petersburg, 1904–1906
Otkrytoe pis'mo. Uman, 1906
Partiinye izvestiia. Saint Petersburg: Izdanie Tsentral'nogo komiteta partii Sotsialistov-Revoliutsionerov, 1906–1907
Piatnitsa. Saint Petersburg, 1907
Pochtovo-telegrafnyi zhurnal. Otdel neofitsial'nyi. Saint Petersburg: Tipografiia Ministerstva vnutrennikh del, Various dates.
Pulemet. Saint Petersburg, 1905
Revoliutsionnaia Rossiia. Kuokkala, Tomsk, Geneva, 1900–1905
Rus'. Saint Petersburg, 1906
Simplicissimus. Munich, 1904–1906
Strely. Saint Petersburg, 1906
Svet i teni. Moscow, 1881
The Illustrated London News. London, 1905
The Sphere. London, 1905
Trud. Saint Petersburg: Izdanie Peterburgskogo komiteta i soveta rabochego soiuza, 1906–1908
Volia. Nagasaki: Izdanie Sotsialistov-Revolutsionerov, 1906–8
Vestnik zhizni. Saint Petersburg, 1906
Volna. Saint Petersburg, 1906
Vpered. Saint Petersburg, 1906
Zhalo. Moscow, 1905
Zhupel. Saint Petersburg, 1905–1906
Zritel'. Saint Petersburg, 1905–1906

BOOKS

Alfavitnyi ukazatel' knigam i broshiuram, arest na kotorye utverzhden sudebnymi ustanovleniiami po 1-e ianvaria 1910 goda. Saint Petersburg: Tipografiia Ministerstva vnutrennikh del, 1910
Ascher, Abraham. *The Revolution of 1905: Russia in Disarray*. Stanford: Stanford University Press, 1988
Ascher, Abraham. *The Revolution of 1905: Authority Restored*. Stanford: Stanford University Press, 1992
Balmuth, Daniel. *Censorship in Russia, 1865–1905*. Washington: University Press of America, 1979
Bel'gard, A. V. *Vospominaniia*. Moscow: Novoe literaturnoe obozrenie, 2009
Benua, A. N. *Moi vospominaniia*. Kniga IV, Moscow: Nauka, 1980
Bonch-Bruevich, Vladimir. *Kak pechatalis' za granitsei i taino dostavlialis' v Rossiiu zapreshchennye izdaniia nashei partii*. Moscow: Zhizn' i znanie, 1924
Bonch-Bruevich, V. D. *Bol'shevistskie izdatel'skie dela v 1905–1907 gg: Moi vospominaniia*. Leningrad: Leningradskoe oblastnoe izdatel'stvo, 1933
Botsianovskii, V and E. Gollerbakh. *Russkaia satira pervoi russkoi revoliutsii 1905–1906 gg.* Leningrad: Gosudarstvennoe izdatel'stvo, 1925
Brooks, Jeffrey. *When Russia Learned to Read*. New Jersey: Princeton University Press, 1993
Chapkina, Mariia. *Khudozhestvennaia otkrytka. K stoletiiu otkrytki v Rossii*. Moscow: Galart, 1993
Chernov, V. M. *Pered burei*. New York: Izdatel'stvo imeni Chekhova, 1953
Dayot, Armand. *La Révolution Française*. Paris: Flammarion, 1896
Dayot, Armand. *Journées révolutionnaires, 1830–1848*. Paris: Flammarion, 1897
Dayot, Armand. *L'Invasion. Le Siège 1870, La Commune 1871*. Paris: Flammarion, Undated
Demchenko, E. P. *Politicheskaia grafika Kieva perioda revoliutsii 1905–1907 gg.* Kiev: Naukova Dumka, 1976
Demchenko, E. P. *Politicheskaia grafika v pechati Ukrainy 1905–1907*. Kiev, 1984
Doklad delegatsii Rossiiskoi Sots.-Dem. Rabochei Partii Amsterdamskomu Mezhdunarodnomu Sotsialisticheskomu Kongressu (14–20 August 1904). Zheneva: Izdanie Rossiiskoi Sotsial'demokraticheskoi Rabochei Partii, 1904
Dreiden, Sim. *V zritel'nom zale – Vladimir Il'ich*. Moscow: Iskusstvo, 1967
Dreiden, S. and K. Chukovskii. *Russkaia revolutsiia v satire i iumore*. Moscow: Izvestiia TSIK SSSR I VTSIK, 1925
Dul'skii, P. *Grafika satiricheskikh zhurnalov 1905–1906 gg.* Kazan: Tatgosizdata, 1922
Durand, Kellogg. *The Red Reign*. London: Hodder and Stoughton, 1907
Engelstein, Laura. *Moscow, 1905. Working-Class Organisation and Political Conflict*. Stanford: Stanford University Press, 1982
Fainshtein, E. B. *V mire otkrytki*. Moscow: Planeta, 1976
Figner, Vera. *Polnoe sobranie sochinenii v semi tomakh*. Moscow: Izdatel'stvo Vsesoiuznogo obshchestva politkatorzhan i ssyl'no-poselentsev, 1932
Gebhardt, Manfred. *Ein Hauch von Maienblüte: Postkarten der deutschen Arbeiterbewegung zum 1. Mai*. Berlin: Verlag Tribüne, 1989
Geifman, Anna. *Thou Shalt Kill, Revolutionary Terrorism in Russia, 1894–1917*. New Jersey: Princeton University Press, 1993
Geifman, Anna. *Death orders: The Vanguard of Modern Terrorism in Revolutionary Russia*. Santa Barbara: Praeger, 2010
Golubeva, O. D. *V. D. Bonch-Bruevich, izdatel'*. Moscow: Kniga, 1972
Gor'kii i Leonid Andreev: Neizdannaia perepiska. Moscow: Nauka (Literaturnoe nasledstvo Tom 72), 1965
Gor'kii, Maksim. *Sobranie sochinenii*. Tom 28, Moscow, 1954
Harcave, Sidney. *First Blood. The Russian Revolution of 1905*. London: The Bodley Head, 1964

Hildermeier, Manfred. *The Russian Socialist-Revolutionary Party Before the First World War*. Palgrave Macmillan, 2000

Iliushin, Aleksandr (Ed.). *Pochtovye kartochki Rossiiskoi imperii s reklamnymi ob'iavleniiami / Tsel'nye veshchi*. Kirov: Izdatel'skii dom 'Krepostnov', 2014

Isakov, S. *1905 god v satire i karikature*. Leningrad: Priboi, 1928

Ioffe, A. M. *Izdatel'skaia deiatel'nost' bol'shevikov v 1905–1907 gg.* Moscow: Kniga, 1971

Ivan Platonovich Kaliaev. Paris: Partiia Sotsialistov-Revoliutsionerov (otdel'nyi ottisk iz 'Rev. Ross'), 1905

Izveshchenie o vtorom ocherednom s"ezde rossiiskoi sotsialdemokraticheskoi rabochei partii. Zheneva: Izdanie tsentral'nogo komiteta RSDRP, 1903

Lane, David. *The Roots of Russian Communism. A Social and Historical Study of Russian Social-Democracy, 1898–1907*. Assen: Van Gorcum, 1969

Larina, Anna Nikolaevna. *Dokumental'naia otkrytka kontsa XIX-nachala XX vv. kak istochnik po istorii i kul'ture Moskvy*. Ph.D. Dissertation, Moscow: Rossiiskii gosudarstvennyi gumanitarnyi universitet, 2004

Larina, Anna. *Istoriia Moskvy v pochtovoi otkrytke*, Moscow: Moskvovedenie, 2010

Lenin, N. *Chto delat'*. Stuttgart: Verlag von J. H. W. Dietz Nachf., 1902

Levitt, Marcus and Oleg Minin (Eds.). *The Satirical Journals of the First Russian Revolution, 1905–1907*. Experiment, Volume 19, Issue 1, 2013

Maiskii, Ivan. *Pered burei, Vospominaniia*. Moscow: OGIZ, 1944

McReynolds, Louise. *The News Under Russia's Old Regime. The Development of a Mass-Circulation Press*. New Jersey: Princeton University Press, 1993

Minin, Oleg. *Art and Politics in the Russian Satirical Press, 1905–1908*. Ph. D. dissertation. University of Southern California, 2008

Moskovskoe vooruzhennoe vosstanie. Vypusk 1-i. Moscow: Letopis', 1906

Mozokhina, Natal'ia. *Otkrytki Obshchiny Sv. Evgenii kak khudozhestvennyi proekt masterov ob"edineniia 'Mir iskusstva'. Problemy istorii i khudozhestvennoi prakitiki*. Ph.D. dissertation. Rossiiskaia akademiia khudozhestv, Moscow, 2009

M. Gor'kii na rodine: Sbornik vospominanii o zhizni M. Gor'kogo v Nizhnem Novgorode. Gor'kii: OGIZ, 1937

Nashchokina, Mariia. *Khudozhestvennaia otkrytka russkogo moderna*. Moscow: Zhiraf, 2004

Norris, Stephen. *A War of Images: Russian Popular Prints, Wartime Culture, and National Identity*. DeKalb: Northern Illinois University Press, 2006

Obzor khudozhestvennykh izdanii Obshchiny Sv. Evgenii. Saint Petersburg, 1909

Otkrytye pis'ma i drugie khudozhestvennye izdaniia Krasnogo kresta. Izdanie vtoroe. Saint Petersburg, 1903

Ouspensky, Leonid and Vladimir Lossky. *The Meaning of Icons*. Crestwood, New York: Saint Vladimir's Seminary Press, 1982

Pamiatnaia knizhka Sotsialista-revoliutsionera. Vypusk 1, Paris, 1911

Pares, Bernard. *My Russian Memoirs*. London: Jonathan Cape, 1931

Politicheskaia grafika vremeni revoliutsii 1905–1907 gg v zhurnalakh i na otkrytkakh: katalog vystavki. Kiev, 1980

Programma i organizatsionnyi ustav Partii Sotsialistov-revoliutsionerov, utverzhdennye na pervom partiinom s"ezde. Izdanie Tsentral'nogo komiteta P. S-R., 1906

Rice, Christopher. *Russian Workers and the Socialist-Revolutionary Party through the Revolution of 1905–07*. New York: Saint Martin's Press, 1988

Rowley, Alison. *Open Letters. Russian Popular Culture and the Picture Postcard 1880–1922*. Toronto: University of Toronto Press, 2013

Ruud, Charles. *Fighting Words: Imperial Censorship and the Russian Press, 1804–1906*. Toronto: University of Toronto Press, 1982

Samuilikovich, N., N. Shmitt-Fogelivich and S. Mianik. (Eds.). *Peterburg – Petrograd – Leningrad v otkrytkakh 1895–1945*. Leningrad: BAN, 1984

Shleev, V. V. *Revoliutsiia 1905–1907 godov i izobrazitel'noe iskusstvo*. Moscow: Izobrazitel'noe Iskusstvo, 1987

Shleev, V. V. *Iz istorii russkoi revoliutsionnoi otkrytki*. Vypusk 1. Moscow: Izobrazitel'noe iskusstvo, 1974

Shleev, V. V. *Revoliutsiia 1905–1907 godov i izobrazitel'noe iskusstvo: Peterburg*. Moscow: Izobrazitel'noe iskusstvo, 1977

Shleev, V. V. *Revoliutsiia 1905–1907 godov i izobrazitel'noe iskusstvo: Moskva i rossiiskaia provintsiia*. Moscow: Izobrazitel'noe iskusstvo, 1978

Shleev, V. V. and E. B. Fainshtein. *Khudozhestvennye otkrytki i ikh sobranie*. Moscow: Izobrazitel'noe iskusstvo, 1960

Shliapnikov, Aleksandr. *Nakanune 1917 goda*. Moscow, 1920

Skipton, David and Peter Michalove. *Postal Censorship in Imperial Russia*. Volume 1. Urbana: John H. Otten, 1989

Spravochnik filokartista. No. 1. Moscow: Prilozhenie k zhurnalu dlia kollektsionerov otkrytok 'Zhuk' No. 2–3 (10–11), 2006

Spektor, U. M. *Severnoe izdatel'stvo V. O. Zheglinskogo*. Moscow: Vsesoiuznoe dobrovol'noe obshchestvo liubitelei knigi, 1988

Spiridovich, A. I. *Partiia Sotsialistov-Revoliutsionerov i ee predshestvenniki 1886–1916*. Izdanie vtoroe. Petrograd: Voennaia tipografiia, 1918

Stasova, Elena. *Stranitsy zhizni i bor'by*. Moscow: Gosudarstvennoe izdatel'stvo politicheskoi literatury, 1960

Stasova, Elena. *Vospominaniia*. Moscow: Mysl', 1969

Stepniak, Sergei. *Underground Russia*. London: Smith, Elder and Co., 1890

Sverchkov, D. *Na zare revoliutsii*. Izd. tret'e. Leningrad: Gosudarstvennoe izdatel'stvo, 1925

Tagrin, N. *V poiskakh neobychnogo: iz zapisok kollektsionera*. Leningrad: Lenizdat, 1962

Tagrin, N. *Mir v otkrytke*, Moscow. Izobrazitel'noe iskusstvo, 1978

Tret'iakov, V. P. *Otkrytye pis'ma Serebrianogo veka*. Saint Petersburg: Slaviia, 2000

Tret'ii s"ezd RSDRP: Protokoly. Moscow: Gosudarstvennoe izdatel'stvo politcheskoi literatury, 1959

Vitte, Sergei. *Vospominaniia tsarstvovaniia Nikolaia II.* Tom. I. Berlin: Slovo, 1922

Vladimirov, V. E. *Mariia Spiridonova: S portretom i risunkami, s predisloviem ot Soiuza ravnopraviia zhenshchin.* Moscow: Tip. A. P. Poplavskogo, 1906

Wortman, Richard S. *Scenarios of Power: Myth and Ceremony in Russian Monarchy from Peter the Great to the Abdication of Nicholas II.* Princeton: Princeton University Press, 2006

Zabochen', Mikhail. *Filokartiia.* Moscow: Sviaz', 1973

Zavarzin, P. P. *Rabota tainoi politsii.* V dvukh chastiakh. Paris: Izdanie Avtora, 1924

Zelikson-Bobrovskaia, Ts. (Ed.). *Pervaia russkaia revoliutsiia v Peterburge 1905 g. Sbornik statei, vospominanii, materialov i dokumentov.* Moscow/Leningrad: Gosudarstvennoe izdatel'stvo, 1925

Zelikson-Bobrovskaia, Ts. (Ed.). *Pervaia russkaia revoliutsiia v Peterburge 1905 g. Sbornik 2-oi: Po fabrikam i zavodam.* Leningrad: Gosudarstvennoe izdatel'stvo, 1925

Zhirkov, G. V. *Istoriia tsensury v Rossii XIX–XX vv.* Moscow: Aspekt Press, 2001

ARTICLES

Anonymous. 'La rage des cartes-postales'. *Domashnii muzei.* No. 1, Saint Petersburg, April 1904, pp. 5–6

Anonymous. 'Nashi izdaniia'. *Domashnii muzei.* No. 2, Saint Petersburg, October 1904, p. 5

Anonymous. 'Nasha fabrika'. *Domashnii muzei.* No. 2, Saint Petersburg, October 1904, pp. 6–7

Anonymous. 'Voina!'. No. 1, Saint Petersburg, April 1904, pp. 6–7

Anonymous. 'O geroiakh'. *Pulemet.* No. 1, Saint Petersburg, 1905, p. 9

Anonymous. 'Zagranichnaia pechat' o polozhenii otkrytochnoi torgovli'. *Otkrytoe pis'mo.* No. 1, Uman, 1906, p. 5

Ashbee, F. 'Fotograf s Maloi Morskoi'. *Iunost'.* No. 7, 1976, p. 102

Avel'-Avok, A. L. 'Satira v zhurnalakh i gazetakh'. *Vestnik znaniia.* No. 2, Saint Petersburg, 1906, pp. 382–393

Belopol'skii I. P. 'Vospominaniia uchastnikov Pervoi russkoi revoliutsii'. *Voprosy istorii,* No. 12, 1955, pp. 42–44

Bonch-Bruevich, Vladimir. 'Biblioteka i arkhiv RSDRP v Zheneve'. *Krasnaia letopis'.* No. 3 (48), 1932, pp. 110–115

Boniece, Sally A. 'The Spiridonova Case, 1906: Terror, Myth and Martyrdom'. *Just Assassins: The Culture of Terrorism in Russia.* Evanston: Northwestern University Press, 2010, pp. 127–151

Botsianovskii, V. 'Karikatura i tsenzura v nachale XX veka. Iz vospominanii redaktora satiricheskogo zhurnala'. *Byloe* No. 26, Leningrad, 1924, pp. 177–206

Carlson, John. 'Postcards and Propaganda: Cartographic Postcards as Soft News Images of the Russo-Japanese War'. *Political Communication.* Volume 26, No. 2, 2009, pp. 212–37

Cherepov, V. L. 'Revoliutsionnye satiricheskie otkrytki v Ekaterinburge'. *Iz istorii khudozhestvennoi kul'tury Urala.* Sverdlovsk. 1980, pp. 60–75

Daly, Jonathan W. 'On the Significance of Emergency Legislation in Late Imperial Russia'. *Slavic Review,* Vol. 54, No. 3, 1995, pp. 602–629

Dediukhina, V. 'Fotografii A. K. Zavadskogo po vooruzhennomu vosstaniiu v Moskve (dekabr' 1905 g.).' *Trudy Gosudarstvennogo Istoricheskogo Muzeia,* Vyp. 41, 1967, pp. 19–24

Doroshevich, Boris. 'Knizhnoe delo v epokhu Pervoi russkoi revoliutsii (1905–1907 gg.)' *Katorga i ssylka.* No. 1 (74), 1931, pp. 163–180

Druzhinin, N. 'Doktor Chemodanov'. *Kommunist.* No. 1, Moscow, 1982, pp. 63–66

Felitsin, S. Untitled article on Valerii Karrik. *Vestnik literatury.* No. 3, Saint Petersburg, 1910, pp. 57–61

Ferenczi, C. 'Freedom of the Press Under the Old Regime, 1905–1914'. *Civil Rights in Imperial Russia* (Eds. Crisp, O. and L. Edmondson). Oxford: Clarendon Press, 1989, pp. 191–214

Golubeva, O. D. 'Izdatel'skoe delo v Rossii v period Pervoi russkoi revolutsii (1905–1907)'. *Kniga: Issledovaniia i materialy.* No. 24, 1972, pp. 115–41

Gorodetskii, Ig. 'Podpol'naia karikatura epokhi pervoi revoliutsii'. *Rezets,* No. 3, Leningrad, 1931, p. 13

Gorodskii, I. 'Podpol'nye otkrytki 1905 g.'. *Rabochii i teatr,* No. 3, 1931, pp. 8–9

Gorodskii, Ig. '1905 g. v podpol'noi karikature'. *Stroika,* No. 5, 1931, p. 15

Grjébine, Hélène. 'Z. I. Grzhebin – izdatel' (po dokumentam i vospominaniiam ego docheri)'. *Solanus,* Vol. 1, 1987, pp. 4–40

Guzikov, S. M. 'V poiskakh novykh putei v zhivopisi'. *Vestnik znaniia,* No. 4, 1905, pp. 135–146

Knight, Amy. 'Female Terrorists in the Russian Socialist-Revolutionary Party'. *Russian Review.* No. 38 (2), April 1979, pp. 139–159

Korolenko, V. 'Svoboda pechati'. *Russkoe bogatstvo,* Nos. 11–12, 1905, pp. 195–207

Kovalev, I. 'Tsarizm v bor'be s revoliutsionnoi pechat'iu v 1905 g.'. *Krasnyi arkhiv.* No. 105, 1941, pp. 140–155

'Pis'mo S. M. Kravchinskogo k V. I. Zasulich ot 24 iiulia 1878 g.'. *Krasnyi arkhiv.* No. 19, 1926, pp. 195–197

Krupskaia, Nadezhda. 'Chto nravilos' Il'ichu iz khudozhestvennoi literatury'. *Udar: Al'manakh.* Moscow: Novaia Moskva. 1927, pp. 124–128

Kushnerovskaia, G. 'Karikaturist M. M. Chemodanov (1856–1906)'. *Iskusstvo.* No. 6, Moscow, 1955, pp. 70–73

Lenin, N. 'Partiinaia organizatsiia i partiinaia literatura.' *Novaia zhizn'.* No. 12, November 13, 1905, p. 1

Levi, A. 'Kak kollektsionirovat' otkrytki'. *Otkrytka.* No. 1, Kaluga, March 1907, pp. 4–6

L-skii, M. A. 'Vo vlasti gluposti'. *Istoricheskii vestnik,* No. 4, April 1912, p. 99

Maiskii, S. '"Chernyi kabinet": Iz vospominanii byvshego tsenzora'. *Byloe*. No. 13, Kn. 7, Petrograd, July 1918, pp. 185–97

Maliazh. 'Nedavnee i nastoiashchee. Kharakteristika satiricheskikh zhurnalov'. *Otkliki khudozhestvennoi zhizni*. No. 2, Saint Petersburg, 1910, pp. 70–75

Mintslov, S. R. '14 mesiatsev svobody pechati. 17 okt. 1905 g. – 1 ianv. 1907'. *Byloe*. No. 3/15, Saint Petersburg, March 1907, pp. 123–148

Mozokhina, Natalia. 'K istorii izdaniia v Rossii otkrytykh pisem s portretami chlenov imperatorskoi familii'. *Filokartiia*. No. 1 (36), Moscow, 2014, pp. 20–23

Nepein, B. 'Izdano v Vologde'. *Al'manakh bibliofila*. Vypusk VIII, Moscow, 1980, pp. 193–194

Nikotin, Georgii. 'K chitateliu'. *Domashnii muzei*. No. 1, Saint Petersburg, April 1904, p. 4

O. P. 'Kollektsionirovanie otkrytok'. *Otkrytka*. No. 1, Kaluga, January 1909, pp. 2–6

Ossipoff, Nicolas and Bruno de Perthuis. 'Le Dimanche rouge'. *Cartes postales et Collection*, No. 207, 2003, pp. 8–16

Paichadze, S. A. and G. I. Kan. 'Russkoe izdatel'stvo 'Volia' v Nagasaki (1906–1908gg.)'. *Kniga i knizhnoe delo v Sibiri: Istoriia, sovremennost', perspektivy razvitiia*. Novosibirsk: GPNTB SO AN SSSR, 1989, pp. 74–77

Perrie, Maureen. 'Political and Economic Terror in Russia pre-1914'. *Social Protest, Violence and Terror in Nineteenth- and Twentieth-Century Europe* (Eds. Mommsen, Wolfgang J. and Hirschfeld, G.). New York, 1982, pp. 63–79

Podol'nyi, I. A. 'Otkrytki Eserov'. *Zhuk*. No. 3 (07), Moscow, 2005, pp. 17–22

Podol'nyi, I. A. 'Otkrytki Valeriia Karrika'. *Zhuk*. No. 4 (08), Moscow, 2005, pp. 24–26

Podol'nyi, I. A. 'Otkrytki rossiiskikh sotsial-demokratov'. *Zhuk* No. 1 (09), Moscow, 2006, pp. 36–39

Poliak, L. V. and I. I. Palkin 'Politicheskaia deiatel'nost' M. M. Chemodanova (K 80-letiiu so dnia smerti)'. *Stomatalogiia*. No. 2 (68), 1989, pp. 92–94

Riabov, G. 'Vrach-revoliutsioner'. *Zdorov'e*. No. 2, 1956, p. 25

Roshchupkin, S. N. 'Zhurnal 'Kramola' i ego illustrator'. *Iskusstvo*. No. 1, Moscow, 1969, pp. 64–67

Roshchupkin, S. N. 'Dekabr'skoe vooruzhennoe vosstanie v Moskve v risunkakh E. V. Orlovskogo'. *Iskusstvo*. No. 11, Moscow, 1975, pp. 56–59

Rubakin, N. 'Knizhnyi priliv i knizhnyi otliv'. *Sovremennyi mir*. No. 12, Saint Petersburg, 1909, pp. 1–25

Ruud, Charles A. 'The Printing Press as an Agent of Political Change in Early Twentieth-Century Russia'. *Russian Review*. Vol. 40, No. 4, October, 1981, pp. 378–395

Rykachev A. 'Tseny na khleb i trud za 58 let.' *Vestnik finansov, promyshlennosti i torgovli*. No. 31, Saint Petersburg, 1911, pp. 200–206

Shabel'skaia, N. 'Novaia otrasl' khudozhestvennoi promyshlennosti'. *Iskusstvo i khudozhestvennaia promyshlennost'*. No. 8, Saint Petersburg, 1899, pp. 670–682

Shleev, V. 'Otkrytki v zhizni i revoliutsionnoi deiatel'nosti V. I. Lenina'. *Sovetskii kollektsioner*, No. 6, Moscow, 1968, pp. 123–134

Smith, Steve and Kelly, Catriona. 'Commercial Culture and Consumerism.' *Constructing Russia in the Age of Revolution: 1881–1940* (Eds. Kelly, Catriona and Shepherd, D.). Oxford: Oxford University Press, 1998, pp. 106–164

Starikov, S. V. 'Esery na otkrytkakh: vzgliad istorika'. *Filokartiia*. No. 1, Moscow, 2006, pp. 14–18

Teterevleva, T. P. 'V. V. Karrik (1869–1943): emigrant iz Peterburga v Norvegii'. *Sankt Peterburg i strany severnoi Evropy: Materialy 5-oi ezhegodnoi mezhdunarodnoi konferentsii (23–25 aprelia 2003)*. Saint Petersburg, 2004, pp. 11–51

Tret'iakov, V. P. 'Russko-iaponskaia voina na otkrytkakh'. *Russkoe iskusstvo*. No. 4, Moscow, 2005, pp. 120–125

Turmov, G. P. 'Pesni i stikhi o russko-iaponskoi voine 1904–1905 gg.' *Filokartiia*. No. 4 (29), 2012, pp. 22–25

Lansere, Evgenii. 'Khudozhniki o revoliutsii 1905 goda'. *Iskusstvo*. No. 6, 1935, pp. 39–46

Vasil'ev, A. N. 'Kul'turnoe znachenie otkrytogo pis'ma'. *Otkrytka*. No. 1, Kaluga, March 1907, pp. 3–4

Vasil'ev, A. N. 'Pora sorganizovat'sia'. *Otkrytka*. No. 2, Kaluga, April 1907, pp. 18–19

Vasil'ev, A. N. 'Kakie kollektsionirovat' otkrytki'. *Otkrytka*. No. 7, Kaluga, September 1907, pp. 85–6

Waldron, Peter. 'States of Emergency: Autocracy and Extraordinary Legislation, 1881–1917'. *Revolutionary Russia*. Vol. 8, No. 1, 1995, pp. 1–25

Zabochen', M. 'Illiustrirovannaia khronika pervogo dnia revoliutsii'. *Filateliia SSSR*. No. 4, 1975, pp. 53–54

Zabochen', Mikhail. 'Oruzhiem iskusstva. Izdaniia po izobrazitel'nomu iskusstvu partiinogo izdatel'stva "Vpered"'. *Iskusstvo*. No. 11, 1979, pp. 60–68

Zabochen', M. 'Otkrytki partiinogo izdatel'stva "Vpered" (1906–1907 gg.)'. *Sovetskii kollektsioner*, No. 18, Moscow, 1980, pp. 53–76

[illegible] *Black Hundreds Follower (Latest Call up)*. No publication details, late 1905.

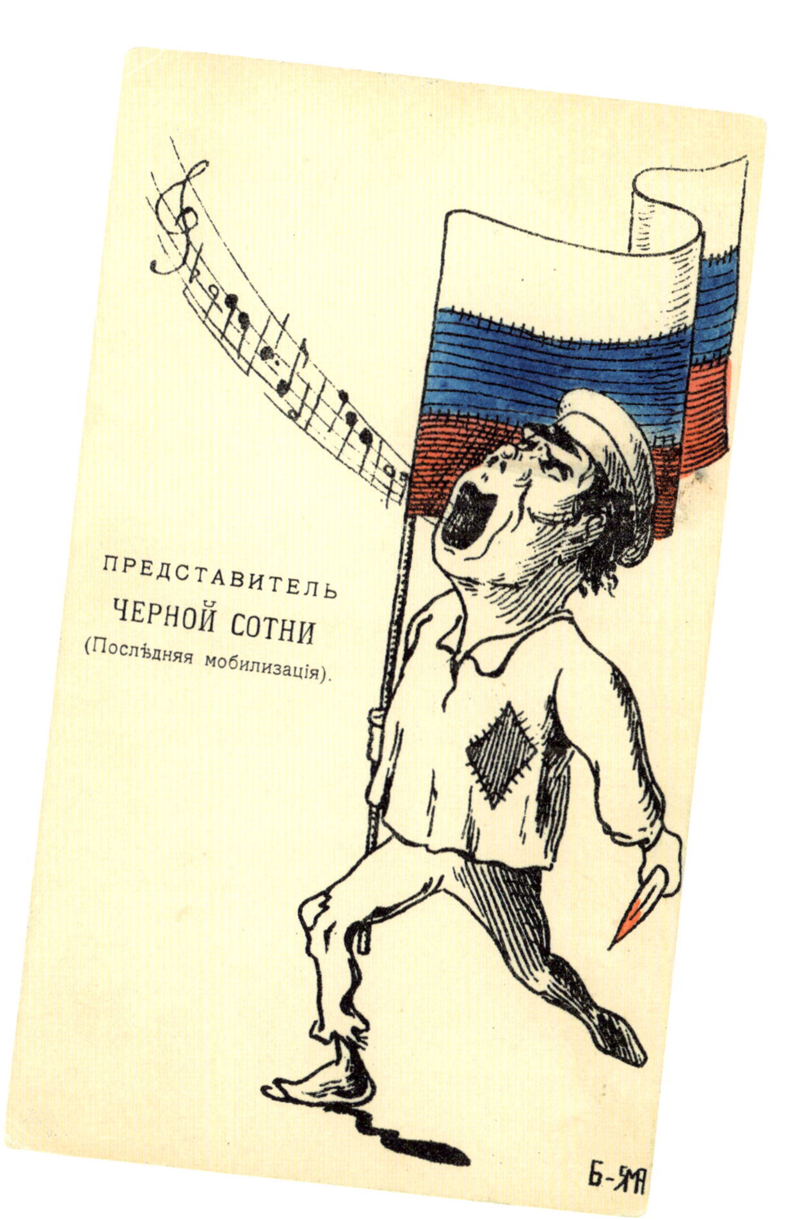
ПРЕДСТАВИТЕЛЬ
ЧЕРНОЙ СОТНИ
(Послѣдняя мобилизація).
Б-ЯМ

Notes

AUTHOR'S NOTE

1 Pakhomov, V. 'Rabochie o 9-m ianvariia 1905 goda'. Zelikson-Bobrovskaia, Ts. (Editor). *Pervaia russkaia revoliutsiia v Peterburge 1905 g. Sbornik statei, vospominanii, materialov i dokumentov.* Leningrad/ Moscow: Gosudarstvennoe izdatel'stvo, 1925, p. 27.

PROLOGUE

1 TsDIAK, f. 275, op. 1, d. 938, ll. 12–14; TsDIAK, f. 318, op. 1, d. 688, ll. 2–5.

2 The earliest articles on anti-government postcards date from the 1930s (see: Gorodetskii, Ig. 'Podpol'naia karikatura epokhi pervoi revoliutsii'. *Rezets*, No. 3, Leningrad, 1931, p. 13; Gorodskii, I. 'Podpol'nye otkrytki 1905 g.'. *Rabochii i teatr*, No. 3, 1931, pp. 8–9; Gorodskii, Ig. '1905 g. v podpol'noi karikature'. *Stroika*, No. 5, 1931, p. 15). However, detailed research into the subject was only undertaken in the 1960s, largely within the framework of broader investigations into the 1905 Revolution. This corresponded to rising interest in postcard collecting in general, prompted by a more indulgent attitude towards such materialistic endeavours. From the time of Khrushchev's Thaw onwards, several books and guides to the hobby were published, as were numerous articles, the majority of which appeared in the journals *Sovetskii kollektsioner* [*Soviet Collector*] and *Filateliia* [*Philately*]. In respect of anti-government postcards, three historians led the way, Emmanuil Fainshtein, Vladimir Shleev, and Mikhail Zabochen'. Their key works are: Fainshtein, E. 'Russkie revoliutsionnye otkrytki. (Delo No. 933… Sekretno)'. *Sovetskii kollektsioner*, No. 5, Moscow, 1967, pp. 83–90; Shleev, V. V. *Revoliutsiia 1905–1907 godov i izobrazitel'noe iskusstvo*. Moscow: Izobrazitel'noe Iskusstvo, 1987; Zabochen', M. 'Otkrytki partiinogo izdatel'stva "Vpered" (1906–1907 gg.)'. *Sovetskii kollektsioner*, No. 18, Moscow, 1980, pp. 53–76.

3 Mariia Chapkina was the guiding light of post-Soviet postcard research. See, in particular: Chapkina, Mariia. *Khudozhestvennaia otkrytka. K stoletiiu otkrytki v Rossii*. Moscow: Galart, 1993. More recently Anna Larina (Larina, Anna. *Istoriia Moskvy v pochtovoi otkrytke*, Moscow: Moskvovedenie, 2010), Natalia Mozokhina (Mozokhina, Natal'ia. *Otkrytki Obshchiny Sv. Evgenii kak khudozhestvennyi proekt masterov ob"edineniia 'Mir iskusstva'. Problemy istorii i khudozhestvennoi prakitiki*. Ph. D. dissertation. Rossiiskaia akademiia khudozhestv, Moscow, 2009), Mariia Nashchokina (Nashchokina, Mariia. *Khudozhestvennaia otkrytka russkogo moderna*. Moscow: Zhiraf, 2004), and Vitalii Tret'iakov (Tret'iakov, V. P. *Otkrytye pis'ma Serebrianogo veka*. Saint Petersburg: Slaviia, 2000) have taken up the mantle. Articles in the journals *Filokartiia* [*Deltiology*], *Zhuk* [*Beetle*], and publications from the Krepostnov Publishing House have also added to the historical record. Recent

Russian research, however, has focused almost exclusively on artistic postcards; few articles have been written on political subject matter, and none that have offered any significant new insights. See, for example: Podol'nyi, I. A. 'Otkrytki Eserov'. *Zhuk*. No. 3 (07), Moscow, 2005, pp. 17–22; Podol'nyi, I. A. 'Otkrytki Valeriia Karrika'. *Zhuk*. No. 4 (08), Moscow, 2005, pp. 24–26; Podol'nyi, I. A. 'Otkrytki rossiiskikh sotsial-demokratov'. *Zhuk*. No. 1 (09), Moscow, 2006, pp. 36–39; Starikov, S.V. 'Esery na otkrytkakh: vzgliad istorika'. *Filokartiia*. No. 1, Moscow, 2006, pp. 14–18.

4 See, for example: Carlson, John. 'Postcards and Propaganda: Cartographic Postcards as Soft News Images of the Russo-Japanese War'. *Political Communication*. Volume 26, No. 2, 2009, pp. 212–37; Jahn, Hubertus. *Patriotic Culture in Russia during World War I*. Ithaca, N. Y. and London: Cornell University Press, 1995; Rowley, Alison. *Open Letters. Russian Popular Culture and the Picture Postcard 1880–1922*. Toronto: University of Toronto Press, 2013. In regards to non-Russian postcards, see, in particular: Eds. Mendelson, Jordana and Prochaska, David. *Postcards: Ephemeral Histories of Modernity*. University Park: Pennsylvania State University Press, 2010.

5 On postcards not getting their historical due, see: Gorodetskii, Ig. 'Podpol'naia karikatura epokhi pervoi revoliutsii', p. 13; *Politicheskaia grafika vremeni revoliutsii 1905–1907 gg v zhurnalakh i na otkrytkakh: katalog vystavki*, Kiev, 1980, p. 5.

6 Levi, A. 'Kak kollektsionirovat' otkrytki'. *Otkrytka*. No. 1, Kaluga, March 1907, pp. 4–5; Vasil'ev, A. N. 'Kakie kollektsionirovat' otkrytki'. *Otkrytka*. No. 7, Kaluga, September 1907, pp. 85–6; O. P. 'Kollektsionirovanie otkrytok'. *Otkrytka*. No. 1, Kaluga, January 1909, p. 2.

7 The main revolutionary parties referred to postcards as: kartiny [pictures], kartochki [cards], portrety [portraits], and otkrytki [postcards]. The term 'kartina' was also used to refer to prints, while in the nineteenth and early twentieth centuries 'kartochka' could mean carte de visite. The words 'otkrytki' and 'kartochki' were used interchangeably with no indication as to whether the image was a cartoon, caricature, photograph, or reproduction of a painting. Government documents labelled opposition postcards in similarly broad terms, referring to then as 'anti-pravitel'stvennye otkrytki' ['anti-government postcards'] or 'otkrytki tendentsioznogo kharaktera' ['postcards of a tendentious nature'].

8 I have not, for example, discussed the Ukrainian nationalist postcards drawn by Vladimir Riznichenko in around late 1903, even though he also produced cartoons for the Social Democratic newspaper *Iskra*, under the pseudonym 'Gaid' (For more information on this, see: Demchenko, E. P. *Politicheskaia grafika Kieva perioda revoliutsii 1905–1907 gg.* Kiev: Naukova Dumka, 1976, pp. 21–34; TsDIAK, f. 275, op. 1, d. 222, l. 7).

THE PICTURE POSTCARD

1 GARF, f. 102, op. 203, d. 2 ch. 34 t. 1, ll. 724–725.

2 GARF, f. 102, op. 203, d. 2 ch. 34 t. 1, l. 698.

3 Article from *Deutsche Verkehrszeitung*. No. 33, Berlin, 1902, reprinted in *Pochtovo-telegrafnyi zhurnal. Otdel neofitsial'nyi*. Saint Petersburg: Tipografiia Ministerstva vnutrennikh del, October 1902, p. 766

4 RGIA, f. 1289, op. 1, d. 2992, l. 2

5 RGIA, f. 1289, op. 1, d. 2992, l. 11

6 At the Second Postal Union Congress, in 1878, standard sizes for postcards were adopted, and the name of the international body changed to the Universal Postal Union.

7 Tagrin, N. *Mir v otkrytke*, Moscow: Izobrazitel'noe iskusstvo, 1978, p. 33.

8 RGIA, f. 1289, op. 1, d. 2992, l. 62.

9 RGIA, f. 1289, op. 1, d. 3615, l. 21.

10 RGIA, f. 1289, op. 1, d. 3615, ll. 24–25.

11 RGIA, f. 1289, op. 1, d. 3615, l. 27; Published in *Pravitel'stvennyi vestnik*. 25 August 1873, No. 202, front page.

12 RGIA, f. 1289, op. 1, d. 3615, ll. 28–29

13 For example, see postcards sent by the Saint Petersburg Post Office to the Postal Department on 4 September 1873, the last of which is described as politically suspect. In the covering letter, postal officials also complain about the difficulties caused by the need to inspect so many messages (RGIA, f. 1289, op. 1, d. 3615, ll. 52–56).

14 GARF, f. 109, op. 3a, d. 3149, ll. 1–2.

15 GARF, f. 124, op. 8, d. 232, l. 10.

16 GARF, f. 124, op. 8, d. 232, ll. 10, 12.

17 The postcards, which were sold in black-and-white and colour versions, were printed by I. N. Kushnerev, and sold exclusively through the Zaks and Iarres Department Store in Moscow.

18 Among the largest firms were Lapin (France), Granberg (Sweden), and T. S. N. (Germany).

19 Some of the Society of Saint Eugenia's postcards were also printed abroad, particularly in the early years.

20 These envelopes were designed for carrying calling cards. Karazin's postcards, meanwhile, were produced for the Easter Holidays, a reflection of increasing commercial intrusion into Russian tradition.

21 The Society was also awarded the non-exclusive rights to reproduce images of the exteriors of the Imperial palaces, as well as pictures and artworks in the Hermitage, Russian Museum, Academy of Arts, and the Moscow Kremlin's Faceted Palace and Armoury (RGIA, f. 776, op. 21 ch. 1, d. 583, ll. 11–13, 14–16).

22 The new press laws were seen in some quarters as politically restrictive; nonetheless, they laid for the groundwork for the continued expansion of the printing industry, which had grown exponentially since Alexander II's accession to the throne.

23 Cited in Brooks, Jeffrey. *When Russia Learned to Read*. New Jersey: Princeton University Press, 1993, p. 110.

24 Anonymous. 'La rage des cartes-postales'. *Domashnii muzei*. No. 1, Saint Petersburg, April 1904, p. 5.
25 RGIA, f. 776, op. 8, d. 1763, l. 2.
26 Shabel'skaia, N. 'Novaia otrasl' khudozhestvennoi promyshlennosti'. *Iskusstvo i khudozhestvennaia promyshlennost'*. No. 8, Saint Petersburg, 1899, p. 671.
27 *Obzor khudozhestvennykh izdanii Obshchiny Sv. Evgenii*. Saint Petersburg, 1909, pp. 15–16.
28 For more, see: Smith, Steve and Catriona Kelly. 'Commercial Culture and Consumerism.' *Constructing Russia in the Age of Revolution: 1881–1940* (Eds. Kelly, Catriona and David Shepherd). Oxford: Oxford University Press, 1998, pp. 106–164.
29 Anonymous. 'La rage des cartes-postales'. p. 5.
30 *Otkrytka*. No. 2, Kaluga, April 1907, p. 2.
31 Shabelskaia does not mention the Society of Saint Eugenia explicitly, but she undoubtedly had the charity in mind when writing her article.
32 RGIA, f. 776, op. 21 ch. 1, 583, l. 12.
33 *Otkrytoe pis'mo*. No. 1, Saint Petersburg, 1904, p. 2.
34 For Alexandra Fedorovna's copy of the journal, see: GARF, f. 640, op. 2, d. 130.
35 Vasil'ev, A. N. 'Kul'turnoe znachenie otkrytogo pis'ma'. *Otkrytka*. No. 1, Kaluga, March 1907, p. 3.
36 Vasil'ev, A. N. 'Pora sorganizovat'sia'. *Otkrytka*. No. 2, Kaluga, April 1907, p. 18
37 *Otkrytka*. No. 2, Kaluga, April 1907, p. 24; *Otkrytka*. No. 6, Kaluga, August 1907, p. 77.
38 TsGIA SPB, f. 202, op. 2, d. 1159, l. 46.
39 *Domashnii muzei*. No. 2, October 1904, p. 13.
40 Levi. 'Kak kollektsionirovat' otkrytki?', pp. 4–5
41 Vasil'ev. 'Kakie kollektsionirovat' otkrytki', p. 85.
42 *Otkrytka*. No. 6, Kaluga, August 1907, pp. 71–2.
43 Anonymous. 'Nasha fabrika'. *Domashnii muzei*. No. 2, Saint Petersburg, October 1904, p. 6.
44 Anonymous. 'Nashi izdaniia'. *Domashnii muzei*. No. 2, Saint Petersburg, October 1904, p. 5; Nikotin, Georgii. 'K chitateliu'. *Domashnii muzei*. No. 1, Saint Petersburg, April 1904, p. 4.
45 Contemporary postcard journals contain many letters and articles that make suggestions as to how postcards might be used to educate children from less well-off families. 'Postcards with images of animals, plants, flowers, different peoples, town views, and local areas can serve as a wonderful and easily affordable school text book,' wrote one critic, adding, 'postcards with photographs of paintings can also serve as a good and cheap guide to learn about art history.' (Vasil'ev. 'Kul'turnoe znachenie otkrytogo pis'ma,' p. 3; For a letter from a teacher, see *Otkrytka*. No. 1, Kaluga, March 1907, p. 10).
46 Shabel'skaia. 'Novaia otrasl' khudozhestvennoi promyshlennosti', p. 677.
47 Shabel'skaia. 'Novaia otrasl' khudozhestvennoi promyshlennosti', p. 671.
48 *Otkrytoe pis'mo*. No. 5, Saint Petersburg, 1905, p. 143.
49 The growth in public spirit that accompanied Alexander's reforms found an outlet in many different areas, and it is no coincidence that one of these would be revolution.
50 For more information on early advertising postcards see: Iliushin, Aleksandr (Editor). *Pochtovye kartochki Rossiiskoi imperii s reklamnymi ob"iavleniiami/Tsel'nye veshchi*. Kirov: Izdatel'skii dom 'Krepostnov', 2014; Larina, Anna Nikolaevna. *Dokumental'naia otkrytka kontsa XIX-nachala XX vv. kak istochnik po istorii i kul'ture Moskvy*. Dissertation, Moscow: Rossiiskii gosudarstvennyi gumanitarnyi universitet, 2004, p. 93.
51 Around the same time, a French bookseller in Sillé-le-Guillaume named Léon Besnardeau started printing propaganda postcards for soldiers of the Breton Army. It is not clear, however, whether these were ever sent through the post.
52 May Day had been inaugurated as a worker's holiday the previous year, at the Congress of the Second International. One of the Vienna postcards illustrates the defeat of Mammon, while the other shows an allegorical female figure rising up against the backdrop of a factory. Their German titles are: *Die Bezwingung Mammons*. Wien, Verlag der 'Neuen Glühlichter', Druck von Johann N. Vernay, circa 1890; *Völkermai*. Wien, Verlag der 'Neuen Glühlichter', Druck von Johann N. Vernay, circa 1890. For more on May Day postcards, see: Gebhardt, Manfred. *Ein Hauch von Maienblüte: Postkarten der deutschen Arbeiterbewegung zum 1. Mai*. Berlin: Verlag Tribüne, 1989.
53 Pochtovo-telegrafnyi zhurnal. Otdel neofitsial'nyi. Saint Petersburg: Tipografiia Ministerstvo vnutrennikh del, December 1900, pp. 1333–4.
54 'Ustav o tsenzure i pechati'. *Svod zakonov*. Tom XIV, 1890.
55 In regards to postcards, the requirement to include publication details caused difficulties for both publishers and officials. In 1900, the police complained to the Press Administration that postcards were regularly being offered for sale without a censor's mark. Some of these cards, undoubtedly, had not been officially approved, but as the Society of Saint Eugenia later pointed out, adding the necessary details was a time-consuming and fiddly enterprise, so rather than put them on each individual card, most firms instead put them on the larger printed sheets. This practice was eventually sanctioned by the Administration (GARF, f. 102, op. 57, d. 87, l. 54; RGIA, f. 776, op. 21 ch. 1, d. 583, ll. 6–8).
56 From 1865, there were regional censorship committees for the inspection of secular works in: Saint Petersburg, Moscow, Warsaw and Tiflis. There were also individual censors in: Riga, Reval, Iuriev, Mitava, Kiev, Vilnius, Odessa, Kazan and Łódź. After 1903, there were also individual censors in: Vladivostok, Ekaterinoslav, Nizhnii-Novgorod, Rostov on Don, Saratov, Tomsk and Kharkov. Religious works and foreign publications came under the aegis of different branches of the censor's office ('Ustav o tsenzure i pechati'. *Svod zakonov*. Tom XIV, 1890).

57 For more information on restrictions governing portrait postcards of the Imperial Family see: GARF, f. 102, op. 117, d. 139; Mozokhina, Natalia. 'K istorii izdaniia v Rossii otkrytykh pisem s portretami chlenov imperatorskoi familii'. *Filokartiia*. No. 1 (36), Moscow, 2014, pp. 20–23.

58 The censors were guided in their work by specific articles relating to the press in the Russian Criminal Code (principally Articles: 103, 106, 107, 111, 128, 129, 132, and 133).

59 RGIA, f. 777, op. 5 (1904), d. 3, l. 18.

60 RGIA, f. 777, op. 27, d. 69, ll. 32–33.

61 The other works were: Jacopo Sansovino's *Bacchus*, and Jean-Antoine Houdon's *Diana*. (RGIA, f. 777, op. 21 ch. 1, d. 583, l. 32; *Obzor khudozhestvennykh izdanii Obshchiny Sv. Evgenii*, p. 8). It appears, in the latter case at least, that permission was later granted to reproduce images of the sculptures in postcard form.

62 The postcards were published by Mikhail Stoshch, who was based in Irkutsk. Two of the images, titled: *Dom dekabristov* [*House of the Decembrists*] and *Chasovnia vystroennaia dekabristami v 1826* [*Chapel Built by the Decembrists in 1826*] were eventually banned (RGIA, f. 776, op. 21 ch. 1, d. 692, ll. 1–2).

63 See, for example: RGIA, f. 777, op. 27, d. 69, l. 207 (portraits of Herzl and other Zionists); RGIA, f. 777, op. 27, d. 69, l. 243 (portraits of N. A., A. A. and M. A. Bestuzhev, Ogarev, Herzen, Prince S. G. Volkonskii, and Chernyshevskii); RGIA, f. 777, op. 27, d. 69, ll. 32–33 (Surikov's *Boyarina Morozova*); RGIA, f. 777, op. 27, d. 69, l. 244 (chromolithographic reproductions of *Boyarina Morozova*).

64 It appears from the Saint Petersburg Censorship Committee's records that the Society of Saint Eugenia was one of the only publishers to be scrupulous about submitting all of its postcards for inspection.

65 There were inspectorates in: Saint Petersburg, Moscow, Warsaw, Vilnius, Kiev, Łódź, Odessa, Riga and Tiflis. In other areas, dedicated officials were appointed by the regional governor.

66 For pornographic images, see: GARF, f. 102, op. 57, d. 87, ll. 56–57, and for numerous examples of all of the above, see: RGIA, f. 776, op. 21 ch. 1, d. 467, ll. 1–83.

67 King Alexander I of Serbia had been assassinated in a military coup earlier that month (GARF, f. 102, op. 200, d. 1746, l. 4).

68 Other 'Black Offices' may also have existed in Tiflis, Riga, Vilnius and Kharkov. Less sophisticated operations were in place in towns throughout the Russian Empire (Skipton, David and Peter Michalove. *Postal Censorship in Imperial Russia*. Volume 1. Urbana: John H. Otten, 1989, pp. 78–80).

69 Zavarzin, P. P. *Rabota tainoi politsii*. V dvukh chastiakh. Paris: Izdanie Avtora, 1924, pp. 42–43; Maiskii, S. '"Chernyi kabinet": Iz vospominanii byvshego tsenzora'. *Byloe*. No. 13, Kn. 7, Petrograd, July 1918, p. 196.

70 Rataev, Leonid. *No. 107*. 24 May 1905/Intercepted letter addressed to Vladimir Vladimirovich in Moscow. HIWRP OA, Paris Office – Outgoing Dispatches, 1905, Volume 1, No. 107.

71 Chernov, V. M. *Pered burei*. New York: Izdatel'stvo imeni Chekhova, 1953, p. 175.

72 Shleev, V. 'Otkrytki v zhizni i revoliutsionnoi deiatel'nosti V. I. Lenina'. *Sovetskii kollektsioner*, No. 6, Moscow, 1968, pp. 123–134.

73 Anonymous. 'La rage des cartes-postales', p. 5.

OPPOSITION VISUAL PROPAGANDA

1 Stepniak, Sergei. *Underground Russia*. London: Smith, Elder and Co., 1890, pp. 200–202.

2 The first uncensored Russian newspaper, *Kolokol* [*The Bell*], was founded in London in 1857 by Alexander Herzen and Nikolai Ogarev. Copies were regularly smuggled into Russia, where it was widely read in the upper echelons of society.

3 For more on cartes de visite of the revolutionary Dmitrii Karakozov and the Tsar's alleged saviour Osip Komissarov, see: GARF, f. 109, op. 1a, d. 270, l. 17; Verhoeven, Claudia. *The Odd Man Karakozov. Imperial Russia, Modernity and the Birth of Terrorism*. Ithaca and London: Cornell University Press, 2009, pp. 66–84.

4 These cartes de visite were presented in evidence against the revolutionaries at the so-called Trial of the 193, in 1877–1878 (GARF, f. 112, op. 2, d. 1983; GARF, f. 112, op. 2, d. 820).

5 The firm Vezenberg and Ko. [Wesenberg and Co.] was founded in Saint Petersburg in 1865 by Wilhelm Wesenberg, a Russified German. It remained in operation following his death in 1880, before closing sometime in the early twentieth century.

6 According to a Social Democratic Party report published in 1904, it was popularly believed that the revolutionaries 'spent all their time in endless talk, when what was needed was action.' (*Doklad delegatsii Rossiiskoi Sots.-Dem. Rabochei Partii Amsterdamskomu Mezhdunarodnomu Sotsialisticheskomu Kongressu (14–20 August 1904)*. Zheneva: Izdanie Rossiiskoi Sotsial'demokraticheskoi Rabochei Partii, 1904, p. 26).

7 'Pis'mo S. M. Kravchinskogo k V. I. Zasulich ot 24 iiulia 1878 g'. *Krasnyi arkhiv*. No. 19, 1926, p. 196. Despite regular setbacks, the revolutionaries retained a firm belief that if the masses were made aware of their downtrodden position, they would immediately rise up against the government. This conviction remained central to their propaganda, which deployed a combination of fact and theory to convince the people of the despotism of the regime and the surety of its eventual downfall.

8 The source for this story is Lenin's wife, Nadezhda Krupskaia. She uses the Russian word 'kartochki' to describe the images, literally meaning 'cards.' In previous studies this has been taken to mean photographic postcards, but the date of Lenin's exile (1897–1900) makes it far more likely that they were small format cabinet cards or cartes de visite (Krupskaia, Nadezhda. 'Chto nravilos' Il'ichu iz khudozhestvennoi literatury'. *Udar: Al'manakh*. Moscow: Novaia Moskva. 1927, p. 125).

9 Revolutionary cartes de visites later became comparatively widespread. The Perm Administration of Gendarmes, for example, reported that in September 1889, a certain Vladimir Iatsenko-Khmelevskii had bought a library off Nikita Vsevolozhskii at a public sale. It later came to Iatsenko-Khmelevskii's attention that the collection included an album containing 428 cartes de visite of individuals whom he believed 'belonged to anti-government parties.' This he duly handed over to the authorities, sparking a police investigation (GARF, f. 102, op. 87, d. 552).

10 For images of the Tsar's assassination, see: *Zlodeiskoe pokushenie na sviashchennuiu osobu, nyne v boze pochivshogo, Gosudaria Imperatora Aleksandra IIgo, 1 Marta 1881 g.* [*The Despicable Assassination Carried Out on the Holy Person of the Sovereign Emperor Alexander II, Now Reposed in the Lord, 1 March 1881*], Golike Printworks, Saint Petersburg, 6 March 1881; *Zlodeiskoe pokushenie na zhizn' v boze pochivshogo Gosudaria Imperatora Aleksandra IIgo 1 Marta 1881 goda* [*The Despicable Assassination on the Life of Sovereign Emperor Alexander II, Now Reposed in the Lord, I March 1881*], Iakovlev Lithography, Moscow, March 1881 (Both contained in RNB OE, Ė Al Ir 4–1/3). The author's collection includes two contemporary cartes de visite of the assassination, one by Wesenberg and Co., and the other unmarked.

11 Following their trial and execution, the revolutionaries made a conscious effort to find and reproduce portraits of the Tsar's assassins (Figner, Vera. *Polnoe sobranie sochinenii v semi tomakh.* Tom piatyi: *Ocherki, stat'i, rechi.* Moscow: Izdatel'stvo Vsesoiuznogo obshchestva politkatorzhan i ssyl'no-poselentsev, 1932, pp. 318–21).

12 The Okhrana was the name given to the Department for the Protection of Public Order and Security, a branch of the police established in 1880 to deal with crimes against the state.

13 Engelstein, Laura. *Moscow, 1905. Working-Class Organisation and Political Conflict.* Stanford: Stanford University Press, 1982, p. 40.

14 For more information on the origins and beliefs of the Socialist-Revolutionary Party, see: White, Elizabeth. *The Socialist Alternative to Bolshevik Russia, The Socialist-Revolutionary Party 1917–1939.* London and New York: Routledge, 2010, pp. 1–14.

15 The Union of Social Democrats Abroad, founded in 1894, was a competing organisation to the League of Russian Revolutionary Social Democracy Abroad. It was disbanded in 1903.

16 GARF, f. 124, op. 11, d. 1646, ll. 12–13.

17 *Doklad delegatsii Rossiiskoi Sots.-Dem. Rabochei Partii Amsterdamskomu Mezhdunarodnomu Sotsialisticheskomu Kongressu*, p. 74.

18 The League effectively replaced the Union of Russian Social Democrats Abroad, which had been set up under the direction of the Emancipation of Labour Group (the first Marxist organisation in Russia), but later went its own way.

19 The cartoons Belozerov found depicted a version of Nikolai Lokhov's *The Pyramid* (GARF, f. 124, op. 11, d. 1814, ll. 1, 16).

20 Stepan Balmashev shot and killed Interior Minister Dmitrii Sipiagin in April 1902.

21 GARF, f. 102, op. 200, d. 580, ll. 4–5, 13–14, 20.

22 GARF, f. 102, op. 200, d. 580 ch. 1, l. 3; Gorodnichev was released from police surveillance following a political amnesty enacted in August 1904 (GARF, f. 102, op. 200, d. 580, l. 53).

23 GARF, f. 124, op. 11, d. 1646, l. 16.

24 GARF, f. 124, op. 11, d. 1814, l. 15.

25 See, for example: GARF, f. 124, op. 12, d. 2518, l. 8.

26 Output centred on the assassins of Tsar Alexander II (the author's collection, for example, contains a group of cartes de visite printed in Berlin, which reproduce drawings from *The Illustrated London News.* No. 2188, April 23 1881, p. 385). There were, however, also images produced depicting Populist activists from the 1870s and 1880s.

27 There were undoubtedly other postcards printed prior to the Perovskaia image. For example, an entry in *Revoliutsionnaia Rossiia* (No. 23, Geneva, 1 May 1903, p. 20) lists funds raised in aid of political exiles and prisoners between 1 June 1900 and 31 December 1901 from selling 'cards P. L.' – the initials might stand for Petr Lavrov, or for the name of the person selling the cards.

28 The postcard was sent from Paris in March 1902 by 'Jacques', to the French historian and one-time Socialist, Maurice Reclus.

29 For a discussion of the Party's use of terrorism, see: *Revoliutsionnaia Rossiia.* No. 7, June 1902, pp. 2–7.

30 Hildermeier, Manfred. *The Russian Socialist-Revolutionary Party Before the First World War.* Palgrave Macmillan, 2000, p. 52.

31 Perrie, Maureen. 'Political and Economic Terror in Russia pre-1914'. *Social Protest, Violence and Terror in Nineteenth- and Twentieth-Century Europe* (Eds. Mommsen, Wolfgang J. and Gerhard Hirschfeld). New York, 1982, p. 65.

32 Spiridovich, A. I. *Partiia Sotsialistov-Revoliutsionerov i ee predshestvenniki 1886–1916.* Izdanie vtoroe. Petrograd: Voennaia tipografiia, 1918, p. 118.

33 Gershuni made Balmashev write a short autobiography before carrying out the attack, and this was later used for propaganda purposes (Spiridovich. *Partiia Sotsialistov-Revoliutsionerov i ee predshestvenniki*, p. 117).

34 The strikes started out as a dispute over pay among railway workers but soon spread. It took three weeks for the demonstrations to be fully suppressed, by which stage many lives had been lost and numerous workers had been dismissed from their jobs. It was subsequently seen as a defining moment of the early revolutionary movement, when for the first time large groups of workers had raised political questions about the nature of their existence. (*Doklad delegatsii Rossiiskoi Sots.-Dem. Rabochei Partii Amsterdamskomu Mezhdunarodnomu Sotsialisticheskomu Kongressu*, p. 31).

35 *Revoliutsionnaia Rossiia*. No. 18, 15 February 1903, p. 20.
36 After being arrested and expelled from Russia, Bliumenfeld worked in Vienna and Paris, before moving to Geneva. There he joined the Emancipation of Labour Group, rising to become head of its printing department. When, in 1900, Lenin helped to set up *Iskra*, Bliumenfeld was put in charge of technical matters.
37 *Otchet gruppy za vremia ot 17 noiabria po 17 dekabria* and *Za mesiats ot 17 dekabria po 17 ianvaria 1901–1902 goda*, HIWRP BN, Box 184, Folder 3.
38 Receipt from Imprimerie Typografique Edouard Pfeffer in Geneva made out to Boris Ginzburg (who took over printing activities from Bliumenfeld after his arrest in March 1902), 30 April 1902, HIWRP BN, Box 184, Folder 3.
39 *Iskra*. No. 24, Munich, 1 September 1902, p. 6.
40 Lenin argued that the Party should be limited to a small band of professional revolutionaries, operating with the support of much larger numbers of sympathisers. Opposing him was Iulii Martov, who wanted to keep membership of the Party open to all comers. Relations between the two camps became increasingly bitter, and although the Party remained united under a Social Democratic roof, the division was later formalised.
41 *Izveshchenie o vtorom ocherednom s"ezde rossiiskoi sotsialdemokraticheskoi rabochei partii*. Zheneva: Izdanie Tsentral'nogo komiteta RSDRP, 1903, p. 29. Throughout the 1905 Revolution, the Party's Technical Bureau remained the key body in charge of all the practical aspects of propaganda production and distribution.
42 Bonch-Bruevich, Vladimir. *Kak pechatalis' za granitsei i taino dostavlialis' v Rossiiu zapreshchennye izdaniia nashei partii*. Moscow: Zhizn' i znanie, 1924, p. 42.
43 The publishing house started operations in March 1904. Works were issued under the name: Izdatel'stvo V. Bonch-Bruevicha i N. Lenina [V. Bonch-Bruevich and N. Lenin Publishing House].
44 Bonch-Bruevich. *Kak pechatalis' za granitsei i taino dostavlialis' v Rossiiu zapreshchennye izdaniia nashei partii*, p. 97.
45 Bonch-Bruevich, V. D. *Stenogramma vystypleniia Vl.Bonch-Bruevicha v DDRI na iubilee MKhAT (dlia gazety 'Trud')*. 20 October 1948, RGASPI, f. 4, op. 2, d. 3042, l. 33; Dreiden, Sim. *V zritel'nom zale – Vladimir Il'ich*. Moscow: Iskusstvo, 1967, p. 106.
46 However, Bonch-Bruevich claims elsewhere that it was he who had the idea to reprint the postcards (Bonch-Bruevich, Vladimir. *Stenogramma vystypleniia Vl.Bonch-Bruevicha v DDRI na iubilee MKhAT*, RGASPI, f. 4, op. 2, d. 3042, l. 33).
47 Bonch-Bruevich. *Stenogramma vystypleniia Vl.Bonch-Bruevicha v DDRI na iubilee MKhAT*, RGASPI, f. 4, op. 2, d. 3042, l. 37.
48 An advertising leaflet issued by the Social Democratic Transportation Office [Ekspeditisiia] lists nineteen of the postcards by name. For copy of leaflet, see: Dreiden, p. 104.
49 Bonch-Bruevich. *Stenogramma vystypleniia Vl.Bonch-Bruevicha v DDRI na iubilee MKhAT*, RGASPI, f. 4, op. 2, d. 3042, l. 37.
50 Bonch-Bruevich, V. D. *Zhenevskie vospominaniia (iiul' 1902-dekabr' 1904 g.g.)*. GBL OR, f. 369, k. 9, d. 1, l. 397.
51 Bonch-Bruevich, Vladimir. *Otnoshenie Vladimira Il'icha k teatru, k tsene, k khudozhnikam (iz moikh vospominanii)*. 26.XII, 1933, RGASPI, f. 4, op. 2, d. 3042, l. 5.
52 Bonch-Bruevich, Vladimir. *Liubimyi teatr Lenina*, Undated, RGASPI, f. 4, op. 2, d. 3042, l. 43.
53 *Iskra*. No. 56, Geneva, 1 January 1904, p. 8; *Iskra*. No. 62, 15 March 1904, p. 8; *Iskra*. No. 68, 25 June 1904, p. 8; *Iskra*. No. 77, 5 November 1904, p. 8.
54 In 1904, there were over twenty 'Contributing Party groups' [Gruppy sodeistviia partii] controlled by the League, through which Party literature was distributed to the centres of Russian emigration. (*Doklad delegatsii Rossiiskoi Sots.-Dem. Rabochei Partii Amsterdamskomu Mezhdunarodnomu Sotsialisticheskomu* Kongressu, p. 96)
55 The Foreign Committee was elected annually from regional members of the Foreign Organisation. Its duties were to edit *Revoliutsionnaia Rossiia*, oversee Party propaganda, and maintain links with the Central Committee in Russia (Hildermeier. *The Russian Socialist-Revolutionary Party Before the First World War*, p. 112); *Z. K. No. 3. Kassovaia kniga Z. K. P. S. R. 1904 g.*, IISG PSR, Index 212; *Revoliutsionnaia Rossiia*. No. 39, 1 January 1904, p. 22; *Revoliutsionnaia Rossiia*. No. 41, 15 February 1904, p. 21; *Revoliutsionnaia Rossiia*. No. 46, May 1904, p. 23; *Revoliutsionnaia Rossiia*. No. 50, 1 August 1904, p. 21; *Revoliutsionnaia Rossiia*. No. 52, 15 September 1904, p. 24; *Revoliutsionnaia Rossiia*. No. 55, 20 November 1904, p. 24.
56 Bonch, Bruevich, Vladimir. *Lenin v Zheneve v 1904 i 1905 gg.* RGASPI, f. 4, op. 2, d. 2994, l. 131; Accounts in *Revoliutsionnaia Rossiia* also show money raised from sales of literature in America.
57 *Otchet biblioteki-chital'ni Z. K. P. S. R. (s noiabria 1904 po avgust 1905)*. IISG PSR, Index 211; Bonch-Bruevich also mentions selling literature in the entrance of the Party's 'Bibliothèque Centrale Russe' in Geneva (Bonch-Bruevich, Vladimir. 'Biblioteka i arkhiv RSDRP v Zheneve'. *Krasnaia letopis'*, No. 3 (48), 1932, p. 112).
58 Sverchkov, D. *Na zare revoliutsii*. Izd. tret'e. Leningrad: Gosudarstvennoe izdatel'stvo, 1925, p. 65.
59 Bonch-Bruevich. *Kak pechatalis' za granitsei i taino dostavlialis' v Rossiiu zapreshchennye izdaniia nashei partii*, p. 6.
60 Letter from the Acting Chief of Police to Petr Rachkovskii. 26 August 1900, HIWRP OA, Index XVIIf (1), Folder 5k.
61 Rataev, Leonid to Director of Department of Police. *Doklad 120*. 7–20 June 1904, HIWRP OA, Index XXIVe, Folder 1.
62 Bonch-Bruevich. *Kak pechatalis' za granitsei i taino dostavlialis' v Rossiiu zapreshchennye izdaniia nashei partii*, p. 91.
63 Bonch-Bruevich. *Kak pechatalis' za granitsei i taino dostavlialis' v Rossiiu zapreshchennye izdaniia nashei partii*, p. 22.

64 Rataev, Leonid. *Doklad 172*. 28 June – 11 July 1904, HIWRP OA, Index XXIVe, Folder 1; Bonch-Bruevich. *Kak pechatalis' za granitsei i taino dostavlialis' v Rossiiu zapreshchenny izdaniia nashei partii*, pp. 14–15.

65 648 of the postcards reproduced *Est' na Volge utes* [*There Is a Cliff on the Volga*], 150 the *Rabochaia marseleza* [*Worker's Marseilleise*], 199 the *Pesnia rabochikh* [*Song of the Workers*], and 690 carried a poem in Polish titled *Rytsari dukha* [*Knights of the Soul*] (GARF, f. 102, op. 102, d. 2893, ll. 2–4, 22).

66 The discovery in Irkutsk of a Social Democratic postcard reproducing *The Pyramid* in May 1902 shows that postcards were already circulating around the country (GARF, f. 124, op. 11, d. 341, l. 1).

67 *Otchet ob dostavlennoi v Rossiiu literatury cherez odnu iz granits ot noiabria 1903 do iiulia 1904 (za 8 mesiatsev)*. IISG PSR, Index 212.

68 There are five different types of illustrated propaganda that appear in revolutionary financial accounts. They are: graviury [prints], kartiny [pictures], kartochki [cards], otkrytki/otkrytye pis'ma [postcards], and portrety [portraits]. I have discovered next to nothing about the 'prints' and 'pictures', and have not seen an example of either that can be conclusively dated to the pre-1905 period.

69 *Iskra*. No. 24, Munich, 1 September 1902, p. 6; *Iskra*. No. 56, Geneva, 1 January 1904, p. 8 (two mentions); *Iskra*. No. 62, 15 March 1904, p. 8; *Iskra*. No. 68, 25 June 1904, p. 8; *Iskra*. No. 77, 5 November 1904, p. 8; *Iskra*. No. 78, 20 November 1904, p. 8; *Revoliutsionnaia Rossiia*. No. 18, 15 February 1903, p. 20; *Revoliutsionnaia Rossiia*. No. 23, Geneva, 1 May 1903, p. 20 (two mentions); *Revoliutsionnaia Rossiia*. No. 37, 1 December 1903, p. 24; *Revoliutsionnaia Rossiia*. No. 39, I January 1904, p. 22; *Revoliutsionnaia Rossiia*. No. 41, 15 February 1904, p. 21; *Revoliutsionnaia Rossiia*. No. 46, May 1904, p. 23 (two mentions); *Revoliutsionnaia Rossiia*. No. 50, 1 August 1904, p. 21 (two mentions); *Revoliutsionnaia Rossiia*. No. 51, 25 August 1904, p. 24; *Revoliutsionnaia Rossiia*. No. 52, 15 September 1904, p. 24; *Revoliutsionnaia Rossiia*. No. 55, 20 November 1904, p. 24.

70 Lenin, N. *Chto delat'*. Stuttgart: Verlag von J. H. W. Dietz Nachf., 1902, p. 124.

REVOLUTION AND REFORM

1 Intercepted letter from Leonid Baron to Luri, 11 January 1904, HIWRP OA, Index XVIII (2), Folder 1a.

2 Vitte, Sergei. *Vospominaniia tsarstvovaniia Nikolaia II*. Tom. 1. Berlin: Slovo, 1922, p. 262.

3 Anonymous. 'Voina!' *Domashnii muzei*. No. 1, April 1904, p. 6.

4 In total, the Society printed 201 postcards on the Russo-Japanese War. Sixty-four of these were general views of the Far Eastern region and the rest, which are roughly split between drawings and photographs, comprise: portraits of army and naval officers, pictures of the fighting, soldiers, medical wards, and images of the Pacific (Mozokhina. *Otkrytki Obshchiny Sv. Evgenii kak khudozhestvennyi proekt masterov ob"edineniia 'Mir iskusstva'*, pp. 90–91; Tret'iakov, V. P. 'Russko-iaponskaia voina na otkrytkakh'. *Russkoe iskusstvo*. No. 4, Moscow, 2005, p. 122).

5 The appearance of cartoon postcards in Russia was likely the result of print industry initiative, rather than regulatory adjustment as there is nothing in the archives of the Press Administration to indicate an official change in policy towards such works.

6 The censor found that the image, titled *Kovarnyi vyzov* [*A Devious Challenge*] was inadmissible because it suggested 'a lack of Russian vigilance' (RGIA, f. 777, op. 27, d. 69, l. 100).

7 For more on lubok imagery of the Russo-Japanese War, see: Stephen Norris. *A War of Images: Russian Popular Prints, Wartime Culture, and National Identity*. DeKalb: Northern Illinois University Press, 2006, pp. 107–134.

8 This set of around fourteen postcards was published in Saint Petersburg by A. K. Veierman. The images passed the censor on various dates between 19 February and 18 April 1904. For examples see: Turmov, G. P. 'Pesni i stikhi o russko-iaponskoi voine 1904–1905 gg.' *Filokartiia*. No. 4 (29), 2012, pp. 22–25.

9 Benua, A. N. *Moi vospominaniia*. Kniga IV, Moscow: Nauka, 1980, p. 400.

10 Sverchkov. *Na zare revoliutsii*, p. 69.

11 *Otchet Bakinskoi gruppoi Partii Sotsialistov-Revoliutsionerov za mai/iiun' 1904*, IISG PSR, Index 481; *Revoliutsionnaia Rossiia*. No. 51, 25 August 1904, p. 24.

12 *Denezhnyi otchet Nizhegorodskogo komiteta Partii Sotsialistov-Revoliutsionerov za 1904*, IISG PSR, Index 344.

13 The Nizhnii Novgorod Committee was formed in May 1903, and the Baku group in May 1904 (Hildermeier. *The Russian Socialist-Revolutionary Party Before the First World War*, p. 101).

14 None of these images were unique to the Socialist-Revolutionary Party.

15 Photographic apparatuses did not require a special license to own, and so were widely used by underground groups to reproduce anti-government postcards (GARF, f. 102, op. 117, d. 139, l. 17).

16 Felten initially came under suspicion in connection with an intercepted letter sent to a revolutionary in Paris – the same incident that ensnared Valerii Karrik. The investigation into Felten was eventually closed without charges being brought (GARF, f. 102, op. 102, d. 2933, ll. 8, 9, 19, 128).

17 The method of reproduction is typical – an ink drawing tacked to a wall and then photographed, pins and all, showing the necessarily amateur nature of revolutionary propaganda at this time.

18 Even though only one of the images is signed ('Izd. PSR' [Pub. Socialist-Revolutionary Party]), they are identifiable as a group both on stylistic grounds and by the wallpaper backdrop. The images are not mentioned explicitly in any of the financial accounts published in *Revoliutsionnaia Rossiia*, but they were likely printed by the Saint Petersburg Committee. Their titles are: *Biurokraticheskii Press* [*The Bureaucratic Press*]; *Venchanie novogo konstitutsionnogo samoderzhavtsa* [*Marriage of the New Constitutional Autocrat*]; *Konovalov i svobododeistvuiushchie* [*Konovalov and the Free Wheelers*]; *Rossiia nakanune konstitutsii sverkhu* [*Russia on the Eve of a Constitution from Above*]; *Eto khorosho chto im sdelali krovopuskanie – dolgo budut pomnit' – Prof Dem'ianov* [*It's Good That They Were Bled – They'll Remember It for a Long Time – Prof. Dem'ianov*].

19 In the cities, a few larger enterprises benefited from government contracts, but the effect was uneven. Increased demand in textile production for uniforms actually depressed prices and wages, and jobs were still being lost from many smaller workshops as Russia struggled to recover fully from recession (Engelstein. *Moscow, 1905*, p. 42). For more information on police activity, see: Spiridovich. *Partiia Sotsialistov-Revoliutsionerov i ee predshestvenniki*, pp. 130–132; Rice, Christopher. *Russian Workers and the Socialist-Revolutionary Party Through the Revolution of 1905–07*. New York: Saint Martin's Press, 1988, p. 52.

20 Lane, David. *The Roots of Russian Communism. A Social and Historical Study of Russian Social-Democracy, 1898–1907*. Assen: Van Gorcum, 1969, p. 71.

21 Chemodanova, E. M. *Zhizn' i tvorcheskii put' M. M. Chemodanova 1856–1908*, Unpublished typescript, circa 1935, p. 8, MM FC, f. 22, op. 1, d. 6, OF 9823/41–13.

22 The image is titled *Na rasput'e. Na levo ili napravo?* [*At the Crossroads. Left or right?*]. It is signed 'M. Chemodanov', and dated 9/XII 1904. The composition is modelled on Viktor Vasnetsov's painting *Vitiaz' na rasput'e* [*A Knight at the Crossroads*].

23 Chemodanov's first works of the new period appeared in *Novosti dnia* [*News of the Day*], a liberal newspaper published in Moscow (No. 7760, 9 January 1905, p. 2). For background to these cartoons, see: Smirnov, A. V. *Vospominaniia o M. M. Chemodanove*, unpublished one-page typescript, undated, MM FC, f. 22, op. 1, d. 6, OF 9823/41–10.

24 Estimates of the numbers vary, but it is thought that 50,000–100,000 people took part (Ascher, Abraham. *The Revolution of 1905: Russia in Disarray*. Stanford: Stanford University Press, 1988, p. 90).

25 Gapon's petition expressed the workers' loyalty to the Tsar and appealed for 'justice and protection' from 'despotism and lawlessness'. However, it also contained radical political proposals, including a plea for popular representation, and civil liberties for all citizens. Gapon's own motives are unclear, but the act of holding an unsanctioned protest and the petition itself was seen as constituting a direct challenge to Imperial authority (Ascher. *The Revolution of 1905: Russia in Disarray*. p. 90).

26 Razorenov. 'Rabochie o 9-m ianvariia 1905 goda'. Zelikson-Bobrovskaia, Ts. (Editor). *Pervaia russkaia revoliutsiia v Peterburge 1905 g. Sbornik statei, vospominanii, materialov i dokumentov*. Leningrad/Moscow: Gosudarstvennoe izdatel'stvo, 1925, p. 18.

27 There is no consensus on the numbers. Official figures reported 130 were killed and 299 seriously injured, but other estimates were considerably higher (Ascher. *The Revolution of 1905: Russia in Disarray*. pp. 91–92).

28 Letter from Rataev to the Department of Police, 28 December – 15 January 1905, HIWRP OA, Index XXVb, Folder 1.

29 Letter sent by Iulii Martov and Georgii Plekhanov to Victor Servy, Geneva, January 1905, author's collection.

30 *Tovarishchi rabochie!* Saint Petersburg Socialist-Revolutionary Party Committee, Undated but early 1905, IISG PSR, Index 325.

31 Klaas, G. 'V organisatsiiu, v organizatsiiu'. Zelikson-Bobrovskaia, Ts. (Editor). *Pervaia russkaia revoliutsiia v Peterburge 1905 g.* Sbornik 2-oi: *Po fabrikam i zavodam*. Leningrad: Gosudarstvennoe izdatel'stvo, 1925, p. 105.

32 Razorenov. 'Rabochie o 9-m ianvariia 1905 goda', p. 19.

33 RGIA, f. 777, op. 6, d. 9, l. 14.

34 The only items that were allowed to be published legally were official reports and government communiqués passed by the censor. However, in practice many editors found a way to sneak in references to these issues (Zhirkov, G.V. *Istoriia tsensury v Rossii XIX–XX vv*. Moscow: Aspekt Press, 2001, p. 187).

35 Korolenko, V. 'Svoboda pechati'. *Russkoe bogatstvo*, Nos. 11–12, 1905, p. 198.

36 TsDIAK, f. 275, op. 1, d. 734, l. 37.

37 For mentions of Socialist-Revolutionary postcards, see: *Z. K. No. 4 Zagr. Kom. 1905 g.*, IISG PSR, Index 212; *Revoliutsionnaia Rossiia*. No. 60, 5 March 1905, p. 24; *Revoliutsionnaia Rossiia*. No. 64, 15 April 1905, p. 16.
For Social Democratic postcards, see: *Iskra*. No. 86, 3 February 1905, p. 8; *Iskra*. No. 90, 3 March 1905, p. 8; *Iskra*. No. 92, 10 March 1905, p. 8; *Iskra*. No. 94, 25 March 1905, p. 6.

38 TsDIAK, f. 275, op. 1, d. 661, ll. 9–10.

39 In the factories, this process of transformation was by no means instant or universal. Most workers remained loyal to the Tsar, and resistant to anything they construed as interference in their affairs. But as they became aware of concerns that were greater than their own, their demands for economic change became increasingly political in character. And in looking around them, the workers became more cognisant of the power that they held, of their ability and right to demand. By the year's end they had become a more socially conscious group, often far more effective at organising themselves than at being organised by the revolutionaries.

40 Later in the year, some of these cartoons were reproduced in Russia with Russian captions. One example is Félix-Antoine Marmonier's *Le sang du peuple Russe crie vengeance… [The Blood of the Russian People Cries Out for Revenge]*, first published in the Paris-based satirical journal *L'Arc en Ciel*, and reprinted in France as a postcard in a limited edition of 100. This image was reproduced photomechanically from a hand-drawn Russian copy, bearing the title: *Krov' russkogo naroda vopiet o mshchenii… [The Blood of the Russian People Cries Out for Revenge…]* (The hand-drawn original of the Russian edition is in the Museum of Contemporary History, Fond Grafiki, 36/369).

41 Accounts for the Saint Petersburg Socialist-Revolutionary Party Committee between December 1904 and February 1905 show an income of seven roubles derived from selling postcards of Sazonov (*Revoliutsionnaia Rossiia*. No. 61, 15 March 1905, p. 20).

42 *Otkrytoe pis'mo*. No. 5, 1905, p. 129.

43 Untitled leaflet. Saint Petersburg Socialist-Revolutionary Party Committee, Undated but circa February 1904, IISG PSR, Index 325.

44 See entry in the Foreign Committee accounts book for May 1905, where 'cards of Kaliaev' are listed under expenses for 'library' (*Z. K. No.4 Zagr. Kom. 1905 g.*, IISG PSR, Index 212).

45 The Kobeko Commission ended its work in November, by which stage the political situation was completely different. The press reforms enacted after the October Manifesto were, however, based on some of the ideas put forward by the commission.

46 The Pirogov Society Conference on cholera took place on 21–23 March 1905. The drawings displayed at the conference were among those later reproduced in postcard form by Dmitrii Peschanskii (Smirnov, A.V. *Vospominaniia o M.M. Chemodanove*, p. 1).

47 Chemodanova, E. M. *Khudozhnik Russkoi Revoliutsii – M.M. Chemodanov*. Unpublished typescript, circa 1935, p. 8, MSI KF.

48 See, for example, copy of this postcard sent in March 1905 to Karrik's cousin Nevill Forbes by his aunt (LRA FA, MS1496, Box 5).

49 Bel'gard, A. V. *Vospominaniia*. Moscow: Novoe literaturnoe obozrenie, 2009, p. 211.

50 GARF, f. 102, op. 233a, d. 80 ch. 20, l. 96.

51 The images were originally submitted to the censor in February 1905 (RGIA, f. 777, op. 27, d. 82, ll. 9–10; RGIA, f. 777, op. 27, d. 518, l. 220.

52 RGIA, f. 777, op. 27, d. 518, l. 280.

53 See also three drawings for postcards titled *Krasnyi smekh [Red Laughter]*, which were turned down by the Moscow Censorship Committee in June 1905 (TsDIAK, f. 294, op. 1, d. 380, l. 72).

54 RGIA, f. 777, op. 27, d. 518, l. 535.

55 The Press Administration sent a circular about the Warsaw postcards in early July 1905, but it was not until 29 September that the city's censorship committee acted upon it. It was then another few weeks before another circular reporting the decision was sent out to other regional censors (TsDIAK, f. 294, op. 1, d. 380, l. 89). As for the Svedomskii and Kalinichenko postcards, the delay was even greater. The cards were banned in May, but it was only in September that the Kiev Committee received a list of prohibited works that included the images (TsDIAK, f. 294, op. 1, d. 380, l. 80). Reports in the Press Administration archives show that they were aware of the issues caused by the delays, but there was little they succeeded in doing about it (See, for example: RGIA, f. 776, op. 9, d. 65, l. 125). A few weeks, let alone four months, was quite sufficient for postcards to have been distributed across the Empire.

56 The best known images are a set of four postcards published by a firm named *Iskra* or *Iskry* (grammatically it is unclear which). Three reproduce photographic images of the Battleship Potemkin, and one a drawing of Seaman Vakulinchuk's corpse by the illustrator Louis Sabattier. The latter, which was also reproduced photomechanically by other publishers, was originally published in the French journal *L'Illustration* (Louis Sabattier. *Le Corps du Matelot Omeltchouk Exposé, le 28 juin, sur le Nouveau Mole D'Odessa. L'Illustration*. No. 3255, Paris, 15 July 1905, pp. 40–41).

57 Spiridovich. *Partiia Sotsialistov-Revoliutsionerov i ee predshestvenniki*, p. 177–8.

58 The Bloody Sunday postcards were by Georges Scott: *The Cossacks' Onslaught*, and Samuel Begg: *Martyrs in the Cause of Freedom: The Massacre of Strikers at the End of the Troitzky Bridge* (GARF, f. 63, op. 25, d. 466, ll. 20, 23, 29).

59 RGIA, f. 777, op. 27, d. 518, l. 322.

60 This was the so-called Bulygin Duma, named for the ineffectual Interior Minister who replaced Sviatopolk-Mirskii in the wake of Bloody Sunday.

61 The postcards were printed by A. A. Levenson, one of the largest printing houses in Moscow. Their titles are: *Na rasput'e napravo ili nalevo [At the Crossroads – Left or Right]*, 9.XII.1904; *Kto kogo [Who Will Defeat Whom]*, 12.XII.1904; *Molodets rastet ne po dniam a po chasam…*

[*The Good Fellow Grows Not by the Day but by the Hour*], 9.1.1905 (Marked on reverse as having passed the censor on 11 August 1905). Like most of the drawings he made in 1905, all are signed 'M. Chemodanov'.

62 RGIA, f. 777, op. 27, d. 518, ll. 383–384.
63 Ascher. *The Revolution of 1905: Russia in Disarray*, p. 215; Bel'gard. *Vospominaniia*, p. 252.
64 RGIA, f. 776, op. 16 ch. 1, d. 17, l. 411.
65 RGIA, f. 776, op. 16 ch. 1, d. 17, l. 411; Bel'gard, p. 253.
66 *Knizhnyi vestnik*. No. 47, Saint Petersburg, November 1905, pp. 1314–1315.
67 Bel'gard. *Vospominaniia*, p. 260.
68 Bel'gard. *Vospominaniia*, pp. 266–267.
69 Effectively, Belgard was attempting to create the right conditions for the continued growth of the print industry, while at the same time endeavouring to ensure that this expansion did not come at the expense of the government's political security. It was a delicate balance to tread (Bel'gard. *Vospominaniia*, p. 261).
70 Mintslov, S. R. '14 mesiatsev svobody pechati. 17 okt. 1905 g. – 1 ianv. 1907'. *Byloe*. No. 3/15, Saint Petersburg, March 1907, p. 125.
71 Maliazh. 'Nedavnee i nastoiashchee. Kharakteristika satiricheskikh zhurnalov'. *Otkliki khudozhestvennoi zhizni*. No. 2, Saint Petersburg, 1910, p. 70.
72 In Saint Petersburg, students and teachers from the Imperial Academy of Arts, the Stiglitz Technical School of Drawing, and in Moscow, from the Stroganov School of Arts and Industry, and the School of Painting, Sculpture and Architecture, became closely involved in the revolutionary movement (Shleev, V. V. *Revoliutsiia 1905–1907 godov i izobrazitel'noe iskusstvo: Moskva i rossiiskaia provintsiia*. Moscow: Izobrazitel'noe iskusstvo, 1978, p. 5).
73 See, for example *Burelom*. No. 1, Saint Petersburg, 1905, p. 8; *Bureval*. No. 1, Saint Petersburg, 1906, p. 8 etc.
74 Maliazh. 'Nedavnee i nastoiashchee. Kharakteristika satiricheskikh zhurnalov', p. 71.
75 Maliazh. 'Nedavnee i nastoiashchee. Kharakteristika satiricheskikh zhurnalov', p. 70.
76 Rubakin, N. 'Knizhnyi priliv i knizhnyi otliv'. *Sovremennyi mir*. No. 12, Saint Petersburg, 1909, p. 6
77 Bonch-Bruevich, V. D. *Bol'shevistskie izdatel'skie dela v 1905–1907 gg: Moi vospominaniia*. Leningrad: Leningradskoe oblastnoe izdatel'stvo, 1933, p. 85.
78 RGIA, f. 776, op. 29, d. 29, l. 5.
79 Rubakin. 'Knizhnyi priliv i knizhnyi otliv', pp. 3–4.
80 RGIA, f. 776, op. 23, d. 10, l. 13.
81 Avel'-Avok, A. L. 'Satira v zhurnalakh i gazetakh'. *Vestnik znaniia*. No. 2, Saint Petersburg, 1906, p. 384
82 Gulak, Vasil. *Osnovy grazhdanskoi svobody* [*The Principles of Civil Freedom*]. K. V. Bykov, passed by censor on 9 November 1905.
83 RGIA, f. 777, op. 27, d. 257, ll. 564–5.
84 In Kiev there were at least three publishers that printed Gulak's postcards: K. V. Bykov, D. T. Markov and I. Richter. In Moscow, they were printed by I. N. Kushnerev, in Saint Petersburg by the Smirnov Printing House, and in Odessa by the Grinbau Printing House (Demchenko, E. P. *Politicheskaia grafika v pechati Ukrainy 1905–1907*. Kiev, 1984, p. 187).
85 TsGIA, f. 706, op. 1, d. 3, l. 6.
86 Golubeva, O. D. 'Izdatel'skoe delo v Rossii v period Pervoi russkoi revolutsii (1905–1907)'. *Kniga: Issledovaniia i materialy*. No. 24, 1972, p. 116.
87 It does not appear that opposition parties other than the revolutionaries had much involvement in the production of anti-government postcards. There is only one image that I can link unequivocally to the Kadets, a postcard listing the First Duma results in the Moscow region, which extols the Party's 'brilliant victory' in the election.
88 Garting, Arkadii to Petr Rachkovskii. *Otpusk 121*. 26 October – 13 December 1905, HIWRP OA, Index XXIVh, Folder 4c.
89 Chernov. *Pered burei*, p. 257.
90 Korolenko. 'Svoboda pechati', p. 198.
91 Garting, Arkadii to Petr Rachkovskii. *Otpusk 121*. 26 October – 13 December 1905, HIWRP OA, Index XXIVh, Folder 4c.
92 *Moskovskoe vooruzhennoe vosstanie, vypusk I-i*. Moskva: Letopis', 1906, p. 22.
93 Engelstein. *Moscow, 1905*, p. 220.
94 Bel'gard. *Vospominaniia*, p. 262.
95 *Knizhnyi vestnik*. No. 47, December 1905, p. 1450.

CONCESSION AND REPRESSION

1 Prior to the October Manifesto, revolutionary or reformist subject matter was printed in *Iskry* only when it touched the ruling classes directly, or was initiated by them. For example: photographs from the scene of Grand Duke Sergei's assassination were printed in *Iskry*. No. 7, 13 February 1905, p. 50; street scenes of people reading the announcement of the so-called Bulygin Duma were published in No. 32, 14 August 1905, pp. 252–253, 256, and No. 33, 21 August 1905, pp. 260–261. For images relating to the post-Manifesto unrest, see: No. 41, 30 October 1905, pp. 321–326, which includes photographs of barricades and demonstrations in Moscow on 18 October, as well as photographs of Nikolai Bauman's funeral; No. 42, 6 November 1905, pp. 330–331, 334–336, shows the aftermath of a pogrom in Ekaterinoslav and Mikhailovsk, and an 18 October Demonstration in Warsaw; No. 43, 13 November 1905, pp. 339, 343, carries pictures of pogroms in Kaluga, a funeral of pogrom victims in Sebastopol, and unrest in Kronstadt. The front page of the following number has a sculpture of Maxim Gorky on the front page, and a picture of Father Gapon by Bulla on the back page (No. 44, 20 November 1905). Schmidt's mutiny is given half a page of photographs in No. 45, 27 November 1905, p. 358, and three and a half pages in No. 46 from 4 December 1905, pp. 363–366.

2 See, for example, entry in the Saint Petersburg Censorship Committee's register for 3 November 1905 granting *Niva* permission to print 'images of the revolt in Kronstadt and other recent events' (RGIA, f. 777, op. 27, d. 82, ll. 117–118).

3 RGIA, f. 777, op. 27, d. 82; Bel'gard. *Vospominaniia*, p. 259.

4 One banned postcard, looked at by the Committee on November 2 1905, was titled *Edinomyshlenniki* [*Kindred Spirits*]. It depicted 'an officer arm in arm with a ragamuffin, who has a bottle emerging from his pocket' (RGIA, f. 777, op. 27, d. 518, l. 590).

5 For example, on 11 May 1905, Vera Vodovoza was stopped from publishing a portrait of the theorist Petr Lavrov. In March 1906, she was given permission to print images of Kaliaev and Polivanov, and shortly afterwards, was allowed to publish a far more extensive series of anti-government portraits. These were possibly prints as opposed to postcards (RGIA, f. 777, op. 27, d. 518, l. 220; RGIA, f. 776, op. 9, d. 43, ll. 10–11; RGIA, f. 777, op. 27, d. 538, ll. 98–100).

6 RGIA, f. 777, op. 27, d. 82, ll. 181–2; RGIA, f. 777, op. 27, d. 83, ll. 1–2

7 RGIA, f. 776, op. 9, d. 43, ll. 1–2.

8 RGIA, f. 776, op. 9, d. 43, ll. 3, 8.

9 RGIA, f. 776, op. 9, d. 43, ll. 14–15.

10 For adherence to the criminal code, see: Bel'gard. *Vospominaniia*, p. 269.

11 RGIA, f. 776, op. 9, d. 43, ll. 5, 12.

12 RGIA, f. 777, op. 7, d. 24, l. 2.

13 RGIA, f. 776, op. 9, d. 43, l. 25.

14 The postcard is undated but likely dates to around spring 1906 (Private collection, Moscow).

15 For examples of banned images, see: RGIA, f. 777, op. 7, d. 24, l. 2; RGIA f. 777, op. 27, d. 84, ll. 11–12; RGIA, f. 777, op. 27, d. 519, l. 283; RGIA, f. 777, op. 27, d. 86, l. 34.

16 Although periodicals, particularly satirical journals and revolutionary newspapers, were badly affected by repression in early 1906, this assessment also broadly applies to the much of the rest of the print industry.

17 RGIA, f. 776, op. 16 ch. 1, d. 17, l. 411.

18 Bel'gard. *Vospominaniia*, p. 266.

19 Vasil'ev, A. N. 'Kul'turnoe znachenie otkrytogo pis'ma.', p. 4.

20 Anonymous. 'Zagranichnaia pechat' o polozhenii otkrytochnoi torgovli'. *Otkrytoe pis'mo*. No. 1, Uman, 1906, p. 5.

21 Anonymous. 'Zagranichnaia pechat' o polozhenii otkrytochnoi torgovli'. *Otkrytoe pis'mo*. Uman, No. 1, 1906, p. 5.

22 TsGIA SPB, f. 202, op. 2, d. 1261, ll. 3–4.

23 Ioffe, A. M. *Izdatel'skaia deiatel'nost' bol'shevikov v 1905–1907 gg.* Moscow: Kniga, 1971, p. 160.

24 There is no reference to Shipovnik's postcards in the Saint Petersburg Censor's journals, but this may be because they came under the aegis of the Foreign Censor.

25 Publishers of politically-themed postcards who operated openly included: (Saint Petersburg) A. Freinkel (also 'Freikel'), Nikolai Merder, Vasilii Metalnikov, Nikolai Martynson, Mysl, Novyi mir, Shipovnik, August Tsenter, and A. K. Veierman. (Moscow): D. P. Efimov, LUMO, Nachalo, and N. V. Vasilev. (Kiev) K. V. Bykov, D. T. Markov, and I. Richter. For printing houses that either received commissions to produce postcards on contemporary political themes or printed their own: (Saint Petersburg) Ia. Balianskii, Golike and Vilborg, Kordovskii and Dressler, I. N. Kushnerev, Sherer and Nabgolts, Smirnov Printing House. (Moscow) R. Bakhman, E. Kudinova and A. Lezina, A. A. Levenson, Russkoe tovarishchestvo pechatnogo i izdatelskogo dela. (Kiev) S. V. Kulzhenko. (Odessa) Grinbau Printing House, Lopshits Printing House.

26 See, for example: *Volna*. No. 2, Saint Petersburg, 27 April 1906, p. 1 for an advertisement by the Social Democratic orientated Novyi mir [New World] bookshop and publisher offering May Day postcards; *Novaia zhizn'*. Moscow, No. 5, 10 June, 1906, p. 4 for 'a large selection of portraits and postcards' offered by the bookstore and publisher Mysl [Thought]; *Novaia mysl'*. Moscow, No. 25, 10 August 1906, p. 1 for reproductions of pictures by 'Iaroshenko, Shlugleit, Vladimirov, Geller, Maimon, Mazurovskii and many others', Shipovnik postcards, and self-published 'postcard portraits of civic activists' offered by Nachalo [The Beginning] bookshop. For Shipovnik postcards see also: *Adskaia pochta*. No. 2, Saint Petersburg, 1906, p. 12; *Adskaia pochta*. No. 3, p. 7; Kautskii, Karl. *Nauka, zhizn' i etika*, advertisement on inside back cover. All these postcards would have been legal to print. With the exception of Shipovnik, I have found no contemporary advertisements for satirical cartoons.

27 By contrast, Black Hundred publications were heavily subsidised and many were disseminated free, due to lack of demand (Rubakin. 'Knizhnyi priliv i knizhnyi otliv', p. 16).

28 *Partiinye izvestiia*. Saint Petersburg: Izdanie Tsentral'nogo komiteta partii S-R, No. 3, December 1906, p. 4

29 Rubakin. 'Knizhnyi priliv i knizhnyi otliv', p. 3.

30 RGIA, f. 776, op. 29, d. 25, ll. 9–11; RGIA, f. 776, op. 29, d. 29, ll. 3–4; RGIA, f. 776, op. 29, d. 30, ll. 5–7.

31 Quoted in: Ascher, Abraham. *The Revolution of 1905: Authority Restored*, p. 118.

32 *Otkrytka*. No. 1, Kaluga, 1907, p. 2.

33 Zabochen', Mikhail. *Filokartiia*. Moscow: Sviaz', 1973, p. 36; *Otkrytoe pis'mo*, No. 1, Uman, 1906, p. 4.

34 Report sent by Head of Paris Okhrana Office to Director of Department of Police. *No. 97*. 23/10 March 1907, HIWRP OA, Index XXIVe, Folder 2c.

35 Their titles are: *Orator 18 Oktiabria 1905 g.* [*An Orator on 18 October 1905*]; *Ne smei bit' – neprikosvennost' lichnosti* [*Don't Dare to Beat – Inviolability of the Person*]; *Besplatnaia vydacha lekarstv* [*Free Distribution*

of Medicine]; *Podvigi synov Marsa* [*The Feats of the Sons of Mars*]; *Vpered rebiata, Da zdravstvuet svoboda* [*Forward Lads, Long Live Freedom*]; *Russkaia konstitutsiia 1905 g.* [*The Russian Constitution of 1905*]; *Portret Spiridonovoi* [*Portrait of Spiridonova*] (RGIA, f. 776, op. 9, d. 43, ll. 16, 17).

36 Tsenter was at this time printing his own photomechanical postcards (most of which related to the Duma), and he did later go on to publish cartoons, but it appears that officials were correct in saying that he was not responsible for these particular images.

37 RGIA, f. 776, op. 9, d. 43, l. 24.

38 The comparative availability of printing facilities inside the country after the October Manifesto would have made producing such postcards abroad counter-productive, both due to time and expense, as well as the complications of smuggling them into the country.

39 Bonch-Bruevich. *Bol'shevistskie izdatel'skie dela v 1905–1907 gg*, p. 113; Bonch-Bruevich, V. D. *Otryvki iz vospominanii o rabote tipografii*. RGASPI, f. 4, op. 2, d. 3107, l. 1.

40 *Knizhnyi vestnik*. No. 26, 1906, p. 635.

41 *Alfavitnyi ukazatel' knigam i broshiuram, arest na kotorye utverzhden sudebnymi ustanovleniiami po 1-e ianvaria 1910 goda*. Saint Petersburg: Tipografiia Ministerstva vnutrennikh del, 1910, pp. 67–8.

42 The first two anti-government postcards, published by Metalnikov and titled *Pamiati 9go ianvaria* [*In Memory of 9 January*] and *Prestuplenie i nakazanie* [*Crime and Punishment*], were both banned by the courts in 1907 (RGIA, f. 776, op. 9, d. 1026, l. 3; RGIA, f. 776, op. 9, d. 983, l. 2). The third postcard, which reproduced a picture by an unidentified artist named 'Kolen', titled *Revoliutsiia* [*Revolution*] was banned in 1909 (RGIA, f. 776, op. 9, d. 1805, l. 5).

43 There were also numerous other small establishments where printed works were sold. For full list see: RGIA, f. 776, op. 29, d. 30, l. 2.

44 RGIA, f. 776, op. 23, d. 10, l. 120.

45 RGIA, f. 776, op. 9, d. 43, l. 20.

46 GARF, f. 102, op. 63, d. 101, l. 1.

47 Vasiliev. 'Kul'turnoe znachenie otkrytago pis'ma', p. 4.

48 RGIA, f. 776, op. 23, d. 10, l. 13.

49 Many of the illegal postcards confiscated by Vinogradov were Polish nationalist images. (RGIA, f. 776, op. 23, d. 10, ll. 22–25).

50 For more on the trade in illegal material, see: RGIA, f. 776, op. 23, d. 10, l. 14.

51 In regards to the disparity of approaches, note the Odessa Inspector's suggestion in March 1906 that the police confiscate images of Lieutenant Schmidt – at exactly the same time that the Administration was pronouncing them legal (Demchenko. *Politicheskaia grafika v pechati Ukrainy 1905–1907*, p. 185). On occasion, Belgard would even write to check with governors under what pretext material was being confiscated. See, for example: RGIA, f. 776, op. 16 ch. 1, d. 16, l. 229.

52 GARF, f. 102, op. 203, d. 2 ch. 34 t. 1, l. 334.

53 For examples of individuals prosecuted under these Articles, see: GARF, f. 58, op. 2, d. 656, ll. 1–30; GARF, f. 102, op. 204, d. 5164, l. 11; GARF, f. 102, op. 203, d. 2 ch. 34 t. 1, l. 700; GARF, f. 102, op. 203, d. 11968, ll. 30–31.

54 See, for example: GARF, f. 58, op. 3, d. 400, ll. 1–61; GARF, f. 102, op. 203, d. 6048, ll. 20–21; GARF, f. 102, op. 204, d. 2330, l. 1.

55 GARF, f. 102, op. 204, d. 2 ch. 34, l. 46.

56 *Knizhnyi vestnik*. Nos. 22–23, 1906, p. 561.

DUMA AND DEMISE

1 Romanova's political outlook appears to have been fluid. In one Interior Ministry document, she is described as being close to the Social Democrats, while in another she is reported to be a member of the Socialist-Revolutionary Party (GARF, f. 63, op. 26, d. 237, ll. 31, 107).

2 GARF, f. 63, op. 26, d. 237, ll. 1, 15.

3 Chemodanov was accused of Criminal Code Articles 128 (showing disrespect to the Supreme Power or system of government) and 129 (publicly displaying or distributing an image that incites the overthrow of the system) (GARF, f. 102, op. 203, d. 2 ch. 34 t. 1, l. 700).

4 GARF, f. 102, op. 203, d. 11968, ll. 14, 16, 21.

5 GARF, f. 102, op. 203, d. 2 ch. 34 t. 1, l. 729.

6 Demchenko, E. P. *Politicheskaia grafika v pechati Ukrainy 1905–1907*, p. 185.

7 Vasil'ev. 'Kul'turnoe znachenie otkrytogo pis'ma', p. 4.

8 Witte's attainment of a foreign loan in mid-April had removed a major source of concern for the government, one greater even than the threat of internal disorder. Salaries could now be paid and state mechanisms would continue to function. After agreeing the loan, Witte was replaced by Ivan Goremykin, a non-entity with a strongly conservative outlook. Largely thanks to his predecessor's success in securing credit, Goremykin was able to act without any obligation to the new legislature. Once convened, his way of dealing with the Duma was to ignore it.

9 GARF, f. 102, op. 203, d. 9631, l. 2; GARF, f. 124, op. 45, d. 1713, l. 2.

10 Ascher, Abraham. *The Revolution of 1905: Authority Restored*. Stanford: Stanford University Press, 1992, pp. 245–8.

11 *Knizhnyi vestnik*. Nos. 22–23, June 1906, p. 562.

12 RGIA, f. 776, op. 9, d. 43, l. 25.

13 RGIA, f. 776, op. 9, d. 43, l. 26. For example, in June 1906, following the appearance of images of Schmidt and the aftermath of an unrelated pogrom, the temporary governor of Odessa used the pretext of martial law to order the Senior Inspector 'to arrest all portraits and photographs related to the revolutionary movement' (RGIA, f. 776, op. 16 ch. 1, d. 16, l. 229).

14 By March 1906, sixty out of eighty-seven provinces and regions in the Russian Empire were under some form of emergency regulation. For full list, see: *Pravo*. No. 10, March 1906, pp. 909–916. See also: Waldron, Peter. 'States of Emergency: Autocracy and Extraordinary Legislation, 1881–1917'. *Revolutionary Russia*. Vol. 8, No. 1, 1995. p. 4; Daly, Jonathan W. 'On the Significance of Emergency Legislation in Late Imperial Russia'. *Slavic Review*, Vol. 54, No. 3, 1995, pp. 602–629.

15 See, for example, use of emergency regulations in September 1906 against a Jewish bookseller in Odessa who was caught selling pornographic postcards and revolutionary portraits. This case reportedly acted as a (possibly only temporary) deterrent against other booksellers carrying out similar activities (TsDIAK, f. 335, op. 1, d. 59, ll. 5, 18, 19).

16 GARF, f. 102, op. 236, d. 829, l. 1.

17 TSGIA SPB, f. 202, op. 2, d. 1261, l. 230.

18 Druzhinin, N. 'Doktor Chemodanov'. *Kommunist*, No. 1, 1982, p. 66.

19 Mintslov. '14 mesiatsev svobody pechati. 17 okt. 1905 g. – 1 ianv. 1907', p. 129.

20 In his letter to Petr Stolypin, Chemodanov claims that he returned from the Caucasus in October after a three-month stay. This would make departure date around August (GARF, f. 102, op. 203, d. 2 ch. 34 t. 1, l. 725). A police report from 28 October, however, says that he only left for the Caucasus on 25 September (GARF, f. 63, op. 26, d. 933, l. 2). It is unclear which is correct.

21 Druzhinin. 'Doktor Chemodanov', p. 66.

22 The letter was from one of Chemodanov's former postcard distributors, who was writing to advise of his recent return to Russia after fleeing abroad, and of his readiness to devote himself again to revolutionary activity (GARF, f. 63, op. 26, d. 1123, l. 2; GARF, f. 102, op. 203, d. 7546, l. 18).

23 GARF, f. 63, op. 26, d. 933, l. 1.

24 Following the initial discovery of Chemodanov's postcards in May, he was made subject to 'unconditional arrest', so it is not immediately obvious why he was not detained on 31 October. Fainshtein claims that it was because he was away at the time, but the official protocol on the search not only attests to his presence, but also includes his signature. The Okhrana search warrant carries a handwritten note reading, 'not arrested, nothing found,' suggesting that lack of evidence precluded his arrest (Fainshtein. 'Russkie revoliutsionnye otkrytki', p. 89; GARF, f. 63, op. 26, d. 933, ll. 4, 5).

25 GARF, f. 63, op. 26, d. 933, l. 7a.

26 GARF, f. 63, op. 26, d. 933, l. 41.

27 GARF, f. 102, op. 203, d. 11968, l. 22; GARF, f. 63, op. 26, d. 933, ll. 41–42.

28 GARF, f. 102, op. 203, d. 2 ch. 34 t. 1, l. 674.

29 Chemodanov's arrest is variously described in Interior Ministry reports as having taken place on either 3 or 4 December. The police protocol records it as having taken place on 3 December. Chemodanov himself writes that it took place on the night of the 3–4 December (GARF, f. 63, op. 26, d. 933, ll. 9, 10; GARF, f. 102, op. 203, d. 2 ch. 34, t. 1, l. 725).

30 GARF, f. 102, op. 203, d. 2 ch. 34 t. 1, ll. 674–5

31 GARF, f. 63, op. 26, d. 933, l. 15; GARF, f. 102, op. 203, d. 11968, l. 22.

32 GARF, f. 58, op. 2, d. 1165, ll. 30, 38.

33 GARF, f. 58, op. 2, d. 1165, l. 79; GARF, f. 102, op. 203, d. 11968, l. 22.

34 GARF, f. 102, op. 203, d. 2 ch. 34 t. 1, l. 725.

35 GARF, f. 102, op. 203, d. 2 ch. 34 t. 1, ll. 724–725.

36 GARF, f. 102, op. 203, d. 2 ch. 34 t. 1, l. 698.

37 In fact, an order was given by Stolypin to release Chemodanov after his first letter, but bureaucratic procedures led to delays (GARF, f. 102, op. 203, d. 2 ch. 34 t. 1, l. 698; GARF, f. 58, op. 2, d. 1165, l. 6).

38 GARF, f. 102, op. 203, d. 2 ch. 34 t. 1, l. 701; GARF, f. 63, op. 26, d. 933, ll. 36, 44.

39 Chemodanov, M. M. *Pis'mo k advokatu*, 11 January 1907, MM FC, f. 22, op. 1, d. 2, OF 9823/13–14a.

40 Chemodanov, M. M. Zapisnaia knizhka, 1907, MM FC, f. 22, op. 1, d. 6, OF-9823/12; Zubovrachebnaia zapisnaia knizhka za 1903 god, 1907, MM FC, f. 22, op. 1, d. 6, OF-9823/11.

41 Chemodanova. *Khudozhnik Russkoi Revoliutsii – M. M. Chemodanov*, p. 12.

42 *Russkoe slovo*. No. 15, 18 January 1908, p. 5.

43 GARF, f. 63, op. 26, d. 237, l. 62.

44 Evreinov's death presents something of a mystery. In February 1907, he was summoned to a duel by an anarchist named Vladimir Glubokovskii. On 30 March, he received a gunshot wound and died in hospital on 2 April. Glubokovskii was arrested, but was not prosecuted after the police concluded that Evreinov had committed suicide. However, Glubokovskii was given a minimum five-year term of exile in 'Asiatic Russia' for unrelated political misdemeanours (GARF, f. 63, op. 26, d. 1123, ll. 23, 56); Morozova was sentenced to five years' hard labour in 1907, also on an unrelated matter (GARF, f. 58, op. 2, d. 656, l. 27).

45 Antonina Romanova and Aleksandra Petrovna were convicted of Criminal Code Articles 128 (showing disrespect to the Supreme Power or system of government) and 132 (anyone guilty of Article 128 who did not succeed in distributing the works in question, or who stored such works). While awaiting trial, Antonina Romanova had been arrested at a meeting of railway workers in July 1907, and again in February 1908, for her part in a robbery on a post office. In June 1908, she was exiled for five years to Yakutsk Province. The one-and-a-half-year term she received in the Chemodanov case in May 1909, however, took precedence, and this she completed in November 1910. In December that year, she was put on trial for her involvement in the robbery, and was sentenced to twelve years' hard labour (GARF, f. 102, op. 203, d. 11968, ll. 30–31; GARF, f. 63, op. 26, d. 237, ll. 107–108, 128, 138).

46 Anna Romanova had been accused of Article 128.

47 GARF, f. 102, op. 203, d. 11968, l. 34; GARF, f. 58, op. 2, d. 656, l. 46.

48 Zhirkov. *Istoriia tsensury v Rossii XIX–XX vv*, p. 191.

49 None of the documents relating to the case make any reference to how the postcards were produced.

50 28 November 1906: *Lidvaliada* [*Lidvaliada*], *Gurko Lidval' opravdyvaiushchiisia* [*Gurko Lidval Looking for Excuses*] (RGIA, f. 777, op. 27, d. 93, l. 121); 7 December 1906: *K vyboram. Pamiati pervoi gosudarstv. Dumy* [*Commemorating the Elections in Memory of the First State Duma*], *Golod v derevne* [*Famine in the Countryside*], *Pokushenie na Admirala Dubasova* [*Assassination Attempt on Admiral Dubasov*], *Zhertvam nashikh dnei* [*The Victims of Our Days*], *V nashe vremia (rasstrelivaiut)* [*In our Time (Executions are Taking Place)*] (RGIA, f. 777, op. 27, d. 94, ll. 49–50); 15 December 1906: *Istinno-russkii patrevot* [*True Russian Patriot*], *1906 i 1907 Rozhdestvenskii gus', sokrashchenie smet, prazdnichnykh net* [*1906 and 1907, Christmas Goose, the Budgets are Being Tightened, No Holidays*] (RGIA, f. 777, op. 27, d. 94, ll. 80–81).

51 These were not the type of images previously covered by Belgard's concessions and their approval in the midst of widespread repression is surprising. Metalnikov's postcards, however, were not the only examples of Press Administration latitude at this time. On 30 November, the Department of Police sent a letter to press officials querying twenty-eight postcards that they believed might be illegal. This was passed on to the Saint Petersburg censor for further verification. The content of these postcards is unspecified, but the censor replied to say that the images concerned had all been passed fit for publication. Thus, even as Cossack whips were swirling overhead, anti-government images could still be legally produced and sold (RGIA, f. 776, op. 9, d. 65, ll. 115–116, 124).

52 RGIA, f. 777, op. 10, d. 59, ll. 1, 4.

53 TsGIA SPB, f. 706, op. 1, d. 244, l. 10; RGIA, f. 777, op. 10, d. 15, ll. 1, 3.

54 The case of *In Memory of 9 January* came before courts on 20 November 1907, and on 27 May the following year it was reported that the drawing, negative and all copies of the postcard had been destroyed (RGIA, f. 776, op. 9, d. 1026, ll. 3, 6). The decision on *Crime and Punishment* was made on 24 February 1907, and the court order was carried out on 1 August i n the presence of Metalnikov's representative Mark Goldberg (RGIA, f. 776, op. 9, d. 983, ll. 2, 7).

55 10 February 1907: *Golod v Rossii* [*The Famine in Russia*], *Posledstviia Gurko, Lidval', Frederiks i Ko.* [*The Repercussions of Gurko, Lidval, Frederiks and Co.*] (RGIA, f. 777, op. 27, d. 96, ll. 34–35); 16 May 1907: *Trud i kapital* [*Labour and Capital*], *Purishkevich v vide Lenskogo* [*Purishkevich in the Guise of Lenskii*], *Son Purishkevicha* [*Purishkevich's Dream*], *Strashnye prizraki goloda* [*The Terrifying Spectres of Famine*], *Purishkevich v Dume* [*Purishkevich in the Duma*] (RGIA, f. 777, op. 27, d. 99, ll. 37–38, 40).

56 RGIA, f. 777, op. 27, d. 97, ll. 33–34.

57 *Domashnii muzei*. No. 8, February 1907, p. 12.

58 RGIA, f. 776, op. 9, d. 43, l. 35.

59 Report sent by Head of Paris Okhrana Office to Director of Department of Police. *No. 97*. 23/10 March 1907, HIWRP OA, Index XXIVe, Folder 2c.

60 RGIA, f. 776, op. 16, d. 1400, l. 1; *Domashnii muzei*. No. 8, February 1907, p. 12.

61 The latter series, dated 1 April, includes one of the few anti-government postcard caricatures of Stolypin as premier.

62 The postcard is titled *Progress* [*Progress*] and bears the caption 'Krushi ego, rebiata. Khvatai i ne pushchai' ['Destroy it Lads! Grab it and Don't Let it Go'] (RGIA, f. 776, op. 9, d. 1063, ll. 1, 3).

63 RGIA, f. 777, op. 27, d. 99, ll. 45–46, 48.

64 Pares, Bernard. *My Russian Memoirs*. London: Jonathan Cape, 1931, p. 135.

65 Pares. *My Russian Memoirs*, p. 55.

66 On 11 June, the Interior Ministry issued a circular linking recent disorder with the press, and asking governors to take all possible measures to crack down on anti-government periodicals.

67 RGIA, f. 777, op. 27, d. 99, ll. 69, 70.

68 The postcards were titled: *V nashe vremia… na rassvete prigovor proizveden v ispolnenie* [*In Our Time… The Sentence is Carried out At Dawn*] and *Zaspirtovannaia golova ubiitsy S.-Peterburgskogo Gradonachal'nika fon der Launitsa* [*The Preserved Head of the Killer of Saint Petersburg Governor von der Launitz*]. They were passed by the censor in December 1906, and January 1907 respectively (GARF, f. 102, op. 236, d. 829, ll. 2, 7–8).

69 GARF, f. 102, op. 236, d. 829, ll. 2–7.

70 RGIA, f. 776, op. 9, d. 43, l. 36.

71 RGIA, f. 776, op. 9, d. 43, ll. 38–39.

72 The Administration reported that while it lacked information on several of the postcards, two were definitely illegal (*Crime and Punishment* and *In Memory of 9 January*). The eventual outcome of Legasova's complaint is unknown (RGIA, f. 776, op. 9, d. 43, ll. 33–34).

73 The postcards were arrested under Article 129, Section 1 (inciting rebellious action). Their titles were as follows: *S 1 maia, tovarishchi! Proletarii vsekh stran soediniaites!* [*Happy 1 May Comrades! Proletarians of the World Unite*]; *S 1 maia! My trebuem: 8 chasov dlia raboty, 8 – dlia sna i 8 svobodnykh!* [*Happy 1 May, We Demand an 8 Hour Working Day, 8 Hours to Sleep and 8 Hours of Free Time*]; *K svobode* [*Towards Freedom*] (RGIA, f. 777, op. 11, d. 14, ll. 1–3).

74 I can find very little information on Freinkel (also Freikel) – even his first name is a mystery. He appears to have been a Social Democratic-orientated publisher, and may possibly have been a Party member named Aleksandr Romanovich (also Rakhmilevich) Freinkel (also spelt Frenkel and Frankel in police records), who was well-known to the police for his revolutionary activities.

75 RGIA, f. 777, op. 11, d. 14, l. 8.
76 *Literaturno-khudozhestvennye al'manakhi izdatel'stva Shipovnik*. Kniga Pervaia, Saint Petersburg, 1907, unpaginated advert at rear.
77 *Otchet Votkinskoi gruppy Partii Sotsialistov-Revoliutsionerov za sentiabr' mesiats 1908 goda*. IISG PSR, Index 369.
78 A questionnaire sent to Socialist-Revolutionary cells abroad ahead of the Third Party Congress in July 1907 asks if activists had 'published any cards, portraits, prints, etc.', or 'received any cards, portraits etc. for sale from other groups' (*Otchet 'gruppy Zagranichnoi Organizatsii' P. S.-R.* 1907, IISG PSR, Index 228).
79 *Z. K. No. 4 Zagr. Kom. 1905 g.*, IISG PSR, Index 212; Various financial accounts of the Oblastnoi zagranichnyi komitet, IISG PSR, Index 220.
80 *Finansovyi otchet Oblastnogo Komiteta Zagranichnykh Organizatsii Sotsialistov-Revoliutsionerov Za tri mesiatsa – s 15 marta po 15 iunia 1908 g./Raskhod po Oblastnomu Zagranich. Komitetu za tri mesiatsa, 15 marta po 15 iunia 1908 g.* IISG PSR, Index 220; *1907 g. v 15 fevralia po 15 oktiabria 1907, zagranitsei.* IISG PSR, Index 191. The images of Akatui were possibly printed in Geneva by the Atar Printing House.
81 *Spisok knig imeiushikhsia dlia prodazhi v ekspeditsii*, undated, IISG PSR, Index 191.
82 *Finansovyi otchet Oblastnogo Komiteta Zagranichnykh Organizatsii Sotsialistov-Revoliutsionerov Za tri mesiatsa – s 15 marta po 15 iunia 1908 g./Raskhod po Oblastnomu Zagranich. Komitetu za tri mesiatsa, 15 marta po 15 iunia 1908 g.* IISG PSR, Index 220.
83 Receipt from L. Desvignes. Paris, 24 October 1910, IISG PSR, Index 224.
84 But not all. Around this time, the journal *Byloe* printed a series of portrait postcards featuring Socialist-Revolutionary terrorists.
85 Letter to 'Dear Comrades' from Secretary of the Bern Group R. Lieberberg, Bern, 10 October 1907, IISG PSR, Index 243.
86 *Izvestiia Oblastnogo Komiteta Zagranichnoi Organizatsii*, No. 8, 1 July 1908, p. 15.
87 Povolzhskii. 'Nekotorye vnutrennie prichiny partiinogo krizisa'. *Izvestiia Oblastnogo Komiteta Zagranichnoi Organizatsii*, No. 9, February 1909, p. 4.
88 GARF, f. 102, op. 101, d. 2031, l. 19.
89 They included images of Nikolai Chernyshevskii, Friedrich Engels, Alexander Herzen, Ferdinand Lassalle, Petr Lavrov, and Georgii Plekhanov.
90 *Knizhnaia letopis'*. No. 25, 27 June 1909, p. 51.
91 RGIA, f. 776, op. 16 ch. 1, d. 17, ll. 414–415.
92 GARF, f. 102, op. 236, d. 829, l. 18.
93 GARF, f. 102, op. 236, d. 829, l. 25.
94 RGIA, f. 776, op. 9, d. 1805, ll. 2, 4, 5.
95 RGIA, f. 776, op. 9, d. 2125, ll. 1–3, 5.
96 *Letuchii listok No. 1: Krizis revoliutsii*. Izdanie gruppy sotsialistov-revoliutsionerov. S.-Peterburg, 12 March 1910, IISG PSR, Index 327.
97 In March 1912, for example, a certain Aleksei Kononov submitted seven postcards depicting 'scenes of revolutionary speechmaking, strikes, and protests.' These images, which were from the same series as those confiscated from August Tsenter in 1906, were swiftly rejected, impounded and destroyed. Their titles are: *(Orator) 18 Oktiabria 1905 g. 'Grazhdane! Slushaite da pogliadyvaite* [*(Orator) 18 October 1905. Citizens! Look Here and Listen*]; *Vpered Rebiata! Da zdravstvuet svoboda! Ved' Ia liberal* [*Forward Lads! Long Live Freedom! Sure, I'm a Liberal*]; *Narodnyi miting* [*Popular Rally*]; *Tovarishchi, zabastuem!!!* [*Comrades! Let's Strike!!!*]; *Svoboda slova – govori!!* [*Freedom of Speech – Well, Go on Speak!!*]; *Zhenskii miting. I my zabastuem* [*Women's Political Rally. And We're Going on Strike*]; *Zabastovali* [*They've Gone on Strike!*] (RGIA, f. 777, op. 18, d. 41, ll. 1, 5). These postcards subsequently appeared in the official list of banned publications (*Alfavitnyi ukazatel' knigam i broshiuram, a takzhe numeram povremmennykh izdanii, arest na kotorye utverzhden sudebnymi ustanovleniiami po 15-e aprelia 1914 goda*. Saint Petersburg: Tipografiia Ministerstva vnutrennikh del, 1914, p. 50).
98 For comparison to Bloody Sunday see leaflet: *Tovarishchi!* Biuro predstavitel'nogo organa i studentcheskaia fraktsiia S.-R., 17 April 1912, IISG PSR, Index 327.
99 The caption to one postcard reads: 'The Lena Shootings, 4 April 1912, illegally photographed a few hours after the shooting. Copyright MOPR.' MOPR is the acronym of Mezhdunarodnaia organizatsiia pomoshchi rabochim [The International Society for the Aid of Workers] – not to be confused with the later Soviet charitable organisation helping former revolutionaries.
100 The postcards were: Nikolai Iaroshenko's *Zakliuchennyi* [*The Prisoner*], Nikolai Verkhoturov's *1905 god* [*1905*], Ivan Vladimirov's *Ne vynes* [*He Could Not Stand it*], Evgenii Zarin's *Na katorgu* [*To the Hard Labour Camps*], Ruvim Shereshevskii's *V tiur'me* [*In Gaol*]. (GARF, f. 102, op. 70, d. 42, l. 1.)
101 For a list of Zlotnikov's postcards, see advertisement in: *Pauk*, No. 4, Saint Petersburg, 21 January 1912, p. 7.
102 GARF, f. 102, op. 69, d. 7 ch. 50, l. 11.
103 The postcards were banned under Article 96 of the Law Code Statute on Censorship and the Press (printing an item that causes hatred between different social estates) (GARF, f. 102, op. 69, d. 7 ch. 50, ll. 13, 29, 32).
104 In December 1916, the head of the Military District sent a secret communiqué to Petrograd's governor with orders to remove any postcards carrying German symbols, and to 'bring the owners to book for distributing such openly Germanophile publications.' A few days later, it was reported that over two hundred postcards had been confiscated from two different shop owners, each of whom were fined a thousand roubles (TsGIA SPB, f. 706, op. 1, d. 2124, ll. 3–5, 33).

105 Shliapnikov writes elsewhere: 'In Saint Petersburg alone, five thousand cards of the deputies exiled to Siberia sold out in two months, at a cost of between 0.25 and 1.50.' (Shliapnikov, Aleksandr. *Nakanune 1917 goda*. Moscow, 1920, pp. 138, 165–166).

106 Lenin was also involved in the production of a postcard cartoon directed against rival Georgii Plekhanov, titled: *My vozbudim techenie, protiv techeniia* [*We Will Stir up the Current, against the Current*] (Shleev. 'Otkrytki v zhizni i revoliutsionnoi deiatel'nosti V. I. Lenina', pp. 130–131).

107 Shleev. 'Otkrytki v zhizni i revoliutsionnoi deiatel'nosti V. I. Lenina', pp. 132–133.

108 Letter in English from Georgii Chicherin as head of the Russian Political Prisoners and Exiles Relief Committee to the Secretary of the Independent Labour Party, 24 July 1915, author's collection.

109 It has been claimed that illegal pornographic postcards of Rasputin and Alexandra were circulated widely in the lead up to 1917, but there is no evidence to suggest this was the case. While there were illegal journal illustrations made, all the postcards that I have seen were printed after the February Revolution.

110 For a contemporary observation of the continuing power of anti-government works, see: Rubakin. 'Knizhnyi priliv i knizhnyi otliv', pp. 23–24.

THE SOCIAL DEMOCRATIC PARTY

1 GARF, f. 102, op. 203, d. 6048 ch. 1, ll. 1, 3; GARF, f. 102, op. 203, d. 6048 ch. 2, l. 1; GARF, f. 102, op. 203, d. 6048 ch. 3, l. 1.

2 TsDIAK, f. 318, op. 1, d. 688, l. 2.

3 TsDIAK, f. 318, op. 1, d. 688, ll. 2–3.

4 TsDIAK, f. 318, op. 1, d. 688, l. 3.

5 TsDIAK, f. 275, op. 1, d. 938, l. 10.

6 Meznev, Stambulov and Isaak Berliner were charged with membership of a prohibited organisation and the crime of printing 'the illegal cartoon journal *Rassvet* [*Dawn*], and manufacturing postcards with criminal content.' Meznev and Stambulov received two years' imprisonment in a fortress prison, and Berliner one year and four months. Efroim Berliner was never caught, and the police later came to the conclusion that he had fled abroad (TsDIAK, f. 275, op. 1, d. 938, l. 10; GARF, f. 102, op. 203, d. 6048, ll. 12, 20–21).

7 *Tret'ii s"ezd RSDRP: Protokoly*. Moscow: Gosudarstvennoe izdatel'stvo politcheskoi literatury, 1959, p. 424

8 Efforts to expand Bolshevik publishing dovetailed with broader efforts to use existing legal and semi-legal structures in order to bring Social Democratic activities out into the open, effectively the Party's attempt to transform a small conspiratorial group into a mass public organisation.

9 At the same time as Vpered was in operation, the Odessa Committee was also working in partnership with another left-leaning commercial publisher named Burevestnik [Storm petrel]. In July 1905, Burevestnik organised the first legal publication of Lenin's pamphlet, *The Agrarian Question and the Critics of Marx*.

10 As banned organisations, the revolutionary parties could not act without some form of cover, but activists proved adept at setting up publishing firms using false documentation and proxy owners. There is some confusion over exactly when Vpered started its operations. Belopolskii claims that it was in early 1905, while Ioffe says that the first books only appeared in July (Belopol'skii I. P. 'Vospominaniia uchastnikov Pervoi russkoi revoliutsii'. *Voprosy istorii*. No. 12, 1955, p. 43; Ioffe. *Izdatel'skaia deiatel'nost' bol'shevikov v 1905–1907 gg*, p. 114).

11 Belopol'skii, I. P. *Pervoe legal'noe bol'shevistskoe izdatel'stvo 'Vpered' v Odesse 1904–1905 godakh. Lichnye vospominaniia. K 50-letiiu Pervoi russkoi revoliutsii 1905–1907 gg.* Vypusk I, Leningrad, 1955. GBL OR, f. 369, k. 377, d. 5, l. 10.

12 Belopol'skii. *Pervoe legal'noe bol'shevistskoe izdatel'stvo 'Vpered' v Odesse 1904–1905 godakh*, GBL OR, f. 369, k. 377, d. 5, l. 13.

13 Belopol'skii, I. P. *Legal'noe bol'shevistskoe knigoizdatel'stvo 'Utro' v Peterburge 1905–1906 g. Lichnye vospominaniia. K 50-letiiu Pervoi russkoi revoliutsii 1905–1907 gg.* Vypusk II, Leningrad 1955 g. GBL OR, f. 369, k. 377, d. 5, ll. 20–24.

14 Little is known about Petukh beyond the fact that it was run by the architects Vladislav Karpovich and Aleksandr Rozenberg. Karpovich was the secretary of the Committee for the Improvement of the Welfare of Construction Workers at the 'Rossiia' Insurance Association, as well as a committee member of the Imperial Society of Architects. According to Belopolskii, much of the practical work at Petukh was done by a young civil engineer, whose name he could not recall. None of the Petukh postcards have been identified, but it appears that the enterprise was legally registered, with profits going towards the Party. For more information, see: Belopol'skii. *Legal'noe bol'shevistskoe knigoizdatel'stvo 'Utro' v Peterburge 1905–1906 gg.*, GBL OR, f. 369, k. 377, d. 5, ll. 24–25; Belopol'skii. 'Vospominaniia uchastnikov Pervoi russkoi revoliutsii', p. 44; Zabochen', Mikhail. 'Oruzhiem iskusstva. Izdaniia po izobrazitel'nomu iskusstvu partiinogo izdatel'stva "Vpered"'. *Iskusstvo*. No. 11, 1979, p. 62.

15 Initially, Petukh formed a separate entity within Utro, with all postcards marketed under the Petukh brand. See, for example, advertisement on the inside back cover of: Kautskii, Karl. *Nauka, zhizn' i etika*. No. 34, Saint Petersburg: Vpered, 1906.

16 There were other more or less closely affiliated groups printing postcards in the capital, but where possible official propaganda output followed a tightly monitored, vertical power structure, similar in formation to the Party itself.

17 Lenin, N. 'Partiinaia organizatsiia i partiinaia literatura.' *Novaia zhizn'*. No. 12, 13 November 1905, front page.

18 The postcards were printed at the Kordovskii and Dressler Printing House, a legally registered firm with no obvious links to the Party. This prominent enterprise also printed postcards for the Society of Saint Eugenia. (See, for example: TsGIA SPB, f. 202, op. 2, d. 1257, l. 14.) The prints were 'the size of a large letter sheet,' while the phototype images ranged in size from 18 cm × 25 cm to 26 cm × 34 cm (*Mezhdunarodnye sotsialisticheskie kongressy*, Saint Petersburg: Utro, 1906, unpaginated advertisement on back covers).

19 Belopol'skii. 'Vospominaniia uchastnikov Pervoi russkoi revoliutsii', p. 44.

20 Utro's postcards included portraits of: August Bebel, Louis-Auguste Blanqui, Friedrich Engels, Joseph Fourier, Jules Guesde, Karl Kautsky, Petr Kropotkin, Paul Lafargue, Ferdinand Lassalle, Petr Lavrov, Wilhelm Liebknecht, Karl Marx, Robert Owen, Georgii Plekhanov, Petr Schmidt. Its picture reproductions included: Victor Adam's lithographs *Saint Antoine Street, 28 July 1830* and *Bastille Square*, Léon Cogniet's *Bravery and Humanity*, Michele Loffredo's *The Widow*, Otto Marcus' *The Last Shot*, Ernest Meissonier's *Barricades*, Mihály Munkácsy's *Strike*, Iegoshua Shlugleit's *The Search*, and two anonymous pictures: *9 January 1905* and *Socialism – Liberator* (Zabochen'. 'Oruzhiem iskusstva', p. 63).

21 The postcards were advertised for: six kopecks each for individual examples, four kopecks each for up to 100, three kopecks fifty for up to 500, and three kopecks for more than 500. These amounts would have required print runs stretching into the tens of thousands (*Volna*. No. 19, 17 May 1906, p. 4).

22 Belopol'skii. *Legal'noe bol'shevistskoe knigoizdatel'stvo 'Utro' v Peterburge 1905–1906 gg.*, GBL OR, f. 369, k. 377, d. 5, l. 29.

23 Belopol'skii. *Pervoe legal'noe bol'shevistskoe izdatel'stvo 'Vpered' v Odesse 1904–1905* godakh. GBL OR, f. 369, k. 377, d. 5, l. 32.

24 See advertisement for the competition in: *Zodchii*. No. 6, Saint Petersburg, 5 February 1906, p. 54.

25 In March 1899, the Society of Saint Eugenia launched the first Russian postcard design competition, which was won by Fedor Bernshtam's *Judgement of Paris* (*Otkrytye pis'ma i drugie khudozhestvennye izdaniia Krasnogo kresta*. Izdanie vtoroe. Saint Petersburg, 1903, p. 5).

26 Zabochen'. 'Oruzhiem iskusstva', p. 62.

27 Bonch-Bruevich. *Bol'shevistskie izdatel'skie dela v 1905–1907 gg.*, p. 16.

28 This legal facility was set up with the involvement of sympathiser I. Ia. Lvov (Bonch-Bruevich. *Bol'shevistskie izdatel'skie dela v 1905–1907 gg.*, pp. 18–19).

29 Bonch-Bruevich. *Bol'shevistskie izdatel'skie dela v 1905–1907 gg.*, pp. 22–25.

30 Bonch-Bruevich. *Bol'shevistskie izdatel'skie dela v 1905–1907 gg.*, p. 33.

31 *Biblioteka nashikh chitatelei*. No. 2, Saint Petersburg, 20 May 1906, unnumbered advertisement at rear; *Vestnik Zhizni*. No. 7, Saint Petersburg, 3 June 1906, p. 62.

32 See advertisements in: *Biblioteka nashikh chitatelei*. No. 1, Saint Petersburg, 26 April 1906, back cover; *Volna*. Saint Petersburg, No. 1, 26 April 1906, front page.

33 Bonch-Bruevich. *Bol'shevistskie izdatel'skie dela v 1905–1907 gg.*, p. 19.

34 Bonch-Bruevich claims that the books he used were: Dayot, Armand. *La Révolution Française*. Paris: Flammarion, 1896, and Dayot, Armand. *L'Invasion. Le Siège 1870, La Commune 1871*. Paris: Flammarion, Undated. However, there do not appear to be any images in these books that were reproduced as postcards. Another work by Dayot, titled *Journées révolutionnaires, 1830–1848* (Paris: Flammarion, 1897) does, however, contain four pictures that were reproduced by Vpered in postcard form: Adam, Victor. *Place de la Bastille*, p. 31; Adam, Victor. *Rue Saint-Antoine, Le 28 juillet 1830*, p. 38; Delacroix, Eugène. *La Liberté Guidant la Peuple*, p. 65; Cogniet, Léon. *Courage et Humanité*, p. 71 (Bonch-Bruevich. *Bol'shevistskie izdatel'skie dela v 1905–1907 gg.*, pp. 19–20).

35 They included: 'Homeless People – a scene from the life of the Italian proletariat, portraits of Karl Marx, G.V.Plekhanov, the leader of the uprising in the Black Sea, Petr Schmidt, a group of old émigré figures: Herzen, Bakunin, Ogarev, and several other pictures and portraits' (Bonch-Bruevich. *Bol'shevistskie izdatel'skie dela v 1905–1907 gg.*, p. 32).

36 Utro postcards are marked: 'Fototipiia Kordovskogo and Dresslera S. P. B.' ['Collotype printed by Kordovskii and Dressler Saint Petersburg']. It is not known for sure where Vpered's postcards were manufactured, but they may have been produced at the Party's 'Delo' printing house, founded in spring 1906.

37 *Biblioteka nashikh chitatelei*. No. 2, 20 May 1906, unnumbered advertisement at rear.

38 Vikent'ev. *Kak frantsuzy dobyvali sebe svobodu*, Vpered No. 33, circa late 1906, advertisement on inside cover.

39 The 'stamp-portraits' were sold as a sheet of sixteen images for twelve kopecks. Vpered also offered phototype pictures for between ten and thirty kopecks, and prints 'the size of a letter sheet' for between five and ten kopecks (See: Vikent'ev. *Kak frantsuzy dobyvali sebe svobodu*, advertisement on inside cover).

40 Vpered, although a legal enterprise, sailed very close to the wind, issuing many of its printed works semi-legally, publishing them under fictitious imprints, disguising the name of the author, and distributing editions before the authorities had time to arrest the work in question.

41 Report sent by Head of Paris Okhrana Office to Director of Department of Police. *No. 97*. 23/10 March 1907, HIWRP OA, Index XXIVe, Folder 2c.

42 Bonch-Bruevich. *Bol'shevistskie izdatel'skie dela v 1905–1907 gg.*, p. 33–36.

43 Bonch-Bruevich. *Bol'shevistskie izdatel'skie dela v 1905–1907 gg.*, p. 61.

44 Bonch-Bruevich. *Bol'shevistskie izdatel'skie dela v 1905–1907 gg.*, p. 41.

45 Vpered postcards carried no identifying features. This may have helped them avoid excessive scrutiny, but it meant that they were in effect blunt implements, serving only to spread a generic idea of Marxist opposition, rather than to increase support for the Party itself. Postcards were thus a financial and ideological complement to the revolutionaries' other activities rather than a precision weapon in their own right.

46 Zabochen'. 'Otkrytki partiinogo izdatel'stva "Vpered"', pp. 75–76.

47 TsGIA SPB, Saint Petersburg, f. 487, op. 1, d. 2406A.

48 Mikhail Zabochen' wrote that: '[Their postcards] were the first extensive grouping of fine art reproductions on a revolutionary theme produced in Russia.' (Zabochen'. 'Oruzhiem iskusstva', p. 67).

49 Lenin. 'Partiinaia organizatsiia i partiinaia literatura', front page

50 For a list of fellow-travelling publishers issuing Social Democratic works during this period see: Bonch-Bruevich. *Bol'shevistskie izdatel'skie dela v 1905–1907 gg.*, pp. 86–87.

51 Bonch-Bruevich. *Bol'shevistskie izdatel'skie dela v 1905–1907 gg.*, p. 33, Note 1.

52 M. M. Chemodanov. *Avtobiografiia*. 1903, GRM OR, f. 44, d. 1, l. 1.

53 Maiskii, Ivan. *Pered burei, Vospominaniia*. Moscow: OGIZ, 1944, p. 72.

54 Chemodanov. *Avtobiografiia*. GRM OR, f. 44, d. 1, l. 9.

55 Chemodanov described himself as unique at this time in using satire to critique the political system in Russia. Prior to 1905, he contributed drawings to: *Budil'nik [The Alarm Clock]*, *Falanga [The Phalange]*, *Gusli [The Dulcimer]*, *Oskolki [Chippings]*, *Razvlechenie [Entertainment]*, *Russkii satiricheskii listok [The Russian Satirical Sheet]*, *Pchelka [The Little Bee]*, *Strekoza [The Dragonfly]*, *Svet i teni [Light and Shadows]*, *and Zritel' [The Spectator]*. He was extraordinarily prolific, and his notebooks from the 1880s are filled with sketches and ideas for cartoons. He used a variety of pseudonyms, including M. Lilin, Struna, Emche, Zh-d-va, Dobromyslov, and claimed to have submitted up to 10,000 drawings to these journals, comprising around 2,000 printed pages (Chemodanov. *Avtobiografiia*. GRM OR, f. 44, d. 1, ll. 26–27, 32).

56 *Svet i teni*. No. 19, Moscow, 16 May 1881, back of front cover (unpaginated).

57 The cartoon depicts a desk, piled high with papers, framed by two inkwells containing quills. In the original sketch submitted to the censor, the caption was located below the inkwells, but when Chemodanov worked up the drawing for publication, he placed it above, forming a link between the quills, and thus giving the appearance of a gallows. The letters themselves were refashioned into small soldiers, and the cedilla of the letter 'Щ' was curled into a loop to form a hangman's noose. The 'weapon' for resolving pressing issues was no longer the censor's pen, but the military and, more seriously, the death penalty – the latter, a reference to the recent executions of Alexander II's assassins (Chemodanov. *Avtobiografiia*. GRM OR, f. 44, d. 1, ll. 30–31).

58 Chemodanov. *Avtobiografiia*. GRM OR, f. 44, d. 1, l. 4.

59 *Doklad Ministra Vnutrennikh Del o priostanovlenii izdanii Svet i teni na 6 mesiatsev*. 23 May 1881, MM FC, f. 22, op. 1, d. 2, OF 9823/37–18.

60 GARF, f. 102, op. 203, d. 2 ch. 34 t. 1, l. 674.

61 Chemodanov. *Avtobiografiia*. GRM OR, f. 44, d. 1, l. 20.

62 The only source for this quotation is Chemodanov's daughter. There is no particular reason to doubt its authenticity, but I could find no record of it among his papers (Chemodanova. *Khudozhnik Russkoi Revoliutsii – M. M. Chemodanov*, pp. 6–7).

63 Chemodanov had continued to practice medicine while working as an illustrator, spending a long stint in Viatka province in 1886–7. His rate of production dropped dramatically in 1893 as dentistry began to take over. He finally stopped drawing for publication in around 1898 (M. M. Chemodanov. *Zapisnaia knizhka*, 1891–7. MM FC, f. 22, op. 1, d. 1, OF 9823/9; Chemodanov. *Avtobiografiia*. GRM OR, f. 44, d. 1, l. 32).

64 Chemodanova. *Zhizn' i tvorcheskii put' M. M. Chemodanova 1856–1908*, p. 7.

65 Riabov, G. 'Vrach-revoliutsioner'. *Zdorov'e*. No. 2, 1956, p. 25.

66 Chemodanova. *Khudozhnik Russkoi Revoliutsii – M. M. Chemodanov*, p. 5.

67 Smirnov. *Vospominaniia o M. M. Chemodanove*, p. 1.

68 See, for example: *Novosti dnia*. No. 7760, 9 January 1905, p. 2.

69 The journal was shut down after only one issue when the censor found fault with three of its illustrations: *V kadetskom korpuse [In the Cadet Corps]*, *Iz Krylovskikh basen [From Krylov's Tales]* and *Druzheskaia beseda trekh sviatitelei [A Friendly Chat between Three Saints]*. None of these were by Chemodanov (RGIA, f. 776, op. 8, d. 2179, l. 1).

70 *Kramola* also only lasted for one issue.

71 *Na rasput'i*. No. 1, Moscow, 1906, pp. 1, 2, 3, 4, 6, 7, 8, 9, 14, 16. Not all were recent creations – his three cartoons reproduced in postcard form in August 1905 were also published in the journal.

72 The image is uncaptioned but was later reproduced in postcard form, titled: *K pravitel'stvennomu rassledovaniiu Kurskogo izbieniia 12 Fevr. [In Commemoration of the Government Investigation into the Kursk Massacre on 12 February]* (*Na rasput'i*, No. 4, Moscow: Sergei Serebrovskii, 1906, p. 5.).

73 Grinberg worked as the head of the Moscow branch of the bookshop Novyi mir (Golubeva, O. D. 'Izdatel'skoe delo v Rossii v period Pervoi russkoi revolutsii (1905–1907)', p. 133).

74 Chemodanova. *Khudozhnik Russkoi Revoliutsii – M. M. Chemodanov*, p. 10.

75 Quoted in Kushnerovskaia, G. 'Karikaturist M. M. Chemodanov (1856–1906)'. *Iskusstvo*. No. 6, Moscow, 1955, p. 72. This quotation comes from Peschanskii's own account of the period, which is purportedly held in the Chemodanov family archive. I could find no trace of it.

76 Advertisement for Khudozhestvennaia fotografiia [Artistic Photograph], *Otkrytka*. No. 10, December 1907, p. 142; Zabochen', M. 'Illiustrirovannaia khronika pervogo dnia revoliutsii'. *Filateliia SSSR*. No. 4, 1975, p. 54.

77 Chemodanova claims that the network was established in late 1905, a claim backed up by Peschanskii. Police reports, however, say that production started in February 1906 (Chemodanova. *Khudozhnik Russkoi Revoliutsii – M. M. Chemodanov*, p. 10; *Spravka (svidetel'skie pokazaniia) Vsekopromsoveta Borisa Iakovlevicha Grinberga, Prepodovatelia Komenko, Petra Nikiforovicha i Peschanskogo, Dmitriia Ivanovicha*. 1948, MM FC, f. 22, op. 1, d. 9, OF 9823/36–3; GARF, f. 102, op. 203, d. 2 ch. 34 t. 1, l. 700).

78 For example, the finished drawing for *Staraia basnia na novyi lad* [*An Old Song Played to a New Tune*] measures 24.4 cm × 34.4 cm (MSI FG, Inv. 36/1642), and the drawing for *K voprosu o narodnom predstavitel'stve v Rossii bez razlichiia pola* [*On the Question of Popular Representation in Russia without Gender Discrimination*] measures 23.1 cm × 33.8 cm (MSI FG, Inv. 36/421). There are also seven sketches for his cartoons in RGALI, which measure circa 22 cm × 35.5 cm (RGALI, f. 907, op. 1, d. 1–7).

79 In regards to pseudonyms, Chemodanov had already used 'Cherv' ['Worm'], for the drawings published in *Na rasput'i*, but the others ('IKS' ['X'], 'Y' ['U'], and 'I. Grek' ['Y']) are only present in his postcard work.

80 Druzhinin. 'Doktor Chemodanov', p. 65.

81 Following the publication of an initial clutch of images, there appears to have been a hiatus, likely because Chemodanov was in Yalta. When he was back in Moscow over the Summer (June/July 1906), he produced a second set of drawings, many of which concern the First Duma and its subsequent dissolution. There was then a further break, when Chemodanov was again away, before he produced his final and most subversive group of illustrations in October 1906.

82 The Chemodanov Family archive in the Museum of Moscow contains three postcards printed by A. A. Levenson in August 1905, twenty-seven numbered postcards (Nos. 2–28) printed by Peschanskii in 1905–6, plus a further four unnumbered postcards dating to around 1906. Comparison of his postcards shows that certain examples of the same images bear different pseudonyms, suggesting multiple editions.

83 They are: *Final zemskogo (noiabr'skogo) s"ezda v Moskve* [*The End Result of the (November) Zemstvo Congress in Moscow*] in *Kramola*. No. 1, 1905, p. 1; *Staraia basnia na novyi lad* [*An Old Song Played to a New Tune*] in *Zhalo*. No. 1, 1905; *Ustoi samoderzhaviia* [*The Buttress of Autocracy*] in *Na rasput'i*, No. 1, 1906, p. 9; *K pravitel'stvennomu rassledovaniiu Kurskogo izbieniia 12 Fevr.* [*In Commemoration of the Government Investigation into the 12 February Kursk Massacre*] in *Na rasput'i*, No. 4, 1906, p. 5.

84 Kushnerovskaia. 'Karikaturist M. M. Chemodanov', p. 72; Shleev. *Revoliutsiia 1905–1907 godov i izobrazitel'noe iskusstvo. Moskva i rossiiskaia provintsiia*, p. 5.

85 A work from Peschanskii's collection titled *Krasnoe znamia* [*Red Flag*] has the name 'Komenko' written on the reverse (MSI FG, Inv. 13/4654); A later Soviet document drawn up by Peschanskii, detailing his involvement in the reproduction of Chemodanov's cartoons, is signed by Petr Nikiforovich Komenko – perhaps a brother, or an indication that one of the Komenko's forenames has been wrongly recorded (MM FC, f. 22, op. 1, d. 9, OF 9823/36–3).

86 Roshchupkin, S. N. 'Zhurnal "Kramola" i ego illustrator'. *Iskusstvo*. No. 1, Moscow, 1969, p. 66.

87 Roshchupkin, S. N. 'Dekabr'skoe vooruzhennoe vosstanie v Moskve v risunkakh E. V. Orlovskogo'. *Iskusstvo*. No. 11, Moscow, 1975, p. 57.

88 The collection contains several original drawings and approximately eighty-six postcards. The original accession notes are scant, but most of the images carry Peschanskii's signature on the reverse (MSI KF, GIK 158/1–88).

89 For hand-drawn copies of French satirical postcards, see: *Vtoroi Port Artur* [*A Second Port Arthur*] (MSI FG 36/420); Félix-Antoine Marmonier (Mille). *Kartina bez slov* [*No Comment*] (MSI FG, 36/422) – originally published as *Les Massacres de Saint-Pétersbourg ont creusé une fosse entre le peuple et le Tsar*; Félix-Antoine Marmonier (Mille). *Krov' russkogo naroda vopiet o mshchenii…* [*The Blood of the Russian People Cries out for Revenge…*] (MSI FG, 36/369). For a hand-drawn copy of a *Simplicissimus* cartoon see Olaf Gulbransson's *Der letzte Romanow verläßt sein Land* [*The Last Romanov Leaves His Country*] (MSI FG, 13/4336). This cartoon originally appeared in: *Simplicissimus*. No. 21, August 1905, p. 248. For a photomontage design, see work commemorating Lieutenant Schmidt (MSI FG, 13/4335).

90 Mintslov, S. R. '14 mesiatsev svobody pechati. 17 okt. 1905 g. – 1 ianv. 1907', p. 129.

91 In his memoirs, however, Bonch-Bruevich (perhaps unfairly) dismissed Molot's proprietor S. A. Baliev, as only in it for the money (Bonch-Bruevich. *Bol'shevistskie izdatel'skie dela v 1905–1907 gg.*, pp. 85–86). Ioffe, is kinder (Ioffe. *Izdatel'skaia deiatel'nost' bol'shevikov*, pp. 92–98).

92 E. M. Alekseeva was a largely Menshevik-orientated publisher. She also owned the publishing firms Demos in Odessa, and Novyi mir in Saint Petersburg and Moscow.

93 RGIA, f. 776, op. 23, d. 10, ll. 14–18.

94 Roshchupkin. 'Dekabr'skoe vooruzhennoe vosstanie v Moskve v risunkakh E. V. Orlovskogo', p. 56.

95 Stasova, Elena. *Vospominaniia*. Moscow: Mysl', 1969, pp. 41–2.

96 Spiridovich. *Partiia Sotsialistov-Revoliutsionerov i ee predshestvenniki*, p. 163; Harcave, Sidney. *First Blood. The Russian Revolution of 1905*. London: The Bodley Head, 1964, p. 175.

97 Zabochen'. 'Oruzhiem iskusstva', p. 62.
98 According to one police report, the postcard packets were sold for either one rouble fifty or two roubles fifty (GARF, f. 102, op. 203, d. 2 ch. 34 t. 1, ll. 674, 700). Druzhinin and Chemodanova, however, both claim they were sold for three roubles. It is possible the postcards were sold for different amounts at different times (Druzhinin. 'Doktor Chemodanov', p. 64; Chemodanova. *Khudozhnik Russkoi Revoliutsii – M. M. Chemodanov*, p. 10).
99 The postcard sellers made no direct reference to the Social Democratic Party, only to suffering political activists (Druzhinin. 'Doktor Chemodanov', p. 64).
100 Chemodanova writes that money was given to the Bolshevik Party Finance Committee and to the Political Red Cross. Druzhinin and police sources mention only 'political prisoners and exiles' (Chemodanova. *Khudozhnik Russkoi Revoliutsii – M. M. Chemodanov*, p. 10; Druzhinin. 'Doktor Chemodanov', p. 63; GARF, f. 102, op. 203, d. 11968, l. 24).
101 Druzhinin was working for *Svetoch* [*The Lantern*], a legally published Social Democratic newspaper (Druzhinin, N. 'Doktor Chemodanov', pp. 63–64).
102 Cherepov, V. L. 'Revoliutsionnye satiricheskie otkrytki v Ekaterinburge'. *Iz istorii khudozhestvennoi kul'tury Urala*. Sverdlovsk. 1980, pp. 60–75.
103 Lenin. 'Partiinaia organizatsiia i partiinaia literatura', front page; Bonch-Bruevich, B. D. *Bol'shevistskie izdatel'skie dela v 1905–1907 gg*. 1933, p. 85.
104 As with all efforts to uncover the past, lack of information puts considerable barriers in the way of any attempt to provide a full assessment of Social Democratic postcard production. All the relevant memoirs were written by Bolshevik participants, who have inevitably bigged themselves up at the expense of their revolutionary rivals. I have barely mentioned the Mensheviks in this study, simply because I have no information on what role they played, even though it is clear that they worked closely with the Bolsheviks in many aspects of propaganda production and distribution.

THE SOCIALIST-REVOLUTIONARY PARTY

1 GARF, f. 102, op. 237, d. 9 ch. 34, l. 230.
2 GARF, f. 102, op. 237, d. 9 ch. 34, ll. 230–231.
3 GARF, f. 124, op. 48, d. 958, l. 23.
4 GARF, f. 102, op. 237, d. 9 ch. 34, l. 231.
5 GARF, f. 102, op. 204, d. 2330, l. 12.
6 GARF, f. 102, op. 204, d. 2330, ll. 20–21. Vinogradov, who was a friend of the artists Natalia Goncharova and Mikhail Larionov, went on to become a celebrated Soviet architect, photographer, and collector. He was born in 1885 and died in 1980.
7 Doroshevich, Boris. 'Knizhnoe delo v epokhu Pervoi russkoi revoliutsii (1905–1907 gg.)' *Katorga i ssylka*. No. 1 (74), 1931, p. 172; Golubeva, O. D. 'Izdatel'skoe delo v Rossii v period Pervoi russkoi revolutsii (1905–1907)', pp. 134–135.
8 There were also firms belonging to the Union in Briansk, Kiev, Nizhnii Novgorod, Odessa, and Vilnius.
9 GARF, f. 102, op. 237, d. 9 ch. 34, ll. 4–8.
10 *Trud*. No. 6, December 1906, p. 13.
11 Bonch-Bruevich B. D. *Bol'shevistskie izdatel'skie dela v 1905–1907 gg*. Moscow, 1933, pp. 86–87.
12 In the words of *Partiinye izvestiia*: 'The centre has put a great deal of effort into streamlining and strengthening Party publishing, but the periphery has done the opposite, facilitating its destruction' (*Partiinye izvestiia*. No. 3, December 1906, p. 4).
13 *Partiinye izvestiia*. No. 3, December 1906, pp. 4–5.
14 It should be pointed out that there is another possible reason for the Party's empty coffers – over-reliance on private enterprise. If the firms in the Union were largely fellow-travelling commercial publishing houses as opposed to the Party's own ventures, then over the long term, dependence on their manufacturing facilities and distribution networks would have resulted in reduced profits, limited control over production, and greater difficulty in getting their wares published in a time of repression. It is possible, therefore (if the Party did indeed fail to set up its own independent legal publishers and printers), that the leadership bore much more responsibility for its publishing difficulties than it ever admitted. However, it must be stressed, there is no firm proof of this.
15 *Partiinye izvestiia*. No. 3, December 1906, p. 3.
16 These measures were introduced at the Second Party Council Meeting, which took place in October 1906. In regards to publishing, provincial cells were instructed to take back control of distribution, ensure that Party literature was being sold in local outlets, and where possible to set up their own shops and kiosks. Free distribution was to be stopped in all but exceptional circumstances, and a commission set up to kick-start regional production (*Partiinye izvestiia*. No. 3, December 1906, p. 3).
17 The long-term implications for the Party as a whole, however, were profound. For a more extensive discussion of its internal difficulties, see: Povolzhskii. 'Nekotorye vnutrennie prichiny partiinogo krizisa'. *Izvestiia Oblastnogo Komiteta Zagranichnoi Organizatsii*, No. 9, February 1909, pp. 4–7.
18 *Trud* listed the ways in which the Party's Finance Committee made money as: 'Publishing books, cards depicting the better known faces of the revolutionary movement, artistic and political-satirical postcards, organising the sale of books, [membership] dues, lotteries, lectures, performances, concerts and so on.' (*Trud*. No. 8, January 1907, p. 15).
19 GARF, f. 102, op. 233a, d. 80 ch. 20, ll. 96, 107.
20 RGIA, f. 777, op. 27, d. 518, l. 220.

21 It is not clear which of these images are prints and which are postcards (RGIA, f. 776, op. 9, d. 43, ll. 10–11; RGIA, f. 777, op. 27, d. 538, ll. 98–100).

22 Examples of postcards published by Vodovozova in my collection all bear the stamp of the P. N. Chelli Photographic Studio in Kiev. It is not clear, however, whether Chelli was the printer or the retailer.

23 The Populist revolutionary Vera Figner mentions sending her portrait to Vodovozova for the *Shlissel'burgskaia galereia* [*Shlisselburg Gallery*] in letters to Afanasii Spandon in March 1906, an indication of how close Vodovozova was to revolutionary circles (Figner, Vera. *Posle Shlissel'burga*. Leningrad: Kolos, 1925, pp. 165–168, 171).

24 *Byloe*. No. 7, July 1906, p. 343; *Byloe*. No. 8, August 1906, p. 322. Nasha zhizn (circa 1906–1910) was run by Artemii Kotelnikov, an economist, translator and patron of the arts. He also edited an eponymous newspaper, founded in 1904.

25 The postcards depicted Konopliannikova and Perovskaia (TsDIAK, f. 295, op. 1, d. 8, l. 137).

26 GARF, f. P-6317, op. 1, d. 13, l. 1.

27 Figner, Vera. *Polnoe sobranie sochinenii v semi tomakh*. Tom tret'ii: *Posle Shlissel'burga*. Moscow: Izdatel'stvo Vsesoiuznogo obshchestva politkatorzhan i ssyl'no-poselentsev, 1932, p. 227.

28 Orzhikh was active in revolutionary circles from 1880, and a key figure in the attempted revival of Narodnaia Volia. In 1886, he was arrested and condemned to death, but this was later commuted to an open-ended sentence of hard labour. He emigrated to Japan in 1905.

29 Paichadze, S. A. and G. I. Kan. 'Russkoe izdatel'stvo "Volia" v Nagasaki (1906–1908gg.)'. *Kniga i knizhnoe delo v Sibiri: Istoriia, sovremennost', perspektivy razvitiia*. Novosibirsk: GPNTB SO AN SSSR, 1989, pp. 74–75.

30 Volia advertisements mention: 'Portraits of Zinaida Vasilevna Konopliannikova, M. A. Spiridonova, Group of Women Sentenced to Hard Labour: Shkolnik, Bitsenko, Fialka, Ezerskaia, Izmailovich, the Shlisselburg Martyrs, and others.' (*Volia*. No. 86, Nagasaki, 2 December 1906, unpaginated advertisement at rear).

31 Volia's accounts regularly mention sales of postcards (GARF, f. P-6317, op. 1, d. 59, ll. 16–20 etc.; GARF, f. P-6317, op. 1, d. 60, ll. 15, 19, 26, 35 etc.; GARF, f. P-6317, op. 1, d. 64, ll. 7–10 etc.).

32 GARF, f. P-6317, op. 1, d. 61, ll. 1–151; Paichadze and Kan. 'Russkoe izdatel'stvo 'Volia' v Nagasaki (1906–1908gg.)', p. 76.

33 Volia agents had helped organise and set up much of the Party apparatus in the Far East. For more on Volia's political activities see: *Prilozhenie k 11 vypusku sbornika statei*, pp. 1–4, IISG PSR, Index 527.

34 At the Second Party Council meeting there was a deliberate push to improve regional accountability

35 For example, the Saint Petersburg Committee reported that their expenses for January 1907 had been destroyed during a police search (*Trud*. No. 11, March 1907, p. 20).

36 This section looks only at the accounts of local committees based in areas outside Saint Petersburg, Moscow, and the other capitals of the Empire, e.g. Baku, Vilnius, Minsk, Riga, Warsaw and Tiflis. Regional committees, organisations representing workers and peasants, and the Red Cross are also not included.

37 Postcards (otkrytki) or cards (kartochki) are mentioned in accounts from the following committees: IISG PSR Indexes: 311 (Vologda), 314 (Novgorod), 317 (Pskov), 341 (Kostroma), 344 (Nizhnii Novgorod), 351 (Elets), 353 (Tula), 367 (Viatka), 373 (Ekaterinburg), 369 (Votkinsk), 375 (Perm), 380 (Zlatoust), 394 (Vitebsk), 398 (Briansk), 405 (Astrakhan), 420 (Saratov), 429 (Tsaritsyn), 440 (Voronezh), 499 (Krasnoiarsk), 505 (Barnaul).

38 Furthermore, postcards are the only form of visual propaganda to appear by name in the accounts. Hectographic cartoons were also produced, but they are not mentioned, possibly because they were handed out for free.

39 *Otchet po kasse Viatskogo komiteta Partii Sotsialistov-Revoliutsionerov s 1-go iiulia po 1-e avgusta*. IISG PSR, Index 353; *Otchet Tul'skogo komiteta Partii Sotsialistov-Revoliutsionerov, fevral' i mart*. 1907, IISG PSR, Index 367.

40 Hildermeier. *The Russian Socialist-Revolutionary Party Before the First World War*, p. 189.

41 *Otchet kassy Pskovskogo komiteta P. S.-R. s 1-go Dekabria '06 po 1-e maia 1907 goda. Raskhod*. IISG PSR, Index 317; *Denezhnyi otchet Ekaterinburgskogo komiteta P. S. R. s 1-go fevralia po 1-e avgusta 1906 g. Raskhod*. IISG PSR, Index 373.

42 *Partiinye izvestiia*. No. 3, December 1906, p. 5.

43 The Party archives contain a continuous run of the Viatka Committee's financial statements from the beginning of June 1906 to the end of April 1907, as well as several handwritten documents pertaining to the activities of the Viatka Committee, the Viatka Organisation, and other sub-groups in the province.

44 Rice. *Russian Workers and the Socialist-Revolutionary Party through the Revolution of 1905–07*, p. 171.

45 *Oblastnaia org. Ural. Oblasti/Viatskaia guberniia*. Undated, p. 4. IISG PSR, Index 365.

46 Viatka Province was originally administered solely by the Viatka Committee, but at the Third Congress of the Urals Regional Organisation in June 1906, the decision was made to hand over responsibility for three districts (Sarapul, Elabuga, and part of Malmyzh) to the Sarapul Committee.

47 Untitled typescript on structure and activities of the groups making up the Urals Regional Committee. Undated, but circa June 1906, IISG PSR, Index 365.

48 The Urals Regional Committee comprised provincial committees from Viatka, Ufa, Perm and Ekaterinburg, and after June 1906, Sarapul.

49 *Ustav organizatsii Partii Sotsialistov-Revoliutsionerov*. IISG PSR, Index 211.

50 Untitled Organisation Bureau questionnaire filled out by the Viatka Organisation in advance of the Second Party Congress, October 1906. IISG PSR, Index 367.

51 This figure includes all references to production (tipografiia [printing house], bumaga [paper], gektograf [hectograph], tekhnika [equipment] etc.), the purchase of pre-made propaganda, and distribution expenses (raz"ezdnaia propaganda [field propaganda], dostavka knig [book delivery] etc.). Most provincial groups spent around 35–40 percent of total expenditure on propaganda during this period. By way of comparison, the Party's Central Committee spent just under twenty-seven percent on 'literature' in 1906 (*Kratkii denezhnyi otchet Ts. K. P. S. R. za 1906 goda* in *Listki Vilenskogo komiteta PSR*, No. 1, 5 April 1907, unpaginated. IISG, Index 393).

52 Between 1 June 1906 and 26 June 1907, the Viatka Committee spent around eighteen percent of their outgoings on supporting 'comrades' and imprisoned activists. Donations to the Political Red Cross brings the amount spent to just over twenty-two percent of expenditure.

53 The First Congress of the Urals Regional Organisation took place in February 1906 (*Oblastnaia org. Ural. Oblasti/Viatskaia guberniia*. Undated, p. 7. IISG PSR, Index 365).

54 Untitled Organisation Bureau questionnaire, October 1906. IISG PSR, Index 367; Untitled typescript on structure and activities of the groups making up the Urals Regional Committee. Undated, but circa June 1906, IISG PSR, Index 365.

55 According to the census of 1897, the population of Viatka Province was 3,030,831.

56 *Oblastnaia org. Ural. Oblasti/Viatskii uezd*. Undated, IISG PSR, Index 365, p. 11; Untitled Organisation Bureau questionnaire, October 1906. IISG PSR, Index 367.

57 *Postanovlenie III s"ezda oblastnoi Ural'skoi organizatsii PSR*, June 1906, IISG PSR, Index 365.

58 *Viatka, polozhenie krestianskoi raboty k 1 noiabria 1907 g.*, handwritten report, IISG PSR, Index 365.

59 See, for example: *Oblastnaia org. Ural. Oblasti/V Urzhumskom uezde/Kotel'nicheskii uezd/Iaranskii uezd/Slobodskoi uezd*, pp. 12–15a. Undated, IISG PSR, Index 365.

60 *Viatskim Komitetom izdano s 1 maia po 20 avg.* (1906). IISG PSR, Index 367; *Izdaniia Viatskogo Komiteta Partii Sotsialistov-Revoliutsionerov s 1-go ianvaria po 1-e marta 1907 goda*. IISG PSR, Index 367.

61 There were several Socialist-Revolutionary newspapers printed in the provinces during the revolutionary period, most published by the larger regional committees.

62 It appears that at least some of this material exchanged hands for money. For example, in late 1906, the Semiannikovskii Sub-District Committee lists costs for buying copies of *Trud* (*Trud*, No. 11, March 1907, p. 19; *Pamiatnaia knizhka Sotsialista-revoliutsionera*. Vypusk 1, Paris, 1911, pp. 17–18).

63 *Oblastnaia org. Ural. Oblasti/Elabuzhskii uezd*. Undated, p. 18. IISG PSR, Index 365.

64 Untitled Organisation Bureau questionnaire, October 1906. IISG PSR, Index 367.

65 *Partiinye izvestiia*. No. 3, December 1906, p. 5.

66 Buying books amounted to over a quarter of the Viatka Committee's total propaganda spend.

67 *Otchet po kasse Viatskogo komiteta Partii Sotsialistov-Revoliutsionerov s 1-go iiulia po 1-e avgusta*. IISG PSR, Index 353.

68 There is one other entry in the Viatka Committee's accounts relating to manufacturing postcards, but it is outside the time frame covered in this section. In April 1908, the Committee spent seven roubles commissioning postcards of the terrorist Evstoliia Ragozinnikova, and that month recorded a postcard-related profit of ten roubles and seventy kopecks (*Otchet Viatskogo Gubernskogo Komiteta Partii Sotsialistov-Revoliutsionerov za aprel' 1908 g. Prikhod/Raskhod*. IISG PSR, Index 367). One report also makes a passing reference to postcard production in the Iaransk District of Viatka Province (*Oblastnaia org. Ural. Oblasti/Iaranskii uezd*, p. 13, Undated, IISG PSR, Index 365).

69 The Committee's entirely yearly income in 1908 came to 1089 roubles, as compared to 1459 roubles in 1907, and 2189 roubles between June and December 1906 (IISG PSR, Index 367).

70 Put simply, the Socialist-Revolutionaries managed the transition from conspiratorial entity to public Party poorly, remaining reliant on underground printing, and not developing the necessary political and financial mechanisms to reflect the greatly expanded audience that emerged in 1905. In postcard terms this meant that commercial manufacturing remained non-existent outside the major cities, while the Party's core publishing activities were continually undermined by regional inefficiency. The diffusion achieved was impressive, but sales were irregular and financially insignificant.

PRIVATE PUBLISHERS, PRINTERS, AND ARTISTS

1 Shipovnik's postcards were the only high-end cartoons known to have been sold by the revolutionary parties. For more, see Vpered advertisement promoting sales of 'colour postcards by the best German artists' (Kautskii, Karl. *Nauka, zhizn' i etika*, advertisement on inside back cover).

2 The advertised publication date for the postcards was 20 May 1906 (*Adskaia pochta*. No. 2, p. 12). There was another advert for Shipovnik in *Adskaia pochta*. No. 3, p. 7.

3 Grzhebin studied at the Simon Hollósy Art School, along with Dobuzhinskii.

4 Lansere, Evgenii. 'Khudozhniki o revoliutsii 1905 goda.' *Iskusstvo*. No. 6, 1935, p. 41; See also letter from Bilibin about *Simplicissimus* in: *Rech*, Saint Petersburg, No. 32, 24 November, 1912, p. 4.

5 Later advertisements suggest that only forty-one were printed (*Literaturno-khudozhestvennye al'manakhi izdatel'stva Shipovnik*. Kniga 9, 1909, unpaginated advertisement at rear).
6 The majority of the images were by Thomas Theodor Heine. Also involved were Leal Da Camera, Adolf Munzer, Bruno Paul, Wilhelm Schulz, Eduard Thöny and Rudolf Wilke. Heine, Paul and Wilke were included in the list of contributors to *Adskaia pochta*, along with Olaf Gulbransson. It appears that most, if not all the cartoons used for the postcards had previously appeared in *Simplicissimus*. See, for example: Thöny, Eduard. *Einteilung. Simplicissimus*. No. 7, 1903, p. 51; Heine, Thomas Theodor. *Nach der Wahl. Simplicissimus*. No. 13, 1903, front page; Heine, Thomas Theodor. *Arbeiterfürforge. Simplicissimus*. No. 26, 1903, front page; Schulz, Wilhelm. *Großstadt. Simplicissimus*. No. 29, 1903, p. 228; Heine, Thomas Theodor. *Durchs Dunkelste Deutschland. Crimmitschau. Simplicissimus*. No. 43, 1903, front page; Heine, Thomas Theodor. *Nach dem Gittlichfeitstongreß. Simplicissimus*. No. 31, 1904, front page.
7 Some were later reprinted illegally in Russia as postcards. See, for example Gulbransson's *Der letzte Romanow verläßt sein Land.*
8 Letter from Grzhebin to Maxim Gorky, 9 November 1906, reproduced in: Grjébine, Hélène. 'Z. I. Grzhebin – izdatel' (po dokumentam i vospominaniiam ego docheri)'. *Solanus*, Vol. 1, 1987, p. 12.
9 Grjébine. 'Z. I. Grzhebin – izdatel' (po dokumentam i vospominaniiam ego docheri)', p. 11.
10 Grjébine. 'Z. I. Grzhebin – izdatel' (po dokumentam i vospominaniiam ego docheri)', p. 12.
11 *Shipovnik*. Kniga 9, 1909, unpaginated advertisement at rear.
12 TsGIA SPB, f. 202, op. 2, d. 1261, l. 230
13 For more on Merder's background, see: RGIA, f. 776, op. 8, d. 1763, l. 2.
14 Anonymous. 'Nasha fabrika', p. 6.
15 Merder also owned a printing house, taking commis sions from other publishers, as well as printing his own postcards (Anonymous. 'Nasha fabrika', pp. 6–7).
16 Anonymous. 'Nasha fabrika', p. 6.
17 Merder's shop was located at 20 Passazh (Department Store).
18 I can find no record of Merder's postcards in the Saint Petersburg Censorship Committee's journals.
19 *Domashnii muzei*. No. 8, February 1907, p. 12.
20 *Domashnii muzei*. No. 3, February 1905, p. 3.
21 Bonch-Bruevich. *Bol'shevistskie izdatel'skie dela v 1905–1907 gg.*, p. 85.
22 *Novaia zhizn'*, No. 1, 27 October 1905, p. 4.
23 The opposition-themed portraits postcards are likely to have been published by Vera Vodovozova (*Volna*. No. 12, 9 May 1906, p. 4).
24 There are a few photographic postcards of the post-October Manifesto demonstrations marked 'Fot. K. Bulla' [Phot. K. Bulla], but it is not clear whether he was also the publisher.
25 Tsenter was based at No. 15 Srednaia Podiacheskaia Street in the Admiralty District.
26 The date is incorrect, and should read: '18.x.05'. The photograph originally appeared in: *Niva*. No. 45, 12 November 1905, Saint Petersburg, 1905, p. 88.
27 RGIA, f. 777, op. 27, d. 96, ll. 34–35; RGIA, f. 777, op. 27, d. 99, ll. 37–38, 40.
28 It is striking how many publishers and printers at the lower end of the market were of peasant origin, showing that for enterprising individuals, there were many opportunities for advancement (GARF, f. 102, op. 200, d. 580 ch. 9, ll. 1–2).
29 RGALI, f. 552, op. 1, d. 2072, ll. 3–4, 6–7.
30 RGALI, f. 552, op. 1, d. 2072, l. 8.
31 RGALI, f. 552, op. 1, d. 2072, ll. 13, 17.
32 GARF, f. 102, op. 316, d. 168, l. 3.
33 In a letter to the Department of Police, Metalnikov mentions the need to escape from his creditors (GARF, f. 102, op. 316, d. 168, l. 4). Judging by his letters to Chertkov, it appears that Metalnikov had a quick temper, and given his expulsion from Rzhevsk, that he also had motive for revenge (RGALI, f. 552, op. 1, d. 2072, ll. 7, 17).
34 GARF, f. 102, op. 316, d. 168, ll. 3–5, 10–11.
35 The correspondence address provided by Metalnikov in the letter is for the Brekko Drama School, so it appears that he did for a time achieve his wish of becoming involved in the theatre (RGALI, f. 552, op. 1, d. 2072, l. 18). A further layer of complication is added by the fact that Chertkov himself seems to have been cooperating with the Imperial police around this time (See: Alexandra Popoff. Tolstoy's False Disciple. The Untold Story of Leo Tolstoy and Vladimir Chertkov. New York: Pegasus Books, 2014, pp. 125–126).
36 Metalnikov was only questioned about having sent the Tolstoyan literature some months after the event, when he was detained as part of a wider investigation into revolutionary circles in Voronezh. It is possible that the matter was brought up at this time because there were Tolstoyans among the latter revolutionaries, some of whom were in close contact with Chertkov (GARF, f. 102, op. 200, d. 580 ch. 9, ll. 1–3, GARF, f. 102, op. 200, d. 580, ll. 36–39).
37 RGALI, f. 552, op. 1, d. 2072, l. 20.
38 GARF, f. 102, op. 200, d. 580 ch. 9, l. 1.
39 GARF, f. 102, op. 200, d. 580 ch. 9, l. 5.
40 GARF, f. 102, op. 200, d. 580, l. 51.
41 GARF, f. 102, op. 316, d. 168, l. 21.
42 RGIA, f. 777, op. 27, d. 93, l. 121.
43 Metalnikov's firm and the Fuchs Publishing House were both registered as occupying Flat 8. The building at No. 43 Nevskii Prospect was constructed in 1900 for Grand Duke Sergei Alexandrovich, who owned the next door Beloselskii-Belozerskii Palace. After his assassination in 1905, it was inherited by his nephew Grand Duke Dmitrii Pavlovich. Among the other occupants of the building was the printing house of the Holy Synod.

44 In addition to Martens and Stoliarov, Metalnikov's artists included: Aleksandr de Paldo, Sasha Kosoi (pseudonym 'Ksi'), Nikolai Iaroshenko, Z. Shapiro, P. Vorontsov, N. V., G. S. or S. G., A. M., and an artist with the monogram 'D' or 'A' surrounded by a circle.

45 TsGIA SPB, f. 706, op. 1, d. 239, l. 1.

46 RGIA, f. 777, op. 25, d. 523, l. 2.

47 The advertisement is printed on the back of Metalnikov's company letterhead. It also lists large-format prints (content not specified), as well as offering a whole range of services from typing to translation. The wholesale price of Metalnikov's postcards was five roubles for 100 (RGALI, f. 552, op. 1, d. 2072, l. 20).

48 RGIA, f. 777, op. 25, d. 522, l. 4; RGIA, f. 777, op. 25, d. 523, l. 1.

49 See letterhead with list of postcards on reverse in: RGALI, f. 552, op. 1, d. 2072, l. 20.

50 RGB KF.

51 Metalnikov took a close interest in production and even contributed to some of the postcards himself. See, for example: *K vyboram. Pamiati pervoi gosudarstv. Dumy* [*Commemorating the Elections in Memory of the First State Duma*], where the text is signed: 'V. M-v.' In this card, he portrays the assembly as a significant step towards the democratisation of power, and as such an institution on which the very future of Russia depended.

52 Tret'iakov, V. P. (Editor) *Peterburg-Petrograd-Leningrad Al'bom-katalog fotootkrytok 1895–1945. Tom V. Petrograd 1917–1924.* Saint Petersburg: Sad iskusstv, 2016, pp. 378–379.

53 GARF, f. 102, op. 101, d. 2031, ll. 4–21.

54 U. M. Spektor. *Severnoe izdatel'stvo V. O. Zheglinskogo.* Moscow: Vsesoiuznoe dobrovol'noe obshchestvo liubitelei knigi, 1988, p. 28.

55 The postcards were manufactured by the local firm of I. I. Sokolov (Nepein, B. 'Izdano v Vologde'. *Al'manakh bibliofila.* Vypusk VIII, Moscow, 1980, p. 193).

56 They are as follows (publishers or printers in brackets): I. V. Gorelov (no publisher given), Vasil Gulak (K.V.Bykov and others) Nikolai Iaroshenko (Metalnikov), Valerii Karrik (no publisher given), Sasha Kosoi (Metalnikov), Evlampii Kosvintsev (no publisher given), Pavel Martens (Metalnikov and Tsenter), Aleksandr de Paldo (Metalnikov), Iosif Ridiger (no publisher given), Z. Shapiro (Metalnikov), Evgenii Sokolov (E. Kudinova and A. Lezina), Mikhail Stoliarov (Metalnikov and Vpered), P. Vorontsov (Metalnikov), Sergei Zhivotovskii (various publishers). There are several other artists for whom there is nothing more to go on than a set of initials.

57 See, for example, Evgenii Sokolov's caricatures satirising the participants of the First Duma, and Sergei Zhivotovskii's widely ciculated image *Odin s soshkoi – semero s lozhkoi* [*One with a Plough and Seven with a Spoon*].

58 Shleev, V. V. *Revoliutsiia 1905–1907 godov i izobrazitel'noe iskusstvo: Peterburg.* Moscow: Izobrazitel'noe iskusstvo, 1977, p. 113; Zabochen'. 'Otkrytki partiinogo izdatel'stva "Vpered"', p. 75.

59 They include: Mikhail Chemodanov, Valerii Karrik, Evlampii Kosvintsev, Evgenii Orlovskii, Iosif Ridiger, Evgenii Sokolov, Mikhail Stoliarov, and Sergei Zhivotovskii. The artist 'L. Ch' who produced a large series of cartoon postcards in circa 1906, also worked for the satirical journal *Skorpion* [*Scorpion*] (See: *Skorpion.* No. 2, Saint Petersburg, 1906, p. 5).

60 For photomechanical postcards reproducing satirical journal images in Peschanskii's archive, see: MSI KF, GIK 158/1–88. In respect of lithographic postcards, there are only three known journals from which illustrations were widely reproduced: *Pulemet* (published and edited by Nikolai Shebuev), *Nagaechka* (published by Kh. M. Knorring and edited by Arkadii Ivanov), and *Strely* (published and edited by I. M. Knorozovskii). Shebuev's celebrated depiction of the October Manifesto stamped with Trepov's bloody handprint (published in *Pulemet* [*The Machine Gun*]. No. 1, Saint Petersburg 1905, p. 12) is known in at least three different postcard versions, one of which is marked: 'From Shebuev's Pulemet'. Meanwhile, *Nagaechka* published their own postcard version of *Vynos* [*Take-out*] (*Nagaechka.* No. 3, pp. 6–7). And at least five illustrations from *Strely* were reproduced as postcards: *Svoboda sobraniia* [*Freedom of Assembly*] (*Strely.* No. 1, p. 4); *Chto za pritcha? Dymit' da i tol'ko!* [*What's Gone Wrong here? All It Does is Give off Smoke*] (*Strely.* No. 3, p. 3); Sergei Zhivotovskii. *Samyi prochnyi soiuz* [*The Most Steadfast Union*] (*Strely.* No. 7, p. 11); Untitled image of death spearing a revolutionary (*Strely.* No. 9, p. 3); *Apofeoz 17-go oktiabria* [*The Apotheosis of 17 October*] (*Strely.* No. 9, p. 11). Lithographic postcards also exist of Sergei Chekhonin's *V Tsarstve Ptits* [*In the Kingdom of the Birds*], originally printed in *Zritel'.* No. 19, 1905, p. 5, and Ivan Bilibin's *Sic Transit…* (*Zhupel.* No. 2, Saint Petersburg, 1905, p. 5). However, both these works are very rare. For the only known example of *Sic Transit…* see: *Obshchestvo khudozhnikov Mir iskusstva na pochtovykh kartochkakh: katalog.* Sankt Peterburg: Standart-kollektsiia, 2006, p. 32. A few cartoons that appeared in mainstream illustrated newspapers were also printed in postcard form. See, for example: Evlampii Kosvintsev's *Gr. Vitte podkovyvaet 'chetyre svobody'* [*Count Witte Nails on the 'Four Freedoms'*] (*Iskry.* No. 8, 19 February 1906, p. 47); *Gr. Vitte v razdum'e* [*Count Witte Thinking*] (*Iskry.* No. 7, 12 February 1906, p. 22); *Pervye deiateli russkoi revoliutsii* [*The First Activists of the Russian Revolution*] (Iskry. No. 8, 19 February 1906, p. 34), and I. V. Gorelov's *Ekspropriator* [*Expropriator*] (*Iskry.* No. 39, 1 October 1906, p. 541).

61 Felitsin, S. Untitled article on Valerii Karrik. *Vestnik literatury.* No. 3, Saint Petersburg, 1910, p. 57.

62 RGIA, f. 1102, op. 2, d. 527, l. 4.

63 See obituary in: *British Journal of Photography.* 27 December 1879, p. 621.

64 Ashbee, F. 'Fotograf s Maloi Morskoi'. *Iunost'*. No. 7, 1976, p. 102; For Karrik's views on his parents see: Karrik, Valerii. *Syn*. 1940, pp. 18–19, LRA FA, MS1496, Box 1; For more information on Carrick and Markelova, see: Karrik, Valerii. *Mat'*. 1923, LRA FA, MS1496, Box 1, and Karrik, Valerii. *Otets*. 1923, LRA FA, MS1496, Box 1.

65 Karrik, Valerii. *Syn*. 1940, pp. 17–25, LRA FA, MS1496, Box 1. Karrik's aims were not strictly subversive. In his words: 'At that time unauthorised teaching among the peasants was all but a crime against the state, equal to disseminating revolutionary ideas. This was not my intention, because I was not and did not consider myself to be an experienced political operator; nonetheless "God and the Tsar" did not figure in my teaching, and the authorities might well have considered this scandalous enough' (Karrik, Valerii. *Syn*. 1940, p. 25, LRA FA, MS1496, Box 1).

66 Dmitrii Karrik had originally bought the revolver a few years previously because he planned to kill himself over a woman. Exactly why he was carrying it on 17 March 1888 remains unclear, but the police were sure that he was up to no good (GARF, f. 102, op. 228, d. 568, l. 1; GARF, f. 102, op. 84, d. 529 t. 1, ll. 4, 12–13, 34–37, 41–42; GARF, f. 102, op. 84, d. 529 t. 2, ll. 27, 33).

67 GARF, f. 102, op. 84, d. 529 t. 2, l. 24.

68 RGIA, f. 1102, op. 2, d. 527, l. 3.

69 The journal was called: *Vestnik finansov, promyshlennosti i torgovli [The Finance, Trade and Industry Gazette]* (GARF, f. 102, op. 102, d. 2933, l. 125).

70 GARF, f. 102, op. 228, d. 568, l. 3.

71 GARF, f. 124, op. 13, d. 819, l. 1.

72 *M. Gor'kii na rodine: Sbornik vospominanii o zhizni M. Gor'kogo v Nizhnem Novgorode*. Gor'kii: OGIZ, 1937, p. 89; *Gor'kii i Leonid Andreev: Neizdannaia perepiska*, Moscow: Nauka, 1965, p. 261.

73 Gunvor Haavik to Janet Ashbee. 19 September 1947, LRA FA, MS1496, Box 5. Haavik, whom Karrik had helped teach Russian, was exposed in 1977 as an agent of the KGB.

74 In London he met the writer Vasilii Maslov-Stokoz, the revolutionary Feliks Volkhovskii, and the Tostoyan, Pavel Bulanzhe (GARF, f. 102, op. 228, d. 568, ll. 2–3).

75 According to the *Manchester Guardian*, he spent ten weeks in gaol (*Manchester Guardian*. Manchester, 20 July 1908, p. 5).

76 GARF, f. 102, op. 102, d. 2933, ll. 13–14.

77 GARF, f. 102, op. 102, d. 2933, ll. 20, 34, 43, 120, 127, 133–134; GARF, f. 124, op. 13, d. 819, l. 6.

78 In his police file there is a letter from the editor of *Vestnik finansov* to the police, stamped 25 November 1904, requesting that Karrik be allowed to continue working at the journal. The response is not recorded. There is a further letter from December 1907 requesting the same (GARF, f. 102, op. 102, d. 2933, ll. 125, 136).

79 Dating his images is not straightforward, but given that no postcards appear in the list of items found in his flat, it is reasonable to assume that production started in the second half of 1904.

80 Karrik made around 2,500 roubles a year working for *Vestnik finansov* (GARF, f. 102, op. 102, d. 2933, l. 2).

81 Postcards were always his main creative outlet, but during this period, Karrik also published his work in satirical journals (*Leshii*. Nos. 1–4, Saint Petersburg, 1906; *Zhupel*. Nos. 1–2). Karrik is also named as a contributor to *Adskaia pochta*, but I can find no record there of his drawings. In 1907, Karrik contributed cartoons, caricatures and prose works to the short-lived journal *Piatnitsa*, which he also helped edit (*Piatnitsa*. Nos. 1–6, Saint Petersburg, 1907).

82 The Ashmolean Museum in Oxford has a collection of 103 caricature postcards by Karrik. Among the right-wing government figures it holds are images of Aleksei Bobrinskii, Fedor Dubasov, Vladimir Purishkevich, and Prince Sergei Urusov (Ashmolean Museum, Print Room, WA1957.60.8).

83 The postcards were sold for twenty kopecks a piece in: 'Datsiaro, Avantso, and all the best art shops in Saint Petersburg and Moscow.' For a partial list of images, see advertisement in: *Piatnitsa*. Saint Petersburg, No. 3, 1907, p. 7.

84 Karrik met Beerbohm in 1908, but it is almost certain that he either knew Beerbohm's work or was personally acquainted with him prior to this date.

85 One other chromolithographic printed image is known, depicting a revolutionary demonstration. All lack publishing details.

86 Karrik, Valerii. *Syn*, 1940, p. 11, LRA FA, MS1496, Box 1.

87 Letter from Valerii Karrik to S. P. Mel'gunov. 1 December 1931. Mel'gunov Papers, Special Collections, British Library of Political and Economic Science, LSE, London.

88 Carbon copy of letter from Felicity Ashbee to Sigrid Haavik, 15 January 1979, LRA FA, MS1496, Box 5.

89 In June 1907, Karrik took over the running of the satirical journal *Piatnitsa*. For related documents, see RGIA, f. 1102, op. 2, d. 527, ll. 1–17.

90 This article gives a good description of Karrik: 'Physically he is a tall man able to look down on most of his victims and this has a recognisable effect on his representation of them. Like other eminent practioners his profile is cut in bold, pouncing lines, his eyes are prominent, and he meets you with a direct straightforward gaze that is usually taken to express a frank, open nature, until his caricature appears.' Published alongside the article were caricatures by Karrik of 'Mr Haldane, Mr Balfour, Colonel Seely, Mr Cripps K. C.'. (*Manchester Guardian*. 20 July 1908, p. 5). Further caricatures of 'Mr Asquith, The Right Hon. Henry Chaplin, Mr Winston Churchill, Mr M'Kenna' appeared on 3 August, and of 'Lord Wolverhampton, Mr John Burns, Lord Halsbury and Lord Wemyss' on 18 August.

91 Felitsin. Untitled article on Valerii Karrik, p. 61. Karrik also drew a series of postcards for Rishar [Richard], illustrating Russian folk songs.

92 Felitsin. Untitled article on Valerii Karrik, pp. 58–59.

93 RGALI, f. 305, op. 1, d. 392, l. 63.
94 For more information on Karrik's time in Norway and his archive in Oslo, see: Teterevleva, T. P. 'V. V. Karrik (1869–1943): emigrant iz Peterburga v Norvegii'. *Sankt Peterburg i strany severnoi Evropy: Materialy 5-oi ezhegodnoi mezhdunarodnoi konferentsii (23–25 aprelia 2003)*. Saint Petersburg, 2004, pp. 44–54.
95 Ascher. *The Revolution of 1905: Russia in Disarray*, p. 2.

NARRATING EVENTS

1 Shleev. *Revoliutsiia 1905–1907 godov i izobrazitel'noe iskusstvo*, p. 174.
2 Quoted in Minin, Oleg. *Art and Politics in the Russian Satirical Press, 1905–1908*. Ph. D. dissertation. University of Southern California, 2008, p. 33.
3 Lansere. 'Khudozhniki o revoliutsii 1905 goda', p. 40.
4 Artists who drew images of Bloody Sunday in 1905 included Vladimir Makovskii, Ilia Repin, Valentin Serov, and Ivan Vladimirov.
5 Evgenii Lansere wrote that during this period, 'we had no contacts at all among genuine revolutionaries' (Lansere. 'Khudozhniki o revoliutsii 1905 goda', p. 40).
6 Two of the most widely reproduced pictures were pirated from the French journal *L'Illustration*. No. 3231, Paris, 28 January 1905: Scott, Georges. *La Journée du 22 Janvier à Saint-Pétersbourg; Le Conflit entre la troupe et les ouvriers à la Porte de Narva*. Other images were taken from *The Illustrated London News*, which on 4 February 1905 (No. 3433) published four full-page, and one double-page spread devoted to events in Saint Petersburg: R. Caton Woodville. *Sleighs for the Barricades: The Saint Petersburg Sledge Drivers' Futile Attempts to Imitate Parisian Revolutionary Methods*; Samuel Begg. *Martyrs in the Cause of Freedom: The Massacre of Strikers at the End of the Troitzky Bridge*. The journal also reproduced Georges Scott's above-mentioned images under the titles: *The Cossacks' Onslaught: A Furious Charge on Defenceless Strikers; The People's Champion: Father Gapon, the Strike Leader, at the Narva Gate*. Long after Russian alternatives became legally available (following the October Manifesto), postcard manufacturers continued to reproduce these foreign illustrations, primarily because they were readily available, familiar to the population, and cost nothing to commission.
7 *The Illustrated London News*. No. 3433, February 4 1905, p. 161.
8 This message was made explicit in revolutionary printed propaganda.
9 RGIA, f. 777, op. 6, d. 9, l. 67.
10 TsGIA SPB, f. 1648, op. 1, d. 1110, l. 200.
11 Guzikov, S. M. 'V poiskakh novykh putei v zhivopisi'. *Vestnik znaniia*, No. 4, 1905, p. 136.
12 The censor banned a postcard reproduction of *Before the Search* in May 1905 (RGIA, f. 777, op. 27, d. 518, l. 280).
13 *Iskry*. No. 10, 5 March 1906, pp. 72–73, 75, 80.
14 An advert for the publishing house Donskaia Rech' [Don Speech] includes a special section devoted to large format socialist pictures that had been 'shown at salons in 1906.' It included both Geller and Mazurovskii's pictures (*Rech'*. No. 65, 5 (18) May 1906).
15 This mode of depiction owes much to the ideal inspired by Rakhmetov, the ascetic hero of Nikolai Chernyshevskii's novel *What Is to Be Done*; the setting was new, but the motif of a hardened, unemotional revolutionary had long been part of the revolutionary canon.
16 *Nasha mysl'*. Nos. 1–2, Saint Petersburg, 1906, p. 1.
17 The first photographs of the Revolution were taken in January 1905. A substantial number, including images of Bloody Sunday and its aftermath, were subsequently printed in *The Sphere*, a London-based illustrated journal. These are all credited to Karl Bulla, who is described by the journal as their 'special photographer' in Russia (*The Sphere*. No. 262, January 28, 1905, p. 102; Supplement to *The Sphere*. January 28, 1905, pp. i–iii). Six of these images were subsequently reprinted in England as a series of postcards, titled: *The Revolutionary Outbreak in Saint Petersburg* (the publisher is given as Lankester and Co., Tunbridge Wells, but the copyright is credited to *The Sphere*). Other photographs by Bulla, including pictures of Father Gapon, and Imperial troops guarding the streets, also appeared in the French periodical *L'Illustration* that same month (Supplement to *L'Illustration*. No. 3231, 28 January 1905, unpaginated). Some of these images were published in Russia after the October Manifesto (see, for example, Father Gapon with workers from the Putilov Factory in *Iskry*. No. 44, 20 November 1905, p. 352). It is not clear whether Russian journals had their own staff photographers, but it appears that in most cases private photographic studios in Moscow and Saint Petersburg worked as ersatz press agencies, licensing out images to publishers of all types.
18 TsDIAK, f. 294, op. 1, d. 380, l. 79; *Iskry*. No. 42, 6 November 1905, pp. 330–331, 334–335; *Iskry*. No. 43, 13 November 1905, pp. 339, 343.
19 *Niva*. No. 45, 12 November 1905, pp. 881–883.
20 The first image carries no publishing details, but the second was published by August Tsenter.
21 Gor'kii, Maksim. *Sobranie sochinenii*. Tom 28, Moscow, 1954, p. 392.
22 One image of the funeral appeared in *Iskry*, but this was not reproduced as a postcard (*Iskry*. 30 October 1905, No. 41, p. 326). No images of Bauman's funeral appeared in *Niva*.
23 *Izveshchenie o vtorom ocherednom s"ezde rossiiskoi sotsialdemokraticheskoi rabochei* partii, pp. 25–26.

24 *Moskovskii listok*, Pribavlenie k No. 336, Moscow, No. 92, 22 December 1905, pp. 1–8; *Moskovskii listok*, Pribavlenie k No. 342, Moscow, No. 93, 29 December 1905, pp. 1–8; *Moskovskii listok*, Pribavlenie k No. 1, No. 1, 1 January 1906, pp. 4–15; *Moskovskii listok*, Pribavlenie k No. 7, No. 2, 8 January 1906, pp. 1–5. The photographs were also reproduced in: *Iskry*. No. 1, 1 January 1906, pp. 1–8; *Iskry*. No. 2, 8 January 1906, pp. 2–8; *Iskry*. No. 3, 15 January 1906, pp. 1–2. Some were printed in *Niva*, where they are attributed in one issue to 'V. Gribov and our correspondent K. K. Bulla', and in a later number to 'Smirnov, Zavadskii, and M. Gribov' (*Niva*. No. 52, 31 December 1905, pp. 993–996; *Niva*. No. 53, 7 January 1906, pp. 10–11; *Niva*. No. 54, 11 January 1906, pp. 25–27). The original prints of many of Aleksei Zavadskii's photographs are in the State Historical Museum, Moscow: Otdel IZO, Fond Fotografii. For background information see: Dediukhina, V. 'Fotografii A. K. Zavadskogo po vooruzhennomu vosstaniiu v Moskve (dekabr' 1905 g.).' *Trudy Gosudarstvennogo Istoricheskogo Muzeia*, Vyp. 41, 1967, pp. 19–24

25 In *Iskry* the pictures are collectively dated the 7–19 December and credited to correspondents 'M. I. Gribov, S. G. Smirnov, Zheludkov, Zavadskii and others.' None of the postcard reproductions of these images mentions *Iskry*, but there is one showing shell damage to the interior of 'Sassulich's flat' that is signed in the plate 'A. Zavadskii', and several others in the author's collection that have his name handwritten on the reverse. This suggests that the copyright, and thus the decision to reprint the images as postcards, rested with the photographer rather the journal.

26 Sent from Novocherkassk on 9 April 1906 to Marcel Bricogne in Gannes (Picardy Region), author's collection; Efimov, who was a well-established bookseller and publisher, had earlier published large numbers of pictures depicting the Russo-Japanese War, a good illustration of changing the priorities of private publishers. After the October Manifesto, he was included is a list of publishers issuing works in defiance of the censor (under the imprint Trud i volia) (RGIA, f. 776, op. 9, d. 97, l. 11).

PLAYING POLITICS

1 Maliazh. 'Nedavnee i nastoiashchee. Kharakteristika satiricheskikh zhurnalov', p. 70. Photomechanical postcards were occasionally finished by hand to increase their visual appeal, often with a heavy daub of red.

2 Boris Kustodiev made a similar image titled *Resignation from the Left and the Right…*, which depicts Witte holding an Imperial flag in one hand and a red flag in the other (*Zhupel*. No. 2, 1905, p. 10).

3 Quoted in Engelstein. *Moscow, 1905*, pp. 94–5

4 The postcard is titled *Dve perspektivy* [*Two Perspectives*], and is dated 26 October 1906.

5 Hildermeier. *The Russian Socialist-Revolutionary Party Before the First World War*, p. 304.

6 *Trud*. No. 6, December 1906, p. 1.

7 Rata Langa. *Nicholas the Juggler*. *Der Wahre Jacob*. Stuttgart, 14 November 1905.

8 Both *Will He Be Able to Keep it up for Long* and *The Premonition* were reprinted in postcard form by the Nagasaki-based publisher Volia.

9 Images of Nicholas II were also distributed on hectographic leaflets.

10 *Tsar-Famine* [*Tsar-Golod*] was published circa 1907, predating Leonid Andreev's play of the same title.

11 *One with a Plough and Seven with a Spoon* was very widely reproduced. Examples were printed in towns across Russia, from Saint Petersburg to Vladivostok.

12 Liebknecht's *The Spider and the Fly* was published in 1889. August Tsenter published a very similar image that uses an octopus in place of a spider.

13 Zaks, B. *Tvorchestvo Chemodanova i revoliutsiia 1905 goda*, Unpublished typescript, circa 1935, p. 3, MSI KF.

14 Chemodanov's own impoverished upbringing and his work as doctor in the rural backwaters of Viatka Province exposed him to the miseries of life in Imperial Russia. In a short autobiography, composed in 1903, he claimed that the distinguishing feature of his artwork was its 'ideological commitment and unchanging attachment to progressive principles' (Chemodanov. *Avtobiografiia*. GRM OR, f. 44, d. 1, l. 45).

15 For more on right-wing newspapers, see: Kovalev, I. 'Tsarizm v bor'be s revoliutsionnoi pechat'iu v 1905 g.'. *Krasnyi arkhiv*. No. 105, 1941, pp. 140–155.

16 I can find only one reference to right-wing postcards in the Press Administration archives – a set of satirical cartoons submitted to the censor in December 1905 by the Party of Legal Order, a moderate conservative group (RGIA, f. 777, op. 27, d. 257, l. 585).

17 *Gimn za Tsaria* [*Hymn for the Tsar*]. Probably published by the Society of Russian Patriots, Moscow, circa 1906.

18 The Tsar's Manifesto of 18 February 1905 characterised the liberation movement as a non-Russian phenomenon, fomented by outsiders.

19 *Zhidu oshvaboditeliu* [*To the Yid Shliberator*]. Probably published by the Society of Russian Patriots, Moscow, circa 1906.

20 The caption is a modified quotation from Psalms. A similar image with the same title (attributed to Nikolai Remizov) appears on the cover of *Strely*. No. 2, Saint Petersburg, 1906.

21 *Otkrytoe pis'mo*. No. 5, Saint Petersburg, May 1906, pp. 132–133.

22 These postcards were published by Sergei Prokudin-Gorskii. While Bem's other postcards of children were very popular, her Duma images are rarely found, suggesting that they did not find great commercial favour.

23 For an example, see: Shleev, V. V. *Iz istorii russkoi revoliutsionnoi otkrytki*. Vypusk 1. Moscow: Izobrazitel'noe iskusstvo, 1974.

24 Bakhman was a Prussian citizen who owned a typo-lithographic printing shop in Moscow (RGIA, f. 776, op. 29, d. 43, ll. 8–9). He also published a similar series entitled *Duma* [*Duma / Thought*], which appear to be by the same artist. Some are signed with the initials 'I. Ia'.

POPULAR HEROES

1 Anonymous. 'O geroiakh'. *Pulemet*. No. 1, Saint Petersburg, 1905, p. 9.
2 See, for example: Volkenshtein and Morozov in *Iskry*. No. 8, 19 February 1906, p. 45; Kaliaev in *Zritel'*. No. 3, 1905, p. 4; Schmidt in *Zarnitsy*. No 6, 1906, p. 4.
3 Postcards eventually comprised just under a third of the images printed by Bonch-Bruevich between 1906 and 1907 (Zabochen', Mikhail. 'Otkrytki partiinogo izdatel'stva "Vpered"', p. 76).
4 Barring a few notable exceptions (such as Bauman, Schmidt, and Spiridonova), Utro and Vpered produced almost no portraits of contemporary activists. Instead, they published around forty different portraits of European political theorists. Apart from Spiridonova, only two living Russians were featured in their postcard output: Georgii Plekhanov, and Petr Kropotkin. There are no postcards featuring Lenin known to have been produced prior to 1917, and Lev Trotsky only appears in a small handful of images, often alongside other members of the Saint Petersburg Soviet.
5 *Novaia zhizn'*. No. 22, 26 November 1905, p. 4.
6 Numbered series captioned with names of the sitters, no publication details, circa 1905.
7 Zabochen'. 'Otkrytki partiinogo izdatel'stva "Vpered"', p. 76.
8 Boniece, Sally A. 'The Spiridonova Case, 1906: Terror, Myth and Martyrdom.' *Just Assassins: The Culture of Terrorism in Russia*. Evanston: Northwestern University Press, 2010, pp. 135–136.
9 Despite playing the role of victim in public, Spiridonova confessed in private that she had not been raped.
10 All portraits of Schmidt use one of two photographs, the first taken by the Odessa photographer Dimitrii Pudichev showing him standing, and the second by the Sebastopol photographer, Mikhail Mazur showing him sitting (Zabochen'. 'Otkrytki partiinogo izdatel'stva "Vpered"', p. 69).
11 The photographs of Plehve's carriage were taken by Karl Bulla, and originally appeared on the front page of *L'Illustration*. No. 3206, Paris, 6 August 1904. They were reproduced in postcard form in France without publication details.
12 Figner, Vera. *Polnoe sobranie sochinenii v semi tomakh.* Tom piatyi: *Ocherki, stat'i, rechi*. Moscow: Izdatel'stvo Vsesoiuznogo obshchestva politkatorzhan i ssyl'no-poselentsev, 1932, pp. 318–319.
13 Geifman, Anna. *Death Orders: The Vanguard of Modern Terrorism in Revolutionary Russia*. Santa Barbara: Praeger, 2010, p. 110.
14 Spiridonova's statement was originally published in *Rus'*. No. 27, 12 February 1906, p. 4.
15 Vladimirov, V. E. *Mariia Spiridonova: S portretom i risunkami, s predisloviem ot Soiuza ravnopraviia zhenshchin*. Moscow: Tip. A. P. Poplavskogo, 1906, p. 11.
16 *Rus'*. No. 29, 15 February 1906, p. 4.
17 *Rus'*. No. 28, 14 February 1906, p. 6.
18 The paper's editorial was also unequivocal in its condemnation of Spiridonova's deed, but similarly, sought to compare it to the heinousness of her subsequent mistreatment: 'No one disputes the fact that Spiridonova carried out a political crime, as did the party that sent this half-child on such a grievous mission. But do these crimes provide even the remotest justification for a person to be treated in the way that Spiridonova has been?' (*Rus'*, No. 27, 12 February 1906, p. 2).
19 *Rus'*. No. 28, 14 February 1906, p. 6.
20 *Ivan Platonovich Kaliaev*. Paris: Partiia Sotsialistov-Revoliutsionerov (otdel'nyi ottisk iz 'Rev. Ross'), 1905, p. 4.
21 Quoted in Geifman. *Death Orders*, pp. 95–96.
22 Untited postcard depicting Kaliaev, with accompanying text reproducing letter to his mother, circa 1905; Untitled portrait postcard of Spiridonova, with accompanying text reproducing extract from letter explaining her actions, circa 1906.
23 *Rus'*. No. 28, 14 February 1906, p. 6.
24 Geifman. *Thou Shalt Kill, Revolutionary Terrorism in Russia*, 1894–1917, p. 19.
25 Knight, Amy. 'Female Terrorists in the Russian Socialist-Revolutionary Party'. *Russian Review*. No. 38 (2), April 1979, p. 147.
26 Spiridovich. *Partiia Sotsialistov-Revoliutsionerov i ee predshestvenniki*, p. 118.
27 Quoted in Geifman. *Thou Shalt Kill, Revolutionary Terrorism in Russia*, p. 49.
28 Quoted in Geifman. *Death Orders*, p. 110.
29 Stanevich, F. Untitled Article. *Otkrytka*. No. 3, Kaluga, May 1907, pp. 34–35.
30 The two images of Spiridonova in Tambov Prison were likely taken by London-based photographer Nahum Luboshitz during a visit he made with the American reporter Kellogg Durand (Durand, Kellogg. *The Red Reign*. London: Hodder and Stoughton, 1907, pp. 162, 387).
31 There is also a set of fifteen numbered postcards depicting his trial, many of which reproduce photographs taken by defence lawyer Sergei Balavinskii.
32 The other two signatories were the Social Democrat Petr Karpovich, who killed Minister of Englightenment Nikolai Bogolepov in 1901, and Shimel-Leiba Sikorskii, who was involved in killing Plehve in 1904 (Reproduced in: V. M. Lavrov. *Mariia Spiridonova: terroristka i zhertva terrora. Povestvovanie v dokumentakh*. Moscow: Arkheograficheskii tsentr, 1996, p. 88).
33 *Rus'*. No. 28, 14 February 1906, p. 6.

34 A poem in the satirical journal *Zarnitsy* [*Sheet-lightning*] praising Lieutenant Schmidt as a 'perpetual lighthouse' is also illustrated with a crown of thorns (*Zarnitsy*. No. 6, Saint Petersburg, 1906, p. 4).

35 Ouspensky, Leonid and Lossky, Vladimir. *The Meaning of Icons*. Crestwood, New York: Saint Vladimir's Seminary Press, 1982, p. 30.

36 Ouspensky and Lossky. *The Meaning of Icons*, p. 44.

37 Untitled leaflet. Moscow Committee of the Socialist-Revolutionary Party, undated but circa May 1905, IISG PSR, Index 357.

38 RGIA, f. 776, op. 16, d. 17, l. 414.

39 It is interesting to note that the revolutionaries often used the expression 'enemies of the people' in their descriptions of Tsarist officials. See, for example: Untitled leaflet. Tsentral'nyi boevoi otriad Partii Sotsialistov-Revoliutsionerov, circa 1906, IISG PSR, Index 738.

CONSUMPTION AND DISPLAY

1 *Adskaia pochta*. No. 3, p. 7.

2 An eight kopeck price mark is stamped on the back of a copy of *Vittova pliaska* [*Witte's Dance*] in the Russian National Library (RNB OE, Ė OIR 580K/1–213), as well as on *Lekarstva, vydavaemye besplatno iz kazennykh aptek po retseptu professora allopata Trepoff* [*Free Medicine Distributed by State Chemists According to the Prescription of Physician Professor Trepov*], published by Kh. K. and A. G. in Saint Petersburg. For silver bromide reproductions of socialist pictures, see: *Otkrytka*, No. 2, Kaluga, April 1907, p. 26.

3 *Otkrytye pis'ma i drugie khudozhestvennye izdaniia Krasnogo kresta*; the prices were the same in 1905 (TsGIA SPB, f. 202, op. 2, d. 1166, l. 80).

4 *Mezhdunarodnye sotsialisticheskie kongressy*. Saint Petersburg. Utro, 1906, unpaginated advertisement on inside back covers; *Volna*. No. 19, 17 May 1906, p. 4; Kautskii, Karl. *Nauka, zhizn' i etika*, advertisement on inside of front cover.

5 Rozen, M. *Ocherki polozheniia torgovo-promyshlennogo proletariata v Rossii*. Saint Petersburg: Vpered, 1907; for pamphlets see: *Vestnik Zhizni*, No. 7, 3 June 1906, p. 62. By comparison, satirical journals were sold for between five and twenty kopecks.

6 GARF, f. 63, op. 25, d. 466, l. 23.

7 Anonymous. 'La rage des cartes-postales'. p. 5. In Saint Petersburg, the average wage for an unskilled labourer in 1906 was ninety-five kopecks a day, for a carpenter 146 kopecks, and for a metal worker 182 kopecks (Rykachev A. 'Tseny na khleb i trud za 58 let.' *Vestnik finansov, promyshlennosti i torgovli*. No. 31, Saint Petersburg, 1911, p. 201).

8 The extent of their dissemination among the peasantry remains an open question, but the contention that anti-government postcards were bought by workers is corroborated by police reports. In December 1906, for example, around 300 striking ship-workers and sailors gathered in the Novorossiisk University dining halls. A government spy reported that during the meeting, 'two young ladies were sitting behind a table selling illegal newspapers, pamphlets and postcards, the profit from which went towards the needs of revolutionary organisations' (TsDIAK, f. 268, op. 1, d. 49, l. 18).

9 In this sense, the postcard's function was closer to its predecessor, the carte de visite.

10 Quoted in: Shleev, V. V. and E. B. Fainshtein. *Khudozhestvennye otkrytki i ikh sobranie*. Moscow: Izobrazitel'noe iskusstvo, 1960, p. 11. See also, photograph of Vladimir Burtsev, pictured in his office against a backdrop of photographs, prints, and anti-government postcards (GARF, f. P-5802, op. 2, d. 1125, l. 37).

11 I have not been able to identify the exact origin of this quotation, but at least part of it ('every decent man should become a revolutionary') is taken from comments that Lenin made in 1904 in reference to Chernyshevskii's novel *What Is to Be Done*.

12 A. R. *Golutvino*. Saint Petersburg: Vpered, circa 1906, author's collection.

13 The poem is: *Puskai obviniaiut, kleveshchut, braniat* [*Let Them Blame, Slander, and Berate*], 1892; Meisonnier, Ernest. *La Barricade, rue de la Mortellerie*, juin 1848. Saint Petersburg: Vpered, circa 1906, author's collection.

14 Following Schmidt's execution, officials banned all remembrance services and demonstrations.

15 Pudichev, Dmitrii. Lieutenant Schmidt, plain back, circa 1906, author's collection.

16 Mikhail Stoliarov. *K zhertvam nashikh dnei* [*To the Victims of Our Days*]. Saint Petersburg: V. A. Metalnikov, circa 1906, author's collection.

17 Vladimirov, Ivan. *Ne Khodi* [*Don't Go*]. No publisher, author's collection. Staff Captain Ivan Borodin was an officer in the Ust-Dvinsk Fortress Sapper's Company, stationed at Ust-Dvinsk (Dünamünde) Fortress, close to Riga. Borodin was later transferred to the Vyborg Fortress Sappers' Company and promoted to lieutenant-colonel. He was murdered by revolting soldiers in 1917.

18 Maimon, Moisei. *Na rodine* [*Back Home*], no publisher, sent in September 1906, author's collection. The Russian expression used in the message is: 'Koshke igrushki, a myshke slezki'.

19 Sokolov, Evgenii. *Monarkhist* [*Monarchist*]. Moscow: E. Kudinova and A. Lezina Lithography, circa 1907, author's collection.

20 GARF, f. 102, op. 237, d. 9 ch. 34, l. 230.

21 GARF, f. 102, op. 203, d. 2 ch. 34 t. 1, l. 371.

22 Untitled Portrait of Lieutenant Schmidt, no publisher, circa 1906, private collection, Moscow.

23 Levi. 'Kak kollektsionirovat' otkrytki?', p. 21.

24 I. V. Gorelov. Untitled image of a revolutionary expropriator, circa 1906, author's collection.

25 Postcard album belonging to Nevill Forbes, LRA FA, MS1496, Box 12.

26 Perott took the album with him when he emigrated to Finland in 1917, and again when he moved to England two years later. After Perrott's death in 1958, the album came into the possession of the scholar and collector Abram Chimensky. It was sold, along with other items in his collection, on 14 April 2011 at Bassenge Auction House in Berlin. The album came up for sale again at Christie's South Kensington on 15 November 2013, where it was bought by Anthony d'Offay.

27 For more information on Perott, see his obituary in the *British Medical Journal*. 17 May 1958, p. 1182.

28 One untitled postcard shows the Tsar being inoculated against liberalism; another, by the same artist, depicts him being welcomed into hell by a panoply of historical figures. The third card, titled *Shestvie avtokratii* [*The Pageant of Autocracy*], shows officials and members of the Imperial Family indulging in an orgy of violence.

29 GARF, f. 10086, op. 1, d. 34, ll. 1–4.

30 *Otkrytoe pis'mo*. No. 11, Saint Petersburg, 1905, pp. 333–4.

EPILOGUE

1 *Partiinye izvestiia*. No. 3, December 1906, p. 4.

2 It is an open question as to how much the market affected revolutionary postcard output, but it is clear that on occasion both their content and their target audience was influenced by financial considerations. A letter sent by the Socialist-Revolutionary Natalia Kogan-Bernshtein in 1906 shows that postcards did not even have to contain revolutionary subject matter in order to be used for fundraising purposes: 'There is a big demand for picture postcards (especially of prints and sculptures), so please could you buy me a selection of 100–150 different examples [for resale].' (Intercepted letter addressed to Ilia Adol'fovich and Pasha, contained in an envelope sent to Madame Braguinsky by Natalia Kogan-Bernshtein, 2 May 1906, HIWRP OA, Index XXIVE, Folder 1).

3 The nearest competitors to anti-government postcards, in terms of the numbers produced, were satirical journals. According to official figures for Saint Petersburg, 1,361,710 copies of periodicals of all types were sold between January 1905 and January 1907 (RGIA, f. 776, op. 29, d. 29, ll. 3–4; RGIA, f. 776, op. 29, d. 30, ll. 5–7). This does not, of course, take into account the many copies of anti-government journals that were sold illegally. Attempts have been made to put an Empire-wide figure on the overall numbers printed, but the estimates vary so widely as to render them statistically useless (see, for example: M. A. L-skii. 'Vo vlasti gluposti'. *Istoricheskii vestnik*. No. 4, April 1912, p. 99; Botsianovskii, V and E. Gollerbakh. *Russkaia satira Pervoi russkoi revoliutsii 1905–1906 gg.* Leningrad: Gosudarstvennoe izdatel'stvo, 1925, p. 37). Any attempt to calculate postcard numbers is equally futile, but the evidence for their predominance is as follows. According to its chief curator, Moscow's Museum of Contemporary History, which likely holds the world's largest collection of such images, has 4,916 anti-government postcards dating to before 1917 (figure given by Valeria Sergeevna Kagramanova to the author in 2013). Although there are some duplicates in the collection, and their print runs were likely smaller, this is still well in excess of the number of satirical journal titles published. Furthermore, anti-government postcards were printed over a much longer period and over a far wider area than were periodicals. This is by no means conclusive, but it is the closest that I can get to proving the point.

4 Anonymous. 'La rage des cartes-postales', p. 5.

5 Further study is needed to determine the exact role played by ideology in increasing support for the opposition. My own conviction is that Party-guided ideological belief played a rather less important part in convincing the population of the need for change than has previously been claimed, an opinion that is borne out by anti-government postcard imagery.

6 While the government could legislate against new production, it could not curtail the existence of anti-government postcards already in circulation, ensuring that the ideological influence of the medium would continue for years afterwards. (For a similar observation about books, see: Rubakin. 'Knizhnyi priliv i knizhnyi otliv', pp. 23–24).

7 Bonch-Bruevich. *Kak pechatalis' za granitsei i taino dostavlialis' v Rossiiu zapreshchennye izdaniia nashei partii*, p. 97; Belopol'skii. 'Vospominaniia uchastnikov Pervoi russkoi revoliutsii', p. 44. The Social Democratic activist (and member of the Party's Saint Petersburg Finance Committee) Elena Stasova also comments on the economic benefits of postcard production in her memoirs (Stasova, Elena. *Stranitsy zhizni i bor'by*. Moscow: Gosudarstvennoe izdatel'stvo politicheskoi literatury, 1960, p. 24; Stasova. *Vospominaniia*, pp. 49–50).

8 In 1908, Lenin remarked in respect of Social Democratic printed propaganda that: 'It has been seeded and it will grow. Maybe not tomorrow, or in the period after, but it will eventually flower. It is not within our power to change the objective conditions for the growth of a new crisis, but it will produce the goods.' This observation in many ways sums up the 1905 period for the revolutionary opposition. In the short term, it was not a success: the Tsar was not overthrown, and many of the more immediate gains of the revolution were quickly overturned. But as Lenin rightly remarked, the seeds of long-term change had been planted, though in what form they would flower was still by no means certain.

Index

References to illustrations are shown in italics with the caption page in brackets if not on the same page. References to endnotes consist of the page number followed by the letter 'n' followed by the number of the note.

Acknowledgements

I could not have written this book without the support of the many different people who have listened, offered advice, and encouraged me along the way. I am grateful first of all to the staff of the institutions that I visited, particularly in Russia, where I received invaluable assistance in my hunt for postcard-related material. No one would claim that the Russian archives are an easy place to conduct academic research, but once idiosyncrasies have been understood and trust gained, I always found an unfailing readiness to help. Indeed, I recall once complaining to the head of a library in Saint Petersburg that I had not been allowed to see a particular publication. He immediately countermanded the order, saying with a smile, 'God forbid that an Englishman should go back to England and tell all his countrymen that the Russians would not allow a foreigner to see their archives.'

Particular thanks go to: Anna Larina at the Russian State Library, and Natalia Mozokhina at the State Russian Museum, both of whom were extremely generous with their time and knowledge; Valentina Kagramanova, and Vera Panfilova at the Museum of Contemporary History; Aleksandra Tsvetkova at GARF; Zinaida Bakhtina at the Museum of Moscow; Tatiana Saburova at the State History Museum; Aleksandr Tarasov and Natalia Patrusheva at the Russian National Library; Svetlana Khodokovskaia at the Museum of Political History; Richard Davies at the Leeds Russian Archive (who was also kind enough to read the finished text); Bob Henderson and Jon Smele at Queen Mary University; Jill Golden at the Hoover Institution, and Dina Melnychuk, who helped with my research in the United States.

In Moscow and Saint Petersburg, many individuals offered a warm welcome and sage advice. My thanks to: Dmitry Artemyev, Maria Chapkina, Sonia Chapkina, Aleksei Ladyzhensky, Galina Panova, Igor Pugachev, Vitaly Tretyakov, and Mikhail Voronin, all of whom went far beyond the call of duty to help answer my requests. Meanwhile, Hannah Fricker, Pavel Odynin, Semyon Smoliak, Marius Stravinsky, Katya Vidre, and Emma Wells all offered excellent respite after a day's research, not to mention a place to stay. In the Ukraine, Andrew Yatsenko dealt admirably with the Kiev archives on my behalf, while in Berlin, Anna Jouravel helped me to track down many articles on early postcard production. My thanks also to Kaj Jalving and Olaf Koens in Amsterdam, Nicolas Osipov in Paris, and René Nyberg in Finland.

Several people have read the manuscript in whole or part. Rachael Claridge, James Clasper, Anna Geifman, Sam Gordon, Jim Heintz, Hubertus Jahn, Michael Melancon, Edward Posnett, Katya Rogatchevskaia, Alexey Smirnoff, and Oleg Tarasov all made suggestions that helped to improve the text. Special mention also goes to Dick Haddon, Michael Meredith, and Erik Zitser, who each in their own way inspired me to write this work, and to Hugh Aplin, Chris Brown-Humes, and Anthony d'Offay for their generosity in lending images. In the UK, I am indebted to Charlie Gammel, Tom Godsal, Hugo Nickols, Michael Parsons, Alex Scott, Jo Weaver, and my family, who provided a wealth of support during the writing process, which lasted much longer than expected. Thanks also to Helen Allman, Michael Chereisky, Ian Shapiro, Natasha Yarotskaya, and Sergei Yurkov for their help.

Three people have been with the project from the very beginning. Oleg Minin, the leading expert on Russian satirical journals, has been an excellent guide to the period, and was an ever-cheerful companion during my time in Saint Petersburg. It has been both a great help and great pleasure to have been able to exchange ideas with such an enthusiastic and knowledgeable individual. Finally, and most importantly, I am grateful to my very patient publishers Richard Embray and Elinor Jansz at Four Corners Books, who were enthusiastic about the project from the start, and continued to provide support and advice throughout the writing process, despite the many missed deadlines. Without all of the above-mentioned people and, indeed, everyone with whom I have spoken about postcards over the years, this enterprise would have been a whole lot more difficult and a great deal less fun.

Greetings from the Barricades
Revolutionary Postcards in Imperial Russia

First published 2018 by
Four Corners Books
56 Artillery Lane, London E1 7LS
fourcornersbooks.co.uk

Design: John Morgan studio
Reprography: Flavio Milani
Print production: Martin Lee
Printed by Verona Libri, Italy

ISBN 978-1-909829-12-1

The author and publishers would like to thank the following individuals and institutions for allowing items in their collections to be included in this book:

Hugh Aplin (pages 28, 35, 357)
Chris Brown-Humes (pages 18, 98–9)
International Institute of Social History, Amsterdam (page 59)
Leeds Russian Archive, Leeds (pages 91, 273)
Museum of Contemporary History, Moscow (pages 171, 192, 206)
Museum of Moscow, Moscow (page 205)
Anthony d'Offay (pages 109, 235, 311, 383, 410, 418)
Rahvusarhiiv, Tartu (page 122)
Russian National Library, Saint Petersburg (pages 221 (left), 227)
Russian State Archive of Literature and Art, Moscow (page 208)
Russian State Library, Moscow (page 177, 191 (top), 211, 216 7, 249)
State Archive of the Russian Federation, Moscow (page 32)
Andrew Yatsenko (pages 278, 339)
Oleg Zarovchatskii (page 27 (bottom))